CREDITS

1732011

191984

221084

AUX SYS

SYSTEM DESIGN
NATHAN DOWDELL

LINE DEVELOPMENT
DAVE CHAPMAN AND
SAM WEBB

WRITING
DAVE CHAPMAN, JIM
JOHNSON, PATRICK
GOODMAN, ROSS ISAACS,
BILL MAXWELL, JONATHAN
BREESE, NATHAN DOWDELL,
JOHN SNEAD, OZ MILLS,
AARON POLLYEA, ROB
WIELAND, ADE SMITH,
ANTHONY JENNINGS, DAN
TAYLOR, DAYTON WARD,
GARETH-MICHAEL SKARKA,
GILES PRITCHARD, LUKA
CARROLL, STEVEN CREECH,
SHAWN MERWIN, SAM WEBB
AND JACOB ROSS

INDEX BY
BILL HERON

EDITING
SCOTT PEARSON
AND BRIAN CASEY

PROOFREADING
ARIC WIEDER

COVER ARTWORK
GUILLEM PONGILUPPI AND
JOSEPH DIAZ

INTERNAL ARTWORK
TOBIAS RICHTER, MATTHEW
COMBEN, RODRIGO
GONZALEZ TOLEDO,
MICHELE FRIGO, CONNOR
MAGILL, NICK GREENWOOD,
WAYNE MILLER, JOSHUA
CALLOWAY, MARTIN
SOBR, JOSEPH DIAZ,

STEVE STARK, GRZEGORZ
PEDRYCZ, CHRIS ADAMEK,
VITALI TIMKIN, ANGEL
ALONSO MIGUEL, DAVID
METLESITS, ALAIN RIVARD,
TOMA FEIZO GAS, JOSE
ESTERAS, CHRIS WEBB,
JACK KAISER AND
CRISTI BALANESCU

ART DIRECTION
SAM WEBB

LEAD GRAPHIC DESIGN
MATTHEW COMBEN

**ADDITIONAL
GRAPHIC DESIGN**
CHRIS WEBB AND
MICHAL E CROSS

PRODUCED BY
CHRIS BIRCH

OPERATIONS MANAGER
RITA BIRCH

PRODUCTION MANAGEMENT
PETER GROCHULSKI AND
STEVE DALDRY

COMMUNITY SUPPORT
LLOYD GYAN

WITH THANKS TO
GENE RODDENBERRY, JOHN
VAN CITTERS, MARIAN
CORDRY, VERONICA HART,
KEITH LOWENADLER,
DAYTON WARD AND
SCOTT PEARSON

PLAYTESTERS
THE CREWS OF THE:
USS LEXINGTON, USS
VENTURE, USS THUNDERCHILD
AND USS BELLEROPHON

MODIPHIUS® ENTERTAINMENT 2-D20™

Published by Modiphius Entertainment Ltd.
2nd Floor, 39 Harwood Road, London, SW6 4QP, England.
Printed by Standartų Spaustuvė, UAB, Vilnius, Lithuania.

INFO@MODIPHIUS.COM
WWW.MODIPHIUS.COM
STARTREK.COM

Modiphius Entertainment Product Number: MUH051060
ISBN: 978-1-910132-85-2   Forth printing

CONTENTS

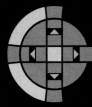

3441A

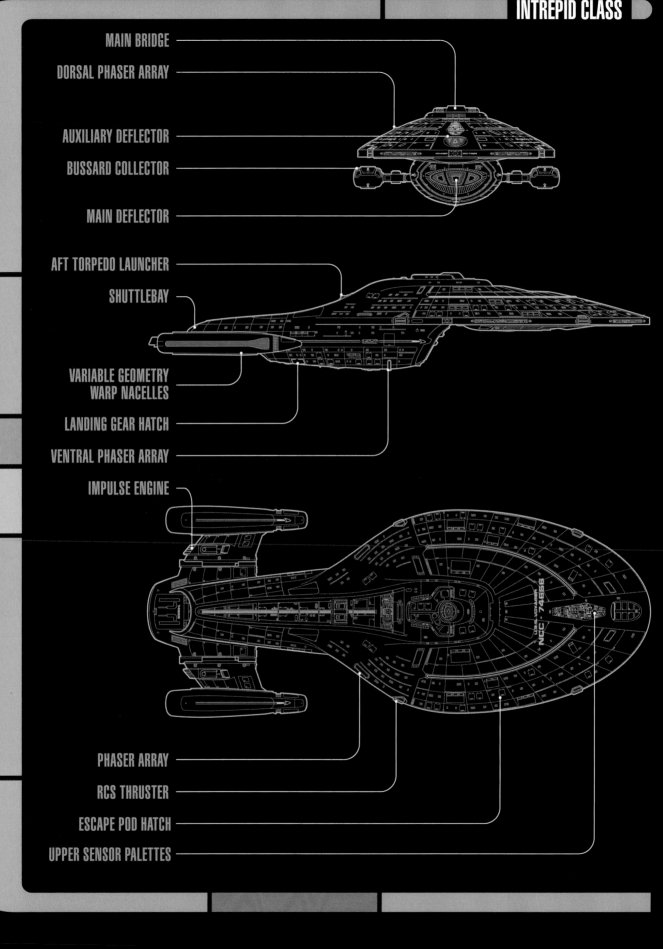

MAIN BRIDGE

DORSAL PHASER ARRAY

AUXILIARY DEFLECTOR

BUSSARD COLLECTOR

MAIN DEFLECTOR

AFT TORPEDO LAUNCHER

SHUTTLEBAY

VARIABLE GEOMETRY
WARP NACELLES

LANDING GEAR HATCH

VENTRAL PHASER ARRAY

IMPULSE ENGINE

PHASER ARRAY

RCS THRUSTER

ESCAPE POD HATCH

UPPER SENSOR PALETTES

CHAPTER 01.00

INTRODUCTION

0221221101181515
020114260109

"SPACE. THE FINAL FRONTIER. THESE ARE THE VOYAGES OF THE STARSHIP ENTERPRISE. ITS CONTINUING MISSION: TO EXPLORE STRANGE NEW WORLDS, TO SEEK OUT NEW LIFE AND NEW CIVILIZATIONS, TO BOLDLY GO WHERE NO ONE HAS GONE BEFORE."

— CAPTAIN JEAN-LUC PICARD

WELCOME TO THE 24TH CENTURY

Humanity always wondered what was out there, beyond our world, in the vastness of space. After one of the most horrific and catastrophic wars in Human history, it was our curiosity about the stars that inspired hope and united the planet to rebuild to make a better world for everyone.

Out in the stars we encountered new life; new allies, and new enemies. We formed an alliance, the United Federation of Planets, with a handful of civilizations and vowed to share our technology to create Starfleet — joined in a mission of peaceful exploration and united defense.

Starfleet ventured further into space, discovering strange new worlds and new civilizations. Vast empires turned against us, powerful forces tried to invade, but our spirit of adventure and wonder drives us to better ourselves and enrich our lives. Even now, we have only charted a quarter of the hundred billion stars and potential planetary systems in our Galaxy.

ADVENTURES BEYOND THE FINAL FRONTIER

Welcome to **Star Trek Adventures**, where Players take on the roles of Starfleet personnel, venturing into the Galaxy to explore, discover, and to encounter the wide diversity the universe has to offer. They can be captains, lieutenants, commanders, ensigns, or cadets. Enlisted or officers, they are Humans, Vulcans, Andorians, Trill, Bajorans, and more, assigned to starships, space stations, research vessels, colonies, and starbases across the Galaxy.

It is an exciting time in Starfleet's history — Earth Year 2371. The *U.S.S. Enterprise* NCC-1701-D will be sent on a mission to the Amargosa observatory, *U.S.S. Voyager* NCC-74656 is about to be sent on a mission into the Badlands to search for a Maquis ship, and the *U.S.S. Defiant* NX-74205 has been assigned to Commander Sisko at Deep Space 9 to assist in the search for the Dominion in the Gamma Quadrant.

Elsewhere, the fragile peace with the Klingon Empire could be jeopardized. Ambassador Spock tries to bring reunification with Vulcans to the Romulans while the Romulans, in turn, plan to join with the Cardassians in a preemptive strike against the Dominion threat.

You may be assigned to a starship caught up in the heart of these events, or sent on a different mission altogether — venturing into unexplored regions of space to make first contact with new civilizations or to chart spatial anomalies that could lead to new information and advances in the sciences.

ENGAGE ROLEPLAYING

There is a good chance that you have experience with roleplaying games, and are familiar with the concepts that we will be using. In its basic terms, roleplaying games are a form of shared storytelling. They are about stretching the imagination to experience exciting adventures out in the vastness of space, on hostile planets, and in exotic locations. With the power of the Player's imagination, they can experience encounters and situations far beyond that of a traditional board or video game.

YESTERDAY'S ENTERPRISE

The default setting of **Star Trek Adventures** is the year 2371 (stardates 48000-48999) but that does not mean that other eras of play are unavailable for the game. Gamemasters can choose to set the game at the dawn of Humanity's exploration into the stars, or during the "Five-Year Mission" period when Kirk commanded the *U.S.S. Enterprise* NCC-1701. Maybe even after Praetor Shinzon's plan to destroy Earth is foiled by Captain Picard and the crew of the *U.S.S. Enterprise* NCC-1701-E. Through wormholes or other temporal anomalies, the crew from one time period can travel to another, even into Earth's past.

Gamemasters wishing to run missions during different time periods will have no trouble using the rules as presented. If an item of equipment or technological advancement is unavailable in a certain era (such as transporters, replicators, etc.) there will be a note in a sidebar like this one. Additional advice for Gamemasters wishing to run games during the classic Kirk era or earlier, or after Shinzon, can be found in *Chapter 10: Gamemastering* (see p. 270) and in future supplements.

There is no formal start or end to the game — the Players and the Gamemaster (see below) get together and the sessions can range in length from a couple of hours to a whole weekend. There is no winning or losing, just a great way to get together, engage in conversation, create a story, and have a good time.

All games, however, have rules. This book provides the rules to help everyone agree on what happens, to avoid dispute over the action, and to help everyone to work together to make sure that the experience is as fair as it is exciting.

PLAYING A ROLE IN STARFLEET

Star Trek Adventures allows you to join Starfleet, take a position on board a starship, starbase, or colony, and discover new and exciting worlds. It is a future of hope, peace, and science. One where the challenge is resolved as much by discussion, diplomacy, and science and research as it is by pointing a phaser.

Missions can be exploratory, unearthing ancient civilizations and finding lost artifacts. They can be diplomatic in nature, making first contact with a new species, or trying to prevent a war between two feuding governments. It could be of a scientific nature, working on a new research project or investigating a temporal anomaly.

What makes *Star Trek Adventures* different from other games is two-fold: the variety of stories, and the depth of character. *Star Trek* is not just about exploring strange new worlds. One mission could be a life or death struggle, stranded on a planet with hostile forces approaching while the crew tries to repair a damaged shuttle. The next could have a medical focus, with a crew member fighting for their life against a strange disease and the medical staff desperate to discover a cure.

However, it is the characters that make *Star Trek* stories special. Behind the main story, through the heat of the action, the characters and their relationships are often the most important element. Frequently, the characters' personal stories come to the fore and become the focus of the adventure, and *Star Trek Adventures* encourages and enables this during play. Player Characters have their own motivations and beliefs, relationships and challenges that make them more than simple numbers on a sheet. With the help of the Players, the characters become three-dimensional — and when the characters are rich and detailed, the sense of tension, drama, and excitement throughout the game will make the experience unique and thrilling.

WHAT YOU WILL NEED

To take your place in Starfleet and to start your adventures across the Galaxy, it is recommended that you assemble the following before you begin:

PLAYERS

Every game needs Players. One of these Players will be the **Gamemaster** (see below), but you will need a handful of Players to take on the roles of the **Player Characters**. The Players work together, just like the crew of a starship, to face the challenges the Gamemaster places before them, explain how their characters act and respond to the encounters, and to ensure everyone is having fun. It is possible to play with six or more Players, but the more Players there are the less time each Player gets to share the spotlight.

Each Player will adopt the role of a crewmember in Starfleet, but there will be times when their character is not the focus of the mission. During these moments, Players will switch to control a **Supporting Character** to play a more active part in the story at that time. That means the chief engineer's Player will not be sitting doing nothing when the security away team beams to the planet for a lengthy encounter.

THE GAMEMASTER

In *Star Trek Adventures*, one Player takes on the role of the Gamemaster — they are the host of the game, the one who sets the scenes, describes the environments, knows the direction the story is designed to take, and poses the dramatic scenes and puzzles that the Players will encounter. They also act as the characters that are not controlled by the Players — **Non-Player Characters**, or **NPCs** for short — whether those are adversaries, their commanding officers, or **Supporting Characters**.

The Gamemaster also acts as referee and adjudicator for the rules of the game. They not only run the game, but also ensure that the game is fun, fair, and exciting. If at any time the rules are contested, or the Players are unsure of the outcome of a Task, the Gamemaster has final say on how the rules of the game are applied. The Gamemaster determines the plot of the mission, how the story unfolds, and sets the scene for the adventures ahead. They describe the setting, what happens and who is talking, and interpret the outcomes of the Players' actions and rolls. The Gamemaster has to be fair and listen to the Players to make sure everyone is enjoying the game. Being the Gamemaster can be a challenge, but a rewarding one. Additional advice for Gamemastering can be found in *Chapter 10: Gamemastering*.

CHARACTERS

Every Player needs a character. *Chapter 5: Reporting for Duty*, presents all of the information Players need to create new characters. They can be cadets in training at Starfleet Academy, ensigns fresh from the Academy on their first assignment, or bridge officers already in command of a ship. They can be crewmembers from Starfleet's dramatic history, or new creations defined by the Players. They can be Human or alien, young or old, and look like anyone you choose.

Players will also have at hand a selection of Supporting Characters that they can control when their Main Character is not currently in the thick of the action. These Supporting Characters can be created by the Players, or supplied by the Gamemaster as the mission dictates.

DICE

Star Trek Adventures uses two common types of dice found in most hobby and game stores. These are twenty-sided dice (abbreviated as **d20**), and six-sided dice (abbreviated as **d6**). Ideally, the group will have at least two d20s per Player, and two or more for the Gamemaster. These d20s are used for many different things, such as attempting Tasks and determining results from tables. The dice are used to help determine the magnitude of certain game effects, such as how effective your solution to the engineering problem was, or how convincing your character was in the sensitive negotiations with a potentially hostile civilization's military leader. More d20s are helpful, as Players and the Gamemaster may need to roll up to five d20s at a time, depending upon the circumstances.

Additionally, you will need at least four d6s for the group. When these dice are used in *Star Trek Adventures* they are called **Challenge Dice** [abbreviated as ⚔ elsewhere in these rules]. It is recommended that the group has a large number of d6 or ⚔ available. Players will generally need three to six to determine the effectiveness of their attempts, whether this is causing damage, or making a scientific breakthrough.

If dice are scarce, they can be shared between Players and the Gamemaster. Additionally, Modiphius produces special *Star Trek Adventures* dice, with certain numbers replaced with the Starfleet delta, though these are not essential.

PAPER AND PENCILS

Having a supply of paper and pencils will be handy for making maps, keeping notes, and tracking various game effects. The Players may need to make note of temporary impairments affecting their characters, the names of characters (both Player and Non-Player), important events, and clues to help them through the mission among other things. The Gamemaster may need it to record the health and status of other beings, and to keep notes of key details from the session. Sometimes the Gamemaster can pass notes to Players, rather than announcing them out loud. It is possible to keep track of all of this with tablets, smartphones, computers, and PADDs, but electronic devices at the game table can be distracting and should only be used with the Gamemaster's consent.

TOKENS, BEADS OR CHIPS

The Players will also need six counters to track Momentum points, while the Gamemaster will also need a dozen or more for the **Threat pool**. Each of these resources is described later in the rules. The more Players, the more of these counters of each type will be needed. These can be similar, but different colors are advised to avoid confusion — from

QUARK'S GAMING EMPORIUM

If you do not have access to a replicator to replicate the necessary dice needed to play the game, Quark has, for a nominal fee, made it possible to acquire official *Star Trek Adventures* Challenge Dice, and special d20s (as well as a wide range of accessories, counters, sourcebooks and supplements). You can order direct online from www.modiphius.com with a credit card or gold pressed latinum, or ask at your local gaming store.

poker chips, coins, glass beads, game counters, kadis-kot pieces, or other chits or tokens. Modiphius Entertainment also sells Momentum tokens, with the Federation symbol, and red alert Threat tokens.

While these different resource pools can be tracked on paper, or by using dice as counters, keeping track of these resources with physical items such as tokens, beads, or poker chips, has a number of advantages. First, it is easier to track the resources by simply adding or removing tokens from each resource pool, and second, it makes it much easier for everyone to know how many of each of these resources remain for every Player and the Gamemaster. Finally, there is an exciting psychological element as the Players watch the Gamemaster's Threat pool increase, heightening the tension and adding a growing sense of unease, as Threat is the resource used by the Gamemaster to make life more difficult for the Player Characters.

BASIC TRAINING

With this book, dice, characters and some Players you are ready to begin, but how do you actually start your mission?

The example of play on p. 7 introduces everything you need to know about how a game works. The Gamemaster describes the scene and what is going on, and the Players describe their action, reacting to the events around them. If a Player decides to do something that they may or may not succeed at — firing a phaser at moving target, struggling to climb up a dangerous cliff, or realigning the plasma conduits — they will need to roll some dice.

At its most basic, when a Player attempts a task like this they will look at their character sheet and determine an **Attribute** and a **Discipline** that best suits the situation. Attributes and Disciplines have scores that define how capable the character is at various actions. The Player rolls two d20s (sometimes more depending upon the situation) and checks to see if any dice roll less than the score of their chosen Attribute and Discipline combined. If a die rolls equal to or under the Target Number, it counts as a success! The more difficult the action, the more successes are needed to accomplish the task, whether it is making a convincing case in a diplomatic debate, leaping into a hovering shuttlecraft, or firing a phaser at the approaching Borg drones.

Roll too high on the dice and you have failed to accomplish the task. It may put the character in danger, or even worse, but it makes the story more exciting. It is often when characters fail or make mistakes that the story really takes a dramatic turn, adding to the sense of threat and tension and making the adventure more compelling.

EXAMPLE OF PLAY

The best way to learn how to play is to get involved in a game, but that is not always possible if there isn't one local to you. Below is an example of play in a typical game of *Star Trek Adventures* to give you an idea of how the game flows.

ABOARD THE KLINGON LANDING PAD...

"I would like to diagnose the Klingon warrior to find out whether he's infected with the virus," states Ashley, playing Dr Anjar Loral, the Thunderchild's *Chief Medical Officer*.

"Okay, he's struggling and doing as all Klingons would and trying to mask his pain. He isn't being all that cooperative. 'Get off me, Human! I will fight this myself!' He yells at you," Sam, the Gamemaster, describes as he figures out the Difficulty of the Task. Normally, this Task would be Difficulty 1, but because of the Klingon's Species *Trait* he is not making it easy for Dr Anjar, so Sam increases the Difficulty to 2. Sam defines the Task as a **Reason + Medicine** Task, so Ashley takes her Reason Attribute of 12 and her Medicine Discipline of 4 to make a Target Number of 16 – she's a medical specialist and knows her stuff, so her Focus of Xeno-Biology applies in this case, giving her a chance of scoring 2 successes if any one of her dice roll below 4.

Ashley scores a 15 and a 3 on 2d20, scoring her 3 successes. That means she diagnoses the Klingon and has one Momentum to spend now or bank for the group. She decides to spend it now, "I want to know how the virus is likely passed between people," she asks.

"Well," describes Sam, *"based on your knowledge of Xeno-biology this particular strain would only be transferred between Klingons. But it has been known to pass to Denobulans as well."* Michael, playing the Denobulan pilot pipes up as the conn officer Lt. Mettus, *"I might stay with the shuttle then, just so there's no risk to the crew and we're ready to leave the station if anything were to happen."*

"What do the rest of you want to do?" Asks Sam.

"I'd like to look around the hanger, to see if there's any signs of a fight, then take up a defensive position," asks Nick playing the chief of security, Lt. Commander Rafael Huerta. That's a fair simple thing

to do so Sam decides that doesn't require a Task to complete and describes how Nick's suspicions are right about there being a fight: *"It looks like someone landed here before you, and there's damage to the control panel on the door. Not sabotage, but definitely battle damage. You'd need to investigate it in greater depth to know more."*

"I'll tell the rest of the Away Team," replies Nick.

"Okay, while he takes up a defensive position at the door at the end of the cargo bay, I'll order our engineering ensign to take a look at the control panel to try and open it," describes Joel, who is playing the Vulcan Commander Sumek, *"It is logical that whoever inflicted the door damage was also the one who infected the landing platform. If we can trace the weapon's energy signature we may understand who the attacker is."* He assists Nikki's **Control + Engineering** Task, as she is playing a Supporting Character for this away team, Ensign Sabu. With a Difficulty of 2 and a Target Number of 13 Nikki wants to make sure she succeeds so she buys one extra d20 with a point of Threat, while Joel rolls 1d20 and is looking for a roll of 11 or under. The Difficulty is 2 as collecting this kind of data will take some care and attention. Nikki scores a 3, 15 and 20, while Joel scores an 11, and because Nikki scored at least 1 success Joel's success also counts, meaning they succeed. *"It's Klingon Disruptor fire,"* describes Sam. As Nikki also scored a 20 on one dice, she gets a Complication. Sam decides to bank 2 Threat instead of creating a Complication, as he has something in mind.

"Can I attempt to take samples from this Klingon Warrior so I can begin tests back on the Thunderchild?" Asks Ashley.

"Are you going to ask him nicely or just go right ahead and work on getting those blood samples?" Asks Sam.

"I don't really have time, we need to work our way through most of the station but I need samples from a lot of different Klingons." She replies, so Sam makes this an Opposed Task, with Ashley looking for one success using **Control + Medicine** while the Klingon opposes that roll using **Fitness + Security**. Ashley decides she really needs these samples so calls on her character's Value "Rough and Tumble

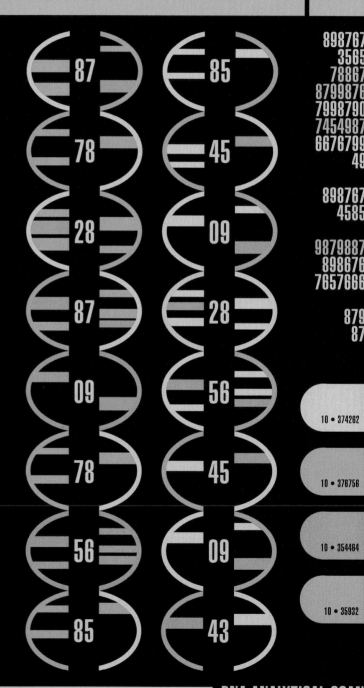

Doctor" to use her Determination to buy 1d20 that has already scored a 1, giving her 2 successes already. She rolls a further success while the Klingon scores 2 successes. Both characters succeed, but Ashley gained 2 Momentum while Sam's Klingon scored 1, meaning Ashley wins the opposed Task and has 1 Momentum to spare. Dr Loral manages to take the sample while the Klingon struggles against her.

"Then suddenly, once the purple Klingon blood sample is safely in the bottle, the alert klaxon of the Klingon station sounds, echoing around the cargo bay and a Klingon voice is translated as 'Self-Destruct Sequence Initiated!'" Sam spends all his remaining Threat to change the scene. "At that point," he continues, "the door opens and three Klingons, step forward, mek'leths and disruptors to hand… 'Step aside Humans, we are destroying this station and its sick inhabitants. This way at least they will die with honor!'"

Joel, as his commander, decides to try and negotiate with the Klingon captain, "Captain, we are here under orders from both your High Council and Starfleet Medical to cure this ailment. Please let us deactivate the self-destruct and continue with our work."

"Never!" Sam shouts, as he describes the Klingon captain aiming to open fire. The scene moves into a Conflict encounter, so the 1 Momentum that had been banked is removed and Sam tells the group that as Nick's character Lt. Huerta was preparing for this, and is in cover, he can act first. Had the group banked more than 1 Momentum they would have had some to help them subdue the Klingons, but from here the group will need to fight them without it and eventually get to the control center to stop the self-destruct sequence from destroying the orbital landing platform they are inside!

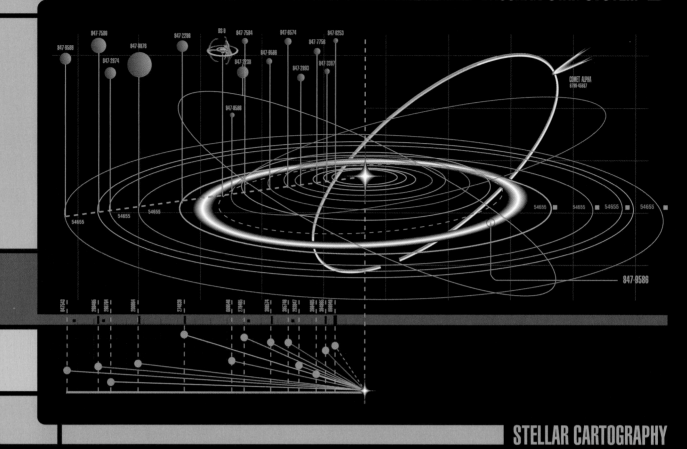

847-9586
847-7506
847-2874
847-9876
847-2298
DS-9
847-2238
847-7584
847-9586
847-8574
847-9586
847-2093
847-7756
847-9253
847-3387

COMET ALPHA
6789-45667

847-9586

54655
54655
54655
54655
54655
54655
54655

847-9586

847542
298495
292784
288894
274928
896698
278985
388574
362748
293847
298495
384985
899849

STELLAR CARTOGRAPHY

AIRLOCK ASSEMBLY	563
CONTROL GONDOLA	68546
SENSOR PALLET	37
DEFENSE SAIL	58456
OPS	9027
DEFLECTOR ASSEMBLY	
DOCKING RING	
PROMENADE	
EXHAUST CONE	
DOCKING PYLON	

DEEP SPACE 9

CHAPTER 02.00

THE UNITED FEDERATION OF PLANETS

1605141425
161809040425

THE UNITED FEDERATION OF PLANETS

OVERVIEW

"STARFLEET COULD'VE SENT A PROBE OUT HERE TO MAKE MAPS AND TAKE PICTURES, BUT THEY DIDN'T.
THEY SENT US SO THAT WE COULD EXPLORE WITH OUR OWN SENSES."

— CAPTAIN JONATHAN ARCHER

BRIEFING FROM STARFLEET COMMAND

Welcome, Captain. Your new assignment awaits. Before you take your place in the captain's chair, we want to bring you up to speed with the current galactic situation. Times are interesting, to say the least, with the discovery of the Dominion in the Gamma Quadrant, the problem with the Maquis in the Cardassian Demilitarized Zone, and the ever-present threat of the Borg's return. We need to make sure you know what to expect once you take your ship out of dock and begin your first mission as captain.

Some of this briefing will seem a bit basic, like we're covering information that you may remember from your days at Starfleet Academy. However, some of it will be new to you — recent intelligence and declassified communications that will help you to better understand the political situation facing Starfleet and the Federation at large.

THE KNOWN GALAXY

Our Galaxy, known as the Milky Way Galaxy, is over 100,000 light years wide and contains over four hundred billion stars. At its center is the galactic core, surrounded by the Great Barrier, which is over 15,000 light years in diameter. At this time, only one Federation starship on record has penetrated that barrier and returned, though you are probably already familiar with the exploits of the legendary Captain James T. Kirk, and we certainly do not expect you to try to copy his rather, ah, reckless style of command. Another barrier, the Galactic Barrier, surrounds the outer rim of the Galaxy. Both barriers contain energy fields that have extreme effects upon starship systems and their crews, and are nearly impossible to navigate.

The Galaxy itself, for the purposes of stellar cartography, is divided into four quadrants: Alpha, Beta, Delta, and Gamma. Each quadrant forms a 90-degree wedge when seen from

above or below the galactic plane. The Sol system, which serves as the center of the United Federation of Planets, is located on the border between the Alpha and Beta Quadrants. All of the other Federation member worlds and protectorates are spread among both quadrants. The Klingon Empire and the Romulan Star Empire are both centered in the Beta Quadrant.

At this time, we have charted only a fraction of the stars and planets within the Alpha and Beta Quadrants, and are only beginning to learn what the Gamma and Delta Quadrants contain. In short, there is a lot of space out there to explore and countless new worlds and civilizations to discover. Even with the challenges here at home in the Alpha Quadrant, Starfleet's primary mission is to explore, so you can be sure the bulk of your missions will take you into uncharted territory.

THE ALPHA QUADRANT

In the early days of Starfleet, we ventured out into the stars only to discover many civilizations that would eventually join us to form the United Federation of Planets. While the details of the Federation, including its foundation, will be covered in detail elsewhere, it is worth noting some of the other major powers and planets within the Alpha and Beta Quadrants, particularly as they stand now, in early 2371. You need to be aware of the bigger political picture, regardless of where your orders send you.

The Alpha Quadrant is home to not only Earth and many other Federation member homeworlds, but also the Cardassian Union, the Tholians, and many other species. The Federation has had a number of encounters with the ever-expanding Orion Syndicate and their criminal dealings within the Alpha Quadrant, and our initial relations with the Ferengi Alliance in the quadrant were hostile, to say the least. Since the Cardassian withdrawal from Bajor, we have had access to the first known stable wormhole, which serves as the gateway to many barely-explored sectors deep within the Gamma Quadrant. Given the recent encounters with the Dominion and the growing importance of the Bajoran wormhole to the Alpha Quadrant and the Federation, it makes sense to discuss Bajor first.

BAJOR

Bajor has been home to a peaceful, religious, and artistic species of humanoids for hundreds of thousands of years. Because Bajor is rich in natural resources, the Cardassian Union recently forcibly occupied Bajor for approximately fifty years, interning entire families into labor camps and stripping the planet of its resources. A fierce resistance fought back until Cardassian forces withdrew just a couple years ago. Now, the Bajorans are working to heal themselves and their planet — with the help of the Federation and others. Despite the appalling casualties and the horrors inflicted upon them during the Occupation, the Bajoran people somehow retained their faith in their Prophets and their love of art and architecture, and have even recently applied for membership to the Federation. However, given the unstable nature of their provisional government and the recurring Cardassian threat, in addition to the ongoing political and religious unrest on their planet, it is unlikely their application will be approved any time soon.

Starfleet Commander Benjamin Sisko is our point man on the station and in the sector. Given the rising importance of the stable wormhole located in the Denorios Belt and the increased focus on Bajor Sector because of that wormhole, I would expect Starfleet to either promote Sisko to captain or replace him with a more politically-seasoned officer. If the rumors about his special relationship with the Bajoran faithful are accurate, though, I suspect Starfleet Command will award him the fourth pip rather than risk installing an officer who does not have the locals' trust.

The Bajorans have a new religious leader, Kai Winn, who has consistently displayed some resistance to the Federation presence on Deep Space 9 and within the sector. She is more conservative than her predecessor, so it's possible that Federation-Bajoran relations may change for the worse in the coming months. Given that, I will let you in on a little secret: Starfleet Intelligence suggests that relations between the Federation and Bajor would improve regardless of who sits as the elected Kai should the Federation find, secure, and return any of the missing eight Bajoran Orbs of the Prophets — religious artifacts stolen by the Cardassians during the Occupation. It is unlikely that Starfleet would authorize any such mission, of course, but should the political balance shift within the Alpha Quadrant, we might just go down that road, no matter how much it might frustrate our Cardassian neighbors. Reliable allies are hard to find and harder to maintain.

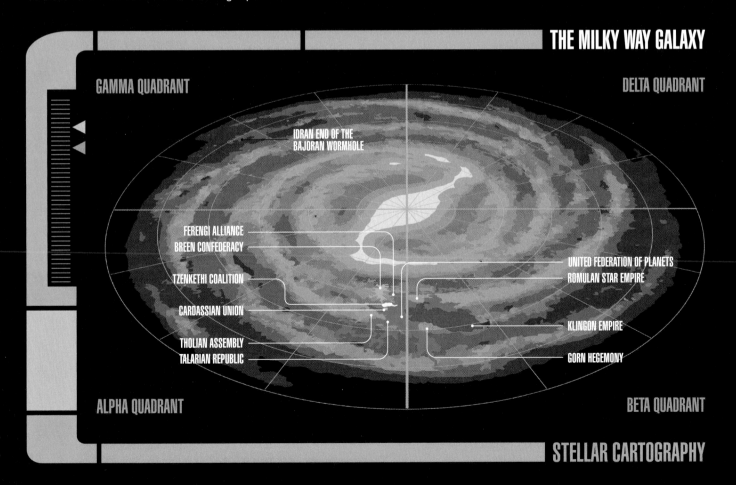

THE MILKY WAY GALAXY

GAMMA QUADRANT

DELTA QUADRANT

IDRAN END OF THE BAJORAN WORMHOLE

FERENGI ALLIANCE
BREEN CONFEDERACY

TZENKETHI COALITION

CARDASSIAN UNION

THOLIAN ASSEMBLY
TALARIAN REPUBLIC

UNITED FEDERATION OF PLANETS
ROMULAN STAR EMPIRE

KLINGON EMPIRE

GORN HEGEMONY

ALPHA QUADRANT

BETA QUADRANT

STELLAR CARTOGRAPHY

CARDASSIAN UNION

It is impossible to discuss Bajor without discussing the Cardassian Union. One of the more powerful forces in the Alpha Quadrant, their war with the Federation formally ended with the truce of 2367 and last year's treaty. The Cardassian Union is made up of the Central Command (the Cardassian military), and the Obsidian Order (Cardassian intelligence), both of which report to the civilian-controlled Detapa Council. How much actual power this civilian council has is debatable, as the Cardassian Union remains an overtly military force. Intelligence reports suggest that the Detapa Council is little more than a figurehead, though there have been rumors that an underground dissident movement on Cardassia is making connections with the Detapa Council. Should they ally, it is possible they could exert enough political and physical force to wrest control from the military.

Until that happens, however, it's the Cardassian military and intelligence operatives we're up against, and individually and together, they pose a significant threat. Cardassian *Galor* class warships, while not a one-to-one match to, say, a *Galaxy*-class starship, carry comparable tactical systems to most of our current ships of the line and are not to be taken lightly. Analysis of recent Cardassian tactical procedures suggest they use a pack formation approach to combat, meaning that any apparent deficiency in one ship's capabilities is minimized by their ability to multiply the threat. Starfleet has too few *Galaxy*-class ships in service as it is, and until more modern Starfleet vessels come off the assembly lines, every captain will have to be careful in any engagement or standoff with Cardassian forces.

As for the Obsidian Order, they are perhaps the most ruthless and efficient intelligence agency in the quadrant, rivaling even the Romulan Tal Shiar in their capability for subterfuge and silent mayhem. It is said that the Obsidian Order has eyes and ears in every Cardassian home, and that even the Cardassian military and leadership are not beyond their reach. Reports indicate that the Obsidian Order is prohibited from owning military hardware and ships, though Starfleet Intelligence is skeptical that such a mandate can be enforced given that the Obsidian Order's stock in trade is finding and keeping secrets. I would not be surprised if there was a stash of Obsidian Order vessels quietly at work out there somewhere.

I cannot stress enough the danger capture by the Cardassians poses. Many of our officers and civilians have been apprehended, detained, and tortured by Cardassian military officers and Obsidian Order operatives, and the techniques they use are horrific, to say the least. They are brutal and cunning in their efforts to extract information from prisoners, every bit as sinister as the Tal Shiar. I would encourage you to offer additional combat training exercises and psychological strengthening regimes to your senior staff and those officers likely to join away teams for any Cardassian-related mission.

Now, all that being said, there is some hope for optimism when it comes to the Cardassians. With the treaty finally signed and the Jankata Accord in place, the Federation and Cardassian Union are formally at peace, despite the ongoing tensions on both sides, particularly those revolving around the Demilitarized Zone. The lines of communication between the Cardassian and Federation science communities are open and operating, and the back-and-forth sharing of data has been encouraging. There is even a preliminary plan on the table for a joint Federation-Cardassian mission to deploy a subspace relay in the Gamma Quadrant. Should the complex details of that mission work out, expect the Federation to take advantage of that foot in the door and begin sending vessels like your own into the Gamma Quadrant to explore and, naturally, to keep an eye on our new neighbors, the Dominion. We will discuss the Dominion in more detail shortly.

MAQUIS AND THE CARDASSIAN DMZ

Though the war with the Federation is over, in order to negotiate the peace treaty, an area of Federation space was surrendered to Cardassian control. Many colonists on the Federation worlds now within the new Demilitarized Zone have resisted the shift to coming under Cardassian rule. These resistance cells, calling themselves the Maquis, have engaged in open terror attacks against the Cardassians, both military and civilian, and are even striking against Federation forces who attempt to maintain the peace. To

OBSIDIAN ORDER REPORT 78871

After the attack on Gul Evek's ship, the *Vetar*, it has come to my attention that many high-ranking Starfleet officers have resigned their posts in order to join the terrorists known as the Maquis. This group of miscreants is responsible for a number of attacks within the Demilitarized Zone. For the record, I would like to voice my concern that having former Starfleet officers, as well-trained as they are, in such close proximity to the Cardassian border puts many of our classified projects in jeopardy.

My recommendation is that our fleet construction in the Omekla system be relocated further within Cardassian space and away from Maquis spies. Of course, false intelligence should continue to be employed to lure any potential Maquis attack to Omekla's shipyards, without jeopardizing the assembly of the fleet for our planned assault on the Founders.

For our sons
– Glinn Sutotk

make matters worse, some Starfleet officers have resigned their commissions or outright abandoned their posts to throw in support to the Maquis; actions which have had severe repercussions in the area and threaten to shatter our nascent treaty with the Cardassians. Needless to say, should you encounter one of these traitors, apprehend them.

In many cases, these Starfleet personnel have taken Federation supplies and weaponry with them and have used that material to further the Maquis efforts. Naturally, this is in opposition to all we hold dear, so should you come across any stolen Federation or Starfleet materiel, recover or destroy it so that it cannot be used against our Cardassian neighbors or fellow Federation members.

It hasn't been announced fleet-wide yet, but the U.S.S. Voyager, under her new captain, Kathryn Janeway, will be heading to Maquis-controlled territory just as soon as the ship is launched from dry dock. I'm not privy to her mission, but given that the new Intrepid-class starships are loaded with the latest sensor systems, I suspect she may be tasked with mapping the gravitational anomalies and plasma storms within the Badlands. Detailed charts would make it easier for our ships to maneuver within that miasma, which could prove useful should the political conditions in the area continue to deteriorate.

BREEN CONFEDERACY

While they have not been designated as a threat, the Breen Confederacy is one of a handful of species that has earned a place on the Security Council's 'must watch' list. While the Federation has had little direct contact with the Breen, our nominal allies, the Klingons, apparently have a long and bloody history with them. The Klingons have been reluctant to share information with us, however; a fact not lost on the diplomatic corps. If I had to guess, I'd say the Klingons are embarrassed about their losses in conflict with the Breen, and the less said about that, the better.

Starfleet Intelligence suspects that the Cardassians maintain an open line of communication with the Breen, and it is believed that the Breen and the Ferengi may have informal trade agreements in place. The Romulans also appear to have a history with the Breen; though, as with the Klingons, we have been unable to gather much in the way of confirmed details regarding relations between the two species.

Our technological evaluation of the Breen is woefully incomplete, but what little we know is that they are a species at or near our own level of capabilities. Starfleet has assets in and near Breen space working to gather intelligence, but, as yet, no clear picture has emerged of the Breen as a people or as a potential threat. We do have confirmed reports of Breen privateers attacking various colonies and transport ships. The information we have is anecdotal, but it's suggested that the Breen possess fast, agile fighters that they use to conduct hit-and-run attacks.

FERENGI ALLIANCE

In the 2360s, our initial interactions with the Ferengi were largely hostile in nature, mostly due to a mutual misunderstanding of each other's species. Since then, the Ferengi have consistently pushed a neutral position in most matters. However, their main focus is the pursuit of wealth, and it is clear that they will work for either or both sides of a conflict if there is gold-pressed latinum to be gained.

Their technology and scientific knowledge is roughly analogous to our own, though as I said before, they are far more focused on the pursuit of wealth than in military conquest or combat. That being said, the Ferengi are fierce negotiators and have dealings with arms traders and merchants throughout the quadrant. I think it is fair to say that if you follow the money from most any military conflict of late, you will probably find a Ferengi holding one end of the purse strings.

Of notable interest to Starfleet Intelligence is the fact that there is a Ferengi presence on Deep Space 9, which puts the Alliance and their insatiable need for the next deal within easy reach of the Gamma Quadrant. Some species that have come through the wormhole have interacted with the Ferengi on the station, and it is possible that the Ferengi are making financial inroads with members of the Dominion. That, coupled with rumors of the Ferengi having trade connections with the Breen, the Cardassians, and the Orion Syndicate, suggests that while they may be presenting an official neutral stance in galactic politics, they're almost certainly working behind the scenes and are more involved than one would normally expect of a truly neutral party.

The Alliance is headed by the Grand Nagus, Zek, who is the political and economic leader of the species. All reports indicate that Zek is both clever and shrewd, even more so than others of his species, which, frankly, is saying a lot. He has been spotted on Deep Space 9 on at least one occasion, lending strength to the rumor that the Ferengi are actively seeking to spread their mercantile grasp into the Gamma Quadrant.

Ultimately, while the Ferengi are not an immediate threat to the Federation, it is advised to keep them at arm's length. Even though Starfleet uniforms don't have pockets, somehow you may find yourself missing something of value after an encounter with them.

MIRADORN

While the Miradorn and their unusual twin-oriented society are generally considered a second-tier species, their technological capabilities and political holdings are sufficient to be influential within the Alpha Quadrant balance of power should they be pushed to pick one side or another. Their Theta class starships are reasonably powerful, able to stand up to many Starfleet and Klingon vessels. Their relatively simple control systems and standard array of starship systems make them popular purchases among independent merchants, and you will find modified versions of the vessel in more than one mercenary fleet.

NYBERRITE ALLIANCE

One of the species the Federation currently enjoys cordial relations with in the Alpha Quadrant is the Nyberrite Alliance. It does not hurt matters that the Klingons also have good connections with them. Nyberrite warships are said to be the equivalent of any Starfleet vessel, and the crews of Nyberrite vessels are often supplemented by officers and crew from other species and political bodies. So far, no Starfleet officers or known Federation citizens have served aboard a Nyberrite vessel, though this may change in the future as our relationship with the Alliance continues forward.

ORION SYNDICATE

Similar in some respects to the Ferengi but far more sinister, the Orion Syndicate has been a fixture of the Alpha and Beta Quadrants since at least the 22nd century. The Syndicate originally held territory near the Klingon Empire in the Beta Quadrant and has had dealings with the Klingons almost continuously for over two centuries. The Syndicate has expanded its reach over the course of those decades, and its criminal activities now stretch into the Alpha Quadrant, touching on Cardassian and Federation space.

The Syndicate is perhaps the premier known criminal organization in the Alpha Quadrant, responsible for countless acts of assassination, extortion, piracy, and racketeering. They operate, either covertly or openly, dozens of gambling halls and slave markets. While most of their crimes are heinous, it is the last that is of the greatest concern to the Federation. The Federation has issued dozens of sanctions against the Syndicate in the last several decades, though the enforcement of those sanctions has been inconsistent from administration to administration.

There have been attempts by Starfleet Intelligence to infiltrate the Syndicate, but every attempt has ended in failure, with the Starfleet operative exposed and eliminated. The Syndicate is very careful who it lets into their confidences, and their membership process is both expensive and time-consuming and not without risk. As yet, Starfleet has been unable to plant a reliable agent into the Syndicate.

It is believed that the Syndicate wields significant power within Orion society and politics, though this has been hard to confirm as officials and civilians both are reluctant to speak out against the Syndicate out of fear of reprisal. The Orion military is modest at best, and they possess little in the way of warships. However, the power and influence they possess is easily worth the power of a dozen warships.

Despite the apparent stranglehold the Syndicate holds over Orion society, there is a small independent group of Orions, called the Free Traders, who conduct intergalactic trade on the open market with the Ferengi and other spacefaring races. Some suspect that the Syndicate created the Free Traders as a front to deflect suspicion, though others believe that they are what they appear to be — independent traders free from their kin's corruption. While the Orion Free Traders have made some useful contacts within the Federation, most representative worlds are hesitant to do business with them because of their suspected ties to the Syndicate. It remains to be seen if the Free Traders can operate effectively and independently of the Syndicate and avoid being absorbed or eradicated by their blood kin.

TALARIANS

The Talarians and Federation currently enjoy a neutral stance, though no formal treaty or agreement is in place. Past skirmishes between our two peoples have largely been forgiven. While they are a warp-capable species, the Talarians currently possess somewhat inferior technology and weaponry in comparison to the Federation's top-tier starships, though they may pose a threat to our smaller

EXCERPT FROM A CLASSIFIED STARFLEET INTELLIGENCE REPORT

…should remain under surveillance. After studying the data on the recent Dominion attack, I think it would be prudent to place one or more assets within Talarian society, specifically a male operative as the Talarians have a strictly patriarchal society and any female operative trying to gather intel would be looked upon with deep suspicion. The goal of any such operative would be to study Talarian military tactics, specifically their guerrilla hit-and-run forays and 'possum' style subterfuges, to determine if Starfleet could adapt any of these tactics for use against the Dominion's Jem'Hadar fighters.

If handled properly, we might not even have to bother with planting an operative — some Talarian captains have proven to be open to cooperation with Starfleet, under the right circumstances and for the right price.

STARFLEET
INTELLIGENCE
OPERATIVE
J-47 ALPHA

scout ships and cruisers. However, the Talarians do employ unconventional tactics such as self-destruct devices used on transports designed to lure in unsuspecting starfarers and liberal use of subspace proximity detonators, so do not dismiss them out of hand.

THOLIANS

The Tholians are a powerful Alpha Quadrant species that are, thankfully, xenophobic through and through. While the Federation and the Tholians have been at conflict in the past, even as recently as the 2350s, we currently enjoy a neutral stance with them. They have also had messy skirmishes with the Klingons that tended to balloon into multi-species conflicts. Recent reports suggest that the Tholian Assembly may soon send an ambassador to reside on Deep Space 9, though it is believed that such an ambassador would be there more to monitor any traffic from the Gamma Quadrant and not to foster better Federation-Tholian relations. Tholian technology is similar to our own, and their unique tractor field energy nets have proven to be the downfall of more than one adversary starship.

TZENKETHI COALITION

The Tzenkethi are one of many species the Federation has had conflict with in the past. Our war with them ended several years ago. Since then, the Tzenkethi have largely been quiet, operating in their space and leaving us to operate in ours. We have a few listening posts in place to monitor their actions, but, for the most part, they seem to want nothing to do with us. A few scientific surveys and mapping missions are planned near the border of Tzenkethi space, so if you are assigned to such a mission, keep your eyes open for anything that might be of interest.

THE BETA QUADRANT

Adjacent to the Alpha and Delta Quadrants, the Beta Quadrant is home to both the Klingon and Romulan Empires, and many Federation worlds, outposts, and protectorates. Even now, much of the Beta Quadrant remains unknown territory, and Starfleet's mandate to explore is naturally oriented, by and large, further into the Beta Quadrant.

Should you and your ship be assigned to a mission in the Beta Quadrant, it is highly likely you will encounter the Klingons and Romulans at some point, so this is a good opportunity for us to briefly detail those two empires, their peoples, and their technological and threat assessments. I will also briefly discuss another species located in the Beta Quadrant, the Gorn Hegemony.

KLINGON EMPIRE

Our alliance with the Klingon Empire has never been what you might call stable. Certainly, there have been moments of very high highs, but plenty of despair and bloodshed as

To all my loyal sub-administrators and associates: We have enjoyed a few years of quiet, profitable growth within the Shackleton Expanse, unfettered by interference from any major political or military body. Save for a few isolated incidents along the border and in the shallow regions of the Expanse, we have been free to build a power base in this little-explored sector of the Beta Quadrant.

I write to you today to warn you that our 'free ride' is nearing an end. This is not cause for sorrow or despair; rather, it is an opportunity for us to flex our newfound muscles. Highly reliable intelligence reports have come to me indicating that the United Federation of Planets and the Klingon Empire have banded together to begin delving deeper into the Expanse, ostensibly to further their respective borders, planetary claims, and resource hoarding. I suspect there is a deeper cause to their expansion into our region, and I suspect it has something to do with the sudden appearance of the so-called Dominion lurking on the other side of the Bajoran wormhole. The Federation and their Klingon lapdogs are likely rushing to find planets they can either strip down for resources or planets they can hide on.

But as they dig deeper into the Shackleton Expanse, they will find us and our blades in the night. Make no mistake — we will not suffer the Federation or the Klingons to challenge us over the claims we have made here. We already have assets in place throughout the Expanse and aboard their Starbase 364, so-called "Narendra Station." Our operatives will continue to work to subvert the alliance between the Federation and the Klingons, and will strive to totter the tenuous balance between the two species aboard the station.

Be aware that the Federation has formally assigned three ships to their starbase, and these three ships, individually and collectively, pose a significant threat to our continued efforts. The *U.S.S. Venture*, *U.S.S. Bellerophon*, and the *U.S.S. Thunderchild* will become our new neighbors in the Expanse, and it is likely that they will be joined by a like number of Klingon vessels in due course. We will need to step up our efforts to acquire more powerful warships and the tested and talented crews to man them.

In closing, I encourage you to continue your initiatives in the name of the Syndicate, and be prepared to step up efforts across the board. While we have enjoyed the freedom to do as we please until now within the Expanse, we are now in a position of power and I am hereby authorizing you all, sub-administrators and associates alike, to flex that power when you see fit.

For the Syndicate.

Administrator Chellix,
Primary Overseer of Syndicate Operations,
Shackleton Expanse

---

well. The recent Klingon Civil War, sparked by the Romulans taking advantage of circumstances revolving around a weakened Klingon High Council, nearly ended in a sudden swing of power in the Beta Quadrant. Had the Romulans and the traitorous Klingon house of Duras succeeded in taking control of the Klingon Empire and its military, the Federation would have suddenly found themselves without a powerful ally and with two powerful adversaries. Fortunately, efforts to block this coup were successful and we managed to maintain the integrity of our alliance with the Klingons.

However, old wounds take the longest to heal, and some wounds simply fester and never recover. Chancellor Gowron might be in command now, with the clone of Kahless the Unforgettable as a figurehead emperor, but intelligence reports indicate that there are still Duras supporters — including his two sisters, Lursa and B'Etor, and his son, Toral — at large throughout the Empire and other dissidents within the Klingon High Council. It's suspected that one strong spark, set off at the right place at the right time, could easily ignite another civil war. A second such internal conflict might well doom the alliance we now enjoy with the Klingons.

The loss of the alliance would almost certainly mean conflict, and the Federation is currently ill-prepared for a stand-up fight with the Klingons. The scientific and technological sharing our two species have enjoyed over the last few decades have left our respective fleets fairly well matched, assuming you do not take their cloaking technologies into account. The Federation, as a general rule, does not use the devices, though the Klingons have no hesitation to do so. Intelligence projections suggest that a protracted Klingon-Federation conflict would result in significant losses of life and matériel on both sides, which would leave both the Federation and Klingons wide open for attack by another species. The last thing we want to do is get into a fight with the Klingons with the Dominion now knocking on the door and the Romulans ever lurking in the background.

But, worst-case scenarios aside, the Klingons are currently our allies, and staunch allies they can be. They have been willing to come to Starfleet's aid on more than one occasion, and we to theirs. The Officer Exchange Program between Starfleet and the Klingon Defense Force continues, though perhaps not quite at the same level as it enjoyed in the 2360s. You may experience the joys of having a Klingon officer serving aboard your starship for a time. Should that happen, you are, of course, encouraged to extend to them every courtesy owed a trusted ally. We also have a strong partnership with the Klingons in the Shackleton Expanse, a little-explored sector of the Galaxy that Starfleet has just recently started to explore in earnest. We will be working with our Klingon allies in the coming months to establish joint ventures into the Expanse.

As for Imperial Intelligence, the espionage arm of the Klingon Empire, surprisingly little is known. Long considered to be an also-ran when compared to such elite organizations as the Tal Shiar, the Obsidian Order, and Starfleet Intelligence, Klingon Intelligence might either be the most efficient intelligence agency, since so little is known about them, or the worst, since there seems to be little notoriety around the organization. Perhaps it is because the Klingons, by and large, are direct with most of their dealings — they may not find working in the shadows to be honorable. Still, it is worth remaining vigilant for signs of Klingons lurking where they are not supposed to.

Klingon relations with other species in the Alpha Quadrant bears mentioning. The Klingons, by their nature a warrior race, have had skirmishes or outright wars with many of the species in the Alpha and Beta Quadrants, and perhaps more than we know given that they're rather close-mouthed about parts of their history. They have had significant dealings with the Breen, have little love for the Ferengi, and look with hunger upon many Cardassian outposts and planets within easy reach. Without the Federation-Klingon treaty in place, a more hawkish Klingon Chancellor and High Council might push for greater imperial expansion, but, Starfleet Intelligence believes that such a scenario is unlikely for as long as Gowron remains Chancellor.

Almost immediately following the discovery of the stable wormhole near Bajor, the Klingons were quick to send survey teams and transport ships into the wormhole to begin their own studies of the Gamma Quadrant. One ship, the *I.K.S. Toh'Kaht*, explored the Gamma Quadrant and then returned to the Alpha Quadrant, only to explode due to sabotage. This has not deterred the Klingons from continuing to push more ships through the wormhole. In public, the Klingons state they are working to explore the Gamma Quadrant much as the Federation desires to do, though it is believed by some that the Klingons have their own agenda for the Gamma Quadrant and might be slipping something past the Federation and Bajorans, right under our collective nose.

With the growing importance of Deep Space 9 to Alpha Quadrant politics, the diplomatic machine has been at work trying to stymie the Empire's request to place a Klingon presence aboard Deep Space 9. As yet, nothing has come of the request, but it's possible that, in the interest of fostering stronger relations between our two peoples, we'll have to assign one or more Klingons to the station.

ROMULAN STAR EMPIRE

Perhaps the most significant adversary the Federation faces today is the Romulan Star Empire. Our two peoples have long been in conflict, either in direct combat or via a drawn-out 'cold war'. While there was a period of time when the Romulans stayed silent on their side of the Neutral Zone, early in the 2360s they decided to remind of us of their presence and have since been a consistent threat to the Federation and to the balance of power across the Alpha and Beta Quadrants.

The Romulans share borders with the Federation and Klingons, and are not all that far from the Cardassians and a number of other less powerful species and political bodies. It is likely that this is one reason their intelligence arm, the Tal Shiar, is so experienced and effective — they have no shortage of foes to infiltrate and spy upon. The Tal Shiar is perhaps the preeminent intelligence force in the Beta Quadrant, and is a powerful military force in its own right.

TAL SHIAR INTERNAL COMMUNIQUE

My esteemed Vice-Chairman Vreenak:

I write to you today with grave misgivings in my heart and the greatest concern for our glorious Empire. My contacts within the Senate's intern echelon have reported that a highly secret request from the Federation for the loan of one of our cloaking devices has not only been considered, but approved! I cannot sit by idly with this information and let it go unchallenged.

My understanding is that our current stance is to monitor the situation between the Federation and the new Dominion threat. I do not believe it is our place to lend any assistance to the Federation — let this be their battle to fight. We can watch and wait and let these two species battle each other and benefit from the wreckage later. Giving one of our long-time enemies one of our most precious of technological devices is a betrayal of all the sacrifices our Romulan brothers and sisters in arms have made over the past century and more. Why would the Senate even consider such a proposal?

I am confident that you, in your position as Vice-Chairman of the Tal Shiar and as the seat-holder in several influential committees, will vigorously challenge this situation and encourage the Senate to overturn their hasty and ill-advised decision. My loyal operatives and I stand ready to support you at a moment's notice.

Jolan tru, Chairman.
Commander Sela

The Romulan military is a potent enough threat, but the Tal Shiar has warships of its own and puts them to sudden, effective use when the need arises for a decisive blow.

Romulan foreign policy has been largely consistent for as long as the Federation has known them: they are devoted to ruining foreign alliances from within, and what they cannot break by subterfuge, they shatter by swift military action. Their cloaking technologies are powerful, though not infallible, and have been used effectively against the Federation and Klingon militaries for decades. Their weapons, defensive screens, and engines are all on a power level comparable to our own, so rest assured that any fight with a Romulan cruiser will be, barring a surprise, a closely-matched effort.

The Romulans have never been comfortable with positive Federation-Klingon relations and have, on more than one occasion, tried to directly or indirectly drive a wedge into the alliance. Their most recent effort, backing the House of Duras and sparking the Klingon Civil War, was nearly successful. While they were defeated, Intelligence is confident that they remain undeterred, and are almost certainly working on the next scheme to destabilize the Federation-Klingon alliance. It's too early to say what the Romulans feel about the sudden appearance of the Dominion, and you can be sure that our Intelligence assets will be keeping a close eye on any Romulan response to Dominion actions, should they arise.

Despite the history of animosity between the Romulans and Federation, there have been, over the last several years, several events that have given cause for hope of a better relationship on the horizon. The *U.S.S. Enterprise-D*, under the command of Captain Jean-Luc Picard, has had a number of encounters with Romulans along the Neutral Zone. While some of these encounters have ended in either a stalemate or a tactical loss, some have resulted in what might be considered the seeds of hope — notably, Picard's involvement with Ambassador Spock and Spock's efforts toward a movement intended to reunite the Vulcan and Romulan peoples. While the mainline Romulan Senate publicly denounces the movement and actively hunts down any members of the underground, Starfleet Intelligence suggests there is quiet support within the Senate to suspect that reunification is a possibility, albeit a long-term one. Spock, in his infinite wisdom, is playing the long game there and it remains to be seen what could come of it. Reunification of the Vulcan and Romulan peoples would certainly affect the balance of power in the Alpha and Beta Quadrants. Starfleet Intelligence is working to determine which other spacefaring species might react negatively to such an event and whether any would attempt to sabotage such a movement. As with all things involving Romulans, this is a waiting game and requires patience and vigilance.

GORN HEGEMONY

While they mostly keep to their own space, Gorn starships ply trading routes throughout the Alpha and Beta Quadrants. They are known to have connections with the Orion Syndicate and the Ferengi Alliance. Other than an encounter with Captain James T. Kirk and some other isolated incidents, Starfleet and the Gorn have had few dealings. We know their technological capabilities are similar to our own, though the Hegemony is dwarfed by the size of the Federation. Still, Intelligence believes that the Gorn could be a useful ally, or, if pressed, a devilish foe.

OTHER THREATS TO THE FEDERATION

There are dangers to the well-being of the Federation even beyond the Alpha and Beta Quadrants. We will discuss some of the more powerful and dangerous of them now.

THE BORG

Perhaps the most powerful and fearsome foe the Federation and Starfleet has ever faced, the Borg have been silent for nearly a year. Their last foray into Federation space was just over a year ago, when Borg led by the Soong-type android, Lore, invaded Federation space but were foiled by the heroic actions of the crew of the *Enterprise-D*.

The Federation has commissioned a new series of deep space probes and listening posts specifically dedicated to monitoring any possible new Borg incursion. We've tended to be a step behind the Borg in most instances, so it is hoped that these probes and posts will serve as an early warning system to give us a fighting chance the next time the Borg invade our space.

And make no mistake, Captain: the Borg will be back. The intelligence communities of the Federation, Romulans, Klingons, and Cardassians agree (shockingly enough) that, now that the Borg know where we are and what we have to offer, they will not hesitate to come back and attempt the final assimilation of all species within the Alpha and Beta Quadrants. While the Federation has been the hardest hit during the previous Borg attacks, both the Klingons and Romulans have admitted to losses at the hands of the Borg, and there have been reports of independent peoples also suffering under the Borg.

If there is one positive note to come from the past Borg attacks, it is that they have forced Starfleet engineers and scientists to get more creative with starship design. There are several new classes of Federation starship on the boards, in the docks, or just now entering service, including the *Akira*, *Intrepid*, *Norway*, *Saber*, *Sovereign*, and *Steamrunner* classes. Perhaps you will be assigned to one of them soon. All these ships were developed following the first Borg invasion and battle at Wolf 359 and carry technological advances sparked in large part by the Borg threat. Hopefully, Starfleet can get enough of these new ships built, manned, and entered into service before the Borg return.

THE DOMINION

The discovery of the stable wormhole near Bajor was a scientific landmark, certainly, but it also serves as a gateway to a whole sector's worth of challenges and threats. While Starfleet Intelligence is still analyzing data secured by the Starfleet crew aboard Deep Space 9 and from other sources, it seems clear that the Gamma Quadrant's Dominion, an organized body of unknown size and strength, may be a clear and present danger to the Federation and other civilizations here in the Alpha and Beta Quadrants.

Our diplomatic corps has been working overtime trying to soothe concerns from some members of the Federation and from unaligned worlds, including Bajor. The Dominion's destruction of the New Bajor colony in the Gamma Quadrant might be considered by some an act of war, but it seems like our diplomats are spinning it as the Dominion protesting an Alpha Quadrant incursion into their territory. No one is sure how it will shake out, but be prepared to answer some hard questions if you find yourself in a discussion about the Dominion and their possible next actions.

Starfleet is woefully short on reliable intelligence on the Dominion and their inner structure, but what we do know is that they are apparently an organization of hundreds of worlds, led by a group called the Founders. For as little as we know about the Dominion, we know even less about the Founders. The Vorta are one of the species within the Dominion, and they appear to be leaders and diplomats. Many of them command squads of Dominion shock troops, called the Jem'Hadar. They are a fierce warrior people, battle-hungry and fearsome in combat. The Klingons regard them as a worthy adversary, though I'm not sure that has done much to put anyone's concerns at ease.

We know that the Dominion collects worlds through a mix of diplomacy, threat, and, in some cases, outright invasion. We have heard rumors that they are willing to wipe out entire populations in order to set an example for other species. It seems that when diplomacy fails, they send in the Jem'Hadar to soften up or eradicate the population of a planet or colony. There are even unsubstantiated rumors suggesting that Dominion science exceeds our own, and that they have the capability to manufacture lethal viruses. The sources of these rumors are unreliable, but Starfleet Command is taking them as seriously as any other rumor regarding the Dominion. Deep Space 9 Chief Medical Officer, Lieutenant Julian Bashir, recently had a Jem'Hadar soldier aboard the station and was able to see it grow from child to maturity. The data he collected was forwarded to several Starfleet divisions and is being examined closely for any useful leads or insights.

In addition, Starfleet Intelligence and the Corps of Engineers are working hard to study all the tactical and technical information they can obtain regarding recent Dominion incursions into the Alpha Quadrant, as well as the battle that resulted in the loss of the *Galaxy*-class *U.S.S. Odyssey* and most of her crew. That a small unit of Dominion attack ships managed to destroy one of the most powerful starships in our fleet has set off alarms through all levels of Starfleet and the Federation. If a few small ships can take out one of our best, we can only imagine what kind of damage one of their battleships, if they exist, could inflict.

The Security Council of the Federation has convened several special sessions to discuss the 'Dominion problem' but, as yet, no formal response has surfaced. We will hear more about the Dominion threat and how we intend to check it in the coming months. Starfleet engineers are already studying the Jem'Hadar phased polaron weapons and figuring out how to adjust Federation shielding technologies to compensate. Further, one of our prototype 'Borg-buster' warships, the *U.S.S. Defiant*, was pulled out of storage, rotated into service, and assigned to Deep Space 9. Its presence on the doorstep of the Gamma Quadrant is meant to send the message that we are not going to take a Dominion threat lightly.

In the meantime, should your missions send you to Bajor Sector or to the Gamma Quadrant, make sure you and your crew are prepared to face unconventional Dominion tactics. A detailed security summary will be made available to you and your senior staff, as well as detailed medical information on the Jem'Hadar once Dr. Bashir's reports are fully analyzed. In addition, an Intelligence briefing will be distributed to you detailing the dangers of a projected Dominion incursion should the Dominion seek a foothold within the Alpha Quadrant. Such a shift of power could threaten the existence of the Federation itself and should be countered if possible.

THE TERRAN EMPIRE
It is not enough that we have plenty of challenges to face within our own universe and reality; but there is at least one alternate universe that we have to contend with, and that is what Starfleet Intelligence still refers to as the 'Terran Empire parallel.' This parallel universe was first encountered by Captain Kirk and his crew in 2267, and while we had thought it would be an isolated incident, recent events on Deep Space 9 confirmed that this parallel universe is still an active concern and poses a threat to the Federation.

By the present day in this parallel universe, the Klingons and Cardassians allied to overthrow the Terran Empire and include the Bajorans as major allies. Humans have been enslaved, though there is a Terran resistance at work that has the technological ability to 'cross over' into our universe and interact with us. Reports suggest that this ability is limited at the moment, though if it can be done once, they will figure out how to do it again and again. We must remain vigilant for apparent doppelgangers and for individuals acting out of character. We cannot afford to accidentally contaminate that universe's timeline any more than we already have, and we need to ensure the safety of our own reality from any possible contamination from their side of the looking glass.

Reports indicate this parallel universe has been in a perpetual state of conflict, and the last thing the Federation needs right now is yet another conflict on another front. If you or your crew are exposed to operatives or technology from this parallel universe, use any means necessary to limit your exposure and contain the threat.

THE Q
One species that the Federation Security Council has marked as a threat is the collective species known as the Q. They are an omnipotent species of beings, residing in an alternate dimension they call the 'Q continuum.' Most of our interaction with the Q has been through one individual of their species who took a strange and special interest in Captain Jean-Luc Picard. Starfleet Intelligence hopes he remains the only curious member of the species, as even that one individual exhibited so many powerful abilities that the Federation would simply be unable to compete.

OTHER STRANGE AND WONDROUS THREATS
As if what we have already talked about was not challenging enough, I have to emphasize that space, for all its apparent emptiness, is rather full. Alien probes, spatial anomalies, time distortion fields, ancient and powerful civilizations lost to time, energy matrices, omnipotent and omniscient beings of all kinds, gateways to alternate dimensions and realities, stable and unstable wormholes to different quadrants and even other galaxies, and more unexplained phenomena than can be properly described or explained, await you out there. Countless vessels from many species have encountered these threats, and many have been lost for all time to the mysteries of space. Exploration is a mission for the bold, the fearless, and the curious, and in this, Starfleet will always lead the way.

INTO THE UNKNOWN...
As mentioned before, the bulk of the Galaxy has yet to be explored. Even close to home, in the Alpha and Beta Quadrants, there are huge swaths of uncharted territory and spatial anomalies and features yet to be catalogued and investigated. Every sector could contain unimagined resources and discoveries, or a sinister alien species that would love nothing more than to destroy the Federation and our way of life. Despite the challenges the Federation faces from the Dominion, the Borg, Cardassians, Romulans, and so many others, we will always explore; we will always continue to seek; and we will always boldly go forward. Good luck, Captain. Fair winds and following seas to you and your crew.

ACCESS GRANTED
LOGIN: 4-7-ALPHA-TANGO

72180	72372	6974	69784	86850
27240	28220	69683	79785	47444
28378	28474	93659	89684	86
92765	38373	90274	79583	48463
7446	38374	85739	78463	9884
97821	20573	798	37454	584T3
55638	66942	6878	77453	37563

LET ME HELP

March 5, 1930

Dear diary,
My life has become positively filled with interesting people the last few weeks. The most recent, I think I've told you already, was a man named Leonard McCoy. He doesn't seem the type we usually see here, but he did stumble into the mission half dead. I suspected then that he'd gotten hold of some bad bathtub gin, but some of the things he's said are making me reconsider.

He talks like the young man I've been seeing, James — no, Jim, he asked me to call him Jim. I must confess, Jim is a mystery to me. He's not like so many of the others at the mission. When I talk about peace and a future without war or hatred, he doesn't roll his eyes. He nods, like he believes in it, too. He seems to see the future more clearly than I do. I think that's what drew me to him in the first place.

He and his friend, Mr. Spock, are clearly in some sort of trouble, though he doesn't want to talk about what it might be. I asked him to let me help the two of them, and he chuckled. He told me that someone a hundred years from now would recommend 'Let me help' over 'I love you,' and I can see how that might be true. I still like the latter more than I do the former, I think, though I believe they're both different ways of saying the same thing.

There was something in the way he looked into my eyes as we were talking about this that has me believing he feels the same way. He's taking me to the picture show tonight (though if I'm honest we're going Dutch treat because neither of us has very much money to spend). But I said his three words, and it made him smile. It might be forward of me, but after the picture show, I think I'll say my three words. One of us has to say them first, after all.

Until then, dear diary!

ARCHIVED DIARY ENTRY

SUBJECT: LATE-TWENTIETH CENTURY EARTH HISTORY LESSON 26

STARFLEET ACADEMY, PROFESSOR WEBB

"The Eugenics Wars represents a dark spot in the history of Earth. Also called the Great Wars, it was fought between 1992 and 1996. Just prior to that, there was an effort to improve Humans through genetic manipulation and selective breeding. This resulted in individuals who were capable of feats of great strength and intellect. While our records are sketchy regarding this period, we know that it took only a few to take control of several countries and nations. They claim to have offered the world order, but as history has shown in the past, such claims are usually met with opposition as people revolted. Most of the augmented individuals were killed. We know some fell from internal faction conflicts while others were killed in the wars by normal Humans resisting their rule.

"Khan Noonien Singh was a force of nature. By 1992 he literally ruled one quarter of the planet. He was able to do what few Augments could and attract other Augments to follow him in an almost religious fervor. They trusted him and willingly followed him without hesitation. His second-in-command, a man named Joachim, chronicled his rise to power and how he tried to be a benevolent ruler at first. According to Joachim, he was concerned for his people's well-being and saw to it that everyone under his rule was fed and received medical care. Ultimately however, the people revolted as they did not like giving up so many rights and Khan was forced to put down their insurgency.

"It was during the end of the Eugenics Wars that we know he commandeered a sleeper vessel named *S.S. Botany Bay* and blasted off from Earth. Eighty-four of his followers joined him in the hopes of finding a planet more fitting to their style of rule. It is pure speculation what might have happened had the *Enterprise* not encountered the *Botany Bay* in 2267 after drifting for over two centuries."

"It is a testament to Khan and his Augment followers that, through their genetic engineering and intellect, they were able to survive on Ceti Alpha V after its orbit was drastically changed upon the destruction of Ceti Alpha VI. The crew of the *U.S.S. Reliant* discovered the remains of the *Botany Bay* and encountered Khan on stardate 8130. Khan and his followers easily took over the Reliant, marooned the crew, stole secretive scientific research at Regula One, and murdered the scientific staff there. If not for the efforts of the *U.S.S. Enterprise* again, we can only speculate what Khan's motives and intentions would have been."

STARFLEET ACADEMY LECTURE

ARES IV COMMANDER LOST, PRESUMED DEAD AFTER FREAK ACCIDENT

NOVEMBER 5, 2032
ERIC CONE, SPACE/AVIATION CORRESPONDENT,
CYGNUS MEDIA WORLDWIDE

Kennedy Space Center, FI – NASA officials have confirmed that Lieutenant John Kelly, leader of the Ares IV expedition currently underway on Mars, was lost and is believed to have been killed in an accident involving the ship's command module in orbit over the red planet. The incident occurred at approximately 4:52pm Eastern Standard Time today, and is believed to have involved some form of spatial anomaly which came into contact with the Ares IV command module. Transcripts of communications between Kelly and his two fellow astronauts on the Martian surface indicate that he attempted without success to maneuver the ship out of danger after detecting the anomaly's approach. Satellites orbiting Mars were unable to confirm whether the ship was destroyed or somehow caught or swept away by the mysterious and still unidentified object.

"We've only just begun our investigation," said NASA Director Amy Sisson, speaking earlier this evening to a pool of journalists at a special press conference. "We'll continue to do everything we can, until we have all the answers as to what happened to Lieutenant Kelly."

Of equal importance, Sisson reminded reporters, was the rescue of astronauts Rose Kumagawa and Andrei Novakovich. Currently stranded at the Ares IV mission site, they now await the arrival of the spacecraft Theseus, which is scheduled to be in orbit over Mars in five days. Their rescue will leave many troubling questions unanswered.

For now, the world mourns the tragic loss of yet another astronaut and hero, Lieutenant John Kelly.

ARCHIVED NEWS REPORT

SOLKAR, CAPTAIN OF THE T'PLANA-HATH

"The detection of the warp signature in the Sol system was unexpected. We were in the outer edges of the system, placing a subspace surveillance array to observe Andorian fleet movements, as ordered. With the revelation that Earth had achieved warp travel, the logical decision was obvious: First Contact, as a means of ensuring that the Humans, and their solar system, more firmly lay within the Vulcan sphere of influence, rather than risking any potential future alliance between the Humans and the Andorians, which could lead to a strategic imbalance.

The discovery that Earth had no central planetary authority complicated matters, to be certain. The launch site, where we landed, was little more than an outpost. The Human responsible for the development of their warp drive, Cochrane, was undeniably a gifted engineer, but, in retrospect, stood as an exemplar of his species: undisciplined, intemperate, and highly illogical."

PERSONAL LOG

HUR'Q SHIP

Colonel,
Agent Firehawk reporting. It's been seven months of cloaked operation, following in the wake of the Klothos and were it not for my duty I'd have gone mad by now. I swear that I can hear those barbaric veruuls barking their "opera" through the void of space.

I finally have some positive results. Yesterday the Klingons happened upon a large derelict. At first I thought it was an older model of the *K't'inga* class cruiser, but from surveillance of Captain Koloth's private channel to Qo'noS, it's something far more valuable.

They believe this to be a Hur'q vessel, which belonged to a species that subjugated the Klingons several centuries ago. Apparently, it was captured Hur'q technology that helped these imbeciles make it into space in the first place.

From what I can tell this ship is more advanced that anything the Klingons have ever been able to scavenge from their old masters. Right now they can't seem to get past the ancient ship's computer lockout, and there are mentions of deadly security countermeasures. It could take decades to hack, but the data in its computer core alone is likely far more advanced than anything we currently possess.

This is a prize that we must bring beneath the raptor's wing. I await further orders.

Jolan tru, Agent Firehawk

INTERCEPTED TRANSMISSION

COUNCILLOR JELOR – KLINGON HIGH COUNCIL

The events involving courier Klaang's crash landing on the planet Earth has revealed more than the Suliban Cabal's efforts to dismantle the Klingon High Council – the Human element. It has become clear that these Humans represent a possible unique threat to the Klingon Empire. While the exploits of the burgeoning United Earth Starfleet are to be acknowledged for abetting in the halting of the Suliban threat, the Empire should take note in the possible menace represented by the Human tenacity and resolve.

tugh qoH nachDaj je chevlu'ta'.

The Vulcan High Command may have inherited more than they bargained for in taking the United Earth and its Starfleet under their wing.

PERSONAL LOG

LAUNCH OF THE ENTERPRISE NX-01

MESSAGE TO VULCAN HIGH COMMAND
FROM AMBASSADOR SOVAL.
EARTHDATE APRIL 11 2151

After a series of last minute discussions, the Humans have decided to ignore our recommendations and launched their experimental ship, the *Enterprise* NX-01. The ship will carry the fallen Klingon who had become stranded upon Earth back to Qo'noS while under the care of the Denobulan Dr. Phlox. We have endeavored to explain that the Klingons venerate their fallen warriors and shun their injured; this has gone unheeded. Thankfully they have accepted the star charts and the Klingon linguistics database that were provided by High Command and allowed Subcommander T'Pol to serve aboard the ship so she may observe and guide their actions. Subcommander T'Pol has an exemplary record from her time aboard the *Seleya* under Captain Voris and as my own personal attaché here at San Francisco so I believe she is well suited to this mission. These safeguards may stop this course of action from having catastrophic repercussions on the security of the Galaxy.

As you may recall this is not the first time Admiral Forrest has ignored our council—his continued support of Captain Archer's erratic actions rather than following the more logical option has occurred on multiple occasions—but this decision may prove to be his most destructive. In the thirty years as the appointed ambassador to Earth I have noted that the Humans seem to have an inherent compulsion to rush into the unknown without any thought for the consequences.

Live long and prosper.

ARCHIVED TRANSMISSION

MILITARY ASSAULT COMMAND OPS

NX-01 ENTERPRISE MISSION PATCH

STARFLEET COMMAND PATCH

MILITARY ASSAULT COMMAND OPS PATCHES

T'LETH, VULCAN PHYSICIAN, EARTH APRIL 15, 2153

The news from areas affected by the Xindi weapon is grave, and my colleagues here at Starfleet Medical are unable to focus their attention away from viewscreens estimating the number of casualties. As volatile a species as all reports indicate, a number of Humans have turned their anger onto us, the obvious aliens, the offworlders. Even those of us who have been here for some time have been the targets of invectives and slurs. No physical altercations have been yet reported, but as the casualty lists continue to tick upwards, it can only be a matter of time before a Human attacks a member of another species in misplaced rage and grief. […]

Participants of the Interspecies Medical Exchange program have been requested to assist in recovery operations. It is not what I expected, to tend the wounded, dying, and dead of the attack. Yet I cannot think of anywhere else I would rather apply my knowledge and skill at this time. My goal was the furthering of my understanding of Human physiology, disease, and treatment techniques, but I realize now how remarkably short sighted the scope of that goal. Though many of our people dismiss Humans as temperamental and violent, as a species they possess an unexpected depth of resilience and determination in the face of catastrophe. A

glimpse into the survival traits of their evolutionary past. A glimpse, perhaps, into our own ancient past. And perhaps, one into their future. […]

I assisted a search and recovery team in the field at a large recreational facility catering to family gatherings. Though not directly in the path of the weapon, the facility suffered infrastructural failure as a result of the fire and aftershocks following the attack. The team recovered sixteen bodies, eleven in unidentifiable condition, and three survivors. One of the survivors is a Human child of no more than eight years who, unfathomably, latched onto my hand while the recovery team carefully removed the debris trapping her. She believes I am a "nice elf lady". I found myself unable to correct her misperception. She asked for a story from "elfland." I instead spoke of Surak's journey across the Plain of Blood, still hot and green from battle, and the logic he used to cool it into stone.

Doctor Vartras, a colleague also attached to the recovery team, commended me for calming the child and keeping her attention focused away from what was no doubt a very painful field amputation, even with pharmaceutical desensitization. I was disconcerted to realize Dr. Vartras, who still insists I refer to her as 'Shanti,' performed emergency field surgery while I was occupied with Surak's story and the child's grip on my hand… […]

It is difficult to maintain my customary decorum amid the raw, untempered emotions of the Humans around me. I have begun to rely on Keethera meditation, as my usual daily meditation does not restore enough equilibrium against their grief and suffering. Shanti has expressed interest in learning the technique to control her own emotional reactions. I have decided to teach her. She will not master the form, as she is only Human, but perhaps the fundamentals will aid her as they have aided me.

UFP WORLD STATUS ADVISORY COMMITTEE MEETING

SPRING SESSION 2311

Topic: Xindi Council application for recognition by and full membership in the United Federation of Planets

Present: Vice President Anaya Chanda, Committee Chair & Moderator; Afia Dakr, United Earth; Sabra Malir, Denobula; T'Prae, Vulcan; Nargl, Tellar; Shrax, Andorian Empire; M'Rissa, Caitian Homeworld; Liarea, Risan Hedony.

[CHANDA]: We have a busy day ahead of us, Senators. Six worlds have applied for Federation status in the last few months. I trust you've all had opportunity to read the information packets?

[SHRAX]: I have, and honestly, I'm astonished that we'd even consider the Xindi application, considering their history with—

[NARGL]: (snort) Oh, let it go, blue-skin. The Xindi Crisis was over a hundred and fifty years ago. Let them through, as far as I'm concerned. Move on to more important matters, before I die of starvation.

[SHRAX]: (angry) Would that we'd be so fortunate to have your corpse stinking up the council chambers. If you've got something to say, Tellarite—

[CHANDA]: Gentlemen…

   [indistinguishable arguing, unable to discern dialogue]

[T'PRAE]: (clears throat) The Xindi application for world status should come as no surprise to anyone on this Committee. When they applied for provisional world status, a number of intelligence agencies investigated thoroughly and uncovered no evidence of wrongdoing since the regrettable incident of 2153.

[DAKR]: That "regrettable incident" cost us the lives of seven million citizens and nearly catapulted us into an interstellar war! Humans may be short-lived, but it's hard to forget a species carving up your planet when the scars are still visible a century and a half after the fact! What should we do, T'Prae? Forget the damage they did?

[T'PRAE]: I am suggesting no such thing, merely that perhaps the time is right to offer the Xindi Council a fresh start. This committee is, itself, the product of many species of former enemies learning to work together for the betterment of all. The Galaxy has changed significantly, Afia, since the days of the Xindi war. Evidence suggests they have as well.

[M'RISSA]: They arrre five species that co-evolved on theirrr homeworrrld? Can they be considerrred separrrately, perrrhaps?

[LIAREA]: That's actually not a bad idea. Weren't the Reptilian and Insectoid the most aggressive of the bunch? And didn't groups from the future manipulate them all anyway? Can we continue to hold them accountable given the extent of the interference some future faction decided to inflict on them?

[MALIR]: For the record, the Xindi have had provisional status for the last quarter century, far longer than any other worlds to date. While caution is certainly warranted by their history, Senator T'Prae is correct. For all our investigations, we've uncovered nothing but regret and a determination to be better than their ancestors. Now we have to answer the same question: are we better than our ancestors?

   [silence, grumbling, papers shuffling]

[CHANDA]: Does anyone else wish to enter a statement into the record? (pause, silence) Thank you, Senators, for your patience and forbearance. Take a few minutes to reread the Xindi Council's packet, and then we'll vote on the matter.

TRANSCRIPT

KLINGON AUGMENTS

Most Glorious Praetor,

The plague that tore through the Klingon Empire in the middle of the 22nd century disfigured and killed most of their people. By now the populace is steadily regrowing, but to fill in gaps in the military the noble houses recruit footsoldiers from the worker caste. Entire fleets along their borders are comprised of conscripts who were too poor to qualify for reconstructive surgery, and led by noble officers who maintain the same appearance to avoid questions and suspicions from neighboring powers.

The fastest way for a low-caste Klingon to ascend to the warrior caste is to volunteer to serve as an infiltrator against an enemy power. Success means that the operative and their family receive corrective care and are given their own minor house.

I mention this now because our loyalty officers just discovered that one of the enlisted techs at the Ara'athal research facility just so happens to be one of these Klingon infiltrators. May she suffer the death of 1,000 traitors, of course, but I have an idea. This individual is attempting to gather all of our notes on the next generation of cloaking devices. If it pleases the Praetor I would beg you that instead of executing her we simply devise new notes with a hidden critical flaw so that if the Klingons ever attempt to go to war with us again we can negate their cloaks. Imagine the look on the Chancellor's face when he hears that his fleet was vaporized because we can track their ships' ionized warp trail.

With Loyalty, General Timnok, Tal Shiar

INTERCEPTED TRANSMISSION

**EXECUTIVE SUMMARY
FOR THE IMPERIAL SENATE**

Presented by Admiral Kylor Jerok,
Intelligence Analyst,
Romulan Imperial Fleet

"Decisive" is a word that historians prefer to avoid. No battle is decisive. One battle is merely the precursor to the next. Was the Battle of Cheron the decisive battle that ended Romulan plans for expansion? Of course not! Nothing has changed except our timing.

The details of the Battle of Cheron, although widely studied, remain a mystery due to the executions of the warbird commanders who allowed the Empire to be humiliated. As a result, conflicting and apocryphal accounts have made their way into the historiography of the battle. The basic facts are simple enough: the Imperial Fleet engaged a smaller Earth task force orbiting Cheron. Confusion about Starfleet's strategy and whether the homeworld itself was in danger sowed doubt and turned the battle and led to a catastrophic defeat and destruction of shipyards.

With our fleet decimated, we expected the Terrans to continue towards Romulus; instead, they sued for peace. Negotiations took place over audio channels only and led to the creation of the Neutral Zone demarcating the Galaxy between ourselves and the nascent Federation.

INTERCEPTED REPORT

INTERCEPTED REPORT

Proconsul,
Despite Major Talok's blunders several decades ago, those of us embedded in other Vulcan agencies remain secure. Per standing orders, I break communications silence to report on a source of potential interest to the Empire. As a member of the Vulcan Science Directorate, I was extended and accepted an invitation to witness the demonstration of a new type of processing technology by the Terran scientist Richard Daystrom, an innovation he terms "duotronic computing."

I must admit, his work is impressive. His technology represents a breakthrough in sensory precision and processing speeds unmatched by even the most brilliant of our scientists. The Vulcans stalled in their creative innovation long ago; their engineers are nowhere close to this kind of technology.

Also in attendance were several high-ranking officials of Starfleet who responded to the demonstration with typical Human exuberance, and immediately engaged in discussions with Daystrom. It is my belief they intend to acquire this technology for their new *Constitution*-class war vessels, bringing their tactical and offensive capabilities to a level on par with the Empire.

Acquiring this duotronic technology is a goal of the highest priority. Not only would its acquisition give the Empire stable, reliable technology to replace our own aging systems, we also gain an immense tactical advantage in understanding the Federation's warships while preventing them from achieving advantage over the Empire.

Intelligence dossier on Daystrom and detailed technical notes to follow.

INTERCEPTED REPORT

Telling someone their loved one has died is the most unpleasant of all the duties I've had to perform. I've just finished composing a message for the parents of Weapons Specialist Robert Tomlinson, and as I sit here, closing out his file, I can't help but thinking of the larger implications his death brings. Along with the men and women serving on the observation outposts along the Neutral Zone, Specialist Tomlinson was the first combat casualty lost against the Romulan Empire in over a hundred years.

The Earth-Romulan War is one of our history's darker periods, and we were the winners. I can only imagine how the Romulans must view it. They've had a century to think about it, and we know from past experience that they're a proud people, unaccustomed to the sort of defeat we handed them. The Federation Council has already sent messages to the Romulan government to lodge formal protests against the unprovoked assaults on our outposts. Will they disavow the actions of a rogue ship captain, or respond in more measured, even provocative tones? Meanwhile, this new attack can't be mistaken for anything but a test, not only of our technology but also our resolve. How far are the Romulans willing to push this? Are they looking to start another war?

Why do I think I'm not going to like the answers to those questions?

PERSONAL LOG

ROMULANS SIGN PEACE TREATY; IMMEDIATELY SEVER ALL DIPLOMATIC TIES

APRIL 23, 2311

In a ceremony that lasted less than five minutes, the Praetor of the Romulan Star Empire met via subspace link with Federation President as each leader affixed their signature to the electronic document representing the Treaty of Algeron. The agreement calls for the cessation of hostilities between the two powers, while reasserting and clarifying the Neutral Zone separating Federation and Romulan Territory.

"As always, we remain committed to the peace process," said Federation President Gan Laikan to small audience on hand to observe his signing. "It is my sincere hope that the steps taken today serve to ensure our continued security and prosperity as we strive to work in partnership with the Romulan Empire."

Critics of the treaty point to concessions made to the Romulans, including the expansion of the Neutral Zone as well as the agreement that Starfleet would not attempt to replicate cloaking technology for use aboard its starships.

"It's like a leash around our necks," proclaimed one high-ranking Starfleet official on condition of anonymity. "Meanwhile, the Romulans will continue to exploit this tactical advantage at every opportunity."

In a terse statement offered just after the signing, Romulan Praetor Dralath said, "So long as the Federation observes all treaty stipulations, so shall we." He offered no further comment about the agreement or any of the Federation concessions before terminating the subspace communications link.

The treaty is already having an effect, with starship commanders along the Neutral Zone reporting the withdrawal of Romulan vessels from the area. Likewise, all Romulan ambassadors and other diplomats working or traveling in Federation space have been directed to return immediately to Romulus.

What any of this might mean for ongoing Federation-Romulan diplomatic relations remains to be seen.

FEDERATION NEWS SERVICE BULLETIN

EXECUTIVE SUMMARY FOR THE IMPERIAL SENATE
Presented by Admiral Kylor Jerok,
Intelligence Analyst, Romulan Imperial Fleet

After the humiliation of the Battle of Cheron, we negotiated the peace treaty with the Federation that created the Neutral Zone, our shield against the Federation. From behind the safety and security of the Neutral Zone, we entered into an unheralded arms race. Our scientists, hidden from the prying eyes of the Federation, developed new starships, better weapons, and the cloaking device. Our admirals developed new tactics. We had also consolidated our hold over the Beta Quadrant and expanded our sphere of influence.

Although the Federation attempted to spy on us with a series of outposts on their side of the Neutral Zone, we could easily slip past the Federation's prying eyes and spy on them thanks to our cloaking devices. We remained a mystery to the Federation until we destroyed several of the Federation's outposts and fought the Federation's flagship, the *Enterprise* NCC-1701. These minor engagements let us test our new ships and tactics. Not every test was a success, but we learned more from those encounters than the Federation did. And we could always slip beyond the Federation's grasp thanks to the Neutral Zone.

INTERCEPTED REPORT

TAL SHIAR TACTICS

Many speak of the glorious victories of the Romulan Star Empire. History is rife with ostentatious verse in tribute to many successes enjoyed by the Senate and Imperial government. Few will speak of the Empire's most colossal blunders. Perhaps it has something to do with the death sentence attached to such, but you are officer candidates of the Tal Shiar. If you crumble under the truth that the Empire is not infallible, your family's genetic line is best served by dragging you outside for immediate execution.

Let us begin with the gravest of the Empire's mistakes: its key role in the formation of the Coalition of Planets.

One hundred and twenty years ago, the Tellarites and the Andorians squabbled over trade disputes and perceived slights. The Senate was concerned about the early signs of alliance between various enemy races, including the Terrans, Vulcans, Andorians, Rigellians, and Tellarites. Seizing opportunity, Senator Vrax authorized Admiral Valdore to construct a series of prototype droneships and covertly destabilize relations between those species. These vessels, able to mimic the appearance of a variety of species' starships, utilized the novel technology of telepresence, acquired from the Andorian species after their abandonment of it.

Here we see Vrax's first mistake: reliance on a disgraced Admiral considered a fool by even his contemporaries, all for the sake of useless friendship. His second mistake: reliance on a technology developed by another species. And in this reliance, his third mistake manifests: though we have the genetic capacity for telepathy, the level of telepathic skill required was beyond any Romulan of the era.

To compensate, Valdore abducted a mutant Andorian with strong telepathic potential. Why he did not draw from the ranks of loyal, telepathic Remans remains a mystery; perhaps his own arrogance and bigotry blinded him to resources already available and less trouble to condition than a pacifistic Andorian mutant.

Valdore enjoyed success, initially, using the mutant to control the drone ships from his command center on Romulus, and seeded dissent and accusations between the Tellarites and Andorians, and later the Vulcans and Rigellians until they stood on the cusp of war. And perhaps Valdore's success would have held firm, had his overconfidence not drowned his sense of judgement and emboldened him to attack the Terran ship *Enterprise* under the guise of an Andorian war vessel.

The captain of the *Enterprise*, carrying both Andorian drone-ship survivors and a Tellarite diplomatic delegation, co-opted the telepresence technology, enabling other Andorian mutants to contact Valdore's captive, and Valdore's plot unravelled as quickly as he had threaded it together. In essence, Valdore led the infant alliance of our enemies into forging stronger and closer bonds, eventually resulting in the Coalition of Planets and its successor, the United Federation of Planets.

Valdore should have been executed for his blunders, and Vrax as well, but the two managed to survive the tender mercies of imprisonment. An equally colossal blunder by our illustrious then-Praetor freed them both to fight the Coalition of Planets they had created, which eventually resulted in Vrax's ultimate achievement: ascension to the rank of Praetor in 2265.

Can you guess how well that upwards failure worked in the Empire's favor?

INTERCEPTED LECTURE

ANDORIAN AMBASSADOR AHRYNN, FEDERATION FOUNDING CEREMONY, 2161

"…and with the goal of this United Federation of Planets being the prevention of conflict through cooperation, I hereby propose that those of us assembled immediately offer membership to the Klingon and Romulan peoples as well. For I fear that without an effort to truly ally all of the major powers, we merely set the stage for future conflicts – and not merely internecine struggles amongst ourselves, but wars which could engulf the Alpha and Beta Quadrants, and eventually the entire Galaxy."

[Audio indicates outcry in the chamber. Indistinct. A gavel can be heard, and a voice (presumably that of Earth Ambassador Vanderbilt) calling "order."]

Footnote: Ahrynn's proposal was rejected. Ambassador Sarahd replaced Ahrynn as head of the Andorian delegation, signing the Constitution, and eventually serving as Federation Vice President.

TRANSCRIPT

ENSIGN RICHARD TRAVERS STARDATE 5632.6

"Hi Mom and Dad. Ship assignments are now posted. Can you believe it? I'm finally going into space! I'm going to be serving on the brand spanking new, yet to be commissioned, *U.S.S. Defiant*. She's the latest *Constitution* class ship to be built. I'm already anxious to get into her engine-room.

She has the most beautiful lines. Her nacelles and support columns have such straight lines. The saucer section is perfectly round. She's downright lovely. I can't wait to see her warp core.

My roommate has teased me about the fact that I already fawn over her like she's my girlfriend. I told him that every chief engineer falls in love with his ship. He reminded me that I wasn't a chief engineer. I laughed and told him not yet.

Mom, I know you're going to worry now that I am shipping out, but I'll be okay. I shouldn't have to be on any landing parties since I'll be serving in the engineering section. So the fact that I'm wearing a red shirt isn't a cause for concern. Good thing I never wanted to get into security, isn't it?

Well, I need to go. We are supposed to report to our senior officer in the morning. I love you both."

PERSONAL LOG

CAPTAIN GARTH

A triumphal procession, just like they used to throw in ancient Rome. That's what they gave me, marched down the Boulevard of Heroes and enshrined forever as Garth of Izar. It nearly made it seem worth it; the applause of the crowd drowned out the screams of my bridge crew and the flashes of recorders brighter than the brief flames of the ships at Axanar disintegrating into nothing.

Unlike the Caesars I didn't need a slave whispering "Remember thou art mortal" into my ear. I realized my mortality when the car carrying my senior staff exploded and tore away half of my body. Forty-one years old, hero of the Federation and all I have left is a trip to a medical research colony where I'll spend the rest of my life as a lab rat for experimental reconstruction procedures that I'm told will end up being half measures at best.

PERSONAL LOG

COMMANDER ARJUN PRAKASH

CO U.S.S. SOLKAR TO DR. DONALD CORY

It seemed like a stroke of the greatest luck when I happened to mention the Antosian Expedition to Doc Le. They've shown some remarkable potential with their nano-medicine breakthroughs, though in the past they never let outsiders have access to their cellular metamorphosis techniques. It took a bit of doing, but I managed to convince their Supreme Fellow that they'd only be treating Captain Garth and that we'd make no efforts to persuade them to share their research with Starfleet. The captain agreed reluctantly and I got permission from Starfleet Command to divert the ship.

Did you know that a caterpillar in a cocoon actually breaks down into a sort of soup, completely recombining its parts into something new? That's the only example I can think of that makes any sense for what happened to my old commander.

We met back up nearly a year after we had left him. On the surface, he looked amazing. No scars, his limbs regrown and he had that same smile that used to make duty shifts more pleasant. Behind his eyes, though, there was something missing. The Antosians told me that he was "awake" during the entire process. I can't fathom what that would do to me, but I saw quickly how soon it changed him.

At our reception in the officer's lounge he spoke in grandiose terms about a "defining new era of man", and how Antosian technology was going to help him reshape the Galaxy. The delegates from planet were appalled, probably as angry as I felt embarrassed. And then he attempted to take command of the ship, ordered me to execute Starfleet General Order 24, the extermination of all life on a planetary surface. I can't state fully my regret. I damned my mentor, destroyed his mind while trying to save his body. Dr. Cory, I'm begging you to please save this man. If there's a sliver remaining of the brilliant tactician, please, rescue him from his personal hell.

TRANSMISSION

DAHAR MASTER KOR, THE ORGANIAN PEACE TREATY

"Do you want to know which Federation captain I respected the most? It was Captain James T. Kirk of the *U.S.S. Enterprise*. There was a man who should have been born a Klingon. He has the heart of a true Suvwl', a warrior. We first met on Organia. I led a force of five hundred Klingons to occupy that backward planet. The people there acted like sheep cowed by the wolf. They promised that we would have no problems. Kirk and his first officer Spock were also there, hidden in plain sight by the village elders. Kirk called himself, Baroner. I could see the hatred in his eyes every time we spoke. It was so refreshing. I installed myself as governor and demanded that he serve as the public liaison.

"It was only after we started to have acts of insurgency against us that it became clear who was behind it. You can imagine my surprise when the Organian elders revealed exactly who Baroner and Spock really were. Elation doesn't cover what I felt. Here was the captain of the Federation's flagship and he was now in my custody! You have to understand that we are two tigers. We were meant for battle. I found myself wishing that we were facing each other on the bridges of our ships locked in combat! We were at war with the Federation and if it wasn't for the fact that the Organians interfered and put a stop to it, it would have been glorious."

COUNCILLOR DEHUS
KLINGON HIGH COUNCIL

The day has finally come. The Klingon Empire and the United Federation of Planets have – not without considerable adversity – negotiated an alliance that promises to provide a cornerstone for roj in the Alpha and Beta Quadrants. Not one Klingon warrior who served on the invasion force on Organia to patrolling the Neutral Zone could have foreseen the concord of the oppositions.

The alliance with the Federation could prove to be a great service to the Klingon Empire, and a considerable shift of power in both the Alpha and Beta Quadrants. It remains to be seen whether the Federation or the Empire benefits the most from the Treaty. As a long-time adversary, the Federation may possess more knowledge about the Empire than any other faction within the Quadrants. While at the same time, is the Empire prepared to allow the Federation know more of our position and role within the Quadrants?

Double-edged? Perhaps. Not unlike the two blades of the single *mevak*.

THE KLINGON HIGH COUNCIL

"Kor, commanding, *I.K.S. Klothos*. All glory to the Empire.

The situation imposed on us by the Organians is infuriating, yes, but I would argue that we are not without an advantage. The terms of the so-called 'treaty' merely prohibit open warfare between the Empire and the Earthers. We already know of the spineless nature of the Federation. They avoid conflict, even before this 'treaty' was put in place.

I say that we continue to be bold, as warriors should be! We push ahead, daring the Federation to fight! It is not within their nature. They are weak, and without honor… and, hiding under the skirts of these advanced aliens, they are even less likely to be prepared to offer any real resistance. They will back down, so no open warfare will occur. We will remain within the letter of the treaty, yet still expand the Empire.

I would also recommend further expansion efforts along the Romulan border, and along the galactic rim headed away from Federation space, which offer many more opportunities for glory, with less interference from god-like interlopers."

On stardate 3045.6 the Gorn ship *Exeron*, under orders from Captain Arijog, eliminated the Federation colony on Cestus III, leaving only one survivor among the hundreds of men and women in the compound.

History tells the tale of the epic duel fought between captains Kirk and Arijog, but the encounter proved to be far more important for the Federation's development than a simple melee. Kirk was able to convince the assembly of admirals to send a diplomatic delegation rather than a punitive expedition to the Gorn homeworld.

The Gorn had been using Cestus III for generations as an integral part of their breeding cycle. Its climate was ideally suited for maintaining the species' optimal male-to-female ratio via temperature-dependent sex selection. A grand tour of Federation worlds convinced the Gorn of the Federation's motives.

In the century since an agreement was signed the two societies proved to be a model for interspecies cooperation. Both maintain unobtrusive colonies on Cestus III, and the Gorn's advanced sensor technology helped Starfleet to make new discoveries and better defend the Federation while Starfleet warp advances made it possible for the Gorn to reach other worlds quickly.

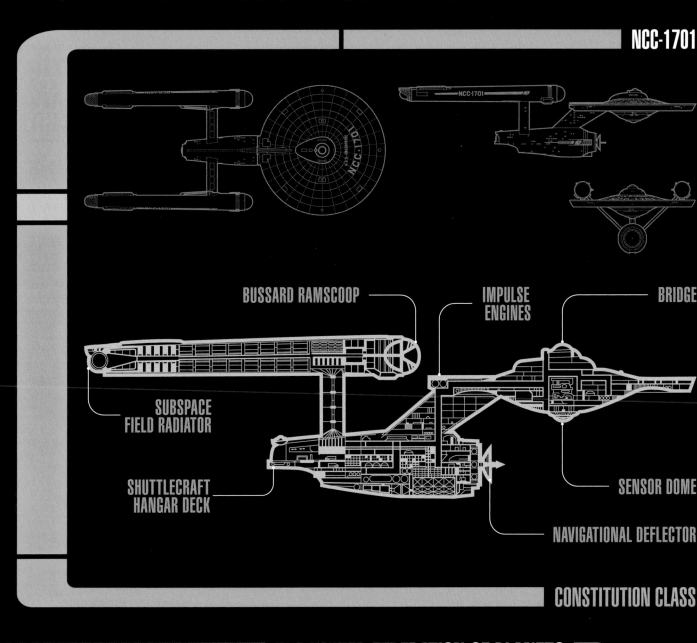

BUSSARD RAMSCOOP — IMPULSE ENGINES — BRIDGE

SUBSPACE FIELD RADIATOR

SHUTTLECRAFT HANGAR DECK

SENSOR DOME

NAVIGATIONAL DEFLECTOR

CONSTITUTION CLASS

Will,
I imagine that Starfleet Command has already contacted you about the loss of the *Constellation*, and your father's death. He died in the line of duty, as I noted in my log, but logs and reports only tell you what happened. They don't always tell you why. There are going to be rumors floating around Starfleet Command about why they happened; I wanted you to hear that from me.

Your dad lost control, Will. He lost his crew under horrific circumstances, and when he tried to redeem himself, he lost himself. Only for a moment, but that's the moment that a lot of people are going to fix on. They won't see the man who fought the Devil for his crew against all odds. They won't even see the man who sacrificed himself to show us how to kill the thing. They'll see the man who turned into Ahab, chasing the white whale through system L-374 at any costs.

They'll also project it onto you in the years to come. "Like father, like son," they'll tell you, "you'll turn out the same way." Hard as it will be to take that, don't let it bother you. There are worse things in life than turning out like Matt Decker. He was a decorated officer, a starship commander, and a Starfleet commodore.

He was a good man, Will, and he died a hero.

Sincerely, Jim

TRANSMISSION

STARDATE 4795.1

TO: **COMMODORE ROBERT WESLEY, SC906-0131-CEC**
        ***U.S.S. LEXINGTON*, NCC-1709**
FROM: **ADMIRAL JAMES KOMACK**
        STARFLEET COMMAND, SECTOR 9

You've already received the official orders, Bob, so let me be the first to congratulate you on your promotion and new assignment. There's no understating the fantastic job you did with the *Lexington*, and I know you've mentioned a desire to stay with your ship now that it's been repaired after everything that happened with the M-5 computer war games. However, Starfleet Command has decided a complete rotation of the entire crew is probably the best way to help everyone get past this horrific incident. The same will be happening with the *Hood*, *Potemkin*, and *Excalibur* once their refits are completed.

You're probably already thinking how much you'll miss that center seat. I know I do, but we go where duty sends us, right? Besides, Starfleet can always use another flag officer who's experienced and been tested by all manner of situations, and I can't think of anyone I'd rather have commanding Starbase 23.

I'm anxious to hear your initial report after you've had a chance to get the lay of the land and consult with the starship captains you'll have under your command. Given our uneasy relationship with the Klingons and even with this Organian Peace Treaty in place, we need someone there who can bring a proper, levelheaded perspective to that whole situation while overseeing and protecting our interests in that region. You're a perfect choice, and I know you'll do us all proud. Komack out.

SUBSPACE TRANSMISSION

COMMANDER CHARVANEK, CHR MEMENDA

STARDATE 5027.4

"I cannot believe I fell for Federation treachery. The *Enterprise* First Officer Spock led me to think he was going to defect to the Empire and deliver us the prize of Starfleet. His captain had ordered the ship to cross into the Neutral Zone. Spock stated the captain had been under duress and his state of mind was fragile. He killed his captain in self-defense except it has become apparent that Spock was a party in the theft of our cloaking device, which he freely admits. The punishment for such actions is death. It is a shame. I had hoped to explore our relationship further on a more personal level. Now, he has not only embarrassed me in front of my crew, but the Praetor will not take kindly to the theft of our cloaking device. We must get it back at all costs even if it means the destruction of the *Enterprise* itself."

INTERCEPTED PERSONAL LOG

"Honesty compels me to admit that I was not a very good person for many years.

"I do not say that lightly. I got by on early breakthroughs for decades, and along the way began to harbor resentment and ill-will against my fellow scientists. My ego, not inconsiderable at the best of times, became virtually unbearable. And unsatisfied. In an attempt to assuage my ego, I tried to become God, to create life, in the form of the M-5 computer. It cost me dearly.

"I am guilty, by proxy, of one murder onboard the *U.S.S. Enterprise*. Fifty-three onboard the *Lexington*. Four hundred and thirty onboard the *Excalibur*. I carry the weight of the souls of almost 500 Starfleet officers on my conscience. I do not say that lightly, either.

"I had a complete nervous breakdown that day, and spent the next decade in a succession of psychiatric facilities. I was thoroughly, properly chastised, even though the murder charges had been dismissed. I expected, and deserved, to be forgotten as a scientist upon my release, remembered only for the tragedy that sprang from my fevered brow.

"I was instead greeted by the very same colleagues I had thought were mocking me all those years. That terrible day had made me Human in a way I had never been before. I was able to resume my work, and now here we are. Today you do me the signal honor of giving these halls of higher learning my name. It is an honor I do not deserve, but I accept it with a grateful and humble heart.

"Thank you, all of you, for your faith in me. Thank you very much, indeed."

STARDATE 48103.9

FROM: JUNEMANN, ADMIRAL L.A.,
UTOPIA PLANITIA FLEET YARDS

TO: SPAIN, CAPTAIN A.J.,
STARFLEET OPERATIONS

Andy, trust me, no one is more ticked off about having to involve the Romulans in the *Defiant* project than I am, but if that piece of junk is going to serve any purpose in the Gamma Quadrant, then it's got to have a cloaking device and for that, it's either the Romulans or the Klingons. In this case, the Romulans were easier to deal with, hard as that might be to swallow.

We had to go to them because every attempt we've ever made to get cloaking technology on our own has met with failure, if not outright disaster. You know James T. Kirk himself stole a cloaking device, right? We should have been home free, but the damned thing worked once for the *Enterprise*, and never again after that.

We spent decades after that trying to reverse-engineer it. We never figured out how to track a cloaked ship because of it, and we lost five ships during various tests trying to make it work before the Tomed incident brought that little experiment to a close.

Don't even get me started on that idiot Pressman and what happened with the *Pegasus*.

Starfleet Command wanted to go to the Klingons; it would have been easier. But the Klingons only use the cloaking device. The Romulans understand them, and with everything else that little ship of Sisko's has going against it, it needs someone on board who understands the thing. So I made the call. I know it doesn't sit well with you, and I'm sorry, but the *Defiant's* mission is too important to the Federation's interests.

Next time you're on Mars, drop by. First round at Amelia's is on me. I owe you that much for all this.

Best,
Laura

THE UNITED FEDERATION OF PLANETS

THE TWENTY-THIRD CENTURY

"YOU KNOW THE GREATEST DANGER FACING US IS OURSELVES, AN IRRATIONAL FEAR OF THE UNKNOWN. BUT THERE'S NO SUCH THING AS THE UNKNOWN — ONLY THINGS TEMPORARILY HIDDEN, TEMPORARILY NOT UNDERSTOOD."

— CAPTAIN JAMES T. KIRK

Always remember, Captain: We're explorers. We may wear a uniform and follow military discipline, but we're not a military force with domination as our aim. Since the first days of Starfleet, even before Captain Jonathan Archer took the *Enterprise* NX-01 out on her maiden voyage more than two centuries ago, ours has been a mission of peaceful exploration. While we've delved deeper into the Galaxy since Captain Archer's time, especially in the last fifty years or so, many in Starfleet look to the 23rd century as the real heyday of Starfleet exploration.

In the middle of the 23rd century, a Starfleet still finding its footing took the twelve *Constitution*-class starships then in service — ships with names like *Enterprise*, *Lexington*, *Excalibur*, and *Defiant* — and sent them out on five-year missions of exploration. Not to push back the boundaries of explored space, though they did that, but to roam the huge sphere of space that the Federation had claimed and find out what was actually there. This initiative captured the imagination of Starfleet — indeed, it captured the imaginations of countless people across the Federation — and established a benchmark against which other exploration missions would be measured for generations to come.

EDGE OF THE FINAL FRONTIER

I'm going to talk a great deal about Captain James T. Kirk and the *Enterprise* here, because their exploits are so well documented, but it's important to remember that she wasn't out there alone. There were eleven other *Constitution*-class starships, which were also sent where no one had gone before. All of them achieved great things. The *Enterprise* shone a little brighter because of the volume of her accomplishments, and the fact that she made it back when several of her sister ships did not. All this was due, in no small part, to Captain Kirk and the crew that surrounded him,

so if my examples lean too heavily on the *Enterprise*, I hope you'll forgive me.

Let's not go the easy route and romanticize things. Let's go strictly by the record. That leaves quite a lot that those ships and their crews accomplished. We can begin by remembering that, by their standards, modern starships would be the height of luxury. The starships of the 23rd century required more crew to support them and their missions, and they really packed them in tightly. The new *Intrepid* class starships, for instance, are about the same size as the *Constitution*-class; the latter, though, has about three times the crew complement of the former.

They also accomplished what they did without our array of technological advancements. While they were hardly primitive, much of the technology we take for granted here in the 24th century was far less advanced in the 23rd, if it existed at all. Their transporters, for instance, were markedly less effective than the modern-day version. Today, we think little to nothing of intraship beaming, or transporting a wounded away team member directly to sickbay; it's simply how things are done. But these processes barely existed in Captain Kirk's day. Sensors were barely accurate enough, and the duotronic computer systems in use at the time, while marvels of the day's technology, were only just up to the task. It was something only done in the direst of emergencies.

THEIR OWN DEVICES

Their missions, like ours, frequently kept them from shore leave and recreation facilities for long periods. Unlike us, they did it without holodecks to provide on-board rest and recreation. While they'd known of the technology for more than a century after the *Enterprise* NX-01's contact with the Xyrillians, making it compatible with the power and computer systems aboard our starships proved to be trickier than our engineers had thought. A prototype of our holodeck was installed aboard Captain Kirk's *Enterprise* late in her five-year mission, but software and safety issues ultimately led to its removal, and there would be decades of additional development before it was tried again.

We also take for granted being able to confer with Starfleet Command when a situation arises. They didn't have that luxury. Subspace communications were slower, and the subspace relay network was a tiny fraction of the size it is now. It could take weeks for a message to reach a starbase and an answer to be received. Kirk and his fellow starship captains, out of sheer necessity, had a great deal more autonomy to make decisions in the field than is generally needed today. They likewise had the responsibility to make the right decision, and more than one would be reprimanded after the fact for errors in judgment.

TESTED IN FIRE

Over the years, Starfleet has developed a battery of psychological tests, designed to gauge an officer's fitness for certain positions. We are especially hard on candidates for command positions. Experience has shown us certain traits that lend themselves to command, and we've come up with ways to measure those traits. Starfleet's first major test of command character originated in the 23rd century: the

Kobayashi Maru simulation. More than one cadet was steered onto a different career path because of how they handled the scenario; a few were cashiered out of the Academy altogether. Every one of the captains on those twelve *Constitution*-class starships endured the *Kobayashi Maru*, several of them more than once. Captain Kirk famously took it three times, and arguably cheated his way through it the third time. He was almost expelled for that, but Starfleet Command saw something in him that they liked: A tenacious will that served him, and the fleet, very well for nearly four decades.

Who was your sacrifice, Captain? When you took your Bridge Officer Examination, who did you send to die that the rest of your crew might live? More than likely, it was your chief engineer; the dozen or so scenarios that the computer chooses from for that test lean heavily on failures in engineering, in my experience. Mine was my security chief, during a boarding action by angry Nausicaans. We've all faced that situation in a simulation, or we'd not be in command now. A hundred years ago, however, they didn't have the Bridge Officer Examination as we know it. Many officers never knew if they could send someone into the jaws of death to save the others under their command. Even the *Kobayashi Maru* doesn't prepare you for that.

I bring this up because Captain Kirk had to face that kind of decision, as his ship sat in orbit over the ore cracking station

at Delta Vega, near the start of his five-year mission. To save his ship, he had to kill his best friend, Lieutenant Commander Gary Mitchell, who had become a menace to the *Enterprise*, and perhaps all of Humanity. Kirk did, in reality, what most of us will never do outside a holodeck. Many other starship commanders of the day had to make similar sacrifices. Starfleet is stronger now because of this. We learn by doing, Captain; we know better how to face these crucibles because of the lessons these officers learned.

MEN FOR ALL SEASONS

Before we'd even really started exploring our corner of the Galaxy, we'd begun colonizing it. Many of the colonies were tiny things, with populations in the hundreds at best. Some were only science stations or archaeological sites with fewer than half a dozen people. Even as they explored, the *Enterprise* and her sister ships visited many of those colonies as part of their duties. They had to; the whole of the fleet was a small fraction of what it is now. Most colonies and outposts didn't have a Federation consulate, or anything else of the sort. Part of the mission for all starships was to put in at these places and reassure the citizens that all was well. They didn't just represent the Federation; on the frontier, for all intents and purposes, they were the Federation.

They had to do a little bit of everything in those days. The ships and the missions weren't so specialized. One day they might be providing routine physical exams to a science team on a remote outpost, and the next making detailed charts of previously unexplored systems. A crew could never be certain of what they might be doing from one assignment to another. Typically, there were three main roles that they took. Sometimes they were diplomats. Sometimes they were peacekeepers. Most often, and most importantly, they were explorers.

DIPLOMATS

During their five-year missions, the *Constitution*-class starships were frequently tasked with establishing diplomatic relations with other cultures. After all, that's more or less what first contact is all about, and during the five-year missions, those twelve starships made dozens of first contacts. While their captains did receive some diplomatic training, and frequently had to use it, quite often their roles in diplomacy were less as ambassadors themselves, but as couriers for dedicated ambassadors, councilors, and other diplomats.

This often required its own special brand of diplomacy, however, because diplomats from opposing sides can be prickly. During the negotiations that admitted Coridan to the Federation, for instance, the *Enterprise* was tasked with transporting several diplomatic parties to the conference site. Captain Kirk had to maintain peace between the Vulcan, Andorian, and Tellarite delegations. These three cultures historically did not get along very well, even a century after they'd founded the Federation together.

That situation very nearly got out of hand, but not all diplomatic missions had the potential for such dire outcomes. The *Farragut*, for instance, played host to the first Procyon Conference, where the worst thing that happened was one of the Rigellian dignitaries discovering she was allergic to walnuts. Most, in fact, went without a hitch, and considering how demanding some diplomats can be, this is noteworthy. Also noteworthy is that, while many diplomatic missions during this period failed, somehow none of them ended in disaster.

WORDS, NOT WEAPONS

As well as people of action, the crew of the *Enterprise* showed an aptitude for diplomacy. They saved the Mantilles colony, for instance, when Commander Spock mind-melded with a gigantic alien that consumed planets for food. They didn't rush in behind a salvo of photon torpedoes. Instead, they showed one sentient being that it was destroying other sentient beings in order to survive.

They overcame the Kelvans the same way, not with phasers and fists, but with ideas. They demonstrated that adapting to a humanoid form had irrevocably made them alien to their own kind. Kirk convinced them to tell their rulers that while we would fight efforts of conquest, the Federation would be open to colonization by friendly visitors.

PEACEKEEPERS

Starfleet might not be a military service, but we are occasionally obliged to act like one. This was even more true in the 23rd century. The *Constitution* class was not just one of the greatest scientific vessels created to that point; it was quite capable of taking care of itself and acting in defense of the Federation and her citizens. It was called on to do so on several occasions.

The fact is, not everybody is friendly. It's unfortunate, but it's true: Sometimes merely showing the flag isn't enough. Sometimes you have to fight. This doesn't have to end badly. For instance, our first encounter with the Gorn Hegemony at Cestus III could have been an absolute disaster. Once a few significant misunderstandings were worked out, though, it became an alliance, however tenuous it might be, which has lasted for decades.

Things didn't always work out that well, however.

ROMULANS

There is no time I can think of when we've gotten along with the Romulan Empire, until now and the new threat from the Dominion. In the 23rd century, we not only didn't get along, we hadn't even had contact with them in over a hundred years.

That ended when they snuck across the Neutral Zone and began destroying border outposts. This was, apparently, a test of our resolve. It very nearly started another war, and helped set the rather bleak tone of our relations with the Empire for decades to come.

Little is known about their goals now, and even less was known then. Tension with the Romulans would remain high throughout the 23rd century, with a small handful of encounters, almost all of which seemed to be like their first incursion, designed to test our resolve. These were mostly with the *Enterprise*, but also occasionally the *Potemkin* and the *Constitution*. It might not have gotten out of hand if Starfleet Intelligence hadn't decided it was a good idea to have Captain Kirk and the *Enterprise* steal a cloaking device for them. This vexed the Romulans considerably, and it was this incident that paved the first steps of the road towards the Tomed incident and the Treaty of Algeron.

KLINGONS

The Romulans may have been mysterious during the 23rd century, but the Klingon Empire was not. Their conquests

FROM: SHRAS, AMBASSADOR,
UNITED FEDERATION OF PLANETS

TO: GHARIS, COMMANDER,
ANDORIAN INTELLIGENCE SERVICE

Commander, by now you have certainly been made aware of the recent incident involving the Orion attack on the *U.S.S. Enterprise* while they were tasked with transporting I and my staff to the Babel Conference to discuss the admission of Coridan to the Federation.

I have been given to understand that it was your office that was responsible for the background investigations into several recent additions of my staff, including one "Thelev." This man, as it turns out, was not even Andorian! He was an Orion spy made to look like one of us! Hundreds were nearly killed and the short-term stability of the Federation itself was put in jeopardy, because you or one of your functionaries failed to do your job properly.

During his tenure with my staff, "Thelev" at least performed his duties adequately. The same cannot be said for you and your staff. I wished to personally express my dissatisfaction, and inform you that I have demanded a full investigation into your office's incompetence!

were well known, their warriors were feared, and Starfleet was the only thing standing between them and domination of much of the Alpha Quadrant as we know it.

Yes, we're allies now; we even have a Klingon in Starfleet. But it took a long time and a great deal of trial and error to arrive at this point. In Kirk's day, they were the enemy, plain and simple. They had been since before the founding of the Federation. The presence of a Klingon battle cruiser could only mean trouble, and more than one Starfleet captain was more than ready to give it to them.

Both sides got more than they bargained for at Organia, though. After more than a century of open hostility towards one another, both sides found themselves powerless to fight each other when the Organians imposed their eponymous peace treaty on both sides.

Of course, even with that treaty in place, it was a long way from there to the Khitomer Accords, and both sides had considerable adjustments to make. Deprived of direct conflict with Starfleet, the Klingons resorted to guile and subterfuge. While this wasn't their strongest suit, by any stretch of the imagination, they proved to be capable students. They interfered with the native culture on the planet Neural, for example, and attempted to wrest away the mineral-rich star systems of Capella and Tellun. These schemes were generally stopped before much damage was done, but tensions and distrust between the Empire and the Federation would continue for decades.

EXPLORERS

The Galaxy was bigger in the 23rd century. Not physically, of course, but it felt larger. It took longer to get from one star to the next, and the Federation's sphere of influence was smaller than it is now. The warp speed scale was different back then, too. While ours is a finite spectrum, with warp 10 as an absolute maximum, the original Cochrane scale was open-ended. While the *Constitution* class had a designed maximum speed of warp 8 on that scale, it wasn't uncommon for other vessels or phenomena to be observed traveling in excess of warp 11. The *Enterprise* once observed one probe approaching them at warp 15 on the Cochrane scale!

ORGANIAN INTERFERENCE

It's maddening, Koloth. Maddening!

I don't know how things have been on the *Gr'oth*, but I've taken the *Klothos* and tried to attack a couple of Federation starships, and it's always the same. The weapon controls are cool to the touch until we actually try to use them, and then they can suddenly melt lead. My weapons officer, Kavin, has tried it with gloves, even tried to fire the disruptors with a stick once. Same thing. Stubborn boy, that Kavin. He can still use that hand, though he's going to have an interesting scar.

I made a recommendation to the High Council. We're going to have to fight the Federation another way for now. No glorious battles, at least until the Organians grow bored and forget about us. We're going to have to wrest planets away from them one at a time, and we're going to have to skulk about like Romulans to do it. It should be easy for you, you talk a lot, but I can't imagine Kang is going to be happy about it....

Duty calls, old friend, as you well know. Qapla'!

Kor

Just because it took longer to get from point A to point B didn't mean there weren't ample discoveries. During their five-year missions, *Constitution* class starships discovered hundreds of worlds. Some were familiar, eerily so — more than one class M planet bore a startling resemblance to Earth, and one such planet encountered by the *Enterprise* early in her mission was actually identical. On most of these worlds, sentient species were discovered, while on others evidence was found of remarkable ancient civilizations. While the *Enterprise* is well known for making discoveries like these, other ships, like the *Lexington* and the *Intrepid*, were also famous for the number of ancient civilizations they uncovered.

As might be imagined with as many M class planets as were found, dozens of first contacts were made with a huge variety of life-forms of every shape and size. Most were humanoids, but many others, such as the Hortas or the Excalbians, were decidedly not so. A few had godlike abilities, and some of those had actually been worshiped as gods, such as the beings who called themselves Apollo and Kukulkan.

Some of these have turned out to be friendly. The Phylosians and the Fabrini have provided us with medical technologies, while the First Federation gives us the liquor *tranya* and other luxury goods. The Hortas from Janus VI have traded their rock-eating metabolisms to mining concerns in exchange for the chance to "taste" other worlds and explore the Galaxy.

Others have been outright hostile, most notably the Tholians. They were not, technically, a first contact — Captain Archer and the NX-01 had that dubious honor — but Captain Kirk's *Enterprise* did have the misfortune of being the first to encounter them in several years. They were just as xenophobic then as they are now, but they seemed much more willing to demonstrate this in the 23rd century.

RISK IS OUR BUSINESS

Do you play "what if?" games, Captain? Have you ever wondered if you could have made it back in the "Golden Age" of Starfleet exploration, serving under men like Matt Decker or Stephen Garrovick? The hazards were very real: neural parasites, dark matter nebulae, random tears in the fabric of space-time — the list goes on and on. It was a risky proposition.

But then, space exploration has always been a risky proposition. A vast emptiness, filled at unexpected times with potentially hostile life-forms or deadly phenomena, is inherently dangerous to the relatively frail humanoid form. In the 23rd century, with its less-developed technologies and limited communications, it was even more so. Exploration in those days was a daunting task, and it took a special breed of person to go out there and do it.

These men and women did it, and did it admirably. The five-year mission initiative wasn't without cost. Three of those *Constitution*-class starships — the *Constellation*, the *Intrepid*, and the *Defiant* — were lost with all hands, while two others — the *Exeter* and the *Excalibur* — suffered complete crew losses. None of the others came back unscathed, yet they never turned back, either. Their captains and crews chose that risk willingly, with their eyes wide open, just as we, their successors, do.

It's a heritage we can take enormous pride in. Say what you will about Captain Kirk and his crew's accomplishments, but nearly everybody recognizes that they were like us in one key respect: They were explorers. And they were exceptional at it.

TO BOLDLY GO: ROLE-PLAYING IN THE 23RD CENTURY

The tone of the original *Star Trek* had a sense of wonder about it; things were new and different, and the Galaxy felt a little less familiar. There were exciting adventures in exotic locales. Roleplaying in the 23rd century should reflect that sense of adventure; your Players should feel that they are experiencing something that is, as Commander Spock often said, unlike anything they have ever encountered. Rather than celebrating the triumph of technology, there should be a greater emphasis on the accomplishments of the crew. The crews of the 23rd century were trained to rely less on their tech and more on their own ingenuity when solving problems. Entire episodes of the Original Series, such as "The Ultimate Computer," were built upon overcoming the limits and failings of

technology. GMs should emphasize this simple premise: It might be the future, but the story is still about the people, not the machines.

The 23rd century was also less focused on politics, and more on the immediate relationships among the crew. While politics do exist, and can either aid or hinder a crew's mission — the entire focus of the episode "Journey to Babel" was about politics, for example — most of a 23rd century crew's missions probably won't involve political intrigue at all. The interplay between cultures tended to be less important than ensuring that the ship's crew worked together as a cohesive unit.

In the 23rd century, the Federation's territory and sphere of influence was substantially smaller than it would be in the 24th century. Warp travel was slower and used a different warp speed scale; subspace communications were also slower and more limited. The slower warp speeds mean that help is frequently less likely to arrive in time, while slower communications mean that contact with Starfleet Command is not as frequent. This means that the PCs are frequently left to their own devices when facing critical decisions.

23RD CENTURY UNIFORM INSIGNIA

   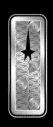  

USS CONSTELLATION NCC-1017

USS EXETER NCC-1672

USS ENTERPRISE NCC-1701

USS DEFIANT NCC-1764

RECENT FEDERATION HISTORY

ADMIRAL WESLEY AND UNKNOWN INDIVIDUAL
STARDATE 8161.8

"Where are the Project Genesis files now?"

"We have them safely secured, sir."

"So they are in your care?"

"Yes, sir."

"And Carol Marcus? Is she also safe?"

"Yes, we have her in a location known only to members of Starfleet that qualify as 'need to know.' We felt it would be better that way."

"Good, we cannot afford for this data to fall into the wrong hands again. We got lucky when that maniac Khan ignited it in the Mutara Nebula rather than on an inhabited planet. Good thing he was so obsessed with Kirk rather than flying straight to a major planet to terraform it to his and his fellow Augments' standards."

"Yes, sir. That will never happen again. Project Genesis is no longer something you or other Starfleet admirals need to worry about again. We've made sure of that."

"Just make sure it stays that way and that Carol Marcus remains safe. She's already lost her son and research team. She's an asset we cannot lose. We need her to continue her research."

"Rest assured, we will see to that."

10 • 0C4404

10 • 35932

RECORDED TRANSMISSION

ORION FREIGHTER

"I still can't believe that Praxis is gone. The Klingons' key energy and mining production facility used to exist there. That was a very lucrative contract. Now, of course, the Federation is involved in providing aide to the Klingons. With the new treaty signed at Khitomer, there are all new regulations I have to follow just to get clearance to cross into Klingon space let alone land on Qo'noS. It was so much simpler without the Federation sticking their noses where they didn't belong. What's an honest Orion trader supposed to do now? The Klingons would have paid handsomely for essential trade goods after the destruction of Praxis. I could have retired in a

matter of months if I wanted too. But no, the Federation had to insert itself into my business dealings. Instead of just being able to bribe a captain or an official to gain passage, now I have to present official documentation of my cargo contents, my intended flight path and the duration of my stay. It's like this new Federation/Klingon alliance is afraid of traders trying to make a living. There are even Federation vessels in orbit. I simply can't stand them. Regulations this, regulations that. I'd rather deal with a hungry targ."

INTERCEPTED TRANSMISSION

KLINGON HIGH COUNCIL
COLONEL WORF AFTER THE KHITOMER ACCORDS

"The Chang House has brought great dishonor upon us as a race. The general conspired with Klingon commanders, Federation officers, and even Romulans to have Chancellor Gorkon assassinated. We are Klingon. We do not use others to do dirty work like General Chang did. He and his conspirators are no better than DenIbya' Qatlhs. Chang did not deserve to die in combat like a warrior. He should have been chased down like the Ha'DIbaH he was and brought back on a leash to answer for his crimes. His actions have now created a power vacuum as other families and Houses are scrambling to position themselves to compete for favor as Gorkon's daughter, Azetbur, has been elevated to High Chancellor. In my opinion, the House of Chang should be stripped of its noble standing and any mention of Chang wiped from the annals of Klingon history."

KHITOMER ACCORDS

FROM: **GOVERNOR JAVEN**
TO: **COMMANDER T'LOR, *I.K.S. S'CHA***

Brother, I trust that this communiqué finds you well, and your command of the *S'Cha* has brought you much honor and success. I have been apprised of your worthy accomplishments along the border. With the signing of the Khitomer Accords it has become apparent that life as we know it will change. Your current assignment as commander of the *S'Cha* will continue to offer much opportunity to prove your worthiness to the Empire, while the High Council's decision to forfeit the Empire's claim to the Archanis Sector to Federation control clearly dictates that my tenure as governor of Archanis has been deemed unworthy and without honor.

I am requesting you to return to Archanis IV and to participate in our time honored tradition of *Mauk-to'Vor*. In accordance of fulfilling your duty as a fellow son of *Jeh'L*, and a Klingon warrior, you restore my honor in the afterlife and ensure my entry into *Sto-Vo-Kor*. I await your arrival.

Qapla'!

SCIENCE REPORT

DR. GILLIAN TAYLOR,
CETACEAN BIOLOGIST,
U.S.S. JOHANNESBURG,
STARDATE 8439.6

"Observation of George and Gracie continue without interference since Gracie gave birth. I continue to receive regular reports regarding their health and welfare. I've accepted a position at the New Cetacean Institute that will start in a few months that will put me back on Earth and in close contact with George and Gracie. I am very excited to see them again. The time spent here on the *Johannesburg* has allowed me to catch up on the three hundred years of history but I'm ready to go back to Earth. Thank God, for my photographic memory. This would not have been as easy without it.

"George and Gracie have adapted well to life in Earth's future. The ecosystem of 23rd century Earth is different than that of the 20th century. Fortunately, krill has not become extinct so there is a vast food supply for them. George and Gracie have already settled into a regular migration pattern along with their new calf. As happy as they seem to be, I expect another calf to be born as soon as Gracie is ready. It will be a very slow process, but I strongly feel that a repopulation of humpback whales will be a success. This is especially important if that Probe ever comes back to Earth to communicate with the whales."

EXECUTIVE SUMMARY

**PRESENTED BY ADMIRAL KYLOR JEROK,
INTELLIGENCE ANALYST, ROMULAN IMPERIAL FLEET**

Narendra III was the single greatest failure in Romulan naval history. Although our task force, consisting of four warbirds, successfully destroyed a Klingon outpost and the *Enterprise*-C, the goal of our attack was to send a clear message to the Klingons who were attempting to assert their superiority in that sector. In that goal, we failed spectacularly. Our victory became the catalyst for a Federation-Klingon Alliance that has dominated the Alpha and Beta Quadrants for over twenty years and isolated us from the rest of the Galaxy.

Reports from the commanders at Narendra III commented on the *Enterprise*-C's resilience after taking sustained fire from their disruptors. Upon further study, the Battle of Narendra III exposed significant deficiencies in the tactical training of our officers. We were fortunate the commanders at Narendra III had the foresight to capture Federation escape pods and take the ship's officers into custody. The interrogation of acting tactical officer Tasha Yar revealed the Federation's training was decades ahead of our own and explained how a single Federation ship was able to defend itself against four warbirds.

"Endless Profits to you, Oh Grand Nagus!

I, DaiMon Tarr, bring to you news of a recent triumph. My efforts in the Delphi Ardu system have confirmed that the so-called 'United Federation of Planets' has no real sense of commerce whatsoever – even less than that of the Klingons, and you know what lobeless fools they are!

The Humans were easily convinced by me to engage in a collaborative venture at Delphi Ardu, in deactivating a dangerous ancient planetary defense system, which presented a hazard to commerce in this region of space. This venture was, of course, a clever ruse, which allowed me to observe them closely – including their perverse habit of working alongside females whom they force to wear clothing – and ended with our taking sole possession of a collection of ingenious hand-restraints ('Chinese finger-traps', as the Humans call them), which we were able to take from them at no cost! (Sadly, the ancient defense system was unsalvageable, but will offer no further threat to bold Ferengi merchants, thanks to me.)

The territory these Humans hold is large, and ripe for exploitation. I'm sure that your keen business sense can derive all manner of profitable ventures that may result from entering into this underdeveloped market. I only humbly ask that a small finder's fee – of whatever amount you deem appropriate, Oh Heavily-lobed One – be bestowed upon Your humble servant Tarr for making the initial overtures.

May the Divine Treasury smile upon our new opportunity… Of course, more upon you in particular, with maybe a little bit for me."

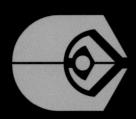

While this institution has consistently recommended a neutral stance when it comes to formal Federation involvement in the Cardassian occupation of Bajor, we have since reconsidered our recommendation. With this report, we hereby inform the Federation Security Council and the Starfleet Chief of Staff that any military involvement against the Cardassians regarding Bajor should absolutely NOT be considered.

While our earlier stance on non-involvement has been consistent over the last 30 years, we are adjusting it due to the recent appointment of one Gul Dukat as the Cardassian prefect of the Bajoran occupation. Data received by us from merchants and other sources indicate Dukat is a ruthless tyrant and a brutally effective administrator. He commands significant forces on and around Bajor and currently has the ability to request additional forces and supplies from Cardassia. Barring a declaration of war, something the Federation can ill-afford at this time, we envision no means by which Starfleet can prevail against the entrenched Cardassian forces on Bajor.

However, we have, as always, carefully considered the variables and believe that there is a 94.7 percent probability that Gul Dukat's methods will only serve to reinforce the Bajoran resistance's resolve and will force a settlement within the next 8 to 12 years. As such, we recommend the Security Council begin to prepare for a contingency in which the Federation steps in to provide food and medical supplies to a broken, but free, Bajor.

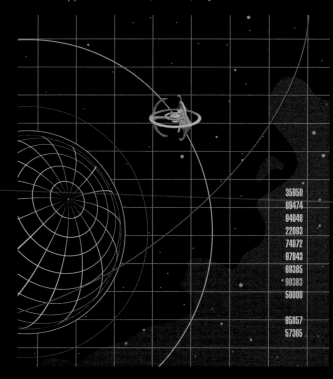

35950
89474
94848
22093
74872
87843
69385
90383
50000

95857
57385

INTERCEPTED REPORT

INTERCEPTED REPORT

Adya,

The enemy has come. The Melbourne has been recalled to Starbase 324, where we've joined three dozen other vessels under the command of Admiral Hanson. In a few hours, we ship out to Wolf 359, where I expect to die. The Borg are powerful and we are laughably unprepared, no matter what the Admiral says with his pretty words.

Remember Crewman Yondar, and his endless complaints about my "offensive bluntness" and "extreme honesty"? Amusingly, he approached me an hour ago to thank me for not blunting the truth of the mission in our staff briefing. "It's much easier," he said, "to not obsess about what could happen, now that you've told us what's most likely to happen." And it's just like I've always said: Humans might prefer someone who'll pet their feelings and tell them what special star-trails they are, but when it's life and death, only honesty does any good.

I have regrets, Adya. I regret I didn't make it home on my last shore leave. I regret that, at long last, I am forced to admit you were always right. Starfleet was a mistake, and I should have stayed on Ricktor Prime. But knowing you were right and knowing that I should have chosen a different life path for our family changes nothing. I am a Starfleet officer, and only honorless cowards flee for safety when the duty they swore to perform results in an unpleasant death. Rejoice in your victory, my love, and curse my name well, but I won't abandon my duty just because survival is impossible.

Tialo, Zeri, if you grow up hating me for dying so early in your lives, I love you anyway. You're going to make bad decisions, and I regret that I won't be there to fight with you about them. Tialo, I completely disapprove of your plans to apply for Starfleet. But you're as stubborn as I am, and if you refuse to be smarter than me, you better choose a field with more career advancement than Security. Zeri, stop listening to your grandfather. He's a bitter old man with nothing but poison in his heart. Go to the Performance Academy. Dance your most flawless, and then kick them all in the teeth if they turn your application down.

Adya… Starfleet will come to you. They'll say I died well. I won't. Most likely, I've been assimilated, and am now enslaved by the enemy. Starfleet will tell you I served with honor and distinction. I did, but they'll get those facts from my service record, not my shipmates, because they'll be dead or assimilated too.

After I finish this message, I'll update my will to demand they send a Vulcan to notify you. Then, you'll get the facts instead of placating lies. You have been the bane of my life, and I love you for it.

Livvia

PERSONAL LOG

TACTICAL ANALYSIS

S02E23

S03E26

S04E01

S05E23

S06E26

58383	HIGH INTENSITY CUTTING BEAMS
83833	MAGNETOMETRIC GUIDED CHARGES
29585	UNKNOWN
60383	MISSILE SYSTEMS
49803	TRACTOR BEAM EMITTERS
86044	UNKNOWN
49000	UNKNOWN
84844	SUBSPACE FIELD GENERATORS
40739	ELECTROMAGNETIC FIELD GENERATORS
84744	REGENERATIVE CAPABILITIES
98394	FORCE FIELD GENERATORS
58383	ADAPTIVE SHIELDING

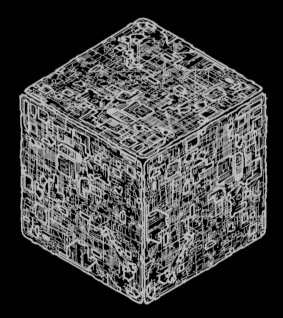

739824
830233   848484
085830

958575
948484   385844
948495   209585
947464   808474
847434   949407
447363

948585
374744   848494
847474   959585
848333   059595
858303   959595

857473
867323

552533
857574
249685
857444

BORG CUBE

WOLF 359

REPORT++++ UPLOAD BEGINS++++
SRC UN ONE OF TEN/PRIMARY ADJUNCT/UNIMATRIX 03++++
TACSUM ENGAGEMENT AT SECTOR 0 0 1 / DESIGNATION WOLF
359++++

WE ENCOUNTERED RESISTANCE / 40 VESSELS OF VARYING
SIZE AND CONFIGURATION / [ATTACHMENT: SENSOR RECORD
45872AA1] / TECHNICAL DATA FROM RECENTLY ASSIMILATED
UNIT LOCUTUS INDICATED EXPECTED OPPOSITION TACTICS
AND CAPABILITIES++++

39 VESSELS DESTROYED / 11230 BEINGS ELMINATED AND
UNAVAILABLE FOR ASSIMILATION / DAMAGE TO CUBE MINIMAL

/ 1 VESSEL NEUTRALIZED AND LEFT FOR EVENTUAL
ASSIMILATION FOLLOWING COMPLETION OF PRIMARY
DIRECTIVE ++++

CURRENTLY ENTERING SOL SYSTEM FOR COMPLETION
OF PRIMARY DIRECTIVE / UNIT LOCUTUS HAS BEEN
REMOVED FROM CUBE / REMOVAL IS FUTILE AND SHALL
NOT EFFECT DIRECTIVE OUTCOME++++

REPORT ENDS++++
[ADDENDUM / CUBE 632 DESTROYED BY CODE
COMMAND ERROR / TIMESTAMP AJ7-5W / PRIMARY
DIRECTIVE FAILURE IN SECTOR 0 0 1 / ALERT]

INTERCEPTED TACTICAL SUMMARY

GUL KALANE

"Those spineless bleeding hearts in the Detapa Council have finally twisted the knife into the back of the Union. Withdrawal from Bajor! I can hardly believe my senses.

With the stroke of a pen, they are giving up a strategic foothold at the very doorstep of the Federation. Madness! Bajor may no longer be producing as much in resources as it once did, but that surely is no reason to abandon the advantage that our presence there gives us, in the event that our treaty with the Federation ends…

But no: the sharp drop in resource extraction, coupled by the cost of fighting the terrorist insurgency, they say. That's the reason for the Detapa Council to blithely give away what Cardassian blood and sweat has secured.

As if they can't see that Bajor will run to the open arms of the Federation, giving Starfleet a base of operations practically inside our borders. This betrayal shall not stand. I hope and pray that some Cardassian patriot saves us from the folly of these weak-willed simpletons."

INTERCEPTED PERSONAL LOG

PERSONAL LOG

In my six-month rotation with disaster relief and trauma teams on the surface of Bajor, I counselled numerous internment camp survivors as well as those termed "collaborators". Thus far, every Bajoran I have encountered has shared one thing with all others: a deep well of violent anger simmering under their skin. It crawls on them, laces each word they speak, twists their smiles and taints their voices until I can hear nothing but their screams for Cardassian blood to be spilled in the streets.

Perhaps that sounds dramatic, but it is quite a dramatic sensation, and I want to describe it as accurately as I can for the sake of non-telepaths' understanding. The lengthy occupation by the Cardassians has left its scars on the planet and her people, a psychic residue that lingers on the soul like the mud lingers on bodies. Stripped bare of its resources, Bajor reflects the pain

of its people, a pain every Bajoran feels in every cell of their beings. Even those accused of colluding with the Cardassians cannot escape it.

Their trauma is far too fresh, their wounds barely closed over. The Bajoran people as a whole need steady hearts and kind hands to help them restore their ravaged, strip-mined world and their decimated society. They need compassion and relief assistance, not power and status. I cannot and will not offer my recommendation for the Bajoran application. Until they begin to heal and let go of their rage and vengeance, it's too soon to welcome them into Federation ranks.

— Jessimi Zikal, Betazoid trauma counselor, in written testimony to the World Status Advisory Committee

PERSONAL LOG

RE: DAYSTROM INSTITUTE ARCHAEOLOGICAL COUNCIL REQUEST TO STUDY HEBITIAN TOMBS

Councilor Pelek:

This issue is one that requires delicacy. The Daystrom Institute is a respected voice across many worlds, including to some within this university, and I am not certain refusing their request will not result in questions being raised. Since we have been making recent overtures to the Federation, any refusal to allow their scientists and archaeologists to study the tombs could be seen as cause for suspicion.

Sura Mekar,
Inquisitor of Culat

RE: DAYSTROM INSTITUTE ARCHAEOLOGICAL COUNCIL REQUEST TO STUDY HEBITIAN TOMBS

Inquisitor Mekar:

You will find a way to dissuade the Daystrom Institute from pressing the issue and coming to Cardassia, and you will do so without arousing the suspicions of Starfleet. Cardassia can ill-afford so-called scientists and archaeologists bumbling around Culat or the floodplains, searching for artifacts and burial sites that are no longer there.

Perhaps you could suggest they purchase rare Hebitian artifacts from Ferengi markets to study. I understand the Ferengi have recently acquired a significant number of them.

Pelek Evim
Detapa Council

"Come now, Gaila. This opportunity should be making your lobes tingle in delight."

"Oh, my lobes are tingling. But in delight, not so much."

"But what is that rule you keep quoting me, the one about war being good for business?"

"Thirty-four. And don't presume to quote the Ferengi Rules of Acquisition to me. I know them all by heart, backwards and forwards."

"But surely you can see the profit potential to be made here. It's not every day the Klingon Empire is shattered by civil war."

"It's happened more than once, and this one has the unmistakable stench of Romulan ale poured all over it."

"Hah! Romulans. They're too busy spying on the Federation across their precious Neutral Zone. Why would the Romulans want to push the Klingons into civil war?"

"Don't be stupid. The Klingons and Federation are two of the three strongest powers in the quadrant, and if one of them collapses, the other will be facing the Romulans on a one to one basis. Now, that, while generally good for my business, is

even more dangerous than arms dealing already is. Playing both sides against the other doubles the chances of getting caught."

"So what's the problem? That sounds like your stock in trade."

"But you're not seeing the whole board, my foolish friend. It's the Klingons. They're far too unpredictable to gauge the odds on how this will turn out. I'm reluctant to sell to them now because their blood is up. Sure, I could make some quick latinum here and there, but I'm playing a longer and more profitable game. Two Klingon fleets happen to be armed with weapons I sold to them months ago."

"You knew this civil war would happen? I find that hard to believe."

"A Ferengi smells profit on the winds of war."

"Is that another one of the damned acquisition rules?"

"No, my friend. That's one of mine. Drink up, and be merry. There's latinum to be made once the Klingons figure out who to fight, other than themselves."

739824
830233
085830

948484
948495
947464
847434
447363

374744
847474
848333
858303

857473
887323

552533
857574
249685
857444

848484

958575
385844
209585
808474
949407

948585
848494

0057

0056

SEC 31

INTELLIGENCE TRANSCRIPT

CAPTAIN ZELNABOG, PAKLED MERCENARY

This was a good day. The comm system my crew stole from a drunken Klingon warrior is strong. Engineer Yaberitog plugged into our ship's power grid with few issues, though after the power surge, I must now seek out a new engineer, one that can make us go better.

We were sneaking past a Romulan outpost when the new comm system made funny noises. It spoke in Klingon, but Officer Turbendadog, who is smart, said that it was actually Klingon translation of a Romulan message. They report that a stable wormhole has appeared in the Bajoran sector; a wormhole that supposedly connects to the Gamma Quadrant. I did not know what

this meant, so I asked my science chief, Otisatasog, who is also smart. He said that a stable wormhole to the Gamma Quadrant meant that a whole lot of space was now open for investigation. There could be many species in the Gamma Quadrant with things we can steal.

I gave Otisatasog extra rations of bu'laq, a painless gesture given that Yaberitog no longer needs them. I have set course for the Bajor system so that we can go to this wormhole and to the Gamma Quadrant. We will be the first Pakled ship to enter the Gamma Quadrant. We will be showered in glory when we return.

PERSONAL LOG

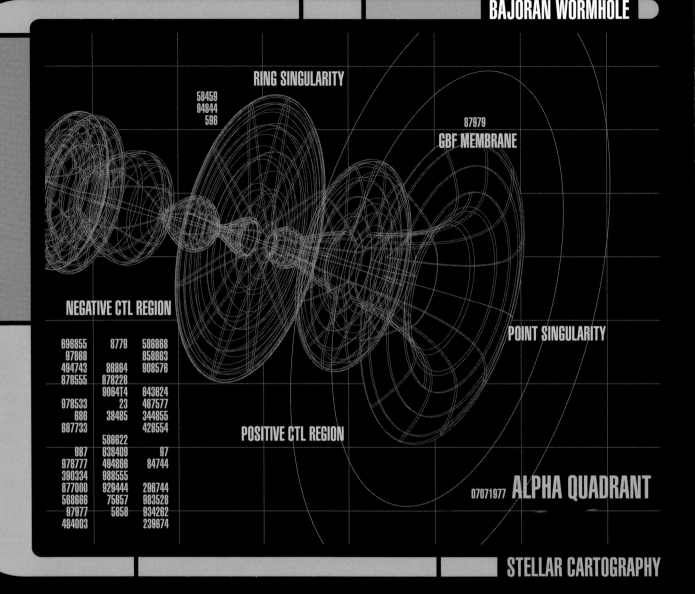

RING SINGULARITY

58459
94844
596

87979
GBF MEMBRANE

NEGATIVE CTL REGION

POINT SINGULARITY

696855	8779	586868
97868		858663
494743	86864	908576
878555	878228	
	9064T4	643624
978533	23	467577
686	38485	344855
687733		428554
	586622	
987	638409	97
978777	494866	84744
390334	988555	
877000	929444	296744
568666	75657	983528
97977	5858	934262
484003		239674

POSITIVE CTL REGION

07071977 ALPHA QUADRANT

STELLAR CARTOGRAPHY

EXECUTIVE SUMMARY

Admiral Kylor Jerok, Intelligence Analyst, Romulan Imperial Fleet

Since the Federation's discovery of the Bajoran Wormhole, Romulan Intelligence has recorded a number of rumors about a powerful, expansionist polity in the Gamma Quadrant known as the Dominion. So far, information on the Dominion is limited to second-hand sources and scattered reports. Some sources report that the Dominion destroyed several Federation outposts in the Gamma Quadrant.

The existence of a new rival to the Federation offers two possibilities:

First, if the Dominion is weaker than the Federation, we should

ally with them. Since the Dominion's only means of travel to the Alpha Quadrant is through the Bajoran Wormhole, then we will have them at a strategic disadvantage. A Romulan-Dominion alliance would allow us the opportunity to exploit the resources of the Gamma Quadrant and develop new allies to combat the Federation-Klingon Alliance.

Second, if the Dominion is more powerful than the Federation, we should incite hostilities between them. Both sides will fight until they have exhausted manpower and resources. The eventual victor will be unable to stop Romulan Empire from ascending to the dominant power in the Alpha, Beta, and Gamma Quadrants.

PERSONAL LOG

YOUR CONTINUING MISSION

YOUR CONTINUING MISSION
STARFLEET'S PURPOSE

"YOU KEEP WONDERING IF MAN WAS MEANT TO BE OUT HERE. YOU KEEP WONDERING; YOU KEEP ON SIGNING ON."

— CAPTAIN JAMES T. KIRK

Starfleet serves a complicated, multi-role purpose within the United Federation of Planets. From the earliest days Starfleet's mission has always been one of peaceful exploration and scientific inquiry. However, because starships venture into unknown, possibly hostile areas, they are armed with powerful defensive weaponry, leading to a secondary, peace-keeping role. It is neither purely scientific, nor purely military, but rather a combination of the two depending on the circumstances.

First and foremost, Starfleet is primarily a scientific and exploratory organization serving on behalf of the Federation government. Back in the late 20th and early 21st centuries, scientific inquiry and exploration were the purview of various private, non-governmental, and governmental organizations. You may recall from your history readings the exploits of Jacques Cousteau exploring the Earth's oceans, CERN's efforts to unlock the mysteries of quantum physics, and NASA's missions to explore the Sol system (and beyond). With the founding of Starfleet, those various independent efforts were centralized and coordinated under Starfleet. After the terrors of the Eugenics Wars and World War III,

humanity had tired of war. First contact with the Vulcans had shown us that we could venture out into space not as conquerors, but as explorers. This idea is embodied in our credo "to seek out new life and new civilizations".

STARFLEET'S NAÏVITÉ

The Earthers say their primary mission is one of peace. But who equips their ships with the power to lay waste to a planet's surface and does not use it?

Starfleet's officers are naïve. And that is something to be exploited. While they prattle on about the right of self-determination and interstellar law, we act. If you can present a starship officer with a *fait accompli*, they will back off and call for some kind of negotiations.

In fact, the only time they will fight is when directly attacked. We fought a war with them once. It was glorious, and they made noble adversaries, but they seem to have lost the taste for war.

They wield awesome destructive power, but hesitate to use it. And that is how you defeat them; never attack a starship directly. Engage them in futile negotiations. Let them talk (starship captains love to talk). Meanwhile, deploy your forces carefully, in secret, and hand them an irreversible situation. Use their peacefulness against them.

Major Rolis, Tal Shiar

Starfleet's secondary function is to defend Federation members and the Federation as a whole from hostile intent. Although every Federation member maintains some kind of planetary defense force to protect their individual star systems, Starfleet vessels patrol ninety percent of the space lanes in between to ensure free and open passage. And our exploratory efforts take us far beyond the boundaries of the Federation into potentially hostile situations. Because starships venture into the unknown, they are equipped not only with sophisticated sensor systems, probes, and drones, but also with powerful defensive systems. Starships patrol along the Klingon and Romulan neutral zones, and in the past have been called upon to investigate the sudden disappearance of Federation colonies, protect Starfleet outposts, defend against hostile alien probes, and serve as peacekeepers between warring alien governments.

Despite the tremendous destructive power a starship can bring to bear, however, Starfleet's role has always been one of peace. Starfleet captains do not start wars, and should never "shoot first and ask questions later."

STARFLEET ORGANIZATION

As an officer in Starfleet, you fit inside a much larger chain of command. Our orders come to us from above — from department heads, who get them from commanding officers, who get them from admirals, who get them from Starfleet Command and, ultimately, from the Federation Council itself. It is our unqualified respect for the chain of command that lets us know that our orders are valid. It is important you understand Starfleet organization and know your place in it.

At the top, ultimate authority rests with the Federation Council and the President of the United Federation of Planets. Both have the power to direct Starfleet to undertake specific missions — say a planetary evacuation, for example — though this has rarely been used.

Next comes the Starfleet commander-in-chief, who is responsible for Starfleet as a whole. The CIC sets the policies and initiatives for the entire organization, keeping in mind Federation needs and priorities and Starfleet's mission statement, regulations, and precedence. They receive a daily briefing on Starfleet's overall disposition as well as any matters that may rise to the level of his or her attention. Examples might include hostilities along the Romulan border or the approach of a potentially hostile alien probe. They are in frequent contact, and consult with, admirals throughout the service. Starfleet monitors all fleet operations through Starfleet Operations, which maintains the present position and disposition of every starship and starbase at the Fleet Operations Center on Earth.

The fleet admirals make up the next level in the chain of command. As their title indicates, fleet admirals are responsible for an entire fleet of starships (and starbases). Typically, this comprises several sectors, such as the region of space along the Klingon border. Their responsibilities include overseeing and directing all the ships within their respective fleets and serving as the link between individual admirals and Starfleet Command.

Admirals command more than one ship. They are typically posted to a starbase (though not always) and command all the Starfleet vessels in their area of responsibility, most often a specific sector. They are the officers most frequently in contact with a starship's captain, with orders and mission assignments coming directly from them.

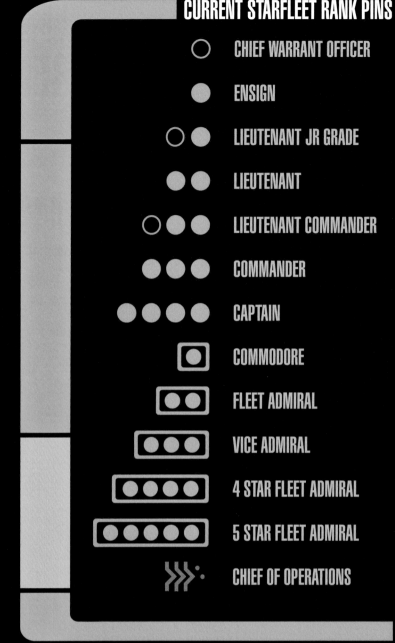

CURRENT STARFLEET RANK PINS

CHIEF WARRANT OFFICER

ENSIGN

LIEUTENANT JR GRADE

LIEUTENANT

LIEUTENANT COMMANDER

COMMANDER

CAPTAIN

COMMODORE

FLEET ADMIRAL

VICE ADMIRAL

4 STAR FLEET ADMIRAL

5 STAR FLEET ADMIRAL

CHIEF OF OPERATIONS

YOUR CONTINUING MISSION
THE PRIME DIRECTIVE

STARFLEET GENERAL ORDER ONE

THE PRIME DIRECTIVE — SUMMARY

"No identification of self or mission. No interference with the social development of said planet. No references to space, or the fact that there are other worlds or more advanced civilizations…

This guiding philosophy prevents Starfleet personnel from interfering in the natural development of other civilizations. It stops them from beaming down to a planet, proclaiming "Behold! I am the Archangel Gabriel!" and using superior knowledge and technology to dominate a less-developed world. Starfleet officers swear to uphold the Prime Directive even at the cost of their own lives, the lives of their crew, and their ship.

The fundamental principles of the Prime Directive existed long before the doctrine itself. Its roots can be seen in the Vulcan practice of avoiding contact with primitive, pre-warp societies. Had Zefram Cochrane failed to make his historic, first faster-than-light trip in the *Phoenix*, the Vulcan survey vessel would have passed Earth by as too primitive, and first contact would not have occurred. Later, early Starfleet crews realized the need for some kind of doctrine establishing what Humans should and should not do while exploring space. Contrary to popular belief, however, application of the Prime Directive is not based solely on warp capabilities. Starfleet Command may, after initial survey missions, determine that a culture possesses significantly advanced technologies to warrant first contact. Similarly, if a civilization contacts the Federation first, then the Prime Directive applies less strictly than it would for a newly discovered world.

Specifically, General Order One prohibits certain actions covering a wide range of activities, which constitutes "interference." You cannot provide knowledge of other inhabited planets or other civilizations. Do not provide knowledge of technologies or science. You may not take actions to generally affect a civilization's overall development. You may not involve yourselves in the internal affairs of another society, such as backing one faction over another.

These prohibitions also include actions that have presented profound moral challenges for both captains and crew — helping a society escape the consequences of their own actions; saving a civilization from a natural disaster (even if inaction would result in the society's extinction); and subverting or avoiding the application of a society's laws. How will you react when you discover a world where capital punishment is the law, and your captain is to be executed for a seemingly minor infraction? Can you sit by and watch a primitive culture be destroyed by an asteroid collision? Since the early days of Starfleet, these kinds of moral quandaries, and many more, have obliged command crews to debate how best to balance competing ethical priorities.

You must determine how to interpret the Prime Directive in any given situation. Starfleet gives commanding officers wide leeway regarding whether and how the Prime Directive applies. In the early years of Starfleet, captains tended to err on the side of intervention, interpreting the Prime Directive to only apply to living, growing, developing civilizations; they interfered in situations where the society fell into a state of arrested development, had been somehow enslaved, or faced mortal danger. The most famous example is Captain James T. Kirk, who has been accused of being slow to invoke the Prime Directive. In later years, officers have taken it as an absolute, and were willing to watch whole societies perish from natural or evolutionary causes rather than interfere. The truth is the application of the Prime Directive exists along a continuum depending on many factors. Is the planet a Federation colony? Has there been prior contamination by Federation citizens or Klingon agents? Is the planet in negotiations with the Federation? Is it possible to intervene without revealing the existence of other spacefaring civilizations? Should an officer violate the Prime Directive, he or she is expected to provide detailed justification in their logs; should Starfleet Command deny the reasons, the penalty for violating the Prime Directive ranges from a reprimand in the officer's permanent record to outright dismissal from the service (and possible imprisonment).

Starfleet recognizes many exceptions to the Prime Directive. These do not revoke the Prime Directive in its entirety, however. If warranted, starship crews are expected to intervene in the least intrusive way possible when the situation calls for it. For example, if required to repair a

I was there when the Federation made first contact with my people. The starship contacted one of our system defense ships at the edge of our star system. We had only just recently developed warp drive, and used it mainly within our system. I was aboard our ship, on the bridge as third mate. I'd never seen anything that big before. It was an *Ambassador* class, the *U.S.S. Resolute*. It took some convincing before our captain believed that your intentions weren't hostile.

We escorted the *Resolute* back to Homeworld. Apparently, our leaders also thought your intentions were hostile, because much of our fleet waited in orbit. That was your first challenge to overcome, but there were others. We didn't like that you'd been spying on us with your long-range probes, secret observatories, and covert agents. We gave your Federation envoy a hard time about that.

Then there was the dislocation you created when we learned we weren't alone in the Galaxy. Some said you intended to assimilate our culture. There was social and political upheaval. We still used money at the time, so news of your replicators caused a lot of fear and anger among our merchants and industrialists. It took time, but you were patient with us. Your envoy negotiated in good faith and addressed our concerns; you let us keep our government, respected our traditions, and phased in those replicators.

Because I was already a military officer and had been on board the ship that made first contact, I was selected to be among the first class from Homeworld to attend Starfleet Academy. That's where I came to better understand your Prime Directive. You do not contact civilizations that aren't ready to accept the idea of the Federation. You don't come to dominate, or impose your ideas or way of life. You knew we were ready to join the larger Galaxy before we did.

And now as a Starfleet officer, I see the wisdom of the Prime Directive. It doesn't only say what we can't do; it tells us what we can do, and when. I don't know where my people would be without the Federation. I've seen the Prime Directive from the other side, and I've seen its value. That's why I proudly swore to uphold its principles, even at the risk of my life.

- Excerpt: Lt. Iekush Fo, Valedictorian Address,
  Starfleet Academy class of 2369

A SWORD OF DAMOCLES

The Prime Directive. Singular and ubiquitous, it governs our approach to how we deal with nascent civilizations and all those we encounter in our journeys between the stars. But every cadet should know, should understand, that this directive, while born of a desire to provide agency to those we encounter and not force them along our path is a Sword of Damocles. It is both the overriding paradigm by which we operate in order to allow freedom, and a burden that at times forces us to stand watching while terrible circumstance wreaks a bloody price.

At the Academy we are taught that to interfere, to bring technology and our definition of civilization to those we encounter almost always leads to chaotic disruption. But it is hardly easy to walk the other route. To follow the Prime Directive means that we must, at times, stand by when problems we could easily solve lead to destruction, suffering, and death. I say this, not to criticize the ideology of our approach, but to ready you for the price this path asks of us. It is no easy thing, our Prime Directive, and while we are right to concede agency to those we encounter, it has a cost. At times we will invest in the circumstances we encounter our emotions, our passions, our hopes; it is only Human to do so. But it carries a heavy price, and that we can bear knowing only that the alternative, to intervene or control, has been demonstrated through history to be disastrous. Between forcing a solution regardless of price and allowing a solution to be discovered and owned by the discoverers, history shows us that there is no truly compassionate choice to make but to follow the Prime Directive.

- Captain Katherine Unmeyer,
  in her lecture series On the Nature of Starfleet,
  Starfleet Academy.

prior cultural contamination, you are expected to do so in a way that does not lead to even greater interference. These exceptions include, but are not limited to: the society already knows about the Federation; they communicate with or attack a Federation vessel; they send a planetary distress signal to any and all spacefaring societies; we are in diplomatic discussions with the society; the civilization was previously contaminated by Federation citizens or non-Federation actors (such as the Klingons or Romulans); compliance with valid, direct orders from Starfleet Command. Doubtless, over the course of your careers in Starfleet, you will encounter many other exceptions to the Prime Directive (and doubtless create a few).

In the end, despite Starfleet's great respect for the Prime Directive, and strict demands that it be adhered to, you must ask yourself how it shapes your personal actions. Do you allow a species to pursue a dangerous political system that oppresses its citizens? Do you allow the extinction of a civilization from a supernova, when you have the power to stop it? Will you sit by and allow Romulan agents to arm one primitive faction against another? There is no question the Prime Directive prevents us from getting involved in situations where we can help. However, we must all consider the unintended consequences of meddling in the affairs of a civilization not yet ready to learn they are not alone in the universe. Are you ready to accept the consequences, whatever your decision? Not every Starfleet officer believes that strict adherence to the Prime Directive is in the best interests of the societies it was designed to protect. You must discover your own personal tolerance for the degree of flexibility you are willing to accept when applying the Prime Directive. You have the power to alter the natural evolution of an entire planet in your hands. You must figure out when to use, or not use, that power. You bear a heavy responsibility.

THOUGHTS ON THE PRIME DIRECTIVE

After the successful completion of our mission to Eudora IV, I find myself thinking about the Prime Directive. Specifically, I'm thinking about all the other species and entities out here in space that do not have a Prime Directive. Of all the spacefaring civilizations, only Starfleet has a non-interference article.

The Romulans, Klingons, Cardassians, and Ferengi don't have one. They interfere all the time. The Borg exist solely to absorb other worlds into their collective. But what about beings who are obviously superior to us — the Organians, the Metrons, the Q Continuum? The Organians intervened in a potential war with the Klingons. The Metrons were prepared to exterminate either us or the Gorn. And Q? He seems to delight in meddling in our affairs.

If the Prime Directive is right and proper, then why don't these more advanced beings have their own version? What does that say about us? Maybe it's our duty to seek out new life-forms and new civilizations, and lift them up. Maybe we should use our power — our science and technology — to do good throughout the universe. End a global epidemic. Stop a world war. Spread our political system. Maybe they're right.

But then I remember that we're not gods. We cannot predict the consequences of our actions. It's just that days like today make it damned hard to obey the Prime Directive.

- Captain Geoff MacIntosh

YOUR CONTINUING MISSION
STARFLEET ACADEMY

THE CALL TO ADVENTURE

Welcome.

Your decisions, from this point on, affect the lives of Federation citizens. Perhaps it will be only a handful — those on your ship or on an away team — or, as experience has shown us, perhaps it will be the lives of us all. Our expectation is that under all these circumstances, you and your crew will represent the finest that Starfleet has to offer.

Due to the overwhelming number of experiential iterations that may have led to your placement in a command position, the Starfleet Office Material Management has compiled the following summary of what to expect from your Academy-trained crew and from later recruits and/or transfers.

WHY WE SEND PEOPLE TO THE STARS

Since duotronic processors gave way to multitronic technology and later to isolinear, there has been a consistent but steadfast group of Federation members who have questioned why Starfleet sends people into space. Why not send drones for exploration and keep people safe? Barring the M-5 incident in 2268, which involved deaths aboard the U.S.S. *Excalibur* and U.S.S. *Lexington*, the types of programs needed to run ships have been technically feasible since the late 23rd century. The question was never "could we?" It has always been "should we?" Is it ethically desirable to promote efficiency over humanity (or, as later argued, over any species)?

This culminated in the famous Soong-Graves debates at the Academy in the early 24th century over the potential development of positronic sentience (later realized in Dr. Noonien Soong's famous creations and others, such as the hologram entity titled "Moriarty") and its impact on the exploration question. The consensus was reached that the answer was embedded in Starfleet's original promise: "to explore strange new worlds, to seek out new life and new civilizations, to boldly go where no one has gone before."

THE EMOTIONAL COST OF EXPLORATION

To be a member of Starfleet already marks you out to be someone special, someone with the fire of curiosity, intelligence to go with it, discipline and courage. But few of us realize, until we have served, the true cost of serving. By setting forth on this path you are choosing the difficult road. You will be away from family and friends, severed from the context of your life before the Academy and sent out journeying. We follow in the greatest traditions of Human endeavor; the exploration of the unknown. But it has a cost, when we leave we will be changed by those things we experience, in ways that our friends and families will not often understand, and as our list of past missions grows, the difference will be greater and greater. Those we leave behind will change as well, and returning to those we love can often be surreal as we, altered by our experiences, meet again people we knew, but who have also changed. It is a difficult thing.

While an often repeated phrase it is also true that the crews you serve with will become your families. Knitted together by circumstance, stressful, at times, and dangerous, you will share a bond with them that we who have served rarely speak about but all understand. Leaving, being away, and coming back, these are hard, but you will have each other and those crews you serve with, bonded by shared experience, a trust like no other and friendships that will last your lives.

- Captain Katherine Unmeyer,
  in her lecture series On the Nature of Starfleet,
  Starfleet Academy.

STARFLEET ACADEMY

EX ASTRIS, SCIENTIA

SAN FRANCISCO · MMCLXI

More notably, each recognized in that debate that, within each species, it is a statistical certainty that people exist who are more curious than average and less averse to risk. In a situation as resource-rich as the Federation, how is their specific potential realized? The answer, of course, is Starfleet. It is reaching out toward the unknown that defines that type of person. It is not the only answer, but it is what defines a starship crew.

Starfleet Academy has been meticulously set up — from our initial public contact with families, through the candidate's initial application, entrance exams, psychological tests, selection committees, preparatory program, curriculum, training cruise, and final placement — to pull through the curious and the brave. While this manifests differently in its outward expression from species to species, it is a virtual guarantee that your crew will exhibit these tendencies.

They are, to date, the reason why the Federation has had unprecedented success in contact with new worlds and new civilizations.

FOSTERING LIFE-LONG LEARNING

Starfleet Academy runs a rigorous academic course, comprised of advanced educational tracks that can take from four to eight years to complete, leaving a cadet with the possibility of graduating holding several degrees in a variety of majors. While there is an incredible variety of majors to be found — advanced theoretical physics, astrophysics, engineering, exo-archaeology, exobiology, probability mechanics, sociolinguistics, and zoology to name a few — all cadets must meet certain requirements.

Cadets are expected to have an exhaustive understanding of Starfleet's General Orders and Regulations, as well as at least a preliminary comprehension of Federation charter law. They must maintain a cross-disciplinary study in the basics of command, astrosciences and navigation, engineering, security, and science and medicine, regardless of their own speciality. The curriculum is deliberately intensive so that graduates from the program may temporarily stand in for any department on a ship, if needed.

Most importantly, though, they are expected to nurture a passion for learning. Memory Alpha contains a wealth of information from across the Federation. Students learn how to access the proper lines of information and formulate novel lines of inquiry at any time, even under severe stress.

In order to promote practicality over the purely theoretical, students are consistently exposed to novel experiences. This is done through bridge simulators, holodeck scenarios, and hands-on missions. The real-world missions are considered especially important because they allow for random variations to enter the scenario. Academy training grounds can be found on various points in the Sol solar system, Beta Aquilae II, Beta Ursae Minor II, Relva VII, Psi Upsilon III, and other locations within Federation space.

THE ACADEMY EXPERIENCE: MAKING CONNECTIONS

Serious attention has been given to the core idea that bold, curious individuals are, above all, the most likely candidates to successfully enter and complete Starfleet Academy. In return, these members from more than one hundred and fifty Federation worlds as well as endorsed individuals from well over a thousand worlds will be in possession of some of the most advanced technology the Federation has to offer.

In the earliest days of multitronic technology, a complex simulation was run to analyze the impact of this combination of individuality and cutting edge technology. Consistently, the simulation predicted the dissolution of Starfleet by rogue action. A copy of this report, adding examples like the Ekos Incident, the fate of the *U.S.S. Exeter*, and Captain Garth's degeneration, was presented to the Federation Council and led to a Vulcan recommendation to scrap Starfleet in favor of a more stable and sedate revision.

The Federation ethos, though, has been one of communication and understanding, building bridges of trust and mutual admiration with disparate, sometimes even hostile, cultures. Effective team-building and the Vulcan tenet of IDIC — respect for infinite diversity in infinite combinations — became the center around which the curriculum was restructured. The hard lessons learned from the earliest days of space exploration to the present were applied to the "rogue officer" problem with unmitigated success.

In brief, the Academy experience became, and is still, focused around the idea of building cooperation among team mates. The more disparate the individuals, the harder the cadets are expected to work at finding connections with their fellow cadets and minimizing the differences. This fosters a pan-universal outlook for their placement in other crews in the future.

This may manifest differently from individual to individual. A person may be socially anxious and possess very view overt friends, but his connection to his work may be where his passions shine. It is the mark of a good commander to actively seek out their crew's proclivities whenever possible. The Academy works hard to push and even exceed the limits of their students through shared experiences. A commander, talking with his crew, may find connections through Academy experiences. For example, how did they handle the difficult experience of the *Kobayashi Maru* test?

HANDS-ON, CUTTING-EDGE RESEARCH

A commonly overlooked asset is that Starfleet Academy, by design, is a research university. It is staffed by leading experts in their fields who are committed to performing cutting edge research while also training the officers of tomorrow. These professors have access to both public and sensitive research and invite students to both learn from them and to also become fresh eyes on the project. It is not unusual for a student to have co-published a discovery or insight in their field before graduation.

New graduates serve as pipelines for new research and insights to migrate to working vessels. While technically, all of their work is available in Memory Alpha, it is the graduate's personal stake that brings it to the attention of others. This level of individual investment has been shown time and again to be invaluable in the variable circumstances a starship crew may find themselves under, whether meeting aliens that masquerade as ancient gods or being able to identify subspace particles only recently isolated by Starfleet.

GRADUATION

Not every person who successfully applies to Starfleet will be able to keep up with its ferocious pace. Many of those who do pass through the initial exams drop out in their first year. There is no attached shame or blame in dropping out. Those who are still committed to serving are channelled into the Starfleet Technical Services Academy on Mars. There is extensive evidence that many of these students require and thrive in an experiential, not academic, environment and it is not unusual to see ship-board promotion, and, for dedicated enlisted personnel, a commission. A commission will require passing the necessary examinations to attend Academy courses, but by this point many enlisted personnel find an achievable challenge simply due to their past experiences.

For those that run the full course of Starfleet Academy, the promise of graduation is that a cadet will receive an officer's commission and assignment to duty. A tremendous amount of effort has been put into this moment and it is often a very emotional time. To best maximize the use of personnel, graduates are offered one to three potential paths.

VALUES AS RELATIONSHIPS

In *Chapter 5: Reporting for Duty*, creating Values for Player Characters is a key part of the character creation process. Values form the key convictions and beliefs of your character, and some of these Values may represent relationships with other characters.

As Starfleet Academy encourages connections between teammates and developing those connections through shared experiences. It could be that during character creation, you and another Player decide they know each other from the Academy – and it is not uncommon for characters on various series of *Star Trek* to know each other before their current assignment. Deciding on a relationship-based Value from the Academy, you should consider how you met, how you'd describe your relationship, and under what circumstances the relationship developed.

"… has always got my back" may come from the lasting support of a fellow cadet at the Academy.

"… is a study buddy" may form a relationship with a colleague with which theoretical work is easier or provides better results.

"Competitive with…" may frame a relationship as one of friendly or fierce competition dating back to days as Academy rivals.

First, as part of the preparation for graduation, a cadet is asked to examine and produce a list of starship postings they would prefer. They must also provide a reason for their request and this will be in their file for you to peruse at your convenience. Postings available to students are ones not already reserved for those of higher rank seeking a transfer, though at least one slot is usually set aside on any ship simply as a courtesy to the Academy.

The cadet is then asked to rank the importance of either research in their speciality or exploration. Their previous experiences are then compared to others to help determine the final state of their commission.

In summary, a graduate is always given the opportunity to shine. Whether it is a posting on a starship they are passionate about, a place where they can research something that they love, or opening up an opportunity for the thrill of adventure, Starfleet Academy is very careful about taking these talented individuals and inserting them into positions that expand their boundaries.

There are only two ways that this traditional system can be circumvented. First, a captain of a vessel may specifically request a recruit. It might be someone with a much-needed expertise or who has published about a desirable subject. Second, a petition can be made through the Federation Council. The Vulcan Science Academy has been known to do this from time to time, with certain promising cadets. Naturally, the student has some say in the matter, but if someone has requested a student to a post, this is generally

seen as a potential for quicker advancement in the ranks in the future. If a placement on your crew seems odd, look at their personnel file. They may be one of the exceptions detailed in this paragraph.

After graduation, Starfleet consistently maintains the chance for rotation between any of the cadet's original career paths. An active alumni database enables officers whose needs may change as they age to select a posting that might be more appropriate. Channels are left open so officers can contact previous instructors from their tenure, to allow quicker access to research that might not otherwise be available. And in return, the Academy receives logs and data from starships that allow them to further their own projects and curriculum.

These robust communication channels allow the Academy to further goodwill with Starfleet and receive constructive criticism as more graduates experience unique adventures.

CONCLUSION

As with everything released by the SF-OMM, we appreciate you taking the time to vet these documents. We respond to any constructive criticism and/or needed addendum as expediently as possible, typically within one standard UFP solar year. Any questions and/or clarifications should be directed to Memory Alpha or one of its sub-annexes for timely answers, and not to this office.

YOUR CONTINUING MISSION
ASSIGNMENT

Your assignment within Starfleet depends on a variety of factors — your course of study at the Academy, the results of numerous tests (of which the *Kobayashi Maru* is only the most infamous), the availability of positions within Starfleet, and the service's needs.

Upon graduation from the Academy, Starfleet Command assigns you to the appropriate division based on your course of study — command, sciences, or operations. If you graduate as a xenobiologist, then you're Assigned to the sciences division. If you're a pilot, then you're assigned as either a navigator or helmsman as part of the command division. Starfleet Command works diligently to ensure that all cadets receive the training they desire (and for which they're qualified), in order to ensure high levels of self-fulfillment, self-actualization, and job satisfaction. You can be sure the crew around you is both highly trained and highly motivated.

When it comes to your duty assignment, Starfleet first asks you what you want to do. What is your preferred posting? Starfleet Command takes these requests seriously, and if there is an opening for your preferred billet then you are assigned to the starship and position of your choice. Not everyone can be chief engineer of a *Galaxy*-class starship, however. If you cannot get the assignment of your choice, Starfleet Command will post you where you are needed: an engineering position on the *Enterprise* might not be available, but there's one open on board an *Akira*-class starship. The needs of the service come first, and you go where you are needed.

There are a number of positions available throughout the fleet. Certainly, assignment to a starship is the most romantic (and everyone's dream). But Starfleet is more than just starships; starbases, dry docks, ship tenders, deep space stations, science stations, and ground facilities — these need personnel, too. Most newly minted cadets are assigned to junior positions where they can do the least damage. Most are assigned either to smaller vessels — like the *Nova* class, *Oberth* class, or *Intrepid* class — or subordinate positions like third engineer on board a *Galaxy*-class starship. Just as likely, cadets are apt to find themselves posted as a transporter operator on a starbase, or chief engineer of an ecological

DEPARTMENT COLORS

Starfleet has largely used three colors to distinguish the three main divisions in the service — gold, blue, and red. (Except for a brief flirtation with additional colors in the late 23rd century, which included orange, white, and green).

In the mid-2260s through the early 2270s, the command branch wore gold shirts, sciences wore blue shirts, and operations wore red. Given the high mortality rate among "red shirts", the operations branch acquired a stigma within the service, and in the mid 24th century Starfleet Command altered uniform colors and some organization within the command division. The command and operations division switched uniform colors, and the positions of navigator and helmsman were moved from command to operations.

testing base on some frozen planet. The type of billet to which you are assigned depends on your performance at the Academy and your service record. For you to be assigned to a prestigious position on board a ship-of-the-line, you must do very well at the Academy indeed.

Lastly, you may be assigned to a position on a per mission basis. This is a temporary assignment. A starship may need a particular specialist to get the job done; for example, a science officer returning to a specific planet who has expertise and experience with the local flora and fauna. Or an expert in multi-dimensional physics assigned to study an unusual quasar. Starfleet Command might send back an officer who previously studied a civilization during an earlier mission in order to conduct first contact. Once the mission is complete, the temporary officer often returns to his or her original assignment (though sometimes a temporary posting can become permanent at the request of the commanding officer or crewman).

YOUR ONGOING MISSION

In the 23rd century, starship tours were limited to a duration of five years. Starfleet's resources were limited. Thus was born the iconic "five-year mission." During those five years, ship and crew were far from Starfleet support. Aside from occasional stops at a starbase for re-supply and repair, it was possible for a starship crew to go for months without seeing another Federation citizen. Even subspace communication might have taken weeks or months to reach Starfleet. The strain on ship and crew could be challenging, and it was decided to limit deployments so ships could be refitted and repaired, and crew could return home for extended shore leave.

DIRECTIVES

Your on-going mission, above, has some great examples of Directives to employ in your game. These Directives can span several individual *Star Trek Adventure* missions. They could be general, in terms of broader edict the Federation holds close, like, "Seek Out New Life," or "Explore Strange New Worlds." While some can be more specific, such as "Catalogue Stellar Bodies of the Shackleton Expanse," or "Discover the Origin of the Strange Readings from Trappist-06."

A good place to start would be the starship's duty role, such as defense, diplomacy, exploration or relief, to establish a key Directive. If any more come to mind, that are a little more specific, add them too.

DILITHIUM REGULATOR CONTROLS **853**

20

860

90

3451

In the 24th century, however, with the advent of new technologies and larger ships, Starfleet mandated long-term, open-ended deep space missions. Improvements in replicator technology and the invention of the holodeck could ease the strain on crewmembers. Advances in communications mean ships are not as out-of-touch as they once were. Whole families could join their Starfleet family member, easing the effects of separation and isolation. Starships could go farther out into space, and for longer periods of time, such that Starfleet personnel might not return home for decades.

When we talk about a starship's mission, we're referring to several things simultaneously. There's the crew's ongoing mission to seek out new worlds and new civilizations — a mission statement for who we are and what we are about. Then there's your specific, long-term, mission; these are typically broad. "Catalog all gaseous anomalies in a particular sector." "Patrol along the Romulan Neutral Zone." "Survey all the star systems in a newly discovered region of space." In addition, before setting out, every starship captain receives a command packet with a list of specific missions to be addressed at specific times. As tradition dictates, this is still printed out on paper and collected into a dossier (though it's available on isolinear chip, as well). These individual missions are based on your projected course and Starfleet's needs — provide medical exams to the members of the archeological base on Talos IV, represent the Federation at the coronation of King Pyrim of Antos IV, transport Ambassador Varik to Argelius, and so forth. Over the course of your mission, you may be contacted by Starfleet Command (through your admiral) to address certain emergent situations we could not foresee, such as diverting a planet-killing asteroid or stopping a Borg incursion. And, of course, you and your crew may stumble upon circumstances that demand your attention; you have the authority as a starship captain to divert to handle these situations (subject to later Command review).

Putting it all together, your overall mission might be to collect samples from comets in the Goodman Cluster; this is what you'll be doing the majority of the time. Inside your command dossier you'll find individual missions that include scheduled stops at Starbase 312 for re-supply, the Harren Colony for their annual medical review, and investigating mysterious RF emissions emanating from a supposedly uninhabited planet. Meanwhile, you could also be diverted by Starfleet Command to study an emergent ion storm and investigate the disappearance of a science station. As you can see, your "ongoing" mission is actually a number of specific missions that fall under your over-arching assignment.

YOUR CONTINUING MISSION
DUTIES

THE MISSION TYPES

Starfleet Command defines many specific mission types. As the Federation's foremost scientific and exploratory organization, Starfleet's missions aren't all that different from those early pioneers in scientific inquiry. We are, at heart, interested in learning more about the universe, and the beings that share it with us. We not only seek out new worlds and new civilizations; we seek knowledge and understanding. These are just some of the kinds of missions you'll engage in during your ongoing mission to explore space.

SCIENCE MISSIONS

Our primary mission is to explore space and expand the boundaries of our knowledge. Despite what the Romulans may think, Starfleet is a scientific organization. Every starship is equipped with powerful sensor arrays and probes that collect a wealth of data. Each is, in many respects, like bringing a powerful telescope farther and farther out into the Galaxy, so that it can see further. Many of your missions will simply be to go where no one else has gone before and see what there is to be seen.

DEEP SPACE EXPLORATION: This is what most people think of when they think of Starfleet — the intrepid explorer going where no one has gone before. You will venture beyond the limits of explored space and expand the boundaries of our knowledge. The most common deep space exploration mission simply involves collecting all the data your long-range scanners can absorb. There is a quark here. There is a nebula over there. The fourth planet orbiting LV-849 is class M. While it may seem boring, your mapping of deep space provides the data necessary for future exploratory missions.

PLANETARY EXPLORATION AND SURVEY: Starfleet's primary goal is to seek out new worlds. Once a noteworthy planet has been identified, it must be explored. Extensive scans of the planet's surface, composition, and atmosphere must be made. Science teams must be sent down to collect samples of flora and fauna. Geological surveys, to determine mineralogical composition and planetary development, have to be conducted. The crew of a starship could spend a lifetime surveying all the plants, minerals, and animals on a single world. And that's in the absence of any intelligent life-forms! The presence of intelligent life only complicates the process, which often leads to covertly monitoring the civilization in order to determine the viability of first contact.

RESEARCH AND DEVELOPMENT: Almost every starship in the fleet has the equipment and personnel to conduct a wide variety of scientific research. In addition to performing routine analysis related to exploration, the science officers aboard typically engage in their own scientific studies, as well as hosting Federation scientists performing independent research. Often, starships provide an excellent testbed for new technological developments, as well — holographic control systems, improved transporters, a new computer system, a more efficient warp drive; whatever new technology or development someone comes up with has to eventually be tested in the field.

STELLAR PHENOMENON SURVEY: Cataloging gaseous anomalies in the Beta Quadrant. Monitoring the planetary collapse of Beta Hydra II. Collecting data on a supernova or black hole. Every stellar phenomenon is different and unique; you never know what new piece of information, what more accurate data, you may retrieve from such an event. Even though we may have witnessed a hundred black holes, there may be something about this one that is somehow different, and scientifically relevant.

DIPLOMATIC MISSIONS

In addition to missions of scientific importance, Starfleet engages in a variety of diplomatic missions. As much as they are mobile scientific platforms, starships are also floating diplomatic outposts, able to conduct first contact assignments, provide neutral ground for negotiations, and transport ambassadors to vital diplomatic conferences.

CONFLICT RESOLUTION: Starfleet's mission has always been one of peace; we seek the peaceful resolution of hostilities first and foremost. Over the course of your travels, you will no doubt encounter conflicts that don't even involve Starfleet or the Federation — you may even somehow become embroiled in these conflicts. But you and your crew are uniquely positioned to put an end to hostilities, separate the combatants, and lend assistance. You may even find yourselves effectively serving as the Federation ambassador to resolve these conflicts, using your starship as neutral ground where compromise can take place. This is an opportunity to demonstrate Federation ideals through the use of your good offices to negotiate a settlement.

DIPLOMACY: Transporting a Federation envoy to negotiations on Parliament. Ferrying the Dohlman of Elas to Troyius. Hosting alien ambassadors on their trip to a conference on Earth. Escorting the Klingon Chancellor to peace talks on Khitomer. You must lend whatever support and assistance is necessary to see these diplomatic missions to their successful completion, up to and including providing security for diplomatic personnel and protecting negotiations from outside meddling. Diplomatic missions can in some ways be more challenging than fighting the Borg — preventing opposing viewpoints from escalating into violence among diplomats, preventing your own prejudices from interfering with your ability to complete the mission (or taint the negotiations), and demonstrating the best of Federation principles in the face of mistrust and even hostility. Our goal is to foster peace and amity throughout the Galaxy, making diplomatic missions perhaps even more important than our scientific endeavors.

FIRST CONTACT: This is the other iconic mission for a Starfleet officer — to seek out new life-forms and new civilizations. Once a new species has been identified, they have to be studied; are they ready to learn about other starfaring races? Are they potentially hostile? Do they possess the necessary technological advancements? After months, or even years, of long-range reconnaissance and clandestine observation, when the time comes, someone has to make first contact. This can be dangerous, with the potential to cause political or religious upheaval, or lead to misunderstanding. Although many times, the Federation Council will send out a qualified ambassador to make first contact, sometimes it will fall to you and your crew to reveal the existence of other planets and civilizations in the Galaxy. First contact missions always require the most patience and gentle diplomacy.

PROTECTION AND SECURITY

In addition to the wide range of sensors, scanners, and probes starships are outfitted with, we also bring with us awesome destructive power undreamed of in earlier centuries. In the 23rd century, a single *Constitution*-class starship could lay waste to a planet's surface. By the 24th century, advances in phaser and photon torpedo technologies only increased a starship's capability to destroy. A starship captain wields more power than all the armies of Earth's history combined, and must use it judiciously.

AID AND RELIEF: Unlike port of call missions, your starship has been tasked with providing aid and relief to a Federation member world or ally, colony, starbase, or other outpost. You may even be tasked with lending aid to a non-aligned world, at the behest of the Federation Council, in the hopes of fostering closer ties or in the name of humanitarian concerns. Possible assignments may include responding to a planetary distress call, providing much-needed medical supplies during a contagion, ferrying a new grain to alleviate a famine, and providing planetary evacuation in extreme emergencies. In many cases, time is of the essence, and you and your crew must remain flexible and improvise.

PATROL: Numerous potential threats confront the Federation — hostilities along the Cardassian and Romulan borders, the Borg, the Nausicaans, an upswing in terrorist activities by the Maquis. In addition, while each Federation member provides for their own planetary and solar system security, Starfleet patrols the routes inside Federation space between member worlds, to ensure the safety and security of civilian traffic. Patrol missions are simple. Patrol the space in your assigned area of operations, scan for unidentified or potentially hostile vessels, and intercept them. Conflict is always a last resort, and oftentimes it is simply enough for a starship to "show the flag."

PORT OF CALL: There are many starbases, science stations, mining facilities, and colonies that require frequent support — supplies to transport, quarterly medical assessments to perform, repairs to make, even shore leave. There are many reasons for a starship to pay a visit to remote, or not-so-remote, Federation installations. Oftentimes, you are there to lend assistance and support in whatever way you can to the local authorities. A port of call mission maintains direct contact with our far-flung outposts across the Galaxy.

TACTICAL: A hostile alien probe enters Federation space. The Romulans attack a starbase along the Neutral Zone. The Borg assimilate a Starfleet outpost. A newly discovered alien species reacts with hostility. A threat to the Federation or its allies emerges, and there is clear and present danger. It is at these times that you and your crew will be called upon to defend the Federation against hostile aggressors. These missions almost always involve the threat of conflict, though we implore you to use minimal force. Often, Starfleet Command will issue you rules of engagement in order to curtail collateral damage and protect as many lives as possible.

YOUR CONTINUING MISSION
AWAY TEAMS

The mission of a captain and their starship to explore new worlds and seek out new civilizations comes in many forms. While a starship is a powerful technological wonder, there is nothing more effective than hands-on exploration. To accomplish the Federation's goals a captain will need to utilize the full skills of their crew.

Away teams staffed by the diverse and skilled members of your crew are key to accomplishing the mission of the United Federation of Planets. Your crew is tasked with a wide variety of missions for the Federation ranging from diplomatic and scientific assignments to military operations. While the Galaxy is full of wonders and new discoveries, it is also rife with danger. When you select an away team for a mission you should make sure to staff it with qualified individuals, and trust your department heads' recommendations for the assignment. For the most sensitive assignments, your first officer will likely lead the away team supported by your second officer. General procedure recommends the captain not accompany an away team.

Make no mistake, when you send your crew on away missions they will be in harm's way. The burden of command means some of your crew might not return from their assignments. Your crew consists of highly trained Starfleet personnel and you must trust in their abilities.

DIPLOMATIC MISSIONS

The core of Starfleet's mission is to promote peace and understanding between all species and a Starfleet vessel acts as a platform for promoting peace. A Federation starship can act as neutral ground for negotiations and diplomatic teams represent the Federation in tense political situations acting as neutral parties negotiating treaties between fierce rivals.

Diplomatic missions at first appear rather straightforward affairs, but cultural mores and traditions of alien cultures are a major factor to consider. Failure to understand the cultures of species involved can disrupt negotiations, exacerbating an already tense situation. This is especially true of peace

negotiations where the diplomats must navigate the complex relationship between embittered enemies. A failure to respect a species' traditions could ruin months of work. It is essential that away team members be well studied in the cultural traditions and expectations of the species.

RELIEF MISSIONS

Away teams will also engage in a wide variety of relief missions: Providing medical aid to a world effected by a plague, delivering food relief, relocating refugees fleeing conflict, constructing emergency shelters for at risk populations, and other relief actions.

Successfully executing relief operations requires constant training and preparation. Tragedies can unfold quickly and an organized response reduces greater suffering and loss of life. Your crew must perform regular drills planning and preparing for every possible situation. There is no certainty regarding what they may face in a dangerous Galaxy.

Medical teams must be prepared to act at a moment's notice to provide medical care. Security teams should expect tense situations where oppressive regimes, terrorists, or other hostile actors target Starfleet personnel and those they have come to help. Engineering teams must be ready to get vital systems on damaged starships and planetary facilities repaired quickly to save countless lives. Practice and preparation will help them face any eventuality.

EXPLORATION & SCIENTIFIC MISSIONS

Exploration is a key mission expanding scientific understanding and knowledge. Survey teams exploring alien worlds conduct geological surveys, catalog new species, study unique plant life, and contact new civilizations. Observation teams will have the opportunity to catalog pre-warp cultures studying their social mores, local customs, and sociological development. The opportunities for expanding knowledge and understanding are nearly limitless.

Survey teams engage in scientific studies of newly discovered planets cataloging unique species of plant and animal life, surveying the planet's mineral resources, and evaluating the planet for potential exploitation and colonization. Survey teams have the opportunity to explore a culture's society, religion, and entertainment. The inherent risk of first contact should be taken into account and the team should avoid violating the social mores and norms of the indigenous culture.

Observer teams explore worlds populated by pre-warp culture and observe their culture without interfering in their natural development. Early pre-warp cultures are watched from concealed, cultural observation posts hidden behind a holographic "duck blind." Anthropologists may get the opportunity to interact and experience the pre-warp society's culture, but, even with the advantage of surgical alterations to disguise their morphology, there are risks of exposing the society to cultural contamination.

Personnel assigned to observation teams should research the local customs to avoid any risk of exposing their presence. Personnel behaving outside local social mores or arrested for violating minor laws exposing the presence of a non-native culture can put the entire mission at risk. Many of these incidents can be explained away with an effective cover story such as being from a distant city or province. Personnel injured may be taken to local medical facilities where local medical personnel can discover their alien biology. It is essential that any cultural contamination is contained and any evidence of your team's presence is destroyed to prevent violations of the Prime Directive. Additionally, outside cultures not bound by the Prime Directive may interfere with the natural cultural development of a culture and it is the duty of Starfleet to protect that natural development.

Upon completion of the survey, the planet's details are gathered in a planetary survey report and sent to Starfleet Command. The Exploration Corps and the Federation Diplomatic Corps will use the information gathered to determine future treaties, locations for new Federation colonies, and evaluate new species for entry into the Federation.

A team well versed in the social and physical sciences is required for executing a successful away mission. You will need to choose members whose skills fit the needs of the mission, but having a team with a wide variety of skills will facilitate success. Exploring an unknown planet can bring a myriad of challenges. Personnel specializing in biology, botany, geology, and other physical sciences will allow your team to effectively catalog the world's wonders and resources. Planets may hold ancient ruins and lost cultures. Personnel competent in history, anthropology, sociology, and archeology will be essential for understanding and recording these discoveries. Lastly, the dangers of investigating unexplored worlds brings a wide variety of dangers ranging from aggressive animal life to hostile indigenous peoples. Security officers will provide protection to away team personnel.

DANUBE CLASS RUNABOUT

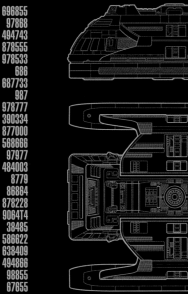

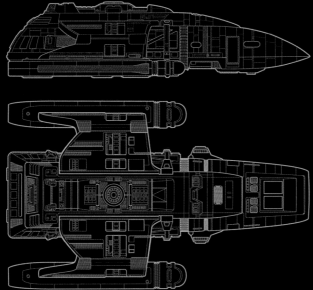

696855
97868
494743
878555
978533
686
687733
987
978777
390334
877000
568666
97977
484003
8779
86864
878228
9064T4
38485
586622
638409
494866
98855
67655

STARFLEET MATERIEL SUPPLY COMMAND
17 SPECIAL DUTY MODULE
SENSOR STATION - 47365

STARFLEET MATERIEL SUPPLY COMMAND
47 SPECIAL DUTY MODULE
RESEARCH LAB - 47365

STARFLEET MATERIEL SUPPLY COMMAND
53 SPECIAL DUTY MODULE
MEDICAL PALETTE - 85647

STARFLEET MATERIEL SUPPLY COMMAND
64 SPECIAL DUTY MODULE
POWER GENERATOR - 47365

RUNABOUT MODULE LABELS

696855	686	877000	86864	638409
97868	687733	568666	878228	494866
494743	987	97977	9064T4	98855
878555	978777	484003	38485	67655
978533	390334	8779	586622	929444

PEACEKEEPING & MILITARY OPERATIONS

Starfleet captains are tasked with protecting the Federation from internal and external threats. While the Federation is not in open conflict with any major power, there are regular risks ranging from Orion pirates to the Borg, and, if war is formally declared, your crew will find themselves on the front lines.

Under the auspices of the Federation Charter, Starfleet is responsible for maintaining the peace within the Federation and assisting its allies in regular peacekeeping and interstellar law enforcement. While the Federation is a society dedicated to peaceful co-existence, criminal enterprises and pirates are an ongoing problem for border colonies and isolated trade lanes. Your crew will be deployed on a variety of away missions maintaining peace and security throughout the Federation. Security teams will find themselves dealing with law enforcement, protecting Federation dignitaries, and defending Federation facilities.

Team members should be skilled in a wide variety of security and investigative fields. Forensics and criminal psychology will reveal the perpetrators of crimes, while knowledge of the local culture and politics will provide insight into local conflicts. In the event of armed conflict, security personnel should have a keen understanding of the area, an awareness of entry and exit points, as well as any security precautions already in place. Military operations will see personnel deployed in a time of war and understanding tactics and strategy is essential for bringing personnel home safely.

COVERT OPERATIONS

Starfleet prefers diplomatic solutions to resolve its problems with rival governments, but Starfleet personnel are required to take on covert missions in the interest of the Federation. Your crew may be called upon to acquire important data, covertly protect foreign dignitaries, rescue hostages, or collect intelligence. You and your crew may be sent on clandestine missions key to the security of the Federation, but a mission's secrecy means the Federation may be unable to acknowledge your crew's activities if captured on the operation. Governments such as the Cardassian Union and Romulan Star Empire do not have the same respect for individual rights and records show they are more than willing to subject captured personnel to humiliation and torture.

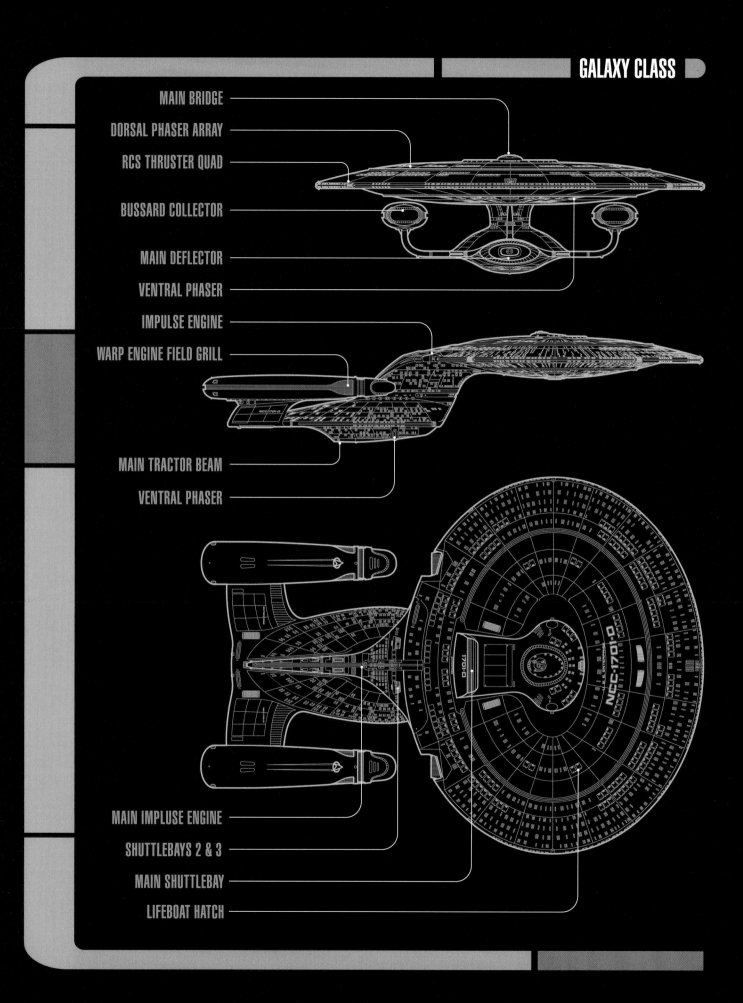

MAIN BRIDGE

DORSAL PHASER ARRAY

RCS THRUSTER QUAD

BUSSARD COLLECTOR

MAIN DEFLECTOR

VENTRAL PHASER

IMPULSE ENGINE

WARP ENGINE FIELD GRILL

MAIN TRACTOR BEAM

VENTRAL PHASER

MAIN IMPLUSE ENGINE

SHUTTLEBAYS 2 & 3

MAIN SHUTTLEBAY

LIFEBOAT HATCH

OPERATIONS

18051415
140522010401

OPERATIONS
INTRODUCTION

"OUT HERE IN SPACE, NO ONE IS COMPLETELY INDEPENDENT. WE ALL DEPEND ON ONE ANOTHER."

— DOCTOR JULIAN BASHIR

Every **Star Trek Adventures** game involves several Players, and their corresponding characters. *Star Trek* is about people first and foremost, and every *Star Trek* story involves a cast of characters, from devious Tal Shiar operatives, to proud Klingon warriors, to the Player Characters themselves.

Player Characters are the protagonists of any **Star Trek Adventures** game, Starfleet officers forming the crew of a starship or starbase operated by the United Federation of Planets. Each Player has a **Main Character** of their own, making decisions for that character, rolling dice, and engaging with the events of the story. Each Main Character has a character sheet, a record of their game statistics, abilities, and other important information. Players may also have **Supporting Characters**, who represent other members of the crew, and whom a Player can control instead of their Main Character as the situation dictates. Player Characters of both kinds are described more fully in *Chapter 5: Reporting for Duty*.

Non-Player Characters are everyone else, from allies and innocent bystanders, to the adversaries the Player Characters face. They are collectively controlled by the Gamemaster.

THE GAMEMASTER

Of the Players gathered for the game, one will be the Gamemaster. This Player has a different set of responsibilities, and interacts with the rules of the game differently. The Gamemaster takes responsibility for Non-Player Characters, is responsible for coming up with the challenging situations and indomitable opponents the Players will face, and oversees the ways in which the Players overcome these problems.

The Gamemaster establishes scenes, building on the actions and choices of the Players to shape the game at every stage, providing a challenge and giving the Player Characters opportunities to shine. They also interpret how the rules apply to a given situation, such as ruling on the Difficulty of Tasks, or adjudicating when unusual situations or

disagreements arise. Above all else, the Gamemaster is not an adversary to the Players — the game works all the better if the Gamemaster is a fan of the Player Characters and their exploits, albeit one who seeks to make those characters' lives as dramatic, exciting, and challenging as possible.

DICE

In many roleplaying games, dice provide the varying chance or probability of an action succeeding; in this way, **Star Trek Adventures** is no different. **Star Trek Adventures** uses three types of dice to resolve the actions a character may attempt, and the situations they may face. In most circumstances, more than once dice of any given type will be rolled at once. These dice collectively are referred to as a "**dice pool**" or "pool".

The first, and most commonly-used, is the twenty-sided die, known throughout this book as a **d20**. D20s are used for resolving **Tasks**, and for rolling on certain large tables. Often, two or more d20s will be required. This is noted as Xd20, where X is the number of dice to be rolled. So, 2d20 denotes that two twenty-sided dice should be rolled.

The second type of die is the six-sided die, or **d6**. These are used relatively infrequently, mainly to roll on certain small tables. If multiple six-sided dice are required, it will be noted as Xd6, where X is the number of dice required — thus, 2d6 indicates that two six-sided dice should be rolled.

CHALLENGE DICE

The third type of dice are **Challenge Dice**, denoted in **Star Trek Adventures** by this symbol: ▲. These six-sided dice are used primarily for inflicting damage and determining how much protection a character receives from cover. Each ▲ has four faces with three possible results — a score of 1, a score of 2, and two faces showing the Starfleet arrowhead, which is an **Effect** — as well as two faces which are blank.

Effects have a score of 1, and additionally trigger special outcomes, which depend on the circumstances. A pool of Challenge Dice is usually rolled all at once, and their results added together, so multiple Challenge Dice are noted as X⚔, where X is the number of Challenge Dice rolled. So, 4⚔ indicates four Challenge Dice should be rolled, and their results added together.

If you don't have special Challenge Dice available, you can use normal six-sided dice instead; treat any die which rolls a 3 or 4 as blank, and any die which rolls a 5 or 6 as an Effect.

Example: Lieutenant Commander Data hits a Borg drone with a blast from his phaser, and rolls 6⚔ for the damage. He rolls 1, 2, and an Effect, as well as three blank faces for a total score of 4 and can activate an Effect.

D6 RESULT	CHALLENGE DICE RESULT
1	1
2	2
3	0
4	0
5	1, plus Effect
6	1, plus Effect

RE-ROLLS

Many circumstances allow a character to re-roll one or more dice. When re-rolling dice the Player chooses the number of dice to re-roll. They roll those dice and the new result replaces the original score. The new results stand, even if they're worse than the original results.

Some situations allow for a specific number of dice to be re-rolled, while others allow all the dice in a pool to be re-rolled. Players may always choose how many dice they wish to re-roll, up to the number of dice listed — in essence, you may always choose not to re-roll a die if you wish to keep that result.

OPERATIONS
BASIC OPERATIONS

The following section covers the core rules of **Star Trek Adventures**, which will be used throughout the rest of the game. These rules are the foundation for the other rules in the game, and every Player should have a basic understanding of these concepts during play.

This section will describe the following rules:

- **Scenes**, which serve as the building blocks of an ongoing story, and a framework within which characters act and react to situations. Some scenes, called **encounters**, are more structured and make greater use of the rules, typically where they deal with a conflict between two or more sides.

- **Traits**, **Advantages**, and **Complications**, which serve to describe scenes, locations, situations, and characters.

- **Tasks**, which are used to resolve a character's activities in situations where the outcome is uncertain.

- **Momentum**, which is generated by Players when they succeed well at Tasks, and which can be used to improve their chances subsequently.

- **Threat**, which is used by the Gamemaster to alter scenes, create complications, and present Players with consequences for their choices.

- **Values**, along with Directives, which allow a character's beliefs, relationships, and orders to impact their choices.

- **Determination**, which is used to gain a positive effect, and is gained when a negative effect is suffered.

SCENES

Just like the events of a TV show or movie, play in **Star Trek Adventures** is structured in scenes. Each scene may cover a few minutes of events, up to an hour or so, during which the characters attempt to achieve a goal, overcome a problem, or otherwise engage in some significant activities. Collectively, scenes are the building blocks of a mission, and serve as the foundation of gameplay.

Anyone familiar with *Star Trek* will have a decent idea of what a scene looks like — the characters talk and act within a single location toward resolving the dramatic conflict present, then move to a new location or new characters when the group has resolved the conflict or decide to move on. The key here is that scenes are the interesting parts of the story, and thus skip past the parts that aren't interesting. Different groups may have different standards as to what is and isn't interesting, so this concept is deliberately flexible.

ENCOUNTERS

Encounters are more tightly structured scenes that deal with a conflict between two or more sides — such as combat — in which the action is divided into **Rounds** and **Turns**. During each Round, each character involved will take a single Turn, handing the action back and forth between sides. During a Turn, a character can attempt a Task, and several **Minor Actions**.

These more structured scenes are described in *Chapter 7: Conflict*.

SETTING THE SCENE

The Gamemaster has the responsibility of setting up the scenes that Players will play through, and on deciding when they end. The Players have free reign to do as they wish within that scene, and the Gamemaster can react through the actions of Non-Player Characters, and by spending Threat to trigger logical and consequential changes in the environment and situation. When things within that scene have concluded, and nothing else can be done in that place right now, the Gamemaster should end the scene and move onto the next one.

TRAITS

Locations, characters, and situations all come in a variety of shapes and sizes, and these differences are handled in-game as **Traits**. Each Trait is a single word or a short phrase, which describes a single significant fact about whatever it is the Trait belongs to.

Because a Trait represents a significant fact, it imposes a context upon the world around it, and upon anything that would interact with whatever possesses that Trait. These are useful for the Gamemaster in adjudicating what is and isn't possible — as well as how difficult those things are to attempt — and for the Players in imagining the scene and figuring out how they can interact with it.

The following rough categories denote what a given Trait applies to and if a character will be impacted by that Trait. These are primarily guidelines for the Gamemaster, but they're useful to know.

- A **situation** Trait is one that applies to the current situation, but which is inherently temporary, lasting no longer than the current scene. Any character in the scene is affected by circumstantial Traits. Darkness is an example of a situation Trait.

- A **location** Trait is one that applies to the current location, and is permanent (or, at least as permanent as the location itself is). Any character in that location is affected by location Traits when they interact with some facet of that location. The construction of a location, or the type of technology present there, are examples of location Traits.

- A **personal** Trait is one that applies to a character or creature, and may be some permanent, innate quality, or it may be something fleeting like a mood or emotion. A character or creature is naturally affected by its own personal Traits, and they may also affect the characters and creatures who interact with them. A character's species is an example of a personal Trait.

- An **equipment** Trait is one that describes a single piece of equipment. It's permanent — so long as the item is functional, it is represented by the Trait — and can be passed freely between characters as needed. An equipment Trait affects any character using that item to perform some relevant activity.

Traits have no specific or exact duration. Instead, they exist so long as they remain true. As soon as a Trait stops being true, it vanishes; conversely, to remove a Trait from the game, it needs to stop being true through the actions of the characters. When establishing a scene, the Gamemaster assigns whatever Traits they feel are appropriate to the scene, thinking of the environment and current

circumstances. The Gamemaster should be open with this process, and allow the Players to suggest Traits at the start of a scene, and allow for the possibility that Traits may change during the scene.

*Example: Chief O'Brien and several other engineers are boarding the abandoned space station, Empok Nor. The Gamemaster decides that the station itself has the Traits **Abandoned Cardassian Station**, and **Power Off-line**. These are both location Traits — they're both facts about the location itself, and they will stay around while they remain true. If the engineers get the power back on-line, the **Power Off-line** Trait will disappear, because it will no longer be true.*

Traits serve one vital purpose for the game: they help the Gamemaster determine what is and what isn't possible. In rules terms, whenever a character seeks to do something, the Gamemaster should consider the Traits present. Each Trait will do one of the following things:

- The Trait would not impact the activity and does not have any effect.

- The Trait is beneficial; it allows the activity to be performed when it might normally be impossible, or reduces its Difficulty.

- The Trait is detrimental; it prevents the activity from being performed when it might normally be possible, or increases the Difficulty.

If a Trait should have a particularly potent or intense effect — a larger effect than those listed above — the Gamemaster should simply make it multiple identical Traits, essentially creating a single Trait that has the impact of many. This can be denoted simply by adding a number after the name of the Trait.

*Example: An unknown phenomenon is causing intense **Subspace Interference**, disrupting communications and the use of sensors. The Gamemaster decides that the effect is severe enough to warrant it counting as two traits: **Subspace Interference 2**. Whenever the Gamemaster considers which Traits are applicable to an activity, it counts as two Traits, and thus could increase the Difficulty of an activity twice.*

ADVANTAGES

An **Advantage** is a Trait which is inherently positive or beneficial, and which will never have a detrimental effect to its owners. Advantages can make an activity possible that wasn't possible before, reduce the Difficulty of a Task (see Tasks, below), or cancel out a **Complication** (below), preventing either from influencing the scene.

COMPLICATION

A **Complication** is a Trait which is inherently negative or problematic, and which will never have a beneficial effect

upon its owners. Complications can prevent a character from attempting something that might otherwise be possible, increase the Difficulty of a Task (see Tasks, below), or cancel out an **Advantage**, preventing either from influencing the scene.

There are numerous ways that Players can produce both Advantages and Complications, which are described later in this chapter.

TASKS

Characters in *Star Trek Adventures* are presumed to be experts, specialists in their chosen fields and with enough breadth of training and practical experience to ensure that they can solve problems and overcome obstacles as a matter of course. However, there are situations where a character's success is in doubt or where failure or Complications are interesting.

A Task will serve one of several basic purposes, and the Gamemaster must have a clear idea of what a Task is for, and what will happen if the Task succeeds or fails. In general, a Task will be for one of the following:

TREKNOBABBLE

Episodes of *Star Trek* often include technobabble — complicated-sounding dialogue that describes fictional science or technology, often to explain a plot development, or a solution to a problem, or simply to add detail to a situation. The sheer bewildering variety of possible technobabble makes it difficult to cover extensively; however, conveniently enough, Traits — and both Advantages and Complications — are extremely useful for representing the kinds of things that technobabble represents.

For the sake of consistency, keep note of Traits that represent technobabble, so that they can be referenced later.

The Task is an attempt to achieve something; there may
be a single activity covered by a single Task, or one Task
may contribute to a larger goal or objective that could
require many Tasks to complete. Success means that the
character achieves what they set out to do, while failure
means the character didn't achieve their goal, though they
might be allowed to try again later, or to succeed at a cost.

- A possible form of this is to create or change a Trait
  currently in play — such as creating an Advantage or
  Complication. Success means the character created
  an Advantage or Complication (or removed one),
  while failure could mean wasted time and effort, or
  entail a success at a cost.

- The Task is to avoid or resist some form of hazard or
  peril. In this case, success means the character is
  unaffected by the hazard or peril, while failure means they
  suffer the full effects.

- The Task is to achieve something, but there is something
  at stake as well. Failure means that not only did the
  character fail to achieve what they set out to do, but they
  suffer some other consequence as well, like rolling to
  avoid a hazard or peril.

The Players should be informed of the potential
consequences for success and failure before they attempt
the Task — Starfleet officers are assumed to be skilled
enough and intelligent enough to know the most likely
outcomes for their actions.

The game presumes that, given sufficient time, the correct
tools, and the ability to concentrate, a character will be able
to succeed at just about anything they set their mind to.
Failure is not a matter of inability, but rather of insufficient
time, inappropriate tools, or some manner of obstacle or
interruption. A course of action may be deemed impossible
not because the character cannot do it, but because they
don't have the means to do it at that moment, and finding out
a way to make the impossible possible is part of a Starfleet
Officer's duties.

ATTRIBUTES, DISCIPLINES, AND FOCUSES

While described in full in *Chapter 5: Reporting for Duty*, it is
nevertheless useful to have a brief overview of these crucial
elements of a character here as well, as they feed directly
into the subject of Tasks.

A character has six **Attributes** — Control, Daring, Fitness,
Insight, Presence, and Reason — which encompass their
innate capabilities. A character's Attributes range from 7 to 12.

A character has six **Disciplines** — Command, Conn,
Engineering, Security, Science, and Medicine — which
cover the character's training and expertise. A character's
Disciplines range from 1 to 5.

A character also has **Focuses**, which are categories of
specialty, representing specialized training and practical
experience in specific fields. Focuses do not have a specific
rating of their own.

For any given Task, a character will combine a single
Attribute, a single Discipline, and may use a single Focus to
establish the **Target Number** (covered below).

OBSERVATION

One of the most common reasons Players may ask to attempt
a Task is to see if their characters notice or find something that
isn't immediately obvious. These will most commonly use Insight
or Reason, as those Attributes are the most associated with
awareness and comprehension. However, which Discipline is
used should vary based on the situation — weighing up a
threat may use Security, while examining technology would use
Engineering, for example.

In any case, the Difficulty of an Observation Task should be low,
with success providing the bare minimum information; Momentum
can be spent to improve upon this (Obtain Information, p. 85). For
vital information — things that the characters must discover for
the plot to continue — use of the Success at Cost rules (p. 83) is
appropriate.

ATTEMPTING A TASK

A Task involves a character's **Attributes**, **Disciplines**, and
Focuses, and requires rolling two or more d20s. Attempting
a Task follows a specific process. The following process
mentions several ideas that will be described fully later in
this section.

1. The Gamemaster chooses which **Attribute** and which
   Discipline are appropriate for the Task being attempted,
   as well as if any of the character's **Focuses** are
   applicable. This might be stated by the rules,
   or the Player may suggest a combination, but the
   Gamemaster has the final say. Add together the Attribute
   and the Discipline chosen. This is the Target Number for
   the Task.

2. The Gamemaster then sets the **Difficulty** of the Task.
   This is normally any number from 0 to 5, but in some

extreme cases can go higher. Some Tasks may have a default Difficulty listed in the rules, but circumstances may affect those basic Difficulties. The Difficulty is the number of **successes** the Player must roll on their d20s to successfully complete the Task.

3. The Player takes two d20s, and may choose to purchase up to three additional d20s by spending **Momentum**, adding to **Threat**, or using **Determination** (see "Improving the Odds", later). Once additional dice have been purchased — if any — the Player rolls their dice pool.

4. Each die that rolls equal to or less than the Target Number scores a single Success.
   A. If there is an applicable Focus, then each die that rolls equal to or less than the Discipline being used scores two successes. There is no extra benefit for having more than one applicable Focus.
   B. If there isn't an applicable Focus, each die that rolls 1 scores two successes.
   C. Each die that rolls a 20 causes a Complication (see "**Complications**", later)

5. If the number of successes scored equals or exceeds the Difficulty of the Task, then the Task is completed successfully. If the number of successes is less than the Difficulty of the Task, then the Task is failed.
   A. Any successes in excess the Difficulty of the Task become **Momentum** (see "Momentum", p. 83).

6. The Gamemaster describes the outcome of the Task, and if the Task was successful, the Player may spend Momentum to improve the result further. After this, the effects of any Complications are applied.

Combinations of Attributes and Disciplines are stated throughout this rulebook, but the Gamemaster may choose to change that combination on a case-by-case basis if a situation seems like it should use a different combination, or if a Player comes up with some ingenious approach that would use a different combination.

Example: Scotty is attempting to squeeze additional power out of the Enterprise's engines. His Target Number is his Control Attribute (11) and Engineering Discipline (4), for a target of 15, and he has a Focus in Starship Propulsion, and the Task has a Difficulty of 2. He rolls two d20s, rolling a 4 and a 19; the 4 scores two successes (thanks to his Focus), while the 19 scores none. With two successes, Scotty is successful.

TASK DIFFICULTY

When the Gamemaster calls for a Task, they set a Difficulty for that Task. Many Tasks detailed elsewhere in this book list a basic Difficulty, which means the Gamemaster doesn't need to determine that baseline, but even those Tasks should

be evaluated in context to determine if other factors impact how difficult the Task is at that moment. The Gamemaster should also determine if the Task is possible or not, given the circumstances and the methods at the characters' disposal.

Unless otherwise noted, most Tasks will have a basic Difficulty of 1, though more routine or straightforward Tasks may have a Difficulty of 0, and more complex or problematic Tasks will have higher Difficulties. After this, the Gamemaster then considers if there are any other factors in the current scene and environment, or affecting the characters involved, which would alter this basic Difficulty.

These factors typically come in the form of Traits, Advantages, and Complications — already described on p. 76 — which will have one of the following effects:

- The Trait would not impact the Task and does not have any effect.

- The Trait is beneficial, and allows the Task to be attempted when it might normally be impossible.

- The Trait is beneficial, and reduces the Difficulty of the Task by one.

- The Trait is detrimental, and increases the Difficulty of the Task by one.

- The Trait is detrimental, and either prevents the Task from being attempted when it might normally be possible, or the situation now requires a Task when one would not normally have been required.

The Players should know the Difficulty of the Tasks they attempt: their characters are skilled professionals, who can easily evaluate how difficult an activity is. This allows the Players to determine what they'll need to do to have the best chance of success.

*Example: Dr. McCoy is attempting to perform complex heart surgery on Ambassador Sarek. This has a basic Difficulty of 2, but there are other factors. Firstly, Sarek is Vulcan, and McCoy's knowledge of Vulcan physiology is limited, which increases the Difficulty by 1. Secondly, without a Vulcan blood donor, the operation can't be performed at all; this Complication is overcome by having Spock donate blood to the procedure, however. Thirdly, the Enterprise is **Under Attack**, which is obviously disruptive, increasing the Difficulty by one. Together, these increase the Difficulty to 4. Fortunately, McCoy has the Enterprise sickbay and Nurse Chapel to assist him.*

IMPROVING THE ODDS

Even the most dedicated Starfleet officers cannot give their full effort one hundred percent of the time; in tense situations, they need to conserve their energy, capitalize on opportunities, and be willing to take risks to triumph. Thus, *Star Trek Adventures* provides several ways for characters to improve their chances of success, by buying additional d20s to roll on a Task. Extra dice allow a character to score more successes, and thus hit higher Difficulties or simply generate more Momentum. However, these extra dice always come with some sort of cost, and which options a character chooses depends entirely upon what costs they are willing and able to pay.

DIFFICULTY ZERO TASKS

Certain circumstances can reduce the Difficulty of a Task, which may reduce the Difficulty to zero. At other times, a Task may be so simple that it does not require dice to be rolled in the first place. These are Simple Tasks. If a Task is Difficulty 0, it does not require dice to be rolled: it is automatically successful with zero successes, with no risk of Complications. However, because no roll is made, it can generate no Momentum — even bonus Momentum from Talents, particularly advantageous situations, etc. — and the character cannot spend any Momentum on the Task either.

At the Gamemaster's discretion, a character can still choose to roll the dice against a Difficulty of 0 and can generate Momentum as normal (because zero successes are required, every success generated is Momentum), but this comes with the normal risk of Complications as well. This sort of Difficulty 0 Task can be quite useful if it's important to see how successful a character is, but there's no real chance of failure.

Example: Lieutenant Paris is piloting the U.S.S. Voyager, maneuvering around a Borg cube during battle. There's no real chance of failure, so the Gamemaster decides that it has a Difficulty of 0. However, it's still valuable to see how well he succeeds, so Paris still rolls for the Task, generating Momentum that can be used to benefit himself and the crew.

SO CRAZY IT JUST MIGHT WORK!

One common element of the exploits and successes of Player Characters is a tendency to employ creative, often bizarre strategies to resolve seemingly-impossible situations. This is the kind and quality of officer that Starfleet trains and employs with determination and ingenuity.

Consequently, when running *Star Trek Adventures*, the Gamemaster should not only expect, but encourage, plans that seem "crazy", though even if a "crazy" plan is possible, that doesn't mean it should be easy. The listed combinations of Attribute and Discipline may not necessarily apply to these unusual approaches, so the Gamemaster should feel free to use a different combination if the situation calls for it. Similarly, entertain the Players' suggestions for Momentum Spends, Advantages, and Complications.

- **MOMENTUM:** The spend Create Opportunity (p. 85) allows characters to buy additional dice, representing coordination, teamwork, and building upon prior successes. A single point of Momentum adds one bonus d20 to a Task; the second bonus die costs 2 Momentum, while the third bonus die costs 3.

- **THREAT:** The Create Opportunity spend can be paid for by adding to Threat (p. 86) instead of spending Momentum, representing taking risks or acting recklessly. This costs the same as buying the dice with Momentum, but a point is added to Threat for each point of Momentum that would have been spent..

- **DETERMINATION:** When spending Determination, the character adds a single bonus d20 to the Task; unlike any other source of bonus d20s, a die bought with Determination is considered to have already rolled a 1 (therefore scoring two successes automatically). Determination may only be spent in certain circumstances, as described on p. 87.

- **TALENTS:** A few Talents (p. 135) that a character may have grant them bonus d20s in specific circumstances. This costs nothing other than being in the correct situation to use, but they still count towards the number of bonus d20s that can be purchased.

Bonus dice bought with Determination or from Talents are applied before any bought with Momentum or Threat, for the purposes of how much Momentum or Threat those dice cost.

In the Gamemaster's case, when buying bonus d20s for Non-Player Characters, there are fewer options — the Gamemaster may spend points of Threat to add dice to a Non-Player Character's Task roll. Non-Player Characters typically do not have Determination.

TEAMWORK & ASSISTANCE

Many Tasks can benefit from teamwork. If the situation allows, several characters can work together as a team when attempting to perform a Task. When more than one character is involved in a Task, one character is the leader, and the other characters are assistants. The Gamemaster has the final say on whether or not a character can assist — there might be only limited space that keeps people from helping, for example — or apply limitations or additional penalties, such as an increase to the Complication range (+1 to Complication range for each assistant after the first). The Gamemaster should be wary of allowing more than one assistant on most Tasks.

To assist with a Task, the Player must describe how their character is assisting the Task's leader. If the Gamemaster agrees, then each assistant rolls 1d20, using their own Target Number, and their own Focus (if any), to determine if any successes are scored. So long as the Task leader generates at least one success, then all successes generated by the

GREETINGS FROM THE DOMINION

To Shiana,
First Secretary for Scientific Developmen of the Mannai People

Greetings from the Dominion! I am Gildar, a humble representative of the Founders. On their behalf I congratulate you on your recent achievement of faster-than-light spaceflight.

Our records show that you've met the Dosi and Karemma, two shining examples of the success that comes with cooperation and peace with the Dominion. We're offering you the hand of peace, support and unity, that you too may one day come to uphold the order that the Founders bring to the cosmos.

First Secretary, the Dominion is the single most advanced civilization in the Galaxy. Our citizens enjoy protection from predation by pirates and rogue nations, disaster relief, and an elevated standard of living, provided that they work their hardest, stay loyal to Dominion ideals, and prove useful to the good of the whole.

Every single planet in Dominion space is free from fear of attack, and its essential citizens are warm and well-fed. A recent survey of planets that declined to join the Dominion showed that they have one and all succumbed to diseases, assault, and the other consequences of chaos. Help us help you to survive and thrive in your transition from backwater world to a vital cog in the Dominion machine.

I can make you a very powerful woman, First Secretary. While your people are robust, healthy and strong, your civilization shows an alarming tendency towards chaos. The lower class's devotion to democratic heresies hold back development by placing too high an importance on the lives and safety of expendable individuals, rather than on the prosperity of the entire nation. I've read your papers, and they show an enlightened attitude towards autocracy.

We're prepared to install you as planetary suzerain of your world. We have the means to do so handily. In return for loyal service we'll send a garrison of our mighty Jem'Hadar soldiers to ensure a secure grasp on your control.

The petty nations who resist a unified world government are no match for our might. We're aware of the terrorist cells who trouble your administration. It's a plague, a plague which we've been able to eradicate from all planets in our space, and will immediately rectify for the Mannai People.

You'll see me personally in three days, escorted by a small task force to make the transition as smooth as possible. You have the choice to leave your people vulnerable and weak or subservient and protected. Make the right one.

Yours with utmost friendship and admiration,

Gildar, Vorta Administrator of Sector

assistants count toward the Task. The Assistants' dice can generate Complications as normal.

Example: Chief O'Brien is attempting to repair a faulty power relay on Deep Space 9, with help from Rom. O'Brien attempts the Task as normal, scoring two successes. Rom rolls 1d20 against his Control + Engineering, and scores one success of his own, which he adds to O'Brien's total, making three successes in total.

Assistants do not have to use the same Attribute, Discipline, or Focus as any other character involved in the Task; indeed, assistance can often be best provided by someone contributing something different. Assistants may only ever roll 1d20 while assisting. In Combat or other encounters assisting a Task is considered to take up a character's Turn.

Example: During a battle against the Borg, Captain Picard points out a specific location on the Borg cube and gives the order to open fire. His specific direction is treated as assistance to Lt. Daniels' attack; Picard rolls 1d20 against Reason + Command, representing the fact that his assistance comes from his direction and leadership skills, rather than from providing direct aid. Any successes that Picard generates are added to Lt. Daniels' Task.

OPPOSED TASK

At times, a character will not simply be trying to overcome the challenges and difficulties posed by circumstances; instead, they may find themselves trying to best an opponent. These situations call for an Opposed Task.

With each Opposed Task, there will be one character attempting to do something, and another seeking to resist or avoid the first character's attempts. These are the active and reactive characters, respectively.

Both characters attempt a Task normally, with a base Difficulty of 1, which may be adjusted by circumstances. If the situation dictates, each character may have a different Difficulty for their respective Tasks. The outcome of the Opposed Task depends on both characters' Task results.

- **ACTIVE CHARACTER SUCCEEDS, REACTIVE CHARACTER FAILS:** the active character achieves their goal, and their Task is successful.

- **ACTIVE CHARACTER FAILS, REACTIVE CHARACTER SUCCEEDS:** the active character fails to achieve their goal, and the reactive character's Task is resolved. Some Opposed Tasks have a specific additional outcome for the reactive character's Task.

- **BOTH CHARACTERS FAIL:** the active character fails to achieve their goal, but the reactive character gains no additional benefit.

EQUIPMENT AND TECHNOLOGY

Starfleet officers make use of a wide range of tools and devices during their duties, and typically have access to whatever items they need to do their jobs. Therefore, the normal Difficulty of a Task assumes that the character has the appropriate tools for that Task, and the Task may become more difficult — or even impossible to attempt — if circumstances dictate that a character lacks those tools.

This is described in more detail in *Chapter 8: Equipment and Technology.*

- **BOTH CHARACTERS SUCCEED:** compare the total Momentum generated on each character's Task. The character with the higher Momentum wins and achieves their goal, but loses one Momentum for each Momentum their opponent scored. The loser then loses all the Momentum they generated, and may not spend any. In the case of a tie, the active character wins, but loses all Momentum they generated.

Example: Worf is locked in hand-to-hand combat with a Jem'Hadar warrior, and Worf lashes out with his mek'leth. This is an Opposed Task, with a Difficulty of 1 for each participant. Worf has Daring 12 and Security 5, for a TN of 17, and is using his Focus in Mok'bara. The Jem'Hadar warrior has Daring 11 and Security 3. Worf rolls an 8 and a 12, scoring two successes, enough to generate one Momentum. The Jem'Hadar rolls a 6 and a 15, scoring only a single success, and no Momentum. After a few moments of struggle, Worf forces his way past the Jem'Hadar warrior's defenses and brings down his foe.

COMPLICATIONS

Things don't always go entirely to plan. When attempting a Task, each d20 that rolls a 20 creates a Complication, which comes into play once the Task has been resolved.

As described on p. 76, Complications are Traits — facts about the scene or situation — that are inherently negative. Suffering a Complication in this way does not prevent a character from succeeding, but they may impede later activities, or they may simply be inconvenient, painful, or even embarrassing. As already discussed, the normal effect of a Complication is to increase the Difficulty of related Tasks by 1, or to make it so that a Task that is normally possible cannot be attempted.

Alternatively, if the Player doesn't wish their character to suffer an immediate Complication, or the Gamemaster doesn't want to inflict a Complication at that point, the Complication can instead be 'bought off' by adding two points to the Threat pool (see below). The Gamemaster may wish to do this to immediately spend the Threat to create a different, more immediate effect. This is discussed in more detail on p. 281.

Some other sections of the rules may suggest specific uses for Complications. Again, these are in place of creating a Trait — each 20 rolled can produce only a single effect, be that a Trait, adding to Threat, or some other result.

*Example: Ezri Dax is trying to help Garak overcome his anxiety and panic attacks from giving information about his people to Starfleet Intelligence. However, Ezri fails her Task, and worse rolls a 20 on one of her d20s, creating a Complication: **Garak's Worsening Anxiety**. In the next scene, Garak acts upon the problems that the Complication represents, attempting suicide.*

COMPLICATION RANGE

Some circumstances can make a Task uncertain, though not necessarily any more difficult. These factors increase the Complication Range of a Task, making it more likely that Complications will occur. A character has a Complication Range of 1 normally. Increasing the Complication Range by one means that Complications occur for each d20 that rolls a 19 or 20 on that Task. Increasing the Complication Range by two means Complications will occur on an 18, 19, or 20, and so forth, as summarized on the following table.

COMPLICATION RANGE TABLE

COMPLICATION RANGE	COMPLICATIONS OCCUR ON. . .
1	20
2	19-20
3	18-20
4	17-20
5	16-20

Complication range can never be increased to more than five.

SUCCESS AT COST

Some Tasks can't really be failed outright; rather, there is uncertainty as to whether the Task can be completed without problems. In such a situation, the Gamemaster may allow characters to Succeed at a Cost, either stating this before the Task is attempted, or providing the option after the dice have been rolled. If this option is provided, then a failed Task still allows the Task to be successful but the character also suffers one automatic Complication, in addition to any caused by 20s being rolled. These Complications function exactly as those generated by rolling a 20, including being able to trade them for 2 points of Threat, or using them to create other effects.

Though the Task has technically been successful, Momentum cannot be spent to improve the outcome of a Task that has succeeded at a cost: Momentum can only be spent if the Task was truly successful. In some cases, the 'cost' can be increased further, at the Gamemaster's discretion, causing the character to suffer more than one automatic Complication on a failed Task. This should be made clear when the option to succeed at cost is presented.

MOMENTUM

Whenever a character attempts a Task and scores a greater number of successes than the Difficulty, then these excess successes become Momentum, a valuable resource that allows characters to complete the Task more quickly or more thoroughly than normal, or otherwise gain additional benefits. Each success above and beyond the Difficulty of a Task becomes one point of Momentum, which the character may use immediately, may save for later, or some mixture of the two.

Some situations and Talents grant a character **bonus Momentum** on specific Tasks. This is added to the amount of Momentum the character generates upon a successful Task of that type. Bonus Momentum may specify that it may only be used in a specific way. Bonus Momentum cannot be saved — if it is not used, it is lost.

Characters do not begin a mission with any Momentum: it only comes from action.

Example: Lieutenant Commander Data performs a scan of a strange spatial anomaly, scoring four successes. As the Task had a Difficulty of 1, this means that he has generated three Momentum.

SPENDING MOMENTUM

The normal use for Momentum is to improve the outcome of a successful Task, such as gaining more information from research, inflicting more damage with an attack, or making more progress with an ongoing problem.

Immediately after determining if a Task is successful, the GM will describe the basic outcome of that Task. Momentum may then be spent to improve this outcome, or provide other benefits. Momentum used in this way doesn't need to be declared in advance, and each point can be spent one at a time as required. For example, a character may see how much damage an attack has inflicted before spending Momentum to inflict more. Thus, Momentum can't be wasted by being used on something that wasn't necessary.

Most uses for Momentum can only be used once on any given Task, or once in any given Round in combat. Some Momentum spends are noted as being **repeatable**, which means that they can be used as frequently as the character wishes and has the Momentum available to spend on them.

Once the character's Task has been resolved, any unspent Momentum is added to the group pool; Momentum that cannot be added to the group pool is lost if it isn't spent.

Example: Lieutenant Commander Data's scan of a spatial anomaly generated three Momentum. He spends the first point to gain additional information from his scan. Not yet having enough information, he spends the second point to get even more information.

SAVING MOMENTUM

As noted above, characters have the option of saving Momentum, rather than letting unspent Momentum go to waste. This saved Momentum goes into a group pool, which can be added to or used by any character in the group, representing the benefits of their collective successes. This pool cannot contain more than six points of Momentum.

During any successful Task, any member of the group may spend points of Momentum from the group pool in addition to those generated during that Task. As normal, Momentum only needs to be spent as needed, so a character does not have to choose how much Momentum they are spending from the group pool until they spend it, nor does it need to be spent all at once.

At the end of each scene, one point of Momentum in the pool is lost; Momentum cannot be saved forever.

Example: Lieutenant Commander Data has one Momentum remaining from his scan. He chooses to save it for later, rather than spending it. It's added to the group pool, and can be used by someone else subsequently.

IMMEDIATE MOMENTUM SPENDS

Some Momentum spends are not tied to a successful Task; rather, they can be used whenever they are required, and may use points directly from the group's Momentum pool rather than waiting for a successful Task. These spends are referred to as Immediate. Immediate Momentum spends often have different restrictions on how and when they can be used, but those restrictions are specific to the individual spends.

Immediate Momentum spends can also be paid for by adding to Threat. Generating a single point of Threat for the Gamemaster provides the same benefits as spending a single point of Momentum. When paying for an Immediate Momentum spend, the cost can be split, paid partly in Momentum and partly in Threat, if the character desires.

Example: Attempting to navigate around the spatial anomaly, the Enterprise's helmsman takes the saved point of Momentum to buy an extra die for their Task, describing it as using the information from Data's scan to plot a better course.

NON-PLAYER CHARACTERS AND SAVING MOMENTUM

Unlike the Player Characters, Non-Player Characters do not have the option of saving Momentum into a group pool. Instead, any Non-Player Character that concludes a Task with Momentum left over can add a single point to the Gamemaster's Threat pool for each point of Momentum they haven't spent on other things.

Non-Player Characters can spend from the Threat pool in the same way as Player Characters spend from the group Momentum pool. The Threat pool is described in more detail later in its own section.

THE TREATY OF ARMENS

There are many cases, and many stories that would-be captains aspire to that demonstrate that creativity, that outside-the-box thinking is what separates good captains from great ones. These stories become legend not because they are especially brilliant, though many of them are, and, I might add, many also carried significant risk at the time. But because they are unusual, they are a step beyond what is expected. Great captains will, in the heat of the moment, when everyone about them is full of doubt, worry and fear, make choices that few would make; that is one of the things that separates them, of course. But less often told and retold, less often remembered, is the fact that great captains are those who also use their creativity to think within the box, to find the unusual or unexpected in the unforeseen places, and that is: plain sight. Take the Treaty of Armens as an example, where Captain Jean-Luc Picard managed to end a protracted conflict, not by enacting an imaginative plan that nobody had seen before, that was not in the play book. But by finding a solution in the expected process. When the Sheliak refused to allow Captain Picard the time required to evacuate a colony, he found his solution in procedure. By selecting third-party arbiters, the Grizzelas, he knew he would be creating more than sufficient time (they were in their hibernation cycle at the time), and that the Sheliak would rather compromise where previously they wouldn't, than follow the process to the letter. Just because the greatest stories of our greatest captains are replete with situations where solutions were found in the unexpected, does not mean that the very greatest will overlook the expected, and seek their solutions there…

- Captain Katherine Unmeyer,
  in her lecture series Captaincy,
  Starfleet Academy.

Example: While firing on the U.S.S. Saratoga, a Borg cube generates two Momentum from the attack. Having no use for the Momentum at that moment, the Gamemaster converts those Momentum to Threat, adding two points to the Threat pool.

COMMON USES FOR MOMENTUM

Players are encouraged to be creative in their use of Momentum. When you score an exceptional success, think in terms of how that superb performance can be reflected in either the result of the immediate Task or in how the outcome of that Task can impact what happens next.

Regardless of how it is used, Momentum spends must make a degree of narrative sense — that is, the benefit gained from Momentum must make sense from the perspective of the characters — and the Gamemaster may veto Momentum spends that do not support or reflect the fiction.

The most common ways to use Momentum are listed below.

- **CREATE ADVANTAGE:** Momentum can allow a character to produce a positive or advantageous circumstance. Spending two Momentum establishes some new Advantage in addition to whatever effect the successful Task had. Advantages created must relate to the nature of the Task attempted, and it must be something that could logically result from the character's actions. This may instead be used to remove a Complication currently in play, or to create a Complication on an adversary.

- **CREATE OPPORTUNITY:** (Immediate, Repeatable). One of the most straightforward uses of Momentum is to add bonus d20s to a Task. The decision to purchase bonus dice must be made before the dice pool is rolled. The cost of this increases for each die purchased (regardless of how those bonus d20s were bought); the first die bought costs 1 Momentum, the second one costs 2 Momentum, and the third die costs 3. As noted on p. 80, no more than three bonus d20s may be bought for a single Task

- **CREATE PROBLEM:** (Immediate, Repeatable). A character can choose to make things more difficult for an opponent, increasing the Difficulty of a single Task by one for every two Momentum spent. The decision to increase a Task's Difficulty **must** be made before any dice are rolled on that Task.

- **OBTAIN INFORMATION:** (Repeatable). Momentum from a successful Task allows a character to learn more about a situation. Each point of Momentum spent can be used to ask the Gamemaster a single question about the current situation, or an item, object, structure, creature, or character present in or relevant to the scene at hand. The Gamemaster must answer this question truthfully, but the Gamemaster does not have to give complete information — a partial or brief answer that leaves room for further questions is more common. The information provided **must** be relevant to the Task attempted, and it must be the kind of information that a character using that skill would be able to determine in that situation — a character could use Medicine to diagnose an illness, or Security to identify a form of ranged weapon from the damage it causes.

THREAT

While not something that the Players will directly interact with, Threat is an integral part of **Star Trek Adventures**. The Gamemaster makes uses of Threat to alter scenes, empower Non-Player Characters, and generally make things increasingly perilous. Threat is a means of building tension — the larger the Threat pool, the greater the likelihood that something will endanger or challenge the Player Characters. Strictly speaking, the characters don't know about Threat, but they will have a sense of the stakes of a situation, and of the potential for things to go wrong, and these things are what Threat represents. Threat is described in full in *Chapter 10: Gamemastering*.

Throughout a game session, the Gamemaster will collect Threat, and spend it to create problems for the Player Characters. In this way, Threat mimics the rise and fall of tension that build throughout a story, eventually culminating in a high-tension finale that exhausts the Threat pool.

Threat comes from action, much as Momentum does. Certain Player options may add to Threat instead of spending Momentum, or allow them to defer a problem until later, while some Player choices can escalate a situation, adding to Threat as they represent a rise in tension and peril. Similarly, adversaries can add to Threat in the way that Player Characters add to their group Momentum. In this way, Threat serves as a visible "cause and effect" for the game, with actions and consequences linked by the accrual and expenditure of Threat.

The Gamemaster typically begins play with two Threat for each Player, though this can be adjusted based on the tone and underlying tension of a given mission.

In game terms, the Gamemaster gains Threat in the following circumstances:

- **IMMEDIATE MOMENTUM:** Whenever the character uses an Immediate Momentum spend — such as to buy bonus d20s — they normally choose to pay that cost in Momentum from the group's pool. However, the character may instead choose to pay some or all that cost by adding one point of Threat to the pool for each point of Momentum that would otherwise have been spent.

- **COMPLICATIONS:** When a character suffers one or more Complications on a Task, they or the Gamemaster may choose not to have the Complication take effect, in exchange for adding two to the Threat pool.

- **THREATENING CIRCUMSTANCES:** The environment or circumstances of a new scene may be threatening enough to warrant adding one or two Threat to the pool automatically. Similarly, some Non-Player Characters — this will be listed in their rules — may generate Threat just for turning up, in response to circumstances, or by taking certain actions. This also includes activities that escalate the tensions of the scene, such as Player Characters using deadly force.

- **NON-PLAYER CHARACTER MOMENTUM:** Non-Player Characters with unspent Momentum cannot save it as Player Characters can — Non-Player Characters don't have a group Momentum pool. Instead, a Non-Player Character can spend that Momentum to add to Threat, adding one Threat for each Momentum spent (Repeatable).

In return, the Gamemaster can spend Threat in a few common ways:

- **NON-PLAYER CHARACTER MOMENTUM:** The Threat pool serves as a mirror for the Players' group Momentum pool. Thus, Non-Player Characters may use Threat in all the ways that Player Characters use group Momentum.

- **NON-PLAYER CHARACTER THREAT SPENDS:** or any action or choice where a Player Character would add one or more points to Threat, a Non-Player Character performing that same action or choice must spend the equivalent number of points of Threat.

- **NON-PLAYER CHARACTER COMPLICATIONS:** If a Non-Player Character suffers a Complication, the Gamemaster may prevent the Complication by spending two Threat.

- **COMPLICATION:** The Gamemaster may create a Complication by spending two Threat.

- **REINFORCEMENTS:** The Gamemaster may bring in additional Non-Player Characters during a scene. Minor Non-Player Characters cost one Threat apiece, while Notable Non-Player Characters cost two. Starship reinforcements cost Threat equal to their Scale.

- **ENVIRONMENTAL EFFECTS:** The Gamemaster may trigger or cause problems with the environment by spending Threat.

Player Characters begin each session with a single point of Determination, and no character can have more than three points of Determination at any time. Using and gaining Determination is tied to a character's Values, and to the Directives in play during a mission.

VALUES AND DIRECTIVES

Values are short phrases or statements that describe the attitudes, beliefs, and convictions of a character while Directives are mission specific Values shared by the characters on that mission. These are covered fully in *Chapter 5: Reporting for Duty*.

USING VALUES

A character's Values can help a character in difficult situations. They often provide an additional push to succeed, as the character's convictions drive them to achieve more than they might have done otherwise. Whenever a character is attempting a Task for which one of their Values would be advantageous, they may spend one point of Determination.

A point of Determination spent provides one of the following benefits:

- **PERFECT OPPORTUNITY:** a point of Determination may be spent to grant the character a single bonus d20. This bonus d20 differs from most in that it is considered to have already rolled a 1, and thus generates two successes automatically. The normal limit of additional d20s bought for a Task still applies.

- **MOMENT OF INSPIRATION:** a point of Determination may be spent to re-roll all the character's dice in their dice pool.

- **SURGE OF ACTIVITY:** the character may immediately perform another Task as soon as this one has been resolved. This is most useful in combat or other situations where the character is under pressure and cannot normally attempt two consecutive Tasks.

- **MAKE IT SO:** the character immediately creates an Advantage that applies to the current scene.

Example: Spock is attempting to uncover the truth behind a conspiracy. Suspecting that the Enterprise's *computers have been tampered with, he sets about testing his hypothesis. This is a Reason + Engineering Task, using his Computers Focus, with a Difficulty of 3. Given the Difficulty, and the urgency, Spock buys an additional d20 for the Task. As Spock is motivated by his Value: "Logic is the Beginning, not the end, of Wisdom," Spock may spend one of his Determination to aid in his Task, which he does to buy an extra d20 that has already rolled a 1.*

However, Values can also hinder a character's judgement, make them biased, blind them to possibilities, or otherwise impair their ability to confront a situation effectively. Nobody is immune to their own preconceptions, as much as they might wish to believe otherwise. If the character is in a situation where one of their Values would make the situation more complicated or more difficult, the Gamemaster may offer the Player one Determination in exchange for suffering a Complication: this may take the form of a course of action, or a decision not to act, but any kind of Complication is suitable so long as it fits the circumstances. The Player can choose not to accept this offer — and Players can choose to suggest situations where their character might face this Complication — but if they accept the Complication, then the setback occurs, without any ability to avoid it. The Gamemaster is the final arbiter of this, but Complications from Values should only ever happen if both Gamemaster and Player agree.

Example: The Enterprise *has rescued an injured Romulan after responding to a distress call in the Neutral Zone. Dr. Crusher is attempting to save the Romulan's life, but the Romulan needs a blood transfusion. Worf is the only member of the crew with the correct cellular factors to help. However, Worf despises Romulans, and this is part of his "Proud and Honorable Klingon" Value; the Gamemaster offers Worf a point of Determination and asks that Worf refuse to help the Romulan. Worf accepts, and the Romulan dies in sickbay.*

In either case, only one Value can be applied to a given Task or situation at once, except when that Value is challenged.

CHALLENGING VALUES

Some situations are not as simple as a Value either helping or hindering the character. Some situations may put a character in a difficult situation, where their Values are sorely tested, shaking their worldview considerably. Maybe the character realizes something about themselves, or learns something important from someone or something they deeply revere or revile.

Once during a mission, if a character has a Value which could affect a Task or situation negatively, they may challenge that Value. The character immediately gains a point of Determination, and then crosses out the challenged Value, meaning that it cannot be used again for the remainder of the mission. If a character has two Values that apply to the situation — one positive and one negative — then the character may apply both Values to the situation, challenging the negative Value and immediately spending the Determination with the positive Value.

Example: Captain Archer, confronting a Xindi Arboreal, finds himself torn between two conflicting Values: "Seek Out New Life, and New Civilizations," and "Angry at the Xindi." While speaking with the Arboreal, Gralik, Archer realizes that not all the Xindi are in support of their war against Humanity, and sets aside his anger; he gains a point of Determination, and crosses out the Value that pertains to his anger, and then spends that point of Determination to try and convince Gralik to help him.

At the end of the mission, the character may alter the Challenged Value to reflect the challenge to the character's beliefs, or replace it with a new Value that represents some other aspect of the character's beliefs. In either case, the new Value can now be used freely.

Directives can be challenged in the same way as Values, but instead of crossing the Directive out, the character who Challenged the Directive should make a note that they have Challenged that Directive. This is likely to have consequences for the character later, as described on p. 142.

THE NEXT STEP

Assimilation. The very word is an anathema to so many coerced by liberal leaning propaganda that any positive implication is sneered at. We exist at a point in our technological capacity where we can intervene on behalf of the haphazard approach of evolution in order to provide order, to better ourselves and our capabilities. To slice away our weaknesses and expand our abilities. The fittest survive, that is an overwhelming fact of biology, and it drives evolution. What the Borg attempt, to make a grasp at greatness, to take the future in their own hands, is nothing to be feared, it is the path any technologically advanced species must take in order to secure their destiny and their survival. While those out there who would protect the integrity of the species abhor the Borg, we have much to learn from their example. At the same time, we must be aware that the path of the Borg is not ideal. There is a middle ground in which, those willing, should have the freedom to extend, augment and improve on the abilities and limitations of our genetics to create something new. We have the technological capability, but we lack the courage, the daring, to make the leap required of us to transcend the hand of base-pair cards we are dealt at birth. We delve the vastness of space, our eyes glowing in the reflected light of the torch we have been handed by thousands of generations of explorers, but we lack the fortitude to explore the possibilities of what we ourselves could become, if only we used our technology to push the frontiers of our innate capabilities…

- Daniel Allers,
  infamous geneticist, outlaw in the Federation.
  Opening words in a speech broadcast
  from his hidden research facility.

This section deals with additional rules that the Gamemaster may wish to use to add extra detail to a scene or situation. These rules are not required, but if used carefully, they can be a valuable way to make a scene more engaging and more memorable.

In that regard, they should be thought of more as tools for the Gamemaster to construct a scene, rather than as ready-made rules to drop into a situation. They will require some consideration and effort on the part of the Gamemaster to use effectively, and they may not suit all groups and all styles of play.

CHALLENGES

A Challenge is any circumstance, situation, or sequence of events which requires multiple Tasks to overcome. There are a few different ways to resolve a Challenge, depending on the nature of the Challenge and how the Gamemaster wishes to present the situation. These different options can be combined as the Gamemaster sees fit, providing a toolbox for structuring a wide range of different problems for the characters to overcome.

BASIC CHALLENGE

A Basic Challenge is, as the name suggests, relatively straightforward for all involved. It consists of two or more Tasks or Extended Tasks, of a type and Difficulty determined by the Gamemaster. These Tasks or Extended Tasks are the core of the Challenge, the crucial activities that must be completed to overcome the Challenge, and they are referred to as Key Tasks. Once all the Key Tasks have been completed successfully, the Challenge is complete.

The Gamemaster may determine that these Key Tasks be completed in order, or otherwise say that Key Tasks cannot be attempted until certain other Key Tasks have been completed. These restrictions should naturally flow from the narrative of the situation — if the Challenge is to reach main engineering and shut down the warp core before it breaches, then the Task to reach engineering must naturally come first.

Characters may, at their option, attempt other Tasks during a Basic Challenge; these won't directly contribute to overcoming the Challenge, but they can be used to remove Complications, to generate Momentum to benefit the group, or, at the Gamemaster's discretion, to reduce the Difficulty of a Key Task (normally by one, but the Gamemaster may permit Momentum to be spent for a greater reduction).

STRUCTURING BASIC CHALLENGES

There are a few different ways that the Gamemaster might structure a Basic Challenge. At the simplest level, having the individual Key Tasks being completely independent of one another requires the least effort in rules terms, but may not be suitable for a lot of different situations. There are a few other common approaches as well:

Linear Challenges arrange the Key Tasks into an order, where each Key Task must be completed before the next can be attempted. These are easy to handle, but they are somewhat inflexible and tend to limit the creativity of the characters in how they approach the Challenge.

Gated Challenges require a little more effort from the Gamemaster to set up, but they're flexible and can be adapted to a range of circumstances. In a Gated Challenge, some of the Key Tasks can only be attempted if one or more other Key Tasks have already been completed; the Gamemaster might want to present this as a chart that clearly denotes which Key Tasks "unlock" the restricted Tasks.

Group Challenges are intended to be completed through collective effort, rather than by a single person. In a Group Challenge, whenever a character attempts or assists a Task, they may not assist any other Tasks during the remainder of the Challenge, and any other Tasks they attempt during that Challenge increase in Difficulty by one. This Difficulty increase is cumulative.

OPPOSITION IN CHALLENGES

In some circumstances, the characters may be working against an opposing force. There are a couple of ways to resolve this, depending on the type of Challenge and opposition.

- **DISRUPTION:** The effect of the opposition is disruptive and distracting, even inconvenient, but nothing more. Task Difficulties may increase by one or two because of the presence of this opposition, representing their interference and the disruption it causes. It might even increase the Complication range of the characters' Tasks.

- **DIRECT OPPOSITION:** The effect of the opposition is to directly act against the Tasks attempted, turning them into Opposed Tasks. This may also add additional hazards or consequences to those Tasks, as the opposition may create additional problems on failed Tasks.

- **CONTEST:** The opposition is attempting to complete the same objective, and to complete them sooner than the characters. Each side attempts a single Task, then hands over to the other side to attempt a Task, regardless of which specific characters attempt each Task. Whichever side completes the Challenge first, achieves some greater advantage. Characters can spend Determination to attempt a second Task before handing over to the other side.

- **CONFLICT:** The opposition have different, mutually-exclusive goals to the characters. This is commonly used in Social and Combat Challenges, where each side has a different goal, and the sequence of events is split into Rounds and Turns. This is described in full in the **Combat** section, later.

TIMED CHALLENGE

Functionally like a Basic Challenge, a **Timed Challenge** adds an additional concern: time.

At the start of the Challenge, the Gamemaster determines the number of intervals that the Challenge must be completed within, and how long a period that each interval represents (ten minutes, an hour, a day, etc). The ideal number of intervals is equal to about 2-3 times the number of Key Tasks involved in the Challenge, with a smaller number of intervals resulting in more time pressure on the characters. The Gamemaster should also determine what happens when time runs out — this should be a severe consequence.

Each Task attempted takes two intervals of time to attempt by default; characters can spend one Momentum on a successful Task to reduce this to one interval. A Complication may cause a Task to take longer, adding a single interval to the Task. This applies equally to both Key Tasks and to any others attempted during the Challenge.

EXTENDED TASKS

Unlike normal Tasks, Extended Tasks cannot be overcome in a single attempt. Extended Tasks should be used sparingly, and only in situations where there is additional pressure or tension, such as during combat, or when there is only a limited amount of time to succeed. Extended Tasks use a mechanism similar to how damage is inflicted in combat, to represent activities which will take an uncertain amount of time and effort to complete, which is ideally suited to situations where there is an increasing peril or risk of harm the longer the activity takes to complete. Additional information on Extended Tasks can be found on p. 282.

Extended Tasks have a few additional factors to consider over normal Tasks, which are described below:

- **WORK:** each Extended Task has a Work track, which is a means of determining how much Work will be needed to overcome the Extended Task. Whenever a character succeeds at a Task as part of an Extended Task, it will make an amount of Work (described below), which is marked off from the Work track. A Work track normally has a value from five to twenty.

- **MAGNITUDE:** each Extended Task has a Magnitude, normally a value from 1 to 5, which represents how large and complex an undertaking the Extended Task is. When a character achieves a number of Breakthroughs (described below) equal to the Extended Task's Magnitude, the Extended Task is completely overcome.

- **RESISTANCE:** some Extended Tasks are particularly arduous to overcome, and making progress is slower. This is covered by Resistance which reduces the amount of Work done from each Task. Most Extended Tasks do not have Resistance, but those that do tend to have no more than 3 Resistance.

An Extended Task also has a base Difficulty, which is used for all Tasks made to overcome the Extended Task. This base Difficulty can be modified on each Task as circumstances (such as Traits) dictate, but they all start from the same place.

Whenever a character succeeds at a Task to overcome an Extended Task, there are a few additional steps to follow over and above the normal procedure for completing a Task.

1. The character rolls 2🅰, plus additional 🅰 equal to the Discipline used for that Task. The total rolled on these dice is the amount of Work done.

2. If the Extended Task has any Resistance, reduce the Work done by the Resistance value. Any remaining Work is marked off from the Work track. Further, the character may have achieved one or two Breakthroughs, if either or both following conditions are fulfilled:

A. If five or more Work is made, after reduction for Resistance, the character also achieves a Breakthrough.

B. If the Work track is filled, or if one or more Work is made after reduction for Resistance, when the Work track was already full, the character achieves a Breakthrough.

3. If the number of Breakthroughs achieved is equal to the Extended Task's Magnitude, the Extended Task is complete. Otherwise, the base Difficulty of the Extended Task is reduced by one for each Breakthrough achieved, to a minimum of 0. If the base Difficulty has already been reduced to 0, each subsequent Breakthrough adds +1▲ to any future rolls for Work on this Extended Task.

EXTENDED TASKS AND MOMENTUM

Momentum generated on the Tasks that comprise an Extended Task can be used in all the normal ways, but there are a few Momentum Spends that apply specifically to Extended Tasks. These are listed in the table below.

EXTENDED TASKS AND MOMENTUM TABLE

NAME	COST	DESCRIPTION
Additional Work	1	Repeatable. Increase the Work done by +1 for this Task, before reductions for Resistance.
Piercing	1	Repeatable. Ignore up to two Resistance for this Task.
Re-Roll Work	1	Re-roll any number of Challenge Dice from the current Task.

EXTENDED TASKS AND EFFECTS

Due to the use of Challenge Dice on Extended Tasks, some consideration needs to be made for what happens when Effects are rolled.

Under normal circumstances, the Challenge Dice used for an Extended Task have no special effects, and thus each Effect rolled simply counts as a 1, without any additional benefits. However, characters can obtain benefits which will trigger when Effects are rolled. If the character has multiple benefits, then all of them are triggered when an Effect is rolled.

- **TRIUMPHANT:** If the character achieves a Breakthrough, and one or more Effects were rolled, then an additional Breakthrough is achieved.

- **SCRUTINIZE X:** The character ignores X points of the Extended Task's Resistance for each Effect rolled.

- **PROGRESSION X:** The character makes an additional X Work for each Effect rolled.

These might be granted by the character using the ideal tools for the situation, by establishing favorable circumstances (such as an Advantage), or by the Talents a character has learned.

EXTENDED TASKS AND COMPLICATIONS

Though Complications generated during Extended Tasks can be used normally, there are a few other ways they can be employed during an Extended Task, representing setbacks during that undertaking. Complications used for one of these purposes don't count as normal Complications in any other way; the Complication is 'spent' to produce the effect chosen.

- **DEAD END:** Unmark four points from the Work track. This is applied after resolving the effects of the Task.

- **UNFORESEEN PROBLEM:** The Extended Task's Resistance is increased by two, to a maximum of four.

If the characters abandon the Extended Task or find themselves unable to overcome it, then the GM may declare that they partially completed it; in this instance, the characters achieve their goal, but suffer one additional Complication relating to the Extended Task for each Breakthrough they failed to gain.

*Example: The Enterprise is attacked by a cloaked mine from an unknown aggressor, which has attached itself to the ship's hull. Lieutenant Reed heads outside the ship to defuse the bomb. Because of the complexity of the device, and the danger of the situation, the Gamemaster determines that this is an Extended Task, with a Work of 12, a Magnitude of 3, a Resistance of 1, and a base Difficulty of 3. The mine has various self-defense mechanisms, so any failed Task will result in a dangerous reaction from the mine. The Gamemaster also notes Reed's preparations and tools, and declares that each Effect on a Challenge Dice ignores 1 Resistance. Reed attempts his first Task, using his **Control 10 + Security 4**, and his Focus of Explosives, and buys two extra dice with some saved Momentum. Rolling 6, 7, 12, and 13, he scores four successes, completing the first Task; he then rolls 6▲ — two, plus four for his Security skill — rolling two 2s, a 3 (ignored), two 4s (ignored), and a 5 (an Effect), for a total of 5, ignoring one Resistance. That's enough for one Breakthrough, and Reed pushes on. His second attempt goes less well; a Complication from Mayweather's attempt to move the ship to safety makes things more difficult for Reed, jostling the mine. Reed's Task fails, and a spike shoots from the mine into the hull, impaling Reed's leg in the process. Reed can no longer reach the mine to defuse it, so Captain Archer must venture out to defuse the mine and save Lieutenant Reed.*

16051806050320
2015131325

REPORTING FOR DUTY
A CAREER IN STARFLEET

"COMMANDER, WE DON'T HAVE TO LIKE EACH OTHER TO WORK WELL TOGETHER.
AS A MATTER OF FACT, I'D LIKE YOU TO CONTINUE TO KEEP ME ON MY TOES."

— CAPTAIN WILLIAM T. RIKER

Welcome aboard. For some of you, this will be your first assignment, fresh out of Starfleet Academy. For others, this will be the next stage in your career within Starfleet. No matter where you are assigned on the ship — whether you are bridge officers, specialists in your fields, researchers who will be assigned to science stations, or operations crew ensuring the safety of the ship or to keep the engines running at peak performance — you all have a vital role to play on board.

A great part of the enjoyment of roleplaying games is in creating original Player Characters and telling their stories, and this chapter describes how to do so. *Star Trek Adventures* provides two distinct methods of creating those original characters, and these methods will produce roughly equivalent characters. Whichever method is used, it should be used for the entire group, to get the same play experience.

ERAS OF PLAY

Broadly speaking, *Star Trek Adventures* games are likely to take place in one of three main eras of play: distinct periods of time where important events are unfolding and where the potential for exciting adventures is at the highest. These are discussed in brief below:

- **ENTERPRISE:** In the mid-22nd century, Humanity started exploring the stars, with the aid of the Vulcans. As the years passed, Earth Starfleet vessels such as the *Enterprise* NX-01 forged friendships and alliances with other species, and in the wake of a destructive war between Earth and the Romulan Star Empire, many of these species forged a stronger alliance: The United Federation of Planets. These early years of exploration can be seen in the series *Star Trek: Enterprise,* and the era continues into the early years of the Federation at the end of the century.

- **ORIGINAL SERIES:** In the mid-23rd century, Starfleet's mission of exploration and discovery reaches new heights, with deep-space voyages such as that of the original *U.S.S. Enterprise* taking years at a time and making first contact with many cultures and civilizations. Amidst this, tensions with the Klingon Empire rise to the brink of war, and the Romulans begin reaching beyond their borders for the first time in a century. The era can be seen in the original *Star Trek* series, and continues

until the closing decades of the century, depicted in the movies *Star Trek: The Motion Picture, Star Trek II: The Wrath of Khan, Star Trek III: The Search for Spock, Star Trek IV: The Voyage Home, Star Trek V: The Final Frontier,* and *Star Trek VI: The Undiscovered Country*.

- **NEXT GENERATION:** In the mid-24th century, the Federation is in a period of unprecedented peace and prosperity, even with border wars against the Cardassians and the Tzenkethi, and political turmoil within the Klingon Empire. However, first contact with the Borg presents a threat to the Federation that requires a greater response than the wars of the past, while war with the Dominion in the 2370s pushes the Federation to its limits and requires alliances with the Klingons and the Romulans. Amidst this, the *U.S.S. Voyager* vanished into the Delta Quadrant, making first contact with species tens of thousands of light years away from the heart of the Federation. This era can be seen in *Star Trek: The Next Generation, Star Trek: Deep Space Nine, Star Trek: Voyager*, and the movies *Star Trek Generations, Star Trek: First Contact, Star Trek: Insurrection*, and *Star Trek Nemesis*. Much of the material in this book is written from the perspective of this era, specifically the year 2371.

The term "character" applies to both Player Characters (those representing and controlled by Players) and Non-Player Characters (characters controlled by the Gamemaster). While Non-Player Characters (NPCs) are treated somewhat differently in some aspects of the game systems, they are otherwise like Player Characters and thus, the use of "character" in this chapter applies to both Player Characters and Non-Player Characters.

CHARACTERS IN STAR TREK ADVENTURES

The Galaxy of *Star Trek* is filled with characters of all kinds, who populate its worlds, crew its starships, and interact with one another in all manner of ways, both mundane and dramatic. To represent this abundance and diversity, characters are composed of a several elements that collectively serve to depict how that individual interacts with the universe, both in game terms, and in story terms. These elements are **Attributes**, **Disciplines**, **Focuses**, **Values**, **Traits**, and **Talents**, and together they paint a picture of who the character is, what they are good at, and how they view the universe around them.

Characters are, broadly speaking, divided into three types for the purposes of play.

- **Player Characters** consist of all the characters used by a Player to participate in the game. Player Characters are split into Main Characters, and Supporting Characters, but whatever type of character it is, while it is being controlled by a Player, it is a Player Character.

- **Main Characters** are the primary focus of this chapter, and can be thought of as the Main Characters of a *Star Trek* series or movie. They're the ones who appear in most episodes, and have the biggest impact upon the story. Each Player in a game of *Star Trek Adventures* will have a single Main Character to control, who will normally be a member of the senior staff of a Federation starship. Each Player decides how their Main Character will act the scenes framed by the Gamemaster. This chapter presents two different methods for creating Main Characters, but whichever method is chosen, it is recommended that all the Players use the same method.

- **Supporting Characters** are like Main Characters in many ways, in that they are controlled by the Players. However, there is no fixed list of Supporting Characters; rather, a Supporting Character is created as-and-when needed to provide aid and assistance in difficult situations, or to allow a Player to take part in a scene if their Main Character is busy elsewhere. Supporting Characters are seldom as complex as Main Characters to allow them to be created swiftly, but a group of Players may find that they want to bring back favourite Supporting Characters

INFINITE DIVERSITY IN INFINITE COMBINATIONS

The United Federation of Planets enshrines the rights and freedoms of all individuals, and forbids all manner of unfair discrimination by species, ethnicity, nationality, spiritual or political beliefs (so long as those beliefs are not harmful to, or unfairly imposed upon, others), gender, sex, sexuality, or a range of other factors, such as disability or neurological variation. Within the Federation, all people are given the means and opportunities to pursue their ambitions and realize their potential, and the differences between individuals are celebrated for their differing perspectives, rather than being ignored or marginalized as they may have been in the past.

To reflect this, characters in *Star Trek Adventures* may be of any ethnicity, religion, sex, gender, sexuality, and so forth, without limit or restriction. Such variations will rarely have any impact upon the character in game terms, though Players may choose to make some facets of the character more prominent (such as in a Value) if they wish to draw attention to them.

time and time again, allowing them to develop and grow into more fleshed-out individuals. Supporting Characters are described more fully in their own section, later.

- **Non-Player Characters** are all those characters that are not controlled directly by the Players. They're normally introduced and directed by the Gamemaster, though if a Non-Player Character — abbreviated to NPC — would be friendly to the Players' characters, the Gamemaster may allow the Players to direct that Non-Player Character during tense situations such as combat. Non-Player Characters are described fully in the section on **Adversaries** (p. 311), and their creation is described in *Chapter 10: Gamemastering* (p. 270).

The elements that comprise a character are described in the sections below.

TRAITS

A character will typically have one or more Traits, one of which will always be the character's Species. Traits are essentially descriptions of important parts of the character, in a single word or a short phrase. Alongside a character's Values — which cover the character's personality, motivations, and beliefs — Traits help define what the character is and what they can do, and they can be employed in the same way as Traits for a location or situation, such as to increase or reduce the Difficulty of Tasks.

First and foremost, we have the character's species. Different species in *Star Trek* vary in many subtle ways, both

PLAYSTYLE

allows him to see, countering the effects of his blindness, but it comes with its own set of potential problems.

There are a great many stories that can be told within the *Star Trek* universe, and not all of them revolve around the senior staff of a Federation starship.

When starting a game of **Star Trek Adventures**, it is a good idea to convene the group and figure out the style of game that everyone wants to play — it does nobody any good if the Gamemaster has one kind of game in mind, and the Players have another. Some groups may be fine with the default presumption of these rules — that the Player's Main Characters are the senior staff of a starship, mirroring the format of the TV shows — but others may wish for a different approach. Specialized problem-solving teams within a ship's crew or groups of lower-ranking officers may be more comfortable for some groups, in which case, ignore the section of these rules that asks the Players to choose a role, as they pertain exclusively to senior staff.

Other styles of game will receive greater focus in other books in the **Star Trek Adventures** range: for example, guidance on games focused on Command, Operations or Science division characters can be found in their relevant division sourcebook.

biologically and culturally, and a Trait can encapsulate those many little differences easily. These are both positive and negative, and influence both how the character interacts with their environment and how characters interact with one another.

A character may obtain additional Traits because of things that happen to them during character creation — life-changing events that will define the character going forwards — and they may occasionally gain more during play. This may be something about the character, such as a debility or impairment the character suffers from, or the influence of some external force, such as the impact of a harrowing experience.

Traits are neutral, and thus able to be applied both positively and negatively. There is no fixed number of Traits a character will have, though every character will have at least one: their species. Traits, and their effects upon play, are described in full on p. 76.

Example: Lieutenant Commander Geordi La Forge has two Traits: Human, and Blind. The first is his species: anything that affects a Human in a specific way, or for which being Human is advantageous or problematic, is impacted by this Trait. The second reflects the fact that Geordi was born without eyesight, and will thus impact any situations where eyesight is necessary or useful. Because of this second Trait, Geordi has a unique piece of equipment: his VISOR. This

VALUES

When a character is created, the character's Player creates statements that describe the attitudes, beliefs, and convictions of that character. These are not simple opinions, but the fundamental structure of the character's morals, ethics, and behavior. They are the things that define who a character is as a person, why they behave the way they do, and what drives them during times of struggle and hardship.

One type of Value is a relationship. Where most Values reflect something internal about the character, a relationship reflects a bond between two characters, or a character and an organization, specifically how the character regards the other party described by the Value. This bond doesn't have to be positive — old grudges and resentments can have a definitive effect upon a character's nature — but it must be something significant, and something that shapes who the character is and how they act.

However, a character's Values are not static. They are potent driving forces for the character; people evolve and grow with their experiences, and in many cases, things that once felt like unshakeable beliefs may come to be seen differently as time passes. There will be opportunities during play to alter a character's Values, and Values are an important part of how characters grow and develop over time.

Values differ from Traits (above) in that they describe what the character believes. They are statements about how the character regards the universe around them, and they are both subjective and potentially changeable. How Values are used in play is described on p. 87.

Example: Captain James T. Kirk has four Values, which define the core of his personality. These are "Doesn't Believe in a No-Win Situation," "There's No Such Thing as The Unknown — Only the Temporarily Hidden," "Married to the Enterprise" and "Risk is Our Business".

ATTRIBUTES

Each character in **Star Trek Adventures** is defined by six Attributes. These are described elsewhere, but they're repeated here as a useful reminder. They embody the character's intrinsic physical and mental capabilities, when compared across species, and the ways they prefer to approach problems. These attributes are **Control**, **Daring**, **Fitness**, **Insight**, **Presence**, and **Reason**. Each attribute has a rating which determines its measure, with higher numbers reflecting greater ability. For humanoids, these attributes range from 7 to 12, with 8 representing average capabilities. Nonhumanoid creatures may have attributes across a broader range, and special abilities that increase their abilities further, though that is described more in the rules for Adversaries.

A character may encounter situations for which more than one of their Attributes are applicable. In these cases, it is important to consider the context of the situation, and how the character is choosing to approach the problem. The Gamemaster may choose which Attribute is most applicable to a situation if more than one could be used.

CONTROL

Control is about the character controlling themselves, and it covers precision, accuracy, and careful timing. It can rely on self-discipline and control of one's emotions to ensure mechanistic precision, or it can be a mixture of fine motor skills, coordination, and familiarity with the activity.

A character might use Control…

- …when performing precise or delicate work.

- …when performing a Task that involves precise timing or accuracy.

- …when giving detailed instructions.

- …to resist mental assault, duress, or other stressful situations through an orderly mind and the application of discipline.

DARING

Daring comes into play whenever a character reacts to a new situation without doubt, hesitation, or caution. It covers circumstances where characters take decisive action without a detailed plan or analysis, and relies on gut instinct and quick reflexes.

A character might use Daring…

- …when responding to an emergency.

- …when attempting to evade or resist some form of immediate danger.

- …when acting aggressively.

- …when acting based on instinct.

- …to resist mental assault, fear, or panic through stubbornness and defiance.

FITNESS

Fitness is about enduring hardship and employing force. It covers physical conditioning, general health and well-being, fortitude, and endurance.

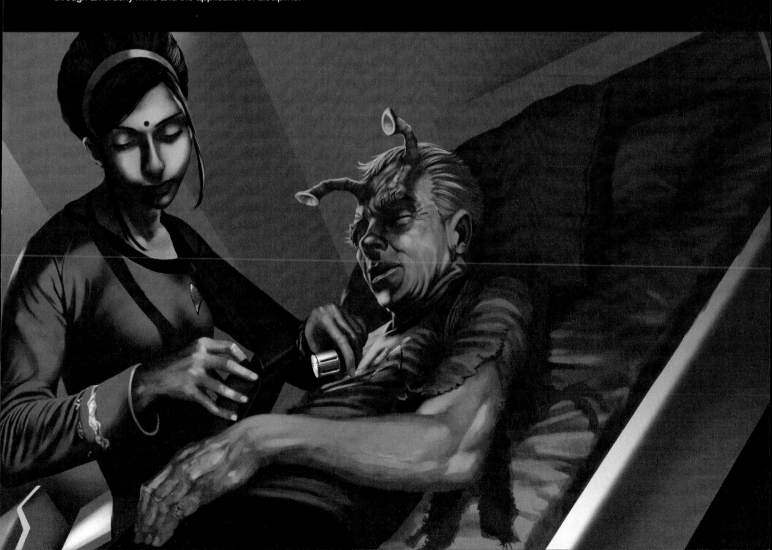

A character might use Fitness...

- ...when attempting to employ raw physical force to a situation.

- ...when performing some strenuous or tiring physical activity.

- ...when trying to resist, or act despite the effects of, some physically debilitating condition, such as poisoning, disease, and extremes of environment.

INSIGHT

Insight is about understanding people and their feelings, and being open to different ideas and ways of thinking. It covers self-awareness, being conscious of a creature's current state of mind, and hard-earned wisdom, and relies upon a person's emotional intelligence, empathy, and experiences.

A character might use Insight...

- ...when attempting to understand the feelings of another creature.

- ...when trying to determine how another creature might think or act, to anticipate or predict its actions.

- ...when trying to overcome their own judgements and preconceptions.

- ...when attempting to calm or reassure others.

- ...when allowing past experiences and instinct to discern changes in the environment around them.

PRESENCE

Presence is power of personality, and the ability to command attention or respect. It's used for being diplomatic during negotiations, giving orders during a crisis, and even being charming or seductive.

A character might use Presence...

- ...to sway the mood or opinion of others through emotive language and rhetoric.

- ...when trying to keep others calm and focused during a stressful situation.

- ...when resisting duress or manipulation by others by maintaining a strong sense of self.

- ...to present a specific appearance or demeanor to others, appropriate to the circumstances.

- ...when seeking to capture and command attention through speech and behavior.

REASON

Reason is about logic and meticulous analysis. It covers forming hypotheses and intricate planning, as well as recall of intricate facts, calculation of complex variables, and it relies on keen observation and a thorough command of the facts.

A character might use Reason...

- ...to study and analyze some unfamiliar phenomenon, and come to a hypothesis about it.

- ...to research a complicated subject, or otherwise interpret large amounts of information.

- ...when trying to sway the opinion of others through facts and logic.

- ...when required to perform complex calculations.

- ...to use observation and rational thought to anticipate and discern changes in the environment around them.

DISCIPLINES

In addition to the six Attributes, each character is trained in six Disciplines, which encompass the broad roles that Starfleet officers are expected to be proficient within. Each Discipline is rated from 0 to 5, with each rating representing a differing level of training, expertise, and natural aptitude. All Main Characters have at least a 1 in every Discipline — Starfleet provides extensive training and expects its officers to have at least basic proficiency in every discipline.

DISCIPLINES TABLE

DISCIPLINE	MEANING
0	Untrained, unskilled, lacking in innate aptitude.
1	Basic training, rudimentary skill, or a raw but undeveloped aptitude.
2	Professional competence, from a combination of training and talent.
3	Experienced and well-trained, or an aptitude developed through study and training.
4	Excellence within the field, achievable through dedication and experience.
5	Exceptional, often a combination of intense training, hard-won experience, and natural aptitude.

The six Disciplines are **Command**, **Conn**, **Engineering**, **Security**, **Science**, and **Medicine** — representing the departments aboard a Federation starship. It's worth noting that many of the Disciplines overlap in a few ways. Each Discipline covers perception, social interaction, and knowledge to some extent, but which Discipline is most applicable to any of those things will depend on circumstances more than anything else — a character with a high Security is quite adept at spotting ambushes and other dangers, but may be less adept at analyzing probe telemetry or experimental data.

As explained in *Chapter 4: Operations*, when asked to perform a Task, the rules or the Gamemaster will choose a single Attribute and a single Discipline — Players may suggest alternate options, though the Gamemaster's word is final — and add their ratings together. This is the Target Number for that Task, and each die that rolls equal to or less than this number scores a success. If the character also has an applicable Focus, any die that rolls equal to or less than the chosen Discipline will score an additional success; if there's no applicable Focus, any die that rolls a 1 will score an additional success.

COMMAND

Command covers a wide range of interpersonal interactions, especially leadership, negotiation, and both coordinating and motivating others. It also includes discipline and resisting coercion, as well as helping others resist fear and panic.

A character might use Command with…

- **Control**, to carefully and precisely coordinate a group of subordinates, or to give detailed orders.

- **Daring**, to make a split-second command decision, or to resist fear or coercion.

- **Fitness**, to coach and guide others performing the same physical activity (such as scaling a cliff, or endurance running), or to coordinate a group all performing related physical activities (such as several people moving a heavy load).

- **Insight**, to judge the mood and morale of a group of subordinates, or to try and assuage the fears of a group.

- **Presence**, to rally or inspire others during a difficult situation, or to command the attention or respect of someone hostile.

- **Reason**, to consider and evaluate the orders given by a superior, or to find a solution to a difficult diplomatic or legal situation.

CONN

A character's ability at the Conn covers piloting craft of all sizes, from ground vehicles and shuttles, to grand starships. It also includes navigation — both on the ground and in space — and an understanding of starship operations, including the procedures and cultures of space travel and exploration.

A character might use Conn with…

- **Control**, to direct a starship or other vessel through a difficult environment, or to operate a craft with such precision as to aid someone else's activities.

- **Daring**, to direct a starship or other vessel to avoid a sudden and imminent danger, or to perform extreme or unorthodox maneuvers with a craft using "feel" or "instinct".

- **Fitness**, to move quickly and effectively in an environment suit, including moving through zero-gravity, or resisting the deleterious effects of extreme acceleration or unpredictable motion without an Inertial Dampening Field.

- **Insight**, to judge the nature or intent of another vessel by the way it is moving, or determining the source of a problem with a familiar vessel.

- **Presence**, to maintain professional decorum and etiquette when representing your ship or Starfleet in formal circumstances, or to argue effectively over a matter of starship protocol, or a course of action.

- **Reason**, to plot a course through a difficult environment, or to determine their location or the location of someone else based on available data.

ENGINEERING

Engineering covers inventing, understanding, designing, repairing, and maintaining technology, as well as using any technology not specifically covered by another Discipline.

A character might use Engineering with…

- **Control**, to adjust or repair a sophisticated device or system, or to operate extremely complex devices like transporters.

- **Daring**, to make improvised repairs to a device in an adverse situation, or to improvise a technical solution to a problem by using technology in an unusual, innovative, or reckless manner.

- **Fitness**, to perform physically taxing, repetitive, or arduous technical activities as efficiently as possible despite physical strain, or to perform a technical activity reliant on the application of physical force.

- **Insight**, to make an "educated guess" about unknown or extremely unfamiliar technology, or to try and understand the behavior of artificial creatures.

- **Presence**, to explain in an engaging manner an extremely complex technical problem or solution to someone with less engineering knowledge, or to argue the merits of a specific approach to a problem with another engineer.

- **Reason**, to study the designs of a device or system and gain additional understanding of its function, or to design a new device or system from scratch.

SECURITY

Security is the use of force during combat — making attacks, essentially — as well as observing and analyzing threatening situations and watching for potential perils. It also encompasses interrogation and intimidation, stealth and infiltration, as well as an in-depth knowledge of weaponry, combat styles, and strategy. It also covers survival skills and athleticism.

A character might use Security with…

- **Control**, to attack an enemy from a distance, or to stay unseen or unnoticed when moving amongst hostile creatures.

- **Daring**, to attack and defend in melee combat, or to scare or intimidate someone with the threat of violence.

- **Fitness**, to restrain an unwilling prisoner, or to climb or swim in difficult circumstances.

- **Insight**, to judge whether an individual is a threat to you or your allies, or to discern if there is the potential for an ambush or trap.

- **Presence**, to question someone suspected of a crime, or to impress upon someone the danger of a course of action or decision.

- **Reason**, to identify the participants of a battle by studying the aftermath, or to devise a plan for a dangerous situation, be it combat, wilderness survival, infiltration, or some combination thereof.

SCIENCE

Science is the understanding of numerous fields of scientific study, both on a theoretical level, and in terms of their practical applications. This does not just cover "hard" sciences like physics, chemistry, and biology, but also social sciences like anthropology. It also covers the application of the scientific method to situations.

A character might use Science with…

- **Control**, to perform a delicate experiment, or to talk someone else through an experimental or complex procedure.

- **Daring**, to devise a solution to a scientific problem without sufficient proof or adequate testing beforehand, or to gather data or perform an experiment under extremely hazardous conditions.

- **Fitness**, to correctly analyze data while fatigued or otherwise suffering from some physical hindrance, or to effectively resist the effects of radiation or other environmental phenomena by knowing how to protect against exposure.

- **Insight**, to gain useful data from witnesses or the subjects of a study, or to devise a rough working hypothesis from incomplete data.

- **Presence**, to explain in an engaging manner an extremely complex scientific problem or solution to someone with less scientific knowledge, or to argue the merits of a theory with another scientist.

- **Reason**, forming a hypothesis from available information, or performing research on an unfamiliar subject.

MEDICINE

Medicine is the understanding of the physical and mental makeup of life-forms, including a knowledge of ailments and diseases that might befall them, the injuries and stresses they can suffer, and the methods for treating those maladies in a wide range of species.

A character might use Medicine with…

- **Control**, to perform delicate procedures, such as surgery, or to talk someone else through providing medical attention.

- **Daring**, to provide emergency medical attention on a patient who is in imminent danger of death, or when resisting fear or panic to protect a patient.

- **Fitness**, to resist the effects of poisons and diseases by knowing how to respond to exposure, or to move or restrain a patient without exacerbating their injuries.

- **Insight**, to diagnose a patient's illness or injury from a description of the symptoms, or to provide therapeutic care for a patient who is traumatized or otherwise in distress.

- **Presence**, to convey to a stubborn or unwilling patient the seriousness of their case or the necessity of the treatment, or to speak on a patient's behalf about their case to convince others of a specific course of action.

- **Reason**, to diagnose a patient's illness from a thorough examination, or to research an unknown disease, procedure, or treatment.

FOCUSES

The Disciplines characters are trained in are broad; Focuses allow a character to demonstrate talent for a narrower set of disciplines, representing specialization and the kind of expertise that comes from deeper study and practical experiences. Focuses are not tied to any specific Discipline, and can thus be applied to any Task a character attempts, so long as the Focus would logically benefit the Task being attempted.

Main Characters will have six Focuses, and they are encouraged to create their own Focuses. Each Focus should be narrower than the six Disciplines that every character is trained in, but they shouldn't be so narrow as to never come up in play. Further, because there is no specific link between Disciplines and Focuses, a Focus may be valuable for Tasks covering more than one Discipline — for example, Astrophysics could easily be used for Science Tasks, but it also has potential uses when trying to plot a course at the Conn. When choosing a Focus, it is still worth considering which Discipline it is most likely to be used with, however.

Example Focuses include:

Anthropology, Astronavigation, Astrophysics, Botany, Composure, Computers, Cybernetics, Diplomacy, Electro-Plasma Power Systems, Emergency Medicine, Espionage, EVA, Evasive Action, Exo-tectonics, Genetics, Geology, Hand Phasers, Hand-to-hand Combat, Helm Operations, Infectious Diseases, Infiltration, Interrogation, Linguistics, Persuasion, Philosophy, Physics, Psychiatry, Quantum Mechanics, Shipboard Tactical Systems, Small Craft, Spatial Phenomena, Survival, Transporters and Replicators, Trauma Surgery, Virology, Warp Field Dynamics, Xenobiology

TALENTS

Talents are additional benefits that a character possesses, that define areas of specialty, the advantages of their personal approach to circumstances, and other decisive abilities. These normally take the form of a bonus — extra d20s, re-rolls, bonus Momentum, the ability to use a different Discipline in a situation, and so forth — that applies when the character is performing a type of Task or taking an approach to a situation.

Many Talents have one or more specific Requirements. These are conditions that must be fulfilled before the Talent can be selected, such as belonging to a specific Species, or having a Discipline at a specific rating or above. A large selection of Talents is provided in its own section, starting on p. 135.

REPORTING FOR DUTY
LIFEPATH CREATION

The default method of creating a character in *Star Trek Adventures* is the **Lifepath**. This is a series of steps that represent important events of the character's life, and the way those events shape the character's nature is reflected in the mechanical choices each step presents.

The Lifepath consists of seven steps, with each step allowing a new choice from a list of options. Each character is made up of the component parts described above, and these will be decided upon with each step of the Lifepath.

These are cumulative gains, and, as a Player works through each step of the Lifepath, the results are added to the character being created. In this way, the character takes shape stage by stage.

While this option presents the steps as a series of tables with results that can be generated by dice rolls, Players may choose to ignore any or all the results rolled, or even to not bother rolling in the first place. In this way, the system never stands in the way of a desired character concept. Some

As the Lifepath consists of many steps and choices, it's useful to have a summary, to provide an idea of the process before Players begin.

At the start of the Lifepath, a character will have a score of 7 in each Attribute, and a score of 1 in each Discipline. Throughout the process, the character will gain an additional 14 points spread across their Attributes, and an additional 10 points spread across their Disciplines.

Additionally, during the process, a character will receive a minimum of one Trait (their Species), as well as four Values, four Talents, and six Focuses.

STEP ONE: Choose the character's species. The options presented in this rulebook are Andorian, Bajoran, Betazoid, Denobulan, Human, Tellarite, Trill, and Vulcan. Each species grants:
- A species Trait
- +1 to each of three Attributes
- Access to Talents unique to that species
- One Talent

STEP TWO: Choose the character's Environment; this is the type of world the character was raised on. Each Environment grants:
- A Value
- +1 to one Attribute, and +1 to one Discipline.

STEP THREE: Choose the character's Upbringing; this is the kind of education the character had during their formative years, and the kind of influence their parents and mentors had. Each gives the character:
- +2 to one Attribute and +1 to a second Attribute
- +1 to a single Discipline
- One Focus
- One Talent

STEP FOUR: The character attends Starfleet Academy, and chooses which track of the Academy they join — command, operations, or sciences. This grants the character:
- One Value
- Three points to spend on two or three Attributes
- +2 to a single Discipline, +1 to two other Disciplines
- Three Focuses
- One Talent

STEP FIVE: Choose how long the character's career has been so far — are they young and inexperienced, seasoned veterans, or somewhere in between? The character gains:
- One Value
- One Talent

STEP SIX: Determine two or more Career Events. Regardless of how many events are chosen, the character gains:
- Two points for Attributes
- Two points for Disciplines
- Two Focuses.

STEP SEVEN: Finishing Touches. Gain:
- One Value
- +1 to two Attributes
- +1 to two Disciplines
- Adjust Attributes and Disciplines that go above the maximum scores for each.
- Record derived scores — Stress, and bonus damage — plus the character's name, rank, role, department, and starting equipment.

Players may begin the process knowing exactly what kind of character they want to create, while others may have part of an idea and use random rolls to fill out the details.

At this stage, anyone wanting to create a character should have a character sheet on hand. These can be found on at the back of this book, and can be downloaded from the Modiphius website. It is, of course, entirely possible to just use a sheet of plain paper, but a character sheet presents the information in an orderly fashion. Also, it's a good idea to use a pencil when writing down information and notes during character creation, as elements are subject to change during the process.

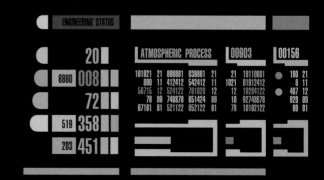

STEP ONE: SPECIES

STARTING POINTS

All characters begin with a score of 7 for each Attribute and 1 for each Discipline. These will be increased during the character's Lifepath. A finished character cannot have more than 12 in any Attribute, may only have one Attribute at 12, cannot have more than 5 in any Discipline, and may only have one Discipline with a score of 5. During the character creation steps a character may end up with scores above these limits, but this will be fixed at Step Seven: Finishing Touches (p. 123).

CHOOSING A SPECIES

The choice made at this stage of the Lifepath is the character's species. There are members of a multitude of species within Starfleet, far too many to list here, but a reasonable selection is provided below. Some species may not be options in earlier eras of play.

Each species provides a few benefits, listed below:

- **ATTRIBUTES:** Each species lists three Attributes. Add +1 to each listed Attribute.

- **TRAIT:** The character gains a single Trait, which is the character's chosen species. This reflects the quirks, strengths, and weaknesses that apply to all members of that species because of their physiology, culture, and shared history. Each species entry provides a few examples of how that Trait may impact situations. A Trait may also serve as a prompt for the Gamemaster to affect a character differently because of a poison, disease, or other hazard.

- **TALENTS:** The character gains a single Talent. This Talent may be chosen freely from any that are available to the character – the main Talent list begins on p. 135. Further, each species has a small number of Talents available to characters of that species, reflecting their physiology or culture in some way.

A Player may choose, or randomly determine, their character's species, from the table below. There are three columns, one for each era of play, each of which lists which numbers on a d20 correspond to each species. Note that, in the *Enterprise* Era, the Federation does not yet exist, so non-human characters will be part of allied organizations — an Andorian may be part of the Imperial Guard, while a Vulcan might report to Vulcan High Command — rather than being Starfleet Officers.

CHOOSING VALUES

Several stages of the Lifepath require that the Player choose a Value for their character. This is sometimes easier said than done: coming up with a suitable phrase on demand isn't always easy, even for highly creative people.

Thus, it's recommended that, where a Player can't come up with a Value for a certain stage, that they make a note that they need to determine a Value for that stage, and move on. The Player can go back and fill in that Value later, even leaving it until the very end of character creation, depending on when inspiration strikes.

If Players are still struggling to come up with a Value during character creation, it is entirely possible to adopt the method used for Creation in Play (p. 131) and leave Values blank even once play has begun, defining them as-and-when required during the game.

RANDOM SPECIES TABLE

SPECIES	D20 ENTERPRISE	D20 THE ORIGINAL SERIES	D20 THE NEXT GENERATION
Andorian	1-2	1-2	1-2
Bajoran	–	–	3-4
Betazoid	–	–	5-6
Denobulan	3-4	3-4	7-8
Human	5-16	5-14	9-14
Tellarite	17-18	15-16	15-16
Trill	–	17-18	17-18
Vulcan	19-20	19-20	19-20

MIXED-HERITAGE CHARACTERS

Many Starfleet Officers have parents from different species. To create characters of mixed-heritage, choose two species, one of which will be the primary species. The character is treated as a member of the primary species for attribute bonuses; most mixed-heritage characters take more after one parent than another. The character gains the species Traits of both parent species, and may select Talents from both parent species.

ANDORIAN

An aggressive, passionate people from the frozen moon Andoria, the Andorians have been part of the United Federation of Planets since its foundation, having been firm allies of Humanity for several years beforehand. Their blue skin, pale hair, and antennae give them a distinctive appearance, and while the Andorian Imperial Guard was demobilized when the Federation was founded, they still maintain strong military traditions, and a tradition of ritualized honor-duels known as Ushaan, using razor-sharp ice-mining tools.

EXAMPLE VALUE: *Proud Son/Daughter of Andoria*

- **ATTRIBUTES:** +1 Daring, +1 Control, +1 Presence.

- **TRAIT:** Andorian. This trait may reduce the Difficulty of Tasks to resist extreme cold, or Tasks impacted by extremely low temperatures. Their antennae aid in balance and spatial awareness; a lost antenna can be debilitating until it regrows. Andorians also have a high metabolism, meaning, amongst other things, that they tire more quickly than Humans; this also makes them more vulnerable to infection from certain types of injury. Before the Federation, Andorians and Vulcans had numerous disputes; though these issues are largely considered to be ancient history, Andorians and Vulcans don't always get along.

- **TALENTS:** The character receives access to the following talents:

PROUD AND HONORABLE
REQUIREMENTS: Andorian, or Gamemaster's permission. Your personal integrity is unimpeachable, and you will not willingly break a promise made. Whenever you attempt a Task to resist being coerced into breaking a promise, betraying your allies, or otherwise acting dishonorably, you reduce the Difficulty by 1.

THE USHAAN
REQUIREMENTS: Andorian, or Gamemaster's permission. You are experienced in the tradition of honor-dueling known as the *Ushaan*, having spilt much blood upon the ice. When you make a melee Attack, or are targeted by a melee Attack, and buy one or more d20s by adding to Threat, you may re-roll the dice pool for the Task. Further, you own an *Ushaan-tor*, a razor-sharp ice-miner's tool used in these duels. The *Ushaan-tor* is a melee weapon with the following profile: Melee, 2▲ Vicious 1, Size 1H.

BAJORAN

A spiritual, dauntless people from the planet Bajor, the Bajorans have lost much after decades of occupation by the Cardassian Union. Many Bajorans were scattered across the Alpha Quadrant during the occupation, while those who remained on Bajor often acted as insurgents or toiled in labor camps under Cardassian rule. The occupation ended a few years ago, but the scars it left will take generations to heal. Bajor is not a member of the Federation, but many Bajorans scattered by the diaspora have found their way into Starfleet. Bajoran culture places a strong belief in the Prophets, celestial beings who are said to have watched over Bajor for millennia; modern religious doctrine states that the Bajoran Wormhole is the Prophets' Celestial Temple.

EXAMPLE VALUE: Faith in the Prophets

- **ATTRIBUTES:** +1 Control, +1 Daring, +1 Insight

- **TRAIT:** Bajoran. For obvious reasons, Bajorans tend to be hostile towards Cardassians, and resentful of those who are dismissive of, or turned a blind eye to, the suffering of the Bajoran people. While not all Bajorans are spiritual or religious to the same degree, most have a cultural understanding of the Prophets' place in Bajoran society.

- **TALENTS:** The character receives access to the following talents:

ORB EXPERIENCE
REQUIREMENT: Bajoran, or Gamemaster's permission.
You have received a vision from the Bajoran Prophets, through one of the Orbs. This rare experience, though confusing at first, has shaped your life and outlook. You have one additional Value, reflecting the insights you received from the experience. The first time this Value is Challenged, roll 1▲; if an Effect is rolled, then some foretold element of the Orb Experience has come to pass, and the Value is not crossed out as it would normally be.

STRONG PAGH
REQUIREMENT: Bajoran, or Gamemaster's permission.
You believe profoundly in the Prophets, and rely heavily upon that faith to see you through hardship. Whenever you attempt a Task to resist being coerced or threatened, you reduce the Difficulty of that Task by 1.

BETAZOID

The peaceful Betazoid people hail from the idyllic, verdant world Betazed. The world is a valued member of the Federation, and its people can be found across Federation space, including Starfleet. Betazoids appear almost identical to Humans, but differ in one major way: they are naturally telepathic, developing mental abilities during adolescence. The potency of this ability varies between individuals, but it has resulted in a culture where honesty and directness are fundamental: it is difficult to keep secrets when everyone around you can read minds.

EXAMPLE VALUE: *Compassion through Understanding*

- **ATTRIBUTES:** +1 Insight, +1 Presence, +1 Reason

- **TRAIT:** Betazoid. All Betazoids are telepathic to varying degrees, and even when not actively using their abilities, they are highly perceptive of others around them, but also highly sensitive to telepathic disturbances and mental assaults. They have little familiarity with lies and deception, due to their open culture and ability to read the thoughts and emotions of others. As they are sensitive to the minds of other living beings, they tend not to be comfortable around animals, for fear of losing themselves in the minds of wild creatures.

- **TALENTS:** The character receives access to the following talents. A Betazoid character must select one of the Betazoid talents at some point during character creation, to reflect their telepathy. Characters who are only partially Betazoid may not select the Telepath talent.

EMPATH

REQUIREMENT: Betazoid, or Gamemaster's Permission. Character creation only. You can sense the emotions of most living beings nearby, and can communicate telepathically with other empaths and telepaths, as well as those with whom you are extremely familiar. You cannot choose not to sense the emotions of those nearby, except for those who are resistant to telepathy. It may require effort and a Task to pick out the emotions of a specific individual in a crowd, or to block out the emotions of those nearby. Increase the Difficulty of this Task if the situation is stressful, if there are a lot of beings present, if the target has resistance to telepathy, and other relevant factors.

TELEPATH

REQUIREMENT: Betazoid, or Gamemaster's Permission. Character creation only. You can sense the surface thoughts and emotions of most living beings nearby, and can communicate telepathically with other empaths and telepaths, as well as those with whom you are extremely familiar. Surface thoughts are whatever a creature is thinking about at that precise moment. The character cannot choose not to sense the emotions or read the surface thoughts of those nearby, except for those who are resistant to telepathy. It will require effort and a Task to pick out the emotions or thoughts of a specific individual in a crowd, to search a creature's mind for specific thoughts or memories, or to block out the minds of those nearby. Unwilling targets may resist with an Opposed Task.

DENOBULAN

Hailing from the planet Denobula, Denobulans are a gregarious, inquisitive people who have been allies of Humanity since the 2130s. Though Denobula was not one of the founders of the Federation, the Denobulans joined soon after. Denobulans are a sociable people, with distinctive expressive features, who are used to living in close, communal conditions, and whose extended family groups are large and complex — a Denobulan may have several spouses, each of whom may have several partners of their own, and dozens of children between them. Culturally, they are intellectually curious, perceptive, and interested in a wide range of philosophies, though their scholarly nature, large families, and gregarious nature means that relatively few of them venture far from their homeworld.

EXAMPLE VALUE: *Safety in Numbers*

- **ATTRIBUTES:** +1 Fitness, +1 Insight, +1 Reason

- **TRAIT:** Denobulan. Denobulans have a robust immune system, but a vulnerability to various forms of radiation poisoning. They are naturally adept climbers, scuttling up sheer walls like some forms of terrestrial lizard. Denobulans do not need to sleep, but must hibernate for several days each year, becoming disoriented if kept awake during this period.

- **TALENTS:** The character receives access to the following talents:

CULTURAL FLEXIBILITY
REQUIREMENT: Denobulan, or Gamemaster's permission.
Your people are friendly, patient, and inquisitive, and you exemplify these traits. You are at ease when meeting new cultures, and adapt to unfamiliar social structures easily. When you attempt a Task to learn about an unfamiliar culture, or to act in an appropriate manner when interacting with members of such a culture, you reduce the Difficulty by 1.

PARENT FIGURE
REQUIREMENT: Denobulan, or Gamemaster's permission.
You have a large family, with many children, nieces, and nephews, and you've learned how to coordinate even the most unruly and fractious of groups when necessary. When attempting or assisting a Task, and two or more other characters are involved in the Task, the first Complication generated on the Task — either by the character attempting the Task, or one of the assistants — may be ignored.

HUMAN

Originating on the planet Earth in the Sol system, Humans are a resilient, diverse, and adaptable species, who developed from fractious, warring nations on the brink of mutual annihilation to a united, peaceful society in less than a century, and managed to forge alliances between former enemies within a century of achieving interstellar space flight. Earth is a founder and pivotal member of the United Federation of Planets, and many of the Federation's institutions can be found on Earth. Humans often exhibit a dichotomy in their nature — being both driven to strong emotion and careful reason — and while they have largely grown beyond their warlike and divisive past, their drive and capacity for aggression are as much a part of their success as their curiosity and analytical minds.

EXAMPLE VALUE: *The Drive for Exploration*

- **ATTRIBUTES:** Instead of the normal Attribute options, choose three Attributes and add +1 to each of them.

- **TRAIT:** Human. Humans are adaptable and resilient, and their resolve and ambition often allow them to resist great hardship and triumph despite great adversity. However, Humans can also be reckless and stubborn, irrational, and unpredictable.

- **TALENTS:** The character receives access to the following talents:

RESOLUTE

REQUIREMENT: Human, or Gamemaster's discretion. You are indomitable, and unwilling to succumb to adversity. You increase your maximum Stress by 3.

SPIRIT OF DISCOVERY

REQUIREMENT: Human, or Gamemaster's discretion. You have the drive, spirit, and courage to voyage into the unknown. You may spend one Determination to add three points to the group Momentum pool. The normal conditions for spending Determination still apply.

TELLARITE

The stout, hirsute Tellarite species comes from Tellar Prime, a temperate planet in the Alpha Quadrant. Theirs is a culture noted for being abrasive and argumentative, with a stubborn pride, quick tempers, and little patience. However, this is only a superficial view: while Tellarites are argumentative, it comes from a sense of intellectual honesty and rigorous skepticism. To a Tellarite, no idea, concept, or person is beyond challenge or analysis, and any notion that cannot stand up to scrutiny is an unworthy one. Tellarites revel in debates, and tend to greet one another with criticisms, complaints, and even insults; failing to respond in kind is poorly-regarded, as it displays a weakness of character and an unwillingness to confront flaws.

EXAMPLE VALUE: All Ideas must Withstand Scrutiny

- **ATTRIBUTES:** +1 Control, +1 Fitness, +1 Insight

- **TRAIT:** Tellarite. Tellarites have a keen sense of smell and a high tolerance for many common drugs, toxins, and inebriants (Tellarites don't get drunk, just feisty). They also have excellent eyesight, and more acute perception of distance, depth, and dimension than Humans.

- **TALENTS:** The character receives access to the following talents:

INCISIVE SCRUTINY
REQUIREMENT: Tellarite, or Gamemaster's permission.
You have a knack for finding weak spots in arguments, theories, and machines alike to glean information from them, learning about things by how they respond to pressure against vulnerable points. When you succeed at a Task using Control or Insight, you gain one bonus Momentum, which may only be used for the Obtain Information Momentum Spend.

STURDY
REQUIREMENT: Tellarite.
You have a blend of physical resilience and mental fortitude such that you're difficult to subdue. You reduce the cost to resist being knocked prone by the Knockdown damage effect by one, to a minimum of 0, and gain +1 Resistance against all non-lethal attacks.

TRILL

The Trill species, from their homeworld of the same name, appear almost identical to Humans, but for rows of spots running down the sides of their bodies, from head to toe. However, this superficial similarity conceals a considerable difference — the Trill are capable of bonding with a symbiotic organism known as a symbiont, creating a distinct being from the two individual creatures. The symbionts can live for many centuries, and are placed with successive hosts, carrying the memories and knowledge of previous hosts into a new joining with each new generation. This fact isn't widely known outside the Trill themselves, but it isn't a secret — it simply isn't widely discussed, and the number of joined Trill is relatively small. The Trill have been part of the Federation for well over a century, with several renowned Trill serving important roles in shaping the Federation. The Trill, as a culture, tend to be focused on intellectual pursuits first and foremost, as learning and wisdom are prized by the symbionts in their hosts.

EXAMPLE VALUE: *Four Lifetimes of Adventure*

- **ATTRIBUTES:** +1 Control, +1 Presence, +1 Reason

- **TRAIT: Trill.** Trill are especially resilient to parasites, as a quirk of their potential to be Joined; Joined Trill are entirely immune to parasitic infection. However, they tend to have strong allergic reactions to insect bites and other forms of venom, which can disrupt their neurochemistry, particularly if they're Joined. As many of the specifics of Trill physiology — especially with regards to symbiosis — are not widely known, this can result in medical complications.

- **TALENTS:** The character receives access to the following talents:

FORMER INITIATE

REQUIREMENT: Trill, may only be taken during Character Creation.
You joined the Initiate Program, hoping to be chosen by the Symbiosis Commission to become Joined. As there are far more Initiates than there are Symbionts, you were one of the many who failed, but the quality of even a failed initiate is enough for Starfleet to recruit you. When you attempt a Task using Control or Reason, and spend Determination to buy a bonus d20 for that Task, you may re-roll your dice pool. Former Initiate cannot be taken if the character has the Joined Talent — they are mutually exclusive.

JOINED

REQUIREMENT: Trill, requires Gamemaster's permission to take this Talent after Character Creation. You have a symbiont, with lifetimes of memories to draw upon. Once per mission, you may declare that a former host had expertise in a relevant skill or field of study; you gain a single Focus for the remainder of the scene, as you draw upon those memories. Additionally, you gain a Trait with the name of the Symbiont; this reflects potential advantages of the Joining, the ability to perform rites and rituals to awaken past hosts' memories, and the vulnerabilities inherent in the connection. Former Initiate cannot be taken if the character has the Joined Talent — they are mutually exclusive.

VULCAN

ALL ERAS OF PLAY

The Vulcans are a stoic, rational people. Widely claimed to be emotionless, in truth the Vulcans feel deeply and intensely, to their own detriment. Their stoicism comes from a culture of logic and self-discipline, where emotions are analyzed and dissected to rob them of their potency, so that they cannot overwhelm or control the individual. Vulcans embrace science and reason, but their lives are not purely devoted to logic: they also have a deeply philosophical side, with art and music as vital to their culture as logic. They are also an intensely private people, with many aspects of their culture — such as the rites of pon farr — which are not discussed amongst outsiders.

EXAMPLE VALUES: The Needs of the Many Outweigh the Needs of the Few, or the One.

- **ATTRIBUTES:** +1 Control, +1 Fitness, +1 Reason

- **TRAIT:** Vulcan. Due to the harsh, arid, high-gravity world they come from, Vulcans are naturally resistant to extreme heat and dehydration; they are also extremely strong, with keen auditory and olfactory senses. They are also telepathic, though this takes training to properly manifest, and they learn mental discipline and emotional control from childhood. However, this control takes regular meditation to maintain, and their controlled nature and desire for privacy can distance them from others, and make interactions awkward.

- **TALENTS:** The character receives access to the following talents:

KOLINAHR
REQUIREMENT: Vulcan, or Gamemaster's permission. You have undergone the ritual journey to purge all emotion. You reduce the Difficulty of all Tasks to resist coercion, mental intrusion, pain, and other mental attacks by two.

MIND-MELD
REQUIREMENT: Vulcan.
You have undergone training in telepathic techniques that allow the melding of minds through physical contact. This will always require a Task with a Difficulty of at least 1, which can be opposed by an unwilling participant. If successful, you link minds with the participant, sharing thoughts and memories; Momentum may be spent to gain more information, or perform deeper telepathic exchanges. This link goes both ways, and it is a tiring and potentially hazardous process for you. Complications can result in pain, disorientation, or lingering emotional or behavioral difficulties.

NERVE PINCH
REQUIREMENT: Vulcan, or Gamemaster's permission.
You have learned numerous techniques for the stimulation and control of nerve impulses — collectively called neuropressure. Some applications of neuropressure can be used to swiftly and non-lethally incapacitate assailants. The nerve pinch counts as a melee weapon with 1▲, Size 1H, and the Intense and Non-lethal qualities. You may use Science or Medicine instead of Security when attempting a nerve pinch Attack, and may increase damage by your Science or Medicine Discipline instead of Security.

UNUSUAL OR UNIQUE CHARACTERS

Starfleet Academy attracts applicants from many worlds, including some that aren't a part of the United Federation of Planets. With a suitable recommendation, anyone can apply, though they're still faced with the same challenging entrance examinations that ensure that only the best of the best become Starfleet officers. The presence of the likes of Lieutenant Commanders Worf and Data, aboard the *U.S.S. Enterprise*, are a testament to the value of this policy, and many Academy graduates are at least passingly familiar with a classmate who wasn't from a Federation world.

At the Gamemaster's discretion, Players may seek to play as any species, even going to far as to create unique species never seen on screen. This requires a little more work, but the results can be well worth the effort. The Player and Gamemaster should confer as to the nature of the species desired, and get a rough idea of what that species is capable of, what their culture is like, and so forth, as well as why the character might seek to join Starfleet. These provide the foundations for how to use the species' Trait in play, as well as generating plot hooks and ideas that can be explored further during play. The Gamemaster should also decide upon three Attributes, each of which are increased by +1. The Gamemaster may also wish to create one or two unique Talents to reflect unique facets of that species' culture, but this isn't essential.

Guidance on creating new species or unique characters is covered in greater detail in *Chapter 10: Gamemastering* (p. 270).

Example: Nathan is creating a character using the Lifepath method. First, he determines the character's species. The game is set in the Next Generation era, so all the species are available to him, and he decides to roll for this choice, to see if that sparks any ideas. He rolls an 18, resulting in a Trill character. Seeing some possibilities with this, he sticks with it. He also selects the Trill-specific Talent "Joined." Nathan decides that his character is joined to the Etahn symbiont, and adds the "Etahn symbiont" Trait accordingly.

This gives the character the Trill species Trait, and means the character now has the following Attribute scores: Control 8, Daring 7, Fitness 7, Insight 7, Presence 8, Reason 8.

STEP TWO: ENVIRONMENT

Regardless of their species, Starfleet officers come from many places, across many worlds. While many Humans (for example) are born on Earth, there are many more who were born on a colonized world elsewhere in the Galaxy, or on a starbase or a starship.

A character's environment grants the character a single Value, one point in a single Attribute, and one point in a single Discipline.

A Player may choose their environment, or randomly determine it from the table below by rolling a d6.

RANDOM ENVIRONMENT TABLE

D6 ROLL	ENVIRONMENT
1	Homeworld
2	Busy Colony
3	Isolated Colony
4	Frontier Colony
5	Starship or Starbase
6	Another Species' World

1. HOMEWORLD

The character comes from the world that birthed their civilization, and has been surrounded by cultural and spiritual legacies their entire life. Species homeworlds are often utopian and idyllic, serving as the platonic ideal of that species' culture. They also exemplify aspects of a culture's most revered traditions, and serve as the heart of that civilization's legal and political landscape.

VALUE: At this step, the character gains a single Value. This Value should reflect the environment and culture the character was raised within. This is a good opportunity to consider how the character views their own culture, and how they connect — or possibly, don't connect — to the philosophies and traditions of their people.

ATTRIBUTE: Choose one of the three Attributes the character's species improves; increase one of those Attributes by +1.

DISCIPLINE: Choose one of Command, Security, or Science; the character increases that Attribute by +1.

2. BUSY COLONY

The character comes from one of their culture's oldest or most prosperous colonies, which may be another world within their home system — such as Luna or Mars for Humans — or one of the first worlds colonized after the culture achieved interstellar flight. These colonies often develop a fiercely independent outlook, often having developed with little direct aid from their homeworld, and a sense of pride that accompanies being amongst the first of their kind to tame another world.

VALUE: At this step, the character gains a single Value. This Value should reflect the environment and culture the character was raised within. This is a good opportunity to consider how the character views their own culture, and

The alien species seen in *Star Trek* are often presented as having a singular culture that spans their entire civilization, while we still see elements of different cultures amongst the Human characters we see on-screen. There's no real need for this to be true except for storytelling convenience; there's room for a variety of cultures and subcultures amongst the Vulcans, or the Andorians, even if these differences might not be immediately recognizable to those not intensely familiar with those peoples. There'll always be a degree of cultural blending within these species anyway — all of them are represented by unified planetary governments, and celebrate individual diversity. Many of the old divisions between cultures are things of the past.

The same can be said of ethnicity and concepts of race. Variation in physiognomy, skin color, and so forth can be found amongst all species, typically because of evolutionary adaptations to specific climates on a species' homeworld. Bajorans, Betazoids, Denobulans, Tellarites, Trill, and Vulcans, all have similar diversity in skin color, hair types, and other such variations as Humans do, and for essentially the same reasons, and Andorians have their own range of variations in the shape of their antennae, the color of their skin (shades of blue and gray), hair, and eyes, and so forth.

how they connect — or possibly, don't connect — to the philosophies and traditions of their people.

ATTRIBUTE: Choose one of the following Attributes and increase it by +1: Daring or Presence

DISCIPLINE: Choose one of Command, Security, or Science; the character increases that Discipline by +1.

3. ISOLATED COLONY

The character comes from a colony that is isolated from broader galactic society. Worlds like the Vulcan monastery on P'Jem use the vast distances between star systems as an opportunity for contemplative isolation, while others are settled because they present unique research opportunities. The cultures of these colonies tend to focus on learning and introspection.

VALUE: At this step, the character gains a single Value. This Value should reflect the environment and culture the character was raised within. This is a good opportunity to consider how the character views their own culture, and how they connect — or possibly, don't connect — to the philosophies and traditions of their people.

ATTRIBUTE: Choose one of the following Attributes and increase it by +1: Reason or Insight.

DISCIPLINE: Choose one of Engineering, Science, or Medicine; the character increases that Discipline by +1.

4. FRONTIER COLONY

The character comes from a colony located on the fringes of known space, either on the edge of uncharted space or on the border with another civilization. Frontier colonists tend to be hardy and determined, even stubborn, and well-prepared for the dangers that their home may pose.

INTERNAL MEMO

... And to those populists seeking to undermine our authority by touting these fallacious studies as fact, I say that they need only consider the recent joining of the Dax symbiont to Joran Belar as a clear cautionary tale.

I personally believe that the Commission may in fact be far too optimistic when we say point-one percent of our population can join with a symbiont. One in a thousand Trill may join with a symbiont, but this number represents only their raw, genetic suitability as a potential host.

Over the years, seeking a more comprehensive understanding of the relationship between our two biologies, joined Trill with scientific and medical backgrounds have provided this Commission with comprehensive and exhaustive studies that suggest, once accounting for the Symbiosis Commission's rigorous vetting and training process, and taking such factors as mental constitution, personality facets, and intended career paths into consideration, the practical number of Trill who will successfully join is much closer to one in ten thousand, not one in a thousand.

Again, one need only look as far as Joran Dax to see the damage that may be done to the symbiont and all its future hosts. Should the high standards for our candidates slip even a fraction, catastrophic damage to our society, our citizens, and our very planet remains the most probable consequence.

Eyes Only Internal memo composed by Loreli Bhar, Senior Joining Counselor of the Trill Symbiosis Commission, 2286

VALUE: At this step, the character gains a single Value. This Value should reflect the environment and culture the character was raised within. This is a good opportunity to consider how the character views their own culture, and how they connect — or possibly, don't connect — to the philosophies and traditions of their people.

ATTRIBUTE: Choose one of the following Attributes and increase it by +1: Control or Fitness.

DISCIPLINE: Choose one of Conn, Security, or Medicine; the character increases that Discipline by +1.

EXAMPLE VALUES

- A Starship is a Home, it's Crew a Family

- Most Comfortable in a Crowd

- Body and Mind Alike Must Be Healthy

- No Stranger to Violence

- Emotion in a Crisis only Makes Things Worse

- Engineer at Heart

5. STARSHIP OR STARBASE

The character grew up in space, travelling aboard a starship or living aboard a space station or starbase. While they're unlikely to have lived aboard a Starfleet vessel — only some of them carry families — many freighters, transports, and other civilian vessels have a tradition of family or generational crews, and many officers with families take postings to starbases rather than ships. Those raised in space learn the ins-and-outs of shipboard life as children, and many are groomed for leadership, or learn to fly a shuttle in their formative years.

VALUE: At this step, the character gains a single Value. This Value should reflect the environment and culture the character was raised within. This is a good opportunity to consider how the character views their own culture, and how they connect — or possibly, don't connect — to the philosophies and traditions of their people.

ATTRIBUTE: Choose one of the following Attributes and increase it by +1: Control or Insight

DISCIPLINE: Choose one of Command, Conn, or Engineering; the character increases that Discipline by +1.

6. ANOTHER SPECIES' WORLD

The character grew up amongst another species. They might have lived amongst a small enclave of their own kind, or they may have been orphaned by some manner of disaster and raised by aliens. Whatever the situation, the character has unique perspectives on their own species and on those they were raised alongside.

VALUE: At this step, the character gains a single Value. This Value should reflect the environment and culture the character was raised within. This is a good opportunity to consider how the character views their own culture, and how they connect — or possibly, don't connect — to the philosophies and traditions of their people.

ATTRIBUTE: Choose or randomly roll another species from Step One, then choose one of the Attributes that species gains a bonus to. The chosen Attribute is increased by +1.

DISCIPLINE: Choose any one Discipline; the character increases that Discipline by +1.

Example: The next step for Nathan's character is Environment. Nathan again rolls for this, to see if it produces any interesting results. He rolls a 3 — Isolated Colony — and sees some interesting possibilities there.

Nathan adds +1 to the character's Reason, bringing it up to 9, and +1 to their Science Discipline, bringing that to 2. He also chooses a Value at this stage: "Understanding is the Purpose of Life".

STEP THREE: UPBRINGING

The nature of a person's family and their surroundings as they grew up can have a massive impact upon them, and, whether they accept this influence or rebelled against it, it will shape the rest of their lives.

A character's upbringing provides them with three points spread across two Attributes. Which Attributes can be increased, and by how much, is determined not only by the upbringing chosen, but also by whether the character accepted their upbringing or rebelled against it.

Each upbringing also gives the character a single point to add to one of their Disciplines, with each upbringing having a choice of which Disciplines can be increased. Finally, the character receives a single Focus, which should relate in some way to the upbringing chosen (a few examples are provided in each case). Finally, each upbringing gives the character a single Talent.

A Player may choose their character's upbringing, or randomly determine it from the table below by rolling a d6.

D6 ROLL	UPBRINGING
1	Starfleet
2	Business or Trade
3	Agriculture or Rural
4	Science and Technology
5	Artistic and Creative
6	Diplomacy and Politics

1. STARFLEET

The character's family may have a strong tradition of Starfleet service, with at least one member of the family in every generation serving the Federation in this way. Perhaps both the character's parents were Starfleet officers, who met in service. Either way, the character's formative years were influenced by Starfleet.

ATTRIBUTES: If the character **accepted** this upbringing, the orderly, purposeful life increases their Control by 2 and their Fitness by 1.

If the character **rebelled** against this upbringing, their bold and self-determined living increases their Daring by 2 and their Insight by 1.

DISCIPLINES AND FOCUS: The character's exposure to the ways and traditions of Starfleet allows them to increase any one Discipline.

The character's Focus should relate to their connection to Starfleet, covering skills learned during the character's formative years. Examples include: Astronavigation, Composure, Extra-Vehicular Activity, Hand-to-Hand Combat (may be renamed to a specific martial art), Hand Phasers, Small Craft, Starfleet Protocol, Starship Recognition, History.

TALENT: The character also gains a single Talent from the list of Talents, see p. 135.

EXAMPLE VALUES

- Serving Starfleet is a Family Tradition
- Indefatigable Confidence
- Proud and Honest
- Insatiable Curiosity
- Understands Technology Better Than People
- A Responsibility to the Truth

2. BUSINESS OR TRADE

The character's family may have connections on countless worlds, overseeing and directing some grand business endeavor. They might have been traders or involved in interplanetary freight. Either way, the character has grown up encountering people from all walks of life, including those from outside the Federation, and their outlook on life has been shaped accordingly.

ATTRIBUTES: If the character **accepted** this upbringing, a cosmopolitan, ambitious lifestyle increases their Daring by 1 and their Presence by 2.

If the character **rebelled** against this upbringing, stepping away from the family business to find their own identity increases their Insight by 2 and their Reason by 1.

DISCIPLINES AND FOCUS: The character's experiences with their family business allows them to increase any one of Command, Engineering, or Science.

The character's Focus should relate to the nature of their family's business, covering skills that are valuable during trade, or which were useful to the family business in other ways. Examples include: Finances, Geology, Linguistics, Manufacturing, Metallurgy, Negotiation, Survey.

TALENT: The character also gains a single Talent from the list of Talents, see p. 135.

3. AGRICULTURE OR RURAL

The character grew up surrounded more by nature than by people, in rural communities, on the frontier, or somewhere else distanced from the bustle of cities. They might be heavily involved in agriculture, growing real food to supplement synthesized or replicated meals.

ATTRIBUTES: If the character **accepted** this upbringing, the tough, practical life on the land breeds a strong work ethic and a healthy body, increasing their Control by 1 and their Fitness by 2.

If the character **rebelled** against this upbringing, they are likely to have embraced science, technology, and the fruits of civilization, increasing their Presence by 1 and their Reason by 2.

DISCIPLINES AND FOCUS: The character's living off the land and growing up on the edge of civilization allows them to increase one of Conn, Security, or Medicine

The character's Focus should relate to the character's rural lifestyle, and the skills they learned there. Examples include: Animal Handling, Athletics, Emergency Medicine, Endurance, Ground Vehicles, Infectious Diseases, Navigation, Toxicology.

TALENT: The character also gains a single Talent from the list of Talents, see p. 135.

4. SCIENCE AND TECHNOLOGY

The character's home was one filled with the potential of science, and cutting edge developments were familiar ground. Perhaps the character was raised by scientists or engineers, or had mentors and teachers who encouraged a talent for the technical.

ATTRIBUTES: If the character **accepted** this upbringing, they are rational, methodical, and precise, increasing their Control by 2 and their Reason by 1.

If the character **rebelled** against this upbringing, they don't lack for technical talent, but they haven't developed that talent and instead rely more on instinct, increasing their Daring by 1 and their Insight by 2.

DISCIPLINES AND FOCUS: The character's familiarity with cutting-edge science and the latest research allows them to increase one of Conn, Engineering, Science, or Medicine.

The character's Focus should relate to the character's favoured fields of study and inquiry. Examples include: Astrophysics, Astronavigation, Computers, Cybernetics, Power Systems, Genetics, Physics, Subspace Communications, Surgery, Quantum Mechanics, Warp Field Dynamics, Xenobiology.

TALENT: The character also gains a single Talent from the list of Talents, see p. 135.

5. ARTISTIC AND CREATIVE

The character's life was filled with arts and creativity of all kinds, and no matter what pursuits the character favors, they are exposed to the great works of many cultures, and given every opportunity to express themselves.

ATTRIBUTES: If the character **accepted** this upbringing, they develop a greater understanding of emotion and communication, increasing their Insight by 1 and their Presence by 2.

If the character **rebelled** against this upbringing, the character is more inclined to action than to expression, increasing their Daring by 1 and their Fitness by 2.

DISCIPLINES AND FOCUS: The character's ease with creativity and self-expression lend themselves to many pursuits, allowing the character to increase one of Command, Engineering, or Science.

The character's Focus should relate to the character's preferred way of applying their skills. Examples include: Botany, Cultural Studies, Holoprogramming, Linguistics, Music, Observation, Persuasion, Psychology.

TALENT: The character also gains a single Talent from the list of Talents, see p. 135.

6. DIPLOMACY AND POLITICS

The character has been exposed to the complexities of political thought and the nuances of diplomacy since they were young, perhaps because a family member was involved in those fields.

ATTRIBUTES: If the character **accepted** this upbringing, they're disciplined and well-versed in the arts of debate, increasing their Control by 1 and their Presence by 2.

If the character **rebelled** against this upbringing, then they've instead sought more tangible things to focus on, increasing their Fitness by 1 and their Reason by 2.

DISCIPLINES AND FOCUS: The character's familiarity with the practices and perils of diplomacy, politics, and the law allow them to increase any one of Command, Conn, or Security.

THE ETHICAL FAMILY UNIT

In the whole of the Federation, there is nothing so unique as the structure the Denobulans have developed to arrange their familial units. Every male marries up to three females. Every female marries up to three males. Though the Vulcans would say it's only logical those three males and three females be the same individuals, making a family unit of six intermarried adults, the Denobulans don't necessarily restrict themselves to sharing the same partners with each other. This leads to convoluted, complicated tanglings of family lineages sure to drive any historian insane. For example, in my research, I studied an image of one family chart that spanned the length of a ten-foot wall.

Despite this, they somehow remain deeply devoted to the many complicated relationships spawned by their family structure. I honestly don't know how they keep it all straight, and I honestly don't know how they refrain from killing each other. If Andorians were to adopt the Denobulan structure, we'd be extinct as a species within a handful of generations because every household would be the site of daily civil warfare. Our technology would no doubt leap forward, however, in those short years our species would have left. I, for one, would need to have the still-theoretical neural link to a dedicated personal data server installed in my antennae just to remember the names of all my in-laws.

Excerpt: "The Ethical Family Unit: a case study of familial culture in Federation species", Interspecies Ethics term paper prepared by Cadet Theven Sth'Zann, Starfleet Academy, Spring 2198

The character's Focus should relate to the character's preferred way of applying their skills. Examples include: Composure, Debate, Diplomacy, Espionage, Interrogation, Law, Philosophy, Starfleet Protocol.

TALENT: The character also gains a single Talent from the list of Talents, see p. 135.

Example: The character is starting to take shape, and Nathan moves on to the next step — determining the character's upbringing. He has an idea of what could work, but rolls the dice to see if that suggests anything. A roll of 3 results in a rural upbringing, which fits the idea of an isolated colony, and creates the potential for a little conflict in the backstory; better than a more straightforward scientific upbringing. He chooses to rebel against this upbringing.

With this choice, Nathan's character now has a Presence of 9, and a Reason of 11, and chooses to increase Medicine to 2 as well. Familiarity with the outdoors provides the character with a Focus of Survival Training. He also selects a Talent, Cautious (Science).

STEP FOUR: STARFLEET ACADEMY

The years spent at Starfleet Academy are some of the most memorable and definitive of an officer's life, shaping the direction of their career going forwards. For those who pass the grueling entrance examinations, the Academy takes four years, covering a mixture of intense training, academic studies, and practical experiences. Much of this takes place within the main Starfleet Academy campus in San Francisco on Earth, but other campuses and annexes exist across the Federation, and a cadet may spend time at any of these before they graduate.

A graduate of the Academy receives a commission as a Starfleet officer, with the rank of ensign, after which they may wait several weeks, or even months, for their first assignment. Some cadets — particularly those pursuing a doctorate — choose a path that requires an additional year or two of training and study, and instead graduate at the rank of lieutenant (junior grade).

A character's time at Starfleet Academy has a significant impact upon them in game terms. The way these improvements are provided is explained in full below.

A Player may choose their character's academy track, or randomly determine it from the table below by rolling a d6.

RANDOM ACADEMY TABLE

D6 ROLL	TRACK
1–2	Command Track
3–4	Operations Track
5–6	Sciences Track

1–2. COMMAND TRACK

The Command track is for those cadets who aspire to command their own starship someday. It focuses on leadership and interpersonal skills, diplomacy, decision-making in crisis situations, an understanding of protocol and procedure, and starship operations, which includes flight control. Many command track cadets begin their careers as flight control officers and pilots, where their training can be put to the test on a smaller scale while they gain the experience necessary for more authority and responsibility. Command track cadets customarily undertake the infamous Kobayashi Maru test during their final year.

VALUE: The character gains a single Value, which should reflect some aspect of the character's beliefs that developed during their time at the Academy.

ATTRIBUTES: The character gains three points, which may be split between two or three Attributes (increase three Attributes by +1 each, or increase one by +2 and another by +1). The character may pick these Attributes freely.

DISCIPLINES: The Player must select either Command or Conn as the character's major — the subject they studied most intensely. This Discipline is increased by 2. Then, the Player selects two other Disciplines — the character's minor subjects — which are increased by 1 each. A character may not have any Discipline higher than 4 at this stage.

FOCUSES: The character selects three Focuses, at least one of which should relate to the character's chosen Track. Examples for command track Focuses include: Astronavigation, Composure, Diplomacy, Extra-Vehicular Activity, Evasive Action, Helm Operations, Inspiration, Persuasion, Small Craft, Starship Recognition, Starfleet Protocols, Team Dynamics.

TALENT: The character also gains a single Talent from the list of Talents, see p. 135.

3–4. OPERATIONS TRACK

The Operations track is practical and hands-on, dealing with many of the realities of Starfleet's mission. Divided broadly into engineering and security divisions, operations track cadets are defined by a sense of pragmatism, whether that applies to the technical or the tactical.

VALUE: The character gains a single Value, which should reflect some aspect of the character's beliefs that developed during their time at the Academy.

ATTRIBUTES: The character gains three points, which may be split between two or three Attributes (increase three Attributes by +1 each, or increase one by +2 and another by +1). The character may pick these Attributes freely.

DISCIPLINES: The Player must select either Engineering or Security as the character's major — the subject they studied most intensely. This Discipline is increased by 2. Then, the Player selects two other Disciplines — the character's minor subjects — which are increased by 1 each. A character may not have any Discipline higher than 4 at this stage.

FOCUSES: The character selects three Focuses, at least one of which should relate to the character's chosen Track. Examples for operations track Focuses include: Computers, Cybernetics, Electro-Plasma Power Systems, Espionage, Hand Phasers, Hand-to-Hand Combat, Infiltration, Interrogation, Shipboard Tactical Systems, Survival, Transporters & Replicators, Warp Field Dynamics.

TALENT: The character also gains a single Talent from the list of Talents, see p. 135.

EXAMPLE VALUES

- Inexperienced and Idealistic

- Threw Out The Handbook and Wrote My Own

- Always Prepared, Always Vigilant

- Precise to a Fault

- Fast Ships and Strange New Worlds

- Exploring to Test New Theories

- A Theory For Every Situation

5–6. SCIENCES TRACK

Somewhat isolated from the other Tracks, the Sciences track is primarily academic, with Starfleet Academy producing many accomplished scientists. Included within the sciences track, but separated by a distinct curriculum, is Starfleet Medical, training doctors, nurses, and counselors to serve aboard Starfleet vessels and facilities across the Federation.

VALUE: The character gains a single Value, which should reflect some aspect of the character's beliefs that developed during their time at the Academy.

ATTRIBUTES: The character gains three points, which may be split between two or three Attributes (increase three Attributes by +1 each, or increase one by +2 and another by +1). The character may pick these Attributes freely.

DISCIPLINES: The Player must select either Science or Medicine as the character's major — the subject they studied most intensely. This Discipline is increased by 2. Then, the Player selects two other Disciplines — the character's minor subjects — which are increased by 1 each. A character may not have any Discipline higher than 4 at this stage.

FOCUSES: The character selects three Focuses, at least one of which should relate to the character's chosen Track. Examples for sciences track Focuses include: Anthropology, Astrophysics, Botany, Computers, Cybernetics, Emergency Medicine, Exo-tectonics, Genetics, Geology, Infectious Diseases, Linguistics, Physics, Psychiatry, Quantum Mechanics, Trauma Surgery, Virology, Warp Field Dynamics, Xenobiology.

TALENT: The character also gains a single Talent from the list of Talents, see p. 135.

Example: Time to join Starfleet Academy. Nathan's character clearly has a talent for the sciences, and thus selects the Science track — no need to roll. Nathan chooses a Value for the character: "Seek Out New Life and New Civilizations". Then, he chooses to increase two of the character's Attributes, adding +1 to Control, and +2 to Insight, so that both have scores of 9. Next, he chooses Science as his major, and Medicine and Command as minors, increasing Science to 4, Medicine to 3, and Command to 2. He then selects three Focuses: Linguistics, Psychology, and Xenoanthropology. Finally, he selects a Talent: Technical Expertise.

STEP FIVE: CAREER

At this stage, the Player has a choice to make about the character. This decision is a clear one: is the character a young officer, fresh out of the Academy, with their whole career ahead of them, have they served in Starfleet for several years, or are they a veteran with decades of experience?

This stage grants the character a Value and a Talent. This stage should always be chosen manually, rather than rolled — if you're creating your character randomly, default to the Experienced Officer option, below.

YOUNG OFFICER

The character is defined by their potential more than their skill. Their raw talent and their expectations of what the universe is like have not yet been tempered by reality.

VALUE: The character receives a Value, which must reflect the character's inexperience and naïveté in some way.

TALENT: The character receives a single Talent: **Untapped Potential**, described below.

EXPERIENCED OFFICER

The character has several years of experience in service of Starfleet, and is enjoying a promising career. This is the default assumption for characters created using these rules.

VALUE: The character receives a Value, and this can be chosen freely.

TALENT: The character receives a single Talent, which may be chosen freely.

VETERAN OFFICER

The character has decades of experience in the service of Starfleet, and has served on many ships, and starbases. The character's judgement and opinions are highly-regarded by subordinates, peers, and even superiors.

VALUE: The character receives a Value, which must reflect the character's years of experience and the beliefs they've formed over their long career.

TALENT: The character receives a single Talent: **Veteran**, described below.

Example: It's now time to look at the length of the character's Career. There's no roll here, and Nathan chooses the Experienced Officer option. From this, he selects the Value "Seen Too Much to be Surprised", and the Talent Intense Scrutiny.

STEP SIX: CAREER EVENTS

The character's career is a tapestry of events and experiences, but amongst this, a few will have been pivotal moments in the character's life. A character defines which moments of their life are important in retrospect, and what seemed definitive to an ensign in their early 20s may be inconsequential to that same officer decades later.

This is defined as two identical steps — the Player rolls or chooses a career event from the following list, gains whatever benefits it provides, and then repeats the process, giving the character two definitive career events.

Each career event increases one Attribute and one Discipline by one point each, and gives the character one additional Focus. Which Attribute and which Discipline are improved — and guidelines and suggestions for Focuses — will be listed in the entries for each Career Event. Each Career Event also includes a few questions to consider about how the event happened and how it affected the character.

Some Career Events also grant the character the option of a Trait, to reflect some major lasting impact on the character's life. These are not compulsory.

AGE

With the Federation's medical science, people can live long, healthy, productive lives. The average life expectancy of a Human being is around 120 years, while some more robust species — such as Vulcans and Denobulans — can live far longer than that. With that increased lifespan and better health comes many years of vitality, allowing people to fulfil their ambitions and better themselves for many decades.

A character can be of any age in *Star Trek Adventures*, though this should normally be guided by the choice made in Step Five: Career of the Lifepath. A Young Officer is likely to be in their early 20s: old enough to have completed Starfleet Academy, but not old enough to have done much else. Whereas Veteran officers are likely to be much older. There is no age requirement for Starfleet Academy, only an entry exam. As such, the Young Officer represents their experience in Starfleet over their physical age. These numbers, naturally, can be adjusted for species that live a particularly long time: a middle-aged Vulcan may be a century old, and as fit as a Human half the age.

UNTAPPED POTENTIAL

REQUIREMENTS: Young Officer (only available during character creation)

The character is inexperienced, but talented and with a bright future in Starfleet. The character may not have or increase any Attribute above 11, or any Discipline above 4 while they have this Talent (and may have to adjust Attributes and Disciplines accordingly at the end of character creation). Whenever the character succeeds at a Task for which they bought one or more additional dice with either Momentum or Threat, they may roll 1🅐. The character receives bonus Momentum equal to the roll of the 🅐, and adds one point to Threat if an Effect is rolled. The character cannot gain any higher rank than lieutenant (junior grade) while they possess this Talent.

VETERAN

REQUIREMENTS: Veteran Officer (during character creation, or at Gamemaster's discretion)

The character is wise and experienced, and draws upon inner reserves of willpower and determination in a more measured and considered way. Whenever the character spends a point of Determination, roll 1🅐. If an Effect is rolled, immediately regain that spent point of Determination. The character has a rank of at least Lieutenant Commander.

The Player may wish to combine multiple career events into a single event in the character's backstory, or have them as distinct moments in their history. Players may also wish to roll more than twice for career events; in this case, the character can mix and match the benefits each career event provides, so long as they do not gain more than two Attribute increases, two Discipline increases, and two Focuses.

For characters that chose Young Officer in Step Five, assume that these career events took place during the character's time at the Academy, perhaps during a field training assignment aboard a starship.

EXAMPLE VALUES

- Holds Everyone to the Highest Standards

- Nothing Better Than Practical Experience

- Understands Machines Better Than People

- Meticulous Scrutiny and Pride in His/Her Work

- The Price of Peace is Vigilance

- Driven to Ease Suffering

- Voice of the Crew

- The Captain's Second Opinion

CAREER EVENT TABLE

D20 ROLL	CAREER EVENT
1	Ship Destroyed
2	Death of A Friend
3	Lauded by Another Culture
4	Negotiate A Treaty
5	Required to Take Command
6	Encounter with A Truly Alien Being
7	Serious Injury
8	Conflict with A Hostile Culture
9	Mentored
10	Transporter Accident
11	Dealing with A Plague
12	Betrayed Ideals for A Superior
13	Called Out a Superior
14	New Battle Strategy
15	Learns Unique Language
16	Discovers an Artefact
17	Special Commendation
18	Solved an Engineering Crisis
19	Breakthrough or Invention
20	First Contact

1. SHIP DESTROYED

The ship the character was serving on was lost, destroyed during a mission, and the character was one of the few who survived.

- What was the ship's mission? Was it something routine that went horribly wrong, or was it something perilous? What destroyed the ship?

How many survivors were there? How long did it take before they were recovered?

ATTRIBUTE: The character's resolve and competence in a crisis increases their Daring by 1.

DISCIPLINE: The character's experiences of a perilous situation increases their Security by 1.

FOCUS: The character gains a Focus, which should reflect the character's experiences. Examples include: Extra Vehicular Operations, Small Craft, or Survival.

2. DEATH OF A FRIEND

During an important mission, one of the character's friends was killed in action.

- Who was the friend? How did the character know them?

- What was the mission? How did the friend die? Who was to blame?

ATTRIBUTE: The character's experience with loss increases their Insight by 1.

DISCIPLINE: The character's understanding of grief and recovery increases their Medicine by 1.

FOCUS: The character gains a Focus, which should reflect the character's experiences. Examples include: Counselling, but it may also represent a skill or pursuit the character takes up in their fallen friend's memory or to prevent the same thing happening in the future.

3. LAUDED BY ANOTHER CULTURE

The character was involved in a mission that earned the official praise of a non-Federation culture; they are now considered to be a friend to that people.

- What culture was aided by this mission? What was the mission? Why was it particularly praiseworthy?

- Does the character have any friends or contacts in that culture who can be contacted for help?

ATTRIBUTE: The character's standing and renown increases their Presence by 1.

DISCIPLINE: The character's broader understanding of the universe and another culture increases their Science by 1.

FOCUS: The character gains a Focus, which should reflect the character's experience with that culture. A Focus of X Culture, replacing the X with the name of that culture, is a good example, as would any that represent skills or techniques specific to that culture.

TRAIT: The character may gain a Trait, which should reflect this event. A good example might be Friend to the X, replacing the X with the name of the culture. This reflects the character's renown amongst that culture, and the benefits and problems such status brings.

4. NEGOTIATE A TREATY

The character was part of a delegation that helped negotiate a treaty, agreement, or alliance with a culture outside the Federation.

- What culture was the treaty with? What was it for?

ATTRIBUTE: The character's familiarity with minutia and the careful work of diplomacy increases their Control by 1.

DISCIPLINE: The character's familiarity with diplomacy and negotiation increases their Command by 1.

FOCUS: The character gains a Focus, which should reflect the character's experience with the negotiations. Examples include: Diplomacy, Negotiation, or Galactic Politics.

5. REQUIRED TO TAKE COMMAND

During a mission, a crisis left the mission's leader unable to lead. This required the character to take command, something they may not have been prepared for.

- What was the mission? What went wrong?

- Was the mission successful despite the loss of the leader?

ATTRIBUTE: The character's need to improvise during a crisis increases their Daring by 1.

DISCIPLINE: Being required to lead increases the character's Command by 1.

FOCUS: The character gains a Focus, which should reflect the character's experiences during the crisis. Examples include: Lead by Example, Inspiration, or Composure.

6. ENCOUNTER WITH A TRULY ALIEN BEING

The character encountered a life-form which is truly alien, something barely within the comprehension of humanoid life. It might have been some godlike entity, or a creature that swims through space, but whatever it was, it was not life as we know it.

- What kind of creature was it? What did the character learn from the experience?

- What happened to the creature afterwards? Has it been seen again?

ATTRIBUTE: The character's encounter with the unknown increases their Reason by 1.

DISCIPLINE: The character comes away from the experience with a greater understanding of, and curiosity for, the universe, increasing Science by 1.

FOCUS: The character gains a Focus, which should reflect the character's experiences with the entity. Examples include: Empathy, Philosophy, Xenobiology

7. SERIOUS INJURY

The character was seriously hurt, and needed to spend a considerable amount of time recovering.

- What was happening when the character was injured? Who was responsible?

- What did the recovery entail? Did the character need a prosthesis or cybernetic afterwards?

ATTRIBUTE: The character's long, arduous recovery forced them to think about their health more, increasing their Fitness by 1.

DISCIPLINE: Being surrounded by doctors for a long time increased the character's Medicine by 1.

FOCUS: The character gains a Focus, which should reflect the circumstances of the character's injury, something that helped them through recovery, or something they took up after recovering. Examples include: Athletics, Art, or Philosophy

TRAIT: The character may gain a Trait, which should reflect some lasting effect of the character's injury or the way they recovered. Examples include: Prosthetic Implant, or some form of disability.

8. CONFLICT WITH A HOSTILE CULTURE

The character was involved in a major battle with a hostile force, and is unlikely to forget the experience.

- Who was the enemy in this battle? Why did the battle occur? Was it fought in space, on the ground, or both?

- What did the character have to do to survive? Was the battle won or lost?

ATTRIBUTE: The character needed to be tough to survive in battle, increasing Fitness by 1.

DISCIPLINE: The harrowing experiences of battle have increased the character's Security by 1.

FOCUS: The character gains a Focus, which should reflect skills they honed during the fighting. Examples include: Hand Phasers, Hand-to-Hand Combat, or Shipboard Tactical Systems.

9. MENTORED

A highly-respected officer took notice of the character's career. For a time, the character served as the officer's pilot and aide, gaining the benefit of the officer's experiences and lessons.

- Who was the officer? Does the officer remain a contact or even friend of the character?

ATTRIBUTE: The officer's lessons came in many forms; increase any one Attribute by 1.

DISCIPLINE: Time spent as the officer's pilot, and studying the structures and procedures of Starfleet, increase the character's Conn by 1.

FOCUS: The character gains a Focus, reflecting the lessons learned. Examples include: Composure or Etiquette, though any Focus reflecting the officer's specialities would be fitting.

10. TRANSPORTER ACCIDENT

The character suffered some manner of strange accident while using a Transporter.

- What happened to the character during the accident? Were there any lasting repercussions?

- How does the character feel about Transporters now?

ATTRIBUTE: The character is cautious and careful after their experiences, increasing Control by 1.

DISCIPLINE: The experience means the character takes shuttles more often now than the Transporter, increasing Conn by 1.

FOCUS: The character gains a Focus, which should reflect something they learned either because of the accident, or in the aftermath. Examples include: Transporters & Replicators, Small Craft, or Quantum Mechanics.

11. DEALING WITH A PLAGUE

The character's starship was assigned to provide aid to a world deal with an epidemic.

- What was the disease that was running rampant? What planet it was affecting?

- Did the character deal directly with the sick? How was the character involved?

ATTRIBUTE: Helping a people in distress during a massive crisis helped the character understand people, increasing Insight by 1.

DISCIPLINE: Dealing with a problem of this nature increases the character's Medicine by 1.

FOCUS: The character gains a Focus, which should reflect how they helped during the crisis. Examples include: Infectious Diseases, Emergency Medicine, or Triage.

12. BETRAYED IDEALS FOR A SUPERIOR
The character was placed in a situation where they had to choose between a trusted superior and their own ideals, and chose to follow the superior.

- Who was the superior? What did they ask the character to do? How does the character feel now?

- What were the repercussions of this? Are the details of this event on record? Was the character right?

ATTRIBUTE: The character learned a lot from the superior on how to command respect, increasing Presence by 1.

DISCIPLINE: Difficult decisions are part of being a leader; the character increases their Command by 1.

FOCUS: The character gains a Focus, reflecting the event and its aftermath. Examples include: Persuasion, Inspiration, Investigation.

13. CALLED OUT A SUPERIOR
The character was placed in a situation where they had to choose between a trusted superior and their own ideals, and chose to follow their ideals.

- Who was the superior? What did they ask the character to do? How does the character feel now?

- What were the repercussions of this? Are the details of this event on record? Was the character right?

ATTRIBUTE: The character learned to evaluate situations on their own merit, rather than blindly trusting others, increasing Reason by 1.

DISCIPLINE: The legal proceedings that followed gave the character a greater insight into Starfleet protocol, increasing Conn by 1.

FOCUS: The character gains a Focus, reflecting the event and its aftermath. Examples include: Uniform Code of Justice, History, or Starfleet Protocol.

14. NEW BATTLE STRATEGY
In combat with a hostile force, the character devised a new strategy or tactic.

- Who was the battle against? Was it in space or on the ground?

- What was the strategy devised?

ATTRIBUTE: The character's creativity under pressure shows boldness and ingenuity, increasing Daring by 1.

DISCIPLINE: The character's combat experience increases their Security by 1.

FOCUS: The character gains a Focus, reflecting their decisive battlefield leadership. Examples include: Combat Tactics, Hazard Awareness, or Lead by Example.

15. LEARNS UNIQUE LANGUAGE
The character encounters a species with an unusual form of communication, and learns to communicate with them.

- Who were the aliens the character encountered? Was the encounter tense, or peaceful?

- What method of communication do the aliens use? How did the character learn it?

ATTRIBUTE: The character learned a lot about understanding others from the experience, increasing Insight by 1.

DISCIPLINE: The character's gains new knowledge and new understanding, increasing Science by 1.

FOCUS: The character gains a Focus, reflecting what the character learned from the event. Examples include: Linguistics, Cultural Studies, or Negotiations.

16. DISCOVERS AN ARTEFACT
During a survey mission, the character discovered a device or fragment of technology from a now-extinct civilization.

- What did this piece of technology do? Does it still function now?

- What is known about the civilization that made it?

ATTRIBUTE: The character's studies of the technology produced numerous theories, increasing Reason by 1.

DISCIPLINE: The character's is more able to understand unfamiliar technology, increasing Engineering by 1.

FOCUS: The character gains a Focus, reflecting the event and its aftermath. Examples include: Ancient Technology, Computers, Reverse Engineering.

17. SPECIAL COMMENDATION

During a crisis, the character saved the lives of several colleagues, helping them to safety. This earned the character a special commendation.

- What was the crisis? Why was the mission in danger?

- What were the repercussions of this? Are the details of this event on record?

ATTRIBUTE: The character's physical conditioning was vital, increasing Fitness by 1.

DISCIPLINE: The character's commendation opened up many avenues of advancement; increase any one Discipline by 1.

FOCUS: The character gains a Focus, reflecting the event and its aftermath. Examples include: Athletics, Survival, or Emergency Medicine.

18. SOLVED AN ENGINEERING CRISIS

The character was instrumental in ending a crisis caused by malfunctioning technology, and saved many lives in the process.

- What technology had malfunctioned, and why was it dangerous?

- How did the character solve the problem?

ATTRIBUTE: The character's precision when dealing with complex technology increases their Control by 1.

DISCIPLINE: The character's familiarity with technology increases their Engineering by 1.

FOCUS: The character gains a Focus, reflecting the technology involved in the event. Examples include: Electro-Plasma Power Systems, Fusion Reactors, or Warp Engines.

19. BREAKTHROUGH OR INVENTION

The character made an important technological discovery, devised a new way of using a particular technology, or invented some new technology that will be invaluable in the future.

- What was the discovery, breakthrough, or invention? How will it be useful?

ATTRIBUTE: An achievement of this nature often comes from an unexpected direction; increase any one Attribute by 1.

DISCIPLINE: This kind of technological achievement does not go unrecognized by Starfleet; increase Engineering by 1.

FOCUS: The character gains a Focus, reflecting the character's achievement. Examples include: Experimental Technology, Invention, or Improvisation.

20. FIRST CONTACT

The character was chosen to be involved in one of the most important of Starfleet's missions: first contact with another culture.

- What culture did the character make first contact with? Did the mission go well?

ATTRIBUTE: The prestige and honor of being involved in a first contact mission is significant; increase the character's Presence by 1.

DISCIPLINE: There are many ways a character can be involved in a First Contact; increase any one Discipline by 1.

FOCUS: The character gains a Focus, reflecting the nature of the mission. Examples include: Cultural Studies, Diplomacy, or Infiltration.

Example: With the character mostly complete, it's now time to roll for a couple of Career Events. Nathan rolls a 13 ("Called Out a Superior"), and an 18 ("Solved an Engineering Crisis"), but isn't sure about the 18, so rolls that one again, getting an 8 ("Conflict with a Hostile Culture").

His "Conflict with a Hostile Culture" increases his Fitness to 8, and his Security to 2, and gives him a Focus of Hand Phasers, representing skills honed during the fighting. Meanwhile, the time he "Called out a Superior" increases his Reason to 12, and his Conn to 2, and gives him a focus of Uniform Code of Justice, from the disciplinary hearings that followed.

STEP SEVEN: FINISHING TOUCHES

At this stage, the character is almost complete, and needs only a few final elements and adjustments. This serves as a last chance to customize the character before play, and cannot not be done randomly.

VALUE: The character receives one final Value. This might reflect the Career Events rolled in Step Six, or it may represent some other element of the character. This Value might be a relationship, connecting the character to another character in the crew, or to another organization or culture in some way.

ATTRIBUTES: A character may not have any Attributes above 12, and may not have more than one Attribute at 12 (if the character has the Untapped Potential talent, from Step Five, they may not have any Attributes above 11 instead).

For any Attribute which has a rating above and beyond those limits, reduce it until it is within the limit. For each point reduced on an Attribute, increase another Attribute by one, though the limits noted above must still be obeyed.

Once this has been done, the character may then increase two Attributes by 1 each; again, the normal limits apply.

DISCIPLINES: A character may not have any Disciplines above 5, and may not have more than one Discipline at 5 (if the character has the Untapped Potential talent, from Step Five, they may not have any Attributes above 4 instead). For any Discipline which has a rating above and beyond those limits, reduce it until it is within the limit. For each point reduced on a Discipline, increase another Discipline by one, though the limits noted above must still be obeyed.

Once this has been done, the character may then increase two Disciplines by 1 each; again, the normal limits apply.

FINAL DETAILS: Finally, there are a few other things that need to be determined:

- **FINAL CHECK:** The character's Attributes, added together, should add up to 56. The character's Disciplines added together should add up to 16. The character should have 4 Values, 4 Talents, and 6 Focuses.

- **STRESS:** A character has Stress equal to their Fitness Attribute, plus their Security Discipline.

- **DAMAGE BONUS:** On all attacks, a character gains bonus ◣ equal to their Security Discipline.

- **PERSONAL DETAILS:** Choose the character's name (discussed below) and age (discussed in the sidebar on p. 118), and decide on a rough description of the character's personality and appearance, if this hasn't been done already.

- **DEPARTMENT:** The character's department will normally be the same as their highest Discipline (in the case of a tie, the Player chooses).

- **RANK AND ROLE:** This should be done with the rest of the group, and is described in more detail below.

- **EQUIPMENT:** The character receives a Communicator, and additional equipment described below.

Once these final details have been resolved, the character is complete!

PERSONAL DETAILS

This step is about turning the choices and numbers of the Lifepath into a person, whose story can be explored as the game progresses.

NAME

Every character needs a name. This can be anything, though it's probably best to avoid anything that would break the mood of the game. A character's name reflects their culture — different species and cultures have different conventions for how they give names, and many cultures ascribe traditional meanings to names, or require that a name take a certain form. For alien characters, the name should fit their species — and some guidance for that is provided here — while for Human characters, their name should be reflective of their culture and upbringing. In any case, it's better to give a character an original name, rather than adopt one from another source, as it's likely to be less distracting to the other Players.

The following list provides a rough overview of each species' naming conventions, sample names (female, male, and family names), as well as a couple of examples of complete names where the species' naming conventions are unusual.

- **ANDORIAN** names tend to be somewhat harsh-sounding, and have a personal name followed by a clan name. Amongst some Andorians, it's common to begin the clan name with a gender-specific prefix: "zh" or "sh" for females, and "ch" or "th" for males. This is placed before the family name, separated by an apostrophe. Longer or more complicated Andorian names are commonly shortened, especially when dealing with other species.

  - **Female:** Athytti, Vryvih, Zyle, Vyssia, Thriras, Shreri, Vrossaan, Itamaan, Ishrelia, Vreraat, Talas, Tarah, Jhamel, Talla,

  - **Male:** Ishrath, Thoss, Shon, Oshrev, Atheth, Tyvaass, Thasiv, Tyssab, Tylihr, Thy'lek, Shras, Thelev, Keval, Gareb

  - **Clan Names:** Tharhat, Qiaqir, Chiaqis, Thenehr, Zynes, Shraviq, Thilrerh, Azonan, Azollarh, Shran

    - *Examples: Ishrelia zh'Azonan (female), Atheth th'Zynes (male)*

- **BAJORAN** names begin with the family name, followed by a personal name. The individual names are normally short — rarely more than two syllables — and with a soft or melodic sound. Bajor Is traditionally matriarchal, with children taking their mother's family name.

  - **Female:** Adami, Chami, Fala, Jaxa, Laren, Lipras, Leeta, Lupaza, Meru, Neela, Nerys, Seriah, Sul, Yesa

  - **Male:** Anaphis, Edon, Essa, Furel, Gel, Holem, Hovath, Kag, Los, Mabrin, Nalas, Reon, Taban, Tennan

  - **Family:** Anbara, Anjohl, Faren, Jaro, Kalem, Krim, Kubus, Latara, Latha, Lenaris, Li, Tahna, Reil

    - *Examples: Reil Yesa (female), Latara Gel (male)*

- **BETAZOID** names tend to have at least two syllables and a melodic sound, with a personal name followed by a family name; of these, the family name tends to have a harder sound. Betazoids are traditionally matriarchal, with children taking their mother's family name.

  - **Female:** Deanna, Ania, Kestra, Lwaxanna, Dalera, Gloranna, Abeana, Pekera, Nissila, Lomestra, Ioza, Pegira, Nemenna, Nerira, Lojeea

  - **Male:** Konal, Reban, Xani, Enon, Dael, Etas, Andal, Kolel, Atani, Devoni, Algar, Jensar, Nikael, Kalos, Rennan

  - **Family:** Grax, Hagen, Morganth, Stadi, Dutrax, Odutan, Nelan, Onovren, Kader, Nostrun, Dulas, Konin, Ebesin

- **DENOBULANS** tend to only have a single name — an individual Denobulan may be part of several overlapping families. Some Denobulans may use the name of one of their spouses as an impromptu surname, however; this is often to indicate association to species that may not understand Denobulan families. Denobulan names tend to be short and hard-sounding, particularly male names.

  - **Male:** Biras, Bogga, Delix, Grolik, Groznik, Nettus, Moga, Morox, Phlox, Rinix, Takis, Tropp, Tuglian, Vinku, Yolen, Zepht, Zinet

  - **Female:** Anari, Andora, Asha, Daphina, Feezal, Forliza, Kessil, Liera, Lusis, Miral, Natala, Ninsen, Henna, Sabra, Secka, Symmé, Trevis, Vesena

- **HUMAN** names vary wildly, and rather than make sweeping generalizations here, it's better that Players seek out other sources for names, considering the vast range of languages, cultures, and traditions Humanity encompasses.

- **TELLARITE** names have considerable variation, but all tend to be composed of harsh, even guttural sounds. Tellarite names consist of a personal name and a family name, though the family name is often a compound, indicating that the family name is a patronym or matronym (the name of a father or mother, respectively), toponym (derived from a place) or similar — in this way, these prefixes are similar to "O'", "Mc", "von", and similar elements in some Human names.

  - **Female:** Pola, Cherthish, Zhuggaa, Torthem, Neshlel, Verg, Kholo, Fratho, Skig, Vaolli, Glavom, Nihraogh, Ghand, Rensh

  - **Male:** Prugm, Brag, Dash, Gisich, Gullerg, Zankir, Hellek, Trar, Jorsh, Geshniv, Tuk, Rinkog, Veth, Cek, Gullak

- **Prefixes:** bav, glov, blasch, lorin, jav, bim, glasch

- **Family:** Gronnahk, Nonkursh, Slaal, Ker, Zhiv, Blav, Zhuffand, Khebloss, Pend, Brin, Wenkurn, Gerkow, Khutohk, Jagh, Krer.

- *Examples: Pola jav Brin (female), Tuk glasch Khutohk (male)*

- **TRILL** names consist of a personal name and a family name, though in the case of a joined Trill, the family name is replaced with the name of the symbiont.

  - **Female:** Audrid, Azala, Emony, Kareel, Lenara, Nilani, Reeza, Zharaina, Koria, Lidra, Diranne, Kimoni, Larista, Vidria, Kehdza

  - **Male:** Arjin, Bejal, Curzon, Hanor, Joran, Malko, Selin, Timor, Tobin, Torias, Verad, Yedrin, Keman, Sabin, Joal, Dorin

  - **Family:** Nedan, Sozenn, Rulon, Les, Tral, Inazin, Hama, Kelen, Imonim, Razix, Idiron, Paron, Tanan, Sulil, Kerev

  - **Symbiont:** Jexen, Del, Ogar, Kyl, Eku, Nala, Cela, Pohr, Ral, Okir, Etahn, Lahl

  - *Examples: Koria Inazin (female, unjoined), Bejal Okir (male, joined)*

- **VULCANS** have only a single name, in practical terms — while they do have family names, these are not discussed amongst other species — and tend to be traditional in the names they use. Male Vulcans often — though far from always — are given names beginning with S, while female names frequently begin with T. These are far from universal, however.

  - **Male:** Aravik, Delvok, Kovar, Muroc, Rekan, Salok, Savel, Sevek, Skon, Soral, Sutok, Syrran, Tekav, Tolek, Velik

  - **Female:** Falor, Metana, Perren, T'Karra, T'Laan, T'Lar, T'Les, T'Mal, T'Paal, T'Pan, T'Rel, T'Vran, Seleya, Simora, V'Lar

PERSONALITY

Once the Players have an idea of what their characters are like, and have thought about what experiences and career choices have shaped their life to date, consider what sort of personality the character has? Are they grumpy, by-the-book? Adventuresome? Wise? Thoughtful? Tired of routine? Calm? Even choosing a few adjectives like this can help in locking down the personality of a character. It doesn't mean they're always like this — the crewmembers should be three-dimensional, complex characters that will make the game more exciting. Characters can evolve and change over time, but it's good to have an idea of how the character will behave from the start.

A character's Values are a good basis for a character's personality, and vice-versa. If a Player has had difficulty devising any of their character's Values during character creation, this is a good opportunity to consider them.

APPEARANCE

What does the character look like? A character's species will give you some idea on what features they will have, but the finer points such as their build, height, or any distinguishing features will give the Players something to picture when thinking of their characters. Are they distinctive or average-looking? Do they have any habits, or behaviour quirks? It's often useful to give characters some sort of visual description.

Given *Star Trek's* history on television and in movies, it may even be useful for Players to think of an actor or actress who they could imagine portraying that character. This can help both with the character's appearance, and with other details like their voice and mannerisms, which can all provide inspiration for a Player.

RELATIONSHIPS

While a character's Values may define some of their relationships, life aboard a starship on a continuing mission of exploration places many people in a confined space for long periods of time. Consider the character's family relationships: where are the rest of their family? Do they have a spouse or partner aboard the ship? Is the character in contact with the rest of their family regularly, and how did they respond to the character being assigned to a mission in deep space?

What about the people around the character? How do the Main Characters get on with one another? How does the character regard the rest of the crew, and how are they regarded by them? Is the character close friends with anyone else on board, relaxing with them when off-duty? Does the character have any enemies or rivals?

These details can make the interaction between the characters more interesting, and add more depth to the character. Like a character's personality, a character's relationships can — and should — evolve over time, and some relationships may become so strong (whether friendly or adversarial) that they can become Values for the character.

RANK AND ROLE

A character's place within the crew of their ship is an important consideration, but it's one that should be left to the end of the character creation process if this method is used.

Role will have a greater impact upon the character in play than Rank will, so this should be determined first. Main

Characters will normally be the senior staff of their ship — the group of personnel who make the important decisions about the ship, and who aid the Captain as department heads, subject matter experts, and trusted advisors.

Main Characters may fill any of the following senior officer roles aboard their ship. Not every ship will have every role, and not every role must be filled by a Main Character. The senior Staff are chosen at the discretion of the captain, so if there are roles not represented in the group, that's not a problem. Some roles are specific to certain departments, which will be noted with each entry.

Each role comes with a distinct benefit in-game, as well as defining what the character's job is on the ship. These in-game benefits are marked in italics in the entries below.

- **COMMANDING OFFICER:** Command department only. The captain. Even if the commanding officer does not hold the rank of captain, they will be referred to as captain by their subordinates. Every ship must have a commanding officer. *The commanding officer may spend a point of Determination to grant any other character they can communicate with one point of Determination; this does not have to be linked to a Value.*

- **EXECUTIVE OFFICER:** Command department only. Second-in-Command. The executive officer is the captain's chief advisor, and takes command in situations where the captain is unable to. If a ship does not have a dedicated executive officer, an officer in another role should be noted as second-in-command, but they will not gain the benefits of this role. *When another character in communication with the executive officer spends a point of Determination, the executive officer may spend 3 Momentum (Immediate) to let that character regain the spent point of Determination.*

- **OPERATIONS MANAGER:** Engineering department only. The operations manager manages and oversees all technical operations aboard or involving the ship, normally from the Operations station on the Bridge, or

DIFFERENT STYLES OF GAME

As noted in the sidebar on p. 95, different styles of game may require slightly different considerations with the rules. If the game being run is not focused on the senior staff of a starship, then choosing roles doesn't make sense. The Gamemaster may choose to skip that part entirely, or they may devise alternative roles more suited to the style of game being run.

in conjunction with the chief engineer (on smaller ships, one officer may fill both roles). This often entails taking on the duties of a science officer, if there is no dedicated science officer in the senior staff. *When the operations manager succeeds at a Task assisted by the ship's Computers or Sensors, or using a tricorder, the character generates one bonus Momentum, which may only be used on the Obtain Information Momentum Spend.*

- **CHIEF ENGINEER:** Engineering department only. The chief engineer is responsible for ensuring that the ship remains operational and functional, and commands the engineering department aboard the ship. *When aboard the ship, the chief engineer always has the Advantage "Engineering Department", which represents the ship's complement of engineers and technicians.*

ENLISTED PERSONNEL

Not everyone in Starfleet is an officer. It employs a considerable number of enlisted personnel who go through different training and have been trained for specific roles and duties instead. Outranked by even the least experienced Ensigns, these personnel are nevertheless vital to the running of a ship or starbase, as they tend to extremely skilled and experienced in their field. Some are even given authority over those who technically outrank them, teaching junior officers the practical skills they'll need to advance, while others can earn a full commission and become officers themselves.

A Player may choose to make their character Enlisted instead of an Officer following the normal procedure, with a few minor changes the character does not attend Starfleet Academy, but instead receives their training elsewhere (this has no effect on the rules, and is purely background), and cannot select Command as their major during that stage. Further, an enlisted character cannot take the commanding officer or executive officer roles. Enlisted personnel have the ranks listed below:

- Master chief petty officer/master chief specialist

- Senior chief petty officer/senior chief specialist

- Chief petty officer/chief specialist

- Petty officer/specialist/yeoman (1st class, 2nd class, or 3rd class)

- Crewman (1st class, 2nd class, or 3rd class)

An Enlisted character with the Untapped Potential talent can only pick the crewman or petty officer/specialist/yeoman ranks. An enlisted character with the Veteran talent may not pick any rank lower than chief petty officer/chief Specialist.

- **CHIEF OF SECURITY:** Security department only. The chief of security oversees the ship's security department, and is responsible for ensuring the safety of the ship and crew during missions, for the investigation of disciplinary and criminal matters, and for overseeing the protection of important persons aboard the ship. On many ships, the chief of security operates from the Tactical station on the bridge. *When aboard the ship, the chief of security always has the Advantage "Security Detachment", which represents the ship's security personnel.*

- **CHIEF MEDICAL OFFICER:** Medical department only. The chief medical officer, also known as ship's surgeon, or ship's doctor, is responsible for the health and wellbeing of the crew and other persons aboard the ship, and leads the ship's medical department. A chief medical officer can order, and countermand the orders of, senior officers where matters of that officer's health are concerned. *When aboard the ship, the chief medical officer always has the Advantage "Medical Department", which represents the ship's medical personnel.*

- **SCIENCE OFFICER:** Science department only. A science officer is responsible for advising the commanding officer of all matters scientific, providing hypotheses in matters concerning the unknown. Not all ships have a dedicated science officer within the senior staff, often having the operations manager take on these duties. *When the science officer succeeds at a Task assisted by the ship's Computers or Sensors, or using a tricorder, the character generates one bonus Momentum, which may only be used on the Obtain Information Momentum Spend.*

- **FLIGHT CONTROLLER:** Conn department only. Not a typical senior staff role, some captains, particularly those operating in uncharted space, choose the most senior helmsman or flight control officer to serve as senior staff as well. *When the flight controller is required to analyze or repair technology related to flight or propulsion, they may use the Conn Discipline instead of Engineering.*

- **SHIP'S COUNSELOR:** Medical department only. On larger ships and starbases, it's common to have personnel dedicated to the mental soak. Some captains regard them as valuable advisors, as their training covers both culture and psychology, making them exceptionally good at reading the moods and intentions of others. *After succeeding at a Task to determine the emotional state or intent of another living creature, the ship's counselor gains one bonus Momentum, which may only be used on the Obtain Information Momentum Spend.*

- **COMMUNICATIONS OFFICER:** More common in the earlier days of Starfleet, dedicated communications officers are typically skilled in linguistics and cryptography, and aided with advanced translation and decryption technologies, and thus valuable during encounters with both new cultures, and with hostile ones. *When a Task attempted by the communications officer is increased in Difficulty because of an unfamiliar language or encryption, ignore that Difficulty increase.*

Once the characters' roles have been determined, the characters should determine their Ranks. A character can be of any Rank, though there are a few restrictions in specific circumstances. The choice made in Step Five: Career may limit which ranks the character may choose from. Starfleet's officer ranks are as follows:

- **CAPTAIN:** This rank can only be selected by the commanding officer, and no more than one character may select it.

- **COMMANDER:** This rank is the lowest rank that the commanding officer may have.

- **LIEUTENANT COMMANDER:** This rank is the lowest rank that may be taken by a character with the Veteran talent.

- **LIEUTENANT**

- **LIEUTENANT (JUNIOR GRADE):** This rank is the highest rank that may be taken by a character with the Untapped Potential rank. It is also the lowest rank that may be taken by any character with the role of executive officer, chief of engineer, chief of security, or chief medical officer, as those roles are only available to experienced personnel.

- **ENSIGN:** This is the lowest rank available to any officer.

EQUIPMENT

Starfleet personnel are extremely well-supplied, receiving the tools they need to do their jobs. The Main Characters are no different.

Firstly, all characters naturally receive their uniforms. The precise style of uniform will vary based on the era, and on the preferences of the Commanding Officer. Individual characters may have alterations or additional elements on their uniforms — such as a devotional earring for Bajorans, or a lab coat for medical personnel — as required. Characters will receive duty uniforms appropriate for their department and their duties, as well as a dress uniform for formal occasions.

Characters also receive a personal subspace communicator as standard — simply referred to as a Communicator. This may take different forms depending on the era; hand-held communicators are commonplace in the 22nd and 23rd centuries, while the 24th century saw the introduction of communicator badges, or combadges, worn on the uniform.

In addition, all characters have access to tricorders. They aren't carried all the time, but tricorders can be found in storage bays across a starship, and are standard issue for away missions, so if a character needs a tricorder, it isn't difficult to obtain one. Characters from the medical department may use a medical tricorder instead.

Beyond that, characters may have common tools on hand for their day-to-day duties. Any character from the engineering department may carry an engineer's toolkit, while characters from the Medical department may carry a medkit. Similarly, a character with a Trait representing a weakness, flaw, or disability, or whose species cannot easily function in an Earth-standard environment, will receive appropriate equipment to allow them to compensate for these difficulties.

Finally, characters receive a sidearm for personal defense. All Starfleet officers receive a phaser type-1 as standard. All security personnel, and all senior officers (lieutenant commander and higher rank) receive a phaser type-2 as their sidearm instead.

Other equipment is either obtained as required by the mission, or forms a character's personal effects, which are described separately.

In summary, a starting character has the following items:

- Uniforms

- Communicator

- Tricorder

- Sidearm (phaser type-1 or type-2 for security and senior officers)

- Tools (by duty; not all characters will have these)

Example: Finally, Nathan puts the finishing touches to the character. First, a final Value: "Living with Your Ideals is Harder than Dying for Them", reflecting his experiences of conflict and the chain of command. Next, Nathan adjusts the character's Attributes. None of them are above 12, and only one is that high, so he doesn't need to change anything there, meaning he can just increase two Attributes by +1 each. He increases Control and Presence both to 10.

Next, he makes similar adjustments for his Disciplines. None of them are at or above 5, so no adjustment is needed, meaning he can just increase two of them by +1 each. Nathan chooses to increase Command to 3, and Science to 5.

Next, the last few details. The character's Stress is 10 — equal to his Fitness of 8, plus his Security of 2 — and he inflicts 2⬦ extra damage with attacks.

Part of the character's name is already decided — a Joined Trill takes their symbiote's name instead of their surname — so Nathan selects the name Joal Etahn for the character, noting that the character's family name is Kerev, should it become important later. He also decides that Joal is in his late 30s, a suitable age for an officer of his experience, and puts some thought into the character's appearance and personality. He's clearly part of the Sciences department as well.

Then, with the rest of his group, Nathan looks over the senior staff roles, and they determine that he'd be most suitable as a Science Officer, and holds the rank of Lieutenant Commander.

Lastly, he notes down starting equipment — uniform, combadge, tricorder, and a phaser type-2. With that done, Lieutenant Commander Joal Etahn is ready for duty.

REPORTING FOR DUTY
SAMPLE CHARACTER SHEET

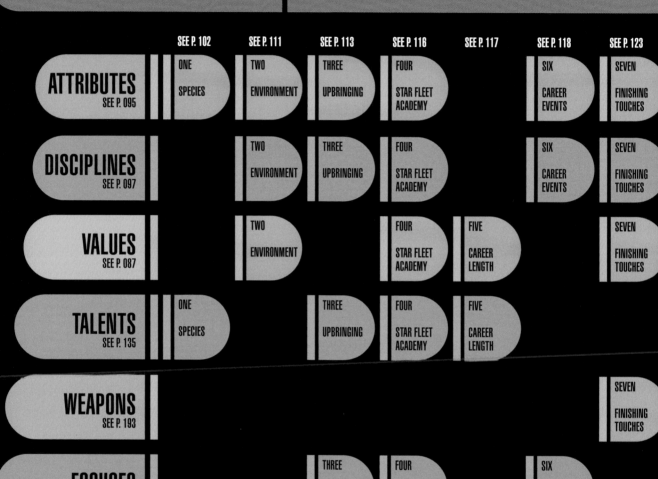

	SEE P. 102	SEE P. 111	SEE P. 113	SEE P. 116	SEE P. 117	SEE P. 118	SEE P. 123
ATTRIBUTES SEE P. 095	ONE SPECIES	TWO ENVIRONMENT	THREE UPBRINGING	FOUR STAR FLEET ACADEMY		SIX CAREER EVENTS	SEVEN FINISHING TOUCHES
DISCIPLINES SEE P. 097		TWO ENVIRONMENT	THREE UPBRINGING	FOUR STAR FLEET ACADEMY		SIX CAREER EVENTS	SEVEN FINISHING TOUCHES
VALUES SEE P. 087		TWO ENVIRONMENT		FOUR STAR FLEET ACADEMY	FIVE CAREER LENGTH		SEVEN FINISHING TOUCHES
TALENTS SEE P. 135	ONE SPECIES		THREE UPBRINGING	FOUR STAR FLEET ACADEMY	FIVE CAREER LENGTH		
WEAPONS SEE P. 193							SEVEN FINISHING TOUCHES
FOCUSES SEE P. 100			THREE UPBRINGING	FOUR STAR FLEET ACADEMY		SIX CAREER EVENTS	
STRESS SEE P. 124							SEVEN FINISHING TOUCHES
OTHER EQUIPMENT SEE P. 128							SEVEN FINISHING TOUCHES

STARFLEET PERSONNEL FILE

NAME: Joal Etahn

SPECIES: Trill

RANK: Lieutenant Commander

ENVIRONMENT: Isolated Colony

UPBRINGING: Agricultural/Rural

ASSIGNMENT: Science Officer

TRAITS: Trill, Etahn symbiont

ATTRIBUTES

CONTROL	10	FITNESS	8	PRESENCE	10
DARING	7	INSIGHT	9	REASON	12

DISCIPLINES

COMMAND	3	SECURITY	2	SCIENCE	5
CONN	2	ENGINEERING	1	MEDICINE	3

VALUES

Understanding is the Purpose of Life

Seek Out New Life and New Civilizations

Seen Too Much to be Surprised

Living with Your Ideals is Harder than Dying for Them

DETERMINATION

TALENTS

Cautious (Science)

Intense Scrutiny

Joined

Technical Expertise

FOCUSES

Survival Training

Uniform Code of Justice

Xenoanthropology

Hand Phasers

Linguistics

Psychology

STRESS

INJURIES

WEAPONS

NAME/TYPE	Phaser type-2		5
QUALITIES	Ranged, Size 1H, Charge		
NAME/TYPE			
QUALITIES			
NAME/TYPE			
QUALITIES			

OTHER EQUIPMENT

Uniform

Combadge

Tricorder

REPORTING FOR DUTY
CREATION IN PLAY

The other method of creating a Main Character is somewhat simpler, but it does require that the Player have a greater understanding of what they want their character to be and do before play begins.

This method allows the Players to partially-create their characters, while leaving many of the details undefined, so that they can be determined during play itself, revealing the character through their actions in the same way that a character's capabilities might be introduced to an audience watching a TV show or movie.

Creating the partial character should be a relatively swift process, but one that requires the Player to know what they want the character to do. For this reason, some elements that are left until last in Lifepath creation are determined up-front with Creation in Play.

This method uses the following steps:

1. Choose the character's Role.

2. Assign the character's Attributes.

3. Choose the character's Species.

4. Assign the character's Disciplines.

5. Choose a single Value.

6. Begin play!

CHOOSE THE CHARACTER'S ROLE

First and foremost, the Player should determine the role they intend the character to fill within the group and aboard the ship. This is the same as choosing the character's Role at the end of Lifepath Creation (p. 126), only the rest of the character's details have not yet been determined. Instead, the character will be created to fill that role, rather than choosing a role once the character has been completed. The Player should also determine the character's Department at

this stage, picking from one of the six Disciplines, and should also note down the equipment the character will start with.

ASSIGN THE CHARACTER'S ATTRIBUTES

Now, the Player should assign the character's Attributes. The Player has the following ratings to assign to the character's Attributes, in any order:

10, 10, 9, 9, 8, 7

CHOOSE THE CHARACTER'S SPECIES

Next, the Player should select the species they wish their character to be. This is a simple matter of choosing from the list of species found in the Lifepath Creation rules, starting on p. 102. The Player then increases their Attributes as described in the entry for the species chosen.

ASSIGN THE CHARACTER'S DISCIPLINES

Next, the Player should choose two Disciplines. One must be the Discipline that matches the character's chosen Department. The other can be chosen freely.

The Discipline that matches the character's chosen department is assigned a rating of either 4, or 5.

The other Discipline chosen at this stage is then assigned a rating based on the choice above: if the department Discipline is a 5, then the second Discipline is a 3, but if the department Discipline is a 4, then the second Discipline will be a 4 as well.

Leave the other four Disciplines blank at this stage. They will be determined during play.

CHOOSE A SINGLE VALUE

Finally, the Player should choose a single Value. This Value should reflect the basic concept the Player has for the character. The character's other Values will be determined during play.

BEGIN PLAY!

At this stage, the character should have their role, their species (including the accompanying Trait), a full range of Attributes, two of their six Disciplines, and a single Value. This is all that's needed to get started.

The Gamemaster should then begin play, devising a basic mission for a group of partially-created characters. This scenario shouldn't be too complex or involved, as it mainly serves as an opportunity to introduce and flesh out the characters. During this mission, each Main Character should have a basic opportunity to show off their skills. Each character will have the following elements left undetermined:

- **VALUES:** The character has three Values left undefined. When attempting a Task, the Player may declare that they're defining one of their remaining Values. The Player chooses a Value applicable to the Task they're attempting, and immediately gains a point of Determination, which may be used with that Value straight away.

- **DISCIPLINES:** The character has four Disciplines left undefined. Whenever called upon to attempt a Task that would use an undefined Discipline, the Player may declare that they're choosing to define that Discipline. The character's remaining Disciplines may be given one of the following ratings: 3, 2, 2, and 1. Each one of those ratings may only be used once. The Task is then attempted using that newly-defined Discipline.

- **FOCUSES:** The character has all six Focuses left undefined. Whenever called upon to attempt a Task, the Player may declare that they're choosing to define one of their Focuses. The Player chooses a Focus applicable to the Task being attempted. The Task is then attempted using the newly-defined Focus.

- **TALENTS:** The character has four Talents left undefined. At any point during the session, the Player may declare that they're choosing to define one of their Talents; this may even be in the middle of resolving a Task. The Player chooses one Talent, for which the character must meet the requirements (if any). Play then resumes with the character gaining the benefits of that Talent. However, the character may not retroactively benefit from having the Talent — they cannot change things that happened before the Talent was gained.

Once the first session is done, the Main Characters should be fully developed and fleshed out. If any characters still have elements undefined, the Players should feel free to decide upon those elements either after the first session, or leave them undefined until subsequent sessions.

CHAPTER 05.40

REPORTING FOR DUTY
SUPPORTING CHARACTERS

As described at the start of this chapter, Supporting Characters are the other type of characters created and controlled by the Players during a game of *Star Trek Adventures*. Supporting Characters are less detailed and are created in a less involved manner than Main Characters, and they are not permanently owned by a single Player. Instead, Supporting Characters are created as and when circumstances require within the game.

Supporting Characters serve the following purposes within *Star Trek Adventures*:

- They represent the rest of the ship's crew in play, giving the Players subordinates to command and provide the experience of being a senior Starfleet officer in play.

- They allow Players to take on different roles in play, allowing them to capitalize on a skillset that doesn't exist amongst the Main Characters, to play a more active role in an adventure that doesn't focus on their Main Character, or account for Players who are absent.

- They allow the Players to split their characters between different activities in different locations without being left out of the game for long stretches: Players can use Supporting Characters in situations where their Main Character isn't present.

- They allow smaller groups of Players to bolster their numbers during challenges, such as by ensuring that enough bridge stations are manned during a space battle.

USING A SUPPORTING CHARACTER

At the start of a scene, a Player may choose which character they are using: their Main Character, or one of the Supporting Characters currently available. For the duration of that scene, that Player will control the character they have chosen — the character chosen is a Player Character.

Where chain of command becomes significant, Supporting Characters are not senior staff, and do not have authority over the Main Characters; beyond that, compare the individual ranks of characters.

The Player, and the Gamemaster, should keep in mind — or keep note of — where the Main Characters and supporting characters are at different times, and it will typically be the case that a Player will choose a character located in the scene being established. However, this means that if the Gamemaster ends a scene, and then establishes the next scene in a location occupied by a different set of characters, the Players can easily switch to the appropriate characters without having to stop and figure out who is involved and who isn't.

If a Player has multiple characters in a single scene, then the Player may not directly control those other characters. Characters which are not under the direct control of any Player cannot perform the full range of actions and Tasks available to a character under a Player's control. Instead, they can do the following things:

- **MINOR ACTIONS:** An uncontrolled character will perform whatever Minor Actions or other incidental activities are needed to keep up with the Player Characters, or to follow the orders of Player-controlled characters with authority over them.

- **TASKS:** An uncontrolled character cannot attempt a Task that has a Difficulty above 0. Uncontrolled characters may, however, use the Assist Task to benefit Player Characters, though they may only do so once per Round in combat.

- **COMBAT:** Uncontrolled characters do not receive a Turn during combat; instead, an uncontrolled character's Minor Actions and Tasks (per the limitations above) are resolved as part of the actions of Player Characters — the uncontrolled characters follow the orders of their superiors immediately.

- **COMPLICATIONS AND INJURY:** Uncontrolled characters can be Injured in combat, and can suffer Complications as normal. However, an uncontrolled character may not spend Momentum or add to Threat to *Avoid an Injury*. Further, in any situation where a Player Character would suffer a Complication or become Injured, and there are one or more uncontrolled characters in the scene, the Player may choose to have the uncontrolled character suffer the Complication or Injury instead. In the case of an Injury, the uncontrolled character cannot be used in any way for the remainder of the scene, and if the Injury was lethal, they will require medical attention or die. If a Player Character suffers an Injury or is otherwise incapacitated, they may immediately choose to take over an uncontrolled character for the remainder of the scene.

Further, uncontrolled characters can be treated as an Advantage, to allow a Task to be attempted which would otherwise be impossible (for activities that would require multiple people), or to reduce the Difficulty of a Task — simply providing an extra pair of hands and an extra set of senses can be valuable.

CREATING A SUPPORTING CHARACTER

The number of Supporting Characters present during any game is variable, and Players do not inherently own any Supporting Characters — though they can lay claim to them during play, for the duration of that adventure.

A group of Players will have a maximum number of Supporting Characters that can be used during a single adventure; this number is the **Crew Support** of the group's ship (Crew Support is described in full in *Chapter 9: Home Among The Stars*). During an adventure, Players may choose to introduce one or more Supporting Characters at the start of any scene, either creating those characters anew or choosing from amongst previously-created Supporting Characters. The total number of Supporting Characters introduced during the adventure cannot exceed the Crew Support.

Note that previously-created Supporting Characters do not count against this number until they are introduced in play, and during a prolonged campaign a group may create many Supporting Characters, not all of whom will appear in every session.

When creating a Supporting Character, use the following procedure:

1. **PURPOSE:** First, determine what purpose the Supporting Character will fill. Are they an engineer, or a doctor, or a scientist, or a security officer? This will shape the rest of the character. This includes choosing a department for the character.

2. **ATTRIBUTES:** Secondly, assign the character's Attribute scores. The character will have Attribute scores of 10, 9, 9, 8, 8, and 7, arranged in any order. Also at this stage, choose the character's species, and note down both their species Trait, and adjust the Attributes accordingly.

3. **DISCIPLINES:** Next, assign the character's Disciplines. The character will have Discipline scores of 4, 3, 2, 2, 1, and 1, arranged in any order. The character's highest Discipline should match up with the department chosen in step one.

4. **FOCUSES:** After this, choose three Focuses for the character. At least one of these should match up with the purpose defined in step one.

5. **FINISHING UP:** Finally, give the character their standard issue equipment (uniform, communicator, tricorder, Phaser, and possibly other tools), and choose an appropriate name and rank for the character. Supporting Characters should never have a rank above lieutenant, and may often be enlisted personnel rather than officers.

Supporting Characters do not have the same level of detail as Main Characters, and initially will lack Values and Talents. Further, a Supporting Character has no Determination to spend (and, lacking a Value, no way to earn Determination either). Supporting Characters can obtain these details and develop during play.

Whenever a Supporting Character is introduced to an adventure, and this is not the first time they have been introduced (i.e., they have been introduced before), the Player introducing them may choose one of the following options:

- **VALUES:** The Supporting Character gains a single Value. This option may be chosen up to four times, gaining a new Value each time.

- **ATTRIBUTES:** The Supporting Character increases a single Attribute by 1. This option may only be chosen once.

- **DISCIPLINES:** The Supporting Character increases a single Discipline by 1. This option may only be chosen once.

- **FOCUSES:** The Supporting Character chooses one additional Focus. This option may be chosen three times, gaining a new Focus each time.

- **TALENTS:** The Supporting Character gains a single Talent that they meet the requirements for. This option may be chosen four times, gaining a different Talent each time.

Once all the options listed above have been taken, a Supporting Character cannot improve further simply by being introduced to an adventure. However, Supporting Characters can also be improved as part of a Main Character's advancement — reflecting a Main Character training and developing the personnel under them.

SUPPORTING CHARACTER OPTIONS

This section describes a few optional rules that affect the way Supporting Characters are used in play.

- **EXTRA PLAYERS:** In a group with a small number of Players, some challenging situations can become more difficult than it otherwise should be. If the group has three or fewer Players, the Gamemaster may allow some or all Players in the group to take control of up to two characters during a scene; this would increase the number of Player Characters, each of whom gets their own Turn during a Round of combat, for example. The Gamemaster may vary this from scene to scene if they wish, or apply it only to specific types of scene (such as space combat, to ensure that all the vital Bridge Stations are filled).

- **MORE ORDERS:** In combat, the Direct Task may be used by any Player Character, so long as they are using it on an uncontrolled character that they have authority over. When used on another Player Character, the normal limits for the Direct Task still apply.

REPORTING FOR DUTY
TALENTS

A character is more than the sum of its parts, and a character's Attributes, Disciplines, and Focuses alone do not give a full picture of what they are truly capable of. Starfleet only accepts the best, and only the best of the best rise to the challenges of command, and it is Talents that set these exceptional individuals apart from the rest. These characters have a particular way of interacting with the world, that lets them overcome impossible odds and triumph when others might falter. These tricks and knacks are Talents.

Mechanically, a Talent gives you a game advantage in specific circumstances. Every Main Character begins play with four Talents, and most are directly related to one of the six Disciplines, enhancing how the character employs their training and expertise.

Some Talents have one or more specific requirements. These are conditions that must be fulfilled before the Talent can be selected, such as belonging to a specific species, or having a Discipline at a specific rating or above.

Beyond that, each Talent has a condition, and a benefit. The condition is the circumstances under which the Talent can be used, and the benefit is what the character gains from meeting that condition. Some of these conditions are mechanical in nature — using a specific game option, like buying bonus d20s, or succeeding at a specific kind of Task — while others may be more narrative.

TALENTS LIST

The following Talents are available to all characters, regardless of species. Unless otherwise noted, each Talent may only be selected once. Players are free to rename the Talents they select to suit their own tastes and the backgrounds of their characters; this will not affect the rules for that Talent in any way.

BOLD
REQUIREMENT: None
You must choose a single Discipline when you select this Talent. Whenever you attempt a Task with that Discipline, and you buy one or more d20s by adding to Threat, you may re-roll a single d20. You may select this Talent multiple times, once for each Discipline. You may not select this Talent for any Discipline for which you already have the Cautious Talent.

CAUTIOUS

REQUIREMENT: None

You must choose a single Discipline when you select this Talent. Whenever you attempt a Task with that Discipline, and you buy one or more d20s by spending Momentum, you may re-roll a single d20. You may select this Talent multiple times, once for each Discipline. You may not select this Talent for any Discipline for which you already have the Bold Talent.

COLLABORATION

REQUIREMENT: None

You must choose a single Discipline when you select this Talent. Whenever an ally attempts a Task using that Discipline, you may spend one Momentum (Immediate) to allow them to use your score for that Discipline, and one of your Focuses.

CONSTANTLY WATCHING

REQUIREMENT: None

When you attempt a Task to detect danger or hidden enemies, reduce the Difficulty by 1.

DAUNTLESS

REQUIREMENT: None

Whenever you attempt a Task to resist being intimidated or threatened, you may add a bonus d20 to your dice pool.

PERSONAL EFFECTS

REQUIREMENT: Main Character

The character possesses some significant and uncommon item or device which is not part of Starfleet's standard issue, but which is nevertheless useful for missions. The character may select one item with an Opportunity Cost of 2, or two items with an Opportunity Cost of 1 each. Neither items may have an Escalation Cost greater than 1. See *Chapter 8: Equipment and Technology* for more details. A character may select this multiple times.

STUDIOUS

REQUIREMENT: None

Whenever you spend one or more Momentum to Obtain Information, you may ask one additional question (in total, not per Momentum spent on Obtain Information).

TECHNICAL EXPERTISE

REQUIREMENT: None

Whenever you attempt a Task assisted by the ship's Computers or Sensors, you may re-roll one d20 (which may be the ship's die).

TOUGH

REQUIREMENT: None

Whenever you *Avoid an Injury*, the cost is reduced by 1, to a minimum of 1.

COMMAND TALENTS LIST

ADVISOR

REQUIREMENT: Command 2+

Whenever you assist another character using your Command Discipline, the character being assisted may re-roll one d20.

DEFUSE THE TENSION

REQUIREMENT: Command 3+

Whenever you attempt a Task to persuade someone not to resort to violence, you may add a bonus d20 to your dice pool.

FOLLOW MY LEAD

REQUIREMENT: Command 3+

Once per scene, when you succeed at a Task during combat or another perilous situation, you may spend one Determination. If you do, choose a single ally. The next Task that ally attempts counts as having assistance from you, using your **Presence + Command**.

SUPERVISOR

REQUIREMENT: Main Character

The ship's Crew Support increases by one. This increase is cumlative if multiple Main Characters in the group select it, but each Main Character may only select this Talent once.

CONN TALENTS LIST

FLY-BY
REQUIREMENT: Conn 2+
Whenever you use the Swift Task Momentum Spend, you do not increase the Difficulty of the second Task if one of the Tasks you attempt is to pilot a vessel or vehicle.

PRECISE EVASION
REQUIREMENT: Conn 4+
Whenever you succeed at the Evasive Action Task, you may spend two Momentum. If you do, the ship does not suffer the increased Difficulty for attacks normally caused by Evasive Action.

PUSH THE LIMITS
REQUIREMENT: Conn 4+
When you attempt a Conn Task that has increased in Difficulty due to environmental conditions or damage to the engines, reduce the Difficulty by 1, to a minimum of 1.

STARSHIP EXPERT
REQUIREMENT: Conn 3+
Whenever you succeed at a Conn Task to identify a type of starship, or to try and understand an unknown form of Starship, you gain one bonus Momentum, which may only be used on the Obtain Information Momentum Spend, or to pay part of the cost of the Create Advantage Momentum Spend (where the Advantage must represent some form of known or observed weakness in the ship being studied).

SECURITY TALENTS LIST

CLOSE PROTECTION
REQUIREMENT: Security 4+
When you make a successful Attack, you may spend one Momentum to protect a single ally within Close range. The next Attack against that ally before the start of your next turn increases in Difficulty by 1.

INTERROGATION
REQUIREMENT: Security 3+
When you succeed at a Task to coerce someone to reveal information in a social conflict, you will gain one bonus Momentum, which may only be spent on the Obtain Information Momentum Spend.

MEAN RIGHT HOOK
REQUIREMENT: None
Your Unarmed Strike Attack has the Vicious 1 Damage Effect.

PACK TACTICS
REQUIREMENT: None
Whenever you assist another character during combat, the character you assisted gains one bonus Momentum if they succeed.

QUICK TO ACTION
REQUIREMENT: Security 3+
During the first round of any combat, you and your allies may ignore the normal cost to Retain the Initiative.

ENGINEERING TALENTS LIST

A LITTLE MORE POWER
REQUIREMENT: Engineering 3+
Whenever you succeed at an Engineering Task aboard your own ship, you may spend one Momentum to regain one spent Power.

I KNOW MY SHIP
REQUIREMENT: Engineering 4+
Whenever you attempt a Task to determine the source of a technical problem with your ship, add one bonus d20.

IN THE NICK OF TIME
REQUIREMENT: Engineering 3+ or Science 3+
Whenever you succeed at an Engineering or Science Task as part of an Extended Task, you score 1 additional Work for every Effect rolled.

INTENSE SCRUTINY
REQUIREMENT: Engineering 3+ or Science 3+
Whenever you succeed at a Task using Reason or Control as part of an Extended Task, you may ignore up to two Resistance for every Effect rolled.

JURY-RIG
REQUIREMENT: Engineering 4+
Whenever you attempt an Engineering Task to perform repairs, you may reduce the Difficulty by two, to a minimum of 0. If you do this, however, then the repairs are only temporary and will last only a single scene, plus one additional scene per Momentum spent (Repeatable) before they fail again. Jury-rigged repairs can only be applied once, and the Difficulty to repair a device that has been Jury-rigged increases by 1.

SCIENCE TALENTS LIST

COMPUTER EXPERTISE
REQUIREMENT: Science 2+
Whenever you attempt a Task that involves the programming or study of a computer system, you may add a bonus d20 to your pool.

IN THE NICK OF TIME

REQUIREMENT: Engineering 3+ or Science 3+

Whenever you succeed at an Engineering or Science Task as part of an Extended Task, you score 1 additional Work for every Effect rolled.

INTENSE SCRUTINY

REQUIREMENT: Engineering 3+ or Science 3+

Whenever you succeed at a Task using Reason or Control as part of an Extended Task, you may ignore up to two Resistance for every Effect rolled.

TESTING A THEORY

REQUIREMENT: Engineering 2+ or Sciences 2+

When you attempt a Task using Engineering or Science, you may roll one additional d20, so long as you succeeded at a previous Task covering the same scientific or technological field earlier in the same adventure.

MEDICAL TALENTS LIST

DOCTOR'S ORDERS

REQUIREMENT: Medicine 4+

When you attempt a Task to coordinate others, or to coerce someone into taking or refraining from a specific course of action, you may use your Medicine Discipline instead of Command.

FIELD MEDICINE

REQUIREMENT: None

When attempting a Medicine Task, you may ignore any increase in Difficulty for working without the proper tools or equipment.

FIRST RESPONSE

REQUIREMENT: Medicine 3+

Whenever you attempt the *First Aid* Task during combat, you gain a bonus d20. Further, you may always Succeed at a Cost, with each Complication you suffer adding +1 to the Difficulty of healing the patient's Injury subsequently.

QUICK STUDY

REQUIREMENT: Medicine 3+

When attempting a Task that will involve an unfamiliar medical procedure, or which is to treat an unfamiliar species, ignore any Difficulty increase stemming from your unfamiliarity.

TRIAGE

REQUIREMENT: Medicine 3+

When you attempt a Task to identify specific injuries or illnesses, or to determine the severity of a patient's condition, you may spend one Momentum (Repeatable) to diagnose one additional patient.

CHAPTER 05.60

REPORTING FOR DUTY
CHARACTER DEVELOPMENT

A character doesn't remain unchanged throughout their career. As they explore strange new worlds and seek out new life and new civilizations, they will be changed by what they learn, and they will grow from their experiences. The adversity these characters overcome, and the challenges they confront, will shape them. Beyond that, the successes and failures of a character will shape how others regard them.

Character development in *Star Trek Adventures* comes in two forms: characters grow and change periodically during their careers, in events called milestones; alongside this,

the character's renown and reputation will change as they complete missions and make important decisions.

Only Main Characters can receive **Milestones**, but the benefit of a Milestone can be used to change a Supporting Character or the ship itself — this represents the Main Character working to improve the crew and the ship. Changes made to Supporting Characters and to the ship must be discussed with the entire group: they belong to everyone, so everyone should have a say.

MILESTONES

A milestone is a meaningful event in the character's life, a point at which the character reexamines themselves and changes in response to what they've experienced. Milestones occur at the end of adventures, though a character will not always have a milestone at the end of every adventure.

There are three kinds of milestones a character can receive. The most common are referred to as normal Milestones, and whenever a character receives a milestone, it will be of this common variety unless otherwise noted. The second type are **Spotlight Milestones**, so-called because they happen at the end of adventures where the character was in the spotlight. The final type are **Arc Milestones**, which come at the culmination of a series of important events for the character.

NORMAL MILESTONES

A Main Character receives a normal Milestone at the end of any adventure in which that Main Character was present in at least half the scenes of the mission, and if that Main Character fulfils one of the following requirements:

- The character challenged a Value or Directive during the mission.

- The character was Injured by an Attack to kill during the mission.

- The character used at least one Value or Directive positively or at least one Value or Directive negatively.

These kinds of milestones are mainly to allow a character to change and adapt to the ongoing game, rather than improving the character's abilities. With a normal Milestone, the Player may choose to do one of the following:

- If a Value was challenged and crossed out, rewrite that Value. The new Value should relate somehow to both what the Value was before, and the circumstances that caused it to be challenged. It doesn't have to be a huge change — and often, it won't be — but the new Value should demonstrate how the character's perspective has changed.

- Choose two Disciplines. Reduce one of those Disciplines by 1 (to a minimum of 1), and increase the other by 1 (to a maximum of 4).

- Choose one of the character's Focuses, and replace it for another Focus.

- Select a Supporting Character that was used during that adventure, and use one of the above options for that Supporting Character.

- Save the Milestone, which may be used in the manner described below.

SAVING A MILESTONE

If a Player doesn't have an immediate use for a Milestone, they may save it for later. A saved Milestone can be valuable to have, as it can be used at a later point to provide a much-needed boost.

When a Milestone is saved, note it down on the Main Character's sheet, with a short description of the mission the Milestone came from, or the event that it represents; if the Gamemaster is using a pre-written adventure, or gives individual mission names, the Player can simply use the adventure's name for this.

At any point during any subsequent adventure, the Player may call back to that saved Milestone and the adventure it came from. The Player describes how a memory of, or lesson from, that adventure relates to the current situation. If the Gamemaster approves, then the Player gains the effects of a point of Determination, as if they had used a Value or Directive in a positive fashion. After this has been resolved, cross out the saved Milestone — each saved Milestone may only be used once.

SPOTLIGHT MILESTONES

A Spotlight Milestone occurs when a single Main Character is particularly prominent and significant during an adventure. At the end of an adventure, the Gamemaster may award a single Spotlight Milestone, though the Gamemaster is not required to do this every mission - one Spotlight Milestone every 2-3 missions is reasonable.

If the Gamemaster chooses to award a Spotlight Milestone, then the Players each vote for which of them will receive it. Players may only vote for Players who would receive a Normal Milestone for that mission, and they may not vote for themselves. The Player who receives the most votes receives the Spotlight Milestone instead of their Normal Milestone. In the case of a tie, the Gamemaster breaks the tie.

With a Spotlight Milestone, the Main Character receives a single choice from the Normal Milestone list, and a single choice from the following list as well:

ARC MILESTONES TABLE

ARC MILESTONES RECEIVED	SPOTLIGHT MILESTONES REQUIRED FOR NEXT ARC MILESTONE
0	2
1	3
2	4
3	5
...each successive...	+1

- Choose two Attributes. Reduce one of those Attributes by 1 (to a minimum of 7), and increase the other by 1 (to a maximum of 11).

- Choose one of the character's Talents, and replace it for another Talent.

- Select a Supporting Character that was used during that mission, and use one of the above options for that Supporting Character.

- Choose two of the ship's Systems. Reduce one of those Systems by 1 (to a minimum of 6), and increase the other by 1 (to a maximum of 12).

- Choose two of the ship's Departments. Reduce one of those Departments by 1 (to a minimum of 1), and increase the other by 1 (to a maximum of 4).

- Choose one of the ship's Talents, and replace it for another Talent.

ARC MILESTONES

An Arc Milestone represents the culmination of a story that drives a single character's growth and development: a story arc. This represents a major change for the character, and Arc Milestones have the biggest impact of all three types of Milestone.

When a Main Character has received two or more Spotlight Milestones, the next Spotlight Milestone they receive will be an Arc Milestone instead. The number of Spotlight Milestones required increases with every Arc Milestone received: the first Arc Milestone is received after the character has received two Spotlight Milestones, and the number required increases by one for every Arc Milestone received.

Receiving an Arc Milestone grants all the benefits of a Spotlight Milestone (which also grants the benefits of a Normal Milestone), and allows the character to select an option from the following list:

- Choose a single Attribute, and increase it by 1. The Attribute cannot be increased above 12.

- Choose a single Discipline, and increase it by 1. The Discipline cannot be increased above 5.

- Select one additional Talent.

- Select one additional Focus.

- Select one additional Value.

- Select a Supporting Character that was used during that adventure, and use one of the above options for that Supporting Character.

- Choose one of the ship's Systems, and increase it by 1 (to a maximum of 12).

- Choose one of the ship's Disciplines, and increase it by 1 (to a maximum of 4).

- Select one additional Talent for the ship; this option may be selected only once for the ship.

REPUTATION

An officer's reputation can make or break their career, for it shapes how their peers and their superiors regard them, and in turn influences the kinds of opportunities and considerations they receive. A certain standard of behavior is expected of Starfleet personnel, and those standards increase with rank and responsibility.

This does not mean that Starfleet personnel are expected to obey orders without thought or question, but they must exercise good sense in their decisions, and take responsibility for their mistakes and failures. Some of the most successful Starfleet officers are known for being bold, even reckless at times, and disobeying the orders of their superiors, but never without good reason and never without a willingness to face the consequences of their actions.

A Main Character has a Reputation score, which is an approximate gauge of how they are regarded by their peers and superiors. Reputation is not just a passive indicator, however: it can also serve as a limited defense against disciplinary actions; a well-regarded officer has more leeway in their actions, particularly where they can provide reasonable justification.

A Main Character begins play with a Reputation score of 10.

Further, a character's rank is an additional factor here, as shown on the table below. A higher rank has privileges, and makes some things easier for the character, but it also comes with responsibilities, which can make things more difficult.

RANK AND REPUTATION TABLE

RANK	PRIVILEGE	RESPONSIBILITY
Ensign	1	20
Lieutenant (junior grade)	1	20
Lieutenant	2	19-20
Lieutenant Commander	2	19-20
Commander	3	18-20
Captain	4	17-20

WHAT REPUTATION MEANS

Under normal circumstances, a character's reputation will serve as a basic guide for how well-regarded they are among the rest of Starfleet, and even beyond. This should serve as a guideline for how other Starfleet personnel – outside the ship – views the character after examining mission reports and other official records. This shouldn't affect the views of people who know the character personally – they'll have their own opinions, for better or worse – but rather it should influence the views of those who haven't yet met the character.

The different levels of reputation should have different effects, as summarized on the table below. These should be viewed within the context of the character's current rank, role, and responsibilities: exemplary performance for an ensign is different to exemplary performance for a captain, after all.

REPUTATION TABLE

REPUTATION	INFLUENCE
0-4	The character's record is poor, and their future in Starfleet is in question. They are viewed as dangerously prone to disobedience, insubordination, and needless recklessness. Further problems actions may result in significant disciplinary action.
5-9	The character's record is somewhat uncertain, and their performance is questionable. They are viewed as being too quick to disregard Starfleet's rules and regulations, occasionally insubordinate, or they have gained a reputation as unnecessarily reckless.
10-14	The character's record is solid and their performance is satisfactory. This is the default state for a character's Reputation.
15-19	The character has a fine record, including a few commendations for exceptional performance. They are viewed as good and dutiful officers, and their expertise and perspectives are worthy of consideration.
20	The character has an exemplary record, including numerous commendations and decorations for acting above and beyond the call of duty. They are the finest that Starfleet has to offer, and given greater discretion in how they carry out their duties.

GAINING AND LOSING REPUTATION

Naturally, a character's Reputation is not fixed, but can change as they face new challenges and the consequences of their decisions. Actions in keeping with Starfleet's values and standards will see an increase in a character's reputation, while choices and outcomes which reflect poorly upon Starfleet will see a character's reputation reduce, and may even see disciplinary action taken against the character.

At the end of an the mission, the Gamemaster should consider the outcome of that adventure, and the decisions that were taken, and decide how those actions will affect the characters' reputation. The Gamemaster should determine which actions and outcomes from the adventure may have a positive or negative influences upon that reputation.

GAINING AND LOSING REPUTATION

PLAYER ACTIVITY OR DECISION	INFLUENCE
Acted in accordance with orders and Directives	Positive
Challenged a Directive	Negative
Prevented combat	Positive
Personnel under your command are killed	Negative; 1 Influence per character (Main or Supporting) killed
Resorted to lethal force without cause	Negative
Established an alliance with an enemy	Positive
Directly contributed to saving lives	Positive, multiple Influences at Gamemaster's discretion
Acted above and beyond the call of duty	Positive, at Gamemaster's discretion
Taking unnecessary risks in the course of the mission	Negative, at Gamemaster's discretion

Once the influences have been chosen, the character makes a Reputation Check. This is resolved in a comparable way to a Task, though it uses different scores and ratings. The character rolls a number of d20s equal to the number of positive influences, with each d20 that rolls equal to or less than the character's Reputation scoring a success. Each d20 that rolls equal to or less than the character's Rank Privilege scores one additional success, for a total of 2.

If the number of successes scored is less than than the number of negative influences, then the character has lost Reputation: reduce the character's Reputation by 1, plus an additional 1 for each die that did not score any successes, and by a further 1 for each die that rolled within the range of numbers indicated for the character's Rank Responsibilities. A character of sufficiently high Reputation is capable of having a die both score a success and fall within the range indicated by their Responsibilities.

If the number of successes scored is greater than the number of negative influences, then the character has gained Reputation: increase the character's Reputation by 1 for each success scored above the number of negative influences.

REPUTATION, RANK, AND DISCIPLINARY ACTION

Reputation is linked to a character's current rank. With each rank attained, the responsibilities and demands placed upon the character change and grow, and a newly-promoted officer will be expected to prove that they are up to the challenge of their new rank.

Reputation can, however, be used as a guide for whether a character is ready for a promotion. Should a character have a Reputation of 15 or higher, and it would increase further, then the captain (or rather, the Player whose character is the commanding officer) or the Gamemaster may offer them promotion instead of an increase in Reputation. If this promotion is accepted, the character's rank increases, representing how they are now faced with a new set of expectations and responsibilities. A character cannot be promoted to captain in this way - only the admiralty can offer such a promotion, which would come with its own command or another posting elsewhere (essentially taking the character out of play).

If a character's Reputation would drop below 0, then the character faces disciplinary action. Prior to this point, issues of conduct and performance will be dealt with in minor ways, and a character losing Reputation may find a reprimand placed in their official record, or be given some unpleasant or menial additional duty, or lose some privilege normally afforded to the crew for a time, or even just a warning from their commanding officer. This should be handled through roleplay, and has no specific game effect other than the loss of Reputation it already represents.

Disciplinary action is when matters need to be taken further. This may be something handled within the ship's command structure, or it may be more serious and require that the character being punished be detained and face a court-martial. The range of possibilities here are broad, and best left to the discretion of both the commanding officer and the Gamemaster, though suggestions are provided here. Punishments that come from disciplinary actions cannot be lethal, or involve harming or permanently marking the accused in any way, per the Federation strictures against cruel and unusual punishment… though some of them may make it so that a character can no longer be used.

Short-term detention is a possible punishment that can be given at the discretion of the commanding officer, confining an officer to their quarters or to the brig for days, weeks, or even a month. Detention longer than this is unlikely – a more severe crime probably warrants a different punishment. A character in detention cannot be used – that character cannot be selected during play for the next adventure (and the Player should use a Supporting Character instead), barring extreme circumstances.

Demotion is another punishment that can be handled at the discretion of the commanding officer. The character's rank is reduced by one step, and their Reputation is reset to 9: the character is on shaky ground, but a demotion at least gives them some opportunity to redeem themselves. This may make the character ineligible for their current role; if this is the case, the group should re-assign roles accordingly.

Court-Martial is the most severe, and the one that can be the most disruptive to an ongoing game, but also the most rewarding if handled well. The character is detained until the ship can reach a starbase or other Starfleet facility where the character will be tried for their crimes. Potential punishments for this are most likely to be dishonorable discharge from Starfleet, or long-term imprisonment in a penal settlement, either of which will make the character unplayable. The advantage of this method is that a court-martial can make for an exciting and dramatic session that allows for plenty of social conflict and investigation. Court-martials do not have to happen exclusively because of this mechanic – any character accused of a serious crime may face court-martial.

Commanding officers are a special case. As they are the top of the chain of command on their ship, their superiors are the admiralty, who aren't present for day-to-day matters. Instead, in the short-term, if a commanding officer loses reputation while already at 0, they should be relieved of duty by the executive officer/second-in-command, and confined to their quarters (short-term detention, above) until the situation has passed. More significant problems are to be handled by the Gamemaster, possibly in a court-martial.

23RD CENTURY STARFLEET FIELD EQUIPMENT

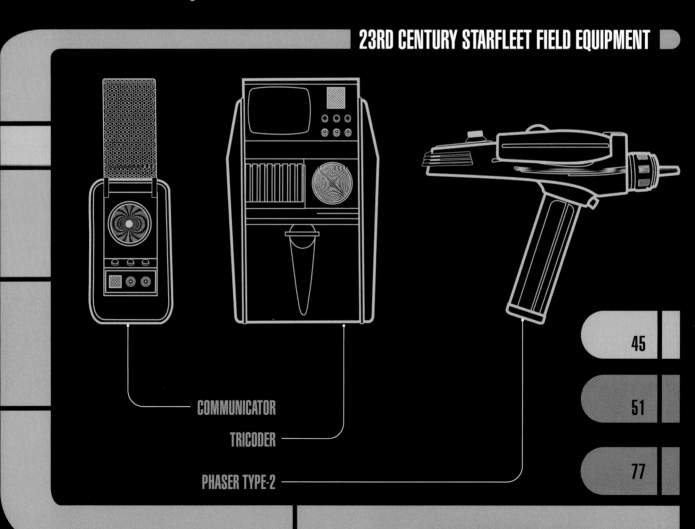

COMMUNICATOR

TRICODER

PHASER TYPE-2

45

51

77

THE FINAL FRONTIER

140523
100518190525

THE FINAL FRONTIER
STRANGE NEW WORLDS

"TO BOLDLY GO WHERE NO MAN HAS GONE BEFORE."

— CAPTAIN JAMES T KIRK

One or more planets surround most stars, and every one of these worlds is utterly unique. All Starfleet personnel should keep in mind that each new world they encounter has the potential to be deadly and, at the same time, home to secrets found nowhere else. However, it is also important to remember that the vast majority of these millions of planets fall into one of a relatively small number of types. All Class J gas giants are relatively similar, as are all Class D planetoids. The following list describes the eight most common classes of planets. Other types of planets exist, but are sufficiently rare or idiosyncratic to defy any type of standard classification. The standard planetary types are:

CLASS D

Class D worlds are the most common planetary bodies, and exist in almost every stellar system. They are all relatively small, airless moons and asteroids that are essentially barren balls of rock. Earth's moon, Luna, is a typical example of such worlds. Almost all of these worlds are lifeless, although a few are home to vacuum-dwelling life or life-forms that live in subsurface cavern complexes. While typically useless for any purpose except mining, some of the larger Class D worlds, like the Andorian world of Weytahn, can be terraformed.

AVERAGE GRAVITY: Negligible to 1G, most are between 0.05 and 0.5 G.

DANGERS: Deadly atmosphere (vacuum), hazardous, hostile, or deadly temperatures, hazardous or hostile radiation.

ENVIRONMENTAL DAMAGE TYPES

Regardless of their source, all environmental hazards are divided into three types, depending on their severity — hazardous (the least dangerous category), hostile, and deadly (the most dangerous).

● **HAZARDOUS ENVIRONMENT:** Any hazardous environmental danger causes damage at a rate of between X/hour and X/day, depending upon the severity of the hazard. Appropriate survival gear permits humanoids to endure this environment indefinitely.

● **HOSTILE ENVIRONMENT:** Any hostile environmental danger causes damage at a rate of between X/minute and X/5 minutes, depending upon the severity of the hazard. Only environment suits permit humanoids to endure hostile environments for more than a few minutes.

● **DEADLY ENVIRONMENT:** Any deadly environmental danger causes damage at a rate of X/Round. Humanoids must

wear space suits to survive in deadly environments. However, while space suits can protect against deadly atmospheres for as long as their life support lasts, extended exposure to deadly temperatures or radiation can cause space suits to malfunction.

● The above damages are cumulative, so a world with a hostile atmosphere and hazardous temperatures would require characters to roll for damage caused by both threats.

Hazardous Atmospheres contain a modest amount of oxygen, but either that amount is insufficient for the long-term survival of humanoids or the atmosphere contains slow toxins, like traces of chlorine or too much carbon dioxide. Respirator masks or specialized medications can reduce or eliminate this damage.

Hostile Atmospheres either contain little oxygen or larger amounts of moderately rapid toxins like high concentrations of carbon dioxide.

Deadly Atmospheres are poisonous or otherwise rapidly fatal, like chlorine atmospheres, extreme atmospheric pressure, or the vacuum of space.

Hazardous Temperatures for humanoids are above 50 C or below 0 C, and include extreme environments on Class M planets, like glaciers and hot sandy deserts. Proper survival gear can completely eliminate this damage.

Hostile Temperatures are above 80 C or below -50 C.

Deadly Temperatures are above 200 C or below -200 C, and include planets covered in lakes of liquid nitrogen or where lead is molten.

Hazardous Radiation includes residual radiation from a nuclear war several decades before, normal stellar and cosmic radiation on an airless world, radiation from natural radioactive materials, and radiation from massive stellar storms on a Class M planet. Anti-radiation suits or an adequate supply of the correct anti-radiation drugs can reduce or eliminate this damage.

Hostile Radiation includes radioactive fallout from recent nuclear explosions, residual radiation from a nuclear war several years before, radiation from stellar storms on an unshielded spacecraft or an airless world, and radiation from unshielded fission reactors or other dangerous radiation leaks.

Deadly Radiation includes radiation from nuclear weapons, radiation from massive stellar storms on an unshielded spacecraft or airless planet, or exceptionally bad radiation leaks.

CLASS J

CLASS K

CLASS H

CLASS D

CLASS L

CLASS H

These are hot, dry terrestrial planets, which have little surface water or ice and are, at best, marginally habitable by humanoids. Although some Class H worlds have oxygen-argon atmospheres, many have atmospheres that are mildly poisonous, making long-term survival impossible. Humanoid colonies have been established on Class H worlds, but they rarely thrive.

AVERAGE GRAVITY: 0.5 to 1.5 Gs.

DANGERS: Hazardous or hostile temperatures, possibly hazardous atmospheres.

CLASS J

Class J worlds are the most common gas giant planets found. These are large worlds that are typically between 3 and 15 times Earth's diameter that have enormous and dense atmospheres primarily composed of either methane (on smaller Class J planets) or hydrogen (on larger Class J planets) and their surface is almost impossible to reach due to the size and density of their atmospheres. No Class J planet is habitable by humanoids and they are impossible to terraform. However, some have their own entirely airborne alien ecosystems and may even be home to exceptionally alien and intelligent creatures. Class J planets can be found anywhere in a star system, from intensely hot worlds close to

their primary to distant frozen worlds. Some Class M planets orbit Class J worlds as moons.

AVERAGE GRAVITY: 0.8 to 3 Gs.

DANGERS: Deadly atmosphere, hazardous, hostile, or deadly temperatures, possibly hazardous, hostile, or deadly radiation.

CLASS K

These frigid worlds include a relatively broad range of planets, from cold, dry worlds like Mars, which typically possess relatively thin carbon dioxide atmospheres, to somewhat larger planets that resemble Saturn's moon Titan or smaller versions of Uranus and Neptune. These frigid worlds have denser atmospheres of methane and nitrogen. These worlds are not gas giants, because they all possess a solid surface, but none are habitable without extensive terraforming and the coldest are simply too hostile to terraform.

AVERAGE GRAVITY: 0.25 to 2 Gs.

DANGERS: Deadly atmosphere, hostile or deadly temperatures, possibly hazardous or hostile radiation.

CLASS T

CLASS M

CLASS Y

ANOMALOUS WORLDS

CLASS L

Class L worlds are marginally habitable planets which contain limited vegetation, but no animal life on land. Most are primitive worlds where life recently evolved and animals have not yet developed the ability to live on land. However, some are simply marginally habitable worlds where land animals cannot survive. Most have atmospheres composed of argon and oxygen, and many have sufficient atmospheric carbon dioxide to cause most humanoids at least mild distress. On some Class L worlds, carbon dioxide levels are sufficiently high enough to slowly poison humanoids.

AVERAGE GRAVITY: 0.5 to 1.5 Gs.

DANGERS: Possibly hazardous atmosphere, possibly hazardous or hostile temperatures, possibly hazardous radiation.

CLASS M

Class M planets are easily habitable by all humanoids, including Humans, Vulcans, Klingons, Andorians, and many others. These worlds possess oxygen atmospheres and a range of temperatures and pressures that allow liquid water to exist over most of their surface. However, this does not mean that the entire surfaces of these planets are pleasant or even survivable. Much of Vulcan is a desert and some Class M worlds are in the midst of frigid ice ages, where

ice sheets a kilometer thick cover more than half their land area. However, all offer locations where humanoid life-forms can thrive with only minimal technology. As a result, the Federation is always looking for uninhabited Class M planets to colonize. Every uninhabited Class M planet you discover may eventually become home to a thriving Federation colony.

Nevertheless, do not forget that even Class M planets can be lethal. In addition to regions that are burning hot or freezing cold, all Class M planets are home to robust ecosystems of animals and plants with biochemistries that are all somewhat similar. As a result, virulent diseases, poisonous or possibly carnivorous plants, and deadly predators can be found on many Class M planets. Starfleet has placed more than a few such worlds off limits for colonization because one or more life-forms were simply too deadly.

AVERAGE GRAVITY: 0.5 to 1.5 Gs.

DANGERS: Localized hazardous or hostile temperatures, possibly localized hazardous or hostile radiation.

CLASS T

These planets are a variety of large gas giant, typically much more massive than Class J worlds. Class T planets are the largest and most massive objects classified as planets, and there remains lively debate surrounding the point where a body is too large to be considered a Class T planet and is instead classified as a brown dwarf star. Some Class T worlds are as much as a dozen times the size of the largest Class J world. Gas giants only remain this large when they have not yet finished forming. The largest Class T worlds are a hallmark of a very young stellar system. All Class T planets possess exceedingly high gravity and pressure. Even a brief artificial gravity failure can incapacitate the crew of a starship in the upper atmosphere of a Class T planet, and venturing deeper than the upper atmosphere of such a world can exceed the structural integrity of almost any starship. Also, they are only found in exceedingly young star systems, which abound with asteroids, dark matter, strong stellar flares, and many other dangers rarely found in older star systems.

AVERAGE GRAVITY:
2 to 10 Gs

DANGERS:
Deadly atmosphere, hazardous, hostile, or deadly temperatures, possibly hazardous, hostile, or deadly radiation.

CLASS Y

Sometimes called "demon planets," Class Y worlds are noted for dense, toxic, highly corrosive atmospheres, surface temperatures that exceed 200 C, and periodic thermionic radiation discharges. These radiation discharges mean that even entering a low orbit around a Class Y world can be hazardous. In addition, both the radiation and dense clouds that surround all Class Y worlds limit the utility of sensor scans from orbit. Because of the multitude of dangers Class Y worlds present, Starfleet considers them to be the terrestrial planets least hospitable to humanoid life. They are almost instantly fatal to unprotected humanoids, and space suits, probes, and even starships must all be protected by specially modified shields in order to survive the thermionic radiation.

AVERAGE GRAVITY:
0.5 to 1.5 Gs

POSSIBLE THREATS:
Deadly atmosphere, deadly temperatures, deadly radiation.

ANOMALOUS WORLDS

While most worlds fall into one of the above standard types, a few do not, and these planets are, by definition, worthy of further investigation. There are many reasons why a world might fall outside the expected range of planetary classification. The Federation's knowledge of planetary formation is large but incomplete. Some naturally occurring worlds may provide opportunities to expand this knowledge. Theoretically possible examples include a pair of planets closely orbiting around one another that share the same atmosphere or exceedingly ovoid or ellipsoidal worlds that have been reshaped by their star's tidal forces or by their own sufficiently rapid rotation.

Often the strangest and most intriguing worlds are those that have been reshaped or even created whole cloth by a technologically advanced sentient species. There are literally no rules for what governs such planets. One may be millions of years old, another might only be several centuries old, and a starship could even encounter a world being constructed. The artificial planet created by the Kalandans and encountered by Captain Kirk's *Enterprise* in 2268 is an excellent example of such a created world. It is several thousand years old, roughly the size of Earth's moon, but with a gravity nearly that of Earth, a Class M atmosphere that supports limited plant life, and no surface water. As far as Federation geologists know, a world like that could never have naturally evolved. It can only exist because a sentient species designed and built it for a specific purpose. The Dyson Sphere discovered by the *Enterprise-D* in 2369 can be considered the most extreme known example of an artificial planet, and other possible options include ring and donut shaped worlds of various sizes.

There are also worlds that were once naturally created planets that have been drastically altered. Terraformed worlds like the Andorian world of Weytahn is an example of such a world. However, more technologically advanced species can perform far more extensive types of terraforming, including so-far theoretical possibilities like building a vast shell around a Class J or T planet and then terraforming the outer surface of this shell to create a Class M planet many tens or potentially even many hundreds of thousands of kilometers in diameter. Remember that if you ever encounter an artificial world or a world that has been radically altered by a more technologically advanced civilization, almost anything is possible.

THE FINAL FRONTIER
ALIEN ENCOUNTERS

During your time in Starfleet, you will often encounter life-forms which are not easy to communicate with. These may be creatures, plants, fungi, or even something completely different and new. Do not underestimate them, Captain. Just because they cannot communicate with you in a manner to which you are accustomed does not mean they should be ignored.

INTRODUCTION

Much as the Prime Directive prohibits interference in other cultures and civilizations, similar Starfleet regulations prohibit significant non-scientific interference with non-sentient species or their environment. That flock of Gunji jackdaws might not look like much today, but, given a few million years of evolutionary advancement, who can say what they may become? They may end up as the backbone of the Federation, or the greatest threat this Galaxy has ever faced, but it is not up to us to decide that now. We cannot know what the future holds, and there is far more out there than we could ever catalogue.

The Vulcan Science Academy celebrates this multiformity in its core tenet, "Infinite Diversity in Infinite Combinations." So, while we celebrate the differences throughout the Galaxy, be ready for anything.

Now, some of your crew may be faster than the rest, while others smarter, and yet more might display extreme strength reserves, but that will mean nothing when facing down a Vulcan *sehlat*, or staving off the mental drain of a neural parasite. Never underestimate what the Galaxy might throw at you, as even the smallest creatures have put the Federation at risk, or must I remind you of the blue gill parasite infestation of 2364?

We shall describe a number of common threats you may face in this section of the briefing. This should come in handy for ninety-nine percent of the situations you find yourself in. If you remember your biology textbooks, A.E. Hodgkin found that many species evolve in parallel across multiple planets; so when you find yourself facing off against a saber-toothed

STARDATE 1691.7

"Now, I'm not sure what kind of joke this is…".

"I am a Vulcan, sir, we do not joke."

"Don't interrupt me, Cadet. Now, I don't know what sort of person you think you are, but I can tell you now that a woman of my age and experience does not appreciate fiction when marking her cadets' essays. I expected more from a cadet such as yourself."

"Fiction, sir?"

"These 'Winged, fire-breathing lizards' you mention. Did one of your fellow cadets put you up to this, or convince you that such things were real?"

"No, sir."

"Then tell me… cadet… where do these creatures come from?"

"Berengaria VII, sir. Discovered by a Vulcan science team. I apologize, sir, but I do not know the exact stardate. If you would like, I can provide citations."

"Please do, cadet"

"Yes, sir. … There. I have sent you a dispatch with the original scans of the creature in the report, as well as information on where to find a detailed biological assessment."

"I see… Well I suppose I have some reading to do tonight."

"Am I dismissed, sir?"

"I suppose you are, cadet… It's not every day I'm proven wrong in such things."

Transcripted from a discussion between Professor Young and Cadet T'Pria at Starfleet Academy.
Stardate 1691.7

cat on a far-flung planet, bear in mind what I am about to tell you....

AGGRESSIVE CREATURES

The most up-front creatures of the Galaxy are often the easiest to deal with. These are animals which are naturally aggressive due to territory, instinct, or because you and your away team appear edible. Even naturally-docile creatures can become aggressive when injured or trying to protect their young.

Fortunately, such situations have a simple resolution. If backing away or scaring the creatures does not work, your response must be swift, else you shall be putting yourself and your crew in mortal peril.

A sample of the away team priority reports which have come across my desk this week include such delights as being trapped in a cave with what can only be described as a horned version of a Vulcan *sehlat*, and a colony which was forced to evacuate when they uncovered a mineshaft infested by some form of cow-sized spiders. Fortunately, the miners evacuated and the mine was closed while the situation was dealt with.

Just one of these creatures, or even a small group of them, is bad enough, but many cultures use such animals in displays of pride, strength, or to aid their hunters. Their usefulness as symbols of their tribe or hold, as gladiatorial opponents, or as weapons of war are enhanced when used alongside trained keepers. I don't think I need to describe how much more dangerous an aggressive bear, or a similar alien creature, would be when fighting alongside a strategically-thinking tribe.

Similarly, if fighting larger animals, be aware that they may be assisted by a herd or group. If you are fighting a parent creature, its offspring may be attempting to move around you. If fighting one creature, others in a symbiotic relationship may choose to attack you at the same time, and that's without even mentioning the possibility of an animal injecting you with an assortment of parasites, or forcing a telepathic link to you, or — I think I've made my point....

LARGE GROUPS

Everyone knows that targs are nasty little creatures, or that the hook spiders of Talaria are easily dealt with. Get a large group of them in one space, however, and things may not go the way you want them to. A herd of *targs* can easily devastate a colony's crops, or otherwise cause irrevocable harm to their infrastructure due to the creatures' movements and appetite. That same colony that dealt with beasts in the summer may find itself infested with insects in the winter, or vice-versa.

Large groups may change their behavior, also. That Gunji jackdaw may be frightened away by a single phaser blast, but a flock is more likely to stampede. Just be careful where that stampede ends up.

PARASITES

Now, I imagine you've seen the old reports from the Deneva colony? Creatures that attach themselves to and within sentient species have proven on multiple occasions the ability to infiltrate settlements or groups with different degrees of success, with our most significant infiltration being that of the neural parasites which infected Starfleet Command in 2364.

Without going into too much detail, as the motivations of any particular alien life are impossible to predict, you should be aware that this kind of infiltration is possible. Aliens you encounter, other Starfleet ships, or even members of your own crew can be infected by such creatures, and you should do everything within your power to save those you find in this condition.

As for their capabilities, be aware that they may retain all abilities their host had, including their memories. There is even a chance that the parasite may push the host's body to feats of strength or endurance far surpassing that of the host's normal abilities.

TERRAIN ADVANTAGE

While it might be nice to think you will always be dealing with the most unknowable creatures in safe environments, chances are that you will be dealing with them on their own turf. After all, a *mugato* is not likely to attack you unless you enter its mountain territory.

Creatures such as spiders — and many others — generally prefer dark places, polar creatures often prefer the cold, and aquatic creatures often have no small amount of trouble on land. If you can find a way to even out that advantage then you are going to be better off, either by removing your disadvantage, or negating their advantage.

You must remember that your greatest advantage is that of your technology. You will always be able to see better with a tricorder, or take action from a distance with a phaser, but officers are often in situations involving dangerous non-sentient life due to being taken out of their comfort zone. Do not become too reliant on that to which you have grown too accustomed.

SPACEFARING CREATURES

Creatures which live in space have often been the bane of starship captains' safety. While we have surrounded ourselves with alloys and warmth, they have grown to adapt themselves to the rigors of space travel. These creatures often have abilities far surpassing those of our own starships. The spacefaring creature Captain Jean Luc Picard's crew dubbed "Junior," the crystalline entity, and various cloud-based creatures have all shown themselves to be more than capable of disabling or placing drains on a starship's ability to function.

As with all non-sentient creatures, these entities will have their own needs and desires, which are often the key to avoiding conflict or preventing their interference with Starfleet operations.

CHAPTER 06.30

THE FINAL FRONTIER
STELLAR PHENOMENA

STELLAR CARTOGRAPHY FOR BEGINNERS

The stars of the Galaxy come in hundreds of forms, from tiny brown dwarfs to massive stars like UY Scuti. The Hertzsprung-Russell Diagram (or HR Diagram) is humanity's best attempt to categorize all observed stars into groups for ease of classification and study. The two axes of this diagram are temperature and luminosity.

Most stars that you and your crew will encounter will fall into seven temperature categories that range from warmest to coolest: O (blue), B (blue-white), A (white), F (yellow-white), G (yellow), K (orange), M (red). Each of these categories is sub-divided into ten fractional numbers to show where in that code the star falls. Sol, our Sun, is a G2 star, thus it is on the warmer end of yellow G-class stars while the primary star of 61 Cygni (the home system of the Tellarites) is a K5 star, in the middle of the orange K class stars. Other temperature

"Just outside a planet's atmosphere is the realm of Stellar Phenomena, or space weather. Early Human manned spaceflight had to deal with dangerous conditions only briefly when in low Earth orbit or on its short journeys to the Moon and back, but longer trips meant more risk of encountering conditions that could prove hazardous to the ship and crew. With the invention of warp drive, Humanity began to discover new, strange, and interesting stellar phenomena they had never encountered before, light-years from home. All UESPA crew members are highly trained on how to deal with space weather, and if you spot something,

ask a crew member on duty to help explain what it is to you, and know that UESPA is on the job! On your first trip to the stars, we are happy to provide you with this spotter's guide for stars and space weather to make your journey more educational."

– Child's Guide to Stars and Space Weather,
United Earth Space Probe Agency Educational
Pamphlet, 2140.

Discovered in 2292 on wreck of United Earth colony ship
S.S. Glukhovsky, Wolf 294 IIg.

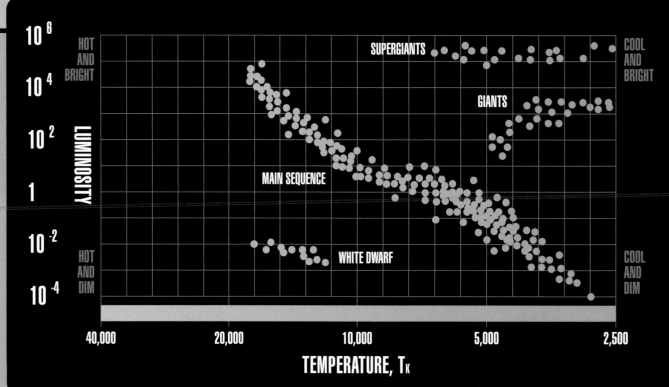

categories include L (cool reds), Y (brown dwarfs), C (Carbon Stars), and D (White Dwarfs) to name but a few. Hotter stars tend to burn quickly and have short lifespans measured in as little as millions of years, and cold red stars burn slowly and can possibly have lifespans reaching trillions of years.

The second axis on the HR Diagram is luminosity. Stars can be split into 7 general categories (with other sub-categories left out for sake of clarity): I (Super-giants), II (Bright Giants), III

(Giants), IV (Sub-Giants), V (Main-Sequence), and VI (Sub-Dwarfs), and VII / WD (White Dwarfs). Most stars in the Galaxy are Main Sequence (V) and fuse hydrogen at their cores to produce energy. The Sun is a G2V. Sub-Dwarfs (VI) are similar to Main Sequence stars, but typically have less heavy elements (greater atomic mass than helium) than Main Sequence and thus burn cooler than Main Sequence. Main Sequence stars tend to be stable, and thus provide planets around them with relatively greater opportunities for life to evolve.

The luminosity classes brighter than the Main Sequence (Super-Giants, Bright Giants, Giants, and Sun Giants) nearly always involves stars that have begun to age out of the Main Sequence. As stars get older they expand as they cool. This expansion, and greater surface area of the star, is what allows these stars to become so bright. Worlds around these stars tend to be lifeless or show the signs of previous life. As these stars are so luminous, radiation can prove to be an extreme hazard around them even for the most well shielded science vessel. As these stars continue to age they will either form a nova or supernova (see The Dangers of Space below). Some examples of these brighter stars include: Pollux (K0III, or an Orange Giant), Rasalgethi (M5Ib, or a Red Supergiant), and Rigel (B8Ia, or a Blue Supergiant).

THE DANGERS OF SPACE

Even the newest recruit to Starfleet understands that space is a dangerous place. Even the smallest Main Sequence stars produce more energy per second than the entire Federation does with its antimatter reactors and fusion power plants. With that kind of energy, both beautiful and dangerous occurrences are commonplace across the Galaxy.

NEBULAE

Nebulae are gas and dust clouds that are left over from stars that have undergone nova or supernova, or even gas clouds hundreds of light years across that still exist from before the formation of the Galaxy. Typically, these clouds are made up of hydrogen and helium, along with trace amounts of heavier elements. Nebulae are lit by ionization and light from stars (or stellar remnants) within them, and flying through such highly-charged clouds of gas tends to disrupt starship sensors. While warp travel through nebulae is possible due to a starships deflector array moving the particles away, slight gravitation eddies and density fluctuations mean cautious starship captains tend to go around nebulae rather than risk damaging their ships. Some nebulae have been in existence for billions of years without collapsing and can be home to strange native life-forms, so exploration of these beautiful clouds is often a priority. Examples of these objects are the Orion Complex, the Mutara Nebula, and the Coalsack Nebula.

FLARES, RADIATION STORMS, AND GEOMAGNETIC STORMS

Flares, **radiation storms**, and **geomagnetic storms** are interlinked. Flares can occur on any star, but more often around small stars such as Class M Main Sequence stars. These bursts of energy erupt out of the star and often outshine the rest of the star for hours at a time. The charged particles and radiation from such flares can cause problems with a starship's shields and sensors, and unprotected crew on the surface of planets without a magnetic field can receive heavy doses of radiation. On worlds that do have a magnetic field, such as Earth, flares cause aurora that have the possibility to destroy large electronic networks, disrupt communications, and even stop transporter operations. Flare stars are stars that tend to have these events occur far more often than others. Examples of stars like this are: Proxima Centauri (home of Earth's earliest colony), Wolf 359 (site of the devastating battle against the Borg in 2367), and II Pegasi.

ION STORMS

Ion storms are severe versions of flares and radiation storms. They start the same way, with a powerful burst of energy from a star or stellar body, powerful enough that the

EFFECTS ON SHIPS

Each type of Stellar Phenomena can be placed into 5 severity categories, from low to high: I, II, III, IV, and V. Difficulty increases by one for each level.

For example: Commander Chekov is attempting to achieve a weapons lock on U.S.S. Reliant while maneuvering in the Mutara Nebula. The Mutara Nebula is considered a Class III Nebula, thus Chekov's Task increases by 3 Difficulty.

The Complication range increases due to Stellar Phenomena in the following starship Systems and Departments, depending on the severity, unless otherwise stated in adventure rules or specific examples:

- **NEBULA:** Sensors, Weapons, Engines

- **ION STORMS / RADIATION STORMS, STELLAR FLARES:** Shields, Sensors, and transporters. Possible radiation damage to crew.

- **NOVA:** Shields and Sensors.

- **SUPERNOVA:** Shields, Sensors, Engines

- **PULSAR / BLACK HOLE:** Shields, Conn, Engines, Sensors, Structure

- **GRAVITATIONAL WAVES:** Conn, Engines.

Other effects and system challenges may be required when a starship first encounters these phenomena.

radiation density of the pulse can ionize interstellar gases and punch through most planetary magnetic fields, causing severe damage to unshielded electronics and delicate ship systems. Ion storms can hold together over decades and travel across light-years before finally dissipating when conditions are right. Numerous examples in Starfleet history record encounters with ion storms, but none so strong as the Halkan Storm of 2267 that focused the subspace scanning array of *Enterprise's* transporter systems in such a way as to accidentally tunnel through subspace into a parallel timeline, beaming alternative versions of members of her bridge crew aboard.

NOVAS

A **nova** is the gradual death of a star as its core contracts and gets hotter, blowing off the outer layers of its atmosphere and that material accreting onto a nearby stellar partner (typically a white dwarf) which then accumulates mass until it explodes in an uncontrolled fusion reaction. As most stars form binary pairs this is an event that is semi-common, but still dangerous. The rapid expansion of stellar material away from the star's core can also result in the beginnings of a stellar nebula. These high-energy events wash out sensors, can sterilize worlds that are even protected by the most advanced shielding, and can pose significant radiation hazards to starship crews. These events can also spawn ion storms, radiation storms, and even geomagnetic events in nearby star systems.

SUPERNOVAS, NEUTRON STARS, AND BLACK HOLES

Supernovas, **neutron stars**, and **black holes** are intrinsically linked. As massive stars begin to run out of hydrogen in their core, there is enough mass and pressure to continue the fusion process using heavier elements such as helium, carbon, and even silicon. Once silicon begins to fuse into iron, the amount of energy produced from trying to fuse iron is not enough to hold back the immense pressures generated from the mass of these large stars, and gravitation collapse begins. Within seconds the star becomes billions of times brighter than it was as the explosive shock wave reaches a significant portion of the speed of light. The mass of the star's core determines if a neutron star or a black hole forms. Regardless, any starship near a star undergoing supernova is doomed to be vaporized even with the best shielding technology. Neutron stars and black holes alike can produce intense gravitational waves, extreme radiation hazards, and ion storm like effects across dozens of light-years, and even cause enough high energy radiation to sterilize worlds a handful of light years away.

PULSARS AND ACTIVE BLACK HOLES

Pulsars and **active black holes** are even more hazardous versions of neutron stars and black holes. Pulsars are rapidly rotating neutron stars with incredibly strong magnetic fields that channel charged particles and radiation into a beam emanating from two sides. Even from lightyears away starships in the path of these 'lighthouse' beams require heavy shielding and typically do not stay in the path for long. Active black holes are black holes that are currently devouring closely orbiting material, such as a star that came too close. The increasing velocities and densities close to the event horizon of the black hole heat the material to the point that it can emit x-rays and gamma rays. This radiation can cause severe damage to starships and star systems even lightyears away, causing intense ion storms, gravitational waves, and other stellar phenomena.

GRAVITATIONAL DISTORTIONS

Gravitational distortion is a catch-all category for gravity waves and other events that cause ripples in space-time. These originate from high energy events such as supernovas, black holes, closely orbiting neutron stars, and collisions between massive objects. While most gravitational distortions occur fairly close (in astronomical terms) to these events, constructive interference of these ripples can sometimes cause 'rogue waves' much like on the oceans of Earth. Rotating massive objects also cause 'frame-drag' which can cause ships passing through such twisted space-time at warp speeds to undergo 'slingshot' time travel. Federation starship captains are ordered to never attempt such a thing, and those that do at best will have a career-ending interview with the Department of Temporal Investigations in whatever time they find themselves in.

EXOTIC EVENTS

In the course of exploration, Starfleet has come across even more exotic events that have little hard scientific data collected about them as they are so rare as to not have been observed enough for proper theories to explain their formation, or close observation and analysis is impossible. **Wormholes** are points in space-time that link across light-years and allow movement of information or even matter through them. Wormholes are always unstable with their ends moving through space and time, except for the notable example of the Bajoran wormhole. **Subspace Rifts** are extreme distortions in space-time, like gravitational distortions and wormholes, but reach into the underlying realm of subspace. These rips can impede warp field stability and even allow for travel between nearby parallel time streams. **Colliding Neutron Stars** have never been observed by Starfleet as this event is thankfully rare. The amount of energy released in a possible neutron star collision would be enough to sterilize all life within a few thousand light-years of the event and cause extinction events in thousands more. **Micro Black Holes** are nearly impossible to detect at long range and can cause severe damage to starships as they pass straight through shielding and matter, devouring everything in its path. A **Vacuum State Change** is only theorized, but any observations of the underlying fabric of space and time changing instantly into another form would likely be the last observation a member of Starfleet ever made. A Vacuum State Change could literally change the laws of physics to the point where atoms themselves fly apart as the strong nuclear force weakens to near zero, or the speed of light slows to a crawl and time dilation effects could occur at walking speeds.

Exotic events should not have specific rules for them as they should only be used for plot hooks, and even then, rarely. Either they can cause the death of trillions of people over thousands of light years, or they can kill a starships crew before they know what hit them. Use these events wisely.

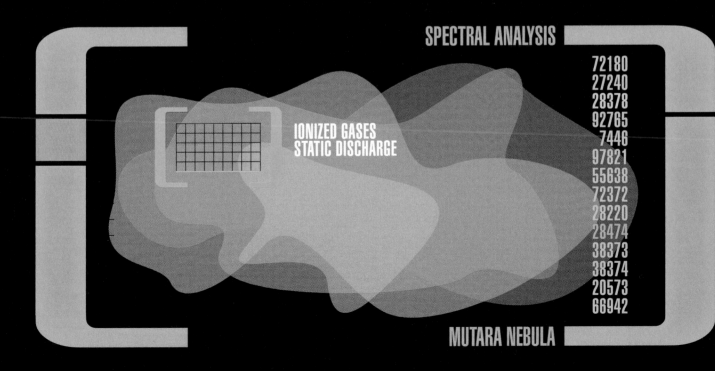

SPECTRAL ANALYSIS

IONIZED GASES
STATIC DISCHARGE

72180
27240
28378
92765
7446
97821
55638
72372
28220
28474
38373
38374
20573
66942

MUTARA NEBULA

THE FINAL FRONTIER
SCIENTIFIC DISCOVERIES AND DEVELOPMENTS

"Every sentient being in the Galaxy has at some point in their existence asked the question, why. This simple question is the beginning of every scientific endeavor from, 'Why do I see the flash of lightning before I hear the thunder?' to 'Why can't I develop a technology to travel faster than light?' When you question something you experience, and try to understand it, you are participating in the Scientific Method. A scientist is just someone highly trained in asking 'Why?' and proving beyond a shadow of a doubt that the conclusion they come to is true."

– Lectures on the Philosophy of Science,
   Dr. Anthony Symmes, 2087.

In this section, we will explore rules to help guide Players and Gamemasters dealing with Research and Development (R&D), technological tweaking, and coming up with new theories and ideas when encountering strange new phenomena.

THE SCIENTIFIC METHOD

Codified since before the Industrial Revolution on Earth, the scientific method is the basis for real life scientific endeavors as well as ones within the *Star Trek* universe. For simplicity's sake, the scientific method can be generalized into three steps: The Question and the Hypothesis, Prediction of a Solution, and Testing. With each of these steps a character gains increasing insight into a scientific problem and a solution to it, or even a breakthrough that could have universe-changing consequences. The game mechanics for this center on the use of Challenges, and specifically **Gated Challenges**.

STEP 1 – OBSERVE

When a scientist is presented with an observation that they do not understand, or an event that is occurring that is not well understood, they must begin to ask questions. Initial observations by the characters will be able to determine what Discipline the observations fit into: Engineering, Science, or Medicine. Any character with Disciplines from those categories may make this Task with a Difficulty of 0 (or 1, if a very bizarre phenomena). Once this category is determined, a character with a high skill level in that Discipline becomes **"Research Lead"**. This character takes lead in further steps and makes any dice rolls needed.

U.S.S. Saratoga is scanning the whale probe as it approaches the Sol System when power begins to flicker. Amy is portraying Lieutenant Scha'ls, the ship's science officer, and is told by the Gamemaster that determining the research category is a Difficulty Zero Task, she does not need to roll to determine success, and is told it is a Science problem. As Scha'ls is the highest skilled science officer on Saratoga, she becomes Research Lead.

STEP 2 – HYPOTHESIZE

At this stage, Players are encouraged to throw out ideas on what might be happening while trying to fit them into the Focuses for the category of the problem. The Research Lead then chooses between 3 and 5 of these ideas to use. These are called **Hypotheses** and the Research Lead may or may not have the skill focus, but they then explain these ideas to the Gamemaster. If the Gamemaster sees a Hypothesis that fits the actual solution to the research problem, they regard that as **'The Right Way'**. They do not inform the Players which Hypothesis is correct. If none of the Hypotheses presented fit the actual problem at all, the Gamemaster immediately gains a Threat and can tell the Players to go back to the drawing board and repeat the process.

Amy comes up with three possible causes to the power disruptions: Quantum Mechanics, Biology, and Theoretical Physics. The Player then explains that it might be Quantum Mechanics because of disruptions to how energy moves, it could be Biology because the probe itself has seemingly biological components, and it could be something totally outside the realm of known phenomena with Theoretical Physics. The Gamemaster thinks two of the presented

Hypothesis are possible, but chooses Quantum Mechcanics as 'The Right Way.' He informs Amy that the correct Hypothesis is indeed in front of her, but not which one.

STEP 3 — TESTING

The Gamemaster now assigns a number of successes needed to determine if the Hypothesis is correct. This is between 1 and 10 depending on the difficulty of the research or the problem. The Research Lead then chooses a direction to focus the research on. Players may pursue the wrong path and, if they are pressed for time, they may need to decide if they should continue to work on the Hypothesis they have chosen, or switch to another (see Timed Challenges). This is to represent the unknowns of research and development. Once the Players reach a total number of successes equal to the Difficulty in the correct research path, the Gamemaster informs the Players of their success. If a character has a Discipline of 2 or greater in the category of the problem (i.e., Engineering, Science, or Medicine) they are allowed to be an **Assistant** in the research regardless of what Focuses they have. This is due to common training amongst scientists and the ability of ideas to cross-pollinate between Focuses.

The Gamemaster informs the Players that the energy disruptions from the whale probe are causing Life Support malfunctions, and time is of the essence. She assigns a Difficulty of 5 to the Research (without informing the Players of the correct choice, or the Difficulty) and says that they

have six intervals (each Task taking two intervals) to find the solution. Leading the research, Lt. Scha'ls has the backing of three other characters that are in the sciences and needs a Target Number of 15. The three assistants (one a Medical Officer with a Science Discipline of 2 that feels they can assist because of the biological nature of the whale probe, an Engineer who has a Science Discipline score of 2 that feels they can assist because of their knowledge of EPS systems, and a newly arrived junior science officer with a Science score of 2 that has a fresh outlook and may see things the others do not) all roll successes and Amy rolls a 5 and 10, getting two more successes for a total of five. A great roll, but the Gamemaster says they have not found the solution. Seeing they have four more intervals, and the roll was as good as it could be, the Player of Lt. Scha'ls decides to change the research direction to Quantum Mechanics. Only one Assistant gets a success (the engineer), and Amy rolls a 10 and 17, for a total of two successes. With two intervals to go, Amy chooses to stick with Quantum Mechanics. Two assistants get successes and Amy rolls a 5 and 18, for three successes and a total of five successes over six time intervals. The Gamemaster informs the nervous Players that Lt Scha'ls has discovered that the whale probe's transmissions are interfering with energy transfer on a quantum level and that she finds a way to dampen the effects enough to get life-support back to minimal levels, allowing the Players to wait out the whale probes visit to the Sol System.

ZEN AND THE ART OF WARP CORE MAINTENANCE

The technology of the *Star Trek* universe, while wondrous, is rooted in concepts that are either understood in the real world, or are theorized as being possible. While some concepts such as the warp drive seem to be out of reach for the moment, much of the science and technology people are comfortable using today have equivalents aboard the Starfleet vessels.

USING THE RIGHT TOOL FOR THE RIGHT JOB

Technology in *Star Trek* can be broken down into three broad categories: *high energy power systems, sensing and computing technology*, and *warp and subspace theory*. While improvements in one category may help make other technologies more efficient or better suited for a particular task, typically, if an engineer wants to improve the sensing capabilities of a tricorder, they do not focus on improving the energy storage capacity of the device. They look at its computing strength, its sensors sensitivity, or the selection of sensors already installed.

High Energy Power Systems include the fusion reactors that power a starship's sublight impulse drive, the matter/antimatter reactors that power ships warp coils, and even the emergency batteries on starships and charge packs of tricorders, phasers, communicators, and PADDs. The improvement of radioisotope thermoelectric generators made these low-power systems highly efficient and are used in emergency situations across colony worlds in the Federation and in starship lifeboats. Channeling the massive amounts of energy these devices generate on Starfleet vessels is done through an electroplasma system, i.e. EPS Conduits.

Sensors and Computing Technology deals with the hardware that absorbs input, processes and catalogs it, and then outputs it in ways people can understand. While Moore's Law broke down during the World War III on Earth, it came back with a vengeance after First Contact, with standard transistor based computers improving until the development of duotronics by Dr. Richard Daystrom in 2243, revolutionizing computing technology for the entire Federation. Sensors and computers continued to get more sensitive and powerful through the 23rd century as warp fields began to be used around duotronic CPUs to allow calculations to occur at FTL speeds. Finally, the development of isolinear processing in the early 24th century continued to make computers able to process vast amounts of information. Even by the mid-23rd century computers were small and powerful enough that handheld tricorders typically had the memory storage of a starships main computer core from the 22nd century, and by the launch of *Enterprise-D* the handheld PADDs used on board had more processing power than the entire *Enterprise* NX-01.

Warp and Subspace Theory is the largest development in Human, or any other starfaring civilization's, history. On Earth this was done by Zefram Cochrane in 2063 and helped end the third World War and initiated First Contact with the Vulcans. Warp and subspace

theory also brought about other developments in science and technology such as subspace communications (which allowed FTL communications across vast distances), FTL sensing and computing systems, transporter systems, and the better understanding of a wide variety of high-energy phenomena linked with subspace and altered physics.

BREAKING THE LAWS OF PHYSICS

Improvements to technology already available to starship crews are part and parcel of many *Star Trek* episodes, from improving the transporter systems so it can lock onto a crew member stuck on the surface of a world in the middle of a heavy ion storm, to cold starting an inactive matter/antimatter warp core, to modifying the warp capabilities of a Klingon bird-of-prey to allow it to time travel.

When time is of the essence, such as cold starting a warp core before a starship crashes onto the surface of a disintegrating planet, it is best to use the methods described in *the scientific method* above. For general improvements to ship systems, or any technology for that matter, the use of a Gated Challenge is recommended with the following changes:

Like *the scientific method*, one Player should be the Research Lead and choose three separate Focuses to use as research and development directions, explaining their reasoning to the Gamemaster. The Gamemaster chooses a '**Good Way**' and may select one other Focus called '**Outside the Box**' only if they feel the character has an interesting idea that could work, but is risky. The Gamemaster does not inform the Player which is chosen. Just like a regular challenge, the Gamemaster assigns a Difficulty to the Task of improving technology or making a breakthrough ranging from 4 to 6 depending on the complexity of the technology and the degree of improvement to existing technology. The number of Tasks that need to be completed before the Gated Challenge is complete should range between 3 and 5. The Player is not made aware of these values as to keep secret if they are on the right track and to know how far along they are. (See the sidebar for an example.)

The Player chooses a Focus from their list and begins the **Extended Task**. A single Task in the Gated Challenge can be completed per story. This prevents improvements and deep research from occurring too rapidly and making further Tasks frivolous, and better matches the pace seen on screen. A character that follows the Good Way will achieve their research goal once the number of Tasks determined by the GM are completed. If a Character is following a path that was not chosen as Good or Outside the Box, they will know they are researching in the wrong direction when they succeed at their first Task and the Gamemaster announces their progress.

When the Challenge is complete, the Gamemaster informs the Player that their Character has achieved what they have been attempting and any benefits and drawbacks it may have if it was Outside the Box.

Lt. Torres of U.S.S. Voyager is attempting to improve the cruising speed of the starship to get them home from the Delta Quadrant faster. As Chief Engineer, she is the Research Lead and chooses Warp Core Engineering, Subspace Theory, and Jury Rigging as the possible paths. The Gamemaster chooses Warp Core Engineering as the Right Way and Jury Rigging as Outside the Box.

The desired improvement to the warp drive Lt. Torres is proposing to research is an increase of cruising speed by 5%. As the warp drive is a known technology, but still very complex, the Gamemaster assigns a Task Difficulty of 4 to the Task. As a 5% increase in speed is an average improvement and concludes that a total of 3 successful Tasks must be completed before the Gated Challenge is finished.

*Lt. Torres chose the Focus 'Jury Rigging' and explains that it makes sense because U.S.S. Voyager is so low on spare parts that they may use scavenged or bartered technology for repairs, and it stands to reason that some of those new parts may be very useful in replacing material in the ships warp coils. The Gamemaster assigned Warp Core Engineering as 'The Good Way', but Jury Rigging as 'Outside the Box'. After the first story, Lt. Torres makes her first roll and succeeds in the Difficulty 4 Task. She is told she **is not** on a wrong path. After the third story, she makes her 3rd successful Task roll and finds that she was on the 'Outside the Box' path. The Gamemaster then determines that not only is Voyager's cruise speed increased by 5%, but the ship gains an extra dice to resist system damage the next time its warp nacelles are damaged! The drawback to an Outside the Box result is that repair Tasks to the Engines System has its Difficulty increased by 1.*

RESEARCH AND DEVELOPMENT GUIDELINES FOR WORK AND MAGNITUDE

Any changes a character proposes should fall within a 0-10% range of improvement in the known statistics of technology. Larger improvements tend to be seen coming out of research institutes and major universities. Like Montgomery Scott's continual tinkering with *Enterprise's* warp drive, the improvements to its speed and efficiency were gradual and in the end made *Enterprise* the fastest ship in Starfleet. Gamemasters should feel free to assign Work Tracks and

Magnitudes for tasks that fit their game's pace and style, but some suggestions can be found below.

SENSORS AND COMPUTING TECHNOLOGY: Technology such as short-range sensors, planetary sensors, tricorders, medical devices, computers (of all scales), holodecks, and light-speed communications equipment. Non-powered technology such as developing stronger alloys or making a better version of transparent aluminum fits into this category.

Work between 5-10, Magnitude 1-3. Difficulty 2

HIGH ENERGY POWER SYSTEMS: Nuclear fission reactors, fusion reactors and impulse drives, EPS conduits, matter/antimatter reactors, weapon systems, shields, structural integrity fields. Miscellaneous technology that requires power fits into this category.

Work between 7-15, Magnitude of 2-5. Difficulty 1

WARP AND SUBSPACE SYSTEMS: Warp coils, subspace communications, transporter systems, tractor beams, deflector beams.

Work between 10-15, Magnitude 4-5. Difficulty 3

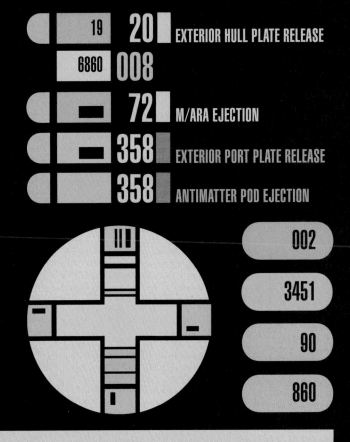

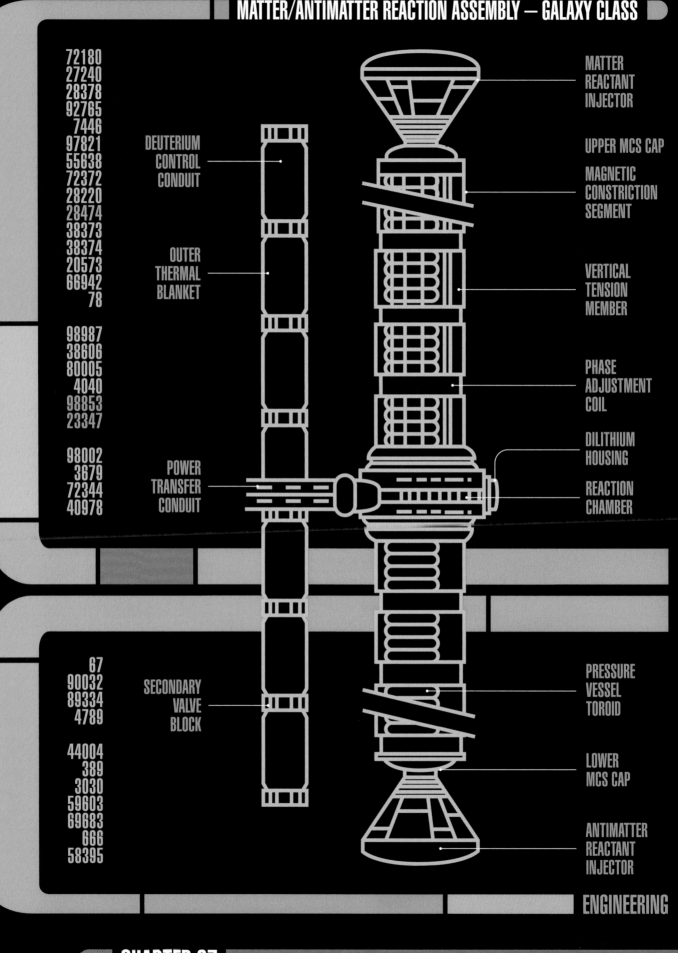

72180
27240
28378
92765
7446
97821
55638
72372
28220
28474
38373
38374
20573
66942
78

98987
38606
80005
4040
98853
23347

98002
3679
72344
40978

67
90032
89334
4789

44004
389
3030
59603
69683
666
58395

DEUTERIUM
CONTROL
CONDUIT

OUTER
THERMAL
BLANKET

POWER
TRANSFER
CONDUIT

SECONDARY
VALVE
BLOCK

MATTER
REACTANT
INJECTOR

UPPER MCS CAP

MAGNETIC
CONSTRICTION
SEGMENT

VERTICAL
TENSION
MEMBER

PHASE
ADJUSTMENT
COIL

DILITHIUM
HOUSING

REACTION
CHAMBER

PRESSURE
VESSEL
TOROID

LOWER
MCS CAP

ANTIMATTER
REACTANT
INJECTOR

ENGINEERING

CONFLICT

1609141125
03011818212008051819

CONFLICT
INTRODUCTION

"DIRECTIVE 010: BEFORE ENGAGING ALIEN SPECIES IN BATTLE, ANY AND ALL ATTEMPTS TO MAKE FIRST
CONTACT AND ACHIEVE NON-MILITARY RESOLUTION MUST BE MADE."

— CAPTAIN KATHRYN JANEWAY

The cultures that make up the Federation have moved beyond the divisive and destructive wars of their pasts, but that unfortunately has not meant an end to strife and conflict. Wherever two intelligent beings exist, there will be differences of opinion and, while a peaceful resolution is ideal, that is not always possible. Starfleet is not a military organization, but its starships and personnel are armed and equipped to defend themselves and the Federation when necessary.

This chapter deals with ways that characters are likely to resolve conflicts in **Star Trek Adventures**. There are two paths to this: social conflict, and combat.

Social Conflict deals with resolving disputes and conflicts through personal interaction. This can take a wide variety of forms, ranging from simple deceptions to achieve short term goals, to protracted negotiations over the fate of worlds.

Combat meanwhile deals with the use of violence to achieve a goal or objective. Characters may engage in combat willingly, or they may be forced to defend themselves or when left with no other course of action. Of course, Starfleet officers are taught that there is always another way, and finding ways to prevent or end the fighting are just as important as having the means to defend themselves and others.

ACTION ORDER

As noted in **Opposition in Challenges** (p. 89), the sequence of events in a Conflict may be split into Rounds and Turns. During a Round, each character takes a single Turn, during which that character can attempt a single Task. In addition, they may also take additional Minor Actions (described on p. 171), which happen separately from the main Task.

At the start of a Conflict, the Gamemaster determines a single character to take the first Turn. This is determined in the following way:

- Unless there are any reasons for an NPC to take the first Turn, the Gamemaster chooses a single Player Character to start the combat. This may be obvious, based on events that occurred prior to the start of combat, but if there is any uncertainty (such as multiple characters who could all justifiably act first), select the Player Character with the highest Daring to take the first Turn.

- If the NPCs have an obvious reason to start the combat, then the Gamemaster should select one of those NPCs to take the first Turn. This should only be done if there is clear justification for that NPC to act first.

- If there is doubt as to who should act first, the GM may spend one Threat to allow an NPC to take the first Turn, instead of choosing a Player Character.

After a character has completed their Turn — attempted a single Task and any Minor Actions they wish to perform — the Player hands the action to the opposing side (typically, but not always, Gamemaster-controlled NPCs), who will choose a single character to act next. Alternatively, the Player may spend 2 Momentum (Immediate) to keep the initiative, handing the action to another Player Character instead. Once a Player has opted to keep the initiative, nobody on that side may keep the initiative again until the opposition have taken at least one Turn of their own. In any case, no character may take more than one Turn in a Round.

Once all characters on one side have taken a Turn, then any remaining characters on the other side take their Turns in any order they choose, one at a time, until all characters on both sides have taken one Turn. Once all characters on both sides have taken a Turn, then the action goes to a character on whichever side did not take the last Turn, and the whole process begins again for the next Round.

Example: A trio of Starfleet officer PCs are ambushed by a pair of Jem'Hadar. The Jem'Hadar are invisible, concealed by their Shrouding ability, so the Gamemaster determines that

they go first. The Gamemaster chooses the Jem'Hadar leader to take the first Turn, killing one of the Starfleet officers in the process. After this, the action passes to the Starfleet officers. One acts, and generates two Momentum from her Task, choosing to keep the initiative and pass to another Starfleet officer, who acts, and then passes to the Jem'Hadar again. As all the (surviving) Starfleet characters have acted, and there is one Jem'Hadar remaining, that Jem'Hadar acts and finishes the round. The next round begins with one of the Starfleet Officers.

CONFLICT
SOCIAL CONFLICT

In Starfleet, an officer's ability to deal with people is an important part of their successes and their failures. Officers of all kinds, but those aspiring to command especially, need to be able to read and deal with people both individually and collectively. This isn't limited only to their subordinates and their superiors, but also to strangers — a Starfleet officer represents all of Starfleet, and so some basic understanding of diplomacy is a necessity.

Social Conflict is the collective term for Tasks and Challenges that are resolved through deception, diplomacy, bargaining, intimidation, and a range of other social skills. Not all

SHIP COUNSELOR'S LOG

USS ENTERPRISE, NCC-1701-D
LIEUTENANT COMMANDER DEANNA TROI
STARDATE 46362.1

I've just completed by first session with Captain Picard following his return from Celtris III. Though Doctor Crusher has informed me that the physical injuries inflicted by his Cardassian captors will leave no lasting effects, it's obvious from our conversation that the captain's emotional healing will take some time. Frankly, I'm amazed he came through the ordeal as well as he did. The torture to which he was subjected would have broken most Humans, regardless of their level of physical fitness and psychological wellbeing.

However, from my private conversations with him, I've come to understand that Captain Picard possesses a mental fortitude that is atypical for Humans. I believe it's this strength which has allowed him to overcome severe trauma on more than one occasion, namely his assimilation by the Borg Collective three years earlier. Of course, we have no other former Borg drones with which to compare his recovery, so we can only speculate as to whether the captain's circumstances are unique.

Doctor Crusher has also shown me another interesting item: Captain Picard's neurological scan graphs from the past three years. There is what appears to be a "refocusing" of thought processes present in his brain activity, which was not there prior to his mind meld with Ambassador Sarek a few weeks before his assimilation. Did the meld have a lasting impact on the captain's mental faculties? Further investigation seems a prudent measure, particularly with respect to monitoring his overall psychological state, though I have to wonder how Captain Picard will feel about it.

personal interactions are Social Conflict, but all Social Conflict is driven by interactions, especially those where each side has different goals or may not wish to yield to the desires of another.

At the heart of Social Conflict is a desire or objective, which takes the form of a request: one side wants something that the other side can help them obtain. So, at its very simplest, it comes down to one character asking another character a question. Once the question has been asked, the Gamemaster needs to decide how reasonable that request is. This depends entirely on what the request is, who is doing the asking, and who is being asked.

- If the request is something trivial, something which requires minimal effort, or which is within the normal activities of the person being asked, then it is likely to be agreed to automatically.

- If the request is something that will take some degree of effort, entails some risk, or which is somewhat unusual for the person being asked, then it is likely to require a Task — the Gamemaster should determine the Difficulty for this as normal.

- If the request is something which will require considerable effort, significant risk, or which is completely contrary to the normal activities of the person being asked, then it is likely to be refused automatically.

- If the request is something which the person asked cannot do or provide, the request automatically fails.

This is called the Persuasion Task. If the Persuasion Task fails — including if it failed automatically — then the asking character not only does not get what they want, but it prevents them from trying again without some change of circumstances (or altering the request). If the Persuasion Task succeeds, then the character receives what they asked for. As a Persuasion Task is driven by its context, what is impossible in one situation, may be entirely feasible in another. It may be useful, then, to break up a goal into smaller, more reasonable objectives, each with their own distinct Persuasion Task, and pursue that goal piece by piece rather than all at once.

This is also where **Social Tools** come in: Social Tools are the methods by which a character can alter the context and circumstances of a Social Conflict, moving things in their favour. This normally comes in the form of applying Traits, and they can be used individually or collectively to shape a Social Conflict.

During a Social Conflict, each side may have different goals, meaning that each side will engage in their own Tasks to further those goals. Even in something as seemingly one-directional as an interrogation, the interrogator will be trying to get information, while the interrogated party may have a goal all their own, such as trying to prove their innocence.

DECEPTION

Falsehoods and deceit can be valuable tools, but they are dangerous ones. Deception can be used by itself to make a request seem more reasonable or palatable, or it can be used in conjunction with other tools to create a more significant impact. However, effective deception requires skill, cunning, and an understanding of who is being lied to.

Successfully deceiving someone convinces them of some fact or facts which are not true; subsequent Persuasion Tasks are then resolved with those fictitious facts in mind. A successful deception applies a Trait to the target, which represents the lie that they now believe to be true and will shape their future actions accordingly. Deception is always an Opposed Task, with the deceiver's Difficulty based on

Social Conflict is meant to be a mixture of roleplayed conversation and game mechanics — Players describe or act out their character's parts of the conversation, the Gamemaster uses that to adjudicate the rules side of things (the Difficulty of Tasks, what Attributes and Disciplines are appropriate, what Traits are created), which sets things up for more dialogue, and so forth.

It is deliberate that the Social Conflict rules do not list a specific combination of Attribute and Discipline for any of the options in this section — these things should be determined by the Players and the Gamemaster on a case-by-case basis, rather than pre-set. Depending on the characters involved, and the nature of the Social Conflict, different combinations of Attribute and Discipline may be viable.

It is also worth remembering that Social Conflict does not exist independently of the other rules in this game — naturally, the normal rules for Tasks apply here, but creative Gamemasters may wish to use the rules for **Challenges** (p. 89), or **Extended Tasks** (p. 90), to expand the scope of a Social Conflict. A Challenge made up of several Persuasion Tasks can easily represent different stages of a negotiation or a trial, culminating in a larger outcome, while using Extended Tasks for part of a Social Conflict could be valuable when trying to defuse a crisis or other high-stakes situation, where time is of the essence or the wrong word could spell disaster. And, as noted later in this chapter, there's nothing to prevent Players or the Gamemaster making use of Social Conflict rules even within a combat.

how reasonable or believable the lie is to the target, and the target's Difficulty being determined by their suspicions.

Usefully, deception can be used to establish lies that are the foundation for other social tools as well. Empty threats can intimidate a foe with a peril they believe is real, and history is full of scams, cons, and tricks where people bargained with things they didn't own.

The problem with deception is, of course, that it's all a lie. If the target discovers that they were deceived, they will hesitate to trust the character in future, and may even seek recompense or retribution. Further, Complications suffered while lying may reveal flaws in a deception, making the target suspicious.

Example: Freshly-recovered from the rapid aging he had been suffering from, Kirk retakes command of the Enterprise *as Romulans move to attack. Outnumbered and outgunned, the* Enterprise *can't fight its way from the situation, even with Kirk back in command. Kirk, remembering that one of their encrypted channels has recently been broken by the Romulans, orders a message to be broadcast, announcing that the vessel will use its "Corbomite Device" to self-destruct, destroying every other vessel nearby. The Gamemaster sets the Difficulty at 2: the lie is somewhat implausible, but the Romulans don't know that Starfleet know the encrypted channel has been broken, so they have little reason to suspect that it's a lie. Kirk succeeds, and creates a Complication on the Romulans — "Believe the Corbomite Device ruse". The Romulans, believing the threat of the fictional device, choose to withdraw of their own volition.*

EVIDENCE

The counterpoint to deception is evidence — offering something that provides certainty and proof of a character's claims. In many cases, providing evidence may be a straightforward affair, automatically successful, but convincing someone that the evidence is legitimate may be difficult, particularly if that person expects deception, which may set a Difficulty for a Task. Each piece of Evidence is a Trait, each of which represents some information proven to be true.

Evidence can be used in conjunction with any of the other Social Conflict tools, and their use often drives uses of those tools: providing proof of your ability to carry out a threat can be vital when intimidating, giving evidence of your ability to pay during negotiations can smooth things along, and even deception can benefit from the right forged documentation if it helps make the lie more believable.

Example: Confronted by the unenviable situation of being worshipped as a god by the Mintakan people, Picard chooses to bring one of their number aboard to try and disprove their belief. Little by little, he reveals facts about his people to her, trying to establish the idea that they are mortal, and just more technologically advanced, without giving too much information and making the situation worse. Each reveal reduces the Difficulty of the Persuasion Task by one, but Picard is wary of exposing the Mintakan to more of his culture than necessary. He reduces the Difficulty down to 3, but fails, and the Gamemaster declares that he'll need something bigger to reduce the Difficulty further, so Picard shows her sickbay, and the death of one of his own people, to prove that he doesn't have control over life and death. This piece of evidence, and Picard's final Persuasion Task are enough to convince the Mintakan. Now they must convince the rest of her people…

INTIMIDATION

A direct and crude method of coercion is to inspire fear, doubt, and uncertainty. Intimidation is the practice by which a person uses threats to compel action, often by convincing others that their non-compliance will be met with force.

Intimidating someone is an Opposed Task, with the Difficulties of each Task are based on the relative perceived strengths of each side: it is easier to intimidate, and to resist intimidation, from a position of strength. Intimidating someone, naturally, requires that they believe that there is a real threat.

Successfully intimidating someone imposes a Trait upon them, representing their fear of whatever the threat was. Failing to intimidate someone makes further attempts to intimidate them that scene more difficult, often requiring even greater threats to compensate for this.

The drawback of intimidation is that it is inherently hostile, which can cause problems of its own. Employing intimidation creates an antagonistic tension between the two sides which can worsen other forms of interactions, cause lingering resentment, or even provoke a target to aggression. Intimidation is not a path to a protracted and stable peace.

Example: Gul Madred has Jean-Luc Picard captive, and wants to learn the Federation's plans. Picard has no intention of giving up these plans, so Madred's initial Persuasion Task is impossible — simply asking for the plans won't work. Instead,

Madred sets about using a range of interrogation techniques on Picard to try and break his spirit — a form of intimidation, to try and make his Persuasion Task possible. Intimidating Picard is difficult — Picard is resolute, loyal to the Federation, and strong-minded. Madred gathers up his dice pool and rolls Control + Security, with his Interrogation Focus, and the Gamemaster sets Madred's Difficulty at 0 — he's in a good position to make his threats, and has all the advantages. Picard gathers up his own dice, and uses one of his Values to spend Determination, rolling Control + Command, with his Composure Focus to stand firm; because complying with Madred would force Picard to break his oaths, the Difficulty is only 1. Picard generates more Momentum, and manages to fend off the first attempt, but Madred will keep trying until he gets what he wants.

NEGOTIATION

Negotiation is a fine art, requiring a keen and perceptive mind and a strong will. Negotiation involves the offering of compensation in exchange for granting a request, and this compensation can take many forms, with different people and different circumstances susceptible to different offers. The Ferengi and many other cultures trade in gold-pressed latinum and other precious goods, continually adjusting their offers until they reach the best deal for themselves. Diplomats mediate disputes, arranging the terms of trade agreements and territorial disputes by securing concessions from each side until everyone is happy (or at least willing to comply).

Regardless of the circumstances, negotiation means creating an Advantage that represents a favorable position created by the offer, and a Complication that represents the cost of that offer. Each new offer is considered a new change of circumstances for the Persuasion Task as well. Negotiation doesn't require a Task by itself — it is more a process of trial and error.

Negotiations may involve a lot of position shifting from both sides, as they make and retract offers, or discover that the other party doesn't have what they want. In some situations, numerous sessions of negotiation may be needed to obtain what one party wants from someone else to progress.

The drawback to negotiation is the cost of success — characters may find themselves offering more than they wanted to give up, or they may find that what they obtained was worth far less than the price they paid for it. Failing to provide what was offered can also produce serious problems, which can be particularly significant if the negotiations were based on a lie.

In some ways, negotiation is the antithesis of intimidation — achieving a goal through offering something productive, rather than threatening something destructive. Certainly, few beings will be amenable to trade and negotiation with those they've been threatened by, and such trades may have a steeper cost because of previous hostilities.

Example: Confronted by thousands of light years of Borg space, and lacking any other route through or around it, Janeway chooses to capitalize on the Borg conflict with Species 8472. While the Borg regard diplomacy and negotiation as irrelevant, the unique situation gives the crew of Voyager an opportunity: they can innovate and devise a means of defeating Species 8472 where the Borg

SOCIAL CONFLICT IN COMBAT

Social Conflict and Combat are not mutually exclusive; indeed, so long as characters can communicate, they can engage in Social Conflict. The most natural uses for Social Conflict in a combat is to try and convince the other side to stop fighting or to surrender, or to try and influence the way the enemy will act.

In these instances, it's worth remembering that communication doesn't have to mean speech, text, or any other form of complex communication. Actions can convey ideas as effectively as words, so long as the ideas aren't particularly nuanced or complex. A blast from a phaser can be a threat, while conveying a false appearance — hidden troops, or a feigned retreat — can be an effective deception. Using these non-verbal cues, as well as more precise forms of communication, can be an effective way of ending a fight.

cannot. Ensuring that the data on this innovation is safe from assimilation, Janeway proposes a trade to the Borg: in exchange for safe passage across Borg space, she will provide the Borg with the technology to win their conflict — this creates an Advantage of "Something the Borg Need" towards this interaction, and a Complication of "Working with The Collective" going forwards that represents the consequences of this deal. Where previously the Persuasion Task would have been impossible, now there is a possibility. The Difficulty of the Task is now 5, allowing Janeway to attempt the Persuasion Task. If this fails, Janeway can alter or adjust the deal she's offering to make a new attempt, possibly at a lower Difficulty.

HOLODECK PROGRAMMING

SIMULATION IN PROGRESS

"THE BIG GOOD-BYE"
DIXON HILL

SAN FRANCISCO, CALIFORNIA, 1941

347683	678933	489700	678443
479800	457930	794843	673822
239706	307689	583933	890484
780933	259794	904585	895733

3445 939

0707 1977

45

CONFLICT
COMBAT

This section deals with situations where violence — hopefully a last resort, or a tool of self-defense — has broken out. Combat does not prevent other methods being used, and any worthwhile battle will have an objective above and beyond simply overcoming the enemy. These goals are normally straightforward: reaching a location, object, or person, or preventing the enemy from doing those things. There may also be a time factor involved in a combat encounter, where achieving the goal in a specific timeframe is necessary, or one side needs to fend off the enemy long enough to complete some other Challenge.

One important consideration for combat in *Star Trek Adventures* is that not all combats are fought to the bitter end — few combatants are willing to die pointlessly, and even implacable foes like the Borg or the Jem'Hadar know the value of regrouping for another attack rather than pushing on against hopeless odds. Instead, combats frequently end in one side or another retreating or withdrawing from the battle. This may involve a fighting withdrawal on foot, the arrival of a transport craft such as a shuttle, or being beamed out.

ENVIRONMENT AND ZONES
In battle, knowing where everyone is can be of vital importance, and determining both absolute position (where you are on the battlefield) and relative position (how far you are from a given friend or foe) is important. Rather than track everything in precise distances, however, *Star Trek Adventures* resolves this matter using abstract zones.

An environment represents the battlefield. This may be a building, a city street, an area of wilderness, part of a starship, or other such areas. An environment is divided into several zones based on the terrain features or natural divisions present in the area. For example, a building or starship interior may treat individual rooms as distinct zones, using the internal walls and bulkheads as natural divisions, while a city street may focus zones around features like parked vehicles, the fronts of buildings, alleyways, and so forth. Zones are often defined in three dimensions, so the Gamemaster may choose to map multiple floors of a building, connected by stairs and elevators, or consider a few 'empty' zones above the battlefield for flying objects. A relatively simple battlefield may consist of three to five significant zones, while complex environments may have

many more. More zones are often more interesting than fewer, as they provide a greater variety of movement options and tactical opportunities, but this can take more planning on the part of the Gamemaster.

Because zones are of no fixed size, they can be varied to accommodate the Gamemaster's preferences for a given scene, and to represent certain other factors. For example, a battle in a forest may be divided into many small zones amongst the trees, and a couple of larger zones representing clearings. The larger size of the clearing zones helps convey quicker movement and easier target acquisition in open areas, while the smaller zones convey cramped conditions and short lines of sight. However, zones should not be too complex a consideration under most circumstances — a few seconds to describe zones and their relative positions, or to sketch out a rough map on a piece of spare paper, is all that's needed for most situations. Of course, this doesn't prevent the Gamemaster from coming up with elaborate environments if he wishes to spend more time coming up with maps.

Individual zones can — and often should — have terrain effects defined when the Gamemaster creates them. This may be as simple as providing cover, or imposing difficult terrain, but the Gamemaster is welcome to devise other terrain effects, such as objects that can be interacted with, hazards to overcome, or even terrain that changes under specific circumstances, such as the expenditure of Threat. Some zones may be defined more by the absence of terrain than its presence, and some environments are enhanced by a few 'empty' zones between obstacles.

Gamemasters who desire concrete values rather than abstract ranges are encouraged to set specific sizes and shapes for individual zones, essentially using them as a large grid.

CHARACTERS AND ZONES
To help Players visualize their characters' place in an encounter, and to manage combat effectively, it's important to keep track of which zone characters are in at any given moment. This should be relatively easy in most cases. As zones are defined by the terrain and around them, tracking a character can be a matter of simple description — an

enemy might be 'behind the control console' or 'standing by the shuttle'. This has the advantage of relying on natural language and intuitive concepts, rather than specific game terms, and avoids the tracking of relative distances which can become fiddly where there are many characters present.

Larger or particularly complex scenes may become tricky to track purely by memory, so the Gamemaster may wish to use something extra to help remind everyone of which character is where. If you're already using a sketched map, then marking character positions in pencil (so they can be easily erased and redrawn) is a simple approach, as is using tokens or miniatures, and moving them around as required.

DISTANCES

Movement and ranged attacks need some sense of distance to make them meaningful. In combat, the relative placement of zones determines this distance. To keep things simple and fluid, range is measured in four categories, and one state.

- The state of **Reach** is when an object or character is within arm's length of the character. Characters enter Reach to interact with objects manually, to attack in close combat, and to perform any other actions where they may need to touch the target or subject of their action. Reach isn't a specific range, but rather is a state that a character can declare when he moves — that is, when a character moves into or within a zone, he may freely declare that he is moving into or out of Reach of a given object or character. Being within Reach of an enemy is quite disruptive and distracting, adding +1 to the Difficulty of any Task that isn't a Melee Attack.

- **Close** range is defined as the zone the character is within at the time. Moving within Close range is a trivial affair. Close range is, in essence, a distance of 0 zones.

- **Medium** range is defined as any zone adjacent to the character's current zone. Medium range is a distance of 1 zone.

- **Long** range is defined as objects and creatures two zones away from a character's current zone. Long range is a distance of 2 zones.

- **Extreme** range is any creatures and objects beyond Long range. Extreme range is a distance of 3 or more zones.

DISTANCE AND PERCEPTION

The further away something is, the harder it is to notice. In game terms, this means that characters in distant zones are harder to observe or identify than those nearby. A character increases the Difficulty of Tasks to try and notice creatures or objects by one step at Medium range, by two when dealing with creatures and objects at Long range, and by three when trying to discern things at Extreme range. A creature that isn't trying to avoid notice requires a Difficulty 0 Task under normal

DISTANCES AND COMMUNICATION

Characters will want to communicate during combat — calls for help, battle-cries, and other dialogue can abound in combat. In most cases, characters can converse normally within Close range — they're near enough to one another to be heard and to make themselves understood without raising their voices.

A character at Medium range can be communicated with, but only at a raised volume — shouting, rather than talking. At Long and Extreme range, you can shout to draw attention, but conveying any meaning or understanding someone is unlikely. Communicators and similar technologies make distance less of a consideration.

OTHER SENSES

Humanoid perception, broadly, is dominated by sight and hearing, and thus these are the senses dealt with most frequently by the rules. However, other senses can come into play at times. Naturally, a character's sense of touch is limited to Reach. The sense of smell is most effective for Humans within Reach, and Tasks made to detect something outside of Reach by smell increase in Difficulty by one step, plus one step for each range category beyond Close.

Naturally, non-human characters and creatures may have different expectations for their senses — for example, Ferengi can often discern details by hearing that a Human cannot. A creature with a particularly keen sense may reduce the Difficulty of all Tasks related to that sense, while dull senses would increase the Difficulty of those Tasks; in any case, this would be covered by the creature's Traits.

Telepathy can be thought of as a sense in this regard, able to discern thoughts and the mental presence of other creatures over a distance. Similarly, the use of scanning equipment, such as Tricorders, can allow a character to detect and discern things that they would be unable to perceive otherwise.

circumstances, while attempting a Task to avoid notice makes things more difficult. Creatures or objects that are particularly noticeable — someone firing a phaser, shouting, or a fast-moving or brightly-colored object — may reduce the Difficulty further.

MOVEMENT AND TERRAIN

Moving to anywhere within Medium range is a Minor Action, rather than a Task. Moving further than this requires a Task, though this has a Difficulty of 0 under normal circumstances.

Moving as a Task increases in Difficulty if the terrain in any of the zones to be moved through is rough, hindering, or hazardous in any way. The consequences of failure vary based on the nature of the terrain: failure may result in the character's movement stopping prematurely outside of the difficult terrain, the character falling prone, or suffering the effects of hazardous terrain, which may include damage or injury.

Movement may take many different forms on this scale; walking, running, jumping across gaps or down sheer drops, swimming through bodies of water, climbing steep or sheer surfaces, and so forth. The Difficulty of these Tasks should be evaluated separately.

OTHER KINDS OF TERRAIN

There are a range of other terrain effects that might be present in a zone, beyond just difficult terrain. The most common are discussed below.

Cover is one of most common terrain effects, representing objects that interfere with a character's ability to see or attack a target clearly. Cover provides additional Resistance against Attacks, as described in the **Damage, Injury, and Recovery** section, below. A zone will either provide cover universally (granting the benefits of that Cover to any creature in the zone), or the Gamemaster may denote features within the zone that grant Cover (requiring that the character be within Reach of that feature to benefit). Each instance of Cover will grant a certain number of ▲ of Cover Dice (normally 1-4),

and may have additional benefits or drawbacks based on the nature of that Cover.

Interactive Objects are any object or terrain feature that a character could conceivably interact with. Doors and windows are a common example, as are control panels and computer terminals. Interacting with these objects may take little time or effort under normal circumstances (a Minor Action), but a complex system might need a Task to interact with properly.

COMBAT TASKS AND MINOR ACTIONS

In any given Turn in a Combat, a character can attempt a single Task, and several Minor Actions. Several common Tasks for Combat are listed in this section, as are a range of common Minor Actions.

MINOR ACTIONS

Minor Actions are activities a character can undertake that do not count as a Task, and do not require dice to be rolled. They are often taken in support of a Task, such as moving into position before an Attack is made. A character can attempt as many Minor Actions as they wish each Turn. However, only the first one comes with no cost, and each Minor Action may only be performed once each Turn. Each Minor Action taken after the first costs one Momentum (Immediate).

As noted above, each Minor Action can only be performed once per Turn. The most common Minor Actions are as follows:

FALLING

Sheer drops, steep slopes, precarious catwalks, deep chasms, and other places where falling is a possibility are one of the most common forms of hazardous terrain. As it's such a common risk, it deserves a little specific attention, which can also serve as inspiration for how to handle other hazards.

The simplest way to consider falling is simply to inflict damage — falling a long way will hurt, and maybe even cause an injury. However, this is probably the least interesting way to approach the situation, and if the group isn't in combat, it can be an inconsequential one. Further, there are a range of other possibilities that could be explored:

- The fall was mostly inconvenient, and the climb back up will slow the group down as they wait for whomever fell.

- The fall was mostly inconvenient, and the character that fell is stuck unless someone figures out a way to get them back up. That might be a Task or Challenge.

- The fall was inconvenient, and the character that fell is separated from the group and must make their own way to their destination.

- The fall was painful, and character that fell suffered a minor injury, like a twisted ankle, or some other inconvenience. This would take medical attention — a Task — once the character has been retrieved.

- The fall was dangerous, and the character that fell suffers an Injury (which cannot be avoided), needing medical attention to stabilize, and needing help to continue.

Also, it's possible to offer Success at a Cost on Tasks to avoid falling; the character may only fall part of the way, but grab onto something on the way down, or lose some important item or piece of equipment in the process. This is especially useful for falls that would otherwise be deadly, where a character would be killed by the fall (or, more properly, by the impact at the end of the fall).

- **AIM:** The character may re-roll a single d20 made on an Attack before the start of their next Turn.

- **DRAW ITEM:** The character may pick up an item within Reach, draw a weapon or other item carried on their person/stowed in their gear. If the item does not require a Task to use, it can be used immediately upon taking this action, allowing a character to draw and use the item with a single Minor Action.

- **DROP PRONE:** The character immediately drops to the ground, making himself a smaller target. While prone, a character may re-roll any number of Cover dice, and increases the Difficulty of all ranged attacks against him from Medium range or further by one step. However, melee attacks and ranged attacks at Close range gain two bonus Momentum against the character, and he cannot attempt any movement-related Tasks. A character may not Stand and Drop Prone in the same Turn.

- **INTERACT:** The character interacts with an object in the environment. Particularly complex interactions may require a Task instead.

- **MOVEMENT:** The character moves to any point within Medium range. This Minor Action cannot be taken if the character performs any movement-related Tasks. This movement is slow and careful enough to move through difficult or hazardous terrain without problem. If there are one or more enemies within Reach of the character, this action cannot be performed.

- **PREPARE:** The character prepares for, or spends time setting up, a Task. Some Tasks require this Minor Action to be taken before the Task can be attempted.

- **STAND:** If the character is prone, he may take this action to stand, losing all the benefits and disadvantages of being prone. A character may not Stand and Drop Prone in the same Turn.

TASKS

A character can attempt a single Task during each Turn, though there are a few ways that a character can attempt a second Task. Regardless of the method used, a character cannot attempt more than two Tasks in a round.

- **DETERMINATION:** A character may spend one Determination to take a second Task during a Turn. Determination may only be used in conjunction with the character's Values, as described on p. 87.

- **MOMENTUM:** A character may spend two Momentum from a successful Task to attempt a second Task; however, this second Task increases in Difficulty by one.

PERSONAL LOG

MARA HOUSE OF KANG

I wonder at the propaganda we're told about the Federation, and especially the Humans.

I've read the histories, like we all have, and I grew up as we all did, assured that the Humans were nothing but cowardly *petaQs*, with no vestige of honor or courage. But that doesn't align with what I saw on board the Federation starship. I don't believe it's what my husband saw there, either.

Oh, yes, they waste time. They don't approach things directly, they look for ways to solve a conflict other than combat, as these things should be solved. But when they do fight ... oh, when they do finally fight, they fight like angry *targs*, with strength and yes, with honor.

They asked no quarter, they gave no quarter, though this was at least in part due to the alien that was manipulating us. That entity, though, worked with what was already within us. The fierceness they showed had to come from within them. They would not have been the glorious warriors we battled otherwise. I don't think they could have been if there wasn't that instinct within them. I believe that there is more in common between us than either side wants to believe; I think Kang believes this also.

I hope to be able to study this further someday, perhaps under more controlled conditions, but it might be some time before this is possible.

LEADERSHIP: Some characters have actions that demonstrate their prowess as leaders, granting an additional Task to characters under their command. This is covered by the **Direct Task**, below.

The following Tasks are common to Combats.

ASSIST: The character performs some activity that will grant an ally an advantage. The character nominates a single ally they can communicate with, and declares how they are giving aid, including which Attribute, Discipline, and Focus (if any) they are assisting with. During the nominated ally's Task, the character assists using the chosen Attribute, Discipline, and Focus, as normal for assisting on a Task.

ATTACK: The character attacks an enemy or other viable target, and attempts to inflict harm. See **Making an Attack**, below, for a full explanation.

CREATE ADVANTAGE: The character attempts to create some favorable circumstance that benefits their side. This is a **Task with a Difficulty of 2**, using Attribute, Discipline, and Focus (if any) based on how they're trying to gain an advantage. If successful, the character creates an Advantage.

DIRECT: This action is available only to one character on each side in a position of authority, such as the commanding officer or a designated mission leader. The character nominates a single other character present, and the nominated character may immediately attempt a single Task, assisted by the commanding character. **The Direct Task may only be used once per Scene.**

GUARD: The character finds some defensible position, focusses on their surroundings, or otherwise gains additional readiness for attack. This is a **Task with a Difficulty of 0**, and success increases the Difficulty of any attacks made against the character by +1 until the start of that character's next Turn. A character may attempt to confer the benefits of this Task to an ally instead of themselves; this increases the Difficulty of this Task by one, and the benefit lasts until the start of that ally's next Turn.

PASS: The character chooses not to attempt a Task. If the character takes no Minor Actions this Turn, then the character does not count as having taken a Turn, and may act later in the Round instead.

READY: The character declares that they are waiting for a specific situation or event to occur before attempting a Task. This situation or event must be chosen when Ready is declared, as must the Task to be attempted when that situation occurs. When this triggering situation occurs, the character with the readied Task temporarily interrupts the acting character's Turn to resolve the reading Task. Once the readied Task has resolved, events continue as normal. If the triggering situation does not occur before the character's next Turn, the readied Task is lost. Characters who take a readied Task can still perform Minor Actions during their Turn as normal.

RECOVER: The character ducks behind cover, and takes a takes a moment to regain their breath, clear their mind, and ready themselves for more fighting. This is a **Difficulty 2 Fitness + Command Task** (reduce the Difficulty by 1 if the character is in Cover). Success means that the character gains one additional Resistance for each Effect rolled on Cover Dice, and regains their ability to *Avoid an Injury* (p. 176). Further, the character may regain 2 Stress per Momentum spent (Repeatable).

- **SPRINT:** The character attempts a **Difficulty 0 Fitness + Security Task**. Success means that the character moves one zone (to any point in Medium range), and one additional zone per Momentum spent (Repeatable). A character may not attempt this Task more than once per Round, and not at all if the character has performed the Movement Minor Action. Terrain and other factors may increase the Difficulty of this Task, and the Task allows Success with Cost (that is, failure means a basic success with no Momentum, but also inflicts a single Complication).

- **FIRST AID:** The character attempts to stabilize an Injured character within Reach. This is a **Daring + Medicine Task with a Difficulty of 1**; success means that the injured character is stabilized and will not die at the end of the scene, but they remain incapacitated. The character may spend 2 Momentum from this to get the patient back into the fighting right away, exactly as if they'd spent Determination to ignore the Injury.

- **OTHER TASKS:** A range of other Tasks can be performed during a combat, the limits of which are left to the discretion of the Gamemaster. Circumstances or objectives may dictate that a character attempts Tasks to repair or disable equipment during a combat (for example), or to perform other activities that don't directly relate to the fighting, and particularly desperate or dangerous situations may require overcoming Extended Tasks or a Challenge while battle rages around them.

MAKING AN ATTACK

Attacks, as the most important and the most direct of Combat Tasks, require a little more discussion than the other Combat Tasks. The process for making an attack is as follows:

1. The attacker chooses the weapon they plan to attack with. This can be a melee weapon, including making an attack with no weapon (an unarmed attack), or a ranged weapon.

2. The attacker then nominates a viable target for that weapon. A melee weapon can only be used to attack enemies and objects within Reach. A ranged weapon can be used to attack enemies that are visible to the attacker.

3. The character declares whether the attack is intended to be **non-lethal** or **lethal**. If the attack is Lethal, add a single point to the Threat pool.

4. The attacker attempts a Task, determined by the type of Attack:
   - A. For a Melee Attack, the attacker attempts a **Daring + Security Task** with a Difficulty of 1, opposed by the target's **Daring + Security** (also Difficulty 1). If the target wins the Opposed Task, then they are considered to have made a successful Attack instead.
   - B. For a Ranged Attack, the attacker attempts a **Control + Security Task** with a Difficulty of 2. This is not an Opposed Task. This Difficulty of this Task increases by +1 if there is an enemy within Reach of the attacker. The Complication range of the Attack increases by 1 if there are creatures within Reach of the target; a Complication may indicate that one of those other creatures are struck by the attack as well.

If the Attack is successful, then the attacker inflicts damage, as described in **Damage, Injury, and Recovery**, below. A successful attack does not necessarily mean an immediate direct hit on the target, but it does mean that the target has been affected in some way by the attack, even if the effect was just wearing down the target's stamina, or forcing them onto the defensive.

*Example 1: Kirk and Spock are on Sigma Iotia II, trying to move amongst the natives. Confronted with a pair of local mobsters, the two officers attempt to subdue them. Kirk's attack is to Stun, and he rolls his **Daring (11) + Security (3)**, scoring only a single success, while the mobster generates one success on his own **Daring + Security** Task. As Kirk was the aggressor here, he wins the tie, and rolls to inflict damage. Not inflicting enough damage to knock out the mobster, the fight continues, and the Mobster attacks back during his own Turn. This time, Kirk buys an extra d20 by adding to Threat, and scores enough successes to not only hit the mobster, but boost his damage so that the mobster is incapacitated.*

*Example 2: Attempting to drive the Borg from the lower decks of the Enterprise, Picard, Data, and Worf along with several other officers find themselves surrounded and under attack. Data declares that he's attacking to Kill (adding one to Threat), buys an extra d20 with Momentum, and opens fire with his phaser type-2, rolling his **Control (10)** and **Security (3)**. He generates the necessary two successes, and the Borg drone is hit. Data rolls for damage, and deals enough to incapacitate the Borg drone.*

DAMAGE, INJURY, AND RECOVERY

When a character is successfully hit by an Attack during combat, a character may become Injured. Some environmental effects also come with a risk of Injury, such as falling from great heights, being set on fire, exposure to hostile environments, industrial or engineering accidents, and a range of other hazards.

Attacks and other hazards have a **damage rating**, which will be a number of Challenge Dice, or ⚔, with the total rolled applied against the character.

Characters have a quantity of **Stress**, representing their ability to respond to peril and avoid the worst of it; Stress functions similarly to the Work track of an Extended Task. A character's normal maximum Stress is equal to the total of the character's Fitness and their Security Discipline. A character's Stress returns to its maximum value after a brief rest, which will normally happen between scenes.

Some characters will also have a quantity of **Resistance**, which reduces this total, allowing them to shrug off certain types of Attacks through protective gear, innate resilience, or circumstantial advantages like Cover. Resistance comes in two forms — static values, which normally represent armor and innate resilience, and numbers of ⋀, which represent inconsistent and circumstantial protection, such as Cover.

MELEE COMBAT OPTIONS

While risky, hand-to-hand combat is a versatile option: a successful Melee Attack can be used not only to inflict damage, but also to disengage from the fighting, and potentially more besides this. The following are the options for a character succeeding at a Melee Attack:

- **DISENGAGE:** The character may move safely away from their opponent. The character moves to any point within Close range, which is outside of their opponent's Reach.

- **GRAPPLE:** The character grabs their opponent. This requires that the character has an empty hand. This places a Grappled Complication on the target, which will prevent them from taking any action other than trying to break free (**Difficulty 2, Fitness + Security**) than attacking the grappling character (which increases in Difficulty by 1). The grappling character gains one bonus Momentum on all melee attacks against the grappled

character. The Complication is removed automatically when the grappling character chooses, or when they move out of Reach.

- **SHOVE:** The character forces their opponent away. The target is moved out of Reach, to any other point within Close range. In addition, the character rolls their normal unarmed strike damage dice, but does not inflict any damage; the damage dice are rolled only to see if the Knockdown effect triggers. If there is a hazard that a character could be pushed over, then they will only fall if they are knocked Prone as part of this attack.

- **STRIKE:** The character harms their opponent. The character rolls their normal melee damage dice, and inflicts damage normally.

Whenever a character suffers damage, follow this procedure:

1. Roll the number of ⚔ for the attack or hazard's damage rating. The total rolled is the amount of damage the attack or hazard inflicts.

2. If the target has any Resistance Dice (⚔ from Cover, etc), roll those, and add the total rolled to any static Resistance the character has. The total is the character's total Resistance for that attack.

3. Reduce the total damage rolled by one for each point of total Resistance. If there's one or more damage remaining after this reduction, the character loses one point of Stress for each point of remaining damage. The character may also suffer an Injury if one or more of the following conditions occur. If two of the following conditions occur, the character suffers two Injuries instead. Injuries are defined below.

   A. If the character suffers five or more damage from a single attack or hazard, after reduction from Resistance, the character suffers an Injury.

   B. If the character is reduced to 0 Stress by that attack or hazard, they suffer an Injury.

   C. If the character had 0 Stress before the attack or hazard, and the attack or hazard inflicts one or more damage, the character suffers an Injury.

When a character suffers an Injury, they are incapacitated, and unable to take any minor actions or attempt any Tasks for the remainder of the scene. If a character would suffer two Injuries from a single attack, resolve those Injuries one at a time (based on whichever condition occurred first).

If a character was already Injured by a non-lethal attack, then another Injury (of any kind) immediately turns that into a lethal Injury instead. If a character has already been Injured by a lethal attack, then another Injury will kill the character instantly. At the Gamemaster's discretion, a dead character may be disintegrated entirely.

Objects have Structure instead of Stress, but this functions in the same way, and most objects will have a small amount of Resistance, representing their durability. Where a character would suffer an Injury, an object will break; walls and barriers are opened, complex systems cease functioning, and so forth.

AVOIDING INJURY

Characters will not sit idly by and suffer injuries, however. Many characters — including all Player Characters — have a limited ability to fend off mortal wounds, by diving aside at the last possible moment, ducking into cover, or otherwise dodging out of the way. This kind of desperate act cannot be done indefinitely, and it always comes at a price — whether giving up on opportunities, giving the enemy an edge, or allowing some other problem to occur.

When a character suffers an Injury, they have the option of avoiding it. Avoiding an Injury prevents the Injury from happening — the character suffers no effects from being Injured, and may continue to act as normal — but it does not remove any other effects from the attack (Stress is still lost, the character may have been knocked prone, etc).

When a character chooses to *Avoid an Injury*, it costs 2 Momentum (Immediate) to do so; remember that an Immediate Momentum spend can be paid for by adding to Threat instead. A character may alternatively *Avoid an Injury* by suffering a Complication, which represents a minor injury, or some other consequence of the attack such as a bystander hit, damage to machinery nearby, etc.

However, **a character may only *Avoid an Injury* once per scene** under normal circumstances, regardless of how the character pays the price. Characters may obtain the ability to *Avoid an Injury* additional times during a scene by succeeding at a Recover Task; a successful Task allows the character to gain one additional chance to *Avoid an Injury* for that scene. A character may not stockpile extra chances to Avoid Injury — if you already have a chance to Avoid Injury, you can't gain an extra chance to use later — and an unused chance left over at the end of the scene is lost.

Example: Major Kira, in hand-to-hand combat with several Klingons, knocks out one of her attackers, but is attacked from behind by another, who stabs her with a D'k tahg knife. The Klingon has one Momentum left from his attack, and rolls 4⚔ for damage (1⚔ for his knife, and another 3⚔ for his Security skill), for a result of 1, 2, 0, and an Effect, for a total of 4 damage. Spending his Momentum to add +1 to the damage for a total of 5, the Klingon inflicts an Injury on the Major. Kira chooses to suffer a Complication to pay for avoiding the Injury, describing it as taking a minor wound. She's hurt, but she can still stand and fight for now.

INJURY AND HEALING

As noted before, an Injured character cannot attempt any Tasks, nor can they perform any Minor Actions. An Injured character is out of the fight, and can't participate in the scene any further. Injured characters cannot be targeted by any further attacks unless the attacker adds one to Threat (or spends one Threat if a Non-Player Character), though the enemy may interact with them in other ways (such as capturing them). Inflicting an Injury on an already-Injured character will kill them immediately, if the attack was lethal: there's only so much a body can take.

If the Injury came from a non-lethal attack, then this is as far as it goes. The character recovers from their Injury — though not any Complications that came from non-lethal attacks — at the start of the next scene automatically. The character regains consciousness, though they might be a little dizzy or disoriented for a few moments. Of course, they may also have been captured while unconscious, which brings a new set of problems.

If the Injury came from lethal attack, then things can only get worse. At the end of a scene in which a character was Injured by a lethal attack, then they will die unless they have received first aid. The Gamemaster is encouraged not to end scenes before characters have had a chance to attempt first aid. If the character has received first aid, they're still Injured, and unable to take Minor Actions or attempt Tasks until the Injury has been healed properly, but they're no longer in immediate danger of death.

There are two immediate ways that Injuries can be dealt with to avoid or lessen their impact.

- A character may spend a point of **Determination** to ignore the effects of an Injury for the remainder of a scene. Unlike most uses of Determination, this doesn't require that the character has a Value appropriate for the situation: this use is always available. It is also risky: the character is still Injured, but they're giving up the 'protection' of being incapacitated (i.e., enemies no longer need to spend Threat to target the Injured character), so another lethal Injury will be fatal. At the end of the scene, the character returns to suffering the effects of the Injury normally, and any Medicine Tasks made to heal the Injury later increases in Difficulty by +1.

- Another character may provide First Aid, performing the First Aid Task on a single Injured character within Reach. This is a **Daring + Medicine Task with a Difficulty of 1**; if successful, the Injured character is stabilized, and will

not die at the end of the scene. The Injured character still requires proper treatment to recover from the Injury fully.

Healing an Injury is a different matter, and cannot be done during combat. An Injured character requires treatment to remove their Injury. This requires a **Control + Medicine Task, with a Difficulty of 2**, though factors such as the tools available, the place where the treatment is being performed, and the number of injury-related Complications the patient is suffering from can all adjust this. It is, naturally, much easier to treat serious Injuries in a well-stocked sickbay than it is to provide that same treatment in a damp cave with a basic medkit. Success on this Task removes the Injury completely, as well as all related Complications.

Healing for injury-related Complications is straightforward — it takes a **Control + Medicine Task with a Difficulty of 2** to remove one such Complication, and additional Complications can be removed for two Momentum each (Repeatable).

NON-LINEAR COMBAT

The use of Advantages and Complications in conflicts can make for interesting action scenes, particularly ones where overcoming an adversary requires more than simply discharging a phaser at them. An opponent may have some innate immunity to physical attack, meaning that a direct confrontation may be completely useless, which forces the Player Characters to consider alternative methods for victory.

This can come about in a few different ways.

- Affecting the opponent with an attack is impossible, and this immunity cannot be overcome. In these situations, figuring out another way to defeat the adversary is necessary, such as using words instead of weapons in the face of mortal peril, or devising some scientific or technological method to thwart the opponent (or both). This is most applicable with godlike entities such as members of the Q Continuum, who cannot be threatened or harmed (though they can still be struck) but who can be reasoned or bargained with.

- Affecting the opponent with an attack is impossible, but this immunity can be overcome. In these situations, coming up with a way to improve upon the methods of attack (creating an appropriate Advantage) or remove the adversary's immunity (creating an appropriate Complication) is the best solution. This is most applicable with encounters with new and unfamiliar alien species, whose technology may initially seem insurmountable. It's particularly applicable with the Borg, where individual Drones adapt to different forms of attack and gain an immunity to them, but this immunity can be overcome with time and effort.

- Affecting the opponent with an attack is possible, but they cannot be defeated that way; attacks have a diminished effect, perhaps only halting the adversary's advance temporarily (the adversary loses their next Turn if one or more Injuries are inflicted). Coming up with a way to confront the opponent may require using a completely different approach, or it may require some adaptation (Advantages and Complications) to overcome their immunity. This is applicable mostly to particularly alien creatures whose nature and physiology aren't like those of humanoid species, but who aren't godlike in nature, such as the Horta, or certain space-borne macro-fauna.

These situations may still warrant the use of the combat rules for the purposes of action order and the options normally available in combat, but attacks themselves may not have any meaningful effect, requiring that characters spend their turns coming up with other approaches, ways to make the target vulnerable (Complications), or ways to make their attacks effective (Advantages).

COMBAT MOMENTUM SPENDS

Momentum is a key tactical resource during combat. When a character generates Momentum in combat, he has numerous options available to him which can help overcome his enemies, empower his allies, and bolster his own prowess.

The following table provides a few additional options available to a character when he generates one or more Momentum in combat. These are in addition to the normal uses of Momentum, and any others that Players or Gamemaster create themselves.

Under Cost, where a spend is listed with an "R", it means the spend is Repeatable. Where the spend is listed with an "I", it means the spend is Immediate. If neither note is present, then the Momentum spend may only be used once per Round at most.

TYPES OF ATTACK

Weapons and other forms attack, as well as the damage caused by hazards, have a few common traits and values that determine the specifics of how they function. The key elements of a weapon are what type of weapon it is, its damage rating, the size of the weapon, and any qualities it possesses that influence how it is used.

- **TYPE:** This will either be Melee or Ranged, determining how the weapon is used.

- **DAMAGE RATING:** This will be a number of 🅰, and possibly one or more Damage Effect that trigger when Effects are rolled. **All weapons gain additional 🅰 to their damage rating equal to the Security Discipline of the character.**

- **SIZE:** Weapons will either be one-handed (1H) or two-handed (2H). A 2H weapon can be used in one hand to make an Attack, but the Difficulty increases by +1.

- **QUALITIES:** These are additional rules, providing additional restrictions or benefits that apply to the weapon's use.

DAMAGE EFFECTS

The following abilities provide additional benefits whenever an Effect is rolled on the 🅰 (see **Challenge Dice** on p. 4). When one or more Effects are rolled, all Damage Effects that apply to that attack are triggered.

- **AREA:** The attack affects a wider area, and can affect several targets at once. The attack automatically affects any character or damageable object within Reach of the initial target, and then one additional target within Close

COMBAT MOMENTUM SPEND TABLE

MOMENTUM SPEND	COST	EFFECT
Bonus Damage	1 R	A character can increase the damage inflicted by a successful Attack, regardless of the type of Attack. Each Momentum spent adds +1 damage.
Disarm	2	One weapon held by the target is knocked away and falls to the ground within Reach.
Extra Minor Actions	1 I R	Take additional Minor Actions.
Keep the Initiative	2 I	Pass the action order to another ally instead of the enemy; may only be done once before the enemy has taken at least one action.
Penetration	1 R	The damage inflicted by the current Attack ignores two Resistance for each Momentum spent.
Re-Roll Damage	1	The Player may re-roll any number of 🅰 from the current Attack
Avoid Injury	2 I	Avoid suffering a single Injury. The cost may be paid by suffering a Complication instead. Other factors may increase the cost further. May only be used once per scene, though additional uses can be obtained.
Secondary Target	2	A second target within Reach of the Attack's target is also affected by the Attack, and suffers half the attack's damage, rounding down.
Swift Task	2	The character may attempt one additional Task, increasing the Difficulty by one over what the Task would normally require.

range of the initial target for each Effect rolled, starting with the next closest (as determined by the Gamemaster). If one or more Complications is rolled when using an Area attack, the Gamemaster may choose to use Complications to have an ally in the area affected by the attack. A target cannot be hit if it would have been more difficult to hit than the initial target.

- **INTENSE:** The attack is designed to inflict massive harm on a target, incapacitating them far more swiftly. The Cost to *Avoid an Injury* caused by an Intense weapon increases by one for each Effect rolled.

- **KNOCKDOWN:** If one or more Effects are rolled on this Attack, then the target is knocked prone. The target may resist this effect by adding a number of points to Threat equal to the number of Effects rolled (for NPCs, spend points from Threat instead of adding to Threat).

- **PIERCING X:** The Attack ignores X points of the target's total Resistance for each Effect rolled.

- **VICIOUS X:** The Attack inflicts X additional damage for each Effect rolled.

QUALITIES

The following additional qualities alter the way the weapon functions, some in positive ways, others by applying restrictions.

- **ACCURATE:** The weapon is especially precise, often incorporating additional sights that allow the user to use the weapon more accurately. If the character performs the Aim Minor Action before making an Attack with this weapon, then any number of d20s may be re-rolled, instead of the normal benefits of aiming.

- **CHARGE:** The weapon has an adaptable energy supply, allowing its potency to be scaled to different levels. If the character performs a Preparation Minor Action before Attacking with this weapon, they may add one of the following weapon Damage Effects to the Attack: Area, Intense, Piercing 2, or Vicious 1.

- **CUMBERSOME:** The weapon takes patience and precision to use effectively. The weapon cannot be used to Attack unless a Preparation Minor Action is performed during the same Turn.

- **DEADLY:** The weapon is designed to be lethal; if the character attempts to make a non-lethal attack with this weapon, the Difficulty of the attack increases by 1.

- **DEBILITATING:** Medicine Tasks to perform First Aid on characters injured by this weapon, or to heal Injuries caused by this weapon increase in Difficulty by one.

- **GRENADE :** The weapon is a throwable explosive or energetic device, normally carried in small quantities. It cannot be used to make attacks against an enemy at Long or Extreme range. A character with a grenade weapon has sufficient grenades to make three Attacks with it during a scene.

- **HIDDEN X:** The weapon is easy to conceal, or designed to be disguised as something else. When the weapon is hidden, any search of the owning character requires an Insight + Security or Reason + Security Task, with a Difficulty of X, to locate the weapon. A character may use a Minor Action to conceal a Hidden weapon.

- **INACCURATE:** The weapon is imprecise and clumsy, and very little can be done to change that. The character gains no benefit from the Aim Minor Action when making an Attack with this weapon.

- **NON-LETHAL:** The weapon is debilitating, rather than deadly; if the character attempts to make a lethal attack with this weapon, the Difficulty of the attack increases by 1.

IMPROVISED ATTACKS

From surprising a foe with a hypospray full of anesthetic, to blasting a cliff-face and causing a rock-slide, to improvising a weapon out of whatever materials are to hand, Starfleet officers may often find themselves devising creative means to incapacitate their opponents.

Improvised attacks of this sort require a little work — they're not as readily usable as proper weapons, and may need to be set up beforehand. This can be represented by an Advantage — the character creates an Advantage to represent the work they've done in advance. This might be loading up the hypospray with the right drugs and dosage, or assembling an improvised weapon, or simply identifying the place where a rock-slide could be caused.

Once the Advantage has been created, the Gamemaster should determine the Type, Damage Rating, Size, and Qualities of the attack, as well as any other limitations. The Gamemaster should also determine what combination of Attribute and Discipline is used to make the attack.

- **TYPE:** This is a simple choice between Melee and Ranged, and it should be evident based on the character's intent. A hypospray is done at Reach, so it's a melee attack, while a rock-slide is Ranged because it effects enemies at a distance.

- **DAMAGE RATING:** In most cases, a basic damage rating of 2⬧ (increased by the character's Discipline as normal) should suffice, though if the Attack is especially large or powerful (and has accompanying limitations), it may be 3⬧, 4⬧, or even more. The Gamemaster may add a single Damage Quality to the Attack as well, if desired (a hypospray may have Intense, while a rock-slide would logically have Area). If the Attack does not use Security, then the Gamemaster may allow a different Discipline to add to the Attack's damage instead (a hypospray could use Medicine, for example, while a rock-slide could use Engineering).

- **SIZE:** If the item used to make the attack is carried in one hand, then the Attack's size is 1H. If it takes two hands to make the Attack, then it's size is 2H. A hypospray is clearly a 1H item; a rock-slide may not be classified this way, but the attack is triggered by a phaser blast, so the phaser's size is what's important.

- **QUALITIES:** All Improvised Attacks have the Cumbersome quality— they're not as easy to use offensively as a proper weapon. The Gamemaster may determine that the attack has other Qualities, from the list above. For example, a hypospray may have non-lethal, while a rock-slide will be lethal.

- **OTHER LIMITATIONS:** The Gamemaster may wish to consider other limitations or restrictions for an Improvised Attack, particularly if the attack is particularly potent. This may be a limit on how often the attack can be used (a rock-slide can only really be "used" once) or lingering consequences from the attack (overloading equipment to make it explode destroys the equipment).

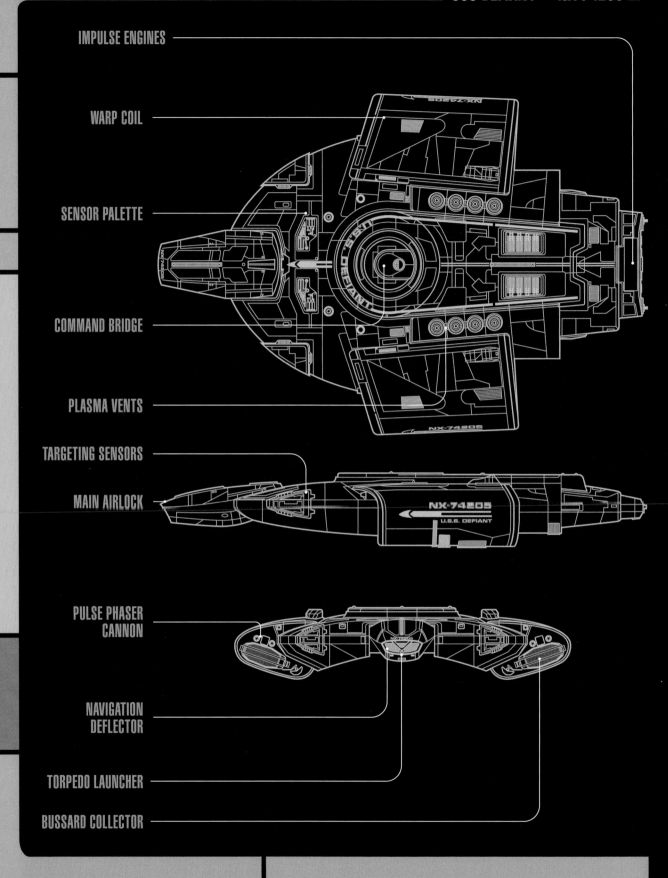

IMPULSE ENGINES

WARP COIL

SENSOR PALETTE

COMMAND BRIDGE

PLASMA VENTS

TARGETING SENSORS

MAIN AIRLOCK

PULSE PHASER
CANNON

NAVIGATION
DEFLECTOR

TORPEDO LAUNCHER

BUSSARD COLLECTOR

TECHNOLOGY AND EQUIPMENT

16180406051919151518
0809112001A

TECHNOLOGY AND EQUIPMENT

INTRODUCTION

"YOU STARFLEET TYPES ARE TOO DEPENDENT ON GADGETS AND GIZMOS. YOU LOSE YOUR NATURAL INSTINCTS FOR SURVIVAL."

— MAJOR KIRA NERYS

TECHNOLOGY: THE RIGHT TOOL FOR THE JOB

The technology of the 22nd, 23rd, and 24th centuries is miraculous, allowing people to test the limits of their individual potential, and explore the unknown frontiers of understanding. But, it must be remembered that technology itself is merely a tool, and like all tools, what matters is how it is used: not only the proficiency with which the tool is employed, but also the purpose the technology is put towards.

Technology in **Star Trek Adventures** is handled with this philosophy in mind: a device is only useful if it enables a person to achieve something useful. *Star Trek* is brimming with a dizzying array of sophisticated technologies, but these technologies are, really, only there to serve the needs of the users.

COMMON EQUIPMENT

The United Federation of Planets is a society where few things are scarce. Many common items can be replicated, or assembled from replicated components, meaning that people are seldom in situations where the right tools for a specific activity are unavailable. They might prefer real, rather than replicated, versions of those items, but that's a matter of preference rather than necessity.

In game terms, most ordinary items of equipment take the form of an Advantage, where the item's name is the name of the Advantage. Advantages are described on p. 76, but in summary, an Advantage allows the owner to attempt Tasks and activities that they would not normally be able to attempt, or reduces the Difficulty of a Task by one. A tricorder, for example, enables the character to try the things that a tricorder would logically let them do, and makes easier the things that a tricorder would assist them with.

Fundamentally, this means that most items of equipment do not have individual or specific rules. Descriptions for a wide range of common items can be found later in this chapter, to provide Players and the Gamemaster with guidance on how they work and what they are capable of.

OBTAINING EQUIPMENT

Acquiring most items is not particularly difficult. Even a small starship is large, and has many conveniently-located storage compartments containing a wide variety of commonly-used tools. Replicators can produce other items, or parts for those items, in a matter of moments.

STANDARD ISSUE

A few items are so ubiquitous amongst Starfleet personnel that the rules assume their presence as a matter of course. The items a character gains as standard issue equipment during character creation are regarded this way.

It falls to the Gamemaster to determine whether a given item's effects are assumed (and thus already included in the Difficulty of a Task, or the ability to attempt the Task in the first place), or if using the item will affect the Task further. If an item's effects are assumed, then the absence of that item will make Tasks more difficult, or even impossible, equivalent to a Complication.

A character always has access to their standard issue equipment: the items that the character is granted as part of character creation. The presence of those items is assumed, and characters don't need to say anything or take any additional action to be carrying those items. In addition, some items will be necessary for the Task ahead; the Gamemaster grants these items for free. A common example of necessary items includes environment or EV suits, without which a character simply cannot survive in certain environments.

Characters wishing to take items beyond this must retrieve them from storage, replicate them, or otherwise spend a little time to collect them.

- If the situation is not time-sensitive, or where the situation cannot get worse by spending time preparing, this can be done for free: the character states which equipment they wish to obtain, and they obtain it.

- If the situation is time-sensitive, or where the situation could deteriorate by spending additional time preparing, obtaining equipment is costly: the character states which items they wish to obtain, and then must spend Momentum to retrieve them.

Spending Momentum to obtain an item is regarded as an Opportunity Cost: time spent gathering extra items steals away potential opportunities that the crew may have, or even creates opportunities for the situation to get worse. Whenever an item has an Opportunity Cost, it will be listed as **Opportunity X**, where X is the amount of Momentum that must be spent to obtain the item. Opportunity Costs are an Immediate Momentum Spend (see p. 84) — the Momentum spent does not have to come from a successful Task, and they can be paid for from the group's saved Momentum, or by adding to Threat.

Some items — most commonly weapons, destructive equipment, or anything that signifies aggression, or preparation for battle — may have an additional or different cost. This is called an **Escalation Cost**, and it is paid by adding to Threat, to reflect potentially escalating an uncertain or dangerous situation. Items with an Escalation Cost will be listed with **Escalation X**, where X is the amount of Threat added when the item is obtained.

Items may have both Opportunity and an Escalation Costs.

CARRYING CAPACITY

Characters can only carry so much at any one time. In addition to their standard equipment, and any equipment the character is wearing, a character may carry up to two items at once, or a single large item (or two-handed weapon). A character may also wear a single suit (armor, or an EV suit). A character may try to carry more than this, but each additional item imposes a Complication ("*Overburdened*" or something similar) on the character, which will hinder the character's physical activities, and may prevent them from taking certain actions (you can't wield a weapon if your hands are full, for example).

OBTAINING MULTIPLE ITEMS

When a character obtains an item, they obtain one copy of that item. If they wish to obtain additional copies, they must pay the Opportunity Cost for each copy of that item individually.

Escalation Costs are not increased in this manner. A single Escalation Cost is paid regardless of how many of a specific item is obtained, but if a character wishes to obtain multiple different items, they must pay the Escalation Cost for each of those different items, where applicable.

PERSONNEL

While not technically equipment, the personnel aboard a starship can be used in a comparable manner — a team of engineers or scientists can help a character, making Tasks easier or allowing them to attempt activities that they could not perform alone. And, just like equipment, characters can obtain assistants like this with relative ease, so long as they're willing to take the time to gather those personnel.

A team of personnel — a half-dozen or so personnel from a single department aboard the ship — can be obtained in the same way as a piece of equipment. It serves as an Advantage in the same way as an item of equipment, with the name of the Advantage noting the primary specialty of the team (such as Science Team, or Medical Team), and has an Opportunity Cost of 1.

Security teams, which are more likely to be useful in combat as they are routinely armed, also have an Escalation Cost of 1.

Personnel used in this way are distinct from Supporting Characters — a team Advantage represents a group of assistants in a simple manner, while a Supporting Character is a distinct individual with more involved rules.

UNUSUAL EQUIPMENT

Some items cannot be obtained quickly or easily. They may require specialized components or rare materials that cannot be replicated, or the designs for them may not be readily available. In some cases, the tools necessary to achieve a specific goal may only be theoretical, requiring someone to invent the technology needed. It may even be that the characters have been isolated from their normal gear, and must spend time and effort fashioning rudimentary tools.

In these situations, obtaining the right equipment for a job is a Task, or perhaps even a Challenge or Extended Task. This is especially the case where an objective cannot be completed, or an activity cannot be attempted at all, without

the use of a specific technology: like most equipment in **Star Trek Adventures**, such an item may only be an Advantage, but gaining that Advantage is a significant hurdle that must be overcome before any progress can be made.

The Gamemaster's discretion applies with regards to unusual equipment of this sort, in determining how the characters may need to go about acquiring or constructing the equipment they need. This could take many forms — negotiating the use of technology from its creator, designing or inventing the technology to fabricate, or figuring out a way to modify existing technology — and doing so could even serve as the core objective of scenes or even entire missions.

INNOVATION

While the equipment aboard a starship, and that carried by its personnel, is capable of being used in a variety of ways, a skilled engineer knows that there's always more to a tool in the right hands. Using technology in an unusual way, or pushing the capabilities of that technology beyond its normal limits, are a common part of an engineer's role. Similarly, devising ingenious solutions to unusual problems is part of the engineer's skill-set. These creative solutions can provide options that a crew might normally not have in a difficult situation.

Innovation is about providing options for other Tasks and Challenges. Innovation allows a character to push the limits of existing technologies, often to create new or greater function for some form of technology, such as using a starship's navigational deflector to project streams of high-energy particles, or increasing the range and effectiveness of a transporter system.

As these uses aren't standard, they can come with some form of cost above and beyond the time and Tasks or Challenges needed to make the changes. These nonstandard uses of technology could draw disproportionate amounts of power, or put a strain on the system being modified, or require that some other systems be disabled to create the new effect.

A need for innovation may stem from a new scientific discovery, such as those explained in *Chapter 6: The Final Frontier*, and technically-minded characters may embark upon an innovation immediately after making a discovery using the Scientific Method guidelines (see p. 157).

This kind of innovation requires a few additional considerations, and has a few steps:

- **Design** — what purpose the innovation will play, what it is intended to do, and the way it fulfils that role.

- **Development** — the Gamemaster defines some condition for the innovation, and then the characters roll to determine the outcome.

• **Prototype** — The innovation is completed, though it will have some manner of cost or consequence.

DESIGN

The first step in any innovation is for the characters to determine what they want to do. They should think about what effect they wish it to have upon the situation, whether enabling some new option or opportunity, removing an option or opportunity from an opponent, or preventing some escalating peril.

Whatever the characters come up with at this point is the basis for everything that follows.

Once the characters have defined the intended purpose of the innovation, they need to define the way it will achieve that purpose. This doesn't have to be precise or accurate science, and should really be some manner of vaguely-intelligible "technobabble" — the most important part is that it makes some sense in story terms, and that the explanation sounds like it makes sense. The accurate science isn't a concern for the Players — the characters should all have expertise enough to know the specifics.

At this point, the characters should define what system or existing technology the innovation will build upon. The further the purpose (what the innovation wants to achieve) or scale (how big the effect is) is from the normal function of that technology, the more difficult everything else in this process will become, and some innovations may be deemed impossible if the technology and the outcome are too far apart in terms of function or scale.

DEVELOPMENT

The Gamemaster then defines a cost for the innovation. This will come in the form of some narrative requirement, an amount of time, the support of personnel, some limited resource, some physical or geographic need (being in the right place), or anything else the Gamemaster feels is appropriate. The type and scope of this cost should partly reflect the difficulty of the overall innovation, and how big a conceptual gap exists between the basic technology and the intended result, and particularly complex innovations could have multiple costs. However, the costs should be achievable — they should make the problem challenging, not impossible.

• **Time:** The innovation may be entirely possible, but it'll take a while, and in that time, the situation may grow worse or other problems may arise. The innovation won't be rendered useless by the time, but the delay can cause other issues, and will require the engineer's attention for the whole duration, preventing them getting involved in other activities.

• **Materials:** Some aspect of the innovation requires a rare, difficult-to-access, restricted, or otherwise hard-to-acquire material resource. Obtaining that resource could end up being a Task or Challenge.

• **Personnel:** The innovation requires more than one person to work on it. In the simplest terms, this might mean obtaining an engineering or scientific team to work on the innovation (see the sidebar), for however long it takes, or using a Supporting Character. It may even require another Player Character or an important NPC to be involved, taking up their time and effort towards the completion of the innovation. In more complicated situations, it might need specialist input, needing the input or even presence of a noted expert in a specific field, and this may pose difficulties if they have conditions for their assistance, possibly requiring Social Conflict to convince them to help.

• **Location:** The innovation can only be done in a specific place, due to being built upon some immobile facility or reliant on certain spatial or subspace conditions, or some other quirk of location. Gaining access to that location may be tricky, but that's not the only way that location can be a problem — it also means that it cannot be relocated in the face of an enemy attack, or that circumstances in that location pose a time limit all their own due to a shifting or perilous environment.

At this point, the characters should attempt to create a final schematic for the innovation. This will invariably be a Task, or perhaps an Extended Task if the work is perilous or time-sensitive, and it should use the Engineering Discipline. It should also use the Success at Cost rules — you can't really fail at this stage, but the result may not be quite as was hoped. The Gamemaster should set the Difficulty as normal, accounting for the costs already paid, and should also determine the number of Complications that occur on a failed Task.

The Gamemaster should keep track of the number of Complications which occur as a result, but should not define what they are immediately: they apply in the next stage.

PROTOTYPE

A prototype of the innovation has been created and assembled, and is ready to be used for its intended purpose. It serves as two Advantages for whatever purpose the device was designed to fulfill, and it can be used as soon as the characters need it. However, nothing created in this way is perfect — the character is using technology in ways outside the normal design parameters, often while under pressure and with limited resources. This is a very different experience to designing a system from scratch under laboratory conditions, and nothing ever goes entirely to plan here. There are invariably some issues that make the innovation less convenient to use, and this is the point where the Gamemaster determines what they are and reveals them to the characters.

The drawbacks are up to the Gamemaster to determine, and the number and severity of these drawbacks should be based on the complexity of the innovation, as well as on the number of Complications generated on the Task or Challenge during the previous stage. Examples include:

- **Extremely large and bulky:** The innovation's final form is big, often to a point where moving it into position becomes difficult. This should require a Task to get the innovation into position before it can be used. The more Complications put towards this drawback, the more difficult the Task.

- **Massive power requirements:** The innovation needs vast quantities of energy to function, and may need to be hooked up to powerful reactors such as a starship's warp core. This could hinder the function of other devices drawing from the same power source — you can't use the warp drive if power from the warp core is being diverted to some innovative-but-power-hungry-creation. Using the innovation should require the expenditure of at least one point of Power from some source. The more Complications put towards this drawback, the more Power the innovation requires.

- **Distinctive energy signature:** The innovation's output products an obvious and easy-to-detect signature that can potentially draw unwanted attention or make stealth impossible. The more Complications put towards this drawback, the more potent the signature and the easier it is to detect.

- **Burn out:** The innovation puts a lot of strain on the systems being used. The innovation can only be used a limited number of times, and in the process, it causes damage to the systems it was built upon. This may mean that the process of using the innovation may require repairs to restore the underlying technologies after the innovation has been used. The more Complications put towards this drawback, the more quickly the system burns out, allowing fewer uses.

- **Mutually exclusive:** The innovation so thoroughly alters the normal function of the underlying technology that it will take time and effort to restore the system to its normal working state after use. This may not require a Task (or require a Difficulty 0 Task), but it will take time, and prevent characters from making use of the technology's normal function until it has been restored. The more Complications put towards this drawback, the more difficult and/or time-consuming it is to restore the system's normal function.

TECHNOLOGY AND EQUIPMENT

ADVANCED TECHNOLOGY

At times, the normal rules for equipment and technology may not be entirely satisfactory. This might be because the technology involved is especially complex or unusual, because it varies from the norm in some notable way, or because it is specialized or especially suited to a certain activity.

This section provides guidance for the Gamemaster, but it is presented here so that Players can see the possibilities and suggest instances where they may be relevant.

GENERATIONS OF TECHNOLOGY

Most of the well-known cultures found in the Alpha and Beta Quadrants have travelled the stars for centuries, and have a long history of both conflict and cooperation, and,

while many staples of modern technology — warp drive, transporters, directed energy weapons — have existed for generations, the sophistication of those technologies has increased over time as new generations have developed and advanced those technologies.

During a normal mission, characters will mostly have access to the technologies of their era: their phasers, tricorders, communicators, and their ship will all use contemporary technology. However, some situations — including the ever-problematic time travel — can bring characters into contact with technology decades or even centuries more advanced, or less advanced, than the devices they are accustomed to.

MORE ADVANCED

Technology from the future is typically far more sophisticated and capable than the devices that preceded it. Similarly, some advanced alien cultures may have technology that appears miraculous even to the most sophisticated devices that the Federation has ever created. This might take a few different forms:

- **Unprecedented Technology:** The device or technology has no equivalent, and achieves something that familiar technology cannot. An iconic example of this would be the mobile holoemitter used by *Voyager*'s Doctor, derived from 29th century technology. This can be achieved with an Advantage, as with most devices — what differs is what the Advantage represents and enables, which is something beyond the reach of the technologies that the characters normally interact with. Where it differs is that this technology may not be easy to reproduce, or it may be difficult or even impossible to repair if damaged.

- **Later Generation Technology:** The device or technology is of a familiar type, but several decades, or even centuries, ahead of familiar examples. This can easily be handled by applying one or more extra Advantages onto the device: it does the same thing as contemporary versions, but better, faster, and more effectively, as well as having features and capabilities that may only be theoretical for a contemporary version. A good example of this would be the tricorders of the 29th century's Starfleet, which can detect and monitor things which a 24th century tricorder cannot, and which is a more effective device overall. Again, this additional advanced functionality may make the device harder, or even impossible to recreate, or it may mean that it cannot be repaired if it malfunctions or suffers damage.

- **Unfamiliar Designs:** A possible consequence of handling advanced technology is that it is unfamiliar — it may have components or design elements that may be partly or entirely unrecognizable to those trying to use or examine the device. This could serve as a Complication, increasing the Difficulty of, or making impossible, certain Tasks involving the device, but that may run counter to the benefits of the technology, and make an advanced device seem less 'special'. Instead, consider increasing the Complication Range of Tasks involving the device: making it more likely that something will go wrong.

LESS ADVANCED

Technology from the past, or from cultures whose technology has not yet reached the level of the major powers of the Alpha and Beta Quadrants, is not commonly used, simply because it is less effective and less functional than the devices that Starfleet officers will normally have access to. However, circumstances may conspire to deprive characters of their customary tools, requiring them to rely on devices that are less sophisticated.

- **Last Generation Technology:** The device or technology is a century or two out of date, or is otherwise equivalent to technology used earlier in Federation history, but it's still the technology of a culture capable of interstellar travel. It might be less refined, or less accurate, less sophisticated, or have a more limited range of functions than its modern counterparts. This can be mostly represented by the Gamemaster applying the device's Advantage in a more limited fashion, but it could also be handled by imposing an increase to the Complication Range of any Tasks involving the device — increase the Complication Range by 1 for each step the Difficulty of the Task is above 1 (so a Difficulty 4 Task would increase the Complication Range by 3), as the more challenging uses are often those that older devices struggle to perform.

- **Pre-Warp Technology:** The technology of pre-warp cultures — and of Federation worlds before they invented the warp drive — covers a broad range of possibilities, but in this context, it applies to technologies roughly equivalent to those of Earth during the 18th, 19th, 20th, and 21st centuries. The likes of tricorders, post-warp computing, subspace radio, and similar advanced devices don't have any direct counterparts, and creating anything more advanced than the "background" level of technology will typically require some manner of invention (using the innovation rules, on p. 185).

- **Primitive Technology:** Pre-industrial technology is even more limited than that of industrialized pre-warp cultures. In these situations, characters may need to work hard to even produce tools equivalent to that of later centuries, turning simple raw materials into basic tools. This may require Tasks, or it may require something more involved — Challenges, Extended Tasks, or use of the Innovation rules.

STARFLEET TECHNOLOGY IN DIFFERENT ERAS

Technology used by Starfleet has varied in sophistication across the centuries, with starship crews often field-testing the latest technologies.

ENTERPRISE ERA

In the 2150s and 2160s, the United Earth Starfleet made use of cutting-edge technology. The *NX* class was the first Human vessel to be able to travel at warp 5. The introduction of phase cannons and photonic torpedoes — predecessors to the phasers and photon torpedoes used in later centuries — gave Starfleet vessels like the *Enterprise* and *Columbia* an edge. However, they had not yet introduced deflector shields, relying instead on polarization of the ship's hull plating to repel fire. Similarly, early Starfleet vessels made use of cable grapplers before the introduction of tractor beams. The *Enterprise* was also the first vessel to be equipped with a transporter capable of transporting people, rather than just cargo.

When it comes to personnel, the phase pistol and particle rifle are the standard weaponry of the time, preceding the introduction of phasers. Early scanners — similar to the more advanced tricorders that would replace them — aid Starfleet officers in studying phenomena and analyzing problems. The universal translator was also invented in this time, but it was experimental at first; the linguacode translation matrix developed by noted exo-linguist Hoshi Sato made the universal translator much more reliable. When it comes to sustaining the crew on a long journey, protein resequencing allowed a starship to synthesize a range of different foods.

ORIGINAL SERIES ERA

A century after the founding of the United Federation of Planets, many of the technologies that were new at that time had become commonplace. Starships capable of achieving warp 8 were Starfleet's ships of the line, and phasers, photon torpedoes, deflector shields, and tractor beams are all part of a ship's standard complement of tools. Transporters capable of transporting people are ubiquitous and personnel transport to and from a planetary surface more often than they use a shuttle.

Personnel carry phasers and tricorders regularly, and the universal translator is much more compact, with versions built into communicators. Food synthesizers allow the near-instantaneous production of a wide range of foods on command.

NEXT GENERATION ERA

By the 24th century, most of the technologies commonplace a hundred years earlier had been refined further. The biggest differences to technology in that time is the introduction of interactive holography and the widespread adoption of replicators.

Holography, specifically aboard holodecks and holosuites, allow realistic simulations of environments, situations, and even people to be created for training, study, or recreation. As the technology grows more advanced, the creation of holographic entities such as the Emergency Medical Hologram becomes possible, and holoemitters can simulate matter on a molecular level, producing near-perfect simulacra of people and places.

Replicators — as an outgrowth of transporter technology — are a revolutionary advantage, allowing inanimate objects to be recreated instantly, accurate to a molecular level. This allows food to be created, but also a great many other common items, and those same items can be recycled by placing them back into the replicator and dematerialized. Replicators are also used to provide life support: dematerializing surplus carbon dioxide and replacing it with oxygen to maintain a breathable atmosphere, and replicating all the water needed aboard ships and starbases, while dematerializing waste. The most sophisticated replicators — operating at the same quantum level as personnel transporters — can even replicate tissue for organ transplants, blood transfusions, and other medical purposes, though this takes much more power and computing power.

TECHNOLOGY AND EQUIPMENT
WEAPONS, GEAR, AND OTHER ITEMS

This section provides descriptions of a range of common items and technologies in use by Starfleet personnel and other cultures in the Alpha and Beta Quadrants. These descriptions both identify what the item is, and are designed to serve as guidance for how an item benefits the user, and what those items can be used for, which is valuable when adjudicating the way that an item's Advantage affects a Task.

COMBAT EQUIPMENT

Weapons, protective gear, and other items used in combat. These have additional rules above and beyond simply being treated as an Advantage.

WEAPONS

While peace is Starfleet's goal, a need for self-defense against aggressors is necessary. Starfleet thus makes use of several different types of weapon.

Weapons and other forms of attack, as well as the damage caused by hazards, have a few common traits and values that determine the specifics of how they function. The key elements of a weapon are what type of weapon it is, its damage rating, the size of the weapon, and any Qualities it possesses that influence how it is used.

- **Type:** Melee or Ranged, showing how the weapon is used.

- **Damage Rating:** A number of $\blacktriangle$, and possibly one or more Damage Effect that trigger when Effects are rolled. **All weapons gain additional $\blacktriangle$ to their damage rating equal to the Security Discipline of the character.**

- **Size:** Weapons will either be one-handed (1H) or two-handed (2H). A 2H weapon can be used in one hand to make an attack, but the Difficulty increases by +1.

- **Qualities:** These are additional rules, providing additional restrictions or benefits that apply to the weapon's use.

DAMAGE EFFECTS

The following abilities provide additional benefits whenever an Effect is rolled on the $\blacktriangle$ (see Challenge Dice on p. 73). Whether one or more Effects are rolled, all Damage Effects that apply to that attack are always triggered.

- **Area:** The attack affects a wider area, and can affect several targets at once. The attack automatically affects any character or damageable object within Reach of the initial target, and then one additional target within Close range of the initial target for each Effect rolled, starting with the next closest (as determined by the Gamemaster). If one or more Complications is rolled when using an Area attack, the Gamemaster may choose to use Complications to have an ally in the area affected by the attack. A target cannot be hit if it would have been more difficult to hit than the initial target.

- **Intense:** The attack is designed to inflict massive harm on a target, incapacitating them far more swiftly. The Cost to *Avoid an Injury* (p. 176) caused by an Intense weapon (p. 179) increases by one for each Effect rolled.

- **Knockdown:** If one or more Effects are rolled on this attack, then the target is knocked prone. The target may resist this effect by adding a number of points to Threat equal to the number of Effects rolled (NPCs spend points from Threat instead of adding to Threat).

- **Piercing X:** The attack ignores X points of the target's total Resistance for each Effect rolled.

- **Vicious X:** The attack inflicts X additional damage for each Effect rolled.

QUALITIES

The following additional qualities alter the way the weapon functions, some in positive ways, others by applying restrictions.

- **Accurate:** The weapon is especially precise, often incorporating additional sights that allow the user to use the weapon more accurately. If the character performs the Aim Minor Action before making an attack with this weapon, then any number of d20s may be re-rolled, instead of the normal benefits of aiming.

Charge: The weapon has an adaptable energy supply, allowing its potency to be scaled to various levels. If the character performs a Prepare Minor Action before attacking with this weapon, they may add one of the following weapon Damage Effects to the attack: Area, Intense, Piercing 2, or Vicious 1.

Cumbersome: The weapon takes patience and precision to use effectively. The weapon cannot be used to attack unless a Prepare Minor Action is performed during the same Turn.

Deadly: The weapon is designed to be lethal; if the character attempts to make a non-lethal attack with this weapon, the Difficulty of the attack increases by 1.

Debilitating: Medicine Tasks to perform First Aid on characters injured by this weapon, or to heal Injuries caused by this weapon, increase in Difficulty by one.

Grenade: The weapon is a throwable explosive or energetic device, normally carried in small quantities. It cannot be used to make attacks against an enemy at Long or Extreme range. A character with a Grenade weapon has sufficient grenades to make three attacks with it during a scene.

Hidden X: The weapon is easy to conceal, or designed to be disguised as something else. When the weapon is hidden, any search of the owning character requires an **Insight + Security or Reason + Security** Task, with a Difficulty of X, to locate the weapon. A character may use a Minor Action to conceal a Hidden weapon,

Inaccurate: The weapon is imprecise and clumsy, and very little can be done to change that. The character gains no benefit from the Aim Minor Action when making an attack with this weapon.

Non-lethal: The weapon is debilitating, rather than deadly; if the character attempts to make a lethal attack with this weapon, the Difficulty of the attack increases by 1.

MELEE WEAPONS

Nearly every sentient species at one time in their history has developed weapons capable of breaking limbs or cutting flesh. Some of these weapons were culturally important to those species and have remained in use even after that culture entered the wider interstellar culture.

While not really equipment, every character has the means to make an **unarmed attack**, striking with fists, feet, knees, elbows, head, or otherwise using brute force without a weapon. Countless martial arts, such as Klingon *mok'bara*, Vulcan *suus mahna*, and Human styles like boxing or *aikido*, exist to allow individuals to hone their ability to disable foes without weapons.

Bladed weapons such as the **knife** or **dagger** continue to be useful as tools or for close combat situations. While projectile weapons and later energy weapons have surpassed the destructive power of hand weapons, developments over the centuries in materials science have given these weapons continued use in nearly every service as backup weapons or as tools that can be used in lieu of more specialist equipment.

WEAPONS TABLE

NAME	TYPE	DAMAGE RATING	SIZE	QUALITIES	COST
Unarmed Strike	Melee	1▲ Knockdown	1H	Non-lethal	–
Knife/Dagger	Melee	1▲ Vicious 1	1H	Deadly, Hidden 1	Opportunity 1
Blade (Sword, *Mek'leth*, etc)	Melee	2▲ Vicious 1	1H	–	Opportunity 1
Heavy Blade (*Bat'leth*, *Kar'takin*, *Lirpa*)	Melee	3▲ Vicious 1	2H	–	Opportunity 1, Escalation 1
Bludgeon	Melee	2▲ Knockdown	1H	–	Opportunity 1
Phaser Type-1	Ranged	2▲	1H	Charge, Hidden 1	Standard Issue
Phaser Type-2	Ranged	3▲	1H	Charge	Standard Issue
Phaser Type-3 (Phaser Rifle)	Ranged	4▲	2H	Accurate, Charge	Opportunity 1, Escalation 2
Pulse Grenade	Ranged	4▲ Area	1H	Charge, Grenade	Opportunity 1, Escalation 2
Andorian Plasma Rifle	Ranged	4▲ Intense	2H	Accurate, Deadly	Not Available
Phase Pistol	Ranged	3▲	1H	–	Standard Issue
Particle Rifle	Ranged	4▲	2H	Accurate	Standard Issue
Disruptor Pistol	Ranged	3▲ Vicious 1	1H	–	Not Available
Disruptor Rifle	Ranged	4▲ Vicious 1	2H	Accurate	Not Available
Jem'Hadar Plasma Pistol	Ranged	3▲ Vicious 1	1H	Debilitating	Not Available
Jem'Hadar Plasma Rifle	Ranged	4▲ Vicious 1	2H	Accurate, Debilitating	Not Available

- Larger **blades** such as the Klingon *mek'leth* or various forms of sword, provide more of a symbolic use, but still are used ritually, in sports, or even in real combat, depending on the skill and inclination of the individual.

- **Heavy blades** like the *bat'leth*, *kar'takin*, and the Vulcan *lirpa* only see use in heavily ritualized combat or in very limited situations where hand-to-hand combat is almost assured.

KLINGON BAT'LETH

SCHEMATICS

- Bludgeons — ranging from improvised blunt objects, to batons, cudgels, and maces — are a useful way of fending off aggressors, or disabling enemies. This profile can also be used for any two-handed ranged weapon, wielded as an impromptu club.

PHASERS

Developed in the mid-22nd century, the hand phaser was an outgrowth from research into focused particle streams for higher efficiency warp cores. Primitive phaser systems, such as the phase pistol and ship mounted phase cannon were refined into true phaser systems by the 23rd century. Like ship mounted phasers, hand phasers use a phased and modulated particle beam that can transmit incredible amounts of energy onto a target depending on the setting of the device and the frequency of the power modulation. Starfleet hand phasers have multiple distinct settings ranging from heating an object or causing light burns to a target, stunning a life-form through 'shorting out' its central nervous system, up to cutting through a target or entirely disintegrating it. All hand phasers use a high-energy density power cell as their power source, and are split into three categories that are dependent on the power storage capabilities of the device. At their lowest settings, all phasers are capable of long term use, but at their highest settings a phaser type-1, the smallest rated as combat effective by Starfleet, may only have enough energy stored for a few seconds of use compared to the phaser type-3, the 'phaser rifle', that may allow for a full minute or more of discharge at the highest settings before the batteries require changing or recharge. 23rd century hand phasers typically only used a single particle emitter on each device, but by the 24th century multiple emitters were in widespread use allowing for redundancy and the weapons targeting systems to get ranges to a target and produce constructive interference of the phased particle streams in a target allowing for a higher destructive potential at lower power emission settings.

- **Phaser Type-1** is the smallest design of hand phaser, a tiny device a few centimeters long, which is the most widely-used form of phaser distributed to personnel for self-defense.

- **Phaser Type-2** refers to the larger form of hand phaser, carried by security personnel and Starfleet officers going into dangerous environments. Versions used in the 23rd century are a pistol grip attachment that can be fitted to a phaser type-1, with a secondary power cell to increase output. 24th century hand phasers are a distinct design, with a curved ergonomic grip.

- **Phaser Type-3**, or phaser rifles, are higher-powered weapons designed for hazardous situations and combat. In addition to a larger power supply, they have numerous targeting and beam-focusing systems that make them more accurate. They are only issued to properly-trained personnel, and only when necessary.

- **Pulse Grenades** work on a similar principle to hand phasers. The user selects a setting and a countdown timer. When the timer reaches zero, the grenade discharges its power cell at once in all directions. After discharge, the grenade's components burn out,

PHASERS

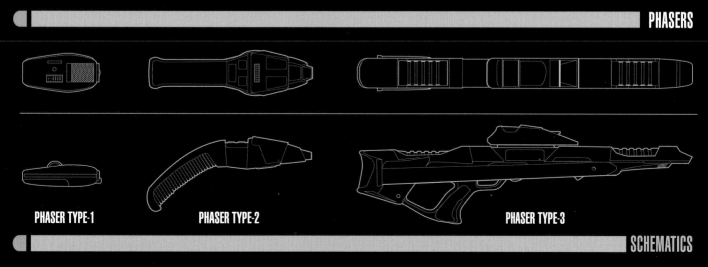

PHASER TYPE-1   PHASER TYPE-2   PHASER TYPE-3

SCHEMATICS

rendering them inert to prevent them being reused. Pulse grenades cover a number of similar technologies used throughout Starfleet's history — from the stun grenades used by United Earth MACO forces, to photon grenades employed in the 24th century.

ENTERPRISE ERA

Phase pistols are standard issue for Starfleet Player Characters in *Enterprise*-era games, while particle rifles are standard issue for MACO Player Characters in that era. Characters from that era cannot take phasers.

EARLY, AND PRE-FEDERATION ENERGY WEAPONS

There are many types of hand weapons that Starfleet crews can encounter traveling across the Federation, but the two most typically seen civilian weapons are derived from the **Andorian plasma rifle** and the 21st and early 22nd century Earth particle rifle. Andorian plasma rifles use similar principles to phasers used by Starfleet with a particle beam as the primary effect. What is different is the particle beam is augmented by an encapsulated plasma discharge that always causes thermal damage to a target. This means that Andorian style plasma rifles are unable to cause a stun effect, and at best can knock a humanoid unconscious through pain. **Particle rifles** and **phase pistols** were early forms of directed energy weapon used before the development of phasers. The most advanced designs of particle rifle were those produced for United Earth MACO forces in the 22nd century, while phase pistols were introduced in 2151 to replace the EM-33 plasma pistol.

ALIEN ENERGY WEAPONS

Like hand phasers, disruptor and plasma weapons typically use a high-density power cell to provide power, or an energy source of similar capacity. Pistols can be held in a single hand, while rifles tend to need the use of two hands to balance and aim the larger device. These weapons are typically less versatile than phasers, but inflict significantly more damage; their brutal simplicity makes them more appealing to those who seek a weapon more than a tool.

- **Disruptor** weapons rely on extremely high energy particle discharges that will burn or boil targets at the lowest settings, and can disintegrate a target if enough energy is applied.

- The **plasma** weapons used by the Dominion's Jem'Hadar soldiers cause severe burns and death through thermal shock, and incorporate an anticoagulant effect that makes injuries inflicted by them far harder to treat.

ARMOR AND PROTECTIVE GEAR

While not a standard part of Starfleet duty uniforms, many cultures make use of metal, ceramic, or other dense materials to provide additional protection from attacks and hazards. In some extreme cases, personal force field projectors are used to protect against severe danger, though these are not particularly efficient.

Armor provides a character with Resistance, which reduces the amount of damage a character suffers from attacks and hazards. A character may only wear a single form of protective gear. Many NPCs wear armored uniforms, particularly those from militaristic cultures like the Klingons and Cardassians.

BODY ARMOR

Body Armor has been issued periodically to Starfleet security at various times in Starfleet's history. In the late 23rd century, it took the form of a bulky vest and helmet, designed to absorb and disperse impacts and energy attacks. By the 24th century, ablative body armor is used mainly by personnel engaged in protracted conflict.

ENVIRONMENT SUITS

Environment Suits or EV Suits are normally used for extra vehicular activities — such as moving in hard vacuum. They provide minimal physical protection, mainly due to being made of tough materials. These suits are issued as and when a mission requires — the Opportunity Cost may be ignored if the mission takes place in an environment that would be deadly without protection. The suits contain magnetic boots, a supply of breathable atmosphere, radiation shielding, and a communications relay more powerful than a normal personal communicator.

PERSONAL FORCE FIELDS

These personal shields were sometimes issued to security and combat personnel, though the power requirements of such devices mean they have limited use in protracted fighting. A character with a personal force field gains the listed Resistance, but must roll 1▲ after each time they are hit by an attack; if an Effect is rolled, the force field loses power for the rest of the scene, and no longer provides Resistance.

ARMOR TABLE

NAME	RESISTANCE	COST
Body Armor	2	Opportunity 1 Escalation 1
Environment Suit	1	Opportunity 2
Personal Force Field	4	Opportunity 1 Escalation 2

TOOLS AND PORTABLE ITEMS

TRICORDERS

'Tricorder' is the label given to a class of versatile devices in use across the Federation. Their name is derived from the original early 22nd century name for the device, 'Tri-function Recorder,' able to sense, record, and analyze data from a variety of sensors attached to the device, dependent on the primary use. During the 23rd century there were two primary versions of the Starfleet tricorder (science and medical), and a single highly specialized version (the psychotricorder). The psychotricorder was primarily used by psychologists and law enforcement agencies as a device to more accurately determine a humanoid's behavioral and emotional state, aiding in helping physicians provide accurate diagnoses of trauma and useful treatments. Law enforcement would use these devices as a way to determine truthfulness of statements or in aiding officers in finding mentally disturbed individuals. The more common medical and science tricorders only differed in the range and scope of their sensors and ability to use tricorder attachments. The medical tricorder typically had fewer sensors and a shorter range as a tradeoff for higher resolution scans more specialized towards biological functions and a greater capacity for specialist attachments. The science tricorder had a large multi-discipline database and a built in sub-space uplink that could connect to nearby Starfleet vessels for main computer access when needed. By the 24th century tricorders were unified into a single design as data storage and sensor design was further miniaturized by the development of isolinear computing technologies, even including more specialist analysis capabilities for engineering teams. Without a tricorder, Starfleet crewmembers would have difficulty diagnosing medical ailments, engineering glitches, or scientific curiosities.

Tricorders are standard issue, and do not have a Cost.

ENGINEERING DEVICES

Chronometer (Opportunity 1): The chronometer is a useful device that has far more functionality than a clock, as its name suggests. A chronometer records the passing of time in the universe outside of the immediate vicinity of the device. This is accomplished by monitoring hundreds of pulsars and standing gravity waves in subspace with accuracy down to nearly Planck-time scales. Comparison of a chronometer and a local 'ships clock' is what allows crews to monitor for relativistic effects and any strange occurrences in space-time. Hand-held chronometers allow for a more localized monitoring of space-time in a smaller more humanoid sized space around the user rather than ship-mounted chronometers.

Engineering Multi-Tool/Engineering Toolkit (Standard Issue for Engineers, Opportunity 1 otherwise): Beginning with the introduction of duotronic computing in the mid-23rd century, analysis of engineering faults in systems controlled by electronics became more difficult due to the high-energy transfer rates and EM interference. The engineering multi-tool was developed and acted as a tricorder like device to detect and diagnose system faults and could be used in a general role as a multi-purpose tool to repair and maintain systems. With the advent of isolinear systems, the multi-tool was rendered obsolete and many of the uses of the device were supplanted by the tricorder, but tools were still needed to maintain and repair damaged equipment, so the Starfleet engineering tool-kit was introduced to provide nearly every tool a damage control or engineering team may need outside of unusual circumstances.

Mass Spectrometer (Opportunity 1): A mass spectrometer is a device that can take a sample of material, break it down, and provide an incredible amount of detail about the matter making it up. While tricorders can provide data similar to this, the mass spectrometers found in engineering sections on starships and specialist devices dedicated to this task are able to provide details on a sample that may be too broad to detect with other devices, such as: getting the accurate age of a sample to within months from carbon dating or a couple of years with other radio-isotope dating techniques, elemental quantities to the parts per quadrillion, and even breakdown of sub-atomic particle deviations.

Plasma Torch (Opportunity 1): Plasma torches are high energy cutting tools powered by an integral energy cell and a compressed helium matter source. The helium is super-heated and ionized before being focused by a magnetic field into a microscopic beam, allowing the beam to cut through all but the strongest of materials. Dependent on availability, other gases and energy sources are used with the same capabilities.

Portable Electron Microscope (Opportunity 1): The portable electron microscope is a name used for any electronic device capable of scanning and imaging objects as small as atomic nuclei, regardless of the sub-atomic particle used. Unlike their larger counter parts, the portable scope is small enough to be carried by an away team member trained in its use and doesn't have the resolution or power to image and analyze sub-atomic particles and quantum structures. These devices are commonly connected to tricorders used by the engineering department to help find structural flaws in bulkheads and hull plating.

MEDICAL DEVICES

If a character is in sickbay at the time a specific medical device is required, reduce the Opportunity Cost by 1, to a minimum of 0. A few of the items listed below are considered part of a standard medkit, which is standard issue for all Starfleet medical personnel. A medkit has a Cost of Opportunity 1 for non-medical personnel.

Monitoring Device (Opportunity 1): The heartbeat reader is a small device that can connect to a medical tricorder or a sick bay bio-bed. This device, placed on the patient, is able to scan a life-form, determine the function of a single vital organ or biological function, and what the physiology of the life-form suggests are normal readings for that organ or function.

Tri-laser Connector (Part of Medkit): Used to heal and repair damaged neurons and nerve tissue, the tri-laser connector uses laser light to stimulate a projected stream of stem cells to specialize into predetermined neural pathways. With a detailed enough scan of a patient, such as one provided by transporter systems, the tri-laser connector is able to repair and reconstruct damaged brain tissue with little to no detectable differences in the patient's cognitive functions if undertaken within days of the last scan.

Anabolic Protoplaser/Dermal Regenerator (Part of Medkit): A common tool in first aid kits on Starfleet vessels, the dermal regenerator allows a physician to stimulate an injured humanoids natural healing process to accelerate the production of new skin cells and connective tissue, effectively healing superficial wounds.

Emergency Surgical Kit (Opportunity 1): The standard Starfleet emergency surgical kit provides single use medical supplies capable of allowing a trained physician the means to perform complex surgical procedures in the field at the expense of equipment durability. The casing contains a built-in PADD that gives readouts on basic biological functions important to physicians such as blood pressure, heartbeat, temperature, etc. The display will also walk even unskilled civilians through steps to triage injured humanoids. An emergency surgical kit is a single-use item, its resources expended after use.

Laser Scalpel (Part of Medkit): Laser scalpels, also known as exoscalpels, are widely used devices that have replaced stainless steel scalpels in hospitals and sickbays across the Federation. The laser scalpel uses a thin low-power laser beam to cleanly cut through tissue to a predetermined depth. The cut is also cleaned and cauterized by the scalpel, allowing dermal regenerators and auto-sutures to more effectively work after the surgery is complete and the patient is healing.

Hypospray (Part of Medkit): In use since before the Eugenics Wars on Earth in the 1990s, hypospray devices provide a high speed and efficient means to deliver drugs that would normally have to be given by hypodermic needle or IV drip. Hyposprays in the 23rd century and beyond have improved far beyond those early models and are able to deliver drugs in a much more efficient way to the patient.

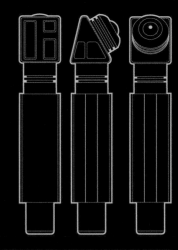

Detronal Scanner (Opportunity 1): The advances in molecular and atomic scanning as well as computing power allowed the development of hand-held genetic analysis devices such as the detronal scanner. This device allows a trained physician to scan the skin and deeper layers of tissue of a humanoid and perform an analysis of the patient's genome. If the patient is of a known and previously studied species, the device can also provide analysis of any genetic drift or damage due to external sources.

Neurocortical Monitor (Opportunity 1): The neurocortical monitor is worn on a humanoids neck and resembles a small disc with pulsing lights. Before the invention of the neurocortical monitor, long-term data collection and monitoring of a patient exhibiting signs of neurological damage or trauma had to be undertaken in controlled environments in sickbays and major hospitals. The introduction of the monitor allowed doctors to collect information about the patient's neurological condition in real time in everyday circumstances where certain symptoms may present more often. Use of the neurocortical monitor allows a patient undergoing observation to continue to perform normal duties, lack of this device means the patient must remain isolated in sick bay and unable to perform any normal ship functions.

CYBERNETICS

These items have no Cost; rather, they are permanent additions to the character, normally connected to a Trait that reflects some disability the character suffers from.

Artificial Organs: Artificial organs have been in use since the mid-20th century. Advances in neuron meshing and cybernetics have improved these devices since their introduction and have made them virtually identical in capability to biological ones. The most common internal organs in humanoids to be replaced are hearts and lungs, nearly always because of severe trauma. Characters who need an artificial organ and do not possess them will die within minutes to days depending on the organ and are typically kept on life support while one is built. A character may have an artificial organ if they have been severely injured in the past.

Prosthesis: Like artificial organs, prosthetic limbs have been in use since the middle of the 20th century, and advances in technology mean that they function identically to the limbs they replace. Arms and legs lost due to trauma can be replaced with relatively little difficulty. Characters who are lacking their prosthetic may find their physical activities are impaired, making some Tasks more difficult, and others impossible.

Artificial Sensory Organs (ASO): Using cutting edge neurological reconditioning and isolinear networks overlaid into a patient's sensory cortex, artificial sensory organs can replace damaged or destroyed senses. This can mean the blind can see, the deaf can hear, and even nerve damaged fingers can once again feel. Depending on when exactly the ASO is built (from about 2350 onwards) the technology can look highly artificial or barely noticeable at all. This technology is highly individual and includes sensors and other devices a person may find useful in their life. It takes years to learn to control the other functions besides the basic sensory input. A Player whose character has an artificial sensory organ should work with the Gamemaster to determine the functionality, look, and usefulness in certain situations of the ASO. It is recommended that while these devices can be advantageous (such as artificial eyes being able to scan across the entire EM spectrum, or touch sensors being able to analyze a surfaces' composition), there are potential disadvantages too, such as needing to charge the device periodically, headaches due to data transfer, or the risk of the device being lost or damaged.

OTHER EQUIPMENT

Anti-grav (Opportunity 1): Anti-gravs are a range of different devices designed to reduce or negate the weight of any object to which they're attached, allowing heavy objects to be moved easily. Multiple anti-gravs are used to provide lift for vehicles like hovercars.

Anti-grav Sled (Opportunity 2): The anti-grav sled resembles a small cart without wheels. On the bottom of the device there are multiple graviton emitters that counter the local gravity field, effectively making the sled and any items placed on it nearly weightless, though not massless. In a natural gravity field the sled is less efficient, while on a vessel that has gravity plating, the sled interacts with the ships computer to lower the artificial gravity around the sled, allowing more mass to be moved and for a longer operational timespan. Versions which double as stretchers for transporting injured personnel are often used in sickbays and hospitals.

Beacons (Opportunity 1): Like most battery powered light sources dating back to the 20th century, the standard issue Starfleet beacon has a wider range of functions including

THE COST OF IMPLANTS

The side effects of having a Visual Instrument and Sensory Organ Replacement (VISOR) are well documented, these can include headaches, migraines, localized and often debilitating pain, nausea, and more. What is less well documented are the side effects of withdrawal. There are few who can cope with the symptoms associated with a VISOR implant for an extended period of time, and fewer still who have managed and have later had the VISOR removed or replaced with synthetic or biological alternatives. This, of course, means a small pool of study samples, of individuals who have maintained the VISOR for an extended period, and then had it replaced or removed. Despite this small sample size there are common experiences documented that are worthy of note in analyzing the effect of withdrawal from this implant. Such effects include disorientation, slower reflex times, shock, pain, and a similar subset of symptoms one would normally associate with drug dependence. Ex-users typically suffer from a range of emotional side-effects, describing such feelings as malaise, depression, hollowness or emptiness, and feeling that they are less without the VISOR than they were with it.

Having a VISOR implant bears a cost, but experiencing one and having it later removed, also has a toll…

Doctor Alberto Mannazzu, in his presentation to the Medical Association on the Effects of Withdrawal from the Visual Instrument and Sensory Organ Replacement (VISOR).

changing the frequency of the light emitted from the near infrared to long-wave ultraviolet or providing a 'white' light for species that evolved with different natural light. Beacons can also be set to emit entirely in the near infrared, providing a short-term heat source in a survival situation. Standard Starfleet beacons are worn on the wrist and are held in place with a strap, but also can be hand-held, mounted on helmets, or fitted to phaser type-3.

Communicator (Standard Issue): The standard Starfleet communicator is a ubiquitous piece of technology. During the 22nd and 23rd centuries, these devices were hand held and allowed the user to communicate with a starship in orbit or another communicator broadcasting on the same series of sub-space channels. By the 24th century the communicator was further miniaturized with the introduction of isolinear technologies, making it small enough to be worn as a pin on the uniform, as well as allowing constant contact with a starships main computer and the ability to communicate directly with any other crew member wearing a similar device. The 23rd and 24th century versions of these devices also include a small, but complex universal translator.

Audio Receiver (Standard Issue for Communications Officer, Opportunity 1 otherwise): The Starfleet ear receiver has fallen out of favor since the 23rd century, but still can be seen in use by specialists in communication technologies, lingual, and other aural sciences. The ear receiver ties directly into shipboard communication networks and allows the user to listen to data coming across both sub-space frequencies typically used for long-range communication and ship to surface, but also listening to computer alerts and data so as not to distract others at nearby stations with the chatter. The receiver can also be programmed to provide aural or vibrational feedback to users allowing sensor operators greater accuracy in their duties.

Emergency Transponder (Opportunity 1): Also known by transporter operation officers as 'The Screamer', emergency transponders are small hand-held devices capable of transmitting very strong sub-space singles with limited amounts of data. This data usually consists of just a wave-guide that allows starship sensors to detect the transmitter from light-years away when there is no interference, and from AU's away with sub-space background scattering. While this does not allow for transporter systems to lock onto and beam a person using the transponder from distances or through material it normally wouldn't (without the aid of pattern enhancers), it does allow for high accuracy in transports and acts as a SOS signal recognized by most governments across the Alpha and Beta quadrants. Characters using an emergency transponder gain the ability to show their position to any vessel currently using sub-space sensors within a radius determined by the GM, but usually very long distances measuring between a few hundred thousand kilometers and light-years.

Holographic Imager (Opportunity 1): Imaging technology has improved dramatically since the invention of the photographic camera. The current state of the art imaging device is the holographic imager, a hand-held multi-spectral camera capable of recording nearly unlimited still and moving images with a resolution down to the micron level. Use of the device can range from recording happy memories from the latest shore leave all the way to recording the behaviors of a new life-form on a newly charted planet. The devices output is detailed enough that the recorded data can be used to recreate the setting inside holodecks, allowing for accurate computer simulations.

PADD (No Cost): The 'Personal Access Display Device' allows Starfleet crew to access the database of the starship or starbase they are currently serving on, tying them into the sub-space network stretching across the Federation. This gives a user as much data access as they have clearance for, access to sub-space communication and the ability to record and transmit text, audio, and video recordings to anyone in the Federation. The primary role of a PADD on a starship is to replace paper books, manuals, technical journals, and act as a personal scheduler and as an aid to complete administrative work. While nowhere near as powerful or complex as the main computer system on a starship, a PADD is able to process and analyze data by itself, or serve as an extension of a main computer to which it is connected.

Pattern Enhancer (Large, Opportunity 1): Used to boost the resolution and strength of a transporter scanning beam, pattern enhancers allow transporter systems to achieve a signal lock even with interference from terrain or cosmic phenomena that normally would prevent a safe transport. These devices are approximately a meter long when deployed on their tripods and require at least three to function when placed equidistant around an away party or other transporter target. Each device's onboard power cell allows for approximately two transports, and additional pattern enhancers can increase the area and number of transports. Pattern enhancers come in sets of three.

PATTERN ENHANCER

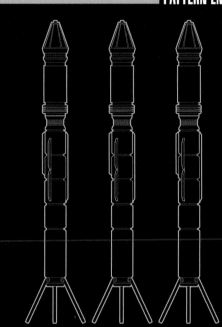

SCHEMATICS

Universal Translator (Opportunity 1): A standard part of Starfleet communicators since the late 23rd century, the universal translator was originally invented before the Earth-Romulan War and has been an integral part of Federation diplomacy ever since. Characters not possessing a universal translator, either through destruction or removal of a communicator, will be unable to converse with beings that do not understand the character's languages past basic hand gestures. Obtaining a separate universal translator provides the character with a stand-alone unit, typically more powerful than the versions found in communicators.

10150813
160118110518

A HOME IN THE STARS
STARSHIPS

"YOU'LL FIND THAT MORE HAPPENS ON THE BRIDGE OF A STARSHIP THAN JUST CARRYING OUT ORDERS AND OBSERVING REGULATIONS. THERE'S A SENSE OF LOYALTY TO THE MEN AND WOMEN YOU SERVE WITH. A SENSE OF FAMILY."

— CAPTAIN HIKARU SULU

Being assigned to your new position within Starfleet can take you anywhere in the Galaxy, and place you aboard one of many possible starships, starbases, or colonies. It will be more than a place to work and sleep, it will be a sanctuary, a base of operations, and a place you can depend upon in the darkest reaches of space. This will be your home for the duration of your mission, and, after a short time, will feel like a part of the crew in itself. A fellow crew member that you will defend and protect, just like any other crewmate. Determining which ship, station, or colony you will be assigned to is almost as important as picking your specialization within Starfleet, and it will depend upon the type of mission you are about to embark upon.

THE MAJOR HERO

"Please remember that a major hero of *Star Trek* has always been the *Starship Enterprise* and her mission. The ship is not just a vehicle — she is the touchstone by which all of our characters demonstrate who they are and what they're up to in the universe."

Gene Roddenberry
– Star Trek: The Next Generation *Writer's/Director's Guide*

YOUR CONTINUING MISSION

Determining what ship or station your characters operate from is almost as important as defining your primary Character.

The first consideration is what types of mission your crew will be undertaking. Some Starfleet vessels are designed for a specific function, whether that is medical or rescue

capabilities, scientific research, stellar cartography, or armed for defense or other military operations.

Some vessels, especially those that become well known as flagships of the fleet, are all purpose — for example, the *U.S.S. Enterprise* NCC-1701-D, is often regarded as one of the flagships. It has specialist scientific research capabilities, is powerful enough to be at the front of some of the major conflicts, and is often sent into diplomatic and rescue situations. It doesn't mean that a *Centaur*-class vessel, normally associated with defensive or military actions, won't be assigned to a rescue mission if they are closest. But the chances of them being sent on a sensitive diplomatic mission will be slim — arriving with a cultural ambassador on a warship does not make for a good first impression.

MISSION TYPES
TO SEEK OUT NEW LIFE, AND NEW CIVILIZATIONS
Exploring the Galaxy — charting and cataloguing the millions of systems, nebula, and other phenomena — is one of the primary missions of Starfleet. Starfleet sends deep-space and planetary expeditions into the unexplored regions of the Galaxy constantly. Each ship charts the undiscovered regions, cataloging the data and feeding information back to Starfleet. If the ship discovers something major, they may be required to investigate further; making first contact, exploring the surface of planets — examining natural flora, fauna, geology or atmospheric conditions — or researching stellar phenomena.

TO PROVIDE SECURITY AND ASSISTANCE TO FEDERATION MEMBERS, COLONIES, AND TRAVELERS
Starfleet is about exploration and defense. Defending the Federation's worlds, members, and those who would fall under the Federation's protection. The Galaxy is filled with hostile species, pirates, and other aggressors who would threaten the Federation's peaceful exploration and expansion. Defense and military missions can be as simple

as patrolling the borders of the Romulan Neutral Zone or the Cardassian Demilitarized Zone, or responding to incursions or threats to specific planets or domains. They could be sent to protect a defenseless research vessel or freighter carrying rare and valuable vaccines venturing into hostile territory for research or relief.

TO BETTER OURSELVES, TO EXPAND THE BODY OF HUMAN KNOWLEDGE

Starfleet conducts many scientific research missions, investigating the new life, new stellar phenomena and new technology discovered during their exploration. Not only are these research missions based upon what they discover, but also acting as a mobile laboratory for a host of experiments and tests of new advances and theories.

TO PUSH THE BOUNDARIES, AND FURTHER UNDERSTAND THE UNIVERSE

Starfleet prides itself with some of the best engineers and technicians in the Galaxy, capable of developing new technology and engineering advances that strive to make space travel faster, easier, and more efficient. Starfleet craft are often called in to test new technology, whether this is computer tech, artificial intelligence, holographic advances, developments in warp field engineering, or repair of ships or stations damaged in the line of duty.

TO HELP THOSE IN NEED, TO RESCUE THOSE IN DANGER

Whether it is the result of a conflict, or a natural disaster such as a solar flare, tectonic shift, or climate disturbance, or a virulent strain of a harmful disease or the effects of a prolonged drought, colonies or entire civilizations can call upon Starfleet for aid. Rescue and relief missions can involve sending medical aid to those suffering from a disease, transporting food and supplies to those stricken with famine, diverting asteroids that would wipe out all life on the planet, or stopping volcanic eruptions. In worst-case scenarios, the inhabitants of a planet can be evacuated and relocated to an uninhabited world.

TO BOLDLY GO WHERE NO ONE HAS GONE BEFORE

Since Zefram Cochrane's first flight, it has been obvious that Earth, and Humanity, was not alone in the Galaxy. When a new civilization is discovered, the Federation has the difficult task of making first contact. However, other diplomatic missions can include negotiating peace treaties, hosting a conference, finalizing trade disputes, or other delicate political situations.

WITH THE STARS AS MY GUIDE

In many cases the ship is capable of adapting to most situations, whether this is a diplomatic mission, the rescue of colonists on a dying world, investigating a strange interstellar phenomenon, or heading into a war zone to liberate a civilization under threat.

STARSHIP NAMES

"Not only does the class of starship the characters are assigned to need to be chosen, but the name of the ship needs to be determined as well. Usually, the first ship of a new class determines the name of the class. For example, the *U.S.S. Akira* NCC-62497 was the first *Akira*-class ship of the line, the *U.S.S. Excelsior* NCC-2000 was the first *Excelsior*-class ship, and so on.

Ships can be named after anything — from cities and towns on Earth (*U.S.S. Portland* NCC-57418 or *U.S.S. Cairo* NCC-42136), famous leaders (*U.S.S. Sarek*, *U.S.S. Crazy Horse* NCC-50446, or *U.S.S. Gandhi* NCC-26632), mythological figures (*U.S.S. Pegasus* NCC-53847 or *U.S.S. Prometheus* NCC-71201), legendary items (*U.S.S. Excalibur* NCC-26517-A) or famous ships (*U.S.S. Challenger* NCC-71099, *U.S.S. Nautilus* NCC-31910, or *U.S.S. Endeavour* NCC-71805).

You could name the ship after your home town or city, the state or county, a figure from history that would be inspirational for the crew's mission, or a naval ship that served in the past.

Take some time over it, and discuss the options with the Players — after all, the Players will be spending a lot of time on the ship, and the name should fill them with pride and a sense of home.

Ships are frequently sent on extended missions, from the legendary five-year mission of the *U.S.S. Enterprise* under the command of Captain James T. Kirk, to even longer missions such as the *U.S.S. Olympia's* eight-year mission, or Captain Jean-Luc Picard's *U.S.S. Enterprise* and its continuing mission. Long missions away from home mean that not only are the crew expected to deal with anything that exploring the uncharted regions of the Galaxy can throw at them, but the ship really becomes a travelling home away from home. The ship must be home, school, work, and recreation for hundreds of personnel.

Such long missions, especially for ships of the line suited to multiple mission-types, means that the crew can expect every possible adventure through the course of their mission. From dealing with a medical emergency with a virulent disease attacking the crew at one moment, to hosting a sensitive peace treaty negotiation for visiting ambassadors the next.

It is this variety of mission that keeps the crew challenged, engaged, and striving to better themselves.

"I think my eyes are going to fall out of my head. Three weeks pouring over the specs and running simulations on the current spaceframe model, but it looks like we've finally got it.

These *Galaxy*-class ships are going to be a lot bigger than older exploration vessels — primarily to make room for families. That necessitates a larger primary hull, which makes the warp field calculations a real bear — the first couple of simulations we ran resulted in a drag on the engine output, barely making warp 6. Not acceptable in a long-range exploration vessel. The next sim solved the output problem, but the ship tore itself apart under the stresses. Not, as Captain T'Len said, "an optimal result."

But it looks like we cracked it — uh, the problem, not the ship. Finally. At times, it felt like pulling all-nighters at the Academy, only for weeks straight — but it will all be worth it.

These things represent an entirely new emphasis on exploration — longer range, and having the crew's families on board means we can send them out for longer missions. Go further out there, to see what's what.

It's been a rough go for a while — but the treaty with the Cardassians puts an end to our last big military problem. It'll be good to get back to a focus on pure exploration."

DECK FOURTEEN

After being assigned to any new ship, it can take a while for the crew to become familiar with where everything is. In most cases, you will not need to know your way around every Jefferies tube or access panel — this knowledge will come over time and experience. For the time being you will only need to know the primary locations — the bridge, your quarters, transporter room, mess hall / recreational lounge, holodeck, and any specialist laboratory or workstation that your position requires.

If the ship comes under fire and sustains damage, the actual location of the damage is not as important as the loss of vital systems, and injuries to the loyal crew. "Captain, we've taken a hit to engineering," means the ship has sustained damage to the integrity of the engineering section, and possibly lost some engineering crew to injury or worse. It's not necessary to know that the impulse drives were housed on decks 23 and 24.

As the missions progress, locations will be used more frequently and the Gamemaster can fill in more detail, gradually making it a real home in the stars that everyone will be familiar with. The more the crew interact at these locations on board the ship, the more the ship will feel like their home, and something to be defended. The chief engineer should feel a sense of relief and familiarity when they return to main engineering.

THE RIGHT CREW FOR THE MISSION

Not only does Starfleet need to assign the right ship for the mission, it also needs to assign the right crew. It is assumed that many of the bridge crew will be Player Characters, but this will probably not be every member of the senior staff.

It could be that the Players and Gamemaster have decided to concentrate on "lower decks" characters, and their interactions during and between missions — in which case it could be that none of the bridge crew are Player Characters.

Look at the list of senior staff and bridge crew listed in the sidebar. Further details of these positions can be found in *Chapter 5: Reporting For Duty*. The crew not being run by Players will need to be created as Supporting Characters (see p. 132) to ensure the ship is properly staffed for the missions ahead. You can also find examples in *Aliens and Adversaries* on p. 314.

Consider who makes up the crew and try to ensure a wide variety of species, genders, professions, and interests. Also, take some time to think about their relationships and how they feel about each other. It could be that the ship's counselor and the first officer had a relationship in the past that they've put behind them due to their professional environment. Maybe the captain has risen through the ranks at a relatively fast rate and is younger than a lot of her bridge crew, and some question her abilities due to her age and experience. Characters will have a number of Values, one of which will be a relationship that will develop and change as their mission continues, and it is little details like this that make the experience of living and working with these crewmembers more engaging.

More specialist missions, such as those carried out by the Corps of Engineers, or a small team of infiltrators from Section 31, will mean the NPCs required to fill the crew will vary. However, most crews — no matter how specialist — will require most of the senior staff to ensure the ship is running smoothly, and the crew are healthy and ready for any action.

While starships come in a variety of classes and designs, there are some key locations that remain constant throughout the Federation, and even non-Federation, starships. They will be the places the crew visit the most. Through their constant interaction at these locations, they can really bring the ship to life in the eyes of the Players, adding depth and a sense of home while on board. This list is just a sample of the most common locations on board, and the crew may find themselves in new locations as their mission dictates.

THE BRIDGE — This is where most of the action takes place. It is where the captain and senior staff control the ship, and is never left unmanned. When the ship is large, the "windscreen" is replaced with a viewscreen that can display and magnify the Galaxy outside, as well as acting as a video screen for communications. It is here that the senior staff crew their stations, advise the captain on suggested courses of action, control the main ship functions, pilot and navigate the ship, and engage in the threats they face.

CAPTAIN'S READY ROOM — The captain often has additional tasks that cannot be dealt with from the captain's chair. Usually off the main bridge, the ready room acts as a private office where the captain can deal with reports, communicate securely with Starfleet, and hold private council with her crew.

MAIN ENGINEERING — While the chief engineering officer can have a post on the main bridge, they are more at home in main engineering. Usually situated at the rear of the ship, it is home to the main matter/anti-matter integrator and the warp core. Most engineering problems or situations can be resolved here, or by crawling through the network of Jefferies tubes that allow engineers access to the inner workings of the ship systems.

SICKBAY — The chief medical officer can also have a post on the main bridge, but more often they can be found in sickbay.

A dedicated area for tending to any injuries, illnesses and diseases that the crew may acquire during their mission. Host to advanced quarantine facilities, advanced diagnostics and biobeds, and sometimes home to the Emergency Medical Hologram (EMH) capable of assisting the chief medical officer, or assuming their role if the CMO is called away.

TRANSPORTER ROOM — Larger starships will have a number of transporter rooms as these are the key means of getting the crew, equipment, and supplies to and from other ships and planetary surfaces. Overseen by a transporter chief or suitably qualified crew, transporters provide quick, efficient and almost instantaneous teleportation to previously scanned locations.

SHUTTLEBAY — When transporting is unavailable due to range or environmental factors, crew and supplies can take a shuttle from the shuttlebay and pilot the craft to the surface, a nearby ship, or on a separate mission.

OBSERVATION LOUNGE — Many larger ships dedicate an area with a particularly good view of the sector outside to a comfortable and spacious meeting room, hosting crew briefings as well as diplomatic negotiations.

HOLODECK — Advances in holographic technology allows a relatively compact area to simulate any environment, from encounters with fictional characters, to meticulous reconstructions of events for research. Holodecks can provide the crew with an endless source of recreation, as well as safe facilities for experiments and investigation.

STELLAR CARTOGRAPHY — A dedicated laboratory responsible for recording, and holographically projecting, detailed maps of the stars, as well as classifying, identifying, and tracking stellar phenomena.

RECREATION LOUNGE — A place for the crew to rest and recover after a long shift, the recreation lounge is often a glorified mess hall, though on some of the larger flagships this takes the form of a bar/restaurant where the crew can socialize and unwind.

CARGO BAYS — With their own dedicated transporter facilities, and often large exterior doors, these areas hold cargo that the ship is transporting to worlds in need of resources, relief supplies, or medical aid. The cargo bay transporters, for security reasons, are usually set to transport non-life-forms only.

CREW QUARTERS / VIP ACCOMMODATION — Each crewmember will have their own private quarters, usually becoming larger depending upon rank and position. Some larger ships in the fleet allow crewmembers to bring their families with them on the mission, and the crew quarters can be a suite with a number of rooms depending upon the needs of the crew and family. Larger quarters are also reserved for VIP accommodation for visiting diplomats, guests, and dignitaries.

BRIG — During the course of the mission the crew may encounter hostile life-forms that may need to be retained for the safety of the rest of the crew. On rare occasions, the brig can become a temporary holding cell for insubordinate or disruptive crewmembers, or prisoners being transported to more secure facilities.

LABORATORIES — The explorative nature of Starfleet's mission means most ships are home to a number of laboratories allowing scientific research and investigation. Whether this is careful examination of artefacts or discoveries from a mission, or a crewmember's own research project, the ship has facilities that can accommodate their needs.

SENIOR STAFF BRIDGE CREW

As a guide, most Starfleet crews are composed of some, if not all, of the following:

COMMANDING OFFICER — Captain or commander of the vessel or station.

EXECUTIVE OFFICER — or First officer, the captain's second-in-command. They may have other duties as well as serving as executive officer.

OPERATIONS MANAGER — responsible for ship's operations, monitoring ship systems.

CHIEF FLIGHT CONTROLLER — Helmsperson and navigator.

CHIEF TACTICAL OFFICER — responsible for ship weaponry, defenses and tactics. A role sometimes taken by the chief security officer.

CHIEF SECURITY OFFICER — head of the security department and responsible for the safety of the crew.

CHIEF ENGINEER — maintains the functionality of the ship, assigning crew for repair and service.

CHIEF MEDICAL OFFICER — responsible for the health and well-being of the crew.

CHIEF SCIENCE OFFICER — head of the science department on the ship, responsible for analysis and research.

SHIP'S COUNSELOR — responsible for the mental health and personal wellbeing of the crew, as well as advisor on diplomatic missions.

AHEAD WARP FACTOR FIVE

With your home constantly on the move, it's difficult sometimes to determine just how far you've travelled on your mission, or how quickly you can get to your next destination. In most cases, travel time is not important. Often, it is purely a case of the ship arriving at the location of a mission, and orbiting the planet they've been sent to investigate.

However, if the time it takes to get to a planet is important, or a matter of urgency, the Gamemaster should determine how long it takes to get there safely, and how long it takes to get there on time. For dramatic purposes, these should be close, but getting

there on time may involve a little risk — overloading the engines, travelling through hostile space, or near a stellar phenomenon that may put the ship in danger. Travelling should take time, but the Gamemaster (and Players) shouldn't be overwhelmed with calculating travel distances and speeds in billions of kilometers per hour.

If the Gamemaster is determined to ensure the accuracy of their travel, a simple chart is provided below. Refer to the map of the known Galaxy to chart your route!

SPEED	KM/H	X LIGHTSPEED	TO NEAR STAR	ACROSS SECTOR
Full Impulse	270 million	0.25	20 years	80 years
Warp 1	1078 million	1	5 years	20 years
Warp 2	11 billion	10	6 months	3 years
Warp 3	42 billion	39	2 months	1 year
Warp 4	109 billion	102	18 days	2 months
Warp 5	230 billion	214	9 days	1 month
Warp 6	423 billion	392	5 days	19 days
Warp 7	700 billion	656	3 days	11 days
Warp 8	1103 billion	1,024	2 days	7 days
Warp 9	1.63 trillion	1,516	1 day	5 days
Warp 9.2	1.78 trillion	1,649	1 day	4 days
Warp 9.6	2.06 trillion	1,909	23 hours	4 days
Warp 9.9	3.29 trillion	3,053	14 hours	2 days
Warp 9.99	8.53 trillion	7,912	6 hours	22 hours
Warp 9.999	215 trillion	199,516	13 minutes	53 minutes
Warp 10	Infinite	Infinite	0	0

A HOME IN THE STARS
STARBASES

LIVING ON THE EDGE

Travelling out into the farthest reaches of space is one of the more common assignments you can expect from a life in Starfleet. However, it is not the only option. Starfleet needs dedicated crewmembers to serve on their many starbases scattered around the Alpha and Beta Quadrants. They act as support for the fleet and are hives of commerce and activity.

Much like the different classes of starships, starbases can have dedicated functions, or act as general support for visiting vessels and personnel. Most common starbases are used for:

STARSHIP MAINTENANCE AND CONSTRUCTION

In the depths of space, starships come under a great deal of strain. Physical damage can come from stellar phenomena, deliberate attack by hostile forces, or general wear-and-tear from the continuing mission. Hull repairs or severe damage cannot easily be carried out by the ship's crew out in deep space, and major repairs need to be carried out within a larger spacestation or drydock. These starbases act as repair and maintenance facilities as well as homes to some of the brightest designers and developers of new starship technology, creating and improving the ships of the line.

DEFENSE, DIPLOMACY, AND COMMAND

Starbases act as strategic positions maintaining the borders of the Romulan Neutral Zone, the edge of the Cardassian Demilitarized Zone, or the extreme reaches of Federation space. They not only act as early warning posts, watching for those who would break the treaties that have been carefully negotiated, but also as listening stations keeping an ear to the comms traffic across the borders for signs of amassing forces or covert operations.

The station also acts as a staging post, assigning the crews and missions for the ships in the sector.

Not only can these starbases act as military and defense for our borders, but also a more diplomatic response for times of tension. Federation starbases can become safe places for diplomatic resolutions to any struggles or conflicts, providing species and cultures a place to voice their concerns, explain their situations, and strive to come to a peaceful solution under the neutral eye of the members of the United Federation of Planets.

SUPPLY, COMMERCE, AND SUPPORT

Starbases are a vital link for essential supplies and services that Starfleet's crews require. Whether this is fresh (unreplicated) food, fuel or goods, advanced medical services for complex or delicate surgical procedures, or administrative and legal services when personnel require legal representation or when the Judge Advocate General (JAG) are called upon. They also provide training and essential recreational services for crews requiring shore leave, with dedicated holosuites, sports facilities, and a variety of traders and restaurants that can help personnel unwind and relax in between missions.

STARBASE ASSIGNMENT

Starbases are usually positioned in locations of high activity — whether this is as a watchful post next to the Bajoran wormhole, or as a staging ground for a number of expeditions into unexplored territory. Life on a starbase is very different to that on board a starship. The adventure isn't out there waiting to be discovered — on a starbase the adventure comes to you.

Starbase assignments are not purely limited to a static post. Most starbases have dedicated smaller ships for exploration, defense, or supply missions that range from shuttles to runabouts or larger craft.

STARBASE PERSONNEL

Just like a starship, starbases have a crew of dedicated personnel who manage, maintain, and staff the station and keep it running smoothly. Just like starships, this crew is given similar positions with a "bridge crew" of senior staff who control things and manage the station. They assign the dozens of crew that work behind the scenes to ensure the base is safe, maintained, and operational.

The positions for the senior staff are similar to that of a starship, requiring a commander or captain to take charge of the base, a second in command or executive officer, and chiefs of departments such as science, medical, security, operations, and engineering. Being assigned to one of these posts is just like taking residence on a starship and your duties will be very fairly similar.

However, a starbase commander's duty can involve a lot more administration, and is often assigned to Starfleet personnel who have a different skillset to those suited to starship command. While they are faced with similar threats and calls for diplomacy, they often need to think for themselves, often isolated from Starfleet. Thankfully, the crew are more likely to have the support of their families and can enjoy a sense of stability and routine without too many sudden surprises.

Crew assigned to starbases often become attached to their base and the community around them, which can easily grow to become a Value.

NARENDRA STATION

An example of one of the most valuable starbases within the Federation is Narendra Station. A staging post for expeditions deep into an area of the Galaxy that has, until now, only been mapped by automated survey probes — The Shackleton Expanse.

Formally designated as Starbase 364, Narendra Station has been operational since 2353. Named in tribute to the Klingon colonists who were massacred during a Romulan sneak attack against the outpost on Narendra III in 2344, the starbase also serves as a reminder of the pivotal shift in Klingon-Federation relations which occurred in the aftermath of the assault. During the attack, the Starfleet vessel *U.S.S. Enterprise* NCC-1701-C commanded by Captain Rachel Garrett answered the colony's distress call, managing to repel the attacking Romulan ships and saving the outpost from total annihilation. The action came at the cost of the *Enterprise*-C and its crew, a gesture of bravery and sacrifice which was not lost on the Klingon Empire's High Council.

Both Federation and Klingon officials have worked to fortify this alliance, working together to expand their territories, research new stellar phenomena, and discover planets rich in needed resources.

Though the Klingon Empire has largely done away with the practice of subjugating other worlds and civilizations, this does not mean that the Klingon High Council and the Federation always see eye to eye.

Narendra Station is home to both Starfleet and Klingon personnel, pursuing missions and goals relevant to their individual governments as well as joint tasks that serve to further support continuing collaborative efforts. Given its location and relative isolation from more populated areas of Federation space, the station's command staff is granted a broad authority to dispatch the vessels in its charge on missions of exploration as well as diplomacy. The starbase also serves as a first line of defense against threats to Federation and Klingon security, whether introduced by a known adversary such as the Romulans, or anyone or anything previously unidentified that might emerge from the unexplored depths of the Shackleton Expanse or points beyond.

REGULA I

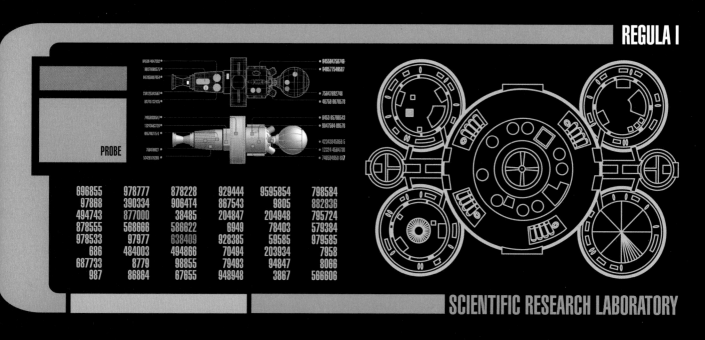

PROBE

696855	978777	878228	929444	9595854	798584
97868	390334	9064T4	887543	9805	882836
494743	877000	38485	204847	204948	795724
878555	568666	586622	6949	78403	579384
978533	97977	638409	928385	59585	979585
886	484003	494866	70494	203934	7958
687733	8779	98855	79493	94847	8066
987	86864	67655	948948	3867	566606

SCIENTIFIC RESEARCH LABORATORY

A HOME IN THE STARS
COLONIES

LIFE ON THE FINAL FRONTIER

In addition to life in the stars, there's a chance that your assignment may place you on a planet's surface. Like the pioneers of the old west on Earth, Starfleet establishes colonies and research facilities on planets on the very edge of Federation space. These planets usually have a particular scientific interest, a strategic location for trade, diplomatic significance, or represent a crucial point of security.

It could be that the colony is nothing more than a tiny research outpost. These posts in the 23rd century were little more than basic living facilities like a shelter, with adjoining laboratory capabilities. Research teams could be a simple family unit with a couple of support staff, living rough on the very edge of the final frontier. Those early days of pioneer science on the fringe of space were dangerous times, with no replicators, and vital supplies being delivered by passing exploratory vessels heading out into the unknown.

Colonies and research posts need to send regular reports by subspace to check in and keep Starfleet updated on their progress and well-being. In those early days, it wasn't unheard of to lose a research team to disease, environmental upheaval, or madness.

Larger colonies range from frontier towns to areas the size of a small city. They can be the thriving hub of commerce, resource acquisition, or scientific breakthroughs.

Just like starships and starbases, larger colonies are run as a Starfleet instillation with staff in positions as before; keeping the colony safe, secure, and running smoothly. As with the larger starships and starbases, colonies are places for Starfleet crews to serve alongside their families.

Much like it was with those pioneers, the colonies that Starfleet helps to create become towns where the role of commander is more like that of town mayor. The security chief becomes the law enforcement, effectively the town sheriff, with security personnel as the police. The chief medical officer can establish a proper medical base of operations that will become the town hospital, while engineering personnel ensure the town's facilities — replicators, vehicles, power supply, and even plumbing, is working efficiently.

The town becomes a real community, rallying together to forge a new life on a new world. They can form relationships, and a sense of duty to the colony that can develop into a Value that ties them to the family they have formed.

COLONIAL RECRUITMENT POSTER

Citizen, does the lure of travel, adventure, and hard work call to you? Are you tired of living in a world that you had no hand in creating? Then join the Federation Colonization Service today and make your own tomorrow!

Colonists are free to democratically select their own level of bureaucracy and economic development. At your new home, you will be responsible for your own success and rise as high as your skills and work ethic can take you.

We're looking for a special breed of person. Someone who prefers to cook their own food and enjoys the craftsmanship of furnishing your own home through your own efforts. If serving as an apprentice until a land allotment opens up for you is too sedentary and slow, then join up and found your own business within months of establishing your colony's infrastructure.

If you feel that this is your true calling, make an appointment at the nearest FCS office today to see our selection of upcoming projects. We're currently offering an extra 50 percent bonus in starting resources for signing up this week. Don't miss your opportunity to get in on the ground floor of Humanity's expansion to a new frontier!

MINING COLONY: A common reason to set up a more permanent base on a strange, new world is for its resources. Many discovered planets have vital and essential natural resources such as dilithium or pergium, as well as precious minerals and metals. However, it is not uncommon for such mining ventures to be at the heart of a political dispute, in dangerous territory, or for the mining itself to uncover a strange and hostile life-form intent on protecting its habitat.

RESEARCH FACILITY: Planets orbiting a particularly interesting star or close to strange or unique stellar phenomena can become homes to longer standing research facilities. It could be that the planet is uninhabited and far enough away from any population that particularly dangerous or volatile research can be undertaken without fear of putting millions of people at risk.

DIPLOMATIC MEETING PLACE: On the edge of a neutral zone, or within the territory of a neutral arbiter, Starfleet can found a colony whose main purpose is to provide a safe and secure meeting place for diplomatic debate and to resolve any political issues that could bring war to the region. It can be a dangerous place to live, with the threat of conflict constantly looming, but what nobler cause for the Federation than to bring peace to the Galaxy?

TRADE STATIONS: Key positions where commonly used routes intersect, or where traders frequently met to exchange goods and services, are prime locations to set up new colonies for markets, traders, and commerce. These marketplaces may specialize in goods, food, repairs or services, or even as recreational resorts for shore leave. However, not every trade is legal, and some market colonies become hives of illegal shipping and trade operating under Starfleet's sensors.

PENAL COLONY: There will always be those who do not respect the rules of society, the rules that keep us safe. When people break the laws, and the safety of those around them are at risk, these criminals can be sent to a penal colony such as Tantalus or the Jaros II stockade. The added security of being isolated on a distant planet means the chance of escape is slim, and being assigned to staff a penal colony can be one of the most challenging positions within Starfleet.

A NEW HOME: Above all, most colonies are simply that — a colony of families hoping to make a new life in the stars, on a new world. They create villages, towns, societies, governments, and trade with their neighbors to thrive and survive. Colonies become homes to farmers, builders, scientists, teachers, and engineers.

A DIFFERENT KIND OF THREAT

Being assigned to a colony can feel very different to a typical Starfleet posting. Colonies require Starfleet to work as engineers to ensure their vital technology keeps running, as security to protect the colonists, as a police force to maintain order, as doctors to keep the colonists healthy, and in a supervisory capacity.

In addition, colony personnel will have to deal with environmental factors, harsh weather conditions, stellar anomalies, tectonic shifts, or hostile flora, fauna, or indigenous people.

Being assigned to a colony, however, is not total isolation. Colonies are allocated shuttles, runabouts, and exploratory vehicles to venture out across the surface of their new home and its neighboring regions in space. They venture into the wild to discover new life-forms.

PLANETARY ADVENTURES

Most *Star Trek Adventures* stories are set on board a starship with regular away teams venturing onto a planetary surface to encounter new adventures and situations. Colony based missions are very similar with these themes reversed. The planet is the "ship", with the colony as their new home, and adventures can either come to them — a threat to the colony, a new visitor, a new scientific breakthrough or discovery, or a social upheaval in the town. Or the team can set out to visit their surroundings or other planets to return to their colony at the end of the mission.

With the planet being the effective ship of the story, the planet should be defined just as much as a Gamemaster would with

their ship. What is the planet like? What is it called? How many moons, or how long is a standard day? What is the environment like, and are there any native species or indigenous life-forms that can help or pose as a threat to their survival.

Gamemasters should look at planet creation in *Chapter 10: Gamemastering* for advice on creating a fitting and exciting location for the crew's assignment. Gamemasters should consider why the colony exists, and what mission the colonists are undertaking.

A HOME IN THE STARS
STARSHIP RULES

STARSHIP FUNDAMENTALS

Operating a Starship is not massively dissimilar to the way characters act and interact normally. The normal rules for Tasks, Extended Tasks, and Challenges still apply to a character aboard a starship, and many of the activities a character engages in aboard ship will be resolved in the same ways that they would be on the surface of a strange new world.

A crucial concept for starship operations is the difference between actions taken aboard a starship, and actions taken with a starship.

- **Actions taken aboard a starship** are no different to actions taken anywhere else. In this context, a starship is essentially just a location within which the action is taking place, rather than an active element of that action. That is not to say that there aren't Advantages to acting aboard ship: the tools and resources available to the crew of a starship can provide a significant benefit that they wouldn't have elsewhere. For actions taken aboard a ship, there are no innate or inherent Advantages, though there may still be benefits depending on where aboard the ship the actions are attempted, and what facilities the ship itself offers. These will be discussed in more detail later.

- **Actions taken with a starship** always benefit from the ship's presence and nature, because the ship is how the actions are taken. These activities are invariably the use of control systems within the ship to make the ship itself do something, such as moving between planets, firing torpedoes, scanning celestial phenomena, and other actions that are performed with the ship's systems directly. These actions normally influence something external to the ship, rather than upon something inside it.

STARSHIP PROFILES

Just as with characters, starships are represented using several Attributes, Disciplines, Traits, Talents, and so forth. Starships, however, use these numbers and rules to reflect different things than they might represent on characters.

TRAITS

A starship will typically have one or more Traits, one of which will always be the name of the civilization which created it. Traits are essentially descriptions of important aspects of the ship's fundamental nature and function, in a single word or a short phrase. Traits help define what the ship is and what it can do, and they can be employed in the same way as Traits for a location or situation, such as to increase or reduce the Difficulty of Tasks.

First and foremost, we have the ship's origin. Different cultures in *Star Trek* manufacture their ships in myriad different ways, and a Trait can encapsulate those many little differences easily. These are both positive and negative, and influence both how the ship interacts with its environment, but also how characters and other ships interact with it.

A ship may have additional Traits reflecting other definitive elements of its construction or purpose, or even the influence of past events.

Traits are neutral, and thus able to be applied both positively and negatively. There is no fixed number of Traits a ship will have, though every vessel will have at least one. Traits, and their effects upon play, are described in full on p. 76.

*Example: The U.S.S. Enterprise, NCC-1701-D, has three Traits: **Federation Starship, Federation Flagship**, and **Fifth Ship to Bear the Name**. The first it's the ship's origin — it is a Federation starship, and anything that affects Federation technology in a certain way, or for which being Federation technology is advantageous or problematic, is impacted by this Trait. The second reflects the fact that the* Enterprise *is an honored and prestigious vessel within the United Federation of Planets, and thus may impact how others perceive her,* *and her crew, whether positively or negatively. The third Trait denotes that the* Enterprise *is the latest vessel to be part of a long and famous history, and those who know of that history may regard the ship and her crew differently.*

SYSTEMS

Each starship in **Star Trek Adventures** is defined by six Systems, which work in a similar manner to a character's Attributes. They embody the intrinsic capabilities of the ship, compared to other vessels, and the ways in which those capabilities are best employed. These Systems are **Communications**, **Computers**, **Engines**, **Sensors**, **Structure**, and **Weapons**. Each System has a rating from 0 to 12 which determines its measure, with higher numbers reflecting greater utility.

Characters may encounter situations in which more than one of their ship's Systems are applicable. In these cases, it is important to consider the context of the situation, and how the character is choosing to approach the problem. The Gamemaster may choose which System is most applicable to a situation if more than one could be used.

COMMUNICATIONS

This System encompasses the transmission, encryption, decryption, and retrieval of subspace signals on a range of frequencies, as well as a range of other forms of signals transmission and reception. Any Task that involves or relies upon communications systems should use Communications.

A character might use a ship's Communications…

- …when attempting to clear up a signal distorted beyond all recognition, to determine its origin or content.

- …when attempting to glean specific information from amongst an abundance of signals.

- …when trying to generate interference to block or jam other signals.

- …when trying to coordinate between many allied vessels during a crisis.

COMPUTERS

This System represents the ship's library and operational computer systems, from the Duotronic systems of the 23rd century, to the Isolinear and Bioneural systems of the 24th century. Any Task that relies on the processing power and data storage of the ship's computers uses Computers.

A character might use a ship's Computers…

- …when attempting to retrieve or research information stored within the ship's library.

- …when analyzing information gathered during an experiment or scan.

- …when creating a simulation of a situation or effect to try to predict how it will unfold.

- …when trying to remotely perform some complex activity using automation.

ENGINES

This System covers the propulsion and power generation systems of the vessel, and its ability to move and maneuver through space. This includes thrusters, impulse engines, and warp drive, as well as reactors, generators, and related systems such as the navigational deflector. Any Task that relies on moving the vessel under its own power uses Engines.

A character might use a ship's Engines…

- …when attempting to maneuver the ship.

- …when trying to increase the ship's power output.

- …when trying to project a particle stream or form of energy from the navigational deflector.

- …when attempting to pursue another vessel moving significantly faster.

SENSORS

This System covers the vessel's sensor suites and probes, allowing it to scan and monitor its surroundings, and the scientific systems that interpret that data. It also relates to transporters, as they are heavily tied into a ship's sensors. Any Task that involves scanning and analysis using the vessel's sensor arrays should use Sensors.

A character might use a ship's Sensors…

- …when attempting to gain information about an object or phenomenon using the ship's sensors or a probe.

- …when attempting to beam a creature or object to or from a location.

- …when using internal analytical systems — such as those found in laboratories, or sickbay — to study an object or creature in depth.

- …when attempting to locate an intruder or foreign force moving within the ship.

STRUCTURE

This System covers the physical construction of the vessel, from its hull and superstructure, to the structural integrity field and inertial dampeners, as well as thermal and radiation

shielding, and all aspects of the ship's basic operational infrastructure, including life support systems, and artificial gravity. Any Task that involves the physical construction of the vessel or its protective systems uses Structure.

A character might use the ship's Structure…

- …when attempting to reinforce the ship against an external threat or hazard.

- …when altering life support to produce specific environmental conditions in a specific compartment or section.

- …when engaged in activity where maintaining the ship's integrity is vital.

WEAPONS

This System covers the tactical and offensive systems of the vessel, normally phasers or disruptors, plus torpedo launchers, and maybe even other weapons besides. Any Task that involves attacking a target use Weapons.

A character might use the ship's Weapons…

- …when attempting to fire on another vessel.

- …when trying to cut or destroy an object or obstacle.

- …when modifying a weapon system to produce an unusual or alternative effect.

DEPARTMENTS

In addition to the six Systems, each ship is equipped to support six Departments, which encompass the various mission profiles, specialties, and personnel each ship carries. Each Department is rated from 0 to 5, with each rating representing variations of resource allocation, technology, and crew proficiency within that field. Federation starships have at least a 1 in every Department — vessels are expected to fulfil a variety of roles and carry out a wide range of missions.

The six Departments mirror the six Disciplines possessed by characters — **Command**, **Conn**, **Engineering**, **Security**, **Science**, and **Medicine** — though they represent how much support those fields receive aboard the ship, as noted above. Each Department covers a wide range of activities, and some activities may fit under more than one Department, so which one is most applicable to any of those things will depend on circumstances more than anything else.

COMMAND

Command is the professionalism and organization of the ship's crew, and its chain of command. It also represents how well the ship represents the virtues and nature of its culture,

DEPARTMENT	MEANING
0	No dedicated facility for this field; improvised capabilities only.
1	Basic, minimum-level capabilities for this department — a small number of personnel and limited facilities.
2	Standard capabilities for this department — moderate facilities and a basic staff.
3	Improved capabilities for this department — large facilities, and experienced personnel
4	Advanced capabilities for this department — expansive, specialized facilities and excellent personnel
5	Top of the line capabilities — state of the art facilities and highly-skilled personnel.

and conveys those things to both allies and outsiders, which can be valuable in diplomatic situations.

A character may use the ship's Command with...

- ...**Communications**, to make an appropriate first impression when contacting others, or to coordinate effectively with other allied vessels during a crisis.

- ...**Computers**, to study the culture of another species for a diplomatic briefing, or to research matters of law and regulation.

- ...**Engines**, to fly in precise formation, or on a precise course laid out by another.

- ...**Sensors**, to scan or monitor a vast area in close coordination with other vessels, or to try and discern the disposition (friend or foe, etc.) of an unknown vessel by its movements and actions.

- ...**Structure**, to present a particular disposition to another vessel or culture, or to adjust the internal conditions of part of the ship to suit a guest or visitor.

- ...**Weapons**, to fire a 'warning shot' to dissuade a hostile vessel, without risk of causing actual harm, or when using weapon systems to produce spectacular displays without inflicting damage.

CONN

Conn is the quality of the ship's flight control and astronavigation systems, as well as the expertise of its flight crews and the maintenance personnel responsible for maintaining those systems.

A character may use the ship's Conn with...

- ...**Communications**, to relay a plotted course, or detailed astrometric data, to another ship, either in advance or in real-time during travel.

- ...**Computers**, to study the astronomical phenomena and spatial variations present within a region, and to plot a course using that data, using the ship's library and records.

- ...**Engines**, for most routine flight and maneuvering operations, as well as emergency maneuvers during a crisis.

- ...**Sensors**, to analyze the astronomical phenomena and spatial variations present within a region, and to plot a course using that data, where the data is obtained in real-time from the ship's sensors.

- ...**Structure**, to effectively adjust the course, heading, and speed of a vessel in a situation where the ship's integrity is under strain, or to alter the ship's orientation to present a more resilient facing to an enemy or hazard.

- ...**Weapons**, to maneuver the ship in such a way as to maximize the effectiveness of the weapons, commonly known as an "attack pattern".

ENGINEERING

Engineering represents the quality and quantity of the ship's engineering and other technical personnel, as well as the tools and facilities they work with.

A character may use the ship's Engineering with...

- ...**Communications**, to alter the communication systems to break through interference or function on a non-standard frequency.

- ...**Computers**, to research technical schematics within the ship's library, or to create a simulation of a device or mechanism to test its function.

- ...**Engines**, to adjust the output of the reactors or the propulsion systems, in order to produce an increased or different effect.

- ...**Sensors**, to perform diagnostics of a particular system on the ship, or to operate the ship's transporter systems.

- ...**Structure**, to reinforce or alter the effects of the ship's defenses, structural integrity, or inertial dampener systems, or to perform significant adjustments to the ship's life support systems.

…Weapons, to alter weapon systems to overcome an unfamiliar form of defense or shielding, or when using weapon systems for precision cutting or demolition of an obstacle.

SECURITY

Security represents the skill, training, and numbers of the ship's security personnel, as well as other on-board security systems such as containment fields, and the refinement and calibration of tactical systems.

A character may use the ship's Security with…

- …Communications, to encrypt or decrypt classified information, or to intercept transmissions from others.

- …Computers, to create combat or tactical simulations, or to use library archives to research the military capabilities of other vessels or cultures.

- …Engines, to overcharge tactical systems (weapons, shields, etc.) to create a greater effect.

- …Sensors, to try and discern the tactical capabilities of another vessel, or to detect the presence of intruders aboard their own ship.

- …Structure, to alter or reinforce the ship's shields against a specific threat, or to control the use of internal force fields to contain intruders.

- …Weapons, to make attacks with the weapon systems against an enemy.

SCIENCE

Science represents the scientific personnel aboard the ship, their laboratories, their analytical facilities, and the other tools and systems available for analyzing data and studying the unknown.

A character may use the ship's Science with…

- …Communications, to attempt to translate or analyze an unknown language or form of communication, or to try and communicate with an unknown entity.

- …Computers, to use the ship's library archives to perform scientific research, or to analyze the results of an experiment or simulation.

- …Engines, to produce a specific, unusual effect with the navigational deflector, the warp field coils, or some other aspect of the power and propulsion systems.

- …Sensors, to scan and analyze spatial phenomena using the ship's sensor arrays or a probe, or to examine and study samples using sophisticated equipment in the ship's laboratories.

- …Structure, to create or implement a theoretical defense against an unusual threat or hazard, or to alter environmental systems to repel a parasite or other hostile entity.

- …Weapons, to find the specific modulation, frequency, or setting for a weapon system to achieve a specific unusual effect.

MEDICINE

Medicine represents the ship's medical facilities (sickbay, and laboratories), as well as the personnel — doctors, nurses, lab technicians, orderlies — who work there. Most of the uses of Medicine are internal to the ship — making use of the facilities in the ship's sickbay — rather than able to be projected outwards.

A character may use the ship's Medicine with…

- …Communications, to transfer large amounts of medical information, such as patient data, or the formula for a cure to a disease, between vessels or other facilities.

- …Computers, to study the ship's medical databases, or to analyze samples and tests taken from a patient.

- …Engines, to ensure a stable flow of power into sensitive medical equipment.

- …Sensors, to diagnose the ailments of a patient using a bio-bed or other sickbay scanner, or to gain more detailed information about the nature of life-forms scanned by the ship's sensors.

- …Structure, to create force fields that can contain or filter airborne pathogens, or to create a controlled environment for quarantine purposes.

- …Weapons, to design a biogenic or biochemical payload for a torpedo.

FOCUSES

Due to their size, advanced technology, and competent crews, starships can easily be adapted to a wide range of activities and operations. As a result, unlike a character, a Starship does not have distinct Focuses, but instead treats every Task it attempts or assists as if it had an applicable Focus. As a result, any d20 rolled on behalf of the ship which rolls equal to or less than the ship's Department scores two successes.

CAPTAIN'S LOG

CAPTAIN WALKER BENNETT
USS LEXINGTON
STARDATE 47935.2

"Three weeks. Three weeks now, the *Lexington's* exploration mission to the Gamma Quadrant has been on hold. Three weeks of extended leave for the crew, as we sit here docked at Deep Space 9. Not doing a damn thing.

Computer — strike that last sentence. Resume recording.

I certainly understand the Federation's desire to avoid tension with the Dominion. The Gamma Quadrant is largely their territory, and there is concern that repeated incursions by vessels from our quadrant would be seen as a threat to their sovereignty, but surely the diplomats can make some sort of allowance for scientific exploration.

Could be worse, I suppose. I hear that the *Merrimac* has been re-assigned from exploration to doing supply runs to colonies. There but for the grace of god….

If I can be forgiven some anthropomorphism, the Lex seems… depressed, somehow. She just doesn't feel like herself. She was made to brave the unknown, not to sit dormant in some dock… and I know that those of us aboard her feel the same way, about ourselves. We weren't made for this.

Computer – end recording."

Example: Ensign Mayweather is trying to steer the Enterprise *through an anomaly-riddled section of the Delphic Expanse. He rolls his Control 9 and Conn 4, and is assisted by the ship's Engines 8 and Conn 2. On the ship's die, any roll of a 1 or 2 — equal to or less than the* Enterprise's *Conn Department — scores two successes.*

TALENTS

Starships have Talents, just as characters do, normally representing areas of design and equipment focus; they provide similar benefits to the Talents of Player Characters, but the context is determined by the starship rather than by character behaviors.

SCALE

Vessels come in a wide range of sizes, from tiny shuttlecraft to stately cruisers and grand battleships. A vessel's Scale is a representation of its size, and it influences several other ratings a starship will use. Scale is a number, typically between 2 and 6 for Starfleet vessels, with larger numbers representing bigger ships. Most vessels fall into this range, though some exceptional craft — such as Borg cubes — may be larger, while Scale 1 is exclusively used for small craft such as shuttles.

A starship's Scale is used to determine a number of other things, but it relates most importantly to the ship's resilience — a ship with a greater Scale can resist attacks more easily, and withstand greater amounts of damage before systems are damaged, disabled, or destroyed. Ships with greater Scale can also project greater offensive power, allowing them to inflict greater damage with energy weapons like phasers and disruptors.

RESISTANCE

Starships are designed to be resilient, for the rigors of space exploration are considerable, and a vessel may have to survive with little or no support for months or even years at a time. This durability — a mixture of the ship's hull and spaceframe composition, the effectiveness of the structural integrity field and deflector shields, redundancies built into vital systems, and sheer size — is expressed as Resistance, which reduces incoming damage suffered by a ship in the same way as it does to a character or creature (though on a much larger scale).

STARSHIP SCALE TABLE

SCALE	EXAMPLE SHIPS
1	Shuttles, Fighters — small craft
2	Runabout
3	*Defiant*-class starship, Jem'Hadar attack ship, *B'rel* bird-of-prey, Maquis Raider
4	*Constitution*-class starship, *Intrepid* class starship, *Galor* class cruiser, Klingon D7 battle cruiser
5	*Akira*-class starship, *Excelsior*-class starship, *K'vort* bird-of-prey, *Vor'cha* attack cruiser
6	*Galaxy*-class starship, *Negh'var* battle cruiser, Jem'Hadar battle cruiser, *Sovereign*-class starship, *D'deridex*-class warbird
7	Borg sphere

A ship's basic Resistance is equal to its Scale, though other factors may modify or replace this.

SHIELDS

Starships and starbases are commonly equipped with powerful layers of deflector shields. These powerful force fields are designed to protect from attacks and hazards, deflecting impacts and absorbing energy discharges. These shields are not impervious to harm, and sufficient force and power can weaken or even break through, damaging the hull and other systems beneath.

A starship or starbase has a Shields rating, and this is reduced when the ship is subjected to damage, and which can be replenished through the actions of the crew and with time. If a vessel suffers too much damage from a single attack or hazard, then it will also suffer serious damage, which impairs the ship's function until repaired.

A ship normally has Shields equal to its Structure plus its Security, though other factors may modify or replace this. In most ways, a ship's Shields are equivalent to a character's Stress. However, ships do not suffer Injuries, as will be described in full later.

POWER

Vessels can generate massive amounts of power, but use much of it powering core systems like propulsion, shields, life support, sensors, computers, and so forth. A ship has a Power rating which represents its reserve and surplus power, which can be spent to boost or support a variety of actions taken with the starship, and which can be lost because of some complications, hazards, and consequences.

At the start of each scene, the ship generates its full capacity of Power, and any Power which remained unused at the end of the previous scene is lost. This provides characters with a pool of points to draw from when attempting actions with the ship, or otherwise using technologies that draw from the ship's power supplies. The basic operation of the ship — life support, communications, computers, and basic maneuvering — are assumed to have already been powered, and do not have to be considered under normal circumstances. Some actions — such as going to warp, or restoring depleted shields — require the expenditure of Power to perform the action (called a Power Requirement), while others can gain a bonus from using additional Power.

If no other benefit for using Power is listed, then the following effect can be used: when attempting a Task with the ship, one or more Power may be spent before rolling, with each point increasing the Complication range of the Task by one. This represents the risk of overloads and problems from putting too much power into a system. If the Task is successful, then the character generates one additional Momentum for each point of Power spent.

Power can also be lost because of Complications, damage, environmental phenomena, unusual weapons, and a range of other effects. If the ship would lose more Power than it

has remaining — that is, if the loss is sufficient to reduce the ship's current Power to less than 0 — then the ship suffers a Complication to a randomly-determined system. This Complication relates to the loss of vital power to some aspect of the ship's operation.

A ship's normal Power capacity is equal to its Engines system, though other factors may alter this.

CREW SUPPORT

Starships require a significant number of personnel, and a skilled officer knows best when to assign those personnel to different problems. Characters often have the advantage of Crew Support, in the form of these personnel. A ship has only a finite supply of Support, representing a small number of the crew available to them.

The total amount of Crew Support available is determined by the ship — each vessel has only a finite amount of crew on hand, most of whom will be busy on routine duties to keep the ship running, and form part of the background of the ship's normal activities. Spending Crew Support brings members of the crew from that mass of background activity into the forefront, putting focus on them and making them an active and significant part of the adventure. Spending Crew Support to bring Supporting Characters into play is described on p. 132.

A ship's normal allotment of Crew Support per mission is equal to its Scale.

OPERATING A STARSHIP

Starship Operations are a straightforward matter, in game terms. Characters will spend a lot of time aboard ship, and they will want to take full advantage of the systems, facilities, and personnel on board. As already discussed, actions involving a starship are split into two broad categories: actions taken on board a ship, and actions taken with the ship.

ACTIONS ABOARD SHIP

A ship is as much a location for action, as it is a tool for the characters. In many situations, characters may be called upon to attempt Tasks while aboard their own ship. These actions are resolved normally, though at the Gamemaster's discretion, the character may treat the ship's facilities and personnel as an Advantage.

This option should be used in any situation where the ship itself is not the means by which the Task is being performed.

SHIP ACTIONS

Conversely, if the character is actively making use of the ship itself to perform the Task — whether in small ways like using the ship's library computer to research something, or in large ways like flying between systems or firing photon torpedoes — then the ship becomes a much more prominent part of the Task.

In these situations, the ship itself assists the character's actions, rolling against a target number made from its own System and Department combination, and using one of its own Focuses, if relevant. It's advisable to get another player to roll the ship's dice for this purpose.

Except with the Gamemaster's express permission, no more than one character may assist on a Ship Action (so the character being assisted is aided by the ship and up to one other character). Ship Actions are typically harder to get assistance for; you can only fit so many officers around a single console, after all.

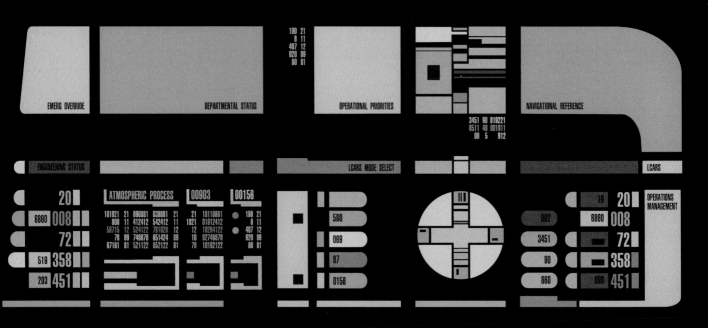

A HOME IN THE STARS
STARSHIP COMBAT

STARSHIP COMBAT

Combat between starships is no less deadly and intense than personal combat, and no less costly, but it is seldom as swift. Large, powerful vessels with powerful shields can weather hostile situations, while nimble craft can maneuver around stellar phenomena and make themselves difficult to attack. Once a vessel's shields are worn down and a target lock gained, grievous damage can be inflicted upon hull and systems, and may result in the deaths of dozens or hundreds of personnel.

Just as with personal combat, at the core of starship combat is the attack, a specific form of Task intended to inflict damage, but successful attacks against starships are seldom so final as against individual characters.

Starship combat uses the same action order as other Conflicts, as described at the start of *Chapter 7: Conflict*.

ENVIRONMENT AND ZONES

For spacecraft, positioning is as important as for individuals, though this applies in a few different ways than it does to people. Still, absolute and relative positioning are important elements to consider, and just as with personal combat, starship combat is resolved across abstract zones.

An environment for starship combat covers a large area — potentially an area tens or hundreds of millions of kilometers across, and even this is only a tiny fraction of the area within a star system. This area may be the edge of a nebula, an asteroid belt, the orbit of one or more small planets, or any other region of space, though it is worth remembering that because battles are always fought for a reason, they are often fought somewhere interesting. The environment is then divided into zones based on physical objects, spatial phenomena, and other details within the area. Starship combat zones can easily be defined in three dimensions, with zones "above" and "below" one another, and with empty zones to provide sizeable gaps between objects and phenomena. A relatively simple battlefield may consist of three to five significant zones, while complex environments may have many more. More zones are typically more

interesting than fewer, as they provide a greater variety of movement options and tactical opportunities, but this can take more planning on the part of the Gamemaster.

As with personal combat, zones have no fixed size, and these can be varied to accommodate the Gamemaster's preferences and needs, and to represent other factors. Zones within a nebula may be smaller, representing more difficult movement and sensor interference, while open space may have larger zones. By and large, the same advice that applies to personal scale zones apply to starship combat as well, and Gamemasters who desire concrete values rather than abstract ranges are encouraged to set specific sizes and shapes for individual zones, using them as a grid.

Individual zones may have terrain effects when the Gamemaster creates them. They may provide concealment or interference, hinder movement, present hazards to overcome, or otherwise alter the way vessels interact with the area.

VESSELS AND ZONES

To help Players visualize their vessel's place in an encounter, and to manage combat effectively, it's important to keep track of which zone each vessel is in at any given moment. This should be relatively easy in most cases. As zones are defined by the bodies and phenomena around them, tracking a vessel can be a matter of simple description — an enemy might be 'behind the moon' or 'on the edge of the gas cloud'. This has the advantage of relying on natural language and intuitive concepts, rather than specific game terms, and avoids the tracking of specific distances which can become fiddly where there are many vessels present.

Larger or particularly complex scenes may become tricky to track purely by memory, so the Gamemaster may wish to use something extra to help remind everyone of which vessel is where. If you're already using a sketched map, then marking vessel positions in pencil (so they can be easily erased and redrawn) is a simple approach, as is using tokens or miniatures, and moving them around as required.

REPORT TO THE ROMULAN HIGH COMMAND

"Under cloak, we trailed the Klingon squadron along the border for three days. Three *K't'inga*-class cruisers. We remained undetected, and the Klingons made no moves to enter Romulan territory. On the third day, the Klingons encountered a vast, luminous energy field, over 300 million kilometers in diameter. Sensors indicated power output beyond the capacity of the entire Romulan fleet emanating from within the cloud-like anomaly. We stayed under cloak, and backed away from the engagement.

The Klingons, typically, opened fire on the cloud, firing photon torpedoes to no effect. The energy field responded suddenly, projecting spherical bolts of high-energy plasma which utterly eliminated each of the cruisers, leaving behind no debris at all. The lead cruiser managed to broadcast a distress signal before it was disintegrated.

We were suddenly hit by a massively powerful scanning beam of some kind, emanating from the cloud. Systems overloaded all over the ship, and our cloak failed. I immediately ordered a full retreat, at maximum warp. The cloud made no hostile action toward us. I was struck immediately with the sense that an intelligence was at work here — an intelligence that had consciously decided to let us go.

Sensors confirmed that the energy field is moving. Extrapolation of its course has it leaving Klingon space, and entering Federation space — on a direct heading for the Human homeworld. Given what I have seen, my recommendation to the High Command is that we move ships and personnel to positions along our side of the Neutral Zone. If this thing is headed for Earth, we may soon be faced with a power vacuum in this quadrant, which could be of benefit to us if we are prepared to move swiftly.

Sensor logs are included in this broadcast. Hail to the Praetor. *Warbird Tovarek*, Captain Xevius commanding."

DISTANCES

Movement and ranged attacks need some sense of distance to make them meaningful. In combat, the relative placement of zones determines this distance. To keep things simple and fluid, range is measured in four categories, and one state.

- The state of **Contact** is when an object or other starship is touching the vessel. This state is used mainly for ships docking with starbases and other facilities, shuttlecraft coming in to land, and similar situations. Contact isn't a specific range, but rather is a state that a vessel can enter when it moves — that is, when a vessel moves into or within a zone, the Helmsman may freely declare that the vessel is moving into or out of Contact of an

object or another vessel. Moving into Contact too quickly can be dangerous, as high-speed collisions can cause considerable damage.

- **Close** range is defined as the zone the vessel is within at the time. Moving within Close range is a trivial affair. Close range is, in essence, a distance of 0 zones.

- **Medium** range is defined as any zone adjacent to the vessel's current zone. Medium range is a distance of 1 zone.

- **Long** range is defined as objects and vessels two zones away from a vessel's current zone. Long range is a distance of 2 zones.

- **Extreme** range is any vessels and objects beyond Long range. Extreme range is a distance of three or more zones.

Communication within a starship combat is a simple matter; subspace communications works at faster-than-light speeds that far exceed the maximum velocity of a starship, meaning that communicating with anyone else in the same combat is instantaneous whether they are within Close range or out at Extreme range.

GOING TO WARP

Starships are capable of travelling extremely quickly, which means they're quite capable of leaving the vicinity of a battle at a moment's notice.

When a ship goes to warp, whichever character is operating the Helm must spend one or more Power, and attempt a Control + Conn Task, with a Difficulty of 0 (modified by terrain as normal), assisted by the ship's Engines + Conn. The Power spent determines how quickly the ship is moving. If this Task is successful, the ship immediately leaves the area, which will normally end the scene, though the enemy may choose to pursue. A ship may not spend more Power to go to warp than its Engines score.

If the enemies wish to pursue, each pursuing ship must spend more Power than the fleeing ship did; if they do, they will quickly catch up with the fleeing ship. Once their pursuers have caught them, the crew of the fleeing ship must choose how they will respond.

DISTANCES AND SENSORS

In ideal circumstances, a starship can scan and detect objects, vessels, and phenomena over a certain size or magnitude for several light years in every direction. Long-range sensors are extremely potent in this regard. The closer an object is, the smaller objects and details can be effectively detected, with the greatest clarity and detail available at ranges of a few thousand kilometers. There are no hard-and-fast rules for this; a starship and its crew will use whatever sensors are most effective at a particular range, though the Gamemaster should adjust the amount of detail provided at different ranges.

MOVEMENT AND TERRAIN

Moving around in starship combat is the responsibility of a vessel's Helmsman, and typically requires a Task, though these Tasks have a Difficulty of 0 under normal circumstances.

Movement Tasks increase in Difficulty if the space the vessel is moving through is hindering or hazardous in any way, or if the vessel itself is being hindered or impaired in some way, such as by a tractor beam. The consequences of failure vary based on the nature of this hindrance or hazard; failure may result in the vessel simply not moving anywhere, in a Complication affecting the engines, the loss of some of the ship's Power, or some similar setback.

Hindering or hazardous terrain will often have a Scale of its own; this represents the maximum Scale of vessel that can traverse that terrain safely. When a ship is within an area of hindering or hazardous terrain, the ship will suffer no penalty for the terrain if its Scale is equal to or lower than the Scale of the terrain. If the ship has a Scale higher than that of the terrain, increase the Difficulty of Tasks to move through that terrain by +1 for each point the ship's Scale is higher than the terrain's.

BRIDGE POSITIONS, COMBAT TASKS, AND MINOR ACTIONS

As with personal combat, in any given Turn, a character can attempt a single Task, and several Minor Actions. Unlike with personal combat, however, the kinds of Tasks a character is likely to perform will vary based on their position on the Bridge (or elsewhere on the ship), and different officers will be given access to different systems as befits their positions.

This section lists the common roles found aboard a starship, the common Tasks they can attempt, and the Minor Actions they can perform.

MINOR ACTIONS

As described in *Chapter 7: Conflict*, Minor Actions are activities a character can undertake that don't count as a Task, and which don't require dice to be rolled. A character can attempt as many Minor Actions as they wish each Turn. However, only the first one comes with no cost. Each Minor Action taken after the first costs one Momentum (Immediate).

The most common Starship Minor Actions are as follows. These are specific to starship operations during combat; a character can perform personal combat Minor Actions (p. 171) if necessary, such as when being boarded.

- **INTERACT:** The character interacts with an object in the environment. Particularly complex interactions may require a Task instead. This covers basic and routine interactions with ship systems that aren't otherwise covered here.

- **CHANGE POSITION:** The character moves to any other station on the bridge, or to any other location on the ship. If that bridge station is unmanned, the character can take control of that station immediately; otherwise, the character takes control whenever the officer already at that station departs. If the character is moving to somewhere else on the ship, they will arrive in that location at the start of their next Turn.

- **PREPARE:** The character prepares for, or spends time setting up, for a Task. Some Tasks require this Minor Action to be taken before the Task can be attempted.

- **RAISE/LOWER SHIELDS:** Tactical only. The character raises or lowers the ship's Shields. If the shields are lowered, then the ship counts as having a Shields of 0. If the shields are raised, they immediately go to either their normal maximum score (if they are being raised for the first time that scene), or to their previous score (if they have taken damage during that scene). A character may not raise and lower shields during the same Round.

- **RESTORE:** The character performs the minor repairs and adjustments needed to restore a system after disruption or minor damage. Certain circumstances will call for the use of this Minor Action.

TASKS

A character can attempt a single Task during each Turn, though there are a few ways that a character can attempt a second Task. Regardless of the method used, a character cannot attempt more than two Tasks in a round.

- **DETERMINATION:** A character may spend one Determination in order to take a second Task during a Turn.

- **MOMENTUM:** A character may spend two Momentum from a successful Task in order to attempt a second Task; however, this second Task increases in Difficulty by one.

- **LEADERSHIP:** Some characters have actions that demonstrate their prowess as leaders, granting an additional Task to characters under their command. This Task is attempted immediately, during the commanding character's Turn, and is considered to be assisted by the commanding character.

The following Tasks are universal and can be attempted by any character during starship combat, regardless of their role. Personal Combat Tasks can also be attempted where relevant, such as when repelling boarders.

- **ASSIST:** The character performs some activity that will grant an ally an advantage. The character nominates a single ally they can communicate with, and declares how they are giving aid, including which Attribute, Discipline, and Focus (if any) they are assisting with. During the nominated ally's Task, the character provides assistance using the chosen Attribute, Discipline, and Focus, as normal for assisting on a Task.

- **CREATE ADVANTAGE:** The character attempts to create some favorable circumstance that benefits their side. This is a Task with a Difficulty of 2, using Attribute, Discipline, and Focus (if any) based on how they're trying to gain an advantage. If successful, the character creates an Advantage. At the Gamemaster's discretion, depending on the nature of the Advantage being created, the ship may assist this Task.

- **PASS:** The character chooses not to attempt a Task. If the character takes no Minor Actions this Turn, then the character does not count as having taken a Turn, and may act later in the Round instead.

- **READY:** The character declares that they are waiting for a particular situation or event to occur before attempting a Task. This situation or event must be chosen when Ready is declared, as must the Task to be attempted when that situation occurs. When this triggering situation occurs, the character with the readied Task temporarily interrupts the acting character's Turn to resolve the reading Task. Once the readied Task has resolved, events continue as normal. If the triggering situation does not occur before the character's next Turn, the readied Task is lost. Characters who take a readied Task can still perform Minor Actions during their Turn as normal.

- **OTHER TASKS:** A range of other Tasks can be performed during a combat, the limits of which are left to the discretion of the GM. Circumstances or objectives may dictate that a character attempts Tasks to repair or disable equipment during a combat (for example), or to perform other activities that don't directly relate to the fighting, and particularly desperate or dangerous situations may require overcoming Extended Tasks or even a Challenge while battle rages around them.

- **OVERRIDE:** The character overrides the controls of another role. The character may attempt a Task from any other role other than commanding officer, but increasing the Difficulty by one, due to the sub-optimal controls.

POSITIONS AND SPECIFIC TASKS

The most important Tasks attempted during starship combat are reserved for characters at particular positions, which are both a physical location and a set of accompanying responsibilities. Each position covers a particular subset of activities important for the operation of the ship. The key positions covered by the bridge are as follows, though these activities are typically grouped together into a smaller number of stations, as determined by the ship's configuration (see p. 257) — for example, a single station may combine both the Helm and Navigator positions into a single Conn station, and any character at that station is both helmsman and navigator.

Certain other element of the Starship Combat rules, particularly the effects of damage, may refer to specific characters by their bridge role. Use the list of roles below, regardless of how they are grouped together in practical terms.

- **COMMANDING OFFICER:** The CO makes the decisions based on the information available.

- **HELM:** The helmsman, or flight controller, is the pilot of the ship, responsible for all Tasks that require the ship's movement and maneuvering.

- **NAVIGATOR:** The navigator is in charge of plotting the ship's course and determining the spatial conditions that would affect the ship along its course.

- **SENSOR OPERATIONS:** Sensor operations — often handled by an officer skilled in Science — are used to control the many and varied external sensor systems the ship contains, used to scan planetary bodies, spatial phenomena, other vessels, and more besides. It also covers interpreting and analyzing that information, and the information retrieved from probes.

- **SECURITY OVERSIGHT:** This station covers all matters of internal security, such as containment fields, deployment of personnel, and internal sensors.

- **TACTICAL SYSTEMS:** This station covers the operation of weapons and shields.

- **COMMUNICATIONS:** This station covers all incoming and outgoing communications, including encryption and decryption of messages.

- **INTERNAL SYSTEMS CONTROL:** This station covers any miscellaneous monitoring and control of internal systems, such as damage control, transporters, and life support.

COMMANDING OFFICER

The following Tasks can be undertaken by characters who have assumed the commanding officer (CO) role. These Tasks do not require being at a particular station; rather, they are the result of status and authority aboard the ship. The commanding officer is the ship's captain, or whichever other character has been given command at that moment (the executive officer, 2nd officer, or any other bridge officer at the discretion of the commanding officer).

- **CREATE ADVANTAGE:** While not unique to commanding officers (this Task is listed on p. 221), it is particularly useful for characters in command, and normally uses one of Control, Insight, or Reason, plus Command, to perform the Task (Difficulty 2, success creates an Advantage).

- **DIRECT:** The CO provides clear, concise orders. Choose one other officer currently on the bridge; that officer attempts a single Task, determined by the CO. The CO assists this Task using the Command skill. **This action may be used once per scene by each character who has access to it.**

- **RALLY:** The CO inspires and coordinates the crew, attempting a **Presence + Command Task** with a Difficulty of 0; this Task is specifically to generate Momentum, either to use straight away or to save for the group.

A secondary commanding officer, common aboard 24th century vessels, cannot take actions that would contradict those of the captain, but can otherwise make use of the commanding officer Tasks, making the ship more efficient in a crisis by spreading the captain's workload.

HELM
The following Tasks can be undertaken by characters who are in the Helm role. Unless otherwise noted, these Tasks all require a **Control + Conn Task** with a Difficulty of 0, assisted by the ship's **Engines + Conn**, though circumstances may increase this Difficulty if there are celestial phenomena or other problematic factors involved.

- **MANEUVER:** The flight controller uses the ship's thrusters to adjust position and moves to anywhere within Medium range.

- **IMPULSE:** The flight controller uses the ship's impulse engines to adjust position and move to anywhere within Long range. This has a Power Requirement of 1.

- **WARP:** The flight controller uses the ship's warp drive to move two or more zones. This has a Power requirement equal to the number of zones to be moved. This represents short — seconds-long — bursts of warp speed, rather than longer journeys. Leaving the battlefield by going to warp is covered on p. 219.

- **EVASIVE ACTION:** The flight controller moves swiftly and unpredictably, attempting to foil enemy targeting. The flight controller attempts a **Daring + Conn Task** with a Difficulty of 1, assisted by the ship's **Structure + Conn**. If successful, until the flight controller's next Turn, all attacks against the ship, and all attacks made by the ship, increase their Difficulty by 1. This has a Power requirement of 1.

- **ATTACK PATTERN:** The flight controller takes a course that will make it easier to target the enemy. The flight controller attempts a **Daring + Conn Task** with a Difficulty of 2, assisted by the ship's **Weapons + Conn**. If successful, until the flight controller's next Turn, all attacks made by the ship reduce in Difficulty by 1 (to a minimum of 1; if already at 1, then gain one bonus Momentum instead). This has a Power requirement of 1.

- **RAMMING SPEED:** The flight controller chooses a single enemy vessel or other target within Long range, and moves towards them at full speed. This is an attack, requiring a **Daring + Conn Task** with a Difficulty of 2, assisted by the ship's **Engines + Conn**. This Difficulty increases by 1 for every range category beyond Close the target is. If successful, the attack inflicts a number of ▲ damage equal to 2 plus the ramming ship's Scale, with the Spread and Vicious 1 effects, and the Devastating quality. However, the ship also suffers a number of ▲ damage equal to the target's Scale, with the Spread and Vicious 1 effects, and the Devastating quality. This has a Power requirement of 1.

NAVIGATOR
The following Tasks can be undertaken by characters who are in the navigator role.

- **PLOT COURSE:** The navigator calculates the best course to the intended destination. This is a **Reason + Conn Task**, assisted by the ship's **Computers + Conn**, with a Difficulty of 3. If successful, the next Task the helmsman attempts reduces in Difficulty by 1. Reduce the Difficulty by a further 1 for every two Momentum spent (Repeatable)

- **CHART HAZARD:** The navigator, using navigational sensors, marks hazards in the vicinity of the vessel and its planned course, and determines the safest route around, past, or through them. This is a **Reason + Conn Task**, assisted by the ship's **Sensors + Conn**, with a Difficulty of 3. If successful, nominate a single hazard or other dangerous phenomenon nearby; the Difficulty of any Task to avoid that hazard is reduced by 2. The navigator can nominate one additional hazard or dangerous phenomenon for every two Momentum spent.

SENSOR OPERATIONS
The following Tasks can be undertaken by characters who are in the sensor operations role.

- **SENSOR SWEEP:** The sensor operator uses the ship's sensors to locate objects or phenomena in space, or otherwise obtain information about something going on outside the ship. This is a **Reason + Science Task**, assisted by the ship's **Sensors + Science**, with a Difficulty of 0. Interference, ambient conditions, or particularly unusual or unfamiliar phenomena should increase this Difficulty. Momentum spent on this Task is normally spent on the Obtain Information Momentum Spend, asking one question to the Gamemaster for each Momentum spent (Repeatable), though this is not required if the Player has some other use in mind for the Momentum.

- **SCAN FOR WEAKNESS:** The sensor operator scans an enemy vessel, looking for vulnerabilities, or attempting to gain some other advantage. The sensor operator chooses a single target they can detect, and attempts a **Control + Science Task** with a Difficulty of 1, assisted by the ship's **Sensors + Security**. This Task increases in Difficulty by 1 for each range category beyond Close between the ship and the chosen target. If this succeeds, then the vessel's next Attack, before the end of the sensor operator's next Turn, gains the Piercing 2 quality, ignoring two of the target's Resistance per Effect rolled. Further, if any bonus d20s are purchased for that next attack, it inflicts +1▲ damage for each bonus d20 purchased.

- **LAUNCH PROBE:** The sensor operator configures and launches a sensor probe in order to study a situation or phenomenon in more depth or from a safe distance. This Task does not require a roll, and has no Difficulty. However, it reduces the Difficulty of Tasks to make a Sensor Sweep with regards to phenomena near the probe by two, determines the range for Scan for Weakness from the probe, and means that hazards that result from proximity to the phenomena affect the probe instead of the vessel. The Probe has a Resistance of 1, and is destroyed if it suffers one or more points of damage.

SECURITY OVERSIGHT

The following Tasks can be undertaken by characters who are in the security oversight role.

- **INTERNAL SENSORS:** The security officer uses the internal sensors to detect the presence or absence of personnel in particular parts of the vessel. This requires a **Reason + Security Task**, assisted by the ship's **Sensors + Security**, with a Difficulty of 1. Momentum spent on this Task is often spent on the Obtain Information Momentum Spend, asking one question to the GM for each Momentum spent (Repeatable) — typically used to ask for precise location, numbers, species, and similar details — though this is not required if the player has some other use in mind for the Momentum.

- **DEPLOY SECURITY:** The security officer dispatches a team of security personnel to a particular location on the ship, possibly to deal with boarders, or some other breach of security. The officer sends a security team to the chosen location, then attempts a **Presence + Security Task**. The Difficulty of the Task is normally 1,

but the Task is opposed by the intruders; if successful, the security breach is contained.

- **INTERNAL CONTAINMENT FIELDS:** The security officer activates containment force fields in a particular section on the ship, to halt the movement of boarders or other unauthorized personnel. This is a **Reason + Security Task**, assisted by the ship's **Structure + Security**, with a Difficulty set by the GM based on the number, resilience, and armament of the intruders. If successful, the intruders are contained. The intruders may attempt a Task of their own to overcome the fields, with a Difficulty equal to 1+ the number of Momentum spent by the security officer on this Task.

TACTICAL

The following Tasks can be undertaken by characters who are in the tactical role.

- **FIRE WEAPON:** The tactical officer nominates a single active weapon system on board the ship, chooses a viable target for that weapon, and makes an attack. This is a **Control + Security Task**, assisted by the ship's **Weapons + Security**. The Difficulty is determined by the type of weapon used, and the conditions of the attack (enemy actions, spatial conditions, etc.).

- **MODULATE SHIELDS:** This Task has a Power requirement of 1, and cannot be attempted if the Shields are at 0. The Tactical officer attempts a **Control + Security Task**, assisted by the ship's **Structure + Engineering**, with a Difficulty of 2. If successful, the ship's Resistance is increased by +1, plus an additional +1 per Momentum spent (Repeatable). This bonus lasts until the next time the ship suffers one or more damage, after Resistance.

- **TRACTOR BEAM:** The tactical officer engages a tractor beam at a nearby object or vessel. This requires a **Control + Security Task**, assisted by the ship's **Structure + Security** with a Difficulty of 2, and can only be directed at a target within Close range. If successful, the target vessel is immobilized and cannot move unless it can break free, using their shield modulations, the raw power of their engines, or disabling the tractor beam emitter (a Task in its own right), with a Difficulty determined by the strength of the ship's tractor beam.

COMMUNICATIONS

The following Tasks can be undertaken by characters who are in the communications role.

- **HAILING FREQUENCIES OPEN:** The communications officer attempts to establish a communications link with a ship, facility, or other place that can receive subspace or similar transmissions. This requires a **Control + Engineering Task**, assisted by the ship's

Communications + Engineering, with a Difficulty of 0. The Difficulty increases based on interference and other factors that would impede communications systems, and the Difficulty will also increase if the message is being encrypted or coded. Success means that a channel has been opened and a hailing signal or message has been sent. Nothing requires that the contacted vessel, etc., respond to a hail.

- **RESPOND TO HAIL:** Functionally the same as the Hailing Frequencies Open action, though this action is taken in response to being hailed. The Difficulty is 0, unless interference or impedance are issues, or if the communications link is encrypted or encoded. Success means that both vessels can communicate visual, audio, and data freely, though Complications or other circumstances may limit some of these.

- **INTERCEPT:** The communications officer seeks to pick up and decipher the transmissions of others; they select a single vessel within Long range to intercept communications from. This is an **Insight + Engineering Task**, assisted by the ship's **Communications + Security**, with the Difficulty set by the Gamemaster based on the level of encryption. The character may use **Control + Engineering** and reduce the Difficulty by 1 if they have up-to-date knowledge of that culture's codes and ciphers. Success means that the message has been successfully intercepted, and its contents revealed.

- **SIGNALS JAMMING:** The communications officer transmits signals to interfere with the target's attempts to communicate. Choose a single vessel or other target within Medium range to jam. This has a Power requirement of 1. This is a **Control + Engineering Task**, assisted by the ship's **Communications + Security**, and the character chooses a Difficulty of 1, 2, or 3. Success means that the target increases the Difficulty of Hailing Frequencies Open or Respond to Hail Tasks by an amount equal to the Difficulty the communications officer chose.

- **DAMAGE REPORT:** The communications officer puts out a call to all decks, and promptly receives reports of damage from across the ship. This is an **Insight + Command Task**, assisted by the ship's **Communications + Engineering**, with a Difficulty of 1. If successful, reduce the Difficulty of one Task to perform repairs by one. Affect one additional Task for one Momentum (Repeatable), or reduce the Difficulty of one Task by an additional one for two Momentum (Repeatable).

INTERNAL SYSTEMS

The following Tasks can be undertaken by characters who are in the internal systems role.

- **POWER MANAGEMENT:** The officer reroutes power from various systems, replenishing reserves or freeing up power for other uses. This requires a **Daring** or **Control + Engineering Task with a Difficulty of 2**, which can Succeed at Cost. On success, the ship gains one point of Power, plus one additional Power per Momentum spent (Repeatable), which may exceed its normal maximum. Complications should represent power being removed from particular systems, increasing the Difficulty of future Tasks, or removing options until systems are repowered.

- **REGENERATE SHIELDS:** The officer routes power to the shield emitters, trying to replenish them. This has a Power requirement of 1. This requires a **Control + Engineering Task with a Difficulty of 1**, assisted by the ship's **Structure + Engineering**; the Difficulty increases by +1 if the ship's Shields are at 0. If successful, the ship regains 2 points of Shields, plus 2 more for each Momentum spent (Repeatable).

- **DAMAGE CONTROL:** The officer sends a damage control team, which attempts to repair a single Breach. The officer chooses a single Damaged or Disabled system, and attempts a **Presence + Engineering Task**, with a Difficulty determined by the system chosen (see p. 230); if successful, the system is restored to function and can be used again normally. This does not remove any Breaches the ship has suffered, only the penalties imposed by damage.

- **TRANSPORTERS:** This Task has a Power requirement of 1. The officer nominates a target (an object, group of small objects, or group of people) and a destination both within Close range of the ship (either or both of which may be within the ship itself). The officer then attempts a **Control + Engineering Task** with a Difficulty of 2, assisted by the ship's **Sensors + Engineering**; this Difficulty increases by +1 if the target is not on a transporter pad, and +1 if the destination is not a transporter pad, and may increase further based on interference or other conditions. The target cannot be transported to or from any location with more than 0 shields. This Task can also be performed from any transporter room, reducing the Difficulty by one.

MAIN ENGINEERING

While not on the bridge — though there is a secondary engineering station on the bridge that controls these functions — main engineering is important for the operation of a starship in battle.

A character in main engineering, or using the engineering station on the bridge, may use the internal systems Tasks, above. Further, any internal systems Task, with the exception of operating transporters, attempted while in main engineering reduces its Difficulty by 1 — accessing these systems is easier from Engineering than from anywhere else.

Characters in main engineering may also be able to handle more complex activities, such as Tasks or Challenges to make significant modifications or come up with unusual solutions to problems. Some complex technical tasks, especially those related to the ship's engines, must be performed in main engineering.

SCIENCE LABS

While most starships have an array of laboratories for scientific research and experiments, they are rarely important within combat.

There is, additionally, at least one sciences station on the bridge, which may use sensor operations Tasks, above. Some bridge configurations may add additional roles to a sciences Station (see p. 257).

NPCS AND STARSHIP OPERATIONS

The normal rules for starship combat are designed from the perspective of Player Characters operating a single ship, which will be the normal situation for most groups of Player Characters. However, this is wholly impractical for NPC ships, where the GM may be running several ships and doesn't necessarily want to track a half-dozen NPC bridge officers per bridge, each with their own rules.

As a result, there are some slightly streamlined rules for NPC starships.

Firstly, an NPC ship does not have specific crew at individual positions on the bridge — this level of detail is unnecessary for running an NPC ship. Instead, each NPC vessel has a **Crew Quality**, which provides ratings which serve as the Attribute and Discipline scores needed by the vessel for any given Task. NPC crew used in this way are always considered to have an applicable Focus.

CREW QUALITY	ATTRIBUTE	DISCIPLINE
Basic	8	1
Proficient	9	2
Talented	10	3
Exceptional	11	4

Because individual NPC crew are not being tracked, each NPC ship takes multiple Turns during each Round — one Turn for each point of Scale the ship has — representing the individual actions of that ship's crew. However, each Task attempted after the first during each Round from any single role increases in Difficulty by 1.

SHUTTLEBAY

Most starships have one or more launch bays for small craft, ranging from work pods to small personnel transports, to larger multi-role support crafts. These vessels are frequently used for transit (when transporters aren't available or suitable), reconnaissance, scientific surveys, and a range of other missions and may often be required to depart or return in hazardous situations.

Small craft may not enter or leave the shuttlebay while the starship's Shields are up, and launching or landing a small craft is a Task for the craft's pilot. Small craft operations are discussed in more detail on p. 232.

SICKBAY

During combat, sickbay prepares for that inevitable consequence of battle — when the fighting starts, people will get hurt. Characters and other personnel may become Injured, or suffer complications representing minor injuries, as a result of damage to the ship.

The Tasks a character performs in sickbay during starship combat are not meaningfully different to those they'd perform in personal combat (p. 172); the biggest difference is that those Tasks take place in sickbay, and can thus be assisted by the ship's **Sensors** or **Computers + Medicine**.

There will also be minor crew injuries throughout the ship, which medical personnel can deal with, quickly patching up the walking wounded and sending them back to their posts. When the ship has suffered one or more Breaches (see p. 227) during a scene, characters in sickbay can choose a single Department, and attempt a **Daring + Medicine Task**, with a Difficulty of 2, assisted by the ship's **Computers + Medicine**. If successful, the next Task which uses that Department may re-roll one d20, as injured personnel from that department rush back to work.

TRANSPORTER ROOMS

A transporter room — and a starship will have at least one of these — serves only one purpose: operating transporters. Each transporter room contains both a transporter pad, normally sufficient for five or six people at once, and all the control systems necessary to operate that transporter with maximum effectiveness.

A character in a transporter room can use the transporters Task (p. 224), but reduces the Difficulty of that Task by 1.

Further, direct access to transporter systems allows them to be altered or adjusted to create a specific effect or to counteract problems, which cannot be done remotely from elsewhere on the ship.

MAKING AN ATTACK

Attacks, as the most important and the most direct of Combat Tasks, require a little more discussion than the other Combat Tasks. The process for making an attack is as follows:

1. The attacker chooses the weapon they plan to attack with. This will be one of the weapon systems the vessel is equipped with — normally a choice between an energy weapons and torpedoes.

2. The attacker then nominates a viable target for that weapon: a single vessel or another viable target visible to the attacker. If the character is attempting to target a specific system, the chosen system should be declared at this stage.

3. The attacker attempts a **Control + Security Task**, assisted by the ship's **Weapons + Security**, with a Difficulty determined by the weapon used. For an energy weapon, the Difficulty is 2. For torpedoes, the Difficulty is 3. If a specific System has been chosen, increase the Difficulty by +1. In addition, if the target is not in the weapon's optimal range, increase the Difficulty by +1 for each range band outside the optimal range.

4. If the Task is successful, then the attack inflicts damage, as described in **Damage and Repairs**, below. If a specific system was not targeted, roll to determine which system was hit on the table below.

SYSTEM HIT TABLE

D20 ROLL	SYSTEM HIT
1	Communications
2	Computers
3-6	Engines
7-9	Sensors
10-17	Structure
18-20	Weapons

DAMAGE AND REPAIRS

When a vessel is successfully hit by an attack during combat, it inflicts damage; first to shields, and then possibly to the ship's systems. Some environmental hazards also come with a risk of damage, such as gravitational stresses, intense radiation, corrosive gases, micrometeors, extreme heat, ionic discharges, and so on.

In most ways, damage for starships is handled similarly to damage for characters. However, for clarity, the full process is described below.

Attacks and other hazards have a **damage rating**, which will be a quantity of Challenge Dice, or $\blacktriangle$, with the total rolled applied against the starship.

Ships have a quantity of **Shields**, representing the defensive fields; Shields function similarly to the Work track of an Extended Task. A ship's normal maximum Shields are equal to the ship's Structure, plus its Security. At the start of a new scene, a ship's Shields returns to their normal value.

Most ships also have a quantity of **Resistance** which reduces total damage received, allowing them to shrug off some of the effect of Attacks. Resistance comes in two forms — static values, which comes from shield strength, armor, and Structural Integrity, and numbers of $\blacktriangle$, which represent inconsistent and circumstantial protection, like Cover.

COVER AND CONCEALMENT

Cover and Concealment are common effects, representing objects that interfere with a vessel's ability to see or Attack a target directly. Cover and Concealment functions the same way for spacecraft as it does for characters — granting a quantity of additional Resistance in the form of one or more $\blacktriangle$. A zone will provide Cover or Concealment to all vessels within that zone. When an attack is made against a ship benefiting from Cover or Concealment, roll the listed number of $\blacktriangle$; the total rolled is added to the ship's normal Resistance, providing additional protection.

Cover or Concealment may have special effects that trigger on each Effect rolled on those $\blacktriangle$, just as attacks do. These should be determined by the Gamemaster in advance, but a few examples of this are:

- **DENSE:** The Cover or Concealment provided here is particularly dense, making it especially hard to score a telling hit. Each Effect rolled generates one additional Resistance.

- **FRAGILE:** The Cover or Concealment provided here is especially inconsistent, and protracted fire will disperse it entirely. Each Effect rolled permanently reduces the number of $\blacktriangle$ that area of Cover or concealment provides by one $\blacktriangle$ (to a minimum 0$\blacktriangle$); apply this effect after the current attack has been resolved.

- **VOLATILE:** The Cover or Concealment is exceedingly volatile, likely to ignite or detonate when exposed to weapons fire. If one or more Effects are rolled, then every vessel within the zone immediately suffers 5$\blacktriangle$ Piercing 2 damage. This damage increases by +1$\blacktriangle$ for each Effect rolled on the cover $\blacktriangle$. The zone does not grant cover or concealment against this attack, and it will not provide cover or concealment for the remainder of the scene.

Whenever any starship suffers damage, follow this procedure:

1. Roll the number of 🅐 for the attack or hazard's damage rating. The total rolled is the amount of damage the attack or hazard inflicts.

2. If the target has any Resistance dice (🅐 from Cover, etc.), roll those, and add the total rolled to any static Resistance the ship has. The total is the ship's total Resistance for that attack.

3. Reduce the total damage rolled by one for each point of total Resistance. If there's one or more damage remaining after this reduction, the starship loses one point of Shields for each point of remaining damage. The ship may also suffer one or more **Breaches** to the system struck, if any of the following conditions occur (if more than one condition occurs, each one causes a Breach). Breaches are defined below.

   A. If the ship suffers **five or more damage** from a single attack or hazard, after reduction from Resistance, the system hit suffers a **Breach**.

   B. If the ship is **reduced to 0 Shields** by that attack or hazard, it suffers a **Breach**.

   C. If the ship **had 0 Shields** before the attack or hazard, and the attack or hazard **inflicts one or more damage**, the ship suffers a **Breach**.

The effect of a Breach to a System varies based on two factors: which system was hit, and how many Breaches that system has already suffered. For each System, a Breach has an immediate impact, a short-term penalty such as being unable to use that System for a Turn. Then, if the number of Breaches suffered to that system exceeds certain Thresholds, the ship suffers additional penalties as well.

If a System has suffered a number of Breaches equal to or greater than half the ship's Scale, then it is **damaged**. If a System has suffered a number of Breaches equal to the ship's Scale, then it is **disabled.** If a System has suffered more Breaches than the ship's Scale, then it is **destroyed**.

What this means for each System is detailed in their individual sections below.

BREACHES TABLE

SCALE	DAMAGED	DISABLED	DESTROYED
1	N/A	1 Breach	2 or more Breaches
2	1 Breach	2 Breaches	3 or more Breaches
3	2 Breaches	3 Breaches	4 or more Breaches
4	2 Breaches	4 Breaches	5 or more Breaches
5	3 Breaches	5 Breaches	6 or more Breaches
6	3 Breaches	6 Breaches	7 or more Breaches
7	4 Breaches	7 Breaches	8 or more Breaches

COMMUNICATIONS DAMAGE

Damage to the Communications system will, obviously, interfere with the ship's ability to communicate, and to perform other activities that relate to communications technology.

IMPACT: Whenever the Communications system suffers one or more Breaches, it disrupts those functions temporarily. Until the communications officer performs the *Restore* Minor Action, the Communications System cannot be used to perform or assist any Tasks; additionally, any ongoing or persistent activities that require Communications Systems — such as transferring information over multiple rounds — are immediately halted, and cannot be resumed until that *Restore* Minor Action has been performed.

DAMAGED: If the total number of Breaches the Communications System has suffered is equal to or greater than half the Scale of the ship, then the System has been significantly Damaged. This increases the Difficulty of all Tasks that involve or are assisted by the ship's Communications by +2 until repaired. The Difficulty to repair this is 3.

DISABLED: If the total number of Breaches the Communications System has suffered is equal to the Scale of the ship, then the system has been Disabled. The Communications system cannot be used to perform or assist any Tasks, and communicating over distances greater than a few kilometers (Close range), using other subspace radios, etc. The Difficulty to repair this is 4, though at the Gamemaster's discretion this may be replaced with an Extended Task (Work 8, Magnitude 2, Resistance 0, base Difficulty 2).

DESTROYED: If the total number of Breaches the Communications system has suffered exceeds the ship's Scale, then the system has been Destroyed and must be replaced. This is identical to the disabled effect, but it cannot be repaired. Further hits on the Communications system damage the Computers system instead.

COMPUTERS DAMAGE

Damage to the ship's Computers will obviously affect the ship's ability to recall library information, and to process data. It will also impede the ship's automation, making other activities more complicated.

IMPACT: Whenever the Computers system suffers one or more Breaches, it disrupts those functions temporarily. Until the officer at the internal systems position (or someone in Engineering) performs the *Restore* Minor Action, the Computers system cannot be used to perform or assist any Tasks; additionally, all other Tasks attempted which are assisted by the ship increase their Complication range by 2, until that *Restore* Minor Action has been performed, due to disruptions in automation.

DAMAGED: If the total number of Breaches the Computers System has suffered is equal to or greater than half the Scale of the ship, then the System has been significantly Damaged. This increases the Difficulty of all Tasks that involve or are assisted by the ship's Computers by +2, and increases the Complication range of all other Tasks assisted by the ship by 1, until repaired. The Difficulty to repair this is 3.

DISABLED: If the total number of Breaches the Computers system has suffered is equal to the Scale of the ship, then the system has been Disabled. The Computers System cannot be used to perform or assist any Tasks, and the loss of automation increases the Complication range of all Tasks assisted by the ship by 3. The Difficulty to repair this is 4, though at the Gamemaster's discretion this may be replaced with an Extended Task (Work 10, Magnitude 2, Resistance 1, base Difficulty 2).

DESTROYED: If the total number of Breaches the Computers system has suffered exceeds the ship's Scale, then the System has been Destroyed and must be replaced. This is identical to the Disabled effect, but it cannot be repaired. Further hits on the Computers system damage the Communications system instead.

ENGINES DAMAGE

Damage to the ship's Engines impacts both propulsion and power generation aboard the ship, and this can be catastrophic if the damage becomes too severe.

IMPACT: Whenever the Engines system suffers one or more Breaches, it disrupts those functions temporarily. The ship loses 2 Power immediately. Further, until the internal systems officer (or someone in engineering) performs the *Restore* Minor Action, all Tasks assisted by the ship's Engines, or which have a Power requirement, increase in both Difficulty and Complication Range by 1.

DAMAGED: If the total number of Breaches the Engines system has suffered is equal to or greater than half the Scale of the ship, then the System has been significantly Damaged. This increases the Difficulty of all Tasks that involve or are assisted by the ship's Engines by +2 until repaired. Further, the ship loses 1 Power at the end of every Round until this is repaired. The Difficulty to repair this is 3.

DISABLED: If the total number of Breaches the Engines system has suffered is equal to the Scale of the ship, then the system has been Disabled. The Engines System cannot be used to perform or assist any Tasks (even those that would normally be Difficulty 0), loss of power generation means that the ship loses 2 Power at the end of every Round. The Difficulty to repair this is 5, though at the Gamemaster's discretion this may be replaced with an Extended Task (Work 10, Magnitude 3, Resistance 2, base Difficulty 2).

DESTROYED: If the total number of Breaches the Engines system has suffered exceeds the ship's Scale, then the system has been destroyed, and cannot be repaired. The ship cannot move or maneuver, it loses 3 Power at the end of every Round, and it has a normal Power capacity of 0 (meaning it will begin the subsequent scenes with 0 Power). Further, roll a number of ▲ equal to the number of Breaches that Engines have suffered beyond the ship's Scale (so, if the ship's Scale is 4, and it has suffered 6 Breaches to Engines, roll 2▲). If any Effects are rolled, the ship's warp engines lose containment, and may explode, as described in the "Warp Core Breach Imminent!" sidebar. Subsequent Breaches caused to Engines trigger another ▲ roll to see if the reactors lose containment.

WARP CORE BREACH IMMINENT!

Catastrophic damage to the engines is a serious matter, increasing the risk of losing containment over the volatile reactors that power the ship. The ships of many cultures, including the Federation, rely on powerful matter/antimatter reactions, which can cause catastrophic explosions if uncontrolled, while the Romulans use a similarly-dangerous artificial singularity to power their warp engines.

If the ship suffers a loss of containment, then the reactors may explode at any moment; roll one or more ▲ at the end of each Round, starting with 1 at the end of the Round in which the containment loss began, and increasing by +1▲ for each successive Round (so, 2▲ for the second round, 3▲ for the third, and so forth). If one or more Effects are rolled, the reactors explode, destroying the ship immediately, killing all aboard, and inflicting 3▲ Piercing 2 damage to all other ships within Close range. Add a number of additional ▲ to this damage equal to the exploding ship's Scale (bigger ships have bigger reactors).

This can, however, be avoided. Characters in engineering may attempt to stabilize the reactor, or they may try to eject the reactor entirely (though not all ships have the capability to eject their reactors, so their crews may wish to abandon ship).

STABILIZE THE REACTOR: This is an Extended Task, with Work 8, Magnitude 3, Resistance 2, and a Base Difficulty of 3. Succeeding at this Extended Task prevents the reactor from exploding. Common combinations for this will be **Daring or Control**, plus **Engineering**.

EJECT THE REACTOR: This is a **Daring + Engineering Task**, with a Difficulty of 2. Success means that the reactor is successfully ejected. If ejected, continue to roll to see if it explodes; when it does, it will not destroy the ship (as it's been ejected and is no longer within the ship), but all ships, including the one that ejected it, within Close range will still suffer damage when it detonates.

SENSORS DAMAGE

Damage to the ship's Sensors hinders the ship's ability to detect and analyze things nearby, which can be particularly troublesome as this also impacts weapons targeting and the ability to navigate.

IMPACT: Whenever the Sensors system suffers one or more Breaches, it disrupts those functions temporarily. Until the sensor operations officer performs the *Restore* Minor Action, no Task can be attempted which will use or be assisted by the ship's Sensors. Further, until that Minor Action is performed, all Attacks made by the ship increase in Difficulty by 1.

DAMAGED: If the total number of Breaches the Sensors system has suffered is equal to or greater than half the Scale of the ship, then the system has been significantly Damaged. This increases the Difficulty of all Tasks that involve or are assisted by the ship's Sensors by +2 until repaired. Further, any Attacks the ship makes increase in Difficulty by +1 until this damage has been repaired. The Difficulty to repair this is 3.

DISABLED: If the total number of Breaches the Sensors System has suffered is equal to the Scale of the ship, then the system has been Disabled. The Sensors System cannot be used to perform or assist any Tasks (even those that would normally be Difficulty 0), and attacks made by the ship increase in Difficulty by +2. The Difficulty to repair this is 4, though at the Gamemaster's discretion this may be replaced with an Extended Task (Work 10, Magnitude 2, Resistance 1, base Difficulty 2).

DESTROYED: If the total number of Breaches the Sensors System has suffered exceeds the ship's Scale, then the System has been Destroyed, and cannot be repaired. This

is identical to the Disabled effect, but it cannot be repaired. Further hits on the Sensors System damage the Weapons System instead.

STRUCTURE DAMAGE

Damage to the ship's Structure impacts the ship's integrity and resilience, as well as functions like life support.

IMPACT: Whenever the Structure System suffers one or more Breaches, the entire ship shudders, power conduits rupture, consoles explode, and personnel are hurled around. Roll 1🅰; if an Effect is rolled, then a random character on the ship (Player Character or important NPC) has been Injured (the character may Avoid the Injury as normal, if they would normally be allowed to). These Injuries are considered to be Lethal. For NPC ships, suffering one or more Breaches to Structure means that the ship has one fewer Turn during the next Round (this is not cumulative).

DAMAGED: If the total number of Breaches the Structure System has suffered is equal to or greater than half the Scale of the ship, then the System has been significantly Damaged. The vessel suffers fires and/or minor hull breaches somewhere on the ship, forcing the area to be evacuated and sealed off. This makes it more problematic to reach parts of the ship in need of repair, increasing the Complication Range of all Engineering Tasks to repair Systems by 2. This also reduces the ship's Resistance by 1. The Difficulty to repair this is 3.

DISABLED: If the total number of Breaches the Structure System has suffered is equal to the Scale of the ship, then the System has been disabled. The vessel has suffered many fires and serious hull breaches, as well as sections losing life support. The extreme disarray of the ship makes it extremely difficult to perform repairs, increasing the

ALL HANDS, ABANDON SHIP!

If a ship has been crippled (has its Structure destroyed), or is at risk of a reactor breach, or is otherwise in some other desperate situation that the ship cannot escape, the commanding officer may give the order to abandon ship. Starships are fitted with large numbers of escape pods, each of which can hold a small number of crew and allow them to either survive in space for a short while, or fly to a nearby planet, and await rescue. These, along with the ship's complement of shuttlecraft — and if near enough to a planet or allied ship, transporters — allows the ship's crew to evacuate quickly and safely.

It requires a Change Position Minor Action, and a **Daring + Conn** Task with a Difficulty of 0, in order to board and launch an escape pod. Each escape pod is designed to carry four individuals

normally, but they can carry up to six if necessary (though more people reduces the life support capabilities of the pod). Launching a Shuttle is covered on p. 232.

For the rest of the crew, it can be assumed that at least 50% of the personnel on board escape the ship by the end of the Round in which Abandon Ship has been ordered. The other 50% will leave in the following Round. Starfleet personnel, and all those who serve or live aboard a starship, have been trained and drilled to respond quickly to emergencies of this sort.

What happens to the ship and her crew after they've abandoned ship… is up to the Gamemaster to determine.

Complication range of all Engineering Tasks to repair the ship by 3, and the Difficulty of all Engineering Tasks to repair the ship by +1. This also reduces the ship's Resistance to half (rounding down) its normal value. The Difficulty to repair this — including the penalty from this damage — is 5, though at the Gamemaster's discretion this may be replaced with an Extended Task (Work 10, Magnitude 3, Resistance 2, base Difficulty 1).

DESTROYED: If the total number of Breaches the Structure System has suffered exceeds the ship's Scale, then the ship's hull integrity has been massively compromised, requiring nothing less than a full rebuild in Spacedock. With hull breaches across the ship, fires raging, and life support systems failing, the ship is crippled. The ship's Resistance is 0, Tasks to repair other systems on the ship can no longer be attempted during combat, and the ship may not move except by thrusters, as rapid movement might tear the ship apart. Subsequent hits to Structure affect the Engines System instead.

WEAPONS DAMAGE

Damage to the ship's Weapons naturally impairs the ship's ability to defend itself, making it harder to make attacks. Severe damage may even result in other problems, as munitions like photon torpedoes are volatile.

IMPACT: Whenever the Weapons system suffers one or more Breaches, it disrupts those functions temporarily. Until the tactical officer performs the *Restore* Minor Action, the ship cannot make any attacks, nor can it attempt any other Tasks which involve or would be assisted by the ship's Weapons System.

DAMAGED: If the total number of Breaches the Weapons System has suffered is equal to or greater than half the Scale of the ship, then the System has been significantly Damaged. This increases the Difficulty of all Tasks that involve or are assisted by the ship's Weapons by +2 until repaired — naturally, this includes attacks. The Difficulty to repair this is 3.

DISABLED: If the total number of Breaches the Weapons System has suffered is equal to the Scale of the ship, then the System has been Disabled. The Weapons System cannot be used to perform or assist any Tasks (even those that would normally be Difficulty 0), which means the ship cannot make Attacks. The Difficulty to repair this is 4, though at the Gamemaster's discretion this may be replaced with an Extended Task (Work 8, Magnitude 2, Resistance 1, base Difficulty 2).

DESTROYED: If the total number of Breaches the Weapons system has suffered exceeds the ship's Scale, then the system has been Destroyed, and cannot be repaired. This is identical to the Disabled effect, but it cannot be repaired. Further, roll 1▲ if the ship fired any weapons during this Turn; if an Effect is rolled, then the ship suffers a single hit from the

weapon used most recently, as energy weapons discharge unsafely or torpedoes detonate. Further hits to the Weapons System will affect the Sensors instead.

REPAIRING DAMAGE

If a ship has been damaged, Tasks can be attempted to try and repair that damage. These will not be full repairs — this would take time and resources not readily available in battle — but starships are designed with redundancies and back-ups, and a skilled engineer can re-route around damaged Systems to create impromptu solutions.

The Damage Control Task listed on p. 224 is a typical way of repairing a damaged System, representing an officer sending a repair team to handle the repairs. However, this is not the only way to repair damage; using the Change Position Minor Action to move elsewhere in the ship, a character can head to the site of the damage, and attempt to perform the repairs personally. This will take a **Daring** or **Control + Engineering** Task.

NPC STARSHIP DAMAGE

NPC STARSHIP DAMAGE

While NPC vessels can make use of the full damage rules, this can become burdensome in larger battles where there are many ships involved. In these situations, the following quick damage rules can be used as an alternative.

If no specific system has been targeted on an NPC ship using these rules, do not roll for which System has been hit. Instead, apply the following effects.

IMPACT: Whenever the ship suffers one or more Breaches, it loses a single Turn during the next Round. This is not cumulative. It also loses 2 Power.

DAMAGED: If the total number of Breaches the NPC ship has suffered is equal to or greater than half the Scale of the ship, then the ship has been significantly Damaged. This increases the Difficulty of all Tasks attempted by the ship by +2 until repaired. The Difficulty to repair this is 3.

DISABLED: If the total number of Breaches the NPC ship has suffered is equal to the Scale of the ship, then the ship has been Disabled. The ship is no longer fully-operational and cannot take any further Turns during this scene.

DESTROYED: If the total number of Breaches the NPC ship has suffered exceeds the ship's Scale, then the ship has been destroyed utterly. The ship explodes in a burst of flame and a shower of scrap metal, though this explosion is not large enough to cause damage to other ships.

Regardless of which method is used, the Difficulty for repairs is set by the damage suffered, as noted in each System's damage section. This will normally be 3 for Damaged Systems, or 4 for Disabled Systems, and the Gamemaster has the option to ask for an Extended Task to repair a Disabled System instead.

Repairs made will remove the penalties and restrictions imposed by Damaged or Disabled Systems, but it cannot actually remove the Breaches that caused those conditions. As a result, if a Damaged System is repaired, and then suffers an additional Breach, it may suffer the Damaged condition for that System again (or worse) for the next Breach. **Breaches cannot be repaired in combat**, or during an adventure; instead, such intensive repairs require days or weeks of work, often at a starbase or other facility, and should be considered to occur between adventures.

During the course of battle or other challenging situations, the ship may also suffer Complications that relate to the condition or function of the ship. These can also be removed by Engineering Tasks, and regarded as repairs. The normal Difficulty to remove these is 2, though this may vary based on the Gamemaster's discretion.

STARSHIP WEAPONS

Starship Weapons have a number of common traits and values that determine the specifics of how they function. The key elements of a weapon are what type of weapon it is, its damage rating, the size of the weapon, and any qualities it possesses that influence how it is used.

- **TYPE:** This will either be Energy or Torpedo, depending on the form the weapon takes and how it is used.

- **RANGE:** This will be one of Close (or C), Medium (M), or Long (L). This is not a maximum range, but rather the optimal range of the weapon. If the target is at that distance, the Difficulty of the attack is unchanged. If the target is closer or further away, increase the Difficulty of the attack by +1 for each category (Close, Medium, Long, or Extreme) away from the weapon's Range.

- **DAMAGE RATING:** This is a number of Challenge Dice, and possibly one or more Damage Effects which trigger when one or more Effects is rolled. The damage of many starship weapons is dependent upon the ship they are installed upon — larger vessels have more power to devote to energy weapons, and a greater number of individual weapons, and combat-focused vessels often use more advanced and powerful systems. Each such weapon rolls a number of Challenge Dice equal to its Scale, plus the ship's Security department. Some systems may have additional modifiers.

- **QUALITIES:** These are additional rules, providing additional restrictions or benefits that apply to the weapon's use.

WEAPON TYPE

There are two types of weapons commonly used aboard starships: directed energy weapons, which project beams or pulses of coherent energy, plasma, or energized particles, and torpedoes, which are heavy projectiles carrying powerful explosive or energetic payloads.

- **Energy** weapons are the primary armament of most vessels, as they are straightforward, effective, and do not require additional heavy munitions stores — only rechargeable power cells and relays that connect to the vessel's power systems. Attacks using energy weapons have a basic Difficulty of 2. Making an attack with an energy weapon has a Power requirement of 1, and may spend up to two additional Power to increase the damage by +1▲ per additional Power spent.

- **Torpedo** weapons, such as the common photon torpedoes employed by vessels of many species, are programmable, self-propelled projectiles with an explosive payload, such as a quantity of antimatter, or some manner of field generator. Attacks with torpedoes do not have a Power requirement, but also cannot use additional Power to add bonus ▲. However, firing torpedoes can be considered to escalate hostilities, so attacking with torpedoes immediately adds 1 to Threat. Characters may choose to fire a torpedo salvo instead of a single torpedo (also known as a "Full Spread"), which adds 2 more to Threat, but which adds +1▲ to the attack's Damage and grants the Spread effect. Attacks using torpedoes have a basic Difficulty of 3.

Additionally, many vessels are equipped with a Tractor Beam Emitter, which has only one value — a strength, which is the Difficulty of Tasks attempted to break free from the beam's effects.

DAMAGE EFFECTS

The following abilities provide additional benefits whenever an Effect is rolled on the ▲ (see *Challenge Dice* on p. 6). When one or more Effects are rolled, all Damage Effects that apply to that attack are triggered.

- **AREA:** The attack affects a wider area, and can affect several targets at once. The attack automatically affects any vessel or damageable object within Contact of the initial target, and then one additional target within Close range of the initial target for each Effect rolled, starting with the next closest (as determined by the GM). If one or more Complications is rolled when using an Area attack, the GM may choose to use Complications to have an allied vessel or neutral bystander in the area affected by the attack. A target cannot be hit if it would have been more difficult to hit than the initial target.

DAMPENING: The attack removes one point of the target's Power for each Effect rolled.

PERSISTENT X: The attack leaves behind a lingering energy field, which continues to damage the target. At the end of each Round, the target vessel suffers an additional X damage. This lasts for a number of rounds equal to the number of Effects rolled.

PIERCING X: The attack ignores X points of the target's total Resistance for each Effect rolled.

SPREAD: The Attack inflicts additional damage elsewhere on the target. If one or more Effects is rolled, the Attack inflicts one additional hit to a random system (even if the Attack was targeting a specific system), which deals half the damage of the initial hit, rounding up, +1 for every Effect rolled after the first. This additional hit is resolved separately, and each hit against the target is reduced by Resistance, reduces Shields, and potentially causes Breaches, individually.

VICIOUS X: The Attack inflicts X additional damage for each Effect rolled.

QUALITIES
The following additional qualities alter the way the weapon functions, some in positive ways, others by applying restrictions.

CALIBRATION: The weapon requires careful calibration before firing. The weapon cannot be used to attack unless a *Prepare* Minor Action is performed during the same Turn.

DEVASTATING: Engineering Tasks to repair Damage caused by this weapon increase in Difficulty by one.

HIDDEN X: The weapon is concealed from scans. When the weapon is hidden, any scan of the vessel to locate the weapon increases in Difficulty by X. A character may use a single Minor Action to conceal a Hidden weapon.

HIGH-YIELD: The weapon inflicts massive damage to enemy vessels; if the Attack inflicts one or more Breaches to a system, it inflicts one additional Breach.

VERSATILE X: The attack gains X points of bonus Momentum if successful.

STARSHIP COMBAT MOMENTUM SPENDS
Momentum is a key tactical resource during combat. When a character generates Momentum in combat, he has numerous options available to him which can help overcome his enemies, empower his allies, and bolster his own prowess.

The following table provides a number of additional options available to a character when he generates one or more Momentum in combat. These are in addition to the normal uses of Momentum, and any others that Players or GM create themselves.

Under Cost, where a spend is listed with an "R", it means the spend is Repeatable. Where the spend is listed with an "I", it means the spend is Immediate. If neither note is present, then the Momentum spend may only be used once per Round at most.

STARSHIP COMBAT MOMENTUM SPENDS TABLE

MOMENTUM SPEND	COST	EFFECT
Bonus Damage	1 R	A character can increase the damage inflicted by a successful attack, regardless of the type of attack. Each Momentum spent adds +1 damage.
Penetration	1 R	The damage inflicted by the current attack ignores an amount of the target's Resistance equal to two for each Momentum spent.
Re-Roll Damage	1	The player may re-roll any number of 🅰 from the current attack
Devastating Attack	2	Roll an additional system; that system suffers an additional hit dealing half the primary attack's damage, rounding up.
Swift Task	2	The character may attempt one additional Task, increasing the Difficulty by one over what the Task would normally require.
Power Loss	1 R	The attack also removes one point of the target's Power.

SMALL CRAFT OPERATIONS

Shuttles and other small craft — also known as auxiliary craft — are commonly found aboard starships and starbases, as well as on a range of other facilities. The terms apply to any small vessel which can function independently of a starship for a short time, and which are employed in circumstances which would be unsuitable for a full-size starship.

Use of Shuttles to move personnel and cargo short distances (between ships) is less common with the use of transporters do fulfil those roles, but it's always valuable to have a few auxiliary craft on board in case of emergencies or unusual situations.

In game terms, Small Craft are Scale 1 and Scale 2 craft, with a few additional considerations.

- **TRAITS:** All Small Craft have the Trait **Small Craft** in addition to any others.

- **SYSTEMS:** Small Craft have the same set of Systems as a Starship, though their scores tend to be somewhat lower as befits their smaller size and more limited capabilities. Unarmed Small Craft have a Weapons System of 0.

- **DEPARTMENTS:** Small Craft have the same set of Departments as a Starship, but their scores are never higher than 2, and are often 0, due to limited facilities and a complete lack of support personnel. The only Department a Small Craft will always have will be Conn, which will always be at least 1.

- **TALENTS:** Small Craft do not normally have Talents. Some advanced, unique, or customizable Small Craft, such as a runabout, or the *U.S.S Voyager's* Delta Flyer, may have one or two Talents as befits their more advanced capabilities.

- **SCALE:** As noted above, Small Craft are normally Scale 1, or Scale 2 at the most.

- **RESISTANCE:** Small Craft have Resistance per their Scale, as normal.

- **SHIELDS:** Small Craft have Shields equal to half their normal values; add together Structure and Security, then halve the total, rounding down.

- **POWER:** Small Craft have much smaller power plants than full-size starships, and only generate Power equal to half their Engines score (rounding up).

- **CREW SUPPORT:** Small Craft do not have Crew Support.

- **MAXIMUM CAPACITY:** Small Craft can only carry a finite number of characters, as noted in each entry.

- **POSITIONS:** Small Craft have two positions: Pilot (covering helm and navigation), and Operations (internal systems, sensors, and tactical if the craft has weapons). There are no other positions aboard.

In addition to the above, when small craft are attacked by any full-size starship (any vessel of Scale 3 or above), the Difficulty of the attack increases by +1.

LAUNCH AND LANDING PROCEDURES

Most starships carry far more small craft, of many different kinds, than can actually be supported at any one time. Ships will hold several shuttles, shuttlepods, work bees, and other auxiliary craft in storage in case of emergencies or to replace lost craft, but only a fraction of the ship's full complement will be ready and available for use most of the time.

A starship can support a number of active small craft equal to its Scale minus 1 at any one time. This number is doubled for ships with the Extensive Shuttlebays Talent, as they're specially equipped to handle large quantities of auxiliary craft. Runabouts and any other Scale 2 craft, being significantly larger than most auxiliary craft, count as two craft towards this limit. Further, only vessels with an Extensive Shuttlebay (as per the Talent) can support runabouts.

Moving to the shuttlebay uses the *Change Positions* Minor Action to relocate to a different part of the ship, and then a *Maneuver* Task (with a Difficulty of 0) to launch and pilot the Shuttle to any point within Close range of the ship (but outside of it). Launching a shuttle cannot be performed while a ship's Shields are up.

Landing a shuttle is similar, requiring a *Maneuver* Task under a few stipulations: the shuttle must be within Close range of the ship, and the ship's shields may not be up. Under normal circumstances, this requires no further Task as the shuttle is guided in by tractor beams and lands safely. In an emergency, a rapid landing may be required, increasing the Difficulty by 2, and causing 6▲ damage to the shuttle (this may Succeed at Cost at the Gamemaster's discretion, allowing the shuttle to crash-land, but the resultant crash-landing means that the shuttlebay cannot be used again that adventure).

SHUTTLES AND RUNABOUTS

OVERVIEW: The need for short range, ship-to-surface shuttlecraft has been a continual one for Starfleet with much of the Federations infrastructure built in orbit around inhabited planets or in orbit around a system's star. Before the 2250s, shuttle design changed quickly and wasn't standardized across the Federation, making maintenance and repair an issue when away from their planet of origin and spare parts that worked. The class-F "Federation" shuttlecraft was the first fully standardized shuttlecraft manufactured by all shipyards and member worlds. But by the early 2300s, Starfleet knew that the class-F shuttlecraft was approaching the end of the design's usefulness. The type-6 shuttlecraft was designed to closely resemble the refitted class-F *Galileo*-type shuttle of the 2280s and the engineers designing it were told to hold very close to the exterior dimensions of the *Galileo*-type. Seeing a need for a larger personnel and cargo transport shuttle after the limitations of the internal space of the type-6 shuttlecraft became apparent, Starfleet issued a directive calling for the design and construction of a larger 'Medium Range Cargo and Personnel Shuttle': the type-7 was still the box-like shape and two nacelles common to all Starfleet shuttles, but in a deviation from what was expected, its edges were rounded and curved, giving it a fluid shape akin to a sea creature or a tear drop. In the early 2360s, Starfleet

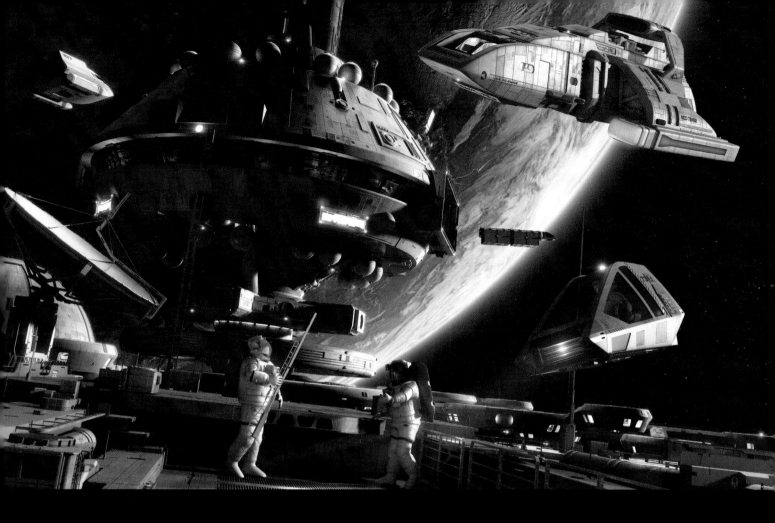

Command saw the need for a vessel that could fill the role of a large shuttlecraft, but also be able to be used in more independent assignments away from parent craft or starbases. The result was the *Danube* class runabout that began production across the Federation in 2368.

CAPABILITIES: The type-6 shuttlecraft upgraded its systems compared to its type-4 predecessor, with the impulse drive having its own fusion power core, and the nacelles on the ventral sides of the shuttle having warp coils that are powered by their own fusion reactors, giving the shuttle a limited FTL capability of slightly over warp 1. Improvements in offensive and defensive technologies allowed the installation of deflector shield emitters, allowing it to survive in more hostile environmental conditions, but still too weak for any real defense against an opponent, with the addition of two modular phaser mounts for type-4 phasers. The *Danube*, however, was capable of warp 5 indefinitely due to its compact warp core and small, but efficient warp coils. This gave the *Danube* class enough range to be assigned to scout duties. The main limitation of the design was the shuttle-sized crew compliment of only four, however, in an emergency, some *Danube* class vessels have been able to handle up to 40 humanoids for up to two hours before life-support systems become overloaded. The typical assignments intended for this class are starbase support, planetary defense, and cargo and personnel transport, and in these roles, they excel. Further assignments can be undertaken due to a modular pod located on the top of a 'roll-bar' and above the primary warp injection manifold. Mission specific pods can include a high-resolution multi-spectral sensor platform for scouting and exploration duties, or a cargo pod able to transport nearly 10% of the vessels mass in dry, liquid, and hazardous materials. Additionally, a weapons pod can be fitted that can include a micro-torpedo launcher or a type-9 phaser array in addition to a small self-contained fusion reactor able to handle the increased power demands. These modular systems are in addition to the vessel's standard equipment that includes a photon torpedo launcher located on the ventral surface of the vessel, four type-6 phaser arrays, a significant shielding capacity compared to many smaller shuttlecraft, and a powerful tractor beam capable of towing much larger vessels at warp speeds. The small size of the vessel meant that starbases and outposts could often produce and maintain at least a single *Danube* class from local materials.

SHUTTLEPOD

A tiny craft, designed to move small numbers of personnel or small quantities of cargo over short distances. They are unarmed, not fitted with a transporter, and not capable of travelling at warp.

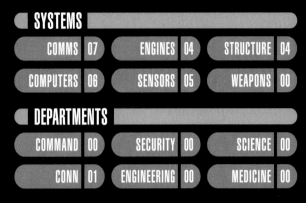

SYSTEMS

COMMS	07	ENGINES	04	STRUCTURE	04
COMPUTERS	06	SENSORS	05	WEAPONS	00

DEPARTMENTS

COMMAND	00	SECURITY	00	SCIENCE	00
CONN	01	ENGINEERING	00	MEDICINE	00

POWER: 2   **SCALE:** 1
SHIELDS: 2   **RESISTANCE:** 1

CREW COMPLEMENT: 1 or 2, plus 1 passenger

ATTACKS: None

SHUTTLECRAFT

A small vessel, designed to move small numbers of personnel or small quantities of cargo over short to medium distances. They are unarmed, but can be fitted with a small phaser bank, and they can travel at low warp (*Next Generation* era only; Original Series era shuttles could not travel at warp speeds).

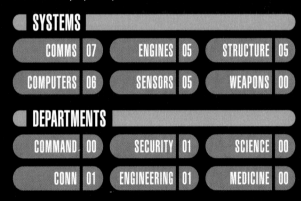

SYSTEMS

COMMS	07	ENGINES	05	STRUCTURE	05
COMPUTERS	06	SENSORS	05	WEAPONS	00

DEPARTMENTS

COMMAND	00	SECURITY	01	SCIENCE	00
CONN	01	ENGINEERING	01	MEDICINE	00

POWER: 3   **SCALE:** 1
SHIELDS: 3   **RESISTANCE:** 1

CREW COMPLEMENT: 1 or 2, plus 6 passengers

ATTACKS: None. The shuttlecraft may be armed, giving the shuttlecraft Weapons 5, and a Phaser Bank (Range Medium, 3▲, Versatile 2). Arming the shuttlecraft has a Cost: Escalation 2 (see p. 184).

DANUBE CLASS RUNABOUT
NEXT GENERATION ERA ONLY

These larger auxiliary craft are used for independent operations from larger starships and starbases. They are capable of warp 5, contain a small transporter and a replicator, and are fitted with phaser arrays for defense. A modular construction allows them to be converted to serve different purposes.

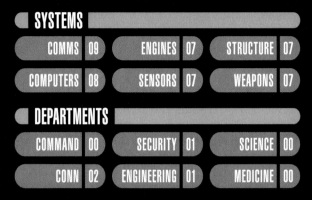

SYSTEMS

COMMS	09	ENGINES	07	STRUCTURE	07
COMPUTERS	08	SENSORS	07	WEAPONS	07

DEPARTMENTS

COMMAND	00	SECURITY	01	SCIENCE	00
CONN	02	ENGINEERING	01	MEDICINE	00

POWER: 4   **SCALE:** 2
SHIELDS: 4   **RESISTANCE:** 2

CREW COMPLEMENT: 1 to 4

ATTACKS:
- Phaser Bank (Energy, Range Medium, 4▲, Versatile 2)

- Micro-torpedoes (Torpedo, Range Long, 4▲ High-Yield)

- Tractor Beam (Strength 1)

CUSTOMIZABLE MODULES: The runabout may be fitted with one of the following modules for additional functionality.
- **PASSENGER TRANSPORT:** The runabout's aft module has been configured for carrying large numbers of passengers. The runabout may carry up to 10 passengers, or up to 40 in an emergency (maximum 2 hours).
- **CARGO TRANSPORT:** The runabout's aft module has been configured to carry cargo.
- **LONG DURATION MISSION:** The runabout's aft module has been configured to serve as a rest area and sleeping quarters for up to four personnel.
- **ATTACKS:** The runabout's aft module has been converted to provide additional, and higher-powered, weaponry. Add +2▲ to damage of the runabout's weapons. This has a Cost: Escalation 2 (see p. 184).

"How would I describe *Danube* runabouts? I'd say they were like Pick-Gnats buzzing around your glass of *rokassa* juice. You wave your hands at them to clear them away, but you never can get rid of them. They just fly away and lazily come back towards their goal. Don't get me wrong, *Danube's* aren't just annoyances, they can be deadly in numbers, and just like Pick-Gnats they can infuriate you and force you into bad decisions. Starfleet's choice to make *Danube's* modular make them even more infuriating since you never know if the runabout is only equipped with sensors or if it has enough weapons installed to menace a *Galor*. Be wary, because some of these Pick-Gnats sting."

Gul Fuhtoh of the 18th Detachment, 3rd Order.

CHAPTER 09.60

A HOME IN THE STARS
STARFLEET SHIPS OF THE LINE

STARSHIP CREATION

Every starship is unique. The specifics of each vessel's mission profile, the legacy of the events they have been party to, the refits and repairs they've undergone, and the requirements of the crews that have served with them make each starship a distinct entity in more than just name. Even two ships of the same class will differ in small but meaningful ways, as the lessons learned in the construction and service of previous ships of that class will shape the way that their sister ships will be assembled.

This is reflected in **Star Trek Adventures**, where the Players' starship will be as unique as their characters, having gone through a similar process of creation. If the Players choose to command a *Constitution*-class starship, theirs will not be a facsimile of the legendary *U.S.S. Enterprise*, but a distinct vessel with its own proud history of exciting adventures.

Starship Creation follows a specific process, which is similar to the Lifepath system used for creating a character, though somewhat shorter. This process is as follows:

1. **SERVICE:** The year in which the ship exists, which will determine how long the ship has been in service for. The Gamemaster and the Players select the year when the game is set, which has bearing on later stages.

STARFLEET SHIP DESIGN DOCTRINE

By this point in the course you've doubtless noticed that Starfleet ships tend to fall into two broad design categories. Vanguard vessels generally consist of a saucer section, two nacelles, and a drive section connecting the two. Support ships have a saucer and nacelles, but usually have no drive section or feature a utility pod.

You've read about legendary ships, the *Constitutions*, the *Excelsiors*, *Ambassadors*, and the new *Galaxies*. Those ships are equipped for long-term exploration and military maneuvers and are equipped to deal with multiple threats and unknown phenomena. Vanguards boldly go; support craft get to bravely follow. *Miranda* and *Nebula* class ships are nearly as fast as their elder sister ships, but they run with a smaller crew. Their modular mission pods are configurable so Starfleet Command can commission specialist ships. A support vessel might begin its service life with an installed sensor package for survey duty, and then get recalled to switch out for a heavy torpedo array or extended shuttlebay module for defense or specialist duty.

- Text from Spacecraft Design 101, 37th Edition, Chapter 2, by Lt. Commander Benjamin Sisko

2. **SPACEFRAME:** The Spaceframe is the ship's basic structure and infrastructure, and the foundation upon which everything else will be laid. At this stage, the Players select a single class, which provides the basic Systems for the ship, as well as its Scale, and its weaponry. Each class also lists the year in which it entered service.

3. **MISSION PROFILE:** The mission profile determines how the ship's facilities and personnel are assigned. The Players select a single mission profile, which provides the basic Departments for the ship.

4. **REFITS:** Each ship receives several refits and upgrades, as determined by its Service and its Spaceframe. A ship receives a single refit for every full ten years between the year in which the Class entered service, and the current year. These provide increases to the ship's Systems and Departments.

SERVICE

First and foremost, the Gamemaster and Players should collectively decide when the game will take place. This, really, should be decided up-front, when everyone agrees to play, as the era in which the game is played will have a broad impact on the kinds of characters involved, the kinds of stories that can be told, and what form the iconic *Star Trek* elements will take.

A timeline of the *Star Trek* universe can be found on p. 3, but it will be common for games to be set in years depicted in the shows and movies, as those years will be the most familiar to Players.

SPACEFRAMES

A vessel's spaceframe is its basic superstructure, core systems, operational infrastructure, and all the other elements that are common to every vessel of the same class.

The Players choose a single class for their starship. This will provide a collection of abilities that will serve as the baseline for the starship — the ship's base scores for its Systems, its Scale, three points towards its Departments, and what weaponry it is equipped with. Each class also lists the year that ships of that type first entered service.

Some classes may also provide Talents, denoting upgrades that are universally applied to ships of that class.

AKIRA CLASS
ENTERED SERVICE: 2368

OVERVIEW: During the aftermath of the Battle of Wolf 359 in 2367, Starfleet saw the need for a more heavily armed vessel capable of patrolling and protecting large volumes of territory against possible Borg incursions, while continuing the primary mission of all Starfleet vessels, exploring the unknown. The Advanced Starship Design Bureau at the Antares Fleet Yards took a concept design, never planned for service, and turned it into the *U.S.S. Akira* in 2368; trial runs were so successful that Starfleet Command immediately ordered full-scale production of the *Akira* class to begin.

CAPABILITIES: Unlike most vessels of its mass, *Akira*-class starships do not have a separate engineering hull, rather the vessel is designed to be as compact as possible to aid in maintaining a strong defensive shield strength over its entire surface area. Other defensive measures included raised pontoon-like structures on either side of the saucer that contained secondary shield generators to help protect vital command and control systems as well as highly sensitive sensor networks for planetary survey and stellar cartography missions that could double as back-up targeting systems for the vessel's weaponry. The *Akira* class was also designed with extensive shuttlebays and attached support and maintenance facilities capable of manufacturing shuttles from scratch with the right raw materials. Capable of deploying shuttles of any size, fighters, and even *Danube* class runabouts, the *Akira* class is superb at space supremacy in combat roles and extensive stellar system survey in peacetime. If the mission assignment requires it, the shuttle recovery and maintenance systems are replaceable with cargo compartments and extra bulk transporter systems or even extra personnel quarters and life support systems to allow the craft to perform rescue and recovery operations. The torpedo pod mounted between the two pontoons aft of the hull isn't as easily replaceable as the shuttlebays in the main hull due to the complex power feeds and targeting system relays that feed up the connecting pylons to the pod. This hasn't stopped ASDB from working on ideas that include making sub-classes of the vessel that would replace the weapons systems with a subspace scanning array equal in size and resolution to ones typically seen in fixed installations. The torpedo pod itself is a unique design in Starfleet vessels, with a series of tubes in a line capable of a nearly continuous barrage as the system staggers the fire of each tube. Each of the standard tubes can be loaded with a store of subspace buoys or sensor probes, but the quantum torpedo systems standard on each vessel are dedicated systems and unable to launch alternate munitions.

SYSTEMS

COMMS	09	ENGINES	10	STRUCTURE	11
COMPUTERS	09	SENSORS	09	WEAPONS	11

DEPARTMENTS

COMMAND	–	SECURITY	+2	SCIENCE	–
CONN	–	ENGINEERING	–	MEDICINE	+1

SCALE: 5

ATTACKS:
- Phaser Arrays
- Photon Torpedoes
- Tractor Beam (Strength 4)

TALENTS:
Akira-class starships have the following Talents:
- Ablative Armor
- Extensive Shuttlebays
- Rapid-Fire Torpedo Launcher

BEING POLITE

"I was first to respond to a general distress call from a Federation colony world in the HR-629 system. There was a 'disagreement' between the colonists and a large number of Ferengi vessels. The Ferengi were claiming the colonists had stolen raw dilithium ore from a visiting merchant, but the colony was set up to mine rich deposits of dilithium already present. The Ferengi were clearly lying and they had fired their particle weapons on the sea as a demonstration of their power. I would later learn the weapon hit too close to the primary settlement, killing thousands. While I was debating if I should call in my concerns' own forces, an *Akira* had dropped out of warp off my starboard and launched a staggering wave of photon torpedoes, dozens...wiping out the attacking vessels in a single swipe. As the smaller ships began to break orbit the Starfleet vessel launched runabouts and fighters, disabling the remaining Ferengi ships and bringing them under control with tractor beams. I'd never seen such deliberate and rapid force used before by Starfleet. When they hailed me to ask for my sensor logs, I made sure I was polite."

Captain Fthi Torvili, Orion Syndicate.

CONSTELLATION CLASS

ENTERED SERVICE: 2285

OVERVIEW: Designed in the mid-2280s in response to increasing tensions between the Klingon Empire and the Federation, the *Constellation* class was originally intended for use as a perimeter patrol vessel and heavy interceptor. The design was not intended as a true warship, therefore, when the initial Khitomer Accords were signed in 2293, the class' production wasn't ceased, but its assignments were changed from being an alert interceptor to an emergency response vessel used to deal with crises that could rapidly spiral out of control without Starfleet's intervention.

CAPABILITIES: Until the deployment of the *Constellation* class, Starfleet had never commissioned a four-nacelle design for general use in the fleet. The intent for the potent combination of four warp nacelles and two separate impulse drive reactor arrays was to provide the craft with the ability to maintain high warp speeds by alternating the use of two nacelles at a time and then switching the active nacelles before the warp coils would overheat and normally require a starship to drop out of warp. While *Constellation*-class vessels were not the highest velocity craft at warp speeds, the maximum sustained cruising speed of the vessel was just over warp 8. All four nacelles could be used to increase warp acceleration or push the maximum velocity of the craft to over warp 9. At sublight speeds, the two impulse arrays would tax the class's structural integrity field by accelerating from full stop to full impulse in less than five seconds, often

surprising non-Federation crews by what was known as the 'Constellation Sprint'. Another tactic developed on *U.S.S. Stargazer* NCC-2893 by then Lieutenant Commander Jean-Luc Picard became known as the 'Picard Maneuver' where the starship would accelerate and jump into warp and then drop back out to nearly full stop so the starship appeared to be in two places at once. This agility and speed lent itself to its re-designation as an emergency response vehicle. In addition, the vessels three large shuttle/fighter bays located along the edges of the saucer were redesigned for use in regular planetary shuttles or cargo shuttles. This made the *Constellation* class ideal for delivering large quantities of emergency supplies to vast areas of a planet's surface, or transporting colonists to newly terraformed worlds. The usefulness of this design has been great enough that Starfleet has kept many of these vessels on active duty, continuing to use them as couriers and rapid response, refitting them with new developments in technology over its decades of service.

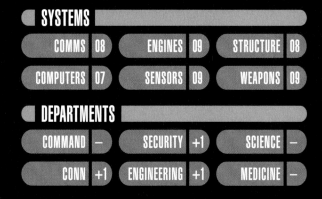

SYSTEMS

COMMS	08	ENGINES	09	STRUCTURE	08
COMPUTERS	07	SENSORS	09	WEAPONS	09

DEPARTMENTS

COMMAND	—	SECURITY	+1	SCIENCE	—
CONN	+1	ENGINEERING	+1	MEDICINE	—

SCALE: 4

ATTACKS:
- Phaser Banks
- Photon Torpedoes
- Tractor Beam (Strength 3)

TALENTS:
Constellation-class starships have the following Talents:
- Improved Warp Drive
- Extensive Shuttlebays

CONSTITUTION CLASS

ENTERED SERVICE: 2243. *Constitution*-class starships were retired from service after 2290.

OVERVIEW: The *Constitution*-class starships defined and helped continue to define Starfleet during the 23rd century and beyond. In 2235 Starfleet decided that, to better expand and protect the Federation as a whole, a more rugged and multi-purpose exploration vessel was needed that was able to stand up to the increasing threat of conflict with the Klingon Empire. The design that resulted would be used in dozens of later classes of starships; a saucer-like primary hull that contained the bridge and the majority of weapon systems, a cylindrical secondary hull that housed the class's warp core, navigational deflector and shuttlebay, and connected to two warp nacelles held far away from the vessel on long struts.

CAPABILITIES: As an exploratory vessel, the *Constitution* class needed the best computer systems available, and was designed to use the newly developed duotronic computer system created by Doctor Richard Daystrom in 2243. This breakthrough in computing technology allowed the computer of *Constitution*-class starships to develop a limited AI-like personality that sometimes became too self-aware and would argue or bicker with officers and crew instead of providing information and analysis. The computer system was able to handle the input from as many sensors as was typically seen on three starships of previous classes, giving *Constitution*-class vessels sensor resolution and accuracy unable to be matched until the late 2290s. To aid in exploration, the design had a large shuttlebay with four class-F shuttlecraft, but in an emergency situation could host six. While the warp propulsion systems were not highly advanced, they were made to be rugged and easily repaired, with many vessels warp coils operating at high subspace field densities for 7–8 times the recommended time for replacement. This resilience allowed *Constitution*-class vessels to operate far above their rated safety limits, with *U.S.S. Enterprise* achieving brief speeds of warp 14.1 in 2268, a speed record that would hold until the 24th century. The warp reactor itself made highly efficient use of antimatter by cycling warp plasma through networked reactor cylinders housed behind main engineering. The class also had a powerful multiple reactor fusion impulse system that was noted to be able to keep the starship aloft even inside planetary atmospheres that the vessels were not designed to enter. Automation of critical systems were not possible with the technology of the time, and the *Constitution* class required over 400 crew members for operation, with two-person teams crewing each of the design's six phaser banks and four-person teams crewing each torpedo launcher. To save on the already high number of crew on board, these teams were made up of crew from the vessel's scientific teams that would not typically be

MAKING A LIVING

"The thrice-damned *Constitution*-class ships! Before it didn't matter if you were in a converted garbage hauler or in a stolen...'borrowed' I should say... Orion raider, when Starfleet came calling you could hide or run and confidently get away. How are things now? An entrepreneur cannot make a living, honest or otherwise! It's all because of those damn...damn *Constitutions* roaming around and acting like oversize nannies! If you want to be left alone, you can't have your breathing space when they're faster at warp or impulse than anything you have. If you want to hide product intended for a more refined taste than your typical do-gooder, no offense intended madam, you simply can't have privacy for your client with how good its sensors are. Moreover, if you want to fight, not that I would ever consider hurting anyone, especially one as beautiful as yourself my dear... Regardless, I doubt the Klingons could hold up against those phasers and tractor beams, all those ships need to do is stop them in their tracks and hold them there while transmitting lectures about proper behavior over subspace until they surrender!"

Rehabilitation interview of Harcourt Fenton Mudd, 2271.

needed during combat operations. The success of the class meant that as further refinements to warp technology and computer systems became available, *Constitution*-class starships were often the first in line for refitting at shipyards across the Federation. The introduction of the *Excelsior* class began the slow decline of *Constitution*-class vessels, as the ships' newer spaceframes and larger size made them better suited for deep space exploration missions.

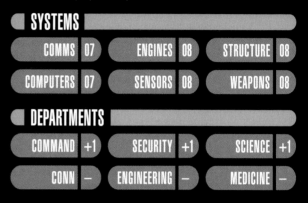

SYSTEMS

COMMS 07	ENGINES 08	STRUCTURE 08
COMPUTERS 07	SENSORS 08	WEAPONS 08

DEPARTMENTS

COMMAND +1	SECURITY +1	SCIENCE +1
CONN –	ENGINEERING –	MEDICINE –

SCALE: 4

ATTACKS:
- Phaser Banks
- Photon Torpedoes
- Tractor Beam (Strength 3)

TALENTS:
Constitution-class starships have the following Talents:
- Rugged Design
- Modular Laboratories

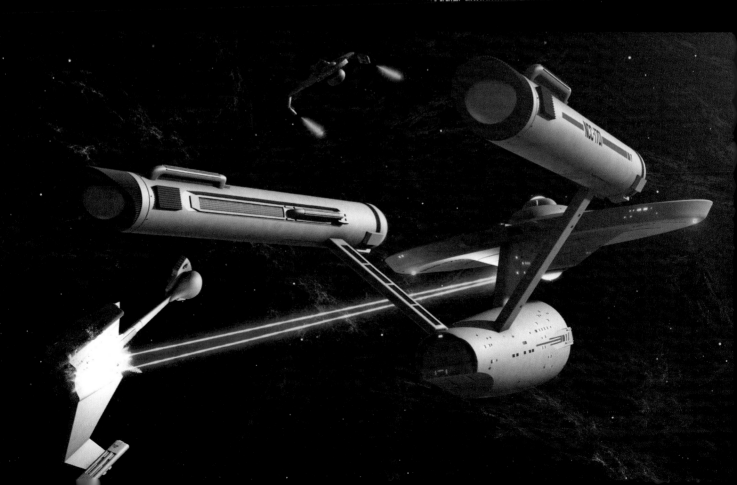

DEFIANT CLASS
ENTERED SERVICE: 2371

OVERVIEW: The primary purpose of Starfleet is science and exploration, with military prowess not being a priority. With some notable exceptions made during the Earth-Romulan War, Starfleet had little experience designing ships specifically made for warfare. The *Defiant* class began development a year before the Battle of Wolf 359, and the starship's development and production was made a priority after the disastrous encounter with the Borg. Initial testing of the prototype showed serious flaws and was mothballed, along with the entire design project. The development of this class halted until 2370 when the commanding officer of Deep Space 9 requested the prototype be assigned to his command to help with the increasing tensions between the Federation and the Dominion.

CAPABILITIES: The prototype (*U.S.S. Defiant* NX-74205) differs significantly from production models of the class by having a Romulan cloaking device. The amount of power required by the starship makes the cloak less effective than if it was used on another starship of similar mass, and careful sensor sweeps are still able to detect *Defiant* at close range. These same power requirements resulted in the shelving of the design due to the extreme power draw required for its weapon systems. The weapon systems installed include four

forward-mounted pulsed phaser cannons, three secondary type-10 phaser strips, and a total of six (four forward and two aft mounted) multi-purpose torpedo launchers able to fire both standard Mark IV photon torpedoes or the newly developed quantum torpedoes. The class's maximum warp speed with weapons charged is warp 7, but with weapons offline *Defiant* class vessels can achieve an impressive Warp 9.5 from warp coils normally unable to produce such a steep subspace gradient. Power draw for propulsion is nearly identical at sublight speeds as the starship's structural integrity field struggles to handle maneuvers normally seen in single crew shuttles or fighters. All of the weapon systems and power generation come at the cost of crew comforts. The *Defiant* class is one of the smallest starships used by Starfleet in an active role with a standard crew size of 50. However, even with this small crew, all crew (except the captain) must share quarters and rely on a single mess hall for any recreation while on board. The interior space did allow the inclusion of a small shuttlebay that is primarily for use when the starship is assigned to reconnaissance duties, and landing struts to facilitate emergency planetary landings or for planetary reconnaissance.

As of 2371 only a single *Defiant*-class starship is in service (the prototype *Defiant*), but the team at Deep Space 9 have overcome many of the prototype's flaws, and several additional *Defiant*-class starships are under construction.

DEFIANCE

"To understand the *Defiant* class, one must understand why Starfleet named it this way. According to the lingual database the word 'defiant' means to be rebellious or insolent against some sort of authority. Naming a vessel like this in the Empire would lead to the 'disappearance' of the engineer who named the vessel. In the Federation the name, and the design, is seen as a way to overturn century-long held ideas about the role of Starfleet as a military body in the Federation. The *Defiant* class has as many weapon systems as the *Galaxy* class and smaller Romulan vessels with pulse phasers and rapid fire quantum torpedoes. I judge that the Federation's request for the inclusion of a cloaking device in the first ship of the class, *U.S.S. Defiant*, be approved on the condition that a Romulan observer be assigned on the ship. This operative will maintain a watch on the vessel and her crew in order to report back how Starfleet will use this new 'challenge to authority', to ensure we know just how well the Federation has kept its killer instinct since our great War so many years ago."

Agent Redacted
Head of *Defiant* class analysis group, Tal Shiar.

SYSTEMS

COMMS	09	ENGINES	10	STRUCTURE	08
COMPUTERS	09	SENSORS	09	WEAPONS	13

DEPARTMENTS

COMMAND	—	SECURITY	+2	SCIENCE	—
CONN	+1	ENGINEERING	—	MEDICINE	—

SCALE: 3

ATTACKS:

- Phaser Arrays
- Phaser Cannons
- Photon Torpedoes
- Quantum Torpedoes
- Tractor Beam (Strength 2)

TALENTS:

Defiant-class starships have the following Talents:

- Ablative Armor
- Quantum Torpedoes

and simulated successes. The first attempted full-scale use of *U.S.S. Excelsior* and its transwarp systems in 2285 resulted in a complete failure of all propulsion systems from a combination of sabotage and failure of the vessel's capability to generate and maintain a transwarp field. The prototype was brought back into space dock for redesign using standard warp propulsion technologies, and by 2290 the 'bugs' had been worked out of the design, resulting in a highly adaptable and capable starship for the late 23rd century and beyond.

CAPABILITIES: The ship-wide failure of *U.S.S. Excelsior* caused engineers at the San Francisco Ship Yards to over-engineer nearly every system on the ship. The design's long transwarp nacelles were no longer needed after the failure of the experiment, but engineers elected to keep them so extra warp coils could be installed, giving the large starship both a robust warp field and a high maximum sustained warp speed. *Excelsior*-class vessels could often sustain dangerous warp speeds for periods long enough that the warp cores would overload or the ship's structural integrity field would begin to fail long before the coils themselves would begin to malfunction. Sublight propulsion was far in excess of what was needed, giving the massive cruiser accelerations typically seen on vessels half its size. The redundant fusion reactors also assisted in powering the ship's impressive shielding systems, capable of greater defensive power absorption than the *Constitution* class over a much greater surface area. Tactical systems were also improved over the older heavy cruiser, with five dual type-8 phaser banks on the primary hull, and a single dual bank tied directly into the impulse reactor array. Further, two phaser banks are located on either side of the 'neck' connecting the primary and secondary hull, and a bank of phasers is located on the dorsal secondary hull between the warp nacelle pylons. Additionally, two forward and two aft mounted photon torpedo launchers gave the *Excelsior* class enough firepower to give pause to any commander of a hostile vessel encountering it, though at least one tube is kept loaded with probes while on exploratory and research assignments. The redesign also allowed the installation of the final generation of duotronic computer processors before the introduction of isolinear systems in the early 24th century. This gave *Excelsior*-class vessels unrivalled sensor and data processing abilities compared to other starships of its era. As the redesign of the class was so extensive, designers on the project ended up inadvertently ensuring the class would be in use even today with large sections of the primary and secondary hull able to be removed and replaced

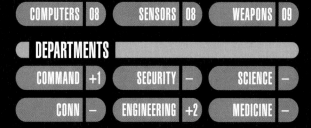

| COMPUTERS | 08 | SENSORS | 08 | WEAPONS | 09 |

DEPARTMENTS

| COMMAND | +1 | SECURITY | – | SCIENCE | – |
| CONN | – | ENGINEERING | +2 | MEDICINE | – |

SCALE: 5

ATTACKS:
- Phaser Banks
- Photon Torpedoes
- Tractor Beam (Strength 4)

TALENTS:
Excelsior-class starships have the following Talents:
- Improved Impulse Drive
- Secondary Reactors

A SIGHT TO REMEMBER

"I had my first encounter with an *Excelsior* class, in fact *Excelsior* herself, in orbit over Khitomer in 2293. I was briefed on Starfleet vessels before my assignment as the lead of our delegation before leaving Romulus, but little was known about this design up until this point. What we did know suggested that the design was a failure of grand proportions, something the Federation was keen to cover-up, so when I saw the ship in orbit I was stunned. The vessel had clearly been in battle, and I saw workbees moving around its exterior giving me its scale; the ship was massive. *Excelsior* was so large it dwarfed my diplomatic vessel and even made *U.S.S. Enterprise* seem small as it orbited close by. My intelligence officer informed me that *Excelsior* maintained an almost incredible speed for over half a standard day before arriving in orbit, something the *Constitution* and any of our vessels would have found impossible. Under the pretense of offering assistance in repairs, I approached and saw its numerous weapon emplacements and its open shuttlebay filled with smaller craft. An impressive ship, a sight I remember clearly even today."

Interview of former Ambassador La'orst, Romulan Empire

GALAXY CLASS

ENTERED SERVICE: 2359

OVERVIEW: Designed to be the best exploration and science vessel ever deployed by Starfleet, the *Galaxy* class was put into service with many of the most advanced technologies available in the late 2350s along with its sister design, the *Nebula* class. It also represented a new philosophy in Starfleet where officers and crew on deep space and long duration assignments could bring along their families and loved ones rather than be apart from them for years. This philosophy meant the starship was one of the largest produced with often over 2000 crew and their family members aboard at any given time, and an emergency evacuation limit of around 15,000, but more typical crew levels numbered near 1000. While non-Starfleet personnel amounted to only between 15-20% of the total crew, each *Galaxy*-class starship had facilities and services onboard to serve Starfleet crew and civilians typically only seen on starbases including schools for children, bars and in some cases restaurants, day-care, and the largest holodecks produced at that time.

CAPABILITIES: With much of the interior space of a *Galaxy* class empty and waiting for mission specific modules to be installed, each vessel quickly became unique compared to others of its class. Often the occupations of the vessel's civilians would dictate what kind of research facilities would be installed. As an example, the civilian husband of a serving science officer may be a metallurgist and request a facility able to handle the specialized needs of his smelting and fabrication research. This adaptability and capability for expansion also meant that these large vessels often ended up with a specialist for any situation, and civilian specialists that Starfleet required the expertise of would receive temporary rank and further space consideration for their facilities and hobbies onboard. Each *Galaxy*-class vessel had the largest warp core then produced by the Federation and designed by the Theoretical Propulsion Group of Mars. This powerplant provided the massive starship with the capability to maintain a cruising speed of warp 6 and an emergency velocity of warp 9.8. Three identical isolinear computer cores with FTL processing capabilities tie the wide variety of scientific sensors, laboratories, and research facilities onboard together. These cores could each take over all computer needs on the ship in the case of the destruction of the other two. This meant that in the case of the destruction of the vessel, the data stored by a *Galaxy*-class starship could be pieced back together based on pieces recovered from each core. Unlike most Starfleet vessels before it, the *Galaxy* class was designed with the ability to separate and reattach its saucer without the need for a return to dry dock, allowing this use for both for emergency purposes and in tactical engagements such as when *U.S.S. Enterprise* NCC-1701-D used the technique against the Borg following the Battle of Wolf 359 in 2367. Auxiliary shuttle craft are located in three separate shuttlebays, and typically include ten Type 6 or 7 personnel shuttles, ten type-9A cargo shuttles, and twelve type-15, 15A, or 16 shuttlepods.

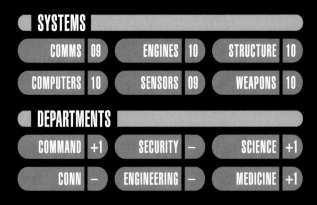

SYSTEMS

COMMS	09	ENGINES	10	STRUCTURE	10
COMPUTERS	10	SENSORS	09	WEAPONS	10

DEPARTMENTS

COMMAND	+1	SECURITY	—	SCIENCE	+1
CONN	—	ENGINEERING	—	MEDICINE	+1

SCALE: 6

ATTACKS:

- Phaser Arrays
- Photon Torpedoes
- Tractor Beam (Strength 5)

TALENTS:

Galaxy-class starships have the following Talents:

- Saucer Separation
- Modular Laboratories
- Redundant Systems

BRINGERS OF HOPE

"When you hear stories from refugees across the Orion Spur, Federation starships have a mythical reputation as bringers of hope to those in need. I had no reason to think of these stories as anything more than tales told to children so they can sleep at night. The day that our star began a series of flares and our orbital infrastructure began to deorbit, the sight of *U.S.S. Cygnus* entering orbit in response to our distress call made me a believer. *Cygnus* was able to tow the largest of our habitats into stable orbits and cut up unmanned satellites with their phasers so they'd burn up safely. After the initial danger for the orbital structures had passed, they stayed in orbit and used all the scientific resources they had to discover why our sun was flaring and then developed a graviton pulse they broadcast through *Cygnus*' main deflector. *Cygnus* not only saved thousands of lives in orbit, it prevented decades of solar instability and increased cancer rates across our planet, but then continued to help by using its small craft and engineering department to rebuild all we had lost."

Prime Minister Mansing or Resgos
Protectorate of the Federation

INTREPID CLASS
ENTERED SERVICE: 2371

OVERVIEW: By the mid-2360s the success and failures of the *Galaxy* class were clear to Starfleet. Its large size and crew along with increasing use as a diplomatic vessel rather than exploratory craft made engineers in Starfleet begin designing the next great explorer, the *Intrepid* class. This first of its class was launched in 2371 to great fanfare and was quickly seen by the Federation Science Council as a valuable resource. It is small compared to the *Galaxy* class, more closely resembling a *Constitution* class, but contains the best technology available to the Federation.

CAPABILITIES: The sleek curves of the *Intrepid* class weren't just a stylistic choice, they assisted the variable geometry warp nacelles in producing a tight warp field over the starship with a steep and stable field gradient in even turbulent space-time conditions, giving these vessels both an impressive warp acceleration and stability. These features, along with the vessels primary class-9 warp drive and its secondary warp assembly allowed the class an impressive top speed of warp 9.975. While its sustained warp speeds are considerably slower, they are still fast enough to allow Starfleet to hail the design as its new deep-space explorer. To aid in this role, *Intrepid*-class vessels are also equipped with the best technology in the Federation, including the newest generation of multi-spectral subspace sensors linked into the most powerful shipboard computer yet in service in Starfleet. This computing power is possible through a breakthrough in the use of bio-neural circuitry, allowing the vessels' computer to form information connections in a faster and more natural way, giving the main computer the unique ability to adapt to new and confusing situations as well as improvise solutions much like sentient life-forms. This increased computer power allows the *Intrepid* class more automation than many Starfleet vessels, keeping the typical crew rosters down to between 130–150 officers and crew. As it's a deep-space exploratory vessel, all *Intrepid*-class starships have an impressive amount of tactical systems as standard, the reasoning being that it would be operating far from any other allied starships and may need to defend itself against multiple attackers. The *Intrepid* class has thirteen type-10 phaser strips, an additional four type 8 phaser emitters, and five torpedo launchers (two forward, two aft, and one ventral launcher that is typically only loaded with probes). To further planetary exploration, all *Intrepid*-class vessels are assigned at least four type-6 or type-8 shuttlecraft in addition to the class-specific aeroshuttle that is located on the ventral side of the primary hull. For crew recreation, new high resolution holo-emitters and integrated replicator systems made holodecks power efficient and able to create permanent matter in the simulation to prevent continual holo-emitter use and degradation. These same holo-emitters are also installed in the sickbay, allowing the new Emergency Medical Hologram system (EMH) to assist medical personnel when they require it.

A LIVING SHIP

"Using the Badlands as cover is something that the Maquis have been doing since before the ink dried on the Federation's treaty with the Cardassians. It's been useful as cover because the plasma storms, gravitational eddies, and ripples in space-time make it difficult for anyone to make their way through that mess at anything faster than a few kilometers per second, unless you know exactly what you're doing. Up until this point it's been the only reason why we've lasted as long as we have with both the spoon-heads and the Feddies hunting us down. I think we might have problems since I've caught wind of a new Starfleet science vessel with variable geometry warp nacelles, adaptive sensors, and a computer that uses living cells to help it learn, change, and improve the performance of the ship. They even have holographic crewmembers if you can believe it! My sources say the ship that's tasked with hunting us down is *Voyager,* and with her in the Badlands, I think our days are numbered."

Ralph Gregori, Maquis resistance leader.

SYSTEMS

COMMS	10	ENGINES	11	STRUCTURE	08
COMPUTERS	11	SENSORS	10	WEAPONS	09

DEPARTMENTS

COMMAND	–	SECURITY	–	SCIENCE	+2
CONN	+1	ENGINEERING	–	MEDICINE	–

SCALE: 4

ATTACKS:
- Phaser Arrays
- Photon Torpedoes
- Tractor Beam (Strength 3)

TALENTS:
Intrepid-class starships have the following Talents:
- Improved Warp Drive
- Advanced Sensor Suites
- Emergency Medical Hologram

MIRANDA CLASS
ENTERED SERVICE: 2274

OVERVIEW: During the mid to late 2260s the Federation saw increasing tensions with the Klingon Empire and many analysts thought that war was inevitable with Qo'noS. The design of the *Miranda* class began as a dual-purpose patrol and combat vessel designed specifically to counter Klingon designs, specifically recent refits of the D7 battle cruiser. A combined team of designers from Starfleet Tactical and the Starfleet Advanced Technologies Group began co-opting and adjusting technologies and systems from the upcoming *Constitution* class refit, producing a heavily armed attack vessel just as peace broke out between the Federation and the Empire in 2267. Production of six spaceframes occurred before further manufacturing was halted while a complete redesign was undertaken. In 2272, the *Miranda* development group had beaten the sword into a plowshare by redesigning nearly 70% of the internal volume of the starship, attempting to make the vessel into a science and survey ship. The result was a highly adaptable starship that continues to be in use nearly one hundred years since its introduction.

CAPABILITIES: The original design of the *Miranda* class had nearly double the amount of weapon systems as the *Constitution* class as well as two large shuttlebays at the aft of the starship. Many of these weapons were removed, leaving three phaser turrets each on the dorsal and ventral sections and two phasers mounted near the vessels impulse deck. A phaser turret on both the port and starboard 'roll-bar' mountings was linked directly into the warp plasma conduits, increasing the firepower significantly at risk of depriving the starship of warp power at critical moments. In addition, a modular torpedo system was installed at the top of the vessels roll-bar, giving two forward and two rear facing launch tubes that could be quickly replaced with probe launchers. Some of the extra power requirements for weapon systems came from the ships compact shape, lacking a secondary hull, the *Miranda* could generate the same defensive shielding power as a *Constitution* class, but for only 70% of the power. The reduction in weapon systems also allowed many of the targeting systems to be replaced by more high-resolution long-range sensors suited for exploration duties. The large shuttle and cargo bays gave the starship an excellent reputation for performing highly detailed planetary surveys, being used for emergency cargo transportation, and a border patrol vessel. The adaptability of the modular systems of the *Miranda* class made it indispensable for assignments to frontier starbases where it could change its modules, and thus what assignments it could perform, with little layover time. This meant that a single *Miranda* could be assigned to a starbase rather than two or three specialized starships. By the mid-2280s the *Miranda* class was in use across the Federation and became the 'Jack-of-all-Trades' of the Fleet, and an overworked one with many *Miranda*-class vessels logging more hours of continual operation than any others. While the *Miranda* class could never achieve the specialization of the *Constitution* class in exploration and science, nor the transport capabilities of the *Ptolemy* class, nor the sheer firepower of

the larger, more advanced *Excelsior* class, it was used for all of these roles. The modular systems that were devised in the 2270s have made this class able to be easily refitted over the century of its service, and many of the starships still in active service today were exploring the Galaxy in the late 23rd century.

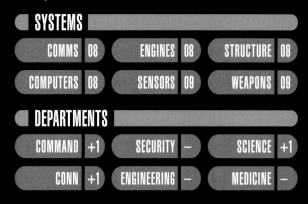

SYSTEMS

COMMS	08	ENGINES	08	STRUCTURE	08
COMPUTERS	08	SENSORS	09	WEAPONS	09

DEPARTMENTS

COMMAND	+1	SECURITY	–	SCIENCE	+1
CONN	+1	ENGINEERING	–	MEDICINE	–

SCALE: 4

ATTACKS:
- Phaser Banks
- Photon Torpedoes
- Tractor Beam (Strength 3)

TALENTS
Miranda-class starships have the following Talents:
- Extensive Shuttlebays

"We rage against the coward Organians that forced an early end of what would be a glorious war against the Federation. We know the Federation was afraid of our mighty warships because of their hasty construction and design of the *Miranda class* as a battleship capable of providing a fight worth the sacrifice of our best warriors and their ships, perhaps even a fight worthy of song and honor to the Federation. But, the Federation dulled the teeth of the *Miranda* and made the vessel less than it could be. The weapons were replaced with little more than sensors and shuttles. Good enough for scientists, but not for warriors! Now I see the Federation tricked us all those years ago as the small pod it carries on its back can be fitted with weapons rather than sensors, and those same shuttlebays can be filled with attack craft! The *Miranda* never lost its heart as a warrior, it just slept until it was again needed by the Federation."

Under-Ambassador to the Federation,
Tal'Q of House Noggra, on seeing the
reactivation of three *Miranda* class vessels
in the aftermath of the Battle of Wolf 359, 2367

NOVA CLASS
ENTERED SERVICE: 2368

OVERVIEW: Starfleet Command and the Federation Science Council formed a committee in 2363 to discuss the state of Starfleet's aging science and exploration vessels. While the *Galaxy* class was considered a success, the amount of personnel and resources required to construct one of the massive exploration cruisers was significant. The end conclusion of the committee was that Starfleet required a new science and exploration vessel that was small, easy to maintain, but had the best sensor and scientific equipment possible in a small spaceframe. The *Nova* class is the result, only entering service in the past few years.

CAPABILITIES: The designers at Utopia Planitia Fleet Yards (UPFY) had been devising various next-generation designs for several years when work began on the *Nova* class. The science vessel was approximately the same size as the *NX* class from the 22nd century and had a similar amount of crew, typically requiring around 80 crew, depending on the assignment. Like many ships designed around this time, the *Nova* class had an integrated secondary hull under its wedge-like primary saucer, capitalizing on both the most recent theories on warp field dynamics and the faster manufacturing that this simpler cross-section would allow. However, though many next-generation technologies were in their infancy at the time, the designers chose to make use of tried, tested, and established components instead, continuing to use an isolinear processing system for both its primary and secondary computer cores and forgoing the use of variable geometry warp drive. The reasoning behind this was that the newer systems were still too bulky for the small vessel and tended to make simulated *Nova* designs far too cramped for even a bare minimum of crew members. Designers at UPFY nevertheless improved upon these basic components by increasing the strength of the warp field around both computer cores, improving the processing speeds by nearly doubling the field strength around the FTL elements. The warp coils needed for the starship were small, and engineers were able to place gimbal and gyroscopic control elements around each of the individual coils, giving the *Nova* class an even greater ability to modify the geometry of its warp field than any other starship of its mass at the cost of maintaining a steep field gradient, i.e. a lower maximum speed. To save space, UPFY engineers compressed the impulse systems into a single unit along the vessels spine and only installed forward facing torpedo systems. The type 10 phaser strips were short, reducing weapon arcs but giving the vessel more interior volume that could be utilized by life support and sensor systems rather than EPS transfer systems and heat exchangers. The small crew size and the slow cruising speed of the *Nova* class mean that its primary assignments are planetary survey and short to mid-range exploration missions lasting no more than six months before crews rotate to larger vessels or facilities.

Since the launch of *U.S.S. Nova* in 2368, three *Nova*-class vessels have been destroyed or are presumed destroyed including *Borealis*, *Equinox*, and *Zodiac*. While the reason for the loss of *Equinox* in early 2371 is not yet known, it is thought to be due to a failure of the anti-matter containment systems when attempting to enter warp while under heavy sublight acceleration. This failure occurred in the other two starships, both in 2371. UPFY engineers are currently studying these failures to determine if there are any serious flaws with the design itself; this may determine whether the *Nova* class has a future within Starfleet.

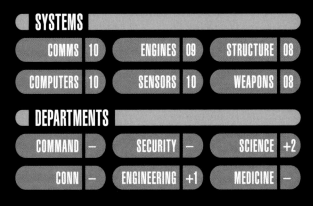

SYSTEMS

COMMS	10	ENGINES	09	STRUCTURE	08
COMPUTERS	10	SENSORS	10	WEAPONS	08

DEPARTMENTS

COMMAND	–	SECURITY	–	SCIENCE	+2
CONN	–	ENGINEERING	+1	MEDICINE	–

SCALE: 3

ATTACKS:
- Phaser Arrays
- Photon Torpedoes
- Tractor Beam (Strength 2)

TALENTS:

Nova-class starships have the following Talents:
- Advanced Sensors

HOW SMALL

"We now must reevaluate what we know of the Earthers and Starfleet. They have changed the rules of the game that we have been playing for a century now with the *Nova* class. The Federation dared the other people of the Galaxy to make ships as big or bigger than them in some form of misguided dominance dance, forcing those that could to match their boasts to build larger and larger. We danced and played in their game, making our ships as big, as advanced, as impressive as theirs. Now the Humans laugh and say, 'Look at our *Nova*, the egg that carries our best and brightest, and see how small we can make it!' My advisors calm me as they have said that it can't range deep into our space as it is too small to be used as a true explorer like starships centuries old. It doesn't even have the power for its propulsion systems to make it safe. I have been told that one destroyed itself trying to flee from one of our Nest-Ships, and this should calm the nerves of even our most frightened nest mates."

Queen Iksytish XXVI
Gorn Hegemony

MISSION PROFILE

A ship's Mission Profile is a key part of what distinguishes one ship of a single class from her sister ships. It determines how the ship will be equipped, what facilities and personnel are assigned to it, and what kind of operations it will be expected to perform.

The Players choose a single Mission Profile for their starship. This will provide the ship's Departments (which are added to those already granted by the class), and a single Talent chosen from a short list.

STRATEGIC AND DIPLOMATIC OPERATIONS

Vessels equipped for Strategic and Diplomatic Operations are often placed under the command of flag officers and used as the heart of squadrons, battle-groups, and even whole fleets. These ships — and the prestige and standing that accompanies them — are also used for major diplomatic engagements, where they can serve as mobile embassies and represent the best of the Federation.

DEPARTMENTS

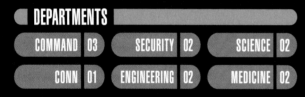

| COMMAND | 03 | SECURITY | 02 | SCIENCE | 02 |
| CONN | 01 | ENGINEERING | 02 | MEDICINE | 02 |

TALENTS:
Select one of the following Talents:
- Command Ship
- Diplomatic Suites
- Electronic Warfare Systems
- Extensive Shuttlebays

PATHFINDER AND RECONNAISSANCE OPERATIONS

Long-range missions often employ the most advanced stellar cartography and astrometric facilities, allowing them to chart and navigate unknown regions of space effectively. These vessels are relied upon for extended exploratory missions, intelligence-gathering military operations, and risky "pathfinder" operations into the unknown.

DEPARTMENTS

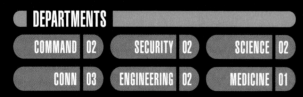

| COMMAND | 02 | SECURITY | 02 | SCIENCE | 02 |
| CONN | 03 | ENGINEERING | 02 | MEDICINE | 01 |

TALENTS:
Select one of the following Talents:
- Improved Reaction Control System
- Improved Warp Drive
- Rugged Design

TECHNICAL TEST-BED

The ship is equipped with an abundance of state-of-the-art or even prototype technologies, allowing them to be tested and studied in practical conditions, so that the flaws can be discovered and overcome, and the systems can be refined and improved upon. These ships are often deployed on a broad range of missions, to provide the most diverse conditions for equipment testing.

DEPARTMENTS

| COMMAND | 01 | SECURITY | 02 | SCIENCE | 02 |
| CONN | 02 | ENGINEERING | 03 | MEDICINE | 02 |

TALENTS:
Select one of the following Talents:
- Advanced Shields
- Backup EPS Conduits
- High Resolution Sensors
- Improved Power Systems
- Improved Warp Drive

TACTICAL OPERATIONS

While Starfleet is not a military, the defense of the Federation is one of Starfleet's responsibilities, and Starfleet has been required to prepare for war on numerous occasions. Thus, many ships are equipped for police and military actions, though the number of vessels outfitted in this manner varies depending on the politics of the day.

DEPARTMENTS

| COMMAND | 02 | SECURITY | 03 | SCIENCE | 01 |
| CONN | 02 | ENGINEERING | 02 | MEDICINE | 02 |

TALENTS:
Select one of the following Talents:
- Ablative Armor
- Fast Targeting Systems
- Improved Damage Control
- Quantum Torpedoes
- Improved Impulse Drive

SCIENTIFIC AND SURVEY OPERATIONS

Starfleet's mission of exploration and discovery means that they employ many vessels for purely scientific missions, studying unknown phenomena or supporting ongoing research. While most Federation starships are expected to have at least some capacity for scientific endeavor, some vessels are equipped specifically for such missions.

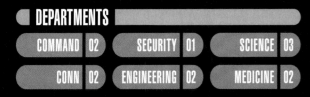

DEPARTMENTS

COMMAND	02	SECURITY	01	SCIENCE	03
CONN	02	ENGINEERING	02	MEDICINE	02

TALENTS:

Select one of the following Talents:
- Advanced Research Facilities
- Advanced Sensor Suites
- High Resolution Sensors
- Modular Laboratories

CRISIS AND EMERGENCY RESPONSE

These vessels are equipped to respond quickly to a crisis, whatever it may be. Normally capable of supporting expansive shuttlebays, they can deploy large quantities of personnel or cargo to, or evacuate large populations from, disaster areas. Such vessels also serve as hospital ships and troop transports during times of war.

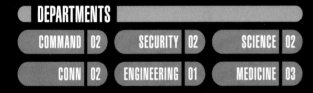

DEPARTMENTS

COMMAND	02	SECURITY	02	SCIENCE	02
CONN	02	ENGINEERING	01	MEDICINE	03

TALENTS:

Select one of the following Talents:
- Advanced Sickbay
- Emergency Medical Hologram
- Extensive Shuttlebays
- Modular Laboratories

MULTIROLE EXPLORER

Some of Starfleet's most renowned and revered vessels have been jacks-of-all-trades, rather than specialized for a single type of mission. This versatility allowed the likes of Jonathan Archer and James Kirk to explore strange new worlds, seek out new life and new civilizations, and to boldly go where no one has gone before.

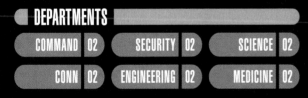

DEPARTMENTS

COMMAND	02	SECURITY	02	SCIENCE	02
CONN	02	ENGINEERING	02	MEDICINE	02

TALENTS:

Select one of the following Talents:
- Improved Hull Integrity
- Improved Power Systems
- Rugged Design
- Redundant Systems
- Secondary Reactors

REFITS

Starships receive periodic refits and upgrades throughout their service. Many of these are tiny adjustments performed as a routine part of the ship's maintenance cycle. Others are significant system overhauls performed at starbases and spacedocks, taking days, weeks, or even months of work. In some cases, ships that have served for decades may receive substantial overhauls, taking a year or more to complete and upgrading or replacing much of the ship.

Whatever the nature of these upgrades, older vessels will have received many of them. Compare the year the ship went into service with the current year of the game. For every full ten years between those two dates, the Players' Starship will have one Refit.

Each Refit increases a single System of the ship by +1. No System may be increased by more than two, or to any score above 12, through Refits (a ship may have a System with a score above 12 before Refits, but Players cannot increase a System to any score above 12).

- **Communications** refits are upgrades of subspace antennae, signals processing protocols, encryption and decryption technologies, and updates for the universal translator.

- **Computer** refits are both software updates that refine and enhance operation, as well as new computer cores and more expansive archive memory.

- **Engines** refits often involve fine adjustments of power generation and propulsion systems, replacing components like field coils and EPS conduits before they wear out, and adopting the latest ideas about warp field theory, intermix ratios, and similar technical subjects.

- **Sensors** refits are a mixture of both new sensor array hardware, and new methods of interpreting and analyzing the data.

- **Structure** refits tend to be adjustments and refinements of structural integrity and inertial dampener systems, updates to life support control systems, and replacement of parts of the ship's internal frame and the outer hull plating. Structure refits can be some of the most intensive and time-consuming to perform.

- **Weapons** refits are a mixture of targeting and control system updates, along with replacements of phaser emitters, torpedo launch mechanisms, and the latest forms of torpedo.

PUTTING IT ALL TOGETHER

Once the game's year and the starship's class, mission profile, and refits have been chosen, it comes time to put all those things together.

- **TRAITS:** A starship has a single Trait — Federation Starship — as standard. It may have others, if the Players and Gamemaster desire. See Traits, below, for more on additional Traits for a Starship.

- **SYSTEMS:** A Starship's Systems are determined by its Class, and then modified by the chosen refits. As noted above, each refit increases a single System of the ship by +1. No System may be increased by more than two, or to any score above 12, through refits (a ship may have a System with a score above 12 before refits, but Players cannot increase a System to any score above 12).

- **DEPARTMENTS:** A starship's Departments are determined by its class and its mission profile. Add these scores together to get the ship's final Department scores.

- **TALENTS:** A starship should have a number of Talents equal to its Scale. Some of these may be determined by class, and at least one should be determined by the ship's mission profile. If, at this stage, the ship has fewer Talents than its Scale, select additional Talents until it has the required number.

- **SCALE:** A starship's Scale is determined by its class.

- **RESISTANCE:** A starship has Resistance equal to its Scale. Talents may modify this further.

- **SHIELDS:** A starship has Shields equal to its Structure plus its Security. Talents may modify this further.

- **POWER:** A starship's normal Power capacity is equal to its Engines. Talents may modify this further.

- **CREW SUPPORT:** A starship's Crew Support is equal to its Scale. This may be modified further by Player Characters taking the Supervisor Talent.

- **ATTACKS:** The weapons a starship has are determined by its class. The damage that energy weapons inflict is equal to the ship's Scale plus its Security, plus additional factors from the type of weapon. The damage that torpedoes inflict is equal to the torpedoes' basic damage plus the ship's Security. These variations are described in Starship Weapons, below.

TRAITS

A Starship is more than just the technologies that went into creating it, or the crew that inhabit and operate it. Starships are symbols, sending a message to all who cross paths with them. Starships are a product of their time, shaped by the circumstances of their creation. Starships represent the nature of their cultures, both in terms of technology but also in the purpose of the ship.

Starships have at least one Trait, representing the culture that created it and the technology base that it was created from. This is the ship's origin, and it serves much the same purpose as a character's species — identifying where the ship came from, and encapsulating all those little quirks and variances peculiar to that origin. In the case of Starfleet vessels, this Trait will always be **Federation Starship**.

Starships may have other Traits beyond this, representing some other aspect of the ship's nature. The Gamemaster should allow the Players to select no more than two additional Traits, and they should ensure that all Traits are fundamentally neutral — neither wholly positive nor entirely negative. A few example Traits (which may be renamed as needed), and what they may represent, are listed below.

- **Prototype** — the ship is the first of its class. It's brand new, highly sophisticated, and not yet fully tested. Foes may underestimate the ship's capabilities, but technical problems with the ship may produce unexpected complications as experimental systems interact strangely.

- **Legacy Vessel** — the ship continues a long and proud legacy, bearing a name that has been used many times before on other starships, and maybe even on ocean-going vessels centuries ago. This legacy may manifest in the pride of the crew to serve aboard the ship, but it may also be found in enemies whose ancestors clashed with a ship of the same name in generations past.

- **Renowned** — the ship and her crew have a proud reputation, but such a reputation also draws the ire of enemies who can gain glory in the defeat of such a prestigious vessel.

- **Long-Serving** — the ship has been a part of the fleet for decades, and she has served with distinction. Even with refits, the older technology isn't quite as capable as the latest designs, but her crew know her systems and her quirks well, and can get the most out of her when it counts.

STARSHIP WEAPONRY

The armaments of Starships have remained largely unchanged for well over a century, with the differences between the weapons of a 23rd century ship and those of a 24th century vessel differing more in refinement and sophistication than in type or function.

These weapons come in two broad categories: energy weapons, and torpedoes.

ENERGY WEAPONS

Directed energy weapons project bolts or beams of focused energy or energized particles at a target. These weapons are commonplace, with most cultures having some form or another of directed energy weapon as the typical armament of their spacecraft, and they draw upon the abundant energy that starships generate as a matter of course.

Energy weapons are composed of a type and a delivery method. These are combined — along with the basic damage from the ship's Scale and Security — to determine how the weapon functions. All the ship's weapons of that type are covered in a single entry: it doesn't matter that a *Galaxy*-class starship has twelve phaser arrays, they're all encompassed by a single profile.

Making an attack with an energy weapon has a Difficulty of 2, and has a Power requirement of 1. An attacker may spend up to two points of additional Power (beyond the requirement) to bolster an energy weapon's attack, adding +1▲ to the damage of the attack for each Power spent.

TYPE: Each type of energy weapon differs by granting a single damage effect or quality to the weapon. Federation starships always use phasers, but others are listed here both for comparative purposes and to illustrate how the weapons of NPC ships are created.

- **PHASER:** Common to Starfleet and Cardassian vessels, phasers are a precise and adaptable weapon. Phasers grant the Versatile 2 Quality.

- **DISRUPTOR:** Used by Klingon and Romulan vessels, disruptors are potent weapons that inflict grievous damage. Disruptors have the Vicious 1 Damage Effect.

- **PHASED POLARON BEAM:** Used mainly by the starships of the Dominion, Phased polaron weapons are especially effective at overwhelming deflector shields. Phased polaron beam weapons have the Piercing 2 Damage Effect.

DELIVERY METHOD: The delivery method of an energy weapon describes how the emitters are arranged, and how the weapon is set-up to fire. Each delivery method defines the Range category of the weapon, and grants some additional benefit on top.

- **Cannons** are close range, rapid-firing weapons that project pulses or bolts of energy rather than consistent beams. These are inaccurate at longer ranges, but the volley of quick pulses can be devastating. Cannons have a Range category of Close, and increase the weapon's damage by +2▲.

- **Banks** are a collection of emitters, designed to fire in unison. They produce a focused beam of energy that can inflict considerable damage. Banks have a Range category of Medium, and increase the weapon's damage by +1▲.

- **Arrays** are long strips of linked emitters that share a power feed, allowing the ship to fire from any point along the strip. This allows the ship to fire in multiple directions at once, or to adjust and fire on moving targets repeatedly in quick succession. Arrays have a Range category of Medium. Further, when declaring the target of an attack with an Array, the attacking character may choose to grant one of the Area or Spread effects to the attack.

Once the type and delivery method have been chosen, combine those with the Scale and Security of the ship. This will determine the weapon's final profile.

- The weapon's Range is determined by the delivery method.

- The weapon's Damage is a number of ▲ equal to the ship's Scale and Security added together, plus any additional damage from the delivery method. This Damage may have an Effect determined by the type, or by the delivery method.

- The weapon may have a Quality, determined by the Type.

Example: The U.S.S. Enterprise is a Constitution-*class starship with a Security of 3, armed with phaser banks. The phaser banks have a Range of Medium, inflict 8▲ damage, and have the Versatile 2 Quality.*

TORPEDOES

Self-propelled projectiles, containing large volatile, energetic, or explosive payloads, torpedoes are a less precise and less subtle weapon than a beam of energy, but they are extremely potent when used correctly.

Torpedoes come in several types, though photon torpedoes are the most common, and the type used as standard aboard all Federation starships. Other types are listed here for comparison. Making an attack with a torpedo has a Difficulty of 3. Torpedoes do not have a Power requirement, and cannot benefit from additional Power spent on their attacks. However, torpedoes are potent enough that they can escalate conflicts, so declaring an attack with a torpedo adds +1 to Threat.

Torpedoes may be fired in a salvo: a volley of several torpedoes, intended to have a much greater effect. Firing a salvo of torpedoes adds 2 Threat to the pool, along with the 1 point of Threat for a torpedo attack, for a total of 3 Threat. Firing a salvo of torpedoes adds +3 to Threat instead of +1, but it increases the attack's damage by +1▲, and grants the Spread effect to the attack.

Unlike energy weapons, torpedoes don't use the ship's Scale as part of their damage value. Instead, they use the damage value listed below, and then add extra ⚔ equal to the ship's Security skill.

All torpedoes have a Range category of Long.

- **Photon** torpedoes use a simple payload of matter and anti-matter to create a large and devastating explosion. They're commonly used by many cultures, including the Klingons, the Cardassians, and the Federation. They have a base Damage of 3⚔, with the High-Yield Quality.

- **Quantum** torpedoes are a recent development by the Federation, though others have made similar developments. They're more powerful than photon torpedoes, though the way they achieve this is classified. They have a base Damage of 4⚔ Vicious 1, with the Calibration and High-Yield Qualities.

- **Plasma** torpedoes have been used by the Romulans have a wider blast, spreading a lingering field of plasma around the target. They have a base Damage of 3⚔ Persistent, with the Calibration Quality.

TORPEDO TABLE

TORPEDO TYPE	RANGE	DAMAGE	QUALITIES
Photon	L	3⚔	High-Yield
Quantum	L	4⚔ Vicious 1	Calibration, High-Yield
Plasma	L	3⚔ Persistent	Calibration

STARSHIP TALENTS

As with the Talents on a character, a starship's Talents provide it with a game advantage in specific circumstances. Every starship begins play with a number of Talents equal to its Scale, some of which may have been provided by the ship's class or its mission profile.

Some Talents have one or more specific requirements. These are conditions that must be fulfilled before the Talent can be selected, such as belonging to a specific species, or having a Department at a specific rating or above. Some of these Requirements are a particular year, where the Talent represents a specific technology introduced in that year — naturally, these Talents cannot be taken if the current date of the game is prior to that year, as the technology hasn't been invented yet.

Beyond that, most Talents have a condition, and a benefit. The condition is the circumstances under which the Talent can be used, and the benefit is what the character gains from meeting that condition. Some of these conditions are mechanical in nature — using a specific game option, like buying bonus d20s, or succeeding at a specific kind of Task — while others may be more narrative. Other Talents may

otherwise provide a flat bonus to one of the ship's functions, such as Resistance, or Shields, or Power.

None of these Talents may be selected more than once, unless otherwise noted. If two different Talents have benefits which can be combined, their benefits stack.

ABLATIVE ARMOR
REQUIREMENT: 2371 or later
The vessel's hull plating has an additional ablative layer that disintegrates slowly under extreme temperatures, such as those caused by energy weapons and torpedo blasts, dissipating the energy, and protecting the ship. This plating is replaced periodically. The ship's Resistance is increased by 2.

ADVANCED RESEARCH FACILITIES
REQUIREMENT: Science 3 or higher
The vessel is equipped with additional laboratories and long-term research facilities, which allow the crew to study phenomena over a protracted period, and thus generate a wealth of useful information. Whenever a character on board the ship attempts a Task to perform research, and they are assisted by the ship's Computers + Science, the character gains one bonus Momentum, which must be used for the Obtain Information Momentum Spend.

ADVANCED SENSOR SUITES
REQUIREMENTS: None
The vessel's sensors are amongst the most sophisticated and advanced available in the fleet. Unless the ship's Sensors have suffered one or more Breaches, whenever a character performs a Task assisted by the ship's Sensors, they may reduce the Difficulty of the Task by one, to a minimum of 0.

ADVANCED SHIELDS
REQUIREMENTS: None
The vessel's shields are state of the art, using developments that other cultures have not yet learned to overcome, or which simply provide greater protection for the same power expenditure. The ship's maximum Shields are increased by 5.

ADVANCED SICKBAY
REQUIREMENTS: None
The ship's sickbay is extremely well-equipped, and larger than is normal for a ship of this size. The ship gains the Advanced Sickbay Advantage, which applies to all Tasks related to medicine and biology performed within the sickbay itself. This Advantage is lost if the ship's Computers System is Disabled.

BACKUP EPS CONDUITS
REQUIREMENTS: None
The ship's power conduits have additional redundancies, which can be activated to reroute power more easily in case of an emergency, keeping it from being lost when the ship is damaged. Whenever the ship would lose one or more Power because of suffering damage, roll ⚔ for each Power lost. Each Effect rolled prevents the loss of that point of Power.

COMMAND SHIP
REQUIREMENTS: Command 3+

The ship has command and control systems allowing it to coordinate easily with allies during a crisis. When a character on the ship succeeds at a *Direct* Task to create an Advantage, they may always be assisted by the ship's Communications + Command, and they may confer the Advantage to allied ships or away teams with whom the ship maintains a communications link.

DIPLOMATIC SUITES
REQUIREMENTS: None

The ship has numerous high-quality staterooms for hosting VIPs, as well as briefing rooms and other facilities that allow the ship to serve as a neutral ground for diplomatic summits, trade negotiations, and similar functions. When hosting negotiations, members of the crew may be assisted by the ship's **Computers + Command** or **Structure + Command**.

ELECTRONIC WARFARE SYSTEMS
REQUIREMENTS: None

The ship's communications systems have been specially-designed to intercept and disrupt enemy communications in battle. Whenever a character on the ship succeeds at the Intercept or Signals Jamming Tasks, they may spend 2 Momentum to select one additional ship to target.

EMERGENCY MEDICAL HOLOGRAM
REQUIREMENT: 2371 or later

The ship's sickbay is equipped with holoemitters and a state-of-the-art holographic doctor, able to assist medical personnel during emergencies. The ship has one additional Supporting Character, an Emergency Medical Hologram, using the Attributes, Disciplines, and so forth as shown in the sidebar, which does not cost any Crew Support to introduce, and which does not automatically improve when introduced. This character cannot go into any location not equipped with holoemitters.

EXTENSIVE SHUTTLEBAYS
REQUIREMENTS: None

The vessel's shuttlebays are large, well-supplied, and able to support a larger number of active shuttle missions simultaneously. The ship may have twice as many small craft active at any one time as it would normally allow, and it may carry up to two Scale 2 small craft. For more on small craft operations, see p. 232.

FAST TARGETING SYSTEMS
REQUIREMENTS: Security 3+

The ship's targeting systems can lock weapons on target much faster and more accurately than other ships of its class, giving it an edge in battle. The ship does not suffer the normal Difficulty increase for targeting a specific System on the enemy ship.

HIGH RESOLUTION SENSORS
REQUIREMENTS: None

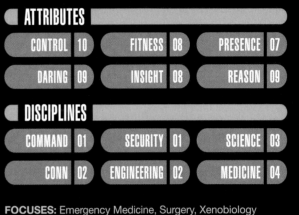

SUPPORTING CHARACTER

EMERGENCY MEDICAL HOLOGRAM
This profile represents a Mark I Emergency Medical Hologram, an acerbic and ill-tempered program often disliked by the crews serving alongside them.

TRAIT: Hologram

ATTRIBUTES
CONTROL 10	FITNESS 08	PRESENCE 07
DARING 09	INSIGHT 08	REASON 09

DISCIPLINES
COMMAND 01	SECURITY 01	SCIENCE 03
CONN 02	ENGINEERING 02	MEDICINE 04

FOCUSES: Emergency Medicine, Surgery, Xenobiology

The vessel's sensors can gain large amounts of accurate data, though they are extremely sensitive. While the vessel is not in combat, any successful Task that is assisted by the ship's Sensors gains one bonus Momentum.

IMPROVED DAMAGE CONTROL
REQUIREMENTS: None

The ship has more efficient damage reporting systems, and better-trained teams of technicians, allowing the crew to respond more quickly to damage during a crisis. When a character takes the *Damage Control* Task aboard this ship, they may re-roll a single d20. If the repairs require an Extended Task, then the characters also gain Progression 1, adding +1 to Work done for each Effect rolled.

IMPROVED HULL INTEGRITY
REQUIREMENTS: None

The ship's hull has been reinforced to hold together better under stress and damage. The ship's Resistance is increased by 1.

IMPROVED IMPULSE DRIVE
REQUIREMENTS: None

The ship's Impulse drives are more powerful than on most ships, allowing the ship to accelerate much more quickly. When the flight controller succeeds at the *Impulse*, *Attack Pattern*, *Evasive Action*, or *Ramming Speed* Tasks, they may spend 2 Momentum to increase the Difficulty of attacks against the ship by 1 until the start of the flight controller's next Turn, due to the ship's rapid acceleration.

IMPROVED POWER SYSTEMS

REQUIREMENTS: None

The ship's power systems are extremely efficient, allowing power to be redirected and rerouted from different systems very quickly. Whenever a character succeeds at a *Power Management* Task, the ship gains 2 Power per Momentum spent (Repeatable) instead of 1.

IMPROVED REACTION CONTROL SYSTEM

REQUIREMENTS: Conn 3+

The ship's maneuvering thrusters operate with greater precision, allowing the ship to adjust its course more carefully. Whenever a Task to move or maneuver the ship would increase in Difficulty because of obstacles or hazards, reduce the Difficulty by 1 (to a minimum of the Task's normal Difficulty).

IMPROVED SHIELD RECHARGE

REQUIREMENTS: Security 3+

The ship's deflector shields have redundant capacitors and emitter arrays that allow the shields to be recharged and replenished much more efficiently. Whenever the *Regenerate Shields* Task is successful, the ship regains 3 points of Shields, plus 3 more for each Momentum spent (Repeatable), instead of the normal amount.

IMPROVED WARP DRIVE

REQUIREMENTS: None

The ship's warp drive is more efficient, capitalizing on improved field dynamics, better control of antimatter flow rates, or some other advancement that allows the ship to expend less energy when travelling at warp. Whenever the ship spends Power to go to warp, roll 1▲ for each Power spent; for each Effect rolled, that point of Power is not spent.

MODULAR LABORATORIES

REQUIREMENTS: Science 2+

The ship has considerable numbers of empty, multi-purpose compartments that can be converted to laboratories as and when required. At the start of an adventure, the crew may decide how the modular laboratories are configured; this configuration counts as an Advantage which applies to work performed within the laboratories.

QUANTUM TORPEDOES

REQUIREMENT: 2371 or later

The vessel has been equipped with the latest in ship-to-ship munitions: the quantum torpedoes. The ship has quantum torpedoes in addition to any other form of torpedo it carries.

RAPID-FIRE TORPEDO LAUNCHER

REQUIREMENTS: None

The vessel's torpedo launchers have been redesigned to allow the ship to fire multiple torpedoes much more quickly and accurately. Whenever the crew add 3 to Threat to fire a torpedo salvo, they may re-roll a single d20 on the attack, and any number of ▲ on the damage roll.

REDUNDANT SYSTEMS

REQUIREMENTS: None

The ship has multiple additional redundancies that allow it to withstand severe damage more easily. Nominate a single System. When that system becomes Damaged or Disabled, the crew may choose to activate the backups as a Minor Action; if the System was Damaged, it is no longer Damaged. If it was Disabled, it becomes Damaged instead. A System's backups may only be activated once per adventure, so subsequent damage will have the normal effect.

RUGGED DESIGN

REQUIREMENTS: None

The ship is designed with the frontier in mind, with a durable construction and easy access to critical systems that allow repairs to be made easily. Reduce the Difficulty of all Tasks to repair the ship by 1, to a minimum of 1.

SAUCER SEPARATION

REQUIREMENTS: *Galaxy* class or Gamemaster's discretion only.

The ship is designed so that the saucer section can be separated from the engineering section, to operate as two distinct ships. Each section has the same Systems, Departments, Talents, and weapons, but their Scale is one lower than the whole ship (recalculate anything derived from Scale), and each section only has half the Power (round down) that the ship had before separation. Further, if the ship has suffered any damage, ongoing effects of that damage apply equally to both sections. The saucer section, which contains the crew quarters and recreational areas, does not have the capacity to go to warp.

Separating is a **Control + Conn Task** with a Difficulty of 3, assisted by the ship's **Structure + Engineering**, performed from the internal systems position or main engineering. Reconnecting requires the same Task with Difficulty 1, but from crew in both parts of the ship; if either Task fails, the reconnection fails. Separating and reconnection cannot be done if the Structure of either ship has been Damaged or Disabled.

SECONDARY REACTORS

REQUIREMENTS: None

The ship has additional impulse and fusion reactors, that allow the ship to generate far greater quantities of energy. Increase the ship's normal Power capacity by 5.

BRIDGE STATIONS

As noted on p. 221, the different bridge positions are normally grouped into a smaller number of stations. This is because the number of officers on the bridge is typically less than the number of positions there would be if the positions were all separate, so it's more convenient and more effective to consolidate positions together.

The commanding officer position is always separate, and staffed by whomever is in the captain's chair. If there's a dedicated executive officer in the crew (common on 24th century starships), then they may take a second commanding officer position on the bridge, though the executive officer can't overrule or contradict the main commanding officer's orders.

Beyond that, the other positions will be grouped into stations, each of which normally covers 2-3 positions, with each position covered by at least one station, but by no more than two. This can be done however the Players wish, but guidelines for common layouts are provided here.

A bridge layout must have the following positions, arranged as the Players desire:

- 1-2 commanding officer positions (the second will be the executive officer)

- 1 helm position

- 1 navigator position

- 1 tactical position (a ship may have a second tactical position, as a separate station, if it has a Security Department of 4 or higher)

- 1 security oversight position

- 1-2 sensor operations positions

- 0-1 internal systems positions

- 1 communications position

The following stations cover the style of bridge most common in the 24th century, as seen on the *Enterprise*-D, and *Voyager*. These are fairly efficient, allowing all the main positions to be handled by four officers (commanding officer, and the three listed below).

- **CONN:** this station consolidates all flight control operations — the helm and navigator positions — into a single station.

- **OPERATIONS:** this station covers the sensor operations and internal systems positions, and should be staffed by an officer well-versed in science and technology.

- **TACTICAL:** this station combines the communications, security oversight, and tactical positions.

The following stations cover the style of bridge common during the 23rd century, as seen on the *Enterprise* and *Excelsior*. Internal systems are either added to one of science (if the science officer is technically inclined) or communications (representing the communications officer calling down to engineering to perform those Tasks), or

handled from main engineering.

- **HELM:** this station naturally covers the Helm position, but also covers either the security oversight or tactical position.

- **NAVIGATION:** this station covers the navigator position, as well as whichever of security oversight or tactical is not covered by the helm.

- **SCIENCE:** this station covers the sensor operations position.

- **COMMUNICATIONS:** this station covers the communications position.

In either case, there will be secondary positions around the bridge which are not constantly staffed.

FINISHING TOUCHES

Once all the rules details are in place, the ship is ready to go… but for a couple of minor details.

Firstly, every Starship needs a name. The Federation has no universal convention for the naming of ships, often naming them after locations, important historical persons (normally only the person's surname), ancient ships, mythical figures, or even more abstract ideals, virtues, or concepts. In many cases, these vague naming conventions overlap — a ship may be named after an ancient ship that was itself named after a location, for example — but this shouldn't cause any issues. The name should ideally be a single word or, more rarely, two.

In all cases, a Federation starship's name will be prefixed with U.S.S.

If the Players are unable to think of a name, perhaps consider looking at Starfleet vessels that have appeared briefly on the shows, or which are mentioned by name but never seen, and using those names — it can add to the feeling of playing in the *Star Trek* universe by playing with a ship that has even a small part in the franchise, without necessarily needing to be aboard an *Enterprise*.

To go with the name, each Federation starship has a registry number. This is a four- (for games set in the Original Series era), or five-digit number (for games set in the *Next Generation* era), prefixed by either the letters NCC, or NX. NCC is used for most ships, but NX is reserved for prototype vessels and the first ship of a class, in honor of the first Human starships able to reach warp 5. Almost any combination of random digits will do, though it's worth double-checking that the ship isn't using an existing number if the Players are sticklers for continuity. In general, registry numbers get higher the newer a ship is, but this isn't applied consistently.

A HOME IN THE STARS
ALIEN VESSELS

KLINGON EMPIRE

D7 BATTLE CRUISER

The D7 battle cruiser was the mainstay of the Imperial Klingon Fleet of the 23rd century, though it began to be replaced by a refitted version, the *K't'inga* class, in 2270. They were so ubiquitous, that technology exchanges between the Klingon and Romulan Empires saw many D7s in Romulan service as well; the same exchange led to Klingons gaining cloaking device technology.

TRAITS: Klingon battle cruiser

SYSTEMS

COMMS	07	ENGINES	08	STRUCTURE	07
COMPUTERS	07	SENSORS	07	WEAPONS	09

DEPARTMENTS

COMMAND	02	SECURITY	03	SCIENCE	01
CONN	03	ENGINEERING	02	MEDICINE	02

POWER: 8   **SCALE:** 4
SHIELDS: 10   **RESISTANCE:** 4

CREW: Proficient (Attribute 9, Discipline 2)

ATTACKS:
- Disruptor Cannons (Energy, Range Close, 9⚔ Vicious 1)
- Phaser Banks (Energy, Range Medium, 8⚔, Versatile 2)
- Photon Torpedoes (Torpedo, Range Long, 6⚔ High-Yield)
- Tractor Beam (Strength 3)

SPECIAL RULES:
- Rugged Design (Talent)
- Some D7s are equipped with **Cloaking Devices** (see sidebar)

K'T'INGA BATTLE CRUISERS

To represent the *K't'inga* class battle cruisers that replaced the D7, the Gamemaster may apply the rules for Refits to the D7; assume that the D7 entered service in 2250.

COMMON KLINGON SPECIAL RULES

The following rules are common to Klingon ships.

CLOAKING DEVICE: The vessel has a device that allows it to vanish from view. Operating the device requires a **Control + Engineering Task** with a Difficulty of 2, assisted by the ship's **Engines + Security** (this is a Task from the tactical position). This Task has a Power requirement of 3. If successful, the vessel gains the Cloaked Trait. While cloaked, the vessel cannot attempt any attacks, nor can it be the target of an attack unless the attacker has found some way of detecting the cloaked ship. While cloaked, a vessel's shields are down. It requires a Minor Action to decloak.

K'VORT CLASS BIRD-OF-PREY

A larger version of the popular *B'rel* bird-of-prey, these cruisers have been a sign of Klingon power and aggression for decades, and make up a sizable portion of the Klingon Defense Force in the 24th century.

TRAITS: Klingon bird-of-prey

SYSTEMS

COMMS	08	ENGINES	09	STRUCTURE	08
COMPUTERS	08	SENSORS	08	WEAPONS	10

DEPARTMENTS

COMMAND	02	SECURITY	04	SCIENCE	01
CONN	03	ENGINEERING	02	MEDICINE	02

POWER: 9 **SCALE:** 5
SHIELDS: 12 **RESISTANCE:** 5

CREW: Talented (Attribute 10, Discipline 3)

ATTACKS:

- Disruptor Cannons (Energy, Range Close, 11🗲 Vicious 1)
- Photon Torpedoes (Torpedo, Range Long, 7🗲, High-Yield)
- Tractor Beam (Strength 4)

SPECIAL RULES:

- Rugged Design (Talent)
- Improved Reaction Control System (Talent)
- Cloaking Device (see sidebar)

B'REL CLASS BIRD-OF-PREY

A light scout vessel, the *B'rel* bird-of-prey is used on long-ranged forays into enemy territory, and to raid poorly-defended outposts and vessels. In larger battles, they are used as escorts and grouped into squadrons.

TRAITS: Klingon bird-of-prey

SYSTEMS

COMMS	09	ENGINES	07	STRUCTURE	07
COMPUTERS	08	SENSORS	09	WEAPONS	08

DEPARTMENTS

COMMAND	01	SECURITY	02	SCIENCE	02
CONN	04	ENGINEERING	02	MEDICINE	02

POWER: 7   SCALE: 3
SHIELDS: 9   RESISTANCE: 3

CREW: Talented (Attribute 10, Discipline 3)

ATTACKS:
- Disruptor Cannons (Energy, Range Close, 7⚶ Vicious 1)
- Photon Torpedoes (Torpedo, Range Long, 5⚶, High-Yield)
- Tractor Beam (Strength 2)

SPECIAL RULES:
- Improved Reaction Control System (Talent)
- Cloaking Device (see sidebar)

VOR'CHA CLASS ATTACK CRUISER

These large vessels were introduced in the 2360s, and were initially limited to serve as the flagships of the Chancellor and other high-ranking officials within the Klingon Empire, who used these vessels to demonstrate their personal power and prestige. Over time, they have become more common in the Klingon Defense Force.

TRAITS: Klingon attack cruiser

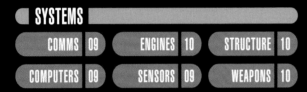

SYSTEMS

COMMS	09	ENGINES	10	STRUCTURE	10
COMPUTERS	09	SENSORS	09	WEAPONS	10

DEPARTMENTS

COMMAND	03	SECURITY	04	SCIENCE	01
CONN	02	ENGINEERING	02	MEDICINE	02

POWER: 10   SCALE: 5
SHIELDS: 14   RESISTANCE: 6

CREW: Exceptional (Attribute 11, Discipline 4)

ATTACKS:
- Disruptor Cannons (Energy, Range Close, 11⚶ Vicious 1)
- Disruptor Banks (Energy, Range Medium, 10⚶ Vicious 1)
- Photon Torpedoes (Torpedo, Range Long, 7⚶, High-Yield)
- Tractor Beam (Strength 4)

SPECIAL RULES:
- Command Ship (Talent)
- Improved Hull Integrity (Talent, included)
- Cloaking Device (see sidebar)

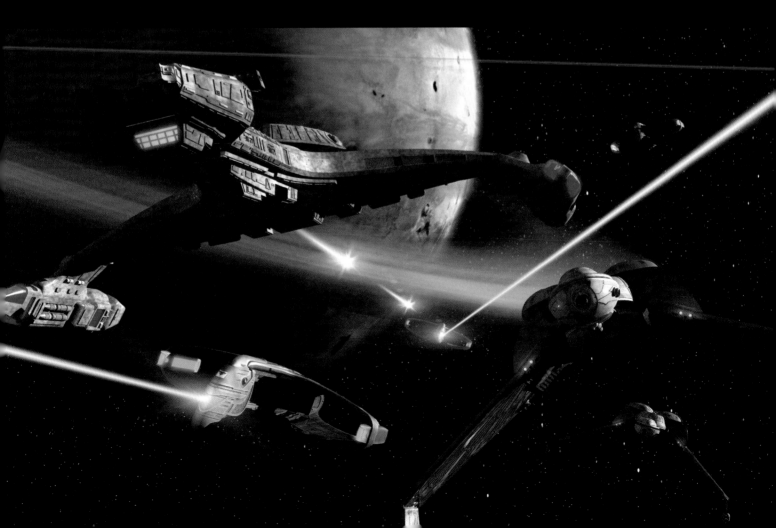

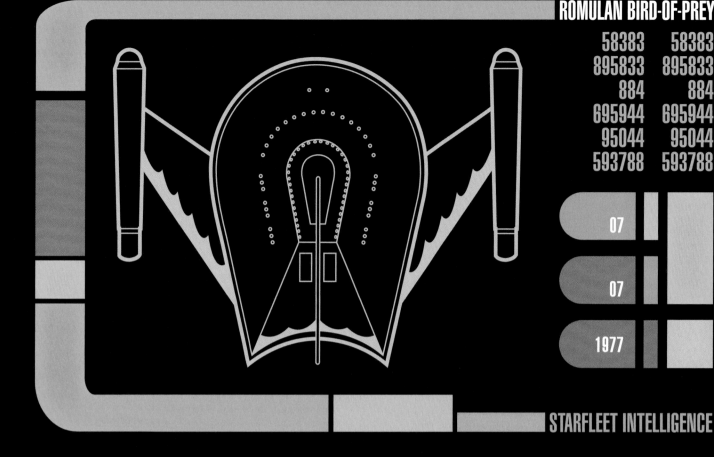

58383	58383
895833	895833
884	884
695944	695944
95044	95044
593788	593788

07	
07	
1977	

STARFLEET INTELLIGENCE

ROMULAN STAR EMPIRE

BIRD-OF-PREY

Little is known about Romulan starships of this sort, which were encountered during the 23rd century, except for limited information gleaned during tense encounters along the edge of Romulan space. Much of Starfleet's knowledge of these vessels is extrapolated from those encounters as well as Romulan technology during the Earth-Romulan war a century earlier.

TRAITS: Romulan bird-of-prey, Prototype

COMMON ROMULAN SPECIAL RULES

The following rules are common to Romulan ships.

CLOAKING DEVICE: Romulan cloaking devices function identically to the same systems on Klingon ships. Use the cloaking device rules from the sidebar on p. 259.

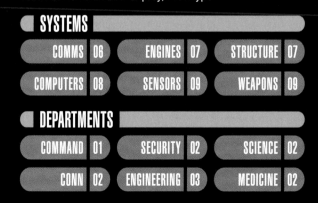

SYSTEMS

| COMMS | 06 | ENGINES | 07 | STRUCTURE | 07 |
| COMPUTERS | 08 | SENSORS | 09 | WEAPONS | 09 |

DEPARTMENTS

| COMMAND | 01 | SECURITY | 02 | SCIENCE | 02 |
| CONN | 02 | ENGINEERING | 03 | MEDICINE | 02 |

POWER: 7 **SCALE:** 4
SHIELDS: 9 **RESISTANCE:** 4

CREW: Talented (Attribute 10, Discipline 3)

ATTACKS:
- Disruptor Banks (Energy, Range Medium, 7▲ Vicious 1)
- Plasma Torpedoes (Torpedo, Range Long, 5▲ Persistent 8, Calibration)

SPECIAL RULES:
- **Prototype Cloaking Device:** This functions as a normal cloaking device (see sidebar), except that the vessel also cannot travel at warp while cloaked, and the Difficulty of the Task to initialize the Cloak increases to 3.

D'DERIDEX CLASS WARBIRD

First encountered in the 2360s, these vessels are the mainstay of the Romulan fleet in the 24th century. These imposing, powerful vessels are powered by an artificial quantum singularity in place of the matter/antimatter reactors that power Federation vessels.

TRAITS: Romulan warbird

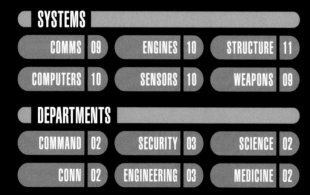

SYSTEMS

COMMS	09	ENGINES	10	STRUCTURE	11
COMPUTERS	10	SENSORS	10	WEAPONS	09

DEPARTMENTS

COMMAND	02	SECURITY	03	SCIENCE	02
CONN	02	ENGINEERING	03	MEDICINE	02

POWER: 10   **SCALE:** 6
SHIELDS: 14   **RESISTANCE:** 6

CREW: Talented (Attribute 10, Discipline 3)

ATTACKS:
- Disruptor Banks (Energy, Range Medium, 10▲ Vicious 1)

- Plasma Torpedoes (Torpedo, Range Long, 6▲ Persistent 8, Calibration)
- Tractor Beam (Strength 5)

SPECIAL RULES:
- Cloaking Device (see sidebar)

CARDASSIAN UNION

GALOR CLASS CRUISER

The core of the Military Orders of the Cardassian Union, the *Galor* class is an unremarkable vessel, normally fielded in squadrons to allow them to overwhelm larger vessels. Numerous variations existed, armed with different weapon configurations, but the most commonly-encountered variant is listed here.

TRAITS: Cardassian warship

SYSTEMS

COMMS	09	ENGINES	09	STRUCTURE	08
COMPUTERS	08	SENSORS	07	WEAPONS	09

COMMAND	02	SECURITY	03	SCIENCE	01
CONN	02	ENGINEERING	02	MEDICINE	02

POWER: 9   **SCALE:** 4

SHIELDS: 11   **RESISTANCE:** 4

CREW: Proficient (Attribute 9, Discipline 2)

ATTACKS:

- Disruptor Banks (Energy, Range Medium, 8▲ Vicious 1)
- Phaser Arrays (Energy, Range Medium, 7▲, Versatile 2)
- Tractor Beam (Strength 3)

DOMINION

JEM'HADAR ATTACK SHIP

Encountered in large numbers in Dominion fleets, and individually on patrols and scouting missions, the Jem'Hadar attack ship is a small, agile warship, though surprisingly heavily-armed for their size. They have a small crew of Jem'Hadar, led by a single Vorta.

TRAITS: Dominion warship

COMMON DOMINION SPECIAL RULES

The following rules are common to Dominion vessels.

ADVANCED TRANSPORTERS: The transporters used by the Dominion are significantly more advanced than those of the Alpha and Beta quadrant cultures, functioning over much longer ranges, and even effective through deflector shields. Vessels with this ability can use their Transporters to beam targets to or from a location within Long range, rather than Close range. Further, they may transport targets to and from locations protected by Shields, though the Difficulty increases by 1 in this case.

ANTI-CLOAK SENSORS: Dominion vessels are fitted with antiproton beam scanners and long-range tachyon scanners, that allow them to reliably detect cloaked vessels. Dominion vessels may always attack cloaked ships, though the Difficulty of attacks against a cloaked ship increases by 1.

SYSTEMS

COMMS	07	ENGINES	07	STRUCTURE	07
COMPUTERS	07	SENSORS	09	WEAPONS	10

DEPARTMENTS

COMMAND	01	SECURITY	04	SCIENCE	01
CONN	04	ENGINEERING	02	MEDICINE	01

POWER: 7   SCALE: 3
SHIELDS: 11   RESISTANCE: 3

CREW: Talented (Attribute 10, Discipline 3)

ATTACKS:

- Disruptor Cannon (Energy, Range Close, 9▲ Vicious 1)
- Phased Polaron Beam Bank (Energy, Range Medium, 8▲ Piercing 2)
- Photon Torpedoes (Torpedo, Range Long, 7▲, High-Yield)
- Tractor Beam (Strength 2)

SPECIAL RULES:

- Advanced Transporters (see sidebar)
- Anti-Cloak Sensors (see sidebar)

JEM'HADAR BATTLE CRUISER

These large warships, often accompanied by a squadron of attack ships, represent the military might of the Dominion, and provide massive power for Dominion fleets during fleet engagements.

TRAITS: Dominion warship

SYSTEMS

COMMS	09	ENGINES	09	STRUCTURE	12
COMPUTERS	08	SENSORS	10	WEAPONS	11

DEPARTMENTS

COMMAND	03	SECURITY	04	SCIENCE	01
CONN	02	ENGINEERING	02	MEDICINE	01

POWER: 9   SCALE: 6
SHIELDS: 16   RESISTANCE: 6

CREW: Talented (Attribute 10, Discipline 3)

ATTACKS:

- Phased Polaron Beam Array (Energy, Range Medium, 10▲ Piercing 2)

- Photon Torpedoes (Torpedo, Range Long, 7▲, High-Yield)
- Tractor Beam (Strength 5)

SPECIAL RULES:
- Advanced Transporters (see sidebar)
- Anti-Cloak Sensors (see sidebar)
- Command Ship (talent)
- Jamming Systems: Any Task which targets a Jem'Hadar battle cruiser, which is assisted by a ship's Sensors, increases in Difficulty by 1.

BORG COLLECTIVE

BORG SPHERE

Spherical, long-range tactical and reconnaissance vessels, Borg spheres are amongst the smaller Borg vessels, yet they still dwarf the starships of other cultures. Crewed with thousands of Borg drones, and capable of travelling via Borg transwarp conduits, they are a deadly threat, only eclipsed by the terror presented by a Borg cube.

TRAITS: Borg vessel

COMMON BORG SPECIAL RULES

The following rules are common to Borg vessels.

ADVANCED TRANSPORTERS: The transporters used by the Borg are significantly more advanced than those of the Alpha and Beta Quadrant cultures, functioning over much longer ranges, and even effective through deflector shields. Vessels with this ability can use their transporters to beam targets to or from a location within Long range, rather than Close range. Further, they may transport targets to and from locations protected by Shields, though the Difficulty increases by 1 in this case.

REGENERATIVE SYSTEMS: Borg technology is highly adaptive and can regenerate from damage very swiftly. When a Borg vessel succeeds at a Task to repair damage, the ship also repairs a single Breach, plus one additional Breach per Momentum spent (Repeatable).

THREAT PROTOCOLS: Borg vessels respond to hostile action with carefully analyzed amounts of force. A Borg vessel will take as many Turns as the combined number of Turns their opponents take — total up the number of Player Characters, plus the Scale of NPC vessels arrayed against the Borg, and this will provide the number of Turns the Borg vessel will take. If there are multiple Borg vessels, this is the number of Turns that the Borg vessels will share between them.

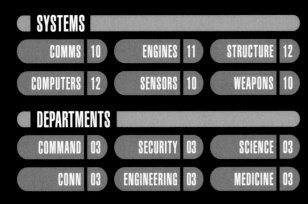

SYSTEMS

| COMMS | 10 | ENGINES | 11 | STRUCTURE | 12 |
| COMPUTERS | 12 | SENSORS | 10 | WEAPONS | 10 |

DEPARTMENTS

| COMMAND | 03 | SECURITY | 03 | SCIENCE | 03 |
| CONN | 03 | ENGINEERING | 03 | MEDICINE | 03 |

POWER: 11   **SCALE:** 7
SHIELDS: 15   **RESISTANCE:** 7

CREW: Exceptional (Attribute 11, Discipline 4)

ATTACKS:
- Cutting Beam (Energy, Range Close, 10▲ Vicious 1)
- Energy Draining Weapon (Energy, Range Close, 10▲ Dampening)
- Tractor Beam (Strength 5)

SPECIAL RULES:
- Advanced Transporters
- Regenerative Systems
- Threat Protocols

BORG CUBE

These massive vessels, over a kilometer long on each side, have been responsible for the destruction and assimilation of whole worlds. A single Borg cube was responsible for the devastation at Wolf 359, and these vessels seem to be unstoppable barring some exceptional circumstances or creative stratagem.

TRAITS: Borg vessel

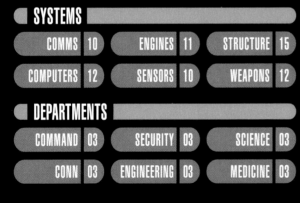

SYSTEMS

| COMMS | 10 | ENGINES | 11 | STRUCTURE | 15 |
| COMPUTERS | 12 | SENSORS | 10 | WEAPONS | 12 |

DEPARTMENTS

| COMMAND | 03 | SECURITY | 03 | SCIENCE | 03 |
| CONN | 03 | ENGINEERING | 03 | MEDICINE | 03 |

POWER: 11   **SCALE:** 13
SHIELDS: 18   **RESISTANCE:** 13

CREW: Exceptional (Attribute 11, Discipline 4)

ATTACKS:
- Cutting Beam (Energy, Range Close, 16▲ Vicious 1)
- Energy Draining Weapon (Energy, Range Close, 16▲ Dampening)
- Tractor Beam (Strength 5)

SPECIAL RULES:
- Adaptive Subspace Field: Whenever a Borg cube suffers one or more Breaches, roll 1▲ for each Breach the cube is currently suffering from. If any Effects are rolled, the cube has adapted to that weapon type (phasers, disruptors, photon torpedoes, etc.), and can no longer suffer any damage from that type of weapon. The vessel may retune their weapons (represented by creating an Advantage) to allow it to damage the cube with that weapon again, but each new retuning can be adapted to as well.
- Advanced Transporters
- Colossal: Borg cubes are huge, dwarfing even the largest Federation starships, and inflicting meaningful damage against them is extraordinarily difficult. No System on a Borg cube can be Destroyed without first locating a vulnerability (normally represented by creating an Advantage, though this Advantage should be especially costly, difficult, or dangerous to create) — without doing this, the ship will continue to regenerate and pose a threat, though it can be temporarily disabled if it turns all of its attention to repairs.
- Regenerative Systems
- Threat Protocols

FERENGI ALLIANCE

D'KORA CLASS MARAUDER

These sizeable craft, utilized mainly by individual Ferengi — the Ferengi Alliance is most accurately described as a collection of culturally-affiliated "businesses" — for defense, trade, salvage, piracy, and any other activities their owners think they can profit from.

TRAITS: Ferengi Marauder

SYSTEMS

| COMMS | 09 | ENGINES | 10 | STRUCTURE | 10 |
| COMPUTERS | 08 | SENSORS | 09 | WEAPONS | 07 |

DEPARTMENTS

| COMMAND | 03 | SECURITY | 02 | SCIENCE | 02 |
| CONN | 01 | ENGINEERING | 02 | MEDICINE | 02 |

POWER: 10 SCALE: 5
SHIELDS: 12 RESISTANCE: 5

CREW: Proficient (Attribute 9, Discipline 2)

ATTACKS:
- Phaser Banks (Energy, Range Medium, 8⚔, Versatile 2)
- Electro-Magnetic Pulse (Energy, Range Close, 10⚔, Piercing 1, Dampening)
- Photon Torpedoes (Torpedo, Range Long, 5⚔, High-Yield)
- Tractor Beam (Strength 4)

THE MAQUIS

MAQUIS RAIDER

Small, maneuverable vessels used by the Maquis rebels in the demilitarized zone along the Federation-Cardassian border, these Raiders are old system defense and patrol craft used by the Federation, repurposed by the disaffected colonists who became the Maquis.

TRAITS: Federation starship

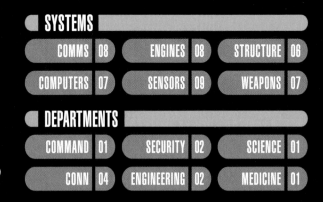

SYSTEMS

| COMMS | 08 | ENGINES | 08 | STRUCTURE | 06 |
| COMPUTERS | 07 | SENSORS | 09 | WEAPONS | 07 |

DEPARTMENTS

| COMMAND | 01 | SECURITY | 02 | SCIENCE | 01 |
| CONN | 04 | ENGINEERING | 02 | MEDICINE | 01 |

POWER: 8 SCALE: 3
SHIELDS: 8 RESISTANCE: 3

CREW: Proficient (Attribute 9, Discipline 2)

ATTACKS:
- Phaser Banks (Energy, Range Medium, 6⚔, Versatile 2)
- Photon Torpedoes (Torpedo, Range Long, 5⚔, High-Yield)
- Tractor Beam (Strength 2)

SPECIAL RULES:
- Improved Impulse Engines (talent)
- Rugged Design (talent)

MAQUIS FIGHTER

Courier ships, light interceptors, training craft, and other agile single- or two-seater light craft are commonly used as Maquis fighters, engaging in raids against Cardassian outposts and cargo convoys.

TRAITS: Federation, Small Craft

SYSTEMS

COMMS 07	ENGINES 07	STRUCTURE 06
COMPUTERS 06	SENSORS 06	WEAPONS 06

DEPARTMENTS

COMMAND 00	SECURITY 01	SCIENCE 00
CONN 02	ENGINEERING 01	MEDICINE 00

POWER: 4   **SCALE:** 1
SHIELDS: 3   **RESISTANCE:** 1

CREW COMPLEMENT: 1 or 2

ATTACKS:
- Phaser Banks (Energy, Range Medium, 3⌁, Versatile 2)
- Photon Torpedoes (Torpedo, Range Long, 4⌁, High-Yield)

030119160518
12091404120525

GAMEMASTERING
RUNNING STAR TREK ADVENTURES

"NOTHING REVEALS HUMANITY SO WELL AS THE GAMES IT PLAYS."

— Q

BEYOND THE FINAL FRONTIER

Everything in this rulebook so far has been directed at the Players, Player Character and Gamemaster. This chapter, however, is entirely for the Gamemaster, the host of the game. It discusses the nuts and bolts of Gamemastering, creating missions, ongoing stories, playing adversaries and gaming in the *Star Trek* universe.

Star Trek, as a collection of television and feature film stories, explores what it means to be Humans of our time, through the voyages of both Human and non-human crews aboard starships, exploring the Galaxy. While the science, technology, and intergalactic setting are of great interest, *Star Trek* stories are always about the crew's personal journeys: Captain Kirk, Dr. McCoy, and Commander Spock's incredible friendship, Lieutenant Commander Data's desire to be Human, Odo's personal journey of self-discovery, Captain Janeway's struggle as a leader far from home. These stories all resonate with us, and tell us something about our lives now — even with the trappings of phasers, photon torpedoes, and the Prime Directive.

Star Trek Adventures aims to provide a tabletop game that evokes those same themes, as well as to experience the excitement of adventure and discovery in the final frontier. This chapter will provide Gamemasters with the tools to facilitate and run game sessions of *Star Trek Adventures* for a new starship and her crew.

LEADING THE ADVENTURE

The Gamemaster is a key role in tabletop roleplaying games, providing the narration, Non-Player Characters' actions, consequence for Players' actions, and facilitating the rules to progress the story being told around the table. They are the one Player around the table who takes the responsibility

to know the rules, prepare the structure of the mission, and run the game. It can be a challenging role, but often hugely rewarding.

A dichotomy also exists for you while sitting in the Gamemaster's chair at the gaming table. You are a storyteller who is framing the adventure your Players are navigating, you help them make informed choices by highlighting their circumstances and ability to act; but you also take charge of the opposition, the antagonists and their plans, actively working against the Player Characters.

This chapter will outline your role as the Gamemaster in *Star Trek Adventures*, how to utilize the rules, structure missions and a continuing campaign, create locations, and provide opposition and adversaries for Players.

TELLING A STORY

Gamemasters are primarily storytellers — they frame the action and show the other Players at the table the challenges present in the unfolding plot. Gamemasters aren't storytellers in a sense that they compose the entire narrative and dictate all the actions that the characters will take in the story. Your role is to create the setting and circumstances for the Player characters to act within. This is called **Framing** a scene. Framing is simply a description of the circumstances the Player Characters find themselves in, introducing the Players to the situation at hand.

Every story contains drama that arises from conflict, whether that's social, political, physical, or intellectual in nature. Problem solving is at the heart of both *Star Trek* stories and tabletop roleplaying. Just as the crew of the *U.S.S. Enterprise* responds to dilemmas as they explore the Galaxy, Players come to the table to engage in their own problem solving. The Gamemaster is the person who presents them with those problems, even creates them, and responds to their solutions creatively and dramatically.

The key difference that a roleplaying game has compared with normal storytelling is the addition of the Players at the table. They collaborate with the Gamemaster, shaping their own character's responses to the unfolding drama by trying to solve the conflicts presented to them. In that sense, it's

key as a Gamemaster to have the structure of the story while leaving space for the Player characters to act. You can do this by having key points of the story prepared — events that would happen regardless of Player intervention — as well as having the beginning clearly prepared while also having in mind possible outcomes of the mission, including what the consequences are for failure.

The rhythm of telling the story at the table goes something like this, depending on the group:

- **Gamemaster frames the action** — The Gamemaster describes the scene or encounter remembering how the following things impact the scene: Who, What, Where, When, and Why. (Though 'Why' is often left for the Players to discover.)

- **Gamemaster establishes Traits** — The Gamemaster notes for the Players any Traits that are affecting the scene or encounter, marking them as Advantages or Complications if necessary.

- **Players take actions** — The Players tell the Gamemaster what they'd like to do within the scene or encounter. In scenes, this will be more freeform, while encounters will be more structured, with an order in which Players act in turn.

- **Player and Gamemaster resolve action** — The Player either rolls some dice or describes how they are going about their desired action. The Gamemaster adjudicates the result.

- **Gamemaster responds to the actions and narrates the consequences** — The Gamemaster then responds to the Players' actions, describing what happens as a result, keeping in mind the consequences for the story and any effect on the scene's Traits.

- **Repeat until the scene or Encounter is resolved** — A scene may feel complete once Players feel they've done everything they want to do or go somewhere else, while an encounter is over once the danger, problem, or conflict has been resolved.

SHOW, DON'T TELL

Another useful dramatic saying that works well for Gamemasters is "Show, don't tell". This simply means describing a scene for the Players without giving away the intentions of the Non-Player Characters or a larger plot point. Instead of saying, "the Romulan commander is angry at you," you could say, "The Romulan commander sneers at you through the main viewer, his eyes burning with intensity as he leans in." This description lets Players come to their own conclusions about how the Commander feels and have more space to roleplay and make choices on how to act next.

Ask any Gamemaster who has run more than a couple of game sessions and they will tell you: "Encounters never survive first contact with the Players." Players will undoubtedly think of a possible solution you haven't planned for, or come up with a completely new use for a Discipline, or succeed against the odds through sheer luck — and even more possibility exists in **Star Trek Adventures** as technology is adapted, jury-rigged, or changed to suit the crisis at hand. Players are inventors as much as the Gamemaster is a storyteller and so your ability to creatively adapt the story in response to the character's actions is key to the fun and progress of the story being told.

RESOLVING THE RULES

The role of the Gamemaster is also one of an adjudicator or arbiter, deciding which rules come into play in scenes and encounters, calling on Players to complete Tasks or engage in Conflict. They are also responsible for interpreting the results of dice rolls for Tasks, Extended Tasks, and Challenges. It is the role of the Gamemaster, along with the Player involved, to decide on which Attribute and Discipline combination is used as a Target Number, with the Gamemaster having the final say. It's also the Gamemaster's responsibility to oversee the results of those dice rolls, checking the Player's successes and failures if they don't do it themselves.

These responsibilities mean that you should be familiar with the rules inasmuch as you can run the game competently. The game will slow down if, in every encounter, you need to reference numerous rules and different chapters of the core rulebook. If a rule does need looking up, then it is always helpful to ask one Player at the table to check those specific rules. One Player may enjoy being designated to do that during game sessions, but, if pressed and not able to look up the rules, it's also fine to "wing it", using your best judgement to keep the action going. Even if you contradict the rules as written, you can always check back to the relevant section of rules before the next session.

The Players at the table are there to enjoy roleplaying as their characters but are also there to play a game — with rules and challenges to overcome. There are some Players who enjoy trying to "beat" the game you run, or "win" the scenario you have written for them. While this is in no way a less valuable way to enjoy playing **Star Trek Adventures** it's important to note that at no time should the Gamemaster be playing **against** the Players. You are still providing a story which is creatively resolved and intended to provide your Players with an entertaining game session.

Deciding on the outcomes of Tasks and dice rolls are the two middle points of encounters, as laid out above, but it's worth examining them in more detail:

- **Player frames their action** — The Players tell the Gamemaster what they'd like to do within the encounter.

- **The Gamemaster asks for the relevant dice roll** — The Gamemaster decides on the best rule mechanic to use to resolve the action, be that a dice roll for a Task, a series of rolls for an Extended Task, or including a Challenge of some kind. The Gamemaster states the Difficulty of the roll (1 or more successes depending on the situation). The Gamemaster always has the final say. It is here you may also want to add any further Difficulty from Complications or Threat.

- **Player and Gamemaster agree on Attribute and Discipline Target Number** — Both the Player and Gamemaster agree on which combination of Attribute and Discipline form the Target Number for the required roll. The Gamemaster always has the final say.

- **Player resolves dice roll(s)** — The Player forms their dice pool and rolls their dice, comparing the results to the Target Number, and declares their successes or failures with the Gamemaster adjudicating.

- **Gamemaster describes the result** — The Gamemaster describes how the success or failure affects the encounter, describing any key story elements if the consequences are far reaching enough. If the Task was successful, the Player may spend Momentum to influence the result. The Gamemaster should describe the basic success, and then allow Players to spend Momentum to influence it further.

Do remember that in all cases, **the Gamemaster has the final say in rules decisions** — even if that decision contradicts a rule in this book. There may come a situation or scenario in which enacting the rules in these chapters to the letter would be either narratively impossible or nonsensical in the *Star Trek* universe.

What happens when characters fail? Failing forward is a fantastic phrase for how a Gamemaster should respond when Players, and therefore their characters, fail or lose a conflict. It represents the idea that even if a dice roll doesn't succeed, that result should still propel the action forward and drive the story to its completion — perhaps tripping the characters up or providing a complication.

A failed Task may not have the desired result, but it may suggest alternative courses of action, such as discovering that a locked door is fused shut and needs to be cut through. Even if an entire away team is defeated by a Klingon war party, it doesn't mean the story should come to a grinding halt. Perhaps the Klingons take hostages, ransoming the Commander and his team to Ferengi

traders who think they could get a good price from Starfleet Command. Perhaps the Klingons leave the team for dead but the medical officer that's part of the team wakes up and is now wrapped up in a high-stakes encounter where she has to save her crewmates.

The 2D20 system has a mechanic in place for increasing the danger to the Players, as well as adding complications too. Should a Player roll a 20 on a D20, a complication develops that is entirely down to the creativity of the Gamemaster. It's up to you what form the complication takes. Threat also adds to the Players' jeopardy, allowing you to add minor obstacles or increasing the abilities of your Non-Player Characters.

STYLES OF PLAY

When beginning a game of **Star Trek Adventures**, you may be about to run a single session, a short series of sessions, or a campaign of missions with no planned end — in all cases you will want to consider carefully what style of game you want to run, its themes, goals, and structure.

Star Trek Adventures presents several styles of play for Gamemasters to consider, mostly tied to the setting of Modiphius' edition of the roleplaying game. The following are different themes or settings a Gamemaster may want to consider when devising the start of their game. You may have a clear idea of the game you want to run, or you may want your Players to give their views and come to a decision. Fundamentally, the style of game the whole group are happy with should be played — that may be found through playing a few sessions, or through group consensus before missions start.

THESE ARE THE VOYAGES...

By default, the Player Characters are senior officers aboard a starship, from captain right the way down to ensign and they operate the starship they are aboard at one of the control stations on the bridge or as heads of department around the ship, like sickbay or main engineering. Whether a new crew to their assignment or a veteran group of explorers, mission by mission the characters are out exploring the Galaxy. The stardate is around 48300, equivalent to Earth year 2371. The Founders have just been located in the Gamma Quadrant, thanks to a successful reconnaissance mission by Commander Benjamin Sisko aboard the *Defiant*. Tensions are high as all the major Alpha and Beta Quadrant powers debate and deliberate over what the Dominion's next move might be. Meanwhile, the Maquis are an ever-present danger around the Demilitarized Zone between the Federation and Cardassian borders, committing acts of terrorism and guerilla

warfare against Cardassian and Federation targets. This year in Starfleet presents Players and Gamemasters a wealth of potential missions and adventures.

2371 EVENTS

A number of key events should be considered when engaging in missions throughout the year 2371. If your game occurs over a number of missions or months, the crew may hear news or even get involved in circumstances surrounding the following events:

- The Dominion and their leaders the Founders have been discovered in the Gamma Quadrant and their only way into the Alpha Quadrant is through the stable wormhole at Bajor and Deep Space 9. Their intentions seem hostile, and Starfleet is worried about a possible invasion force. Exploration into the Gamma Quadrant has been suspended and all major powers within the Alpha and Beta Quadrants are considering how to prepare if the Dominion decide to attempt an invasion.

- The starship *U.S.S. Equinox* disappears followed by *U.S.S. Voyager*, lost in the Badlands on stardate 48315.6. No trace of the starships was found.

- In 48632.4 the *Enterprise*-D is destroyed over Veridian III, as Captain Picard foils a plot by Dr. Tolian Soran to enter the Nexus by collapsing the star of the Viridian system. It will be at least a year before a new *Enterprise* will be launched.

- By the end of the year, stardate 48959.1, a newly promoted Captain Sisko and his crew discover that Changelings have infiltrated the Alpha Quadrant. The security and intelligence ramifications are felt throughout the Federation.

STARFLEET NEEDS A NEW CREW

Later in 2371, the *U.S.S. Enterprise*-D is destroyed over Veridian III. Almost the entire crew survives in the ship's saucer section after the ship's separation, which crash lands on the planet after the ship's stardrive section explodes. While Jean-Luc Picard prevents Dr. Soran from collapsing its star, therefore destroying the Veridian system, the *Enterprise*-D has been lost to Starfleet. It will be more than a year before the newly-commissioned *Enterprise*-E, a *Sovereign* class vessel, can be brought into service.

That leaves a big hole in Starfleet, with the *Enterprise*'s crew on various other assignments or duties before the new ship is built. That hole could well be filled by the Player Characters' new starship. Starfleet needs a new crew and that crew is sitting around your gaming table. Playing **Star Trek Adventures** in the later part of 2371 presents your Players with a higher chance of adventure, being diverted to deal with missions outside of their assignment or even filling in for a Starfleet stretched thin across the Federation. But this is only presented as one style of play, as its understandable that, to a lot of Players, *Star Trek* wouldn't be *Star Trek* without the *Enterprise*.

LOWER DECKS

Another option for Gamemaster and Players is a game based around the lower decks of a starship. Rather than the Player Characters being the command and bridge officers they have duties in the various departments and decks aboard the ship but know each other through a group friendship or through interconnected teams. They could be nurses, scientists, technicians, or security personnel. Or they could even be cadets, still in training, assigned to a starship temporarily for field training aboard one, or even training on board while a family member serves as an officer.

A PORT IN A STORM

Players may want an assignment similar to that of the personnel aboard Deep Space 9. Starfleet personnel aboard starbases provide various roles, with all Starfleet divisions having much to do on board. The command division may take a lead role if the starbase is of high strategic importance or serves as a diplomatic neutral ground for species in its sector of space. The operations division may find assignment aboard drydocks, starship research and development stations, or listening posts, or may provide constabulary duties aboard a larger starship. Those from the science division may be posted to starbases or outposts of scientific value, conducting scans and research on nearby planets that cannot sustain a colony or stellar phenomena, as well as providing more clinical care aboard a larger starbase.

In this style of play, missions and adventure comes to the Players, or is embedded in relationships with regular Non-Player Characters as starships of all civilizations come and go. But that also doesn't stop Player Characters from jumping aboard a shuttlecraft, runabout, or support vessel to investigate local incidents.

LIVING ON THE FINAL FRONTIER

Starfleet personnel may even, on occasion, be assigned to colonies or outposts on a distant planet. The planet may have a certain valuable resource to investigate and mine or harvest, while others may just be a new home for a new community of people. As explorers, Starfleet characters may revel in the experience of living out on the fringes of known space, coming across new flora and fauna and setting up new communities. The struggles and duties on a colony are different, but not so drastically to those aboard a starship. Safety and security of the community is obviously a primary concern, while maintaining or establishing infrastructure is also a priority. Ensuring that order is maintained and expanding the colony or outpost allows it to flourish — it all depends on the objectives of the assignment.

THE 22ND AND 23RD CENTURIES

Setting your **Star Trek Adventures** game in either the 22nd century (*Star Trek: Enterprise*) or the 23rd century (*Star Trek: The Original Series*) is easy as the rules don't need to be adapted or altered in any way. The only considerations need to be how the available technology of the era changes how characters resolve their Tasks in the game as well as the political situation of the Galaxy at the time.

In the 22nd century, Earth Starfleet was venturing out for the first time with the NX-01 *Enterprise* and then the NX-02 *Columbia*. The Federation was either non-existent, or in its infancy, as the Vulcans guided United Earth towards peaceful exploration — although that came with its own complications. Those

complications eventually led to the formation of the United Federation of Planets. An *Enterprise* era game is much more about pioneering adventure and discovery.

In the 23rd century, Starfleet's exploration was led by *Constitution* class vessels pushing the boundaries of discovered space. Of those, the *U.S.S. Enterprise* is the most renowned, Captain Kirk and Commander Spock blazing a path through the stars. Games in the 23rd century are much more about discovery and being on the Final Frontier, months or years away from home, with much more independence as officers. With slower communication with Starfleet command and warp travel not at the scale of 24th century starships, the frontier felt all that further out.

GAMEMASTERING
CHARACTER CREATION

While you, as the Gamemaster, won't be playing the characters created for a game of *Star Trek Adventures*, you should guide the Players through the character creation process, helping them make informed choices about their characters. You should take into consideration the style of play as well as the concept the Player would like to pursue.

APPROACHES TO CHARACTER CREATION

Gamemasters should thoroughly familiarize themselves with *Chapter 5: Reporting to Duty*, which clearly outlines how to create a character from conception to completion. However, you may want to alter the order of that process for your own benefit or the benefit of the Players at your table. There are various starting points as well as a re-ordered process that you can follow if desired.

ROLE CONCEPT

A Player may come to Character Creation with a clear idea of which role they want to fulfill in the group — by default a leadership position aboard their starship. Or the group may have come to a consensus on which Player will fulfil which role. They may want to be the chief medical officer, chief of security, or even the captain. In this case, it may be best to use the Creation in Play rules (p. 131). Knowing which Attributes to increase and which Disciplines to allocate scores to is important when it comes to competently fulfilling their role within the group and aboard the starship. Less important factors for these Players might be Values or even Species, although a character's Species does give benefits to certain Attributes and Disciplines, so to get the most out of their Attributes and Disciplines a Player may want this concept to inform their choice of Species.

SPECIES CONCEPT

A Player may not know what position or rank they wish to play but know they want to play a Vulcan or a Trill character. Naturally the Lifepath approach to character generation on p. 101 would be a great way to make a Player Character as Species selection is the first step. Players who have a firm idea of their Species before creating a character see something interesting in a particular choice and often want to play something other than Human. Often, this means a Value related to their species will be more important to them than any others. All *Star Trek* series have interesting characters from different species: Commander Deanna Troi, Spock,

Worf, Odo, T'Pol, Dax, or B'Elanna Torres. These characters all have a clear identity rooted in their origin species, which, while in the environment of a Federation starship, amplify their differences and celebrate their unique qualities. Players who have a clear idea of which species they want to play may have a Trait they want to highlight and play in contrast to the other Players.

AMBASSADOR'S LOG
FEDERATION AMBASSADOR BALEC
STARDATE 48192.8

Once again, I disagree with the assignment of the *U.S.S. Bashford* to the delicate situation above Tandakkar. Per the Diplomatic Corps rules and regulations Paragraph 87, subsection c, I am sending a request for Captain Jeffrey Deacon's ship to be reassigned immediately and replaced with a more experienced command. I recommend Captain Karen Sarao of the *U.S.S. Brighton* or Captain Liwei Ineti of the *U.S.S. Vera Rubin*.

What Captain Deacon and his crew did for the planet was commendable. I understand why the Tandakkari leader, the Halisst, would feel more comfortable with him at the negotiation table. However, Captain Deacon, as a representative of the Federation's interests, will cause many logical problems for my diplomats and their arguments. The Klingons and Romulans have no such handicap in their entourages. His personal relationship with the Halisst puts me at a grave disadvantage that I fear will be used to great effect by the opposing ambassadors. My aides tell me that the Romulan Ambassador, Ramerak, has already started to suggest an illicit affair between the two.

I think Captain Deacon's exploitation of his familial connections has gone on within Starfleet for far too long. His mother and grandfather are to be respected for their service. His legacy should only get him so far, however. He needs to learn to be an officer on his own merits and skills. Combined with his inexperience, his posting in this capacity is harmful to the Federation's chances of getting the Tandakkari to join us.

VALUES CONCEPT

A Player may come to character creation with a clear Value in mind — about their upbringing, core belief, or motivation for being a Starfleet officer. Two Players may come to the table with a clear idea of creating characters that share a Relationship Value. From this concept, Players and Gamemasters are free to use either the Lifepath or Create in Play methods, but focusing first on where that Value comes from (Species, Environment, or Academy training) then moving back to the remaining steps in order. A Value could inform which role they take aboard the starship, or may inform which division they belong to. It may be a Value chosen from a certain species or related to a certain origin. With a Value as a concept, character creation can be an artistic process, with each decision informing which part of character creation to move onto next.

RANDOMIZATION

Some Players may be averse to creating characters, or parts of their character's history, randomly from the tables presented in *Chapter 5: Reporting for Duty*. However, don't dismiss randomization out of hand as either lazy or uncreative. Some unexpected background details can develop from rolling randomly on the tables for Environment, Species, Upbringing, or Career Events that could even complicate or contradict the character's background so far. A security officer who fled a fight is arguably a more interesting and complex character than one who is incredibly brave, whilst a command division character who has had a problem with authority in their career can provide a roleplaying challenge for the Player. Trying to link random elements or events can be fun and rewarding in themselves, building an interesting history for the character that reflects the sometimes random nature of life itself.

CREATION QUESTIONS

The most creative part of character generation, where the Player has the most originality, is the Values system — developing four Values that describe the core beliefs of their character. But a process like this can be challenging, with Players feeling blocked or short of ideas.

It might be helpful to ask them questions about their developing background so they can frame their Values based on that portion of their life. "How did living on a starbase change your view of Starfleet?" "How did rebelling against growing up surrounded by Science and Technology make your parents feel?" "How did your acceptance into the Command Track affect your friendships with other cadets?" By offering some context to these Values, you limit the unimaginable possibilities the Player can't navigate and give them something concrete to work with.

CREATING VALUES

Creating Values can be challenging. Another variant of the standard Lifepath style of character creation would be to not develop Values for the character until all the steps have been completed and the Player has better idea of who the character is. That's not to say this is a hard and fast rule, instead you can encourage Players to create Values if and when they have ideas for them at any point in character creation, just keep track of how many Values they can create at that step in the Lifepath.

TRAITS

As standard, a Player Character has at least a single Trait — their species — with the potential for others. These Traits — as permanent, or at the very least enduring, elements of the character's nature — are not handed out lightly as part of character creation.

At the Gamemaster's discretion, a Player Character may begin play with Traits in addition to their species. These should have a clear place in representing the nature and experiences of the character, reflecting definitive facets of the character's existence which are unlikely or even impossible to change. This might be something like a disability or injury, such as Geordi La Forge's blindness or Jean-Luc Picard's heart trauma, which requires the use of specialized equipment to overcome. It might be something secret or shameful, like Julian Bashir being genetically-enhanced, or Malcolm Reed being connected to Section 31. It may even represent a reputation or status, and the benefits and problems that accompany them, such as Benjamin Sisko being the Emissary of the Prophets.

Traits of this sort should be neutral where possible — either rarely applicable outside of exceptional circumstances, or applicable in both positive and negative ways. If a Trait is purely negative — essentially a Complication — consider granting an Advantage to balance it out. For disabilities like La Forge's blindness, this can take the form of a piece of equipment that not only helps the character operate normally, but gives them some other benefit too.

Traits like this are normally permanent, as noted above, but this doesn't have to be the case. Some circumstances may change the way a character connects to their Traits, such as Bashir's augmented nature becoming known, or a character may have experiences that leave a permanent mark, such as Picard's traumatic experiences being assimilated by the Borg, or T'Pol's loss of emotional control after becoming addicted to Trellium-D. Changes or additions of this sort should be made only in rare cases, and only where both Player and Gamemaster agree that they are fitting.

GAMEMASTERING
MANAGING THE RULES

While the basic rules for Tasks, and the advanced rules for Extended Tasks and Challenges, are covered in *Chapter 4* and Conflict in *Chapter 7*, knowing when to ask for Tasks, Challenges, or Extended Tasks is always a judgement call for the Gamemaster to make. It may be clear from an already written or structured adventure, but a Player's actions may not present obvious choices or suggest which rules to implement. Always remember that the rules presented in this book are intended as guidance rather than hard and fast rules that must be followed, and it is always your decision, as the Gamemaster, to bend, break, or even abandon certain rules depending on the dramatic situation you would like to frame or the characters find themselves. Playing roleplaying games should always be fun, and if rules get in the way of that, you are at liberty to change them for your own ends.

The following advice should help you decide in which situations certain tests are required from the Players and how to structure those tests, as presented in the rules chapters of this book.

TASKS

Almost any activity where there is doubt in the outcome, where failure or Complications are interesting, or where the degree of success is important can be regarded as one or more Tasks. A single Task represents a single activity that is an attempt to overcome some resistance or conflict. Tasks should, realistically speaking, be actions attempted in one sitting in a short amount of time: scanning for life signs, fixing a replicator, or giving a diplomatic speech are all examples of a single Task.

As outlined in *Chapter 4: Operations*, Tasks require the Player involved to roll two or more d20. It is the Gamemaster, along with advice from the Player involved, who should choose which Attribute and Discipline combination to use as the Target Number. It's also the role of the Gamemaster to decide on the Difficulty of the Task.

TASK DIFFICULTY

Difficulties represent how challenging a Task is, based on environment, opposition, or already established obstacles. Traits are a key part of that and while most basic Difficulties might begin at one or two, it's important to remember that it's you who sets the Difficulty and can demand four, five, or more successes from Players. Traits like hazardous environments, obscurity of information, unprepared characters, or a lack of appropriate tools can all increase the Difficulty of routine Tasks. If it feels appropriate that a situation should increase the Difficulty of the Task at hand, then the Gamemaster has the license to do that.

Structuring the timing of these Difficulties in your game's session should also be a consideration. Don't start a scene or encounter with a Difficulty of four or five successes without the scene warranting that decision or it being an appropriate time in the mission's plot. There is always the opportunity to increase Difficulties as the action progresses from Complications and the use of Threat. It may be that key information or a specific outcome is needed for the story to progress and again, in this case, you should allow the success of the Task, ensuring it is still appropriate to the Player Character's Target Number and the circumstances of the scene.

Environmental Traits also adjust the Difficulty of Tasks, based on whether they are helping or hindering the Player Character. While a character in a spacesuit and a weightless environment may find Tasks involving physical strength significantly easier, the gloves of the spacesuit render the character's dexterous ability much worse off. Think clearly about the circumstances of the scene or encounter, taking particular note of the Traits, Advantages, and Complications, and always be sure to judge the Difficulty appropriately.

Finally, making judgements based on the mood of the group is also key to the Difficulty of tasks. Few groups enjoy constantly having to beat odds of four or five Difficulty Tasks, while some revel in the challenge of beating the game and the Gamemaster. If the group has just faced off against a difficult opponent, tension will have been running high, so easing that with easier Tasks will release that tension and give the Players and the characters a bit of a break from the high stakes of saving the Galaxy. They may also just be having a bad night with some unlucky rolls, and no one will think less of a Gamemaster for allowing success so the story develops and the fun of the game continues.

MOMENTUM

Momentum is a game tool for the benefit of all the Players at the table and rewards Players for rolling well and succeeding with style. Momentum is a group pool that can be used by anyone and helps with group cohesion as one Player's success can help another succeed.

Chapter 4: Operations lists a lot of possible ways to spend Momentum, on p. 85, but that shouldn't be seen as a finite list. At any stage, any Player should be able to propose a new way to use Momentum and providing it is in keeping with a mission, campaign, or the *Star Trek* setting. Encourage unique and creative Momentum spends by Players and always remember a Momentum spend doesn't have to be linked to a Task.

TRAITS

Traits, Advantages, and Complications form a system that assists you while framing a scene, by highlighting the circumstances that may affect characters, benefit them, and also hinder their actions. Traits can do a number of things and a good mix is vital to establishing a scene that characters can navigate effectively.

Traits that aren't inherently advantageous or complicate the scene have the potential to do both, depending on the characters present and the Tasks they want to attempt. Traits will either present the characters with an Advantage, present them with a Complication, or not affect the scene in this circumstance. As Gamemaster, you have the final say in whether they affect the Task or not.

Traits can:

- Increase the Difficulty of a Task

- Decrease the Difficulty of a Task

- Make a Task possible, where it otherwise wouldn't have been possible

- Make a Task impossible, where it otherwise would have been possible

Traits can last for a number of scenes, Rounds or even over several game sessions and their impact may have lasting impact on the characters. They can be introduced either when you are framing a scene (establishing its circumstances and therefore its Traits), through spending 2 Threat points when a scene or encounter is already in play, or by a character through spending Momentum or Threat. Traits should last for as long as they are applicable, but don't necessarily change or go away just because the story moves

away from a location and come back later — a planet's atmosphere doesn't change much in the lifespans of most species, so a Trait linked to a planet's atmosphere will appear as many times as the Player Characters are there.

Traits are broken up into several types, denoting where they show up. Situation Traits tend to only be temporary, while location Traits will come up every time the Players visit that place, and a personal or species Trait reflects a certain character, particularly Non-Player Characters. These types should tell you in what circumstances they come up. Location Traits may affect all Tasks in the area, while character Traits will only affect certain interactions with one character.

Particularly potent Traits may be indicated by a number after them. A "Hazardous Atmosphere 2" Trait will mean it increases Difficulties by 2 rather than just 1 and may even make most Tasks impossible to accomplish without an appropriate Advantage. It essentially counts as two identical Traits, rather than one.

ADVANTAGES

Advantages are Traits that are inherently advantageous to characters and will only ever provide a benefit. Advantages come about mostly from equipment, Momentum spends, or Threat spends in the case of NPCs. They reduce Difficulties for characters attempting Tasks the Advantage relates to or make that Task possible where it normally wouldn't have been. Advantages can be shared, as either a new location or situation Trait, or can be personal to a character as a Character Trait. Remember you can always spend Threat just as Players spend Momentum, creating Advantages for your NPCs during a scene or encounter. Advantages can never be used as a Complication, against a character — they are only helpful.

COMPLICATIONS

Complications are Traits that get in the way or complicate a character's Tasks. They either increase a Task's Difficulty or make it impossible where normally it would have been possible. Complications allow for creative additions or changes to your scenes and is the type of Trait the Gamemaster has most agency over during play. For example, an engineer might succeed in their task but blow out some power relays, blocking them off from their crewmates. In essence, this creates a new obstacle for the Player Characters. Combined with incoming Romulans, it could make for an interesting encounter. Alternatively, it could be saved for later when the Players come to spend Power — it could hinder the Players when they need it most. But Complications aren't as powerful as spending a lot of Threat, and Players should be able to overcome those setbacks with a Task or a short Challenge.

You can also increase the Complication range of a Task, given the circumstances of the scene or the Task. By increasing the Complication range you give more possibility to a Complication arising, letting you either bank two Threat or create a Complication for that Player Character.

COMPLICATION TABLE

COMPLICATION RANGE	COMPLICATIONS OCCUR ON...
1	20
2	19-20
3	18-20
4	17-20
5	16-20

VALUES AND DIRECTIVES

Values form the fundamental aspect of a character's beliefs and personality. They define who the Player Characters are and how they react in any given situation. While Players can use these Values to grant them a use of their Determination, and it gives them a framework to roleplay by, you as the Gamemaster can use those Values against a Player Character, giving them the option of accepting a Complication.

Citing a Value to develop a Complication for a Player uses the character's beliefs against them to develop drama and a mechanical disadvantage within the mission. If a character Value would ever mean that the character would not act as the Player intends or if it brings up dramatic conflict because of the circumstances, then present the Player with a decision:

The Player Character can either:

◾ Accept a Complication about their Value and receive one point of Determination

◾ Decline the Complication

If the Player accepts the Complication, then it could change the scene in one of the following ways: increase the Difficulty of Tasks relating to that Complication or make certain Tasks impossible. In this instance, a Complication may take the form of prohibiting a certain course of action. Complications relating to Values are always personal and don't affect other characters. This could mean that the Player Character finds it more difficult to attempt Tasks relating to that Value or simply won't attempt them at all.

Players should always agree to accept the Complication, and should be aware of the consequences of accepting it: they should know the nature of the Complication they're accepting before they choose to accept it. It is important that Players feel a sense of agency — being able to control their character's actions — and inhibiting them from certain actions may halt the game. Ultimately, Complications of this nature should add drama to a scene or encounter and shouldn't unnecessarily stop Players from acting as they wish.

KEEPING TRACK OF TRAITS

Keeping a track of Traits, Advantages, and Complications should make this aspect of the game accessible and simple. There are a number of playing aids that can be used at the table to do that. Ultimately, Traits should be easy to access and use for both Players and Gamemasters, so having them clearly visible will help the game run smoother.

Having Traits written down in the middle of the table or in the corner of each Zone in an encounter will help everyone track and use Traits to their advantage. Index cards, whiteboards, or gaming matts all fulfil that task and are an easy way to have Traits in play at the table.

Players may wish to challenge the Value that caused them Complications, based on what happened on the mission in which it was invoked against them, which should be encouraged as it lets their character grow and develop, adapting to their circumstances and experiences. This ties directly to a primary tenet of *Star Trek*, that the people of the setting are dedicated to lifelong learning, discovery, and self-improvement.

Directives are a great way to introduce mission specific Values to your game. One Directive is always in play, the Prime Directive, where "No interference with the social development of said planet…" is paramount to all other mission considerations. While this Directive is always in play, it is sometimes worth highlighting to characters before they engage in their mission or certain actions. Other Directives may come into play based on the mission or at your discretion. The *U.S.S. Defiant*'s mission to search for the Founders could be "Co-operative with our Romulan Neighbours," and "Secrecy Above All Else." While the *U.S.S. Voyager*'s mission could have changed from "Apprehension not Assassination," while dealing with the Maquis to "Getting Home," which would remain a permanent fixture throughout a campaign of their journey.

Players have access to all of these Directives at any time, and can call upon them to use Determination and even challenge them to gain points of Determination. The repercussions of challenging them would be up to you at the end of the mission. Equally, you may use any Directive to introduce a Complication for the characters, persuading them to act in a certain way depending on Starfleet's wishes.

Directives are for you to set, or may be present in pre-written mission supplements, and should reflect the ethos of the mission or the orders given by Starfleet Command. Those Directives could remain for one mission, or could form a continuing yard stick by which the crew measures how they act during their on-going missions out on the Final Frontier.

THREAT

Threat provides a unique mechanic to raise the stakes of the scene, encounter, or even the entire mission. It allows you to increase the Difficulty, provide Complications, and change the scene in your favor.

The Gamemaster begins every session with two Threat for each Player at the table. This allows you to have a pool of Threat available at the beginning of the game, but you will also gain Threat in the following ways:

THREAT SPENDS

- **Non-Player Character Momentum.** The Threat pool serves as a mirror for the Players' group Momentum pool. Thus, Non-Player Characters may use Threat in all the ways that Player Characters use group Momentum.

- **Non-Player Character Threat Spends.** For any action or choice where a Player Character would add one or more points to Threat, a Non-Player Character performing that same action or choice must spend the equivalent number of points of Threat.

- **Non-Player Character Complications.** If a Non-Player Character suffers a Complication, the Gamemaster may prevent the Complication by spending two Threat.

- **Complication.** The Gamemaster may create a Complication by spending two Threat.

- **Reinforcements.** The Gamemaster may bring in additional Non-Player Characters during a scene. Minor Non-Player Characters cost one Threat apiece, while Notables cost two. Starship reinforcements cost Threat equal to their Scale.

- **Environmental Effects.** The Gamemaster may trigger or cause problems with the environment by spending Threat.

- **Reversal.** The Gamemaster may end a scene or encounter prematurely, with the situation unresolved, by spending two Threat for each Player Character present in that scene or encounter. The Gamemaster describes the manner in which the situation escalates or deteriorates in a major way — such as large numbers of enemy reinforcements, or some other imminent catastrophe — and then ends the scene. This cannot be used to harm or kill the player characters directly, only to radically change their circumstances, and the Players should be given a few moments to discuss their new situation before the Gamemaster sets a new scene (either with those characters, or, to raise the tension, with other characters elsewhere).

- **Immediate Momentum:** Whenever the character uses an Immediate Momentum Spend — such as to buy bonus d20s — they normally choose to pay that cost in Momentum from the group's pool. However, the character may instead choose to pay some or all that cost by adding one point of Threat to the pool for each point of Momentum that would otherwise have been spent.

- **Complications:** When a character suffers one or more Complications on a Task, they or the Gamemaster may choose not to have the Complication take effect, in exchange for adding two to the Threat pool.

- **Threatening Circumstances:** The environment or circumstances of a new scene may be threatening enough to warrant adding one or two Threat to the pool automatically. Similarly, some Non-Player Characters — this will be listed in their rules — may generate Threat just for turning up, in response to circumstances, or by taking certain actions. This also includes activities that escalate the tensions of the scene, such as Player Characters using deadly force.

- **Non-Player Character Momentum:** Non-Player Characters with unspent Momentum cannot save it as Player characters can — Non-Player Characters don't have a group Momentum pool. Instead, a Non-Player Character can spend Momentum to add to Threat, adding one Threat for each Momentum spent (Repeatable).

When you are framing a scene, it is up to you which Traits you establish affecting how the Player Characters will interact with the scene. Once the scene is underway, the only way to change those circumstances is the use of Threat, or through the actions of Non-Player Characters.

This is very important: **any change the Gamemaster wishes to make to circumstances once a scene has begun must come from either a Non-Player Character or from spending Threat.**

You could bring in reinforcements during an encounter, or increase the Difficulty of curing a virus, but Threat really comes into its own when used as a creative tool to completely change the circumstances the Player Characters find themselves in. From plot twists to unexpected events, Threat can be used to create a shift in the dramatic conflict. You could spend that five Threat to bring in five more Klingon warriors, but what if, instead, the klaxons on board suddenly sounded "Self-destruct sequence initiated, silent countdown begun…" The encounter has changed completely and the Player Characters need to decide how to act next.

Threat also relies on an economy with the Players at the table, as well as the Threat your Non-Player Characters generate through their own 'Momentum'. Remember that Players can always pay for their *Create Opportunity* Momentum spend (p. 85) with Threat. You may also wish to bank two Threat instead of implementing a Complication from a Player's dice roll.

It's especially effective when the way the Gamemaster spends Threat has a clear tie to the way Threat was generated in a scene. If the scene says there's an alarm panel, then a Non-Player Character activating that panel may add to Threat, and then that Threat can naturally be used to bring in reinforcements, creating a sense of cause and effect. This approach can be helpful for making Threat seem like a natural part of the process, rather than something abrupt or intrusive.

OPPOSED TASKS

Opposed Tasks are just like Tasks above, except there is an active, opposite force working against the Player Characters. It's at this point that you can actively roll dice related to the Task at hand, based on your Non-Player Character or other forces working against the Players.

Opposed Tasks, in general, should only be attempted by sentient beings. Environmental factors like freak weather, atmospheric conditions and stellar phenomena only raise difficulties or are forces to be overcome by the Player characters and are covered better with Traits or Complications. It's a great opportunity for Non-Player Characters important to the story to be highlighted through dice rolls as well as roleplay. Main adversaries can be showcased in this way, and it's also a great opportunity to develop some additional Threat if the Non-Player Character does particularly well. You should use Opposed Tasks in moments of direct, non-life-threatening, conflict or where both Player Character and Non-Player Character are striving for the same simple goal within a scene.

Interpreting the results of an Opposed Task calls for a greater degree of bookkeeping because the Gamemaster needs to adjudicate both results and then compare the two, accounting for all the gained Momentum or Complications that may arise. You may even find you need to think on your feet when it comes to narrating the outcome, with the possibility of both sides succeeding on the Task or failing. How should one party win out if both succeed? How do both of the characters acting manage to fail the Task? Opposed Tasks can create a momentary sense of drama or tension as well as having unexpected and exciting consequences for the story.

MELEE ATTACKS IN COMBAT

Melee attack Tasks in combat are always Opposed Tasks and, as such, a number of outcomes can present themselves.

- **Attacker Wins** and inflicts damage to their target — This result is easily adjudicated, track the damage to your Non-Player Character.
- **Target Wins** and inflicts damage to their attacker — In a reversal of fortune, your Non-Player Character wins the fight and can inflict damage on the Player Character.
- **Draw** — No outright winner between the target and their attacker, so what happens now? Could the Player Character succeed at a cost, maybe gaining a Personal Complication? Or does something unexpected happen?

Always remember that you can spend Threat to Create Opportunity and gain more d20s or to increase the Attacker's Difficulty.

EXTENDED TASKS

Extended Tasks provide a greater challenge for the Player Characters than normal Tasks. While Tasks represent attempting to resolve a problem with one approach and in a short amount of time, Extended Tasks give the Gamemaster the opportunity to present problems that require a longer amount of time and greater degree of work to resolve while there is pressure on the characters to achieve the Task. They can be Tasks that last a whole game session, or even extend over several sessions, and often provide slow mounting tension or much more active problem solving from the Players around the table.

Extended Tasks should only be introduced where there is a definitive pressure on the Player Characters to achieve the Task; that ultimately provides excitement and drama. The following suggestions can provide a pacing mechanism rather than a measure of Difficulty — they make the Extended Task longer to complete and the tension should increase because there is some peril or problem that worsens the longer they take.

- Combat: The Extended Task takes place during combat (see the Combat rules for more details). Tasks can only be attempted on a character's Turn, and the rest of combat rages around the characters as they attempt to complete the Extended Task. The dangers inherent in combat offer plenty of risk to make an Extended Task exciting, particularly if overcoming the Extended Task is the objective for the combat as a whole — the combat ends when the Extended Task is completed, and the combat serves to put pressure on the characters while they work towards that goal.

- **Consequences:** The Extended Task itself is risky, with potential consequences either for failed Tasks, or for Complications that occur during attempted Tasks. These consequences may involve damage, or other lingering problems that make it unwise to make too many attempts.

- **Limited Attempts:** The Extended Task can only be attempted a set number of times, normally equal to the Magnitude, or one lower than the Magnitude, depending on how problematic the Extended Task is meant to be (less is more problematic). If the number of attempts are used up without the Extended Task being completed, then the characters suffer some manner of consequence.

- **Peril:** The Extended Task takes place amongst some persistent peril or hazard. This might be a constantly-hostile environment (such as a barely-breathable atmosphere, extreme temperatures, or some other environment that will have a constant effect), or an environment that presents a risk (such as being on the hull of the ship wearing an environment suit, where a suit breach or being knocked away could prove disastrous). If there's a constant peril, the characters suffer a small amount of damage or a Complication with each attempted Task (see Damage, Injury, and Recovery, later), making it dangerous to spend too long attempting the Task. If there's a risky environment, each attempted Task adds one point to Threat, which the Gamemaster may spend to turn that potential for risk into actual danger.

- **Time Pressure:** The Extended Task must be completed within a set amount of time, and exceeding this time limit either makes it impossible to progress or results in some severe consequence. At the start of the Extended Task, the Gamemaster determines the number of **Intervals** that the Extended Task must be completed within, and how long a period that each Interval represents (ten minutes, an hour, a day, etc.). The ideal number of Intervals is about 2-3 times the Extended Task's Magnitude, with a smaller number of Intervals resulting in more time pressure on the characters. The Gamemaster should also determine what happens when Time runs out — this should be a severe consequence. Each Task attempted takes two Intervals, though this can be reduced to one by spending two Momentum on a successful Task, and/or increased by one for each Complication suffered (instead of the Complications' normal effects).

Extended Tasks have several considerations when framing them for Players. You should build your Extended Tasks with the following in mind, and be cautious about when to implement them.

WORK

The Work Track of an Extended Task is a number from five to twenty, which Players progress along depending on the totals scored on Challenge Dice. Progress can be an indication of how much time is required to resolve the Extended Task or how complex the problem is, but care is required when framing this within a mission. If the Extended Task is not of much importance for the ongoing story, but is required in the session, then consider giving it a low Work Track value, between five and ten. Only Extended Tasks that provide genuine tension to Player's engagement with the plot of the mission, or are imperative to resolve the conflict at hand, should be given longer Work Tracks.

There is a danger that longer Extended Tasks could become tedious, as a lot of smaller Tasks and Challenge Dice rolls are required to resolve them, particularly if luck is not on the Players' side. You should always keep in mind the dramatic situation at hand, narrating how progress is being made, rather than relying on the dice and the mechanics to tell the story. How does one success differ from another? How does the character's approach or Discipline being used inform the progress? Are there any specific approaches that should be especially effective, giving the character extra benefits for Effects rolled on their $\blacktriangle$?

MAGNITUDE

The Magnitude of an Extended Task represents how large and complex the Task is, and also provides the Players with the number of Breakthroughs they require. Magnitudes of one or two should be used when a problem or project isn't very complex or outside the normal remit for the characters. Greater Magnitudes of three to five represent very complex problems or situations with newly discovered phenomena or unusual circumstances. Like the Difficulty of normal Tasks, environmental factors or adverse situations may increase the Magnitude by one or two steps, but the Gamemaster should be careful making increases, as repeated Tasks at a Difficulty at 3 or more will drain Players' resources or give you Threat based on their choices. Difficulty can always be increased or reduced through Advantages or Complications.

BREAKTHROUGHS

A Breakthrough represents success in an Extended Task, a point in the scene or encounter where the Player characters both make some progress toward resolving the problem and gain some insight into its nature. Breakthroughs will occur when the Players roll well, when their characters do good work on the problem at hand, or at the end of the Work track when a lot of work has already been done. Breakthroughs early on could be eureka moments, maybe providing the Player characters with some insight into what actions are having the most effect. In a mechanical sense, it reduces the Difficulty by 1. A Breakthrough may also award them additional Momentum in future Tasks relating to this Extended Task or give them a better idea of which Disciplines would be more appropriate or useful. Breakthroughs when

the Work track is full come from a lot of work already being done on solving the problem at hand and so the results ride on the progress already carried out.

RESISTANCE

Resistance should be reserved for the most arduous of Extended Tasks, where obstacles have been placed in the way of the characters by opposing forces, or where environmental factors make progress particularly difficult. Resistance will make the Extended Task longer, so only use it where necessary to the dramatic tension, or as the actions of the Non-Player Characters or situation make things more difficult. Momentum spent by the Players can reduce this value; this can be made sense of dramatically by the characters finding a way around the difficult factor or succeeding at their Task in such a way that it mitigates the obstruction of their attempts.

COMPLICATIONS

When Complications come up in Extended Tasks, they have ramifications for the Work or Resistance of the Task. Narratively this could come down to a number of reasons, such as technology overloading or breaking down due to adaptation, gaffes in political situations, or biology or naturally occurring phenomena adapting to the characters' actions. Complications from Extended Tasks don't usually carry over into the story as a whole unless absolutely appropriate.

PERIL AND TIME

It may be that the Extended Task occurs without constraints on time or without an imminent danger, but, while framing the Extended Task, the Gamemaster should consider the situation around the Task. It may be that the Players only have a certain amount of time to complete their attempts to resolve the problem; meaning limited attempts should be placed on the Players' Tasks, related to the Magnitude. Or the Extended Task may be attempted around an immediate peril or during conflict, in which case the Magnitude may be greater or characters may take damage from attempts or Complications. Framing an Extended Task within a perilous scene or encounter will build the tension and make the Tasks exciting for the Players.

CHALLENGES

An over arcing goal or complex situation may call for a Challenge to be structured by the Gamemaster. Challenges are a series of Tasks, or even Extended Tasks, arranged in such a way as the outcome of one influences or allows for another Task. A Basic Challenge should have its Key Tasks described to the Players, these Key Tasks being the jobs the Player Characters need to complete before the overall problem has been overcome. These Key Tasks can be attempted and completed independently of each other, however, there are a variety of interesting ways to structure Challenges as we'll explore below:

LINEAR CHALLENGES

Tasks in a linear Challenge happen one after the other in a series of rolls. The first Task must be completed before the second can be attempted, and so on. This is a limited way of structuring the Challenge but does give clarity to the Players on what they need to do. While it can be a little uncreative for Players, sometimes situations call for a very specific response or course of action. Linear Challenges are a good way to add a little depth to a Challenge without the need for a lot of bookkeeping.

Example: A group of newly-graduated ensigns are trying to navigate their way through the wilderness after crash-landing on an unfamiliar planet, trying to reach a Federation outpost. Each Key Task in the Challenge represents a single obstacle along their route, which they will logically encounter in a specific order.

GATED CHALLENGES

In a Gated Challenge the Key Tasks can only be attempted once other Tasks in the Challenge have been completed. This provides the Players with a little more flexibility, allowing them to approach the Challenge from a number of angles, or choose from branching options. When building Gated Challenges, you should note your final Task or objective in the middle or at the end of your structure, then place the other Key Tasks around it, indicating what Tasks must be completed before the Players can move onto the others.

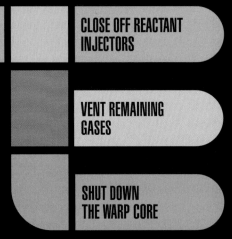

GROUP CHALLENGES

When a whole group is attempting a Challenge, it's important to remember who is helping and where. If a character is Assisting another, then they can't help another character — they can't be everywhere at once! Once a Task has been completed, however, it's feasible that those characters are available to work on another Task. Their attention is also focused on that Task, even if the scene is taking place with the whole group in a confined space. A character who tries to assist on every Task arguably doesn't provide enough help to anyone. Always use common sense and the circumstances to decide if a character can or can't assist or attempt a Task. It may be that completing a Task frees them up for another and you should always let the story inform your choice.

NON-KEY TASKS

Players may want to spend time preparing for a Key Task, making rolls that don't attempt to complete the Key Task but instead prepare for it in some way. That's not a problem and, in this case, you should use your best judgement to frame the Task, and its Difficulty. If successful, completing a non-Key Task could lower the Difficulty of the Key Task or add an Advantage to it, but it alone will never complete the Key Task.

Example: Nikki wants to repair the plasma manifolds in the lower decks of the ship and the first Key Task in this linear Challenge is an assessment of the damage. She wants to prepare by gathering the right tools, calibrating equipment and the like. The Gamemaster asks her to use Reason + Engineering, with a Difficulty of 1. With a Target Number of 15, she rolls 4 and 13 on 2d20, scoring 2 successes. She adds the Advantage "Right tools for the job" to the scene and banks 1 point of Momentum. That gives her an Advantage when attempting the first Key Task in the Challenge.

TIMED CHALLENGES

Combining the pressure of time, or a deadline, to any of the above structures can add tension to the scenes in which the Challenge takes place, and you should always have consequences in mind if time runs out. You should have a clear idea of how many Intervals the Challenge takes, normally around 2-3 times the number of Key Tasks, and you should have a good idea of how long that Interval is: half hour, an hour, a day? Once that's framed, keep a track of how long Task attempts have taken and how long the Player Characters have left — and if they aren't aware of that you can build tension by telling them! Task attempts always take 2 Intervals of time, because Players can reduce that to 1 Interval by spending Momentum. Also bear in mind that if Players wish to prepare for Tasks, that will take time, too. Don't be afraid to tick off some Intervals in the process. Ultimately, a combination of time and the structures above can bring some diversity to your game and add in some tension or climax once the final Key Tasks are being attempted.

OPPOSITION

Your Non-Player Characters may be in a position to interfere with the Player Characters' plans or even to attempt the same Challenge. In this case, you'll want to consider what kind of opposition they provide and how to use that in the Challenge.

Disruption provides an increase in Difficulty but nothing more, and could come in the form of traps or preparations

NPCs have made before the Player Characters attempted the Challenge. This is great if your NPCs knew the Player Characters were coming, or were clever enough to put into place contingencies if they think their plans would be interfered with.

If your NPCs are present and can act at the same time as the Player Characters you may want to make the Tasks in the Challenge Opposed Tasks. This represents the NPCs trying to accomplish the same thing as the Players but for a different reason or end result. It could also be opposition in the form of sabotaging the Players' actions. As with Opposed Tasks, new Advantages or Complications may arise from Momentum or Threat spends, or failed rolls.

Contested Challenges form a race for either the Players or the NPCs to complete the Tasks first. In this case, you should resort to a turn order, much like Conflict in *Chapter 7*. Both sets of characters will attempt a Task but one after the other, back and forth, until every character has been able to act. Take as many rounds as you need for one side to complete the Challenge, at which point the group that didn't complete it has failed. It could be that you lock off Tasks based on who succeeds first — in which case, the side who cannot attempt the Key Task should take appropriate steps and attempt Tasks in order to unlock that Key Task again. In this situation, the groups effectively take control of certain

Tasks once complete, and should only be done if there are multiple ways of completion, as in a Gated Challenge.

Always be mindful that groups of characters attempting the same Tasks can meet and, if they have different goals, will come into some kind of conflict, Social or Combat. Always be ready for the groups to collide in a Combat Encounter to punctuate the overall Challenge.

GAMEMASTERING
PLAYER CHARACTERS

WHAT MAKES US DIFFERENT

Star Trek Adventures and indeed *Star Trek* can be a markedly different experience from other examples of both the roleplay gaming and science fiction genres. Where most science fiction stories focus on conflict, wars, aggressive aliens, and Humanity as heroes, *Star Trek* can be seen, on the whole, to subvert those tropes, leaning more towards a future in which understanding, cooperation, exploration, and discovery is the focus and driving force of the its stories. The opening sequence of the original *Star Trek* series begins with Kirk explaining the five-year mission of the *Enterprise* "to explore strange new worlds, to seek out new life and new civilizations," not for war but for knowledge.

In that sense, *Star Trek Adventures* is not your usual brand of roleplaying game, in which most time spent at the table is engaged in armed conflict with monsters or antagonistic races. *Star Trek Adventures*' missions and campaigns focus on exploration and discovery, with each Player Character having a key role in supporting that effort. This section will tell you, as the Gamemaster, how to highlight those individual roles in a game on the frontier of the *Star Trek* galaxy.

COMMAND ROLE

Those Players taking a role within the group as captains of their vessel or commanders of their officers have made the decision to bring leadership and authority to the Player group dynamic. These Players form the core decision making characters within the group, leading teams and making tough choices.

Command characters often excel in diplomatic situations or scenes which rely on the Presence Attribute and Command Discipline, so make sure those Players are engaged in those scenes. Command characters will have some other, secondary, specialties to their character, placing more importance towards one of the other Disciplines during character creation. Make a note of these abilities and encourage their use or provide opportunities to show how that training might influence the character in the command decisions they make.

Most Player groups are normally governed by group consensus in most roleplaying games and, while this can be true of your missions, there are story elements that may require the captain or commander to make a decision on behalf of their crew. This can always be done in an out-of-character fashion as a discussion in which the whole group has a say, however, the command role really shines when a difficult decision has to be made by one individual, and there may not be time for counsel. Key moments of decision making in the upcoming mission should be marked by you before the session, so that when they come up it is down to the captain or the commander what course of action to take.

In terms of rules, the command role is often one of assistance and guidance. In combat, command characters

ORDERS AND GROUP COHESION

Gamemasters with ranking officers at the table, like captain and commanders, should note that roleplaying is a collective experience of storytelling and most games favor decisions being made by the group as a whole. Captains may order their subordinate characters, but captains such as Jean-Luc Picard and Kathryn Janeway rely on the information of their senior staff. Commanding officers surround themselves with experts and make informed decisions through conference and conversation. This way, a Player group will feel like they have made a group decision, even if the captain's word is final.

may Order their fellow Player Characters, granting them an additional Task in that Round of an encounter, or provide Assist roles in other scenes. They are also the focal point of starship combat, as their orders should be followed by the bridge crew. Command characters can be a lynchpin in tactical play while engaged in starship combat, the one Player who holds a strategy in their head while each other character fulfils a specific duty on the bridge.

Values for command characters will often be strongly phrased towards leadership and core Starfleet beliefs, and thematically it is a captain with strong Values that shapes the ship and their crew to act and react in a certain way to the discoveries they face out on the frontiers of space. It's the command characters' Values that arguably should be the ones of most importance, as these Values will shape the whole group's strategy for completing missions. Challenging these Values may have more impact on the ongoing missions of the crew and, as such, particular attention should be paid to both the commanding officer's, and the executive officer's, Values.

CONN ROLE

Conn roles aboard starships focus heavily on piloting and navigation, and Players who choose this role imagine controlling vast starships, flying shuttles and runabouts, and setting course for the unknown.

Conn characters excel in moments of tense action in which harmful spatial phenomena need to be navigated, shuttlecraft need to be piloted through the tightest terrain, and where Starfleet requires a steady hand and strong nerves at the controls. Their Attributes lean heavily towards Control and Daring, while the Conn Discipline is their most valued, so creating situations in which these are tested, or raising the stakes by increasing the Difficulty of these Tasks, will make the conn officers of your game shine. Conn officers will also have knowledge or even some Focuses in astronavigation or the theory of phenomena and anomalies and this knowledge can be key to the success of a mission or the survival of the crew. Highlighting these challenges for the conn officers provide them some interesting challenges in the game and a chance in the spotlight of a session.

Their Values may be about risk taking or focus and control and challenging those Values may be difficult, but they will give conn Players a needed boost in times of risky maneuvers.

OPERATIONS DIVISION

SECURITY ROLES

Bridge officers who are Player Characters in the security role will most likely be given the task of chief of security, whose responsibility is the protection of the ship and its crew. They will also see action in away missions, particularly when it comes to conflict resolution. Players who choose this role will want to defend their fellow Player Characters and be proficient in both physical and ranged combat.

A chief of security takes the main role in scenes that require feats of physical strength, tests of fitness, or prowess of strategy. They come into their own while in combat encounters, often having the highest potential damage in the Player group, as their score in the Security Discipline is likely to be the highest and directly influences the ▲ they roll for their attacks. In these encounters, the chief of security has the spotlight, often ordering or advising teammates on courses of action while being the key strategist. But while it may seem simple to focus on security officers, what other roles do they fulfil when security is not an issue?

During starship combat, security officers take control of the tactical station, preparing weapon systems, firing phasers and torpedoes, and giving tactical appraisals to the commanding officers. They can also take the lead during investigations of Federation jurisdiction and keep the peace aboard Starfleet vessels and Federation outposts. They could even become wrapped up in a plot within Starfleet Intelligence.

Security officers are prepared to lay down their lives for the Values they uphold and this should be tested as far as it can, depending on the mission. Their Values may also reflect their dedications to particular organizations or individuals, which could change depending on a series of missions or when that faith is tested. Challenging a Value in this way could be a key part of their character development.

ENGINEERING ROLES

Engineering officers are the mechanical bedrock of Starfleet, as experts in their field they have an in-depth knowledge of the technology available to the Federation and aren't afraid to improvise and adapt the technology at their disposal in order to overcome trouble while exploring the edges of known space. Players who choose engineering characters expect get their hands dirty in the engine room of the Players' starship and lead technical Tasks, providing valuable, creative ideas during an away mission.

Chief engineer aboard a starship is a prestigious role and one that shines in times of conflict and times of problem solving. These are the Players that will predominantly manage the power systems of a Starship and push the laws of physics to their very limits. They will, quite obviously, favor the Engineering Discipline but may also have some Science knowledge with their Focuses based around their particular fields of expertise. They will revel in Challenges and Tasks related to repair, reverse engineering or even adaption of current technology. See "So Crazy it just Might Work" in *Chapter 4: Operations* on p. 80 for a little more guidance on handling the rules when your engineers have an

idea they want to try and make a reality. You can challenge these characters by giving them complex mechanical and technological Tasks and mysteries, as well as working on emergency repairs while in starship combat.

An engineer's Values might be tied to a sense of invention and discovery, or they might be more practically applicable. Challenging Values such as these will likely come through new discoveries or adapting technology, or where the engineer has failed to make repairs at the cost of a starship or crewmates' lives.

SCIENCES DIVISION

SCIENCE ROLES

Characters in the sciences division are the Players who revel in the search and discovery of new planets, phenomena and alien life. They work predominantly as advisors to the commanding officers and the rest of the Player group, however they will find their own reward in being the first to make a discovery or even find something that changes their whole perception of the Galaxy.

A career in the sciences at Starfleet is one in which those individuals have excelled in their fields compared to their peers, as all Starfleet cadets receive training in the sciences. Science officers come into their own when knowledge and theories add to the crew's engagement with the mission they

PERSONAL LOG

ROSS, SARAH JANE, STARDATE 47964.7

I'm so excited to see home! I haven't been back to Earth since I graduated three years ago. I guess it's my fault that we need to bring the *Bashford* back for some repairs, but better to fix her up than be marooned in a temporal anomaly. I thought she was running fine, but I think the smell in the engine room was getting to Chief Engineer Sh'thathith.

I'm most excited about seeing Professor Janis again. I've learned so much about practical applications of warp core technology during my first tour. I never would have thought to realign the power transfer conduit on the port side nacelle if she didn't drill the equation into my head for her Astronomic Calculus class. I hope she can spare some time for an old student.

I really hope she can meet Captain Deacon. I think they'd be cute together.

are on. They will revel in the discovery of new phenomena, as well as providing the team with unique insights and possible solutions to the problems they face. Science officers will have high Reason and high scores in the Science discipline and possibly engineering or medicine. Science officers are challenged when they are called upon for new theories and the practical application of those theories. Their Players will want puzzles to solve and new phenomena to study and catalogue, turning the unknown into studied experience.

A sciences officer's Values may be the one of all the Player Characters that is closely tied to exploration and discovery, which means that the development and challenging of those Values can come easily from making those discoveries and finding out something new about the Galaxy.

MEDICINE ROLES

Medical officers are unique within the Player group for being the individuals on the crew to shine in the field of medicine and medical care. Players who have chosen this path have dedicated themselves to the care of the Player Characters' wellbeing and have taken an oath to heal the injured and sick, whoever they are. They will take an interest in several areas of medicine, including xenobiology and be learned in the physiology of many species.

The Player in a medical role should have the highest Medicine Discipline score of the group, which means they are the most qualified individual when it comes to diagnosis, surgery, dispensing medicines, and clinical examination. No other member of the team will be as qualified and any Tasks or Challenges of this nature should go directly to this Player. They will relish challenges of this nature — injured crewmates, discovering and curing new diseases, and investigating medical mysteries. While other Player Characters may have a Medicine score of only 1 or 2 below the chief of medicine, you should reserve key successes and information on progress in certain related Tasks for the chief because of their unique role onboard.

A medical officer's Values will invariably be based in their work, healing others, doing no harm, and saving lives are all common phrases to represent a doctor's ethics. That may come into question when facing an alien species bent on conquering and genocide, or where the cure of a disease may come at the cost of hurting other sentient life.

CHAPTER
10.50

GAMEMASTERING
NON-PLAYER CHARACTERS

The many life-forms that characters are likely to face come in many shapes and sizes, and where some are mighty entities that can stand alone against many foes, others function in coordinated groups. The following categories exist for NPCs.

- **Minor NPCs** are rank-and-file personnel and ordinary people. Minors are the normal type of NPC present in a scene. Minor NPCs cannot spend Threat to resist suffering an Injury. Minor NPCs do not have Focuses. They do not have Values.

- **Notable NPCs** are more dedicated and resourceful characters, often with specialist skills and exceptional talents. Notable NPCs can only spend two Threat once to resist suffering an Injury. Notable NPCs have Focuses and a single Value, relating to their species and affiliation.

- **Major NPCs** are leaders amongst their kind, with a wide range of skills and abilities. Major NPCs have no limit on the number of times they can spend two Threat to *Avoid an Injury* in a single scene. Major NPCs are unique named characters, who have the full range of Focuses, Values, and Talents.

THE CAST OF ADVERSARIES

The Gamemaster also takes on the roles of the various antagonists the Player Characters meet and act against in the missions they devise. At times, you will roleplay and resolve actions for those characters, from friendly Starfleet admirals to hostile Klingon aggressors and inquisitive newly discovered species.

Roleplaying as a Non-Playable Character is one direct way to bring her stories to life. Villains are often remembered for their deeds in *Star Trek*, from Khan to the Borg Queen, Garth of Izar to Data's 'brother' Lore. But they are also remembered for their personalities, which, at the gaming table, can be as fun to watch as the Players' favorite *Star Trek* episode. We're not saying every Gamemaster needs to be able to deliver Oscar-worthy dialogue, but describing what makes your Non-Player Character individual will make your game come to life and engage your Players.

ROLEPLAYING AS ALIEN NPCS

Many *Star Trek* episodes introduce an alien race as the subject of the plotline, just for a single episode. These 'aliens of the week' often have a couple of key qualities that separate them from the regular species of the Federation, the allies and neighbors we are more used to. When it comes to creating these aliens, and roleplaying their various Non-Player Characters, it may be easier to use two or more Traits rather than a one-word species Trait to remind you of what they are like and how they are different. These Traits can be physical, mental, spiritual, or behavioral in nature, but they should always clearly contrast or complement the Player Character species available.

RANDOM PHYSICAL OR MENTAL TRAITS

D20 ROLL	TRAIT	D20 ROLL	TRAIT
1	Protruding spines	11	Breathes a different gas
2	Extremely long tongue	12	Chameleonic skin
3	Low body temperature	13	Multiple stomachs needing constant food
4	Breathes a different element	14	Photosynthesis
5	Sensitive to vibrations	15	Sleeps markedly less than most species
6	Hermaphrodite	16	Empathic
7	Sensitive to light	17	Telepathic
8	Large teeth	18	Strong Willpower
9	Excessive fur	19	Eidetic memory
10	Inhale food whole	20	Multiple personality/identity in one body

RANDOM BEHAVIORAL OR CULTURAL TRAITS

D20 ROLL	TRAIT	D20 ROLL	TRAIT
1	Taste the wrist of the person they meet	11	Will never disagree openly
2	Will only negotiate with one gender	12	Sleep in groups
3	Seal deals in blood	13	Will go into stasis while travelling
4	Worships another species	14	Won't use teleportation
5	Vilifies another species	15	Intensely Honorable
6	High ranking members do not speak	16	One gender dominates the sciences
7	Do not mourn death	17	One gender dominates the military
8	Take trophies of those they kill	18	Pansexuality
9	Will only eat what they kill themselves	19	Will not eat a particular plant / animal
10	Never directly addresses a person	20	Culturally significant clothing item

THE LOOK OF HUMANOID ALIENS

A lot of *Star Trek* humanoid aliens appeared much like Humans, with varied skin tones and two sexes. While that doesn't stop you from inventing strange new life-forms, they do form the backbone of alien civilizations throughout the Galaxy and are the most relatable. They often have variations in their foreheads, brows, noses, mouths, complexions, or even hands and feet, so feel free to add these details when describing your alien species but remember these appearances won't have a direct impact on the character's Traits.

NPCS AS OPPOSITION

Attempting Tasks and acting in combat works exactly the same for NPCs as it does for Player Characters.

Taking damage with Non-Playable Characters and starships on the other hand, is different from the normal rules for Player Characters and their starships. These rules are streamlined for the Gamemaster so you can focus on resolving actions quickly and allowing the Player Characters to have more of the spotlight in scenes and encounters.

During Combat, Non-Player Characters react differently when damage is dealt to them. **Minor** NPCs cannot spend Threat to ignore an Injury, and as such any damage over 5 points of Stress, after Resistance, immediately defeats a Minor NPC. You can spend two Threat for a **Notable** NPC to avoid one Injury, but may not do it again in the same encounter, so the next time the Notable NPC suffers an Injury they are defeated. **Major** NPCs may spend two Threat to *Avoid an Injury* as many times as they like, depending on the pool of Threat available. This gives them an advantage against the Player Characters, who can only avoid their first Injury.

THREAT AS MOMENTUM

The Gamemaster's Threat pool also functions as a pool of Momentum for NPCs, as well as its usual function of allowing the Gamemaster to alter the scene or encounter. As such, when NPCs gain excess successes when attempting Tasks or attacks, those extra successes can be banked just as Momentum can, on a one by one basis, adding to the Threat pool. You may want to immediately spend that Threat, however, depending on the circumstances.

The following Momentum spends (Immediate and Repeatable) are the most utilized when it comes to controlling NPCs:

THREAT SPEND	COST	EFFECT
Create Advantage	2 I	Establish an Advantage in addition to the effect of a successful Task, or remove a Complication affecting the NPC
Create Opportunity	1+ I R	Grants a single bonus d20 to a Task. No more than 3 bonus d20 can be bought
Create Problem	2 I R	Increase the Difficulty of a Task by one for every two Threat spent

COMBAT THREAT SPEND	COST	EFFECT
Bonus Damage	1+ R	A character can increase the damage inflicted by a successful attack, regardless of the type of attack. Each Momentum spent adds +1 damage.
Disarm	2	One weapon held by the target is knocked away and falls to the ground within Reach.
Extra Minor Actions	1 I R	Take additional Minor Actions.
Keep the Initiative	2 I	Pass the action order to another ally instead of the enemy; may only be done once before the enemy has taken at least one action.
Penetration	1+ R	The damage inflicted by the current attack ignores two Resistance for each Momentum spent.
Re-Roll Damage	1	The Player may re-roll any number of ▲ from the current attack
Avoid Injury	2 I	Avoid suffering a single Injury. The cost may be paid by suffering a Complication instead. Other factors may increase the cost further. May only be used once per scene, though additional uses can be obtained.
Secondary Target	2	A second target within Reach of the attack's target is also affected by the attack, and suffers half the attack's damage, rounding down.
Swift Task	2	The character may attempt one additional Task, increasing the Difficulty by one over what the Task would normally require.

NPC STARSHIP DAMAGE

While NPC vessels can make use of the full damage rules, this can become burdensome in larger battles where there are many ships involved. In these situations, the following quick damage rules can be used as an alternative.

If no specific System has been targeted on an NPC ship using these rules, do not roll for which System has been hit. Instead, apply the following effects.

Impact: Whenever the ship suffers one or more Breaches, it loses a single Turn during the next Round. This is not cumulative. It also loses 2 Power.

Damaged: If the total number of Breaches the NPC ship has suffered is equal to or greater than half the Scale of the ship, then the ship has been significantly Damaged. This increases the Difficulty of all Tasks attempted by the ship by +2 until repaired. The Difficulty to repair this is 3.

Disabled: If the total number of Breaches the NPC ship has suffered is equal to the Scale of the ship, then the ship has been disabled. The ship is no longer fully-operational and cannot take any further Turns during this scene.

Destroyed: If the total number of Breaches the NPC ship has suffered exceeds the ship's Scale, then the ship has been destroyed. The ship explodes in a burst of flame and a shower of scrap metal, though this explosion is not large enough to cause damage to other ships.

GAMEMASTERING
EXPERIENCE AND PROMOTION

Character progression and development is a key part of tabletop roleplaying and is also a great strength of the various *Star Trek* stories. The crews of the *Enterprises*, Deep Space 9 and *Voyager* all grow with experience and develop relationships with their fellow crewmates. **Star Trek Adventures** is no different, and focuses its own character progression on significant milestones that signify the growth of your Player Characters and mark changes to starships and their crews, adapting to the on-going mission rather than increasing Attributes and Disciplines. Starfleet already utilizes specialists and talented individuals and, as such, Attributes and Disciplines represent the fact that Player Characters have already reached an excellent level of professional competence. However, there is always room for growth and change.

CHALLENGING VALUES

The simplest way a character progresses is through challenging a Value. This can be done on a game session by game session basis and is led by the Players themselves. Challenging a Value is a core element of developing characters based on their experiences, breaking down prejudices and enhancing their view of the Galaxy.

By Challenging a Value, a Player will lose the use of one of the Values temporarily, but gain one point of Determination to use later in that mission. At the end of the mission, once the story has come to its conclusion, the Player can then reword their Value to reflect the perceived change in their character. The change should be relevant to their experiences and be plausible — unless an incredible personal discovery has been made, completely reversing a prejudice or misconception should be avoided for more natural personal growth.

MILESTONES

There are three types of **Milestones**, all of which take place at the end of an Adventure. A **Normal Milestone** occurs when a Player Character's Values have had an impact on their role in the mission, while a **Spotlight Milestone** is one in which Players vote to highlight a particular character for their actions, and an **Arc Milestone** represents a key developmental point in the life of a Player Character through their missions in Starfleet.

NORMAL MILESTONES

A Normal Milestone occurs at the end of an adventure, you should take note of whether each Player did the following:

- The character challenged a Value or Directive during the adventure.

- The character was Injured by a lethal attack during the adventure.

- The character used at least one Value or Directive positively or at least one Value or Directive negatively.

If they did then award them a Normal Milestone, they then have the option to do one of the following with their Player Character:

- If a Value was challenged and crossed out, rewrite that Value. The new Value should relate somehow to both what the Value was before, and the circumstances that caused it to be challenged. It doesn't have to be a huge change — and often, it won't be — but the new Value should demonstrate how the character's perspective has changed.

- Choose two Disciplines. Reduce one of those Disciplines by 1 (to a minimum of 1), and increase the other by 1 (to a maximum of 4).

- Choose one of the character's Focuses, and replace it with another Focus.

- Select a Supporting Character that was used during that adventure, and use one of the above options for that Supporting Character.

- Save the Milestone, for use when another Milestone is gained.

Most of these options represent a shift in the character's priorities, as their experiences make them evaluate where they focus their time and attention. Maintaining their existing level of competence requires regular study and training, so a shift in priority can see one area of expertise diminish as attention is turned to a different one.

SPOTLIGHT MILESTONES

A Spotlight Milestone works in the same way as a Normal Milestone, only you may wish to highlight one particular character's actions. This Player must already fulfil the requirements for a Normal Milestone, and you may go about the awarding of a Spotlight Milestone in two different ways:

Award the Spotlight Milestone to one character who clearly had a significant impact on the mission, or who's character reached a key stage in development.

When deciding to award a Spotlight Milestone, instead of choosing a Player, let the Players decide who should be awarded the milestone.

Spotlight Milestones should be awarded at least once every two or three missions, but they should not happen every mission. The Gamemaster is, however, free to adjust this level as they see fit — if a group of Players are involved in a deeply character-focused storyline with significant or long-term repercussions, it may be appropriate to award Spotlight Milestones more frequently.

With a Spotlight Milestone, the Main Character receives a single choice from the Normal Milestone list, and a single choice from the following list as well:

- Choose two Attributes. Reduce one of those Attributes by 1 (to a minimum of 7), and increase the other by 1 (to a maximum of 11).

- Replace one of the character's Talents with another.

- Select a Supporting Character that was used during that adventure, and use one of the above options for that Supporting Character.

- Choose two of the ship's Systems. Reduce one of those Systems by 1 (to a minimum of 6), and increase the other by 1 (to a maximum of 12).

- Choose two of the ship's Disciplines. Reduce one of those Disciplines by 1 (to a minimum of 1), and increase the other by 1 (to a maximum of 4).

- Replace one of the ship's Talents with another.

These represent even greater shifts in the character's priorities, making more significant changes to the character. Alternatively, it may represent the character altering, adjusting, or refitting ship systems and retraining personnel, something which takes considerable time and effort in its own right.

ARC MILESTONES

Arc Milestones represent a significant point in the overall continuing mission for the starship and her crew. It represents a major change for the character at a culmination in a story

arc. Awarding Arc Milestones depends wholly on how many Spotlight Milestone's the character has already been awarded.

When a Main Character has received two or more Spotlight Milestones, the next Spotlight Milestone they receive will be an Arc Milestone instead. The number of Spotlight Milestones required increases with every Arc Milestone received: the first Arc Milestone is received after the character has received two Spotlight Milestones, and the number required increases by one for every Arc Milestone received.

Alternatively, the Gamemaster is permitted to award Arc Milestones in a more organic manner, creating distinct character or story arcs across several adventures, and awarding an Arc Milestone to some characters at the conclusion of such an arc.

ARC MILESTONES RECEIVED	SPOTLIGHT MILESTONES REQUIRED FOR NEXT ARC MILESTONE
0	2
1	3
2	4
3	5
...each successive...	+1

Receiving an Arc Milestone grants all the benefits of a Spotlight Milestone (which also grants the benefits of a Normal Milestone), and allows the character to select an option from the following list:

- Choose a single Attribute, and increase it by 1. The Attribute cannot be increased above 12.

- Choose a single Discipline, and increase it by 1. The Discipline cannot be increased above 5.

- Select one additional Talent.

- Select one additional Focus.

- Select one additional Value.

- Select a Supporting Character that was used during that adventure, and use one of the above options for that Supporting Character.

- Choose one of the ship's Systems, and increase it by 1 (to a maximum of 12).

- Choose one of the ship's Disciplines, and increase it by 1 (to a maximum of 4).

- Select one additional Talent for the ship; this option may be selected only once for the ship.

Reputation is a key, thematical mechanic in **Star Trek Adventures** that describes a Player Character's standing amongst their peers and within Starfleet as a whole, and can be found in more detail on p. 141 of *Chapter 5: Reporting for Duty*. Starfleet is made up of exemplary individuals from many different species, all taught its purpose of peaceful exploration. As such, there are rules and Directives to follow, the Prime Directive being the most notable.

It naturally follows that a Gamemaster should have a robust system to reflect the laws and directives of Starfleet Command, and what happens when officers ignore or go against those directives. As a Gamemaster you have several options when dealing with officers who go against their superior officers and Starfleet Command itself, and also for those who go above and beyond the call of their duty or exemplify the code by which Starfleet operates.

At the end of an adventure, the Gamemaster should consider the outcome of that adventure, and the decisions that were taken, and decide how those actions will affect the characters' Reputation. The Gamemaster should determine which actions and outcomes from the adventure may have a positive or negative influence upon that reputation.

Once the influences have been chosen, the character makes a Reputation Check. This is resolved in a comparable way to a Task, though it uses different scores and ratings. The character rolls a number of d20s equal to the number of positive influences, with each d20 that rolls equal to or less than the character's Reputation scoring a success. Each d20 that rolls equal to or less than the character's Rank Privilege scores one additional success, for a total of 2.

If the number of successes scored is less than the number of negative influences, then the character has lost Reputation: reduce the character's Reputation by 1, plus an additional 1 for each die that did not score any successes, and by a further 1 for each die that rolled within the range of numbers indicated for the character's Rank Responsibilities. A character of sufficiently high Reputation is capable of having a die both score a success *and* fall within the range indicated by their Responsibilities.

If the number of successes scored is greater than the number of negative influences, then the character has gained Reputation: increase the character's Reputation by 1 for each success scored above the number of negative influences.

PLAYER ACTIVITY OR DECISION	INFLUENCE
Acted in accordance with orders and Directives	Positive
Challenged a Directive	Negative
Prevented combat	Positive
Personnel under your command are killed	Negative; 1 Influence per character (Main or Supporting) killed
Resorted to lethal force without cause	Negative
Established an alliance with an enemy	Positive
Directly contributed to saving lives	Positive, multiple Influences at Gamemaster's discretion
Acted above and beyond the call of duty	Positive, at Gamemaster's discretion
Taking unnecessary risks in the course of the mission	Negative, at Gamemaster's discretion

PROMOTION

Promotion is a simple way to show how characters are developing and progressing amongst their peers. Should a character have a Reputation of 15 or higher, and it would increase further, then the captain (or rather, the Player whose

BRIDGE OFFICER'S TEST

The Starfleet bridge officer's exam is a series of tests for Starfleet officers who wish to take on greater responsibilities or even transfer to the Command division if they aren't already part of it. The test is most applicable when a Lieutenant Commander is able to gain Commander rank, and should be considered by Gamemasters who wish to reflect the promotion in some form of actual gameplay into their **Star Trek Adventures** game sessions.

The bridge officer's test culminates in a simulated test in which the candidate must deal with a life-threatening situation for the starship and its crew. The lesson of this test is to experience giving a subordinate crewmember an order that sends them to their death — sacrificing themselves for the duty to their ship.

It may be that a scene or Challenge can be played out to reflect this, with the Player Characters as simulations of themselves engaged in the task along with the character up for promotion. Once the candidate has ordered the fellow Player Character to their deaths and seen it happen, they are promoted. The simulation could even be done in secret, the Player not knowing the situation is a simulation until after the character is sent to their death.

character is the commanding officer) or the Gamemaster may offer them promotion instead of an increase in Reputation. If this promotion is accepted, the character's rank increases, representing how they are now faced with a new set of expectations and responsibilities. A character cannot be promoted to captain in this way — only the admiralty can offer such a promotion, which would come with its own command or another posting elsewhere (essentially taking the character out of play).

DISCIPLINARY ACTIONS

If a character's Reputation would drop below 0, then the character faces disciplinary action. Prior to this point, issues of conduct and performance will be dealt with in minor ways, and a character losing Reputation may find a reprimand placed in their official record, or be given some unpleasant or menial additional duty, or lose some privilege normally afforded to the crew for a time, or even just a warning from their Commanding Officer. This should be handled through roleplay, and has no specific game effect other than the loss of Reputation it already represents.

Disciplinary action is when matters need to be taken further. This may be something handled within the ship's command structure, or it may be more serious and require that the character being punished be detained and face a court-martial. The range of possibilities here are broad, and best left to the discretion of both the Commanding Officer and the Gamemaster, though suggestions are provided here. Punishments that come from disciplinary actions cannot be lethal, or involve harming or permanently marking the accused in any way, per the Federation strictures against cruel and unusual punishment — though some of them may make it so that a character can no longer be used.

- **Short-term detention** is a possible punishment that can be given at the discretion of the Commanding Officer, confining an officer to their quarters or to the brig for days, weeks, or even a month. Detention longer than this is unlikely — a more severe crime probably warrants a different punishment. A character in detention cannot be used — that character cannot be selected during play for the next mission (and the Player should use a Supporting Character instead), barring extreme circumstances.

- **Demotion** is another punishment that can be handled at the discretion of the Commanding Officer. The character's rank is reduced by one step, and their Reputation is reset to 9: the character is on shaky ground, but a demotion at least gives them some opportunity to redeem themselves. This may make the character ineligible for their current role; if this is the case, the group should re-assign roles accordingly.

- **Court-Martial** is the most severe, and the one that can be the most disruptive to an ongoing game, but also the most rewarding if handled well. The character is detained until the ship can reach a starbase or other Starfleet facility where the character will be tried for their crimes. Potential punishments for this are most likely to be dishonorable discharge from Starfleet, or long-term imprisonment in a penal settlement, either of which will make the character unplayable. The advantage of this method is that a court-martial can make for an exciting and dramatic session that allows for plenty of social conflict and investigation. Courts-martial do not have to happen exclusively because of this mechanic — any character accused of a serious crime may face court-martial.

Commanding Officers are a special case. As they are the top of the chain of command on their ship, their superiors are the Admiralty, who aren't present for day-to-day matters. Instead, in the short-term, if a Commanding Officer loses Reputation while already at 0, they should be relieved of duty by the Executive Officer/second-in-command, and confined to their quarters (short-term detention, above) until the situation has passed. More significant problems are to be handled by the Gamemaster, possibly in a court-martial.

Naturally, disciplinary action requires a delicate touch in game, and there is a fine line between interesting and dramatic uses of these rules, and abuses of power that may see Players become resentful of one another, or worse.

In the short term, consider that the means by which a commanding officer disciplines their crew is in itself a matter that could affect their reputation, and being excessively harsh or abusive in their authority may see a Commanding Officer's reputation decline. Commanding officers have superiors of their own, and a Gamemaster is free to veto and provide alternatives for any disciplinary actions the commanding officer takes.

Beyond this, however, it comes down to communicating with the Players, and handling things in a considerate manner like reasonable people. If the Players cannot reasonably be trusted not to abuse this power, then the Gamemaster may restrict or even remove the ability to impose disciplinary actions upon other Players. This should be a last resort, however, as this can limit some of the innate drama and tension that comes from things like a court martial.

These situations should also be handled with care as it may spoil the game for the Player involved or the other Players at the table. However, **Star Trek Adventures** is a game about discovery and adventure in line with the guiding principles of the Federation, of peace and furthering knowledge. If one Player is being disruptive to that, it may be more useful to talk to that Player away from the table. A Player Character's punishments should never be used to punish a Player — only provide a good story and interesting character progression.

GAMEMASTERING
CREATING ENCOUNTERS

Missions in **Star Trek Adventures** will be broken up into two types of events; **scenes** and **encounters**. Scenes tend to favor role-playing and drama over rolling dice, while Encounters are where your character puts skills to the test and you put dice to the table. A good mission will usually have a mixture of both types of events. If a mission does end up swaying towards one type of event over the other, consider planning the next mission with an eye to making things even. Follow up a mission focused on starship combat with an intrigue laden ambassador's ball, or vice versa.

PERSONAL LOG

ROSS, SARAH JANE,
STARDATE 47994.6

I've added a couple extra layers of encryption on this entry. I might be paranoid but I'm not quite sure I want these facts to be known by Starfleet. And, honestly, I needed some programming time to think about what happened.

Ryn Janis made contact with me. She's been watching me ever since I left the Astrophysics building at the Academy. She told me that there's something going on here at the Academy, something connected to the Maquis. Or, more specifically, something they will be blamed for to allow Starfleet to take direct action against the resistance. She looked so tired when we spoke and she left before she answered all my questions.

I don't know if I believe her. Even though she's Bajoran, she never really talked about her politics with me or in class. Something must have happened to cause her to resign and she trusts me for some reason. I don't think it's a plot to get on board my ship. I'm programming this log entry to send a copy to Captain Deacon if I'm not back in 12 hours. Sir, I met Ryn Janis near Shuttlebay 42 at 2300 hours.

I have to help her. I joined Starfleet to help people and, real problems or not, she needs my help.

SCENES

The key to making great scenes is figuring out the dramatic question. If a Player wants to do something and there is nothing to be revealed by their action, make a quick judgment and move on. There is a reason *Star Trek* doesn't show every turbolift ride or replicator meal. Those elements add color to scenes, but deciding what gets spotlight time at the table will help the overall pacing of your game. Design scenes that ask a question about the adventure, one of the characters and, preferably, both.

Most scenes have an element of plot development. Whatever adventure you have in mind for your crew requires scenes where they uncover the plot. This means investigating the subspace anomaly or talking to the refugees from the planet and so on. Make sure that whatever information is necessary to move to the next scene is accessible without rolling dice. Dice rolls still cause tension and taking time to explore all the angles can be important, but hiding vital information behind a locked door often ends up an exercise in frustration.

Many scenes also offer character development. This development connects the scene to the characters and engages the Player. Your Players have already given you direction on what character development they wish to see through their character's Values. Values are there to be explored and challenged. A character with a Value connecting them to a rival, for example, should see that rival define the character as the character defines the rivalry. Why are they rivals? Is there something about the rival that the character admires or respects? Is there a step too far that the rival will not take against the characters? These are scenes that should happen during play because they reflect on the Values of the characters at the table.

Scenes are still likely to have dice rolls, just not as many as Encounters. These rolls should not impede the flow of the story but offer interesting directions for the story to go based on the success or the failure of the roll. Failure should not mean the game stalls until a success is rolled. It means the Players might have to choose a different path to get to the end of the adventure. These rolls can also offer additional information that can let Players prepare for later encounters or hint at plot twists. As long as the necessary information to move to the next scene is communicated, it is okay to add in rolls for a little extra tension.

A key element in scene pacing is knowing where to start and where to end. Get right to the thrust of the scene. If the characters are questioning a prisoner, start the scene in the brig with the prisoner offering the information for a price. If the Players have been sent to pick up a passenger, start the scene where they realize the person is not there. Getting to the question keeps Players involved in the scene and pushing toward its resolution. Likewise, once the question is resolved, moving on to the next scene or encounter should happen fairly quickly.

ENCOUNTERS

Encounters are where characters are tested. Dice are rolled, resources are spent and the story changes based on whether the characters succeed or fail. Encounters encompass everything from tense starship battles to dramatic courtroom scenes. These are the moments that turn Starfleet officers into galactic legends. Each of these legends begins with a risk. Sometimes the legend is about a triumph of ingenuity and courage. Sometimes the legend is a cautionary tale about hubris and handling failure.

The first thing a Gamemaster should do when creating an encounter is make sure interesting things happen if the Players succeed and if they fail. The story should not be exactly the same regardless of success or failure because that makes the encounter irrelevant. If the Players rescue the ambassador from the clutches of the Romulans, the negotiations with newly discovered aliens will go smoothly, allowing a backdrop for a Scene of character development. If the Players fail, they might have to take on the negotiations on their own, requiring another encounter.

Use common sense and clear judgment in obvious situations. A *Galaxy*-class starship facing off against a shuttlecraft in a head-to-head battle in the middle of deep space is not going to end well for the shuttlecraft. There are ways to even the odds. The shuttlecraft could lead the starship into a nebula to negate shields and sensors. The shuttle could have access to prefix codes for the larger ship. In these cases, an encounter is interesting, since it will require some good rolls to put those plans into motion.

Gamemasters cannot anticipate every course of action Players might take to resolve an encounter. The discovery of the story between the Players and the GM is part of the fun. Players sometimes come up with a plan that is so crazy it just might work and should be rewarded for their creative thinking. Plots that require Players to fail Encounters, like ambushes, should

SIDE SCENES AND SUB-PLOTS

Scenes don't always need dice to hit the table. Scenes in which one or more characters pursue a hobby together, meet up in 10-Forward, interact with their department staff, or the like without necessarily having a Task to complete or dice to roll, are still great scenes to include because they offer the Players a chance to do some roleplaying involving their character and something meaningful to that character.

They may also offer chances for your NPCs to shine, interacting with the Player Characters for a couple of minutes, to get story details to the group, or highlight certain personality traits before cutting back to the main plot.

be carefully considered. Players do not like to lose and will push harder than Kirk against the no-win scenario.

Instead, Gamemasters should think about multiple solutions to an encounter. There are three general solutions for an encounter; talking through it, thinking through it, and fighting through it. Each of these solutions should be viable, though not necessarily equally so. A captured crew is going to have a difficult time fighting their way out of a Cardassian prison camp, but planning and executing a stealthy prison break seems like a better option. That crew might also try to ply the Gul in charge with information in exchange for freedom which, depending on the character, might be more, or less, difficult. We have classified these solutions along the lines of the branch colors of Starfleet.

Red solutions use command and diplomacy to solve an encounter. Many tense standoffs between enemies are diffused over viewscreen negotiation. It is not always altruistic either; convincing someone you have the upper hand when you do not also falls under this type of solution.

The science of Starfleet is a major component of **Blue** solutions. Technological solutions abound, but sometimes the tech needs to be remodulated, prototyped, or otherwise engineered to fix a problem. Blue solutions also include sneaking into or out of an Encounter and other clever ways of avoiding violence.

Sometimes, action is the best way out. **Gold** solutions come when the shields are up and the phasers are locked. Away teams also get into tactical situations that require some fast action and risky maneuvers. Starfleet crewmembers rarely look forward to combat, but they have been trained to handle fights that are unavoidable.

PACING

Combat encounters are a much more structured version of a scene within **Star Trek Adventures** and role-playing in general. While in a scene, any character can speak or attempt a Task in any order, while encounters require there to be **Turns** and **Rounds** to represent the passage of time as combatants attempt to take each other out simultaneously. Turns allow you to fairly resolve character's actions and Rounds before moving onto the next, representing a short period in which one participant has acted. There are as many Turns in a Round as there are characters able to act.

Turns move back and forth between both the Players and Gamemaster's NPCs. It's always the Gamemaster's decision on which side goes first but the Players should always be favored unless there is a specific reason the NPCs should act first (an unnoticed ambush, for example) or the Gamemaster wants to spend Threat.

ESTABLISHING ZONES

Zones make up the spaces in which a combat encounter takes place. They have no fixed size and it's up to you to determine their shape and size based on the terrain of the combat area. The sizes of Zones may also depend on the features present in the encounter, becoming proportionally smaller or larger depending on the space available for the combatants — moving through a narrow street will have proportionally smaller zones than an open field.

Establishing Zones inside a building will be comparatively easy, as each room can be a zone, while a more open landscape may have a mix of zone sizes based on the obstacles and features of the terrain. The only other factor in defining Zones would then be their relative positions, which can be easily done via a sketch on paper or gaming mat. Once this is done, note how the Zones are connected to one another, whether they are open to move freely between, contain some obstacle between them, have doors between them or whether there are features in place that make moving between them impossible.

TERRAIN

Terrain takes the form of Traits for combat encounters and are specifically linked to location and situation Traits if a scene has already played out in the same location. Each Zone doesn't have to be named, but by doing so it gives a clear idea of what is there.

Marking down Traits in certain Zones can be done directly onto the map available for the Players, and can include things that affect the encounter, like "Smoke" (as a situation Trait), "Lava" (as a location Trait) or "Snow Dunes" (as an environmental Trait).

COMBATANTS

Combatants often, but not always, take two sides, both with rival or conflicting objectives that have led them to fight for those objectives. These two sides are often the Player Characters and the NPCs of your mission, the PCs representing a Starfleet Away Team and your NPCs representing a rival crew or antagonistic beings.

When building a combat encounter's NPC team, you should take note of the circumstances that have brought the conflict to fruition and therefore, how many combatants to have and how those teams are comprised. NPCs might work like a mob, with an irrational mentality to their actions, or they might be calculating, working tactically in small teams. These circumstances should dictate where to place the combatants, noting once again the exact moment that led to a combat encounter starting. Place the Player Characters depending

EXAMPLE MAPS

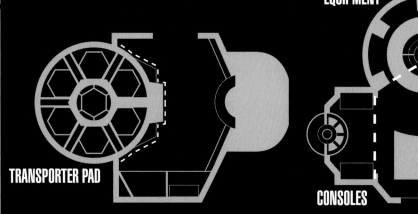

TRANSPORTER PAD

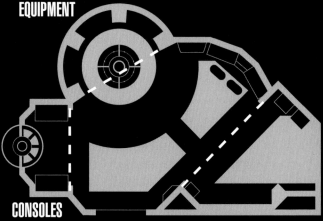

EQUIPMENT

CONSOLES

STORAGE LOCKERS

on where they are at the start of the encounter, then place your NPCs as they either enter or make their violent intent known. The first Round then begins, with the first Turn going to either the Players or, in special circumstances, the NPCs.

The other consideration to have when placing combatant NPCs for a combat encounter is the size of the force you are placing in the encounter and the relative level of threat those NPCs pose. As a rule of thumb, every three Minor NPCs equal two Player Characters, Notable NPCs equal one Player Character, and a Major NPC is powerful enough to represent two PCs in the encounter. So, with a group of five Player Characters, NPCs could be grouped in the following ways:

- **Unorganized Group / Mob** - 8 Minor NPCs

- **Enemy Squad** - 1 Notable NPC, 6 Minor NPCs

- **Two Tactical Teams** - 2 Notable NPCs, 4 Minor NPCs

- **Equivalent Away Team** - 5 Notable NPCs

- **Leader and Guards/Advisors** - 1 Major NPC, 4 Minor NPCs

- **Leader and Lieutenants** - 1 Major NPC, 2 Notable NPCs

- **Leader and Cadre** - 1 Major NPC, 1 Notable NPC, 3 Minor NPCs

COMBAT IN SPACE

PACING

Combat encounters in space work similarly in terms of pacing, but rules for Non-Player Character starships have been streamlined for ease of use at the gaming table. Space combat still takes place over **Turns** and **Rounds** — Turns moving back and forth between both the Players Characters and Supporting Characters in the relevant bridge roles and the Gamemaster's NPC starships.

Individual NPC crewmembers' Turns are not tracked like their Player counterparts. Instead, each NPC ship takes multiple Turns during each Round — one Turn for each point of Scale the ship has — representing the individual actions of that ship's crew. However, each Task attempted after the first during each Round from any single role increases in Difficulty by 1.

Multiple ships may take some effort to track, in terms of number of Turns taken, or Tasks per bridge role, so it's important to note down basic information for each starship you control: number of Turns taken (relating to Scale), number of Tasks attempted per bridge role, Stress, Breaches, Shields, etc.

It's worth noting that starship combat is different than that of personal combat, where each PC acts independently

FIGHTING SMART

Most sentient beings value their lives, and fear of death is a common trait for intelligent species as well — even for the hardened warriors of most civilizations. Of course, species like **Klingons** or the **Borg** don't fear death, particularly if the Klingon lieutenant believes *"Today is a good day to die!"* But most groups, in combat, will either flee or tactically retreat when faced with overwhelming odds or an overpowering foe, and even fearless foes have been known to retreat when success is impossible.

Don't hesitate to finish a combat encounter with an escape or retreat for your NPCs if the story would make sense for them to do so. The use of transporter technology is useful in this regard as, so long as there is nothing stopping transportation, an NPC with a commlink to another location with a transporter pad can ask to be beamed to safety, stopping the combat encounter in its tracks. The use of transporters can also be a useful tool for ambushes and surprise attacks and, used sparingly, these encounters can create a sense of danger and uncertainty for your PC away team.

MINIATURES

Star Trek Adventure miniatures are a great way to track characters' positions during a combat encounter and are available as a line of products to supplement the roleplaying game at www.modiphius.com

following broad orders. Player Character teams will find success much easier if they work more cohesively as a Team, moving the ship into an advantageous position to line up a phaser shot, regulating power to the phasers, then firing, all over the space of a number of Turns. Emphasis should be placed on the Team collectively working and operating one agent within the combat: the starship.

The same can be said for NPC starships. Moving them into a favourable firing arc could show the Players that the enemy ship intends to fire next turn, while evasive maneuvers could show them that the enemy ship is fleeing or wary of their next attack. While under attack in the *Star Trek* series, bridge officers are often heard telling their commanders, "They've raised shields," or "They're powering up their weapons systems." None of these actions should be secret, so long as there is someone crewing an operations, tactical, or science station, so you should declare these actions and events as they appear to the Player Characters' sensors and, vice versa, have your NPC starships react in the same way.

ESTABLISHING ZONES

Establishing Zones for starship combat can be more abstract than personal combat, with zones representing the empty space between planetary bodies in space or other phenomena.

Distances and location are much more important in starship combat, with ships capable of using thrusters when an enemy or object is close, impulse engines around a planet, and Warp into or out of a star system. All these powerful maneuvers mean that distances can be traversed more freely than in personal combat.

As starships can travel between planets at impulse in a matter of minutes and at warp in a matter of seconds, zones are proportionally much larger than the equivalent zones for personal combat.

- Starships at **close** range may be tens of kilometers apart, or in the same Zone.

- Starships at **medium** range may be thousands of kilometers apart, or in the adjacent Zone.

- **Long** range can be thousands to hundreds of thousands of kilometers in distance, or two Zones away (or the distance from Earth to the Moon).

- While **extreme** range represents three to five Zones away, or the distance between two planets within a solar system.

It may be useful for more simple starship combat encounters to keep the 'map' of the encounter based on the descriptions of the bodies and phenomena in the scene, "behind the moon," or "inside the nebula" rather than mapping it out on the tabletop.

OBSTACLES AND PHENOMENA

Chapter 6: The Final Frontier gives excellent examples of phenomena and obstacles that affect starships and their crew while in a combat encounter. On p. 154 you can find great examples of phenomena and their effect on starships.

EXAMPLE MAP

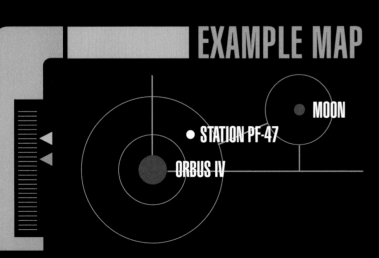

- MOON
- STATION PF-47
- ORBUS IV

These environmental Traits increase Difficulty or make things possible or impossible where they wouldn't otherwise, as well as increasing the complication range of certain Tasks.

Phenomena in space usually form their own Zones, due to the size and nature of spatial bodies, and marking their name as a Trait is simple when mapping out a starship combat encounter, writing them directly onto a map as you would in a personal combat encounter.

COMBATANTS

An NPC ship does not have specific crew at individual positions on the bridge — this level of detail is unnecessary for running an NPC ship. Instead, each NPC vessel has a Crew Quality, that provides ratings which serve as the Attribute and Discipline scores needed by the vessel for any given Task. NPC crew used in this way are always considered to have an applicable Focus.

CREW QUALITY	ATTRIBUTE	DISCIPLINE
Basic	8	1
Proficient	9	2
Talented	10	3
Exceptional	11	4

Starships, on the whole, are similar in strength and capabilities to one another, however certain ships are significantly smaller or less well equipped. A good indication of balance when building a starship combat encounter is the Scale of a ship. Because NPC starships take as many Turns as their Scale value, a starship with a Scale of 3 will take about half as many Turns as the Player Characters. With that in mind, having multiple starships with similar Scale to the number of Players at the table will mean that you take two or three times as many Turns as the Players Characters. Caution should be taken in having too many Turns above the Player's limit, while encounters should be balanced so that smaller Scale ships engage the Players in groups equaling or exceeding the Player's vessel's Scale.

However, as the Security Division statistic of the starship scales the Combat Dice (⚔) rolled for the damage of attacks, NPC ships should be added to balance the threat posed by the Player's vessel. Any Player vessel with a Security above 3 should face additional NPC starships. Likewise, NPC starships with a Security higher than 3 pose more risk to a Player vessel, and the number of them present in the encounter should be reduced to reflect this.

For example, a Player vessel with 5 Players controlling bridge stations could face:

- Several Scale 2 vessels

- Two Scale 3 vessels

- One Scale 4 vessel with Security above 3

- One Scale 5 vessel

Above all, remember that conflict is not always fair or balanced, and there are numerous examples within *Star Trek* of starships being outnumbered or so overpowered in comparison to their opponenets that the antagonists Starfleet face are of no threat. While you should use these circumstances sparingly, missions or storylines may present times in which the odds are stacked against one side or another. In these circumstances, it may be favorable to go back to a normal scene or Social Conflict to resolve the dispute or negotiate with a more powerful enemy.

GAMEMASTERING

CREATING MISSIONS, NPCS, AND LOCATIONS

Once you have a series of scenes and encounters, it is time to put them together into a session. Different groups have different needs for their game sessions. Some meet for short two hour sessions every week. Others meet once a month but play for eight hours or more. Discuss with your Players what sort of session schedule works best for your lives. Plan a scene or encounter for every 30 minutes of playing time, plus two or three extras for maximum storyline flexibility.

Star Trek Adventures can be played in a single session. This happens most often at conventions or demonstrations at gaming stores. However, planning a demo style adventure is also useful for trying out the rules with a gaming group that is already established to see how everyone feels about them. Focus on the parts of the rules you enjoy and can enthusiastically deliver to your Players. Keep the story fairly straightforward and help them wrap up the session on a high note.

Many campaigns are episodic in nature, where each episode contains a story told from beginning to end in a single night. Scenes and encounters naturally occur one after the other, but in a single session it sometimes pays to string several scenes in a row to build up tension that is released in a huge encounter at the end of the episode.

The big advantage to a full campaign is telling stories over multiple sessions. If you have a story that will not fit in a single session, think about how many sessions it might take to tell. If possible, work in a cliffhanger at the end of each session that will keep your Players on the hook to come back next time and see how the story continues. Full campaigns also let you tell stories little by little as time passes and characters learn more about each other. A character that starts out as a cadet in the first episode that grows in skill and rank will make for a tremendous moment in your game if they leave the ship to take command of their own.

While it is important in the short term to give each session a beginning, middle, and an end, consider those elements for the whole campaign. If your campaign is about the return of a new generation of Borg, think about the turning points where the Players discover evidence, where the Borg show up in force, and where the climactic battle takes place. These do not have to be set in stone from the beginning, but knowing the general direction your campaign wants to go will help plot individual sessions. The NPC and locations the Players react to will clue you in on which elements of sessions they want to see again. When you match those elements with important plot moments you will hook your Players in to fight harder to save those things they love and finally defeat the ones they love to hate.

CONTINUING VOYAGES

There are many different ways to start a campaign. Think of the different ways each of the shows started. Is the crew already a few months into a tour? Is the ship full of unproven technology that requires maintenance or unexpected fixes? While Players are making their characters, you should be discussing your ideas for the beginning of the campaign. Many RPGs start with strangers meeting for the first time to go on an adventure, but *Star Trek Adventures* offers opportunities to be different. Your characters may have connections from Starfleet Academy. They may have reputations to live up to — or down from — from other postings. These elements do not have to be fully developed, since half the fun will be exploring them in later sessions, but putting them in place at the beginning of a campaign will let them grow.

Take time to think about the end of the campaign as well. Long term campaigns that last for decades are the stuff of legends. Unfortunately, real life changes often intervene and a game that fades into obscurity can leave everyone feeling unsatisfied. Taking an episode to wrap up questions and plotlines gives everyone a sense of closure and the feeling of a complete story. Do not be afraid to change an ending as a campaign plays out, but having one in mind will help ease the pain of a premature end.

The end of one campaign, however, can mean the beginning of a new one. The *Star Trek* universe offers great precedent in stories involving Starfleet legacies. So many of the films and shows focus on the crew of the *Starship Enterprise*. Other ships also have generational stories to tell with a new campaign set in the halls of an old ship familiar to everyone at the table. Legacy campaigns can also be connected to people. A favorite character with a famous grandfather in Starfleet might find that older character and his crew at the center of a new campaign in an earlier timeline. The end of a campaign often means a new one is ready to begin.

Several Non-Player Characters (NPCs) are presented at the back of this book, in *Chapter 11: Aliens and Adversaries*. However, it may be that you want to create specific NPCs for a scenario, mission, or even a whole campaign. There are a number of methods, depending on the complexity you want to go into. Presented here are a variety of approaches, focused on the mechanics of Attributes, Disciplines, Focuses, Traits, and Talents in order for you to quickly create robust adversaries and allies for your Player Characters.

CREATING MINOR NPCS

Minors form the rank and file members of an organization. They form the nameless extras in missions, as groups of Adversaries to face in a Conflict encounter, or as guards for a Notable or Major level NPC and if encountered alone shouldn't hold up the Player Characters for long.

To create a Minor NPC:

- Begin by describing their species as a Trait (see Step 1: Species on p. 102 for more information)

- Distribute scores of 9, 9, 8, 8, 7, 7 to their Attributes. Then apply increases due to the NPC's species.

- Choose two Disciplines to set to 2, two Disciplines to set to 1, and leave the other two at 0.

- Add one or two special rules, as described below.

- Determine final details:

  - Derive Stress from combining their Fitness Attribute and Security Discipline.

  - Give them weapons and derive their damage (Weapon ▲ + Security Discipline)

The processes here are intended for guidance and are a quick and easy way of developing NPCs either at the table or before a game session. However, you may want to tweak these scores to suit your story, mission, or game difficulty. You can always raise or lower Attributes or Disciplines, but always keep in mind that you should balance those scores: for every point you raise, you should lower another. Also remember that Attributes at creation can only be a maximum of 12 and Disciplines a maximum of 5.

A game is always enhanced for Players if NPCs level up along with them, or become named adversaries that reoccur in later sessions. You may want to promote a Minor NPC to a Notable NPC, or even a Notable NPC to a Major NPC if their interactions with the Player Characters is meaningful enough to earn them promotion within the story.

To quickly promote a Minor to a Notable NPC, add 1 point each to their best two Attributes, add 1 point to every Discipline, give them two Focuses and a single Value. Remember to check their Stress and Weapon damage based on those increases.

To quickly promote a Notable NPC to a Major, add two more Attribute points freely while remembering that Attributes cannot be increased beyond 12, then add 4 more points to their Disciplines while remembering that Disciplines cannot be increased beyond 5. Give them four more Focuses, two more Talents and two more Values. Go through the finishing touches by checking their derived statistics like Stress and Weapon Damage.

CREATING NOTABLE NPCS

Notable NPCs are a cut above Minors and are often Lieutenants to Major NPCs. They are comparable to Supporting Player Characters, and, if encountered as a group or with several Minor NPCs, can form a more formidable obstacle and drain the Player Characters resources, forcing them to use Determination or buy Threat to overcome them.

To create a Notable NPC:

- Begin by choosing the character's species.

- Make their most important/applicable Attribute 10, then distribute scores of 9, 9, 8, 8, and 7 to the remaining Attributes. Apply the character's Species modifiers.

- Make their most important Discipline a score of 3, with two more Disciplines a score of 2, the next two Disciplines a score of 1, and the last Discipline at 0.

- Name two or three appropriate Focuses.

- Add two or three special rules, as described below.

- Give them a single Value.

- Determine final details:

  - Derive Stress from combining their Fitness Attribute and Security Discipline.

  - Give them weapons and derive their damage (Weapon ⒜ + Security Discipline).

CREATING MAJOR NPCS

Major NPCs are the Gamemaster's equivalent of a Player Character. A lot more thought and creativity should be put into creating a Major NPC, giving them names, backgrounds and qualities comparable to the Player Characters at your table that fit with the story they are part of. For this method of NPC creation, you will be drawing from much of the Creation in Play rules from *Chapter 5: Reporting for Duty*.

To create a Major NPC:

- **Concept** – Decide what role your Major NPC will play in the mission, maybe based on their Species, role or position held, or a defining Value that governs their personality.

- **Choose the character's role** – Think about their role in their organization and therefore their rank. You want the Major NPC to command some authority, even if it isn't recognized by an official body. Even rogue Major NPCs command respect from a group of people who follow them and their ideals.

- **Describe Traits** – Note their Species Trait as well as any other Traits that are vital to the nature of the character.

- **Assign Attribute Scores** – Begin every Attribute at a score of 7 and then freely assign 14 more points, with an upper limit on Attributes as 12. Apply the character's Species modifiers to this as normal.

- **Assign Disciplines** – Begin every Discipline at a score of 1 and then freely assign 10 more points, with an upper limit of 5.

- **Choose Focuses** – Create up to six Focuses for the Major NPC.

- **Create Talents** – Create four Talents or special rules as described below.

- **Create Values** – Create four Values as described in *Chapter 5: Reporting for Duty*.

- **Determine final details -**

  - Derive Stress from combining their Fitness Attribute and Security Discipline.

  - Give them weapons and derive their damage (Weapon ⒜ + Security Discipline).

CREATING NPC TALENTS OR 'SPECIAL RULES'

Creating NPC Special Rules can be done easily based on the Talents list beginning on p. 135 of *Chapter 5: Reporting for Duty* or from the list below. When the Special Rule calls for a "particular Task" or "acting in a particular way" it is asking for a limiting factor to the rule. For example, the Special Rule could only apply to **Security** Tasks, or would only apply in circumstances in which the NPC is being threatened by another Character.

- **Proficiency:** When performing a particular Task, in specific way, add one bonus d20.

- **Threatening:** When performing a particular Task, or acting in a specific way, and buying additional d20s with Threat, you may re-roll a single d20.

- **Guidance:** Whenever you assist another NPC in a particular way, re-roll your d20.

- **Substitution:** Whenever you perform a particular Task in a particular way, you may use a specified different Discipline instead of the normal Discipline required, and/ or may use a specific Focus with a different Discipline.

- **Familiarity:** Whenever you attempt to perform a particular Task, you may reduce the Difficulty by one, to a minimum of zero.

- **Additional Threat Spent:** Whenever performing a Task with a particular Discipline, you may spend 1 Threat to gain a specific or unique benefit.

There are also several Special Rules that are available to NPCs only that should be used for exceptionally different or alien adversaries.

- **Extraordinary Attribute X** – An automatic success is added on Tasks using the Attribute defined by X. The number of automatic successes can exceed 1, for example, a creature with Extraordinary Reason 2 gains two success on all Tasks using Reason, in addition to any generated by rolling.

- **Fast Recovery X** - The creature recovers from stress and injury quickly. At the start of each of its Turns, the creature regains X Stress, up to its normal maximum. If the creature is Injured at the start of its turn, it may instead spend two Threat in order to remove that Injury.

- **Immune to X** - The creature is unaffected by conditions caused by a Trait present in the scene, such as: cold, disease, fear, heat, pain, poison, vacuum, etc.

- **Invulnerable:** The creature is impervious to harm, and cannot be Injured in any way; attacks can be attempted and damage is rolled as normal, but it cannot suffer Injuries. This may take different forms; see on p. 313.

- **Machine X** - The creature is not a living being, but a machine, or some form of cybernetic organism. It is highly resistant to environmental conditions, reducing the Difficulty of Tasks to resist extremes of heat and cost by two, and it is immune to the effects of suffocation, starvation, and thirst. Further, the machine's sturdy construction grants it Resistance equal to X.

- **Menacing** - The creature is dangerous, heralding a greater problem for those who confront it. When a creature with this rule enters a scene, immediately add a point to the Threat pool.

- **Night Vision** - The creature has some way of perceiving its environment even in pitch darkness — perceiving infrared or ultraviolet light, echolocation, or some other method. Tasks the creature attempts do not increase in Difficulty as a result of darkness.

- **Threatening X** - The creature is powerful and dangerous, with a vitality and drive that allows it to triumph where others might fail. The creature begins each scene with X Threat, that may only be used to benefit itself, and which are not drawn from the general Threat pool.

CREATING PLANETS

INITIAL IDEAS

Every planet in *Star Trek* should be a locus of adventure. Either someone on that world requires the characters' aid, or there is someone or something on the world that the characters can learn something interesting from. When deciding on what sort of planet you want to create, you should simultaneously think about what sort of adventure you want the characters to get involved in. Are they taking a shuttlecraft down to a hellish Class Y world to discover

the fate of a starship that vanished 30 years ago or are they making first contact with a new alien species that floats in the atmosphere of a Class J gas giant. Will the characters explore alien ruins on a blasted airless world that could provide the Federation with knowledge or valuable new technologies, or have they stumbled upon an ancient artificial world that is now the lair of ancient and deadly menace that they must defeat before it threatens inhabited worlds?

If you are uncertain what sort of planet you want the characters to encounter and what sort of adventure you to have waiting for them on it, you have two options for how to proceed. You can either create the planet first and then decide what's going on, or you can decide what is going on first and then create the planet. The first method is called world-first planet creation, and the second is called adventure-first planet creation. In either case, let the tables in this section help you, but don't allow them to stifle your imagination. If you don't like the result of a particular roll, feel free to roll again, select a different entry, or come up with your own idea. In fact, if you look over one of these tables and one of the entries strikes your fancy, use it and don't bother rolling.

WORLD-FIRST PLANET CREATION

Using the world-first method means you first roll or select what the planet is like using Table 10-1, Table 10-2, or Table 10-3, depending upon whether you are interested in seeing what the dice give you, or if you specifically want either a habitable planet or a hostile planet. Once you have determined what sort of world you are dealing with, you need to decide what's happening there. To determine this, roll twice on Planetary Features of Interest (Table 10-4), and finally roll once on the Planetary Features Table (10-5) to give you, and the Players, a better idea what the planet looks like to visitors.

ADVENTURE-FIRST PLANET CREATION

Using the adventure first method means that you first roll twice on the Planetary Features of Interest table (10-4) to determine what's happening on the planet. Once you know what's happening, it's then time to determine where it's happening. If either of your rolls on Table 10-4 involve intelligent inhabitants on the planet, you should decide if you want to have the characters encountering these inhabitants while wearing environment suits, or for the inhabitants to all live in sealed domes or caverns, protected for the hostile atmosphere outside. Alternately, do you want the characters to beam down to the planet, walk around and meet people and not have to worry about their air supply running out. In this last case, you should roll or select the planet from Habitable Planet Type table (10-2). Otherwise, feel free to roll on the General Planetary Type table (Table 10-1), or if you want an unusual scenario, where the characters are meeting exceedingly alien creatures, roll on the on the Hostile Planetary Type table (Table 10-3). As a final touch, you should roll once on the Planetary Features table (10-5) to give you, and the Players a better idea what the planet looks like to visitors.

PLANET CREATION

Use the following three tables to determine basic information about the planet. See pgs. 145–148 for information about the different classes of planets. You only need to roll on one of these three tables, depending upon what sort of planet you are looking for. The General Planetary Type table (10-1) creates a planet that may or may not be habitable by humanoids, the other two tables (Table 10-2 Table 10-3) creates a planet that is either habitable by humanoids or hostile to humanoid life.

GENERAL PLANETARY TYPE (TABLE 10-1, ROLL 2D20)

ROLL	PLANET
2-5	Artificial planet (non-obvious)*
6-8	Class D planet
9-10	Class H planet
11-13	Class L planet (land life has not yet evolved)
14-16	Class M planet (water world with only small islands)
17-19	Class M planet (verdant jungle world)
20-22	Class M planet (temperate world — like Earth)
23-25	Class M planet (dry desert world — like Vulcan)
26-28	Class M planet (ice age world)
29-30	Class L planet (marginally habitable world)
31	Class K planet (Neptune-like)
32-33	Class K planet (Mars-like)
34-35	Class Y demon planet
36-37	Artificial planet (obvious)*
38-39	Class J gas giant planet
40	Class T huge gas giant planet

* Artificial planets are worlds that were created by powerful intelligent beings. A non-obvious artificial planet is one that superficially looks like a normal world. However, detailed sensors reveal that it's not old enough to be a natural planet, is almost certainly made from different materials, and has a different structure from any ordinary planet. Obvious artificial planets are exotic constructs like Dyson spheres, space stations 2,000 kilometers across, enormous rotating rings where the inner surface looks like a vast strip of a Class M planet, and other equally strange objects that clearly are not natural worlds. Depending upon who created them and what condition they are in, artificial worlds may or may not be habitable, but most are. If you want details on conditions there, roll on Table 10-2 and reroll any result of "artificial planet".

HABITABLE VS. HOSTILE WORLDS

When deciding whether to use either the Habitable Planetary Type table (Table 10-2) or the Hostile Planetary Type table (Table 10-3), one important question to ask yourself is how much do you want the world's physical conditions to impact the scenario. On a temperate, Earth-like world, or even a hot dry desert planet like Vulcan, the characters may face mysteries, intelligent antagonists, or deadly animals, but they can walk around on the planet with minimal difficulty. However, these sorts of worlds are far from the only options available. On an ice-age Class M world, the characters will need cold weather gear to survive for any length of time, and on worlds that are not Class M, characters will require breathing masks or environment suits to survive for any more than a minute or two. Unless there is a habitable region on a hostile planet, such as a domed city, caverns once inhabited by a long-extinct species, or an area mysteriously rendered habitable by aliens with technology far beyond the Federation's, adventures on hostile worlds require the characters to wear bulky environment suits. Hostile worlds are perfect for scenarios about survival, where the characters need to locate a deposit of dilithium crystals to repair their damaged warp drive or obtain a rare life-form because it may provide biological samples that they can use to cure an exceedingly deadly disease. In addition, exploring eons-old ruins on a world that is now an airless rock can be exciting and the difficult conditions help highlight the ancient and inhuman nature of the ruins and make the process of exploration more tense.

However, characters having to clomp around in environment suits while visiting a bustling alien city only serves to isolate the characters from the intelligent beings they are attempting to interact with, which in turn makes these beings seem distant and inhuman. Unless that is specifically a mood you wish to create, you may want to place this alien city on a habitable planet. In general, if you want the characters to be able to easily and freely interact with a planets' inhabitants, they should be able to walk around the city with the aid of nothing more than, at most, drugs they must periodically take to negate mild toxins in the atmosphere.

CONSTRAINED LOCATIONS

One reason to set adventures on hostile planets is to provide a location for an adventure that is exceedingly constrained. If the planet's atmosphere is instantly deadly, or even if the world is sufficiently cold or has atmospheric toxins in it that mean that humanoids cannot safely exist unprotected for more than a few hours, the characters are limited to spending almost all of their time there in locations that provide a Class M environment. For example, if a Class K world has a domed city, or even a small research station in a sealed cavern, the characters will be spending most of their time in this location, unless they wish to return to their starship, which might be temporarily impossible.

They won't be able to leave this city or research station for more than a few hours, and, if they don't have access to environment suits, they won't be able to leave at all. The most extreme version of this sort of constraint is a sealed city floating in the atmosphere of a Class J or Class T gas giant, where the characters cannot safely venture outside at all, since they would fall to their deaths without access to a starship or a shuttlecraft. Also, if the domed city is protected by shields, or the sealed caverns are sufficiently far underground, then the characters cannot even beam up to their ship and may have trouble communicating regularly, meaning that they are now both on their own and restricted to a relatively small location. These types of restrictions can create the ideal setting for facing a dangerous mad scientist, solving a mysterious murder where one of the characters is a suspect, or interacting with two or more mutually hostile factions. In general, constrained locations are a wonderful method of creating a self-contained scenario where the characters are unlikely to wander off towards too many red herrings. They also mean that you don't need to worry too much about what's on the rest of the planet.

HABITABLE PLANETARY TYPE
(TABLE 10-2, ROLL 1D20)

ROLL	PLANET
1-2	Habitable artificial planet (non-obvious)
3-4	Class L planet
5-7	Class M planet (water world with only small islands)
8-10	Class M planet (verdant jungle world)
11-13	Class M planet (temperate world — like Earth)
14-16	Class M planet (dry desert world — like Vulcan)
17-18	Class M planet (ice age world)
19-20	Habitable artificial planet (obvious)

HOSTILE PLANETARY TYPE
(TABLE 10-3, ROLL 1D20)

ROLL	PLANET
1-2	Artificial planet (non-obvious, no breathable atmosphere)
3-5	Class D planet
6-8	Class H planet
9-11	Class K planet (Mars-like)
12-13	Class K planet (Neptune-like)
14-15	Class Y demon planet
16-17	Artificial planet (obvious, no breathable atmosphere)
18-19	Class J gas giant planet
20	Class T huge gas giant planet

PLANETARY FEATURES OF INTEREST

Any planet that's worth the time for the crew of a starship to beam down or head down on a shuttlecraft has something interesting on it, and the most exciting worlds possess multiple features of interest or sources of danger. To find out what's on a planet, roll on the Planetary Features of Interest table (Table 10-4) twice. Apply both rolls and consider how they might interact with one another to produce an interesting situation awaiting the characters. For example, rolling a 3 (peaceful primitive inhabitants) and then a 10 (transcendent inhabitants) could mean that god-like aliens are forcing primitive Humans to fight for their amusement. Similarly, a roll of 12 (ancient ruins or artifacts) followed by a roll of 15 (off-world visitors) could mean anything from the starship visiting an archeological research station in response to a distress call, to the characters discovering potentially valuable alien ruins and then encountering aliens who may be willing to fight the characters for access to these ruins. The same two rolls could even mean that the crew of a previous starship that visited this world has become trapped in an ancient automated alien zoo. If you roll the same result twice, then that's the only thing happening on the world — unless that doesn't work for you and you want to roll on or choose from the table again.

PLANETARY FEATURES OF INTEREST
(TABLE 10-4, ROLL 1D20 - TWICE) *

ROLL	PLANET
1-2	Exceedingly dangerous animal or plant life
3-4	Peaceful primitive inhabitants
5-6	Warlike primitive inhabitants
7	Peaceful technological inhabitants
8-9	Warlike technological inhabitants
10-11	Transcendent inhabitants of great power
12-13	Ancient ruins or artifacts
14-15	Off-world visitors
16-17	Crashed spacecraft
18	Local conditions that limit or prohibit transporter use
19-20	Dangerous natural phenomena

*Note: This table gives a high chance of encountering both animals and intelligent creatures living on a planet. This makes a great deal of sense for Class M planets, but is somewhat less likely on Class D worlds like Earth's moon, Class J gas giants, or on other hostile worlds. If you want to minimize the numbers of intelligent inhabitants on worlds where the characters need to wear environment suits, you should reroll any roll of 1-10 if the planet lacks a breathable atmosphere. However, if the reroll also comes up 1-10, keep the result; since in *Star Trek*, alien life and alien intelligences can appear anywhere, they are just more common on Class M worlds. Also, remember that if you have a planet with a hostile atmosphere, and you roll inhabitants, you don't need to make these inhabitants non-humanoid aliens who can survive on the planet. Instead, perhaps Human or humanoid colonists settled this world long ago and built a large domed habitat or turned deep caverns into a habitable environment. Alternately, maybe this world was once habitable and something happened to it and the survivors have lived in sealed cities for tens of thousands of years.

PLANETARY DETAILS
(TABLE 10-5, ROLL 1D20)

ROLL	PLANETARY FEATURE OF INTEREST
1	Opaque or partially opaque atmosphere (fog, smoke, opaque gasses, swarms of air-plankton)
	(reroll for Class D planets)
2	Perpetual darkness
3	Perpetually dim light
4	Many huge animals (anywhere from the size of a large dinosaur to the size of a large starship)
5	Most animals (and perhaps also plants) are well camouflaged and difficult to notice
6	The air is filled with floating and flying creatures of all sizes (reroll for Class D planets)
7-9	Earth-like vegetation and animals (reroll if planet lacks a breathable atmosphere)
10-12	Most life-forms are unusually colored (blue, purple, bright red, monochromatic…)
13-14	Most life-forms have more or fewer than 4 limbs, perhaps 3, maybe 6, 8, or even more.
15-16	Gelid or blobby life-forms
17-18	Animate plants, sessile animals, or no distinction between plants and animals
19-20	Crystalline life-forms

PLANETARY DETAILS

The final aspect to consider before you introduce a planet to the characters is what it looks like. Are the plants and animals earthlike or is this a world of magenta-colored forests or six-legged animals? Is the world shrouded in perpetual night or does dense fog (or something stranger) reduce visibility to 5 meters or less even in brightly lit conditions? Are the life-forms sufficiently alien that you can't tell the animals from the plants? These sorts of vivid details help a planet come alive for the Players and can also help you come up with a better idea of what else is on the planet. Nothing says to the characters that they are on an alien world than hacking their way through a dense crystalline forest or walking across a field filled with mobile jelly-like blobs. Roll once on the Planetary Details table (Table 10-5) to jumpstart your ideas about the planet. Once you've done that, your new planet should be ready for the characters to beam down.

ALIENS AND ADVERSARIES

19031515200618
12091404120525

ALIENS AND ADVERSARIES

NPCS AND ADVERSARIES

"YOU JUDGE YOURSELVES AGAINST THE PITIFUL ADVERSARIES YOU'VE ENCOUNTERED SO FAR: THE ROMULANS, THE KLINGONS... THEY'RE NOTHING COMPARED TO WHAT'S WAITING. PICARD, YOU ARE ABOUT TO MOVE INTO AREAS OF THE GALAXY CONTAINING WONDERS MORE INCREDIBLE THAN YOU CAN POSSIBLY IMAGINE... AND TERRORS TO FREEZE YOUR SOUL. I OFFER MYSELF AS A GUIDE — ONLY TO BE REJECTED OUT OF HAND."

— Q

This section describes the way in which Non-Player Characters — NPCs — function in game terms, and the means by which a Gamemaster might structure an encounter.

NPC CATEGORIES

The many life-forms that characters are likely to face come in many shapes and sizes, and where some are mighty entities that can stand alone against many foes, others function in coordinated groups. The following categories exist for NPCs.

CATEGORISING NPCS

The clearest way to consider the various categories of NPC is to equate them with the types of character on the shows:

- A Minor NPC is an incidental character; they don't have any dialogue, or they only speak a few lines, and they're mainly there as an extra stood in the background, or an unnamed foe in a battle.

- A Notable NPC might be given a name, or they might speak a few lines of dialogue, or they might get some specific attention in a tense or action-packed scene. They don't appear in more than one or two scenes, though. The extra emphasis on the character means that they get a little more detail.

- A Major NPC is named, developed, receives plenty of dialogue in the scenes they appear in, and they appear in several scenes. They're treated similarly to Player Characters in most ways, as befits characters who may be present in several scenes, or be the focal point of particularly involved or tense scenes. Some Major NPCs may even reappear in subsequent adventures, as a recurring ally or adversary (or even both).

- Minor NPCs are rank-and-file personnel and ordinary people. Minor NPCs are the most common type of NPC present in a scene, significant in groups rather than as individuals. Minor NPCs cannot *Avoid an Injury*. Minor NPCs do not have Focuses or Values.

- Notable NPCs are more dedicated and resourceful characters, often with specialist skills and abilities. Notable NPCs may *Avoid an Injury* once per scene as Player Characters can, but they cannot recover the ability to avoid Injury. Notable NPCs have 1–3 Focuses, and they have a single Value, relating to their race and affiliation.

- Major NPCs are leaders and important individuals, with a wide range of skills and abilities. Major NPCs may *Avoid an Injury* as Player Characters do, and may regain the ability to *Avoid an Injury* in the same was as Player Characters can. Major NPCs are unique named characters, who have four or more Focuses, at least two Values, and other noteworthy abilities comparable to a Player Character's Talents.

While Major NPCs are specifically stated to be unique named characters, that doesn't necessarily mean that Minor or Notable NPCs cannot be named individuals — obviously, each NPC is a person in their own right, but the more important the NPC, the more attention is given to what makes them unique. Major NPCs, thus, must always be unique individuals, and the examples provided later in this chapter serve as starting points for the Gamemaster to create their own cast of memorable allies and antagonists.

NPCS AND VALUES

Typically speaking, Non-Player Characters don't have Determination points to spend; only Major NPCs can gain the benefit of them. However, some NPCs do have Values.

In situations where an NPC's Value create a Complication, or their Values are Challenged, the Gamemaster adds three points to Threat, rather than giving the NPC a point of Determination. Similarly, when their Value would be beneficial, an NPC can gain the effects of a point of Determination by spending three Threat.

COMMON SPECIAL ABILITIES

The following are several common rules and abilities possessed by creatures in *Star Trek Adventures*. These abilities are referred to by name only in the individual NPC entries, and require you to refer here for the specifics of each rule.

EXTRAORDINARY ATTRIBUTE X

One or more of the creature's attributes are far beyond the normal range for humanoids. This is indicated by a number, which is added as automatic successes on Tasks using that attribute. For example, a creature with Extraordinary Reason 1 gains one success on all Tasks using Reason, in addition to any generated by rolling. Extraordinary Attributes, in addition to being noted in a creature's Special Abilities section, will be noted next to the Attribute as an extra value in parentheses.

FAST RECOVERY X

The creature recovers from stress and injury quickly. At the start of each of its Turns, the creature regains X Stress, up to its normal maximum. If the creature is Injured at the start of its turn, it may instead spend two Threat to remove that Injury.

IMMUNE TO X

The creature is unperturbed by conditions and effects caused

ESCALATION

Many of the NPCs presented in this section contain options or rules marked **Escalation**. These represent common variations for that type of NPC that represent response to a greater danger, or which themselves make the NPC more dangerous — it is commonly applied to more powerful weapons for this reason.

NPCs do not have access to **Escalation** options normally. Instead, when an NPC is brought into a scene — either at the beginning, or during the scene — the Gamemaster may spend 1 Threat to add one of the Escalation options to all NPCs of that type. For example, the Gamemaster may spend 1 Threat to have all the Klingon Warrior NPCs in the scene carry *bat'leths* in addition to their other weaponry.

by one of a number of sources of difficulty or hindrance, such as vacuum, extremes of temperature, poison, disease, etc. The most common sources of conditions are described below:

- **Cold:** The creature is unaffected by effects derived from extreme cold, including damage.

- **Disease:** The creature is immune to the effects of disease, and will never suffer the symptoms of any disease. If the creature is exposed to a disease it may become a carrier — able to spread the disease if it is contagious.

NPCS ON EITHER SIDE

Under most circumstances, the rules for NPCs cover adversaries — those who are opposed to the Player Characters' goals in some way. Most of the time, NPCs whose goals align with those of the Player Characters require hard-and-fast rules to the same degree as adversarial NPCs.

That isn't always the case, however. And, in some cases, an NPC's goals may shift — at some points making them an ally, while at others making them an opponent. To handle this, use the following guidelines:

- **If an NPC is an Adversary:** The NPC spends points from the Gamemaster's Threat pool to buy Immediate Momentum spends, and adds surplus Momentum to the Threat pool instead of having a group Momentum pool. Any instance where a Player Character would add to Threat, an adversarial NPC spends from Threat instead. NPC abilities that specifically cost Threat remove points from the Threat pool.

- **If an NPC is an Ally:** The NPC may add to or spend from group Momentum as the Player Characters do (the Gamemaster may wish to let the Players roll for the NPC's Tasks and control their uses of Momentum). Allied NPCs treat instances where they would add to Threat in the same way Player Characters do. NPC abilities that specifically cost Threat add points to the Threat pool.

- **Changing Allegiance:** In any given scene, an NPC is either an adversary or an ally. The Gamemaster determines which is the case for each NPC. This is most likely to be the case where an NPC is regarded as an adversary for some purposes (such as social conflict), and an ally for others (physical challenges, combat). The Gamemaster should try and avoid situations where the NPC must be both adversary and ally simultaneously, to minimize confusion; if an NPC betrays the Player Characters, maybe have this as a Threat spend to emphasize it, while an NPC becoming an ally might be a reward for the Players' successes.

- **Fear:** The creature is incapable of feeling fear, continuing undeterred despite the greatest terror. The creature cannot be intimidated or threatened.

- **Heat:** The creature is unaffected by effects derived from extreme heat, including damage caused by fire.

- **Pain:** The creature is incapable of feeling pain, continuing undeterred despite the most horrific agony. The creature has +3 Resistance against non-lethal attacks, and it is unaffected by any penalties or hindrances caused by pain.

- **Poison:** The creature is unaffected by all forms of poison, venom, and toxin.

- **Vacuum:** The creature suffers no damage from being exposed to hard vacuum, or other extremes of atmospheric pressure, and cannot suffocate.

INVULNERABLE

The creature is impervious to harm, and cannot be Injured in any way; attacks can be attempted and damage is rolled as normal, and the creature has a Stress track, but it cannot suffer Injuries. This can take different forms, as described below. These variations can be combined.

- **Specific Weakness:** The creature has a specific weakness — a weak spot, a certain frequency of energy, a certain material — which can overcome its invulnerability. If this weakness is discovered and employed, then the creature can be Injured by attacks which exploit that weakness (this also bypasses the effects of the other Invulnerable variations). The Gamemaster's discretion applies as to how the weakness may be discovered.

- **Staggered:** The creature cannot be Injured, but it can be hurt. If the creature would ever suffer an Injury, it instead loses the ability to perform any Tasks or Minor Actions on its next Turn. This effect is not cumulative.

- **Wrathful:** The creature grows angry when challenged; if the creature would ever suffer an Injury, it instead adds 2 to Threat.

MACHINE X

The creature is not a living being, but a machine, or some form of cybernetic organism. It is highly resistant to environmental conditions, reducing the Difficulty of Tasks to resist extremes of heat and cost by two, and it is immune to the effects of suffocation, hard vacuum, starvation, and thirst. Further, the machine's sturdy construction grants it Resistance equal to X.

MENACING

The creature is dangerous, heralding a greater problem for those who confront it. When a creature with this rule enters a scene, immediately add a point to the Threat pool.

NIGHT VISION

The creature has some way of perceiving its environment even in pitch darkness — perceiving infrared or ultraviolet light, echolocation, or some other method. Tasks the creature attempts do not increase in Difficulty because of darkness.

THREATENING X

The creature is powerful and dangerous, with a vitality and drive that allows it to triumph where others might fail. The creature begins each scene with X Threat, that may only be used to benefit itself, and which are not drawn from the general Threat pool.

Founded in 2161, the United Federation of Planets consists of over 150 planets plus their affiliated colonies all committed to a single co-operative governmental system. Starfleet is responsible for a majority of their exploratory and defensive capabilities, as well as sometimes diplomatic missions.

The NPCs in this section are all listed as Human, though they do not contain any Attribute increases (+1 to each of 3 Attributes). Changing them to represent any of the other species found within Starfleet requires changing the species Trait, adding that species' Attribute increases, and optionally, adding one of the species' Talents.

STARFLEET CONN OFFICER [MINOR NPC]

The conn officer (abbreviated from flight controller) is responsible for both the helm and navigation systems aboard Federation starships, from *Danube* class runabouts to the colossal *Galaxy*-class vessels. At least one trained Conn officer is present on the bridge at all times.

TRAITS: Human

ATTRIBUTES

CONTROL 10	FITNESS 08	PRESENCE 09
DARING 10	INSIGHT 08	REASON 09

DISCIPLINES

COMMAND 01	SECURITY 01	SCIENCE 01
CONN 02	ENGINEERING 02	MEDICINE 01

STRESS: 9   **RESISTANCE: 0**

ATTACKS:
- Unarmed Strike (Melee, 2▲ Knockdown, Size 1H, Non-lethal)
- Phaser type-I (Ranged, 3▲, Size 1H, Charge, Hidden 1)
- Escalation Phaser type-2 (Ranged, 4▲, Size 1H, Charge)

STARFLEET SECURITY OFFICER [MINOR NPC]

Security officers are found throughout the Federation protecting their installations and serving aboard starships. Security officers protect their ships from both internal and external threats, escort other officers on away missions and are normally responsible for staffing the ship's weapon systems on the bridge.

TRAITS: Human

ATTRIBUTES

CONTROL 10	FITNESS 09	PRESENCE 09
DARING 10	INSIGHT 08	REASON 08

DISCIPLINES

COMMAND 02	SECURITY 02	SCIENCE 01
CONN 01	ENGINEERING 01	MEDICINE 01

STRESS: 11   **RESISTANCE: 0**

ATTACKS:
- Unarmed Strike (Melee, 3▲ Knockdown, Size 1H, Non-lethal)
- Phaser type-2 (Ranged, 5▲, Size 1H, Charge)
- Escalation Phaser Rifle (Ranged, 6▲, Size 2H, Accurate, Charge)

THE MAQUIS

A lot of Maquis terrorists are drawn from the ranks of angry or frustrated ex-Starfleet officers, and as such you can use the Federation NPCs presented here in place of Maquis fighters.

STARFLEET ENGINEER [MINOR NPC]

The Starfleet Corps of Engineers maintain the countless technological devices used throughout the Federation every day. Aboard a starship, the engineers are responsible for the repair of every ship board system, power distribution, and management as well as providing and maintaining any equipment used by the ships' other departments.

TRAITS: Human

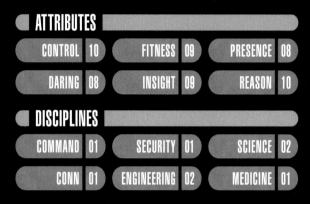

ATTRIBUTES

CONTROL	10	FITNESS	09	PRESENCE	08
DARING	08	INSIGHT	09	REASON	10

DISCIPLINES

COMMAND	01	SECURITY	01	SCIENCE	02
CONN	01	ENGINEERING	02	MEDICINE	01

STRESS: 10   **RESISTANCE:** 0

ATTACKS:
- Unarmed Strike (Melee, 2⚔ Knockdown, Size 1H, Non-lethal)
- Phaser type-1 (Ranged, 3⚔, Size 1H, Charge, Hidden 1)
- **Escalation** Phaser type-2 (Ranged, 4⚔, Size 1H, Charge)

STARFLEET SCIENCE OFFICER [MINOR NPC]

As an integral part of Starfleet, science officers cover the hundreds of areas of expertise essential to the continuation and development of the Federation. Starfleet Medical, a division within the scientific branch is the body responsible for the care and treatment of all Starfleet personnel.

TRAITS: Human

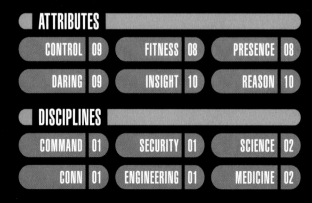

ATTRIBUTES

CONTROL	09	FITNESS	08	PRESENCE	08
DARING	09	INSIGHT	10	REASON	10

DISCIPLINES

COMMAND	01	SECURITY	01	SCIENCE	02
CONN	01	ENGINEERING	01	MEDICINE	02

STRESS: 9   **RESISTANCE:** 0

ATTACKS:
- Unarmed Strike (Melee, 2⚔ Knockdown, Size 1H, Non-lethal)
- Phaser type-1 (Ranged, 3⚔, Size 1H, Charge, Hidden 1)
- **Escalation** Phaser type-2 (Ranged, 4⚔, Size 1H, Charge)

SECTION 31 OPERATIVE [NOTABLE NPC]

Created even before the formation of the Federation, Section 31 is a deep-cover autonomous organization insinuated within Starfleet, largely unknown to all but its members. Unauthorized and unaccountable, it recruits its agents from every branch of service performing illegal black-ops missions throughout the Federation or even within the territories of hostile powers.

TRAITS: Human

VALUE: The Ends Justify the Means

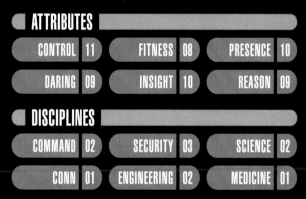

ATTRIBUTES

CONTROL	11	FITNESS	08	PRESENCE	10
DARING	09	INSIGHT	10	REASON	09

DISCIPLINES

COMMAND	02	SECURITY	03	SCIENCE	02
CONN	01	ENGINEERING	02	MEDICINE	01

FOCUSES: Espionage, Infiltration.

STRESS: 11   **RESISTANCE:** 0

ATTACKS:
- Unarmed Strike (Melee, 4⚔ Knockdown, Size 1H, Non-lethal)
- Phaser type-1 (Ranged, 5⚔, Size 1H, Charge, Hidden 1)
- **Escalation** Phaser type-2 (Ranged, 6⚔, Size 1H, Charge)

SPECIAL RULES:
- **Adaptable:** A Section 31 operative may spend 2 Threat to immediately gain a single Focus for the remainder of the scene.
- **Covert:** A Section 31 operative never operates openly, either using an active cover identity or concealing their activities with other duties. Whenever required to attempt a Task to conceal their activities for Section 31 — including to maintain their cover identity — they may roll an additional d20.

CAPTAIN T'MEK [MAJOR NPC]

As high-ranking Starfleet officers, captains are found commanding not only Federation starships but also their various outposts and facilities. Captains may be drawn from any branch of Starfleet and on rare circumstances a ship may have several officers at the rank of captain running their individual departments.

VALUES:
- Wisdom is the Beginning of Logic, Not the End
- A Failure to Act Can Be As Dangerous As Acting Rashly

TRAITS: Vulcan

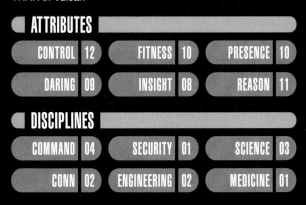

ATTRIBUTES

CONTROL	12	FITNESS	10	PRESENCE	10
DARING	09	INSIGHT	08	REASON	11

DISCIPLINES

COMMAND	04	SECURITY	01	SCIENCE	03
CONN	02	ENGINEERING	02	MEDICINE	01

FOCUSES: Astrophysics, Composure, Diplomacy, Starship Tactics

STRESS: 11   **RESISTANCE:** 0

ATTACKS:
- Vulcan Nerve Pinch (Melee, 4▲ Intense, Size 1H, Non-lethal)
- Phaser type-2 (Ranged, 4▲, Size 1H, Charge)
- **Escalation** Phaser Rifle (Ranged, 5▲, Size 2H, Charge, Accurate)

SPECIAL RULES:
- **Considered Every Outcome:** T'Mek is a keenly analytical commander, regarding every situation from myriad different angles and considering the advice of her senior staff before coming to a command decision. When she succeeds at a **Reason + Command Task**, T'Mek scores one additional Momentum than normal.
- *Kolinahr:* T'Mek has undergone the ritual journey to purge all emotion. Reduce the Difficulty of all Tasks for T'Mek to resist coercion, mental intrusion, pain, and other mental attacks by 2.

REAR-ADMIRAL THYRAN [MAJOR NPC]

These officers form the upper echelons of Starfleet and are ultimately responsible for its day-to-day operations. A majority are based at Starfleet Command in San Francisco on Earth, but they can also be found overseeing starbases and other facilities across the Federation.

VALUES:
- There Is No Higher Calling Than to Serve
- We Endure Hardship, So That Others Do Not Have To

TRAITS: Andorian

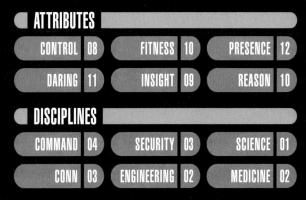

ATTRIBUTES

CONTROL	08	FITNESS	10	PRESENCE	12
DARING	11	INSIGHT	09	REASON	10

DISCIPLINES

COMMAND	04	SECURITY	03	SCIENCE	01
CONN	03	ENGINEERING	02	MEDICINE	02

FOCUSES: Endurance, Fleet Strategy and Tactics, Inspiration, Military History

STRESS: 13   **RESISTANCE:** 0

ATTACKS:
- Unarmed Strike (Melee, 4▲ Knockdown, Size 1H, Non-lethal)
- Phaser type-2 (Ranged, 6▲, Size 1H, Charge)

SPECIAL RULES:
- **Accomplished Strategist:** Admiral Thyran is a skilled commander who learned the arts of warfare commanding ships in battle. Whenever he attempts a Task to formulate, execute, or explain a strategy, he may spend 1 Threat to re-roll his dice pool.
- **Counter-Ploy:** Whenever an enemy attempts a Task to create an Advantage representing some manner of strategy or tactic, Thyran may spend 1 Threat to increase the Difficulty by 1. Further, if this Task then fails, Thyran may immediately spend one additional Threat to create an Advantage of his own, representing his own stratagem.

ALIENS AND ADVERSARIES
KLINGON EMPIRE

Originating from the planet Qo'noS in the Beta Quadrant, the Klingon Empire is a warrior dominated species and one of the major powers in the Galaxy. While there have been hostilities between the Federation and Klingons in the past, since the signing of the Khitomer Accords in 2293 the two powers have been considered allies despite several small skirmishes.

KLINGON WARRIOR [MINOR NPC]

Virtually fearless and trained extensively in various combat techniques, a Klingon warrior (or *bekk*) is a devastating opponent. Ruled by ancient traditions and a strict code of honor, a Klingon warrior does not fear death, but, if they have to die, it should be during battle or in the line of duty.

TRAITS: Klingon

ATTRIBUTES

CONTROL 09	FITNESS 11	PRESENCE 10
DARING 11	INSIGHT 08	REASON 08

DISCIPLINES

COMMAND 01	SECURITY 02	SCIENCE 00
CONN 02	ENGINEERING 01	MEDICINE 00

STRESS: 13   **RESISTANCE:** 1

ATTACKS:
- Unarmed Strike (Melee, 3🗡 Knockdown, Size 1H, Non-lethal)
- *D'k tahg* Dagger (Melee, 3🗡 Vicious 1, Size 1H, Deadly, Hidden 1)
- Escalation *Bat'leth* (Melee, 5🗡 Vicious 1, Size 2H)
- Disruptor Pistol (Ranged, 5🗡 Vicious 1, Size 1H)
- Escalation Disruptor Rifle (Ranged, 6🗡 Vicious 1, Size 2H, Accurate)

SPECIAL RULES:
- *Brak'lul:* A Klingon's Resistance is increased by +2 against Non-lethal attacks.
- Warrior's Spirit: When a Klingon attempts a Melee attack, and purchases one or more additional dice with Threat, the Klingon may re-roll any number of d20s.

KLINGON VETERAN [NOTABLE NPC]

Klingon veterans have not only proven themselves in battle but normally have a long family background of honor and tradition and often serve as officers. A Klingon officer must be seen to be authoritative at all times or they may be forced to prove themselves in a trial of combat by their subordinates.

TRAITS: Klingon

VALUE: Today is a Good Day to Die!

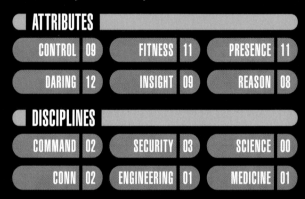

ATTRIBUTES

CONTROL 09	FITNESS 11	PRESENCE 11
DARING 12	INSIGHT 09	REASON 08

DISCIPLINES

COMMAND 02	SECURITY 03	SCIENCE 00
CONN 02	ENGINEERING 01	MEDICINE 01

FOCUSES: Hand-to-Hand Combat, Resilience

STRESS: 14   **RESISTANCE:** 1

ATTACKS:
- Unarmed Strike (Melee, 4▲ Knockdown, Size 1H, Non-lethal)
- *D'k tahg* Dagger (Melee, 4▲ Vicious 1, Size 1H, Deadly, Hidden 1)
- Escalation Bat'leth (Melee, 6▲ Vicious 1, Size 2H)
- Disruptor Pistol (Ranged, 6▲ Vicious 1, Size 1H)
- Escalation Disruptor Rifle (Ranged, 7▲ Vicious 1, Size 2H, Accurate)

SPECIAL RULES:
- **First into Battle:** When the Klingon Veteran makes a successful attack, they may spend 3 Momentum to assist another Klingon's next attack with his **Daring + Command**.
- **Brak'lul:** A Klingon's Resistance is increased by +2 against Non-lethal attacks.
- **Warrior's Spirit:** When a Klingon attempts a Melee attack, and purchases one or more additional dice with Threat, the Klingon may re-roll any number of d20s.

TO GO WITH HONOR

CAPTAIN B'OMA ADDRESSES NEW CREW OF THE I.K.S. RAGOR

Well met, warriors!

The Neutral Zone: the edge of the Klingon Empire. This is the maiden voyage of the spacecraft *Ragor*. Its assigned mission: to patrol Klingon controlled worlds, to seek out new threats and aggressive civilizations, to go with honor in the name of the Klingon Empire.

I am Captain B'Oma. Your lives now belong to me. You few *bekks* have been granted the distinct honor of serving aboard my vessel, the *I.K.S. Ragor*. This duty is not to be taken lightly. We will confront the oppressive Federation and its tenacious Starfleet. Do not, however, take the apparent weaker races of the Federation of Planets for granted. While they can hardly compare to the dominance of Klingons, their perceived vulnerability can be deceiving. When pressed, they too can be as dangerous as a frenzied and cornered *targ*.

Qapla'!

KLINGON CHARACTERS

Klingon characters are typically large, physically powerful, and proud, with an aggressive approach to everything they do, and a propensity for violence that makes them extremely dangerous. They are predatory, with a primarily carnivorous diet, and a preference for either still-living food or wild prey from a hunt. Culturally, Klingons revere physical prowess, victory in battle, and a code of personal and familial honor that influences most of their politics, though not all Klingons live up to this; in some Klingons, this only keeps them from performing shameful acts so long as they can avoid the repercussions. Klingon characters have the following modifiers:

- **ATTRIBUTES:** +1 Daring, +1 Fitness, +1 Presence

- **TRAIT:** Klingon. Klingon physiology is hardy, with many redundant internal organs allowing them to withstand harm and a number of poisons, which would be deadly for many other species. They are significantly stronger and more resilient than Humans, though they have less tolerance for the cold.

MOQ'VAR, SON OF KOLOTH [MAJOR NPC]

The commanding officer of a starship, a Klingon captain is an expert strategist and combatant that has distinguished themselves time and time again in order to rise through the ranks. Weakness is not tolerated in the Klingon military; it is a first officer's duty to assassinate an ineffectual captain.

TRAITS: Klingon

VALUES:
- There is Nothing More Honorable Than Victory
- To Kill the Defenseless is Not True Battle

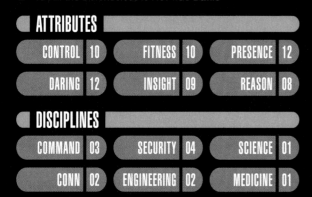

ATTRIBUTES

CONTROL	10	FITNESS	10	PRESENCE	12
DARING	12	INSIGHT	09	REASON	08

DISCIPLINES

COMMAND	03	SECURITY	04	SCIENCE	01
CONN	02	ENGINEERING	02	MEDICINE	01

FOCUSES: Hand-to-Hand Combat, Intimidation, Resilience, Starship Tactics

STRESS: 14   **RESISTANCE:** 1

ATTACKS:
- Unarmed Strike (Melee, 5⚔ Knockdown, Size 1H, Non-lethal)
- *D'k tahg* Dagger (Melee, 5⚔ Vicious 1, Size 1H, Deadly, Hidden 1)
- Escalation *Bat'leth* (Melee, 7⚔ Vicious 1, Size 2H)
- Disruptor Pistol (Ranged, 7⚔ Vicious 1, Size 1H)

SPECIAL RULES:
- **Dauntless (Talent)**
- **First into Battle:** When the Klingon Veteran makes a successful attack, they may spend 3 Threat to assist another Klingon's next attack with his **Daring + Command**.
- **Tough (Talent)**
- *Brak'lul*: A Klingon's Resistance is increased by +2 against Non-lethal attacks.
- **Warrior's Spirit:** When a Klingon attempts a Melee attack, and purchases one or more additional dice with Threat, the Klingon may re-roll any number of d20s.

ALIENS AND ADVERSARIES
THE ROMULAN STAR EMPIRE

The Romulan Star Empire is a reclusive and secretive galactic power that has only recently returned to prominence after a long period of isolationism. Based on the twin worlds of Romulus and Remus, the Romulan Star Empire spans a considerable area of the Beta Quadrant and has clashed with both the Federation and the Klingon Empire on numerous occasions.

ROMULAN UHLAN [MINOR NPC]

The Romulan *uhlan* is the lowest ranking officer in the Romulan Guard and makes up a substantial number of their personnel.

TRAITS: Romulan

ATTRIBUTES

CONTROL 11	FITNESS 09	PRESENCE 08
DARING 08	INSIGHT 10	REASON 11

DISCIPLINES

COMMAND 01	SECURITY 02	SCIENCE 00
CONN 02	ENGINEERING 01	MEDICINE 00

STRESS: 11   **RESISTANCE:** 0

ATTACKS:
- Unarmed Strike (Melee, 3▲ Knockdown, Size 1H, Non-lethal)
- Dagger (Melee, 3▲ Vicious 1, Size 1H, Deadly, Hidden 1)
- Disruptor Pistol (Ranged, 5▲ Vicious 1, Size 1H)
- Escalation Disruptor Rifle (Ranged, 6▲ Vicious 1, Size 2H, Accurate)

SPECIAL RULES:
- **Guile and Cunning:** When attempting to remain hidden or unnoticed, a Romulan may spend one Threat to increase the Difficulty of enemy Tasks to detect them by one.
- **Wary:** Whenever a Romulan attempts a Task to notice or detect an enemy or hazard, they may re-roll one d20.

ROMULAN CENTURION [NOTABLE NPC]

The Romulan centurion is a mid-ranking officer in the Romulan Guard roughly equivalent to a lieutenant commander in Starfleet. They can be found as heads of departments aboard starships and throughout the Empire.

TRAITS: Romulan

VALUE: I Will Not Fail in My Duty to the Empire

ATTRIBUTES

CONTROL 12	FITNESS 09	PRESENCE 09
DARING 10	INSIGHT 10	REASON 10

DISCIPLINES

COMMAND 03	SECURITY 02	SCIENCE 01
CONN 02	ENGINEERING 01	MEDICINE 00

FOCUSES: Paranoid, Guerilla Tactics

STRESS: 11   **RESISTANCE:** 0

ATTACKS:
- Unarmed Strike (Melee, 3▲ Knockdown, Size 1H, Non-lethal)
- Dagger (Melee, 3▲ Vicious 1, Size 1H, Deadly, Hidden 1)
- Disruptor Pistol (Ranged, 5▲ Vicious 1, Size 1H)
- Escalation Disruptor Rifle (Ranged, 6▲ Vicious 1, Size 2H, Accurate)

SPECIAL RULES:
- **Ambush:** When attacking an opponent who is unaware, the Centurion may spend 2 Threat, to allow the Centurion and all Romulans under their command to re-roll any number of d20s on their attack rolls.
- **Guile and Cunning:** When attempting to remain hidden or unnoticed, a Romulan may spend one Threat to increase the Difficulty of enemy Tasks to detect them by one.
- **Wary:** Whenever a Romulan attempts a Task to notice or detect an enemy or hazard, they may re-roll one d20.

ROMULAN CHARACTERS

Romulans are similar, but not quite identical, to Vulcans, having diverged from their common ancestors, though they did not adopt the stoicism and logic of their cousins. Rather, Romulans are a cruel and ruthless people, quick to anger, and easily moved to emotion. A culture of military discipline seems to keep their worst members directed towards useful ends, though paranoia and self-interest motivate Romulan politics as much as a desire for collective benefit; at times, it seems that the only things keeping the Romulan Star Empire together are the fact that they despise other species more than they despise one another. Romulan characters have the following modifiers:

- **ATTRIBUTES:** +1 Control, +1 Fitness, +1 Reason

- **TRAIT:** Romulan. Romulan physiology is not meaningfully different to that of Vulcans, though a portion of the Romulan species exhibits a v-shaped forehead ridge not evident in Vulcans. The largest difference is that Romulans lack the intense mental discipline common to Vulcans. Psychologically and culturally, Romulans prize cunning and strength of will, and are distrustful of other species: this opinion is reciprocated, as Romulans have a reputation for manipulation, deception, and betrayal.

MAJOR VEROHK, TAL SHIAR AGENT [MAJOR NPC]

The Tal Shiar is a secret Imperial Intelligence service that operates autonomously from the Romulan government and is responsible for enforcing the loyalty of its citizens and the security of the Empire. Even a low-ranking Tal Shiar major has the authority to overrule the commanders, generals, and admirals of the Romulan Guard.

TRAITS: Romulan

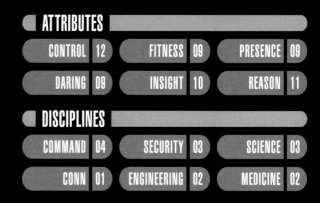

VALUES:
- The Ends Justify the Means
- Everything I Do, I Do for Romulus

ATTRIBUTES

| CONTROL 12 | FITNESS 09 | PRESENCE 09 |
| DARING 09 | INSIGHT 10 | REASON 11 |

DISCIPLINES

| COMMAND 04 | SECURITY 03 | SCIENCE 03 |
| CONN 01 | ENGINEERING 02 | MEDICINE 02 |

FOCUSES: Deception, Infiltration, Interrogation, Paranoid

STRESS: 12   **RESISTANCE:** 0

ATTACKS:
- Unarmed Strike (Melee, 4▲ Knockdown, Size 1H, Non-lethal)
- Dagger (Melee, 4▲ Vicious 1, Size 1H, Deadly, Hidden 1)
- Disruptor Pistol (Ranged, 6▲ Vicious 1, Size 1H)

SPECIAL RULES:
- **Guile and Cunning:** When attempting to remain hidden or unnoticed, a Romulan may spend one Threat to increase the Difficulty of enemy Tasks to detect them by one.
- **Ruthless and Determined:** Major Verohk may spend 2 Threat to gain the effects of a point of Determination, rather than the normal 3.
- **Supreme Authority:** Whenever a Romulan currently under Verohk's command attempts a Task to resist persuasion or intimidation, Verohk may spend 1 Threat to allow that Romulan to re-roll, even if Verohk is not present in that scene herself.
- **Wary:** Whenever a Romulan attempts a Task to notice or detect an enemy or hazard, they may re-roll one d20.

THE BATTLE OF NARENDRA III

EXECUTIVE SUMMARY FOR THE IMPERIAL SENATE
PRESENTED BY ADMIRAL KYLOR JEROK, INTELLIGENCE ANALYST, ROMULAN IMPERIAL FLEET

Narendra III was the single greatest failure in Romulan naval history. Although our task force, consisting of four warbirds, successfully destroyed a Klingon outpost and the *Enterprise*-C, the goal of our attack was to send a clear message to the Klingons who were attempting to assert their superiority in that sector. In that goal, we failed spectacularly. Our victory became the catalyst for a Federation-Klingon Alliance that has dominated the Alpha and Beta Quadrants for over twenty years and isolated us from the rest of the Galaxy.

Reports from the commanders at Narendra III commented on the *Enterprise*-C's resilience after taking sustained fire from their disruptors. Upon further study, the Battle of Narendra III exposed significant deficiencies in the tactical training of our officers. We were fortunate the commanders at Narendra III had the foresight to capture Federation escape pods and take the ship's officers into custody. The interrogation of acting tactical officer Tasha Yar revealed the Federation's training was decades ahead of our own and explained how a single Federation ship was able to defend itself against four warbirds.

ALIENS AND ADVERSARIES
BORG COLLECTIVE

Cybernetic humanoids from the Delta Quadrant, the Borg have travelled the Galaxy assimilating over 10,000 different species to add to their Collective. There is no individuality within the Collective; each drone is linked by a hive mind to one another and given a new designation according to their place within the group.

BORG TACTICAL DRONE [MINOR NPC]

A Borg tactical drone can be any one of the thousands of species assimilated by the Collective but all have the same basic modifications, enhanced strength, a personal force field, a neural transceiver that connects to the hive mind, and an assimilation tubule.

This profile represents an assimilated Klingon, whose size and strength make them ideally suited to becoming Tactical drones. It can be adjusted to represent other species by changing the second species Trait.

TRAITS: Borg, Klingon

ATTRIBUTES

CONTROL 11	FITNESS 12	PRESENCE 06
DARING 09	INSIGHT 06	REASON 12

DISCIPLINES

COMMAND 00	SECURITY 02	SCIENCE 01
CONN 02	ENGINEERING 01	MEDICINE 00

STRESS: 14   **RESISTANCE:** 3 (Exoplating)

ATTACKS:

- Unarmed Strike (Melee, 3⚔ Knockdown, Size 1H, Non-lethal)
- **Escalation** Assimilation Tubules (Melee, 5⚔ Intense, Size 1H, Deadly, Debilitating)

SPECIAL RULES:

- **Adaptive Shielding:** see sidebar
- **Assimilation:** see sidebar
- **Immune to Fear**
- **Immune to Pain**
- **Machine 3**
- **Night Vision**
- **Threat Protocols::** see sidebar

BORG TECHNICAL DRONE [MINOR NPC]

Almost identical to other drones, the Borg technical drone is tasked with the assimilation and modification of any technology the Borg wishes to add to their Collective.

This profile represents an assimilated Vulcan, whose strength and neurological makeup make them well-suited to technical activities. It can be adjusted to represent other species by changing the second species Trait.

TRAITS: Borg, Vulcan

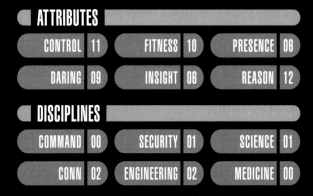

ATTRIBUTES

CONTROL	11	FITNESS	10	PRESENCE	06
DARING	09	INSIGHT	06	REASON	12

DISCIPLINES

COMMAND	00	SECURITY	01	SCIENCE	01
CONN	02	ENGINEERING	02	MEDICINE	00

STRESS: 11 **RESISTANCE:** 2 (Exoplating)

ATTACKS:
- Unarmed Strike (Melee, 2🠔 Knockdown, Size 1H, Non-lethal)
- Plasma Cutter (Melee, 5🠔 Piercing 3, Size 1H, Cumbersome, Deadly)
- **Escalation** Assimilation Tubules (Melee, 4🠔 Intense, Size 1H, Deadly, Debilitating)

SPECIAL RULES:
- **Adaptive Shielding:** see sidebar
- **Assimilation:** see sidebar
- **Immune to Fear**
- **Immune to Pain**
- **Machine 2**
- **Night Vision**
- **Threat Protocols::** see sidebar

BORG MEDICAL DRONE [MINOR NPC]

A Borg medical drone is almost indistinguishable from other members of the Collective except that they are equipped with surgical devices able to make cybernetic modifications to those they have assimilated.

This profile represents an assimilated Cardassian, as their orderly minds and retentive memories make them well-suited to precise technical roles. It can be adjusted to represent other species by changing the second species Trait.

TRAITS: Borg, Cardassian

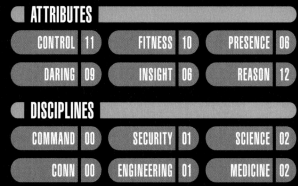

ATTRIBUTES

CONTROL	11	FITNESS	10	PRESENCE	06
DARING	09	INSIGHT	06	REASON	12

DISCIPLINES

COMMAND	00	SECURITY	01	SCIENCE	02
CONN	00	ENGINEERING	01	MEDICINE	02

STRESS: 11 **RESISTANCE:** 2 (Exoplating)

ATTACKS:
- Unarmed Strike (Melee, 2🠔 Knockdown, Size 1H, Non-lethal)
- **Escalation** Assimilation Tubules (Melee, 4🠔 Intense, Size 1H, Deadly, Debilitating)

SPECIAL RULES:
- **Adaptive Shielding:** see sidebar
- **Assimilation:** see sidebar
- **Immune to Fear**
- **Immune to Pain**
- **Machine 2**
- **Night Vision**
- **Reclamation:** A Borg medical drone may attempt a **Reason + Medicine Task** with a Difficulty of 0 on an Injured Borg drone within Reach. If successful, the Injured drone dies, and its parts are reclaimed. Any Momentum generated is added directly to Threat.
- **Threat Protocols::** see sidebar

BORG HAIL

"We are the Borg. Lower your shields and surrender your ships. We will add your biological and technological distinctiveness to our own. Your culture will adapt to service us. Resistance is futile."

Borg is not something that a person is born to, but rather something that they are forced to become — though for infants and children assimilated by the Collective, they may have little or no memory of any other life. The Borg meld biology with technology, and a drone will have countless implants, the result of both invasive surgery and aggressive nanotechnology. As of 2371, only a single individual has ever been removed from the Borg Collective — Jean-Luc Picard, who was captured only days earlier, meaning that his implants were less extensive than those of someone assimilated years or decades before. Borg NPCs are all mixed-species characters — their original species, and their new reality as part of the Collective.

- **ATTRIBUTES:** Borg characters do not receive any specific Attribute increases, nor do they use those of their original species; instead, they increase any three Attributes by +1 each.

- **TRAIT:** Borg. Borg are extremely strong and resilient, owing to their technologically-enhanced physiology. They lack self-determination and intuition, relying on directives and protocols from the Collective, and the gestalt consciousness of countless other Borg drones.

COMMON BORG SPECIAL RULES

Borg NPCs commonly use the following special rules:

- **Adaptive Shielding:** Each time a single Borg drone within a scene is Injured by an energy-based ranged weapon (such as a phaser or disruptor), roll 1▲ for each drone Injured by that type of weapon. If an Effect is rolled, then all Borg drones in that scene become immune to that type of ranged weapon. Melee attacks and projectiles are unaffected by this.

- **Assimilation:** A character Injured by Assimilation Tubules has been injected with Borg nanoprobes, beginning the process of assimilation. This process is extremely difficult to reverse — if the character dies from that Injury, they become a nascent drone. If the character's Injury is stabilized, they must add one to Threat at the start of each scene in order to not succumb to the nanoprobes, until they can have the nanoprobes removed and their Injury healed (a **Control + Medicine Task** with a Difficulty of 4).

- **Threat Protocols:** Borg drones will not attack or take any other hostile or tactical actions unless attacked first, or directed to do so by the Collective. During any scene, it costs 1 Threat to allow a drone to make attacks/take hostile action for the remainder of this scene; this cost is waived for all drones present in the scene (including reinforcements arriving during the scene) if any drone is attacked.

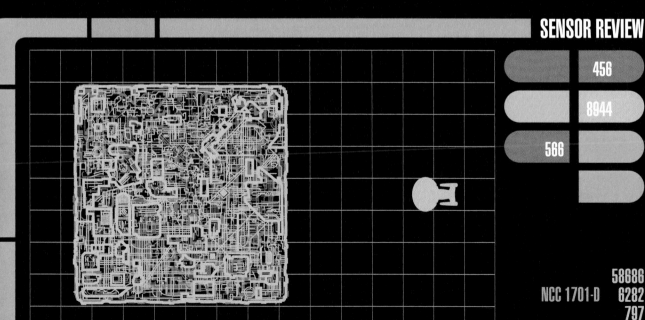

SENSOR REVIEW

456

8944

566

58686

NCC 1701-D   6282

797

SYSTEM J-25   37373

STARDATE 42761.3

FERENGI ALLIANCE

Hailing from Ferenginar, The Ferengi Alliance is a patriarchal civilization whose entire culture is based around trade and profit facilitated by the 285 "Rules of Acquisition." While Ferengi pirates have plagued the Federation even before their first official meeting in 2364, the two powers remain neutral.

FERENGI MENIAL [MINOR NPC]

These Ferengi are the rank and file officers found aboard Ferengi starships including freighters, trade and casino ships, or *D'Kora* class Marauders, as well as the ordinary service staff and petty entrepreneurs found in any place Ferengi gather.

TRAITS: Ferengi

ATTRIBUTES

CONTROL 10	FITNESS 08	PRESENCE 11
DARING 08	INSIGHT 11	REASON 09

DISCIPLINES

COMMAND 01	SECURITY 01	SCIENCE 00
CONN 02	ENGINEERING 02	MEDICINE 01

STRESS: 9 **RESISTANCE:** 0

ATTACKS:
- Unarmed Strike (Melee, 2🗡 Knockdown, Size 1H, Non-lethal)
- Phaser type-1 (Ranged, 3🗡, Size 1H, Charge, Hidden 1)

SPECIAL RULES:
- Greed Is Eternal: When engaged in negotiations that have the potential for the Ferengi to profit financially, they may spend 1 Threat during a Task to re-roll the dice pool.

FERENGI SALESMAN [NOTABLE NPC]

A Ferengi salesman is a master negotiator and trader that can be found across the Galaxy in pursuit of the next big business deal. Where there is latinum to be made, a Ferengi salesman is not far away.

TRAITS: Ferengi

VALUE: First Rule of Acquisition — Once You Have Their Money, Never Give It Back

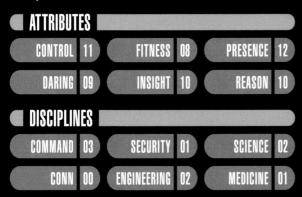

ATTRIBUTES

CONTROL	11	FITNESS	08	PRESENCE	12
DARING	09	INSIGHT	10	REASON	10

DISCIPLINES

COMMAND	03	SECURITY	01	SCIENCE	02
CONN	00	ENGINEERING	02	MEDICINE	01

FOCUSES: Economics, Negotiation

STRESS: 9 **RESISTANCE:** 0

ATTACKS:

- Unarmed Strike (Melee, 2⚔ Knockdown, Size 1H, Non-lethal)
- **Escalation** Disruptor Pistol (Ranged, 4⚔ Vicious 1, Size 1H)

SPECIAL RULES:

- **Greed Is Eternal:** When engaged in negotiations that have the potential for the Ferengi to profit financially, they may spend 1 Threat during a Task to re-roll the dice pool.
- **Free Advice Is Seldom Cheap:** Increase the Difficulty of all Social Conflict to persuade a Ferengi Salesman by 2. This Difficulty increase is removed as soon as the Ferengi is offered something in trade.

FERENGI CHARACTERS

Ferengi are short, unimposing beings, noted more as merchants and traders than as warriors, scientists, or engineers. Their culture promotes the acquisition of material wealth, and their society is extremely capitalistic, with most routine activities accompanied by the exchange of a precious, non-replicable substance called latinum (a room-temperature liquid metal, often stored within gold "slips," "bricks" or "bars"). Ferengi discriminate between their genders considerably, with female Ferengi not being permitted to own property or wear clothing; enterprising female Ferengi invariably find a way around these restrictions. Ferengi characters have the following modifiers:

- **ATTRIBUTES:** +1 Control, +1 Insight, +1 Presence

- **TRAIT:** Ferengi. Ferengi physiology does not lend itself to physical activity, nor does their culture value such hardship, though they have a high resistance to many common diseases. Ferengi have exceptionally keen hearing, and highly-sensitive ears, though this also means that intense sounds (and physical force applied to the ears) can inflict debilitating pain. Their unusual brain structure means that telepaths cannot read Ferengi minds. Culturally, Ferengi are acquisitive, regarding the accumulation of wealth as the highest virtue, and while this has given them a reputation as cunning negotiators, they are also often seen as duplicitous and manipulative as well.

PERSONAL LOG

BROCK, FERENGI MERCHANT

The Federation; a force confused about what success means. With ample wealth comes health and comfort, happiness, and fulfilment. Yet the Federation is mystified as to how health, comfort, happiness, and fulfilment are obtained. Instead of allowing citizens to pursue these goals, they stretch thin their resource base in attempting to supply it for them. What merit is there in disempowering their people?

So much money spent on worthless endeavours, exploration without acquisition, contact without commerce, where the profits are clearly outweighed by the costs, what nation can support such ostentatiousness? To spend regardless of benefit returned?

The vaunted Prime Directive; a symbol for everything wrong with the Federation. If an encounter leads to an arrangement where both parties are happy, where is the problem? Supply and demand!

How the Federation expect to survive as a viable economic force with such a corrupted ideology is beyond me!

DAIMON SKEL [MAJOR NPC]

DaiMon is a purchasable military, mercantile, or political rank that allows for command of a starship and the conducting of trade negotiations or even piracy on behalf of the Ferengi Alliance. DaiMon found using methods unapproved (or which are not adequately profitable) by the Alliance or their investors may lose command and be stripped of their rank.

TRAITS: Ferengi

VALUES:
- 48th Rule of Acquisition — The Bigger the Smile, the Sharper the Knife
- 211th Rule of Acquisition — Employees are the Rungs on the Ladder to Success; Don't Hesitate to Step On Them

ATTRIBUTES

CONTROL 10	FITNESS 08	PRESENCE 11
DARING 11	INSIGHT 10	REASON 10

DISCIPLINES

COMMAND 04	SECURITY 02	SCIENCE 01
CONN 03	ENGINEERING 02	MEDICINE 01

FOCUSES: Deception, Extortion, Negotiation, Weapons

STRESS: 10   **RESISTANCE:** 0

ATTACKS:
- Unarmed Strike (Melee, 3🅰 Knockdown, Size 1H, Non-lethal)
- Energy Whip (Ranged, 5🅰 Intense, Size 1H, Non-lethal)
- Phaser type-1 (Ranged, 4🅰, Size 1H, Charge, Hidden 1)

SPECIAL RULES:
- **Greed Is Eternal:** When engaged in negotiations that have the potential for the Ferengi to profit financially, they may spend 1 Threat during a Task to re-roll the dice pool.
- **Free Advice Is Seldom Cheap:** Increase the Difficulty of all Social Conflict to persuade DaiMon Skel by 2. This Difficulty increase is removed as soon as Skel is offered something in trade.
- **You Can't Make a Deal If You're Dead:** Skel will never make a lethal attack. Further, whenever attempting a Task to make a deal or otherwise persuade an enemy who he has previously incapacitated, or an enemy who obviously outmatches him, he may add a bonus d20 to the roll.

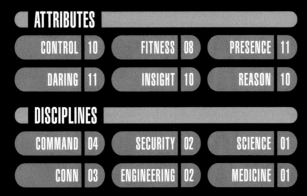

ALIENS AND ADVERSARIES
CARDASSIAN UNION

The Cardassian Union was a once peaceful civilization that developed into a militaristic power to acquire new territories to support their resource-poor world. Three decades of hostilities with the Federation have only recently ceased with a signing of a treaty that established a demilitarized zone between the two powers.

CARDASSIAN SOLDIER [MINOR NPC]

The Cardassian soldier can be found operating in many different posts throughout the Union such as ground troops, crewman, or enforcing laws across their territories.

TRAITS: Cardassian

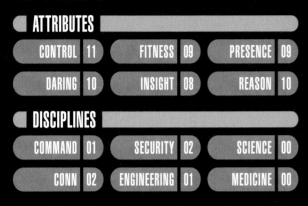

ATTRIBUTES

CONTROL	11	FITNESS	09	PRESENCE	09
DARING	10	INSIGHT	08	REASON	10

DISCIPLINES

COMMAND	01	SECURITY	02	SCIENCE	00
CONN	02	ENGINEERING	01	MEDICINE	00

STRESS: 11   **RESISTANCE:** 1

ATTACKS:

- Unarmed Strike (Melee, 3🔺 Knockdown, Size 1H, Non-lethal)
- Disruptor Pistol (Ranged, 5🔺 Vicious 1, Size 1H)
- **Escalation** Disruptor Rifle (Ranged, 6🔺 Vicious 1, Size 2H, Accurate)

SPECIAL RULES:

- **Ambushes and Traps:** Whenever a Cardassian uses the Ready Task to ready a Ranged attack, that Ranged attack gains one bonus d20.
- **Loyal and Disciplined:** Whenever a Cardassian receives assistance from a superior on a Task, the Cardassian may re-roll a single d20.

CARDASSIAN GLINN [NOTABLE NPC]

The Cardassian glinn is a high-ranking Union officer fulfilling a post equivalent to a Starfleet commander. The Cardassian military structure has two glinn reporting to each gul with their duties shared between them.

TRAITS: Cardassian

VALUE: Cardassians Did Not Choose to Be Superior, Fate Made Us This Way.

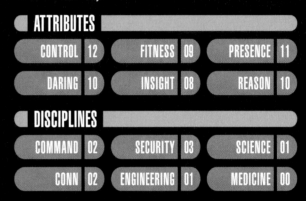

ATTRIBUTES

CONTROL	12	FITNESS	09	PRESENCE	11
DARING	10	INSIGHT	08	REASON	10

DISCIPLINES

COMMAND	02	SECURITY	03	SCIENCE	01
CONN	02	ENGINEERING	01	MEDICINE	00

FOCUSES: Military Tactics, Willpower

STRESS: 12   **RESISTANCE:** 1

ATTACKS:

- Unarmed Strike (Melee, 4🔺 Knockdown, Size 1H, Non-lethal)
- Disruptor Pistol (Ranged, 6🔺 Vicious 1, Size 1H)
- **Escalation** Disruptor Rifle (Ranged, 7🔺 Vicious 1, Size 2H, Accurate)

SPECIAL RULES:

- **Ambushes and Traps:** Whenever a Cardassian uses the Ready Task to ready a ranged attack, that ranged attack gains one bonus d20.
- **Expects Success:** Whenever a glinn uses the Direct or Assist Task to aid a subordinate, that Task may always Succeed at Cost.
- **Loyal and Disciplined:** Whenever a Cardassian receives assistance from a superior on a Task, the Cardassian may re-roll a single d20.

GUL TREMAK [MAJOR NPC]

A Cardassian gul is the commanding officer of a starship or installation within the Cardassian Union. Experienced Guls may be assigned increased duties such as planetary governor to any one of their annexed planets.

TRAITS: Cardassian

VALUES:
- Cardassia Expects Everyone to Do Their Duty
- Knowledge is Power, and Power is Everything

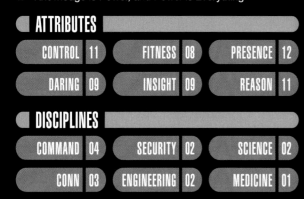

ATTRIBUTES

| CONTROL | 11 | FITNESS | 08 | PRESENCE | 12 |
| DARING | 09 | INSIGHT | 09 | REASON | 11 |

DISCIPLINES

| COMMAND | 04 | SECURITY | 02 | SCIENCE | 02 |
| CONN | 03 | ENGINEERING | 02 | MEDICINE | 01 |

FOCUSES: Debate, Military Tactics, Politics, Willpower

STRESS: 10   **RESISTANCE:** 1 (Armor)

ATTACKS:
- Unarmed Strike (Melee, 3▲ Knockdown, Size 1H, Non-lethal)
- Disruptor Pistol (Ranged, 5▲ Vicious 1, Size 1H)
- Escalation Disruptor Rifle (Ranged, 6▲ Vicious 1, Size 2H, Accurate)

SPECIAL RULES:
- **Ambushes and Traps:** Whenever a Cardassian uses the Ready Task to ready a ranged attack, that ranged attack gains one bonus d20.
- **Cultured:** When engaged in Social Conflict, and given an opportunity to speak at length on a subject, Gul Tremak may re-roll his dice pool if he purchases any bonus d20s.
- **Loyal and Disciplined:** Whenever a Cardassian receives assistance from a superior on a Task, the Cardassian may re-roll a single d20.
- **Ruthless:** Gul Tremak may re-roll any d20s in his dice pool when making an attack against an enemy that was not aware of or prepared for an attack, or against an enemy that is defenseless.

CARDASSIAN CHARACTERS

Cardassians are tall, grey-skinned humanoids with pronounced ridges on their bodies and faces. Their culture demands absolute loyalty to family and to the state — with Cardassian morality plays often depicting conflicts between familial loyalty and loyalty to the state — and they prize individual cunning, self-control, and the ability to endure hardship. Cardassians are a secretive people, even amongst close friends and family, and being suspicious and skeptical of others is regarded as wise and prudent. They value educational attainment and knowledge, and they are fond of conversation and lively debate. They are frequently regarded as domineering, ruthless, arrogant, and duplicitous. Cardassian characters have the following modifiers:

- **ATTRIBUTES:** +1 Control, +1 Presence, +1 Reason

- **TRAIT:** Cardassian. Cardassians possess extraordinary mental discipline, and commonly have photographic memories, the result of intense training during childhood. They are intolerant of cold environments, but quite comfortable at higher temperatures. Cardassian hearing is slightly less acute than that of Humans, and they are uncomfortable in bright light. Cardassians have a negative reputation amongst many Alpha Quadrant cultures, particularly Bajorans, whose homeworld they occupied for decades.

ALIENS AND ADVERSARIES
THE DOMINION

Established over 10,000 years ago, the Dominion is an interstellar power originating in the Gamma Quadrant that seeks to bring order to the Galaxy through diplomacy and subjugation. Ruled by the Founders, a species of shape changing aliens, and served by their genetically engineered subordinates, the Dominion has influence over hundreds of worlds and their civilizations.

JEM'HADAR WARRIOR [MINOR NPC]

Created solely for combat, the Jem'Hadar are the Dominion's main military force. Each warrior is reliant on ketracel-white, an addictive narcotic supplied by the Vorta that provides them with all their nutritional needs. Withdrawal from this drug causes pain, madness, and eventually death ensuring the absolute loyalty of the Jem'Hadar to the Dominion.

TRAITS: Jem'Hadar

ATTRIBUTES

| CONTROL | 10 | FITNESS | 12 | PRESENCE | 07 |
| DARING | 11 | INSIGHT | 10 | REASON | 07 |

DISCIPLINES

| COMMAND | 01 | SECURITY | 02 | SCIENCE | 00 |
| CONN | 02 | ENGINEERING | 01 | MEDICINE | 00 |

STRESS: 14   RESISTANCE: 2

ATTACKS:
- Unarmed Strike (Melee, 3🅐 Knockdown, Vicious 1, Size 1H)
- Blade (Melee, 4🅐 Vicious 1, Size 1H)
- Escalation *Kar'takin* (Melee, 5🅐 Vicious 1, Size 2H)
- Plasma Rifle (Ranged, 6🅐 Vicious 1, Size 2H, Accurate, Debilitating)

SPECIAL RULES:
- Immune to Fear
- Immune to Pain
- Brute Force: Jem'Hadar add the Vicious 1 effect to their Unarmed Strike, and remove the Non-lethal Quality.
- The Shroud: A Jem'Hadar may spend 2 Threat as a Minor Action to become virtually invisible, increasing the Difficulty of all Tasks to observe, locate, or target the Jem'Hadar by three. This effect ends when the Jem'Hadar makes an attack, or takes a Minor Action to end the effect. The Jem'Hadar loses this ability when deprived of ketracel-white.

JEM'HADAR FIRST [NOTABLE NPC]

Each unit of Jem'Hadar is commanded by a First who reports directly to the Vorta. While still held under the sway of ketracel-white addiction, a Jem'Hadar First is authorised to distribute the drug to its unit, when it is provided by their Vorta.

TRAITS: Jem'Hadar

VALUE: We Are Now Dead; We Go into Battle to Reclaim Our Lives

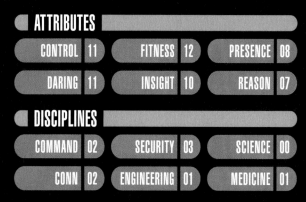

ATTRIBUTES

CONTROL 11	FITNESS 12	PRESENCE 08
DARING 11	INSIGHT 10	REASON 07

DISCIPLINES

COMMAND 02	SECURITY 03	SCIENCE 00
CONN 02	ENGINEERING 01	MEDICINE 01

FOCUSES: Combat Tactics, Hand-to-Hand

STRESS: 15   **RESISTANCE:** 2

ATTACKS:
- Unarmed Strike (Melee, 4▲ Knockdown, Vicious 1, Size 1H)
- Blade (Melee, 5▲ Vicious 1, Size 1H)
- Escalation *Kar'takin* (Melee, 6▲ Vicious 1, Size 2H)
- Plasma Rifle (Ranged, 7▲ Vicious 1, Size 2H, Accurate, Debilitating)

SPECIAL RULES:
- **Immune to Fear**
- **Immune to Pain**
- **Brute Force:** Jem'Hadar add the Vicious 1 effect to their Unarmed Strike, and remove the Non-lethal quality.
- **The Shroud:** A Jem'Hadar may spend 2 Threat as a Minor Action to become virtually invisible, increasing the Difficulty of all Tasks to observe, locate, or target the Jem'Hadar by three. This effect ends when the Jem'Hadar makes an attack, or takes a Minor Action to end the effect. The Jem'Hadar loses this ability when deprived of ketracel-white.
- **Victory is Life:** Whenever a Jem'Hadar First or one of its subordinates inflicts an Injury or achieves an objective, add 1 to Threat.

TARIS, VORTA OVERSEER [MAJOR NPC]

The Vorta are a genetically engineered race created by the Founders to act as diplomats, scientists, and commanders for the day to day running of the Dominion. Through a complex cloning process, any Vorta killed can return with all its original memories although its personality may change.

TRAITS: Vorta

VALUES:
- I Live to Serve the Founders
- There Is Nothing I Will Not Do to Succeed

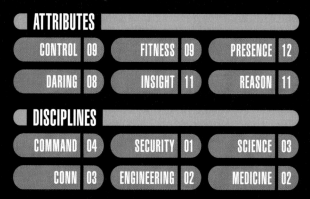

ATTRIBUTES

CONTROL 09	FITNESS 09	PRESENCE 12
DARING 08	INSIGHT 11	REASON 11

DISCIPLINES

COMMAND 04	SECURITY 01	SCIENCE 03
CONN 03	ENGINEERING 02	MEDICINE 02

FOCUSES: Deception, Diplomacy, Observation, Psychology

STRESS: 10   **RESISTANCE:** 0

ATTACKS:
- Unarmed Strike (Melee, 2▲ Knockdown, Size 1H, Non-lethal)

SPECIAL RULES:
- **In the Name of the Founders:** When using the Direct or Assist Task to command other servants of the Dominion, a Vorta may roll 2d20 instead of 1d20.
- **Manipulative:** If Taris purchases one or more d20s when attempting a Task to deceive or intimidate another, she may re-roll her dice pool.
- **Termination Implant:** If a Vorta is captured, they may commit suicide by triggering a termination implant. This requires a Minor Action, and kills the Vorta immediately.

The Dominion is made up of many worlds and many species, but the most prominent are beings created by the Founders themselves, engineered to serve specific roles within the Dominion. These are the Jem'Hadar and the Vorta.

JEM'HADAR

The Jem'Hadar are genetically-engineered life-forms, created to serve as the military of the Dominion. Bred in birthing chambers, rather than born naturally, they grow to maturity in three days, developing complex reasoning and language skills within a day of birth. Once mature, they do not eat, drink, or sleep, taking all nourishment from the drug ketracel-white, often simply known as "the white," which is distributed to them by their Vorta overseer as a means of ensuring loyalty. Few Jem'Hadar live for longer than fifteen years due simply to battlefield casualties, with those living to twenty being regarded as 'Elders.' Jem'Hadar characters have the following modifiers:

- **ATTRIBUTES:** +1 Daring, +1 Fitness, +1 Insight

- **TRAIT:** Jem'Hadar. Individual Jem'Hadar are physically powerful, and far stronger and more resilient than Humans. They also have exceptionally keen eyesight, and act utterly without fear or hesitation in battle. They do not regard death with any apprehension, and are extremely aggressive, limited only by their absolute obedience to the Founders and the Vorta.

VORTA

The Vorta are genetically-engineered life-forms, created to serve as advisors, scientists, diplomats, and overseers for the Dominion, acting as the Founders' closest servants and foremost representatives. Vorta are cloned, in batches of identical beings, with a new clone being activated and placed into service upon the death of a predecessor, receiving the memories of those that came before them, though each clone is nevertheless a distinct individual. Vorta are extremely cunning and clever, but have little creativity or sense of aesthetics. Vorta characters have the following modifiers:

- **ATTRIBUTES:** +1 Insight, +1 Presence, +1 Reason

- **TRAIT:** Vorta. Vorta have extremely keen hearing, but relatively poor eyesight. They are immune to most forms of poison. Vorta are absolutely loyal to the Dominion, revering the Founders as living gods. Those who encounter the Vorta often regard them as insincere or manipulative.

UNKNOWN ALIEN ARTIFACT ANALYSIS

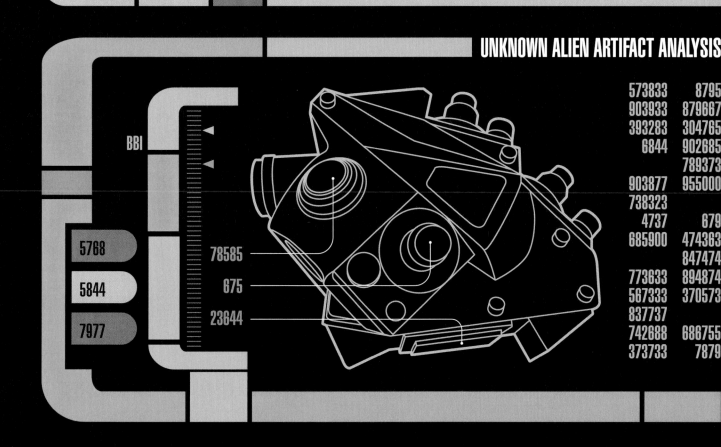

BBI

5768

5844

7977

78585

675

23644

573833   8795
903933   879667
393283   304765
6844   902685
  789373
903877   955000
738323
4737   679
685900   474363
  847474
773633   894874
567333   370573
837737
742688   686755
373733   7879

ALIEN ARTIFACTS

Countless sentient species have existed in our own Galaxy and presumably in many other galaxies. The oldest evolved billions of years ago, and many have become extinct, evolved beyond physical bodies, or vanished to some unknown fate. Some of these species never managed to travel beyond their own world, others could traverse thousands of light years in less than a second, but all of them were as unique, complex, and diverse as any of the species in our own Federation.

Most of these species left behind artifacts, ranging in complexity from stone tools to vast constructs well beyond our ability to duplicate or even fully comprehend. While universities and institutes within the Federation regularly send out archaeological expeditions to search for ruins and artifacts, Starfleet also maintains an interest in alien artifacts, both because of their archaeological importance and because some can provide valuable information about new technologies. One of the duties of any Starfleet crew is identifying and preserving newly discovered alien artifacts, and when possible, entire archaeological sites.

ANCIENT TECHNOLOGY

While many archaeologists are thrilled to find alien pottery or hand-made gears, Starfleet, and many other organizations both inside and outside of the Federation are most interested in alien artifacts created by civilizations that were either more technologically advanced than the Federation or had made discoveries that the Federation missed. Even a civilization or species considerably less advanced than the Federation may have learned techniques or developed technologies unknown to anyone else. For example, while the inhabitants of the now destroyed world of Sarpeidon lacked warp drive or most other technologies related to space travel, they excelled at time travel technologies. Entire academic disciplines, like archaeological medicine, focus on understanding and learning to use these alien discoveries.

Of course, many of these rediscovered techniques and technologies are quite valuable. In addition to Starfleet and professional archaeologists, smugglers, collectors, revolutionaries, and operatives of governments that are not allied with the Federation also regularly investigate potentially useful alien technologies. Starfleet personnel who encounter ancient technologies must be prepared to defend them, or, if no other option exists, to destroy them to prevent them from falling into the wrong hands. The following are some of the more impressive examples of alien technology discovered by the Federation.

EXO III ANDROID DUPLICATOR

Originally discovered in 2261 by renowned medical archaeologist Doctor Roger Korby, the Federation only learned of this device 5 years later, on Stardate 2712.4, when Captain James T. Kirk and Nurse Christine Chapel visited Exo III and learned the fate of the Korby expedition. This device was constructed millennia ago by the inhabitants of Exo III and possesses several different modes of operation. In its simplest mode, it can be used to create androids that seem sentient, but are bound to obey orders from authorized personnel. These androids can be made as exact physical duplicates of specific individuals or the creator can set their appearance as desired. The creator can then either give the android general programming or provide the android with the memories of a single individual who must be scanned by the android duplicator. These non-sentient androids have a relatively limited range of behaviour. Also, while initially emotionless, over time they can develop rudimentary, but erratic emotions, but possess no moral sense at all, making them potentially quite dangerous.

The android duplicator can also be set to physically copy an individual and then download the individual's consciousness into it. This process is fatal to the individual, but the android produced using this process is mentally far more complex than the other androids the device can produce. In most ways, it seems and acts just like the original person, but suffers from impaired conscience and morality, as well as an overly mechanistic and deterministic style of thought.

Creating an android using this device is a relatively straightforward process. The duplicator itself is a rotating circular platform that is divided in two halves. On one half, the operator places a roughly humanoid shaped android template. If the operator wishes to physically or mentally duplicate a person, that person must be placed on the other half of the platform. Using the control panel located nearby, the operator first either shapes the android's body based on specifications he inputs or transforms the android template into an exact physical duplicate of the individual being duplicated. The android seems to possess the same pulse, body temperature, skin texture, and all other external features of the duplicated person. Next, the operator can choose to copy the memories of the individual being duplicated. This process causes the subject pain, but no significant or lasting harm. Transferring the subject's consciousness into the android is a more extensive procedure, but the operator can perform this transfer immediately following memory duplication. While all active androids were destroyed when the *Enterprise* visited Exo III, the duplicator and the entire underground complex it is in remains intact and deactivated androids may remain in remote portions of the underground complex.

Ongoing Research: Science teams began studying the android duplicator shortly after the *Enterprise* visited Exo III in 2266, and now know a great deal about the duplicator and the androids it produces. However, they have made little progress in understanding why the process of transferring sentient consciousness into an android body compromises both morality and mental flexibility. All that is currently known is that androids like Lieutenant Commander Data are significantly more mentally complex than the most sophisticated androids this device can produce. However, records of the *Enterprise*'s visit indicate that at least some of the androids produced by the alien "Old Ones" who created this device may have been fully sentient beings. Other than the ancient android Ruk, who was destroyed, no such androids have yet been found and, so far, and researchers have been unable to produce one. If discovered, approach these androids with extreme caution, they are substantially stronger, faster, and more agile than most humanoids and can be exceedingly deadly.

ICONIAN GATEWAY

More than 200,000 years ago, aliens known as the Iconians created a series of gateways that allowed them to see or travel anywhere in the Galaxy. The Federation has discovered two working Iconian gateways, one on the dead world of Iconia, and another on Vandros IV in the Gamma Quadrant. Until the discovery of the first gateway, the Iconians were believed to be mythic beings, called "demons of air and darkness" in ancient legends. The Federation now knows that the Iconians used their gateways to build a vast interstellar empire. The two gateways discovered so far were quite different in design, but identical in function. Each could create a field that served as a window or doorway to another location. Passing through this doorway only required stepping through it and the doorway was visible and useable from the other side, appearing as a faintly glowing rectangle though which the gateway room could be seen. In its default configuration, the gateway rapidly cycled through a series of different destinations, but the operator can tune it to any location within the Galaxy. As a possible security feature, the gateway on Vandros IV was located in a pyramid made of neutronium, which protected it from all known forms of orbital attack. Also, the gateway generated a damping field that prevented the use of energy weapons in or near the pyramid.

Ongoing Research: Both gateways were destroyed to prevent them from falling into enemy hands. In addition, all information other than the memories of those who encountered the first gateway was deliberately erased, and only limited knowledge was gained from the second gateway before it too was destroyed. Federation researchers look forward to discovering a third functional Iconian gateway, since it might lead to important advances in transporter technology, possibly including transporters with an interstellar range. However, the presence of even a single functional Iconian Gateway is both an important opportunity for the Federation and also a grave danger if it falls into the hands of a hostile species.

KALANDAN OUTPOST

A humanoid species known as the Kalandans constructed this outpost and the planet it is on several thousand years ago. Starfleet believes the Kalandans became extinct soon after this, because of a deadly plague accidentally created on this world. The planet is roughly the size of Earth's moon, but of much greater mass and so possesses earth-like gravity and a breathable Class M atmosphere. However, the world is not considered habitable, because the vegetation is poisonous and there is no easily available water, except within the Kalandan outpost, located beneath the world's surface. This world and the outpost were discovered by the *Starship Enterprise* in 2268.

The entire world was constructed by the Kalandans. Except for a layer of soil on the surface, the entire world is made from an exceptionally durable alloy of diburnium-osmium that interferes with sensor scans of the outpost. While superficially resembling a waterless world with sparse vegetation, this planet contains a concealed subsurface base that utilizes an immense, but so-far unknown, power source. This base is run by a computer that seems to be almost sentient. When fully operational, this computer could transport a starship almost 1,000 light years away in an instant, understand and sabotage complex machinery, and create temporary animated physical projections programmed to kill a single individual by disrupting all of their cells with a single brief touch. The computer used these abilities to execute the outpost's automated defense routines.

This computer also seems to have been able to either read minds or access Starfleet data banks. Also, all of the physical projections it created were based on a single individual, Losira, the station's long dead commander, and included an excellent simulation of her thoughts, memories, and emotions, indicating that the computer was exceptionally complex. When the crew of the *Enterprise* encountered this world, Captain James Kirk was forced to order the computer partially disabled, which prevented it from creating additional projections or transporting starships, but it still maintains a minimal level of function.

STONE OF GOL

The Stone of Gol is not like most weapons. Only psychics can use it, and in the hands of a psychic it is simple to use. If the wielder can clearly see or otherwise sense the target, she can use the weapon on the target and only needs to succeed at a **Control + Science Task** with a Difficulty of 1 to hit any visible target. No form of armor or force shield can protect the target from harm. If the target is wielding a weapon, arguing loudly, or otherwise experiencing strong violent thoughts or emotions, the weapon is automatically fatal, with no need for a damage roll. The only defense is for the target to calm their thoughts and emotions and be at peace. To accomplish this, the target cannot hold a weapon, act or speak in an aggressive fashion, or perform any action more strenuous than talking calmly or moving at a normal walking pace. The target must also succeed at a **Control + Command Task** with a Difficulty of 0. Not attempting to resist this weapon is automatically fatal. Using this weapon requires no effort unless the target manages to successfully resist the attack. If this happens, the wielder automatically suffers one point of Stress, which recovers at the end of the scene.

Ongoing Research: While the computer is damaged, some of the outpost's equipment still functions and the outpost is currently being studied. In addition, Federation geologists are examining this world in an effort to learn more about how the Kalandans managed to construct an entire planet.

MIND SWAP DEVICE

Located on Camus II, in the largely intact ruins of an ancient civilization, this device appears to be a large carved panel, roughly 2 meters wide and almost 3 meters high. This device is capable of temporarily transferring the minds of two subjects. This transference normally lasts for slightly less than 50 hours and the only method of prolonging it, short of a second use of the device, is the death of one of the subjects, at which point the other subject remains in their new body permanently.

It appears that this device was designed so it could be used without the permission of both subjects. When activated, the panel's carvings light up and the device instantly immobilizes anyone who comes too close to the front of the panel. The device then forces this person's body against this panel. To effect the transfer, the other subject first operates the controls on the side of the device and then stands next to the trapped subject on the panel. At this point, the device rapidly switches the two subjects' minds. The device is sufficiently precise that subjects immediately understand how to use each other's bodies, and retain none of the body's original memories. This device was originally discovered by disgraced scientist Janice Lester and she used it to temporarily steal Captain James T. Kirk's body on Stardate 5928.5.

Ongoing Research: This device, along with the other ruins on Camus II are part of an ongoing archaeological investigation, and while Federation researchers can operate this device, they have yet to understand how it functions. The abundant deposits of celebium, a highly radioactive material that is deadly to almost all humanoids, hampers research on this world.

THE STONE OF GOL

Named for the ancient Vulcan city of Gol, this psychic weapon was created long before Surak led the Vulcan people into their Time of Awakening. This weapon can be safely disassembled into three pieces, and when assembled forms a relatively flat, wide device that requires two hands to operate and is approximately 25 cm in diameter and 8 cm thick. This weapon creates a wave of psychic force that appears in front of the target and amplifies the target's violent thoughts and emotions. These emotions then boost the wave of psychic force until it overwhelms the target's body, killing the target and hurling their body backwards. Only psychics can operate this weapon. However, it can be used against any living being, and cannot be stopped by walls, force fields, or any other physical defenses. Given the great range of most psychic powers, it is also likely that this weapon could be lethal even if the wielder was far from the target, but the wielder must be able to see or otherwise sense the target's presence, and it can only be used against one target at a time.

The only defense against the Stone of Gol is to calmly cease all thoughts of anger or violence, at which point the weapon cannot harm the target. A hint about this defense is revealed by the fact that the main body of the device contains three glyphs representing the Vulcan gods of war, peace, and death, with the glyph for peace located between the other two, symbolizing that peace is the only way to survive an attack with this weapon. Successful attacks do not seem to exact any price from the user, but failed attacks, where the target resists the weapon's effects, seem at least moderately tiring or stressful, perhaps due to some form of psychic feedback.

Ongoing Research: Captain Picard of the *Starship Enterprise* turned the Stone of Gol over to the V'Shar (Vulcan Intelligence), who claimed they would destroy it. However, its discovery renewed interest in psychic devices. Many researchers have requested information about it and hope to find other psychic devices created during Vulcan's ancient warlike past. Legends seem to indicate that the Stone of Gol was unique, but there is no proof of this.

ALIEN ARTIFACTS

While many researchers dream of unearthing new technologies that can save lives, advance science, or even revolutionize the entire Federation, some artifacts created by species with advanced technologies are either too advanced, no longer functional, or are otherwise not suitable for any current researchers to learn how they work. However, this limitation does not mean that these artifacts are devoid of interest. Some can be useful as they are, while others may eventually provide information about lost cultures or sentient species very different from any the Federation has contact with. In addition, just because no one can currently understand an artifact does not mean that some future researcher will not be able to. Also, never forget that knowledge is valuable even if it does not provide immediate benefit. Every new artifact you recover and every extinct culture you discover enriches the Federation's knowledge of the universe and of the many sentient species that have inhabited it.

AMUSEMENT PARK PLANET

Located in the Omicron Delta region, this planet was first discovered on stardate 3025.3 by the *Starship Enterprise*, commanded by Captain James T. Kirk. To all but the most intensive scans, this world appears to be a pristine, almost park-like planet that would be considered Class M, except for its lack of all forms of animal life. With its pleasant

SUPPLEMENTAL REPORT

DEPARTMENT OF TEMPORAL INVESTIGATIONS
LIEUTENANT COMMANDER ROBERTA TANAKA
STARDATE 28063.6

Further investigation has revealed that the three individuals who were apprehended while attempting to gain access to the Guardian of Forever were all Vulcan separatists. The jury-rigged cloaking device used by their shuttle may hint at some connection to the Romulans. None of the three have revealed what time and place they were attempting to gain access to, and continued investigation of this incident seems to me to be a high priority.

temperatures, clean air and water, and lush vegetation, it is ideal for visitors from Earth or similar planets.

During the course of the crews shore leave it was discovered that an unknown species massively altered this planet. Beneath its surface lie vast caverns filled with complex machinery, all of which is dedicated to providing for the needs, wishes, and entertainment of visitors. Using highly advanced technology, the planet can create anything from a delicious picnic lunch to an army of well-armed pre-Industrial Klingon warriors. Objects created by the planet appear to be completely real; food is edible and nutritious, devices are fully functional, and created sentient beings seem intelligent, if also singularly focused on fulfilling the purpose they were created for.

The machinery on this planet learns visitors' desires using detailed automated telepathy, which is undetectable by any Federation telepaths. Because it creates anything visitors are thinking intently about, this planet is not without temporary risks. If someone sees a rock formation that vividly reminds them of the time they were pursued and almost eaten by a large carnivorous theropod, they are almost certain to find themselves pursued by an equally hungry-seeming duplicate of that creature. However, while the planet's machinery contains no safeties to prevent injury or even death, the subsurface complexes also contain exceedingly advanced medical facilities that can swiftly repair any injuries or illnesses suffered on the planet, and even revive the recently deceased. Visitors who are killed or badly injured soon regain consciousness in one of these subsurface complexes. Researchers are uncertain exactly how these patients and the objects and people that the planet creates are moved so rapidly.

Ongoing Research: In addition to remaining a popular destination for tourists and starship crews on shore leave, this planet is also subject to ongoing research. Unfortunately, the world's caretaker is unwilling to share this planet's technology with the Federation or any other species known

to have visited it. Visitors who either request admittance to the subsurface caverns or who suffer injury or death are allowed to marvel at the wonders of the vast underground machines, but powerful force fields prevent anyone from getting too close or using advanced sensors to gain detailed knowledge of the technology.

D'ARSAY ARCHIVE

This ancient archive initially appeared to be a rogue comet that left the D'Arsay system more than 87 million years ago and was discovered by the *Starship Enterprise* on Stardate 47615.2. During its long years in space, it became surrounded by a shell of ice and frozen gas, but the archive itself is an angular, three-dimensional construct that looks like a series of platforms, constructed from fortanium and a variety of unknown materials. The archive is slightly more than 1.5 kilometres high and roughly 900 m wide and 600 m deep. While the archive's full contents remain uncertain, it is known to contain extensive information on at least one D'Arsay mythological cycle. This myth cycle focuses on the cruel and regal sun-goddess Masaka and the moon god Korgano who hunts and pursues her. The archive contains

detailed simulations of the personalities of hundreds or perhaps thousands of different mythic figures that live in or are associated with Masaka's city. The archive seems unwilling or unable to create the bodies of sentients, but can imprint these personalities on an android.

Before the *Starship Enterprise* disabled the transformation program, the archive was able to use sensor scans to imprint its knowledge on the starship scanning it, use the starship's replicators to create artifacts from Masaka's city, and eventually, to use an unknown and highly advanced technology to transform the material of that starship into duplicates of portions of Masaka's city. Shutting down the transformation program did not harm the archive or the information contained within it, but it did prevent the archive from being able to suborn Federation technology and transform nearby matter into duplicates of the locations and objects in the mythological locations it records. The purpose of the archive is currently unknown, as is the reason it was sent into space and the fate of the species who created it.

Ongoing Research: A Federation archaeological team is currently examining the D'Arsay archive and hope to be able to find a way to safely access it. One plan involves attempting to connect it to a holodeck or holosuite, while isolating this holosuite from all other systems.

DYSON SPHERE

First discovered by the *U.S.S. Jenolan* in 2294, this vast construct was first reported to the Federation 75 years later, on Stardate 46125.3. This object is the largest artificial construct known to the Federation, with a diameter of 200 million kilometers. It is built around G class star LV426 and has a surface area more than 250 million times that of Earth. Constructed by an unknown species, the sphere's age is currently uncertain, but it is believed to be exceedingly old. The sphere's interior surface was designed to be habitable. It has artificial gravity, a breathable, Class M atmosphere, vast oceans, and land that shows evidence of thriving vegetation and presumably abundant animal life. However, there is no evidence of sentient inhabitants, presumably because they evacuated when LV426 became exceedingly unstable and began producing frequent flares and coronal mass ejections. If any sentient beings remain on the interior of the Dyson sphere, they have found a way to protect themselves from the flares. Unless visiting when the star is relatively quiet, any starship venturing inside the sphere will need to maintain full shields during periods of stellar instability.

The sphere is constructed from carbon-neutronium, and is several kilometers thick. The sphere also possesses several enormous access portals. Each one is roughly two kilometers wide and contains an automated entry system that uses four powerful tractor beams to bring nearby ships inside when the portal detects broadcasts directed at it. Researchers have not yet learned how to open these doors from the inside, meaning that any ship entering will need another ship or shuttlecraft outside that can open the doors for it. Also, the tractor beams' resonant frequency is incompatible with Federation power systems, necessitating special precautions to avoid serious damage to the power systems of any starship entering the sphere.

Ongoing Research: The Dyson sphere is currently under study, but the instability of the interior star, combined with the object's massive size has caused progress to be quite slow. Even the most preliminary sensor scan of the interior requires more than 7 hours, and a detailed scan of the entire interior would require many years. Any inhabitants who have sheltered themselves from the stellar flares would likely only be detected with such a detailed scan.

THE GUARDIAN OF FOREVER

The Federation made one of its greatest finds in 2267, when the *Starship Enterprise* discovered the Guardian of Forever. The Guardian of Forever is located on an ancient Class M planet that was last inhabited many millions, or perhaps even billions of years in the past. Although it appears to be a roughly carved ring of stone in the middle of vast ruins, it can allow visitors to view or travel to any time and space in the Galaxy. Because of the vast potential for misuse or accident, access to the Guardian is strictly controlled by the Department of Temporal Investigations.

GOMTUU

Gomtuu is a living starship, created or perhaps befriended by an unknown humanoid alien species. It is a slightly flattened ovoid approximately half a kilometer long and 300 meters wide. Its interior contains many passages and chambers, which have a Class M atmosphere. Gomtuu can alter its interior to suit the needs and wishes of its crew, creating furniture and changing its interior structure at will. It is also a starship of remarkable power. Gomtuu can create shockwaves capable of destroying starships or deliberately moving them unharmed at warp speeds and can also create powerful shields and produce a transporter-like effect that functions through Federation shields and has a range of more than a billion kilometers. While it was created, or perhaps evolved, as a vessel, Gomtuu is also a fully sentient organism. It is many thousands of years old and may be from another Galaxy. It remembers millions of its kind, but has not seen any in millennia, either because they are extinct or perhaps because they are a in another Galaxy. Gomtuu was last seen in the company of Betazoid telepathic savant Tam Elbrun. Elbrun chose to remain on board Gomtuu, replacing its long dead crew, whose loss Gomtuu mourned.

Ongoing Research: Because of its highly-advanced technology, many Federation researchers wish to examine Gomtuu's interior and learn how its various systems function. However, Gomtuu's current location is unknown. At this point, researchers hope that Gomtuu either decides to communicate with the Federation or that Starfleet encounters another living spacecraft of the same type, which is more interested in permitting examination and sharing technological information.

PLANET KILLER

The *Starship Enterprise* encountered this ancient and devastating weapon on Stardate 4202.9. It was approximately four kilometers long, one kilometer in diameter at its widest point, and roughly cone-shaped. Its hull was made of solid neutronium and is impenetrable to all known weapons, including quantum torpedoes. The planet killer also generated intense subspace interference throughout the star system it is currently in. This interference blocks all interstellar communications and reduces the range and clarity of sensors. This field also dampens energy and transforms antimatter to normal matter. The planet killer's only vulnerability is that it is designed to consume rocks and other materials, including starships. Setting off a vast explosion inside it by allowing it to engulf a starship whose impulse engines were set to overload rendered it harmless by destroying all components, except its neutronium hull.

The planet killer appeared to be ancient, fully automated and entirely self-sustaining. It was programmed to fire a massive anti-proton beam at habitable or inhabited planets, reducing them to rubble and then scooping up this rubble to refuel its total conversion drive, which transformed matter to energy without requiring the addition of antimatter. It was also attracted to relatively nearby starships and similar objects that emit large amounts of energy and could defend itself against attack. Starfleet believes that this device was created as an automated weapon in a genocidal war that continued destroying planets long after this war ended. Its course indicates that it came from another Galaxy, but no other information about its origin is known. Although Captain James T. Kirk destroyed the one known planet killer, some Starfleet officials worry that the Federation may someday encounter another.

Ongoing Research: While the explosion destroyed all of the planet killer's weapons, power, and control systems, its vast neutronium hull remains intact, and researchers have extensively explored it. This research focuses on attempting to learn more about how the planet killer functioned and other means of deactivating it, as well as discovering how a civilization managed to create such a vast structure from neutronium.

PLANET KILLER

Planet killer's neutronium armor is completely immune to all Federation weapons. Also, the planet killer's maw can absorb almost any energy or matter. However, extremely large explosions, like overloading a starship's impulse engines or detonating a large starship's warp core just inside the planet killer's maw will destroy it. The only other techniques that might destroy it require extreme stellar events, like supernovas, black holes, or causing the planet killer to crash into a star.

TRAITS: Planet Killer, Living Ship, Impervious

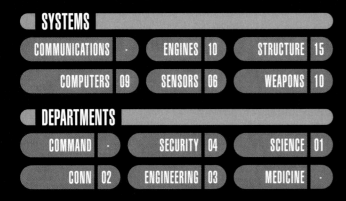

SYSTEMS

| COMMUNICATIONS | - | ENGINES | 10 | STRUCTURE | 15 |
| COMPUTERS | 09 | SENSORS | 06 | WEAPONS | 10 |

DEPARTMENTS

| COMMAND | - | SECURITY | 04 | SCIENCE | 01 |
| CONN | 02 | ENGINEERING | 03 | MEDICINE | - |

POWER: Infinite **SCALE:** 12
SHIELDS: None **RESISTANCE:** Infinite

CREW: Special

ATTACKS:
- Anti-Proton Beam (Energy, Range M, 12▲ Vicious 1, Devastating, High-Yield)

SPECIAL RULES:
- **Invulnerable:** The Planet Killer cannot suffer any damage or Breaches from attacks from outside the hull. Only massive explosive forces – such as a warp core or reactor explosion – inside it, or extreme stellar conditions such as a black hole or supernova, can destroy it. This may require a Task, Challenge or Extended Task to arrange.
- **Living Ship:** The Planet Killer does not have a crew; any Task it performs uses only its Systems and Departments, rolling 3d20 instead of the normal 2d20 (bonus dice can be purchased as normal). If the Task it performs would not normally be assisted by a ship, roll using the Planet Killer's Computers and Engineering.
- **Power Source:** The Planet Killer has an unlimited amount of Power. Further, it generates massive amounts of interference, counting as a complication: *Subspace Interference 3*, which applies across the entire star system the Planet Killer is currently in. Finally, that interference produces an energy dampening effect, causing any ships within Long range to lose 2 Power at the start of each Round.

ALIENS AND ADVERSARIES
BEASTS OF THE GALAXY

Finding yourself at the mercy of life in the Galaxy is never a position a starship captain should find themselves in. This section should help you understand a creature's strengths and weaknesses, including how to exploit them.

TARG [MINOR NPC]

Akin to large, furry terran boar, *targs* are known for being vicious and destructive animals, perfect as Klingon pets. When not kept as companions, the targ is known to be a Klingon delicacy, with the heart being eaten as a traditional dish known to bring courage. *Targs* have long lifespans, living for upwards of multiple decades if not hunted, and are traditionally known for hiding in dirt when threatened.

TRAITS: Targ

ATTRIBUTES

CONTROL 04	FITNESS 11	PRESENCE 08
DARING 10	INSIGHT 05	REASON 02

DISCIPLINES

COMMAND 02	SECURITY 02	SCIENCE -
CONN -	ENGINEERING -	MEDICINE -

STRESS: 13   **RESISTANCE:** 0

ATTACKS:
- Tusks (Melee, 3▲ Knockdown, 1H)
- Bite (Melee, 3▲ Vicious 1, 1H, Cumbersome)

SPECIAL RULES:
- **Boar Rush:** The *targ* charges at the character, attempting to knock them to the ground. As a Task, the *targ* moves to within Reach of an enemy within Long range, and makes a melee attack with its Tusks.

SEHLAT [NOTABLE NPC]

Large, furry creatures; The *sehlat* is a large bear-like creature from the planet Vulcan. While a traditional pet for vulcan children, their six-inch fangs and predatory nature make them a danger to unwary travelers through the deserts of its home planet.

TRAITS: Sehlat

VALUES: Territorial Predator

ATTRIBUTES

CONTROL 08	FITNESS 12	PRESENCE 09
DARING 11	INSIGHT 05	REASON 02

DISCIPLINES

COMMAND 02	SECURITY 03	SCIENCE -
CONN -	ENGINEERING -	MEDICINE -

FOCUSES: Stalking, Clawing and Biting

STRESS: 15   **RESISTANCE:** 2

ATTACKS:
- Claws (Melee, 5▲, Piercing 1, 1H)
- Teeth (Melee, 5▲, Vicious 1, 1H, Cumbersome)

FOCUSES: Melee, Tracking

STRESS: 13 RESISTANCE: 0

ATTACKS:
- Claws (Melee, 4▲ Intense, 1H)
- Bite (Melee, 5▲, Vicious 1, 1H, Cumbersome, Deadly, Debilitating)

SPECIAL RULES:
- **Inject venom:** When biting a victim, the *mugato* may choose to inject them with a venom. This venom will cause a slow, painful death to the victim should they not be cured.

TALARIAN HOOK SPIDER [MINOR NPC]

With legs approaching a half-meter in length and curved hook-like appendages at the end of their legs, the Talarian hook spider is known for being accidentally brought onto ships in cargo crates. The hooks on the spiders' legs allow them to nimbly travel throughout the innards of a spacefaring vessel without requiring traditionally insect-like methods of attaching to a surface such as setules on their legs. Hook spiders are not much more dangerous than a medium-sized dog on their own, but large groups can quickly become a danger to a wayward engineer.

TRAITS: Talarian Hook Spider

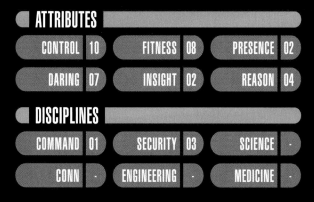

ATTRIBUTES

| CONTROL 10 | FITNESS 08 | PRESENCE 02 |
| DARING 07 | INSIGHT 02 | REASON 04 |

DISCIPLINES

| COMMAND 01 | SECURITY 03 | SCIENCE - |
| CONN - | ENGINEERING - | MEDICINE - |

STRESS: 11 RESISTANCE: 1

ATTACKS:
- Hook (Melee, 4▲ Knockdown, 1H)
- Bite (Melee, 5▲, Intense, 1H, Deadly)

SPECIAL RULES:
- **Web:** Should the hook spider be given enough time in a location, they will fill it with a sticky web-like substance. Characters moving through this substance cannot move more than one zone per turn.

MUGATO [NOTABLE NPC]

The *mugato* of the planet Neural is a white-furred carnivorous ape. Regularly attacking humanoids who stray too close to their mountain home, the *mugato* are known for biting its prey, injecting them with a fatal poison.

It will generally choose to use its poison if it perceives the threat as a future food source, due to the slow-acting nature of the poison. The primary cure for this poison is the local *mahko* root, the use of which is known to locals.

TRAITS: *Mugato*

VALUES: Territorial Predator

ATTRIBUTES

| CONTROL 06 | FITNESS 11 | PRESENCE 10 |
| DARING 08 | INSIGHT 04 | REASON 06 |

DISCIPLINES

| COMMAND 02 | SECURITY 02 | SCIENCE - |
| CONN - | ENGINEERING - | MEDICINE - |

BERENGARIAN DRAGON [MAJOR NPC]

At over two hundred metres in length, and having an innate ability to breath fire, the reptiles of Berengaria VII were a curiosity to the Vulcan science team who first studied them. Berengarian dragons are known to roost primarily in forest regions, using their fire breath to scorch areas of foliage and causing animals within to attempt to escape, which the dragons then hunt for food.

Being so large, the Berengarian dragon also uses its fire breath to herd flocks of birds, which it then devours in a manner similar to Earth's whales, gorging on whole flocks at a time as they attempt to escape its maw.

TRAITS: Berengarian Dragon

VALUES: Arboreal Hunter, Pays Small Creatures Little Heed

ATTRIBUTES

CONTROL	10	FITNESS	12	PRESENCE	10
DARING	13	INSIGHT	05	REASON	04

DISCIPLINES

COMMAND	03	SECURITY	02	SCIENCE	-
CONN	-	ENGINEERING	-	MEDICINE	-

FOCUSES: Hunting, Melee, Observant

STRESS: 28   **RESISTANCE:** 5

ATTACKS:
- Claws (Melee, 5▲ Area, Vicious 1, 1H)
- Teeth (Melee, 6▲, Piercing 2, Vicious 1, 1H, Debilitating)
- Fire breath (Ranged, 5▲ Area, Intense, 1H)

SPECIAL RULES: The creature is massive. It has twice as much Stress as normal. Further, it takes 8 Stress to inflict an Injury, instead of 5.

DENEVAN NEURAL PARASITE [MINOR NPC]

Small, jelly-like creatures, roughly disc-like and flat; The Denevan neural parasite is generally part of a group of such creatures which travel through space, planet to planet, infecting and feeding off of the creatures on whatever planet they visit.

On infecting its host, the parasite attaches itself to the victim's nervous system and very quickly becomes unremovable. It shall then pressure its host to perform tasks by emitting vast amounts of pain if the victim does not do as the parasite wishes. When encountered by the *U.S.S. Enterprise* NCC-1701, they were found to be susceptible to the effects of UV radiation, allowing the crew to deal with these creatures on a planetary level.

TRAITS: Denevan Neural Parasite

ATTRIBUTES

CONTROL	09	FITNESS	08	PRESENCE	05
DARING	04	INSIGHT	04	REASON	06

DISCIPLINES

COMMAND	01	SECURITY	01	SCIENCE	-
CONN	-	ENGINEERING	-	MEDICINE	-

STRESS: 9   **RESISTANCE:** 0

SPECIAL RULES:
- **Attach:** Should the Neural Parasite become attached to an area on a host creature large enough to hold it (i.e., a humanoid torso), the parasite shall quickly become fused with the creature's nervous system, in essence controlling the creature.

NOVA DIGGER [MINOR NPC]

One of the first animals encountered by humanity on a new colony, the Digger of Terra Nova is a large turtle-like creature almost a meter in length known to burrow through the ground. Shortly after landing on Terra Nova, its settlers also found this creature was useful; having a tough shell good for making clothes and equipment from, as well as having a nutritious body.

TRAITS: Nova Digger

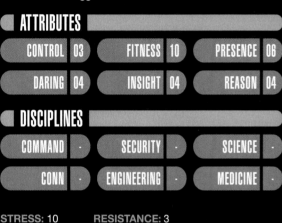

ATTRIBUTES

CONTROL	03	FITNESS	10	PRESENCE	06
DARING	04	INSIGHT	04	REASON	04

DISCIPLINES

COMMAND	-	SECURITY	-	SCIENCE	-
CONN	-	ENGINEERING	-	MEDICINE	-

STRESS: 10   **RESISTANCE:** 3

ATTACKS:
- Bite (Melee, 1▲, 1H)

SPECIAL RULES:
- **Burrow:** So long as not engaged in melee, a Digger can burrow underground over the course of its turn.

GUNJI JACKDAW [MINOR NPC]

This large, flightless bird from Gunji is known for its high-pitched squeal and docile nature. Large groups of them can quickly become a problem by kicking up significant amounts of dust as they cross an open landscape during migratory periods, but on their own are not formidable.

The jackdaw is most often found in pairs. They are known to mate for life and can often be seen in the deserts of Gunji nesting in shallow holes they dig using their clawed feet.

TRAITS: Gunji Jackdaw

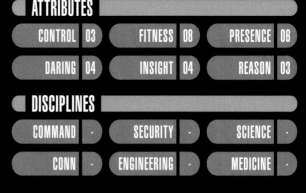

ATTRIBUTES

CONTROL	03	FITNESS	08	PRESENCE	06
DARING	04	INSIGHT	04	REASON	03

DISCIPLINES

COMMAND	-	SECURITY	-	SCIENCE	-
CONN	-	ENGINEERING	-	MEDICINE	-

STRESS: 8   **RESISTANCE:** 0

ATTACKS:
- Claw (Melee, 2▲, 1H)

PALUKOO [MINOR NPC]

Native to the moons of Bajor, the *palukoo* is an oversized spider. Docile and prone to running from intruders, they nevertheless provided ample nutrition for the Bajoran resistance movement while they were stationed on the moons.

TRAITS: Palukoo

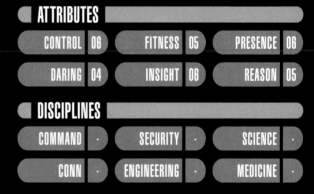

ATTRIBUTES

CONTROL	06	FITNESS	05	PRESENCE	06
DARING	04	INSIGHT	06	REASON	05

DISCIPLINES

COMMAND	-	SECURITY	-	SCIENCE	-
CONN	-	ENGINEERING	-	MEDICINE	-

STRESS: 5   **RESISTANCE:** 0

ATTACKS:
- Bite (Melee, 1▲, 1H, Deadly)

SPECIAL RULES:
- **Web:** Should the *palukoo* be given enough time in a location, they will fill it with a sticky web-like substance. Characters moving through this substance cannot move more than one zone per turn.

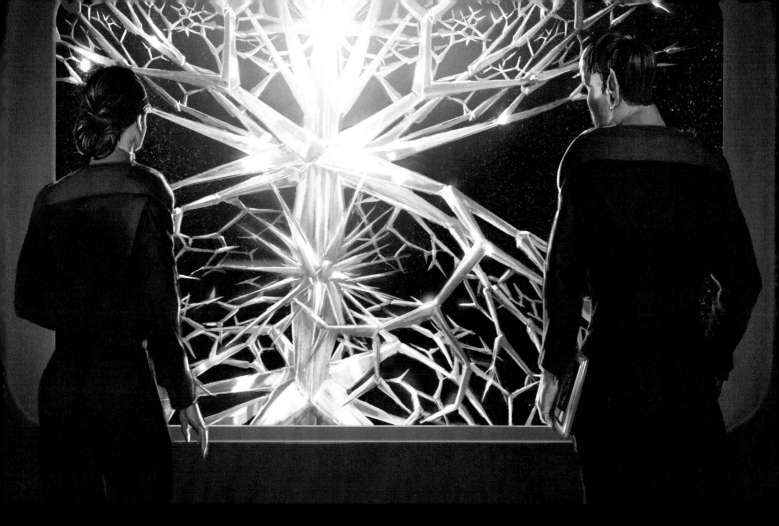

CRYSTALLINE ENTITY [MAJOR NPC]

The Crystalline Entity was a large, dangerous creature which had the ability and propensity to consume all life on a planet. When finding a source of food, the entity would strip it of all nutrients — this includes a planet's natural resources and all life that exists on it.

The entity was encountered by the *Starship Enterprise* NCC-1701-D on multiple occasions and communication was introduced to it, but it was destroyed before formal first-contact procedures could be established. It may not be the only such creature in the Galaxy, and so this briefing serves as a warning. A Crystalline Entity is a very dangerous creature which could cause untold destruction if left unchecked.

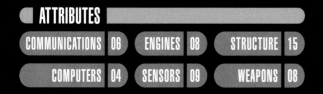

ATTRIBUTES

| COMMUNICATIONS | 06 | ENGINES | 08 | STRUCTURE | 15 |
| COMPUTERS | 04 | SENSORS | 09 | WEAPONS | 08 |

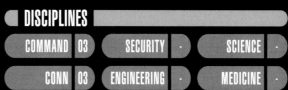

DISCIPLINES

| COMMAND | 03 | SECURITY | - | SCIENCE | - |
| CONN | 03 | ENGINEERING | - | MEDICINE | - |

SHIELDS: 15   **RESISTANCE:** 10
POWER: 8   **SCALE:** 10

CREW: Exceptional (Attribute 11, Discipline 4)

ATTACKS:
- Particle Beam (Energy, Range M, 6⚔ Persistent 5)

SPECIAL RULES:
- **Harmonic Resonance:** The Crystalline Entity's particle beam gains the Vicious 2 effect against ships with maximum Shields of 13 or less.
- **Crystalline structure:** The Crystalline Entity's physical structure means that all damage from energy weapons is reduced to zero. Any damage which would have been done is added to the damage inflicted by the next attack with the particle beam.
- **Organic Ravager:** When a ship with 0 Shields is hit by the particle beam, all characters on the ship suffer 2⚔ Piercing 1 damage. Organic vessels count as having Resistance 0 against the particle beam.

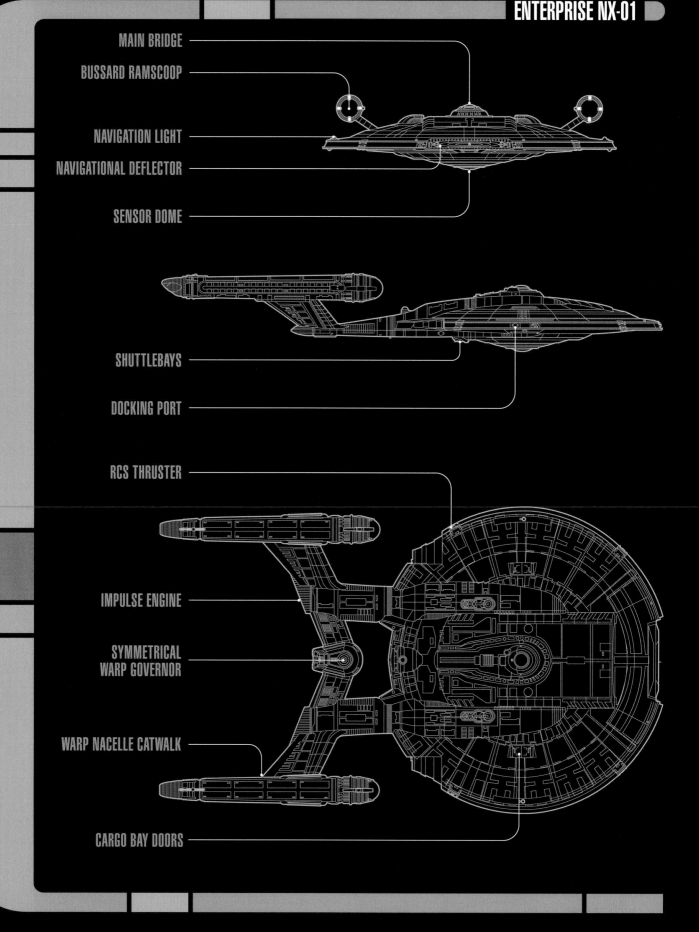

MAIN BRIDGE

BUSSARD RAMSCOOP

NAVIGATION LIGHT

NAVIGATIONAL DEFLECTOR

SENSOR DOME

SHUTTLEBAYS

DOCKING PORT

RCS THRUSTER

IMPULSE ENGINE

SYMMETRICAL
WARP GOVERNOR

WARP NACELLE CATWALK

CARGO BAY DOORS

12.10   MISSION   347

12151804
10150814
23081518060914

THE RESCUE AT XERXES IV
MISSION

The *Rescue at Xerxes IV* was the first mission in the **Star Trek Adventures** Living Campaign playtest series, and it is being included in this book as an excellent starting point for a campaign, or simply as a way to introduce Players to the game. This mission is meant to be played by a Gamemaster (GM) and 3-7 Player Characters.

SYNOPSIS

The Player Characters are newly deployed crew members heading toward Narendra Station on a runabout for assignment to their various commissioned vessels. During the trip, they receive a distress call from a science outpost on a planet that's been struck by a highly irradiated ion storm. The runabout crash-lands on the surface, and the crew is attacked by primitive hostile humanoid creatures wielding clubs and rocks.

After dealing with the primitives, the crew can make the journey from the crash site to the science outpost, overcoming various obstacles along the way. At the science outpost, the crew learns that the members of the science team have been exposed to environmental effects that cause them to devolve into Neanderthal creatures.

The crew must rescue the remaining scientists, find the parts needed to repair the runabout, and decide whether to risk remaining on the planet to gather the flora that could be used to treat a terrible disease. They must also use their social skills to convince the remaining scientists to accompany them off the planet.

Back at the runabout, it is a race against time, the elements, and the devolved scientists to repair the damage and escape before the ion storm destroys all life.

The GM begins this mission with two points of Threat for every Player Character in the group.

SCENE 1: UNWELCOME RECEPTION

When the Player Characters are ready, read:

Your runabout trip to Narendra Station to take your assignment on your commissioned starship has turned out to be more eventful than you anticipated.

As you and your fellow Starfleet graduates chatted about your bright futures, you received a distress signal from Xerxes IV, an uninhabited Class M planet containing no sentient life except for a Federation science team. The distress signal offered no information except that the science team stationed there was in danger.

As you guide the runabout toward the planet's surface, you are caught in a violent ion storm that knocks out navigation and other systems. With systems failing and the planet's surface rising quickly toward you, the situation is grim.

The mission begins with the Player Characters' runabout hurtling toward the surface of Xerxes IV. They should choose among themselves who is at the runabout's controls – only two of them can be seated in the cockpit: one at the Conn, and one at Ops. Ideally, the character with the highest Conn Discipline should be at Conn, while the character with the highest Engineering Discipline should be at Ops, and the characters would know this.

Getting the runabout down safely requires a single Task from the character at the Conn. This will be a **Daring** or **Control + Conn Task**, with a Difficulty of 2. The character at Ops may attempt to assist this, rolling against **Control + Engineering** to keep the runabout's systems working longer, or **Reason + Science** to locate the best place to land within the ion storm. Complications may mean that a random Player Character is a little bit battered and bruised during the crash.

GM Guidance: *This is the first opportunity for the Players to attempt a Task and see how the game works, as well as their first opportunity to try out the rules for assistance. It's worth dwelling on this event a little longer than usual, because the rules here are the foundation of everything else. Establish* *how to attempt a Task: a target number made from one Attribute and one Discipline added together, roll 2d20, and count each die that rolls that number or less scores as one success. Each die that rolls a 1, or equal to or less than a relevant Focus scores two successes instead. Check to see if the total number of successes beats the assigned Difficulty. Don't worry too much about them buying extra dice at this point – this is a basic test to show them how the game works. If the Task generates any Momentum, allow them to spend two to get the runabout closer to the science station, letting them skip the Hazard section of Scene 2, below. If they still have Momentum, encourage them to save it for later in this scene. They'll need it.*

Describe their landing based on the number of Successes and any Momentum or Complications. Describe the runabout as being heavily damaged but potentially reparable if some replacement parts can be located. After everyone takes in the situation and is ready to leave the runabout, read:

As you exit the damaged runabout to reconnoiter the surroundings, you hear strange grunts and shrieks. A group of strange Neanderthal humanoids surrounds the runabout. They throw rocks and lope toward you, raising clubs above their heads threateningly. All of your attackers wear the tattered remnants of Federation-issue uniforms that a science team might wear, and it appears one of the creatures wields a phaser, although it doesn't appear to know how to fire it accurately… yet.

Currently, four of these Neanderthal creatures are attacking. Three throw rocks and carry clubs, while a fourth also carries a phaser type-1. A profile for these creatures is presented below.

The purpose of this encounter is to acclimate the Player Characters (and yourself) to the combat system. The environment for this scene contains three zones: inside the runabout, near the runabout, and the forest a short distance from the runabout.

The runabout is damaged and cannot be used offensively or defensively, except as cover – taking cover behind part of the runabout provides Heavy Cover, granting 4▲ of Cover Dice. The crew cannot, for example, enter the runabout and close the hatch to afford complete protection. Characters who run for the forest at medium range from the runabout have Light Cover from the concealing foliage, granting 2▲ of Cover Dice.

Any Player Characters who were battered and bruised by the runabout crash (from a Complication) start the fight with three less Stress than normal.

GM Guidance: *As noted, this is an opportunity for the Players to try out the combat rules. This shouldn't be a particularly challenging battle, and you shouldn't spend more than one Threat per Player Character on the fight in total – uses of Threat here should be more to illustrate what the GM can do rather than to make the fight too difficult.*

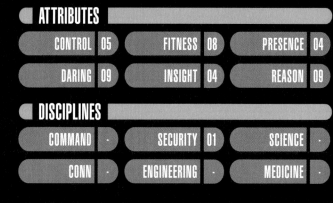

These primitive humanoids are clad in the ragged remains of uniforms and clothing that would be worn by a Federation science team.

TRAITS: Human, De-evolved, Feral

ATTRIBUTES

CONTROL 05	FITNESS 08	PRESENCE 04
DARING 09	INSIGHT 04	REASON 09

DISCIPLINES

COMMAND -	SECURITY 01	SCIENCE -
CONN -	ENGINEERING -	MEDICINE -

STRESS: 9   **RESISTANCE: 0**

ATTACKS:
- Unarmed Strike (Melee, 2▲ Knockdown, Size 1H, Non-lethal)

SPECIAL RULES
- **Aggressive and Fearful:** The Neanderthals only attack to kill – they don't have sufficient self-control to stun or disable.
- **Phaser:** A Neanderthal with a Phaser cannot use it under normal circumstances, as they do not understand how the weapon works. However, the GM may spend two Threat at the start of a Neanderthal's action to allow it to fire the Phaser once, set to stun. If it fails to hit with this attack and scores a Complication, it'll hit one of the other Neanderthals instead. Once the Phaser has been fired in this way, it cannot be used again during that scene, as the power cell is depleted.

These Minor NPCs cannot spend Threat to avoid suffering an Injury, so they should be taken out swiftly. Once each of the Player Characters has taken a turn, check to see if the Players understand how things work, and if they do, have the remaining Neanderthals retreat into the forest.

RESOLUTION

This combat is not meant to be deadly for the Player Characters. After the mechanics of combat are clear to the Player Characters, the remaining Neanderthals flee into the surrounding area. At the end of the fight, the Player Characters have the chance to take a breather, recovering all their lost Stress. Any injured characters can be patched up enough to get them moving (requiring an **Reason + Medicine Task** with a Difficulty of 1 for each injured character), but a Complication on this Task means that character's injuries have a lingering effect, adding +1 to the Difficulty of any Tasks they attempt until they receive proper treatment.

Any foes who have been killed or knocked unconscious can be examined more carefully. Given the tools at hand, it is a **Reason + Science** or **Reason + Medicine Task** with a Difficulty of 2 to learn that these creatures have the genetic makeup of Humans, but something has caused their genes to revert to that of their evolutionary ancestors.

An examination of the runabout, either now or before the encounter with the Neanderthals, reveals that the vessel can be fixed without much problem, but a few new parts are needed to make those repairs. The science outpost on Xerxes IV would have all the parts needed. The science station can be seen on a rocky bluff a few kilometers in the distance.

SCENE 2: THE MARCH

Once the Player Characters begin their trek toward the science station, read:

It is obvious that the march to the science outpost is no simple stroll. The journey covers several kilometers, and the terrain between you and your goal is rough and rocky, with strange and abundant flora blocking the path.

This scene contains several Challenges and Extended Tasks. The purpose of this scene is to introduce the idea of overcoming Challenges, banking Momentum, or adding to Threat to deal with potential calamities.

GM Guidance: The GM shouldn't need to use Threat during this scene, instead saving it for the later scenes when the tension ramps up and problems start to crop up. Any extra Threat the Players generate – either voluntarily or through Complications – adds to this pool of potential problems.

CHALLENGE: THE RAVINE

Early in the trek to the science station, the crew comes to a deep but narrow ravine in the ground. On the far side of the ravine is a long piece of fallen wood that can be placed across the ravine. Crossing the ravine alone is a **Fitness + Security Task** with a Difficulty of 4 – difficult, but not impossible. Once across, characters can attempt to shift the wood into place as a makeshift bridge, requiring a **Fitness + Security** or **Control + Science Task** with a Difficulty of 3. Once the wood is in place, it requires only a **Control + Security Task** with a Difficulty of 1 for each remaining character to balance across the rock.

All these Tasks use the *Success at a Cost* rule, so failing the Task doesn't mean the character hasn't crossed the ravine or moved the wood, only that they've paid some additional cost to do so, suffering an automatic Complication as a price for the most basic level of success. These Complications can either produce an effect now – perhaps making things trickier, hindering the character in some way, causing them

to lose a piece of equipment (a tricorder or phaser falls down the ravine), suffering a minor Injury (+1 Difficulty on all Tasks until treated), or something similar – or cause problems later by adding two points to Threat.

*GM Guidance: This is an ideal opportunity to emphasize the Improving the Odds options, on p. 80 – buying extra dice by spending saved Momentum, adding to Threat, spending Determination, and so forth. The high Difficulty of the first Task makes buying some extra dice particularly important, so it's important that the Players know that hitting a Difficulty of 3 or higher is quite unlikely without extra dice. It's also the first instance of a Challenge – a series of linked Tasks to overcome a single problem, with each Task representing a discrete stage of the problem. Challenges are a potent tool for GMs in **Star Trek Adventures**.*

EXTENDED TASK: POISONOUS PLANTS

Between the crew and the science station are fields of local vegetation. Some of this flora is harmless, while others give off poisonous spores. The crew can evaluate the plants, attempting to determine which plants are safe and which are toxic. This is an Extended Task, with a Work Track of 10, a Magnitude of 3, and with a basic Difficulty of 2 for Tasks to overcome it.

As the crew are trying to maintain a decent pace, they can only attempt a maximum of three Tasks to overcome this Extended Task: if they haven't completely overcome the Extended Task after the third Task, then some of the group have stumbled into something poisonous and begin to sicken soon after. Further, because of the amount of ground to cover, it's difficult for any one person to evaluate everything, so each successive Task attempted by the same character to overcome this Extended Task increases in Difficulty by 1: it's better to spread the workload.

The default Task for this is **Reason + Science**, but there are other possibilities for this. **Presence + Medicine** is a good alternative quickly recalling and using medical knowledge and what substances are toxic to different species, as is **Control + Security** for basic vigilance and field survival skills.

If the Extended Task is successfully overcome, the crew can avoid the dangerous areas and suffer no negative consequences. If the Extended Task hasn't been completely overcome, roll 1▲ for each Player Character in the group: anyone who rolls an Effect (a 5 or 6) has been exposed to poison and starts to sicken. Characters who have a Fitness of 9 or higher may re-roll this die.

A character with the 'Poisoned' Complication adds +1 to the Difficulty of any Tasks they attempt until the poison has been treated, and the GM may cause them to worsen as a Complication on any Task the sickened character attempts, adding an extra +1 to the Difficulty of the character's Tasks for each time their condition worsens. If the Complication would increase beyond 'Poisoned 3' then the character falls unconscious.

GM Guidance: *The first introduction to Extended Tasks, which are a way for a single problem to require protracted effort to overcome. Remember that the Difficulty of Tasks to overcome an Extended Task are reduced by achieving Breakthroughs, and that a particularly successful roll can cause more than one Breakthrough at once, allowing this Extended Task to be completed in only two Tasks if the characters push for it... but it could take much longer. The pressure of a limited number of attempts also adds some extra tension.*

HAZARDS: PRIMITIVE FEARS

As the crew continues their march toward the science outpost, the devolutionary effects of the planet begin to affect them. If the crew managed to crash-land closer to the science station at the start of Scene 1, ignore this Challenge. If not, read the following to the group.

The strong winds caused by the ion storm and the strangeness of the landscape begin to play tricks on your mind. Flashes at the corners of your eyes hint at lurking terrors hiding in the cracks in the ground. Are the wind-whipped plants moving on their own, approaching you? The occasional gnawed carcass of a dead animal suggests that a large predator may be in the area. Soon, you find your heart racing and your breathing heavy.

The dangers the crew sense are (mostly) imaginary, caused by the triggering of their more primitive instincts. To maintain composure, each crew member must attempt a **Control + Command Task** with a Difficulty of 2 to maintain their composure.

Success means that character remains calm, and Momentum can be used to immediately assist other crew members in holding their composure as well. If any crew member fails, their nerve breaks and they become increasingly wary and fearful of their surroundings, gaining the 'Paranoia' Trait. Each character whose nerve has broken in this manner increases the Complication Range of all Tasks they attempt for the remainder of the adventure: now, any d20 that rolls a 19 or a 20 causes a Complication instead of just a 20.

GM Guidance: *These Tasks are purely to avoid suffering an ongoing penalty, rather than to achieve anything. Momentum gained here should be saved, particularly to help those Player Characters who aren't so strong-willed. In this way, it's useful for the group to determine the order in which the characters attempt this Task, and how they use the resources available to them – those less likely to succeed require more dice to increase their odds of success, while those with better chances might be better at generating Momentum that the rest of the group can benefit from. Also encourage the Players to roleplay these effects, whether they shake them off or succumb to them.*

SCENE 3: DEVOLUTION

When the Player Characters arrive at the station, read:

The science station is intact, but heavy damage is evident along the structure's exterior: mostly dents and punctures mar the surface, but a few areas of phaser fire are evident as well.

Inside the outpost, the place has been vandalized. From the living quarters to the kitchen to the laboratories, it is obvious someone or something wrecked the place without regard. All communication devices have been smashed.

As you are ready to give up on your search for life, you find one last storage area with the door closed and locked. You hear a muffled voice inside.

The lock is a simple one, easily bypassed, requiring a **Reason + Engineering** or **Reason + Security Task** with a Difficulty of 0 – that is, characters can succeed automatically without rolling dice, though they may still roll if they wish to generate some extra Momentum (at the risk of Complications). When the crew opens the door, continue:

On a cot at the back of the storage area sits a middle-aged Human. She cradles in her arms a man. It is hard to tell his age because of his strange appearance. His sweat-soaked face is covered with hair, and even as you watch, the ridges of his eyebrows twitch and pulse, as if changing in sporadic fits.

When you enter, the woman looks up at you, her eyes unfocused and filled with tears. "It's too late. They are all gone, and Jasper is..." She cannot finish her thought through her sobbing.

The woman is Dr. Heidi Schipp, the Federation scientist leading this science team. When the crew can calm her – which doesn't require a Task, just a little time – she can supply the following information:

- The science team of 13 members has been here for just over a year. They have been examining the unique flora and fauna of this planet to see if it offered any scientific or medical uses.

- The ion storm has been ravaging the planet for over a week, and something about it has caused the living inhabitants to go through a process of devolution.

- Some of the science workers were more susceptible to the effects, changing almost immediately into Neanderthal versions of themselves. Others took longer but still transformed. She has held out the longest, but she is still starting to feel the effects on her mind.

Just before the ion storm struck, they had made a breakthrough in their research, discovering that a combination of some of the genetic material from the flora and fauna could be useful in the treatment of, and possible a cure for, Irumodic Syndrome.

⬛ Her assistant and lover, Dr. Jasper Conrad, was beaten severely by the transformed scientists. Not only is he suffering from terrible wounds, he is now also transforming into a Neanderthal creature.

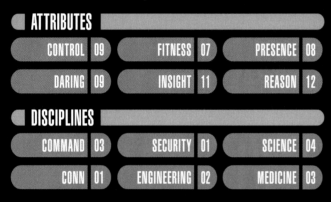

DR. HEIDI SCHIPP [NOTABLE NPC]

TRAITS: Human, De-evolving

ATTRIBUTES

CONTROL	09	FITNESS	07	PRESENCE	08
DARING	09	INSIGHT	11	REASON	12

DISCIPLINES

COMMAND	03	SECURITY	01	SCIENCE	04
CONN	01	ENGINEERING	02	MEDICINE	03

STRESS: 8   **RESISTANCE:** 0

ATTACKS:

⬛ Unarmed Strike (Melee, 2⬛ Knockdown, Size 1H, Non-lethal)

⬛ Phaser Type-I (Ranged, 3⬛, Size 1H, Charge, Hidden 1)

HEALING

Though it has been ransacked, the outpost still has useful medical facilities, allowing injured and poisoned characters to be treated properly. A character suffering lingering injuries from the fight with the Neanderthals, or from crossing the ravine, or who was poisoned by the plants in the forest, can have their ailments healed. An **Insight + Medicine Task** with a Difficulty of 1 is sufficient to treat injuries, while treating a case of poisoning requires a **Reason + Medicine Task** with a Difficulty of 1, +1 for each time the poisoning has worsened.

Jasper's injuries can also be healed by the characters, though Heidi's mind is changing to a more primitive state, making her unhelpful in this process. Healing Jasper's injuries requires minor surgery, which can be performed with a **Control + Medicine Task** with a Difficulty of 2.

A search of the laboratory areas reveals notes relevant to two different issues: the research for the Irumodic Syndrome

treatment, and the observations and theories on the devolutionary transformations.

Dr. Schipp refuses to leave with the Player Characters until they collect specimens as potential treatments for Irumodic Syndrome, and until they find a way to reverse the devolution in Jasper Conrad. Attempting to persuade her to leave is a difficult prospect: A Difficulty 5 Persuasion Task is required if the crew haven't performed either of the activities she wants completed. Completing one of those activities reduces this Difficulty to 3, while completing both reduces the Difficulty to 0. Other social conflict methods – intimidation, deception, and so forth – can be attempted to reduce the Difficulty of this further, though she'll respond poorly to intimidation (she's already terrified and devolving, and more fear may just make her incoherent rather than compliant), and is single-minded at this point.

GM Guidance: Here's a chance to try out the Social Conflict rules, if the Players are inclined to push Dr. Schipp to leave with her work incomplete. The basic Difficulty listed above is for straightforward persuasion, with deception, intimidation, negotiation, and evidence used to shift the context to try and make things easier. Once a Persuasion Task has been attempted, another cannot be attempted without changing the context. Intimidation makes a situation hostile if it wasn't already, but it can be effective in the right situations. Deception is tricky, but can be effective if a character is sufficiently convincing or is careful about the lies they tell. Negotiation involves offering something in return for compliance. Evidence involves finding something to prove why someone should comply or agree. Individually or in conjunction with one another, they're powerful tools. Importantly, each of those tools requires roleplay to function – a Player can't simply say "I deceive them" and gain an effect.

OPTIONS

At this point, the characters have a variety of options:

⬛ **Immediate Escape:** The main objective should be to collect the parts needed to repair the runabout and escape the planet before being transformed. Choosing this option means ignoring the other options.

⬛ **Irumodic Syndrome:** Based on Dr. Schipp's knowledge and notes, she believes that 3 species native to this planet have genetic potential to treat the disease. But if un-devolved specimens are not found and removed from the planet soon, the cure will be lost as the plants undergo the same transformation as the animals.

⬛ **Devolution:** Dr. Schipp made some initial notes on potential cures for the devolution process. Finding this would be much more difficult, especially within the time frame that the devolution might affect everyone on the planet. However, doing so would save Jasper and possibly the other scientists who have already transformed.

Each of these options is covered in more detail below. Note that they are not mutually exclusive, and the characters may attempt to do all three simultaneously by splitting their efforts.

During these scenes, it is likely that the crew encounters one or more Neanderthals in the area. Use the statistics from the first encounter to add them to proceedings and add extra conflict to the scene. Adding a Neanderthal to a situation requires that the GM spend one point of Threat at the start of the round. The presence of Neanderthals doesn't prevent characters from continuing with their other activities – one character may spend their turn salvaging parts to repair the runabout while another fends off an attack.

PLOT COMPLICATIONS

To add some of the moral and ethical complexity to the game that makes *Star Trek Adventures* what it is, consider adding these two plot complications to the situation:

- One of the characters has a loved one who is in the early stages of Irumodic Syndrome. Finding even a treatment, not to mention a cure, for the disease would potentially eliminate pain and suffering for hundreds of thousands of people.

- While checking the records of the science outpost staff, a character learns that one of the scientists at the outpost was a former mentor named Dr. Helena Burlette. Dr. Burlette was instrumental in helping that character during a rough spot in their life. Dr. Burlette has transformed and will be lost forever without a way to reverse the devolution.

These complications can be used to drive roleplaying. Mechanically, they can be used in the same ways that Values or Directives are used: providing bonus Momentum when accomplishing Tasks, or adding Complications when the relationship is strained by taking actions that would harm the relationship.

GM Guidance: Here's where we start putting it all together – Challenges, Extended Tasks, combat, hazards, and the other parts of the game we've already introduced. The traditional notion of "don't split the party" doesn't apply here – the group can split off to do different things, relying on their communicators to keep in contact, and the GM should ensure that everyone gets a chance to do different things, moving from Player Character to Player Character to see what each is doing. Using the turn order for combat for everyone can be helpful here: everyone gets to perform one Task each round, and once everyone has had a turn, start again. This also helps integrate any wandering Neanderthals into the scene smoothly – just add their turns to each round. Judicious use of Threat here can push up the tension and pile on extra pressure.

SCENE 4: OPTIONS

OPTION 1: GATHERING COMPONENTS

To leave the planet, the characters must find replacement parts for the runabout in the science outpost. The damage in the outpost is significant, but many salvageable parts are available. Finding these parts is a timed Challenge, with enough parts found after 3 successful Tasks to find and acquire those parts.

The default Task for this is **Reason + Engineering**, but there are other possibilities for this. **Reason + Conn** is a good alternative covering knowledge of propulsion and power systems, as is **Control + Science**. Other ideas may occur to the Player Characters, and any reasonable suggestions should be fine so long as the Players can make a decent case for them. **Medicine** may help with pulling parts from medical equipment, or **Security** for salvaging components from defensive systems. Each Task takes 2 intervals of time, with the Players having an available 15 intervals of time until the ion storm hits the planet.

Complications on these Tasks may result in power surges, which inflict 3▲ Stun damage to the character performing the Task, and an additional 2▲ Stun damage to anyone assisting them.

GM Guidance: This is a straightforward activity to perform… but the potential threat of attack while it's happening ups the tension and the difficulty, by splitting the characters' attention between salvaging the parts they need and defending themselves. If the group have split up to handle multiple activities, this may become even more pressing.

OPTION 2: GATHERING SPECIMENS

Based on Dr. Schipp's notes, the characters know exactly which types of flora and fauna must be collected to have a viable sample for study. To collect them, however, the characters must venture out into the storm. The samples are only found deeper into the wilderness of the planet, so they cannot be collected on the way back to the runabout from the outpost.

There are three samples to be located and collected. However, the same phenomenon affecting the scientists is also affecting many of the plants and animals on the planet as well, so finding samples that haven't yet been mutated is tricky.

This is a Timed Challenge, with a minimum of six Tasks. These Tasks are split into two types – locating samples and collecting samples. Locating a sample requires an **Insight** or **Reason + Science Task** with a Difficulty of 2, with success allowing that sample to be collected. Collecting a sample requires a **Daring or Control + Security Task** with a Difficulty of 3. Once three samples have been collected, the

Challenge is complete. Each Task takes 2 intervals of time, and the characters have a total of 15 intervals until the ion storm wreaks havoc on the planet.

A Complication on either of these Tasks results in the character encountering some devolved – and dangerous – flora or fauna, inflicting 3▲ Vicious 1 damage to the character.

GM Guidance: If combat occurs here, then it may be useful to devise a quick map – a woodland clearing and a few nearby paths, with numerous potential samples scattered across the area to be analyzed and (if suitable) collected. This compels characters to move around to find and collect the samples, which becomes more challenging if there are enemies around as well. Combat takes 1 interval of time to resolve.

OPTION 3: CURING DEVOLUTION

Curing the devolution is the most difficult problem facing the crew. Normally such an undertaking would require weeks of work, and the characters have neither sufficient time nor the best equipment for the job. However, only the best and brightest are accepted by Starfleet, so anything is possible!

Finding and administering a cure for the devolutionary phenomenon is a linear, timed, Challenge which contains several Tasks, which must be completed in order. Each Task listed takes 2 intervals of time to attempt, and the crew have a total of 15 intervals of time before the ion storm hits the planet surface.

- **Identify the Cause:** A character must locate the source of the devolutionary phenomenon, which is a result of the unique – and typically benign – radiogenic properties of the planet interacting oddly with the encroaching ion storm. This requires a **Reason + Science Task** with a Difficulty of 3.

- **Study the Symptoms:** A character must study those affected to determine how living cells are affected by this phenomenon, now that the cause has been identified. As with many problems of this sort, the more information the better. This is a **Control + Medicine Task** with a Difficulty of 3, which can be performed multiple times if there are multiple subjects available for study – each Task requires the study of a different subject. Completing this Task once allows the character to continue to the next stage, while each additional performance of this Task reduces the Difficulty of the next Task by 1, to a minimum of 1.

- **Devise a Cure:** A character must now use that information to devise a means of stopping and reversing the effects. This is a **Daring + Medicine** or **Daring + Science Task** with a Difficulty of 4 (which may have been reduced by additional Tasks in the previous stage). Success means that a cure has been created, but it now needs to be administered.

- **Administer the Cure:** There are two possibilities here, each of which have their own advantages and problems.

  - **Individual Cures:** Loading up hyposprays with a curative is quick and efficient… but it requires each patient to be cured one at a time. This requires an **Insight + Medicine Task** with a Difficulty of 1 for each individual patient, who must be within Reach (this is an Opposed Task if the patient is still hostile; if the patient wins, they hit the character with a melee attack).

  - **Mass Curative:** Jury-rigging a device to generate a pulse that counteracts the phenomenon can affect everything within a few kilometers of the science station… but it's a lot more difficult. It requires a **Daring + Engineering** and **Daring + Medicine Task** with a Difficulty of 4 to complete, after which it cures every affected being within extreme range of the science station.

Complications on any of these Tasks can produce awkward setbacks, increase the intervals of time taken to complete the Task, create flaws in the characters' understanding of the situation, problems with their solution, and so forth. These shouldn't halt progress, but they can easily slow it down or create a less effective outcome. Also bear in mind the potential for Neanderthals to attack during these activities, creating a serious distraction from the complex and hurried work being performed.

If the Challenge is completed successfully, the resulting cure ceases the transformations of those who receive it. Anyone affected stops transforming immediately (and, for any Player Characters affected during **Hazards: Primitive Fears** in Scene 2, removes the penalty imposed there), and begins to return to themselves, though this restoration takes hours, maybe even days (and Complications may increase how long this takes).

Cured Neanderthals cease their hostile behavior, becoming docile and compliant, though still unable to understand more than simple commands. (Complications may result in the cured being rendered unconscious instead, or the cure having some other behavioral effect.) Regardless, the cure isn't permanent – it'll hold back the effects of the phenomenon for a few days at most but confers no long-term immunity, and anyone cured should be removed from the planet soon to avoid devolving again.

GM Guidance: This takes place mostly within a single lab within the station, where the potential for attack is relatively low – they only have a limited number of ways in, which can be defended by a crewmate if needed. However, the Tasks themselves are difficult, which may require some help or plenty of bonus d20s, and the potential usefulness of multiple subjects to study may make capturing a stunned Neanderthal a valuable course of action.

SCENE 5: BACK AT THE RUNABOUT

The specifics of the encounter(s) on the trip back to the runabout vary depending on what happened at the science outpost.

If the characters created individual cures for the devolution, they can use it on any Neanderthals they encounter during the trip. This essentially eliminates that threat. If they did not, several Neanderthals – ones who were out of range of the mass cure, if that was created, ambush the group once they return to the runabout.

If the Neanderthals have been eliminated as a threat, you can use the Xerxes Panther, a native to this planet, as a combat threat instead.

The Xerxes Panther is cunning enough to go for weakened creatures first, killing them and dragging them to safety to consume at a leisurely pace.

When the Player Characters arrive back at the runabout, they find everything as they left it. At this point, all that remains is protecting against any remaining threats (any remaining Neanderthals or the panther) while the runabout is repaired.

The storm worsens as the repairs begin, forcing the characters to come to the realization that unless they get off the planet and outside of the storm area quickly, they may be trapped here for days, meaning they may eventual succumb to the devolution.

The repairs are an Extended Task with a Work Track of 12, a Magnitude of 3, and with a base Difficulty of 2 for each Task to overcome it. The default Task to overcome it is **Control + Engineering**, though there may be other creative solutions.

In addition, someone needs to plot a course up and out through the ion storms, requiring a **Reason + Science Task** with a Difficulty of 2. Two Momentum may be spent from this Task to reduce the Difficulty of the pilot's Task (below) by one.

Unfortunately for the character, at the same time, the final batch of Neanderthals (or the Xerxes panther) decides to make a last-ditch attack on the ship. Those not performing the repairs or charting the course must hold off the attackers. Complications during the attack can affect the scope and difficulty of the repairs, such as a blow from a Neanderthal smashing a recently repaired component.

When the repairs are done and the course is charted, all that remains is for the group to board the runabout, and the pilot to succeed at a **Control + Conn Task** with a Difficulty of 3 to pilot the runabout successfully through the storms with patched-up power, propulsion, and navigation systems.

The Xerxes Panther is the elite hunter, the top of the food chain of all the animals in the Xerxes star system. It's arguably more dangerous now, having devolved somewhat and become larger and more savage.

ATTRIBUTES

CONTROL 10	FITNESS 12	PRESENCE 06
DARING 12	INSIGHT 08	REASON 02

DISCIPLINES

COMMAND -	SECURITY 03	SCIENCE -
CONN -	ENGINEERING -	MEDICINE -

VALUE: Nothing is Safe While I Prowl

FOCUS: Teeth

STRESS: 15   **RESISTANCE:** 0

ATTACKS:
- Claw (Melee, 3▲ Knockdown, Size 1H)
- Teeth (Melee, 5▲ Vicious 1, Size 1H)

SPECIAL RULES:
- Immune to Fear
- Immune to Pain

GM Guidance: *Another "a little of everything" scene, with a mixture of technical and tactical activities, that helps keep combat and non-combat characters alike engaged. Most importantly here, because this is the end of the adventure, there should be nothing stopping you from burning through all your Threat to keep the pressure up to the very last moment. Try to spend at least one or two points each round, and aim to keep the fighting going on until the characters are aboard the runabout and flying away.*

CONCLUSION

Once the runabout has escaped the atmosphere of Xerxes IV, the crew can call for assistance and limp onward toward Narendra Station.

The following officers and enlisted personnel commended themselves in the shakedown cruises and subsequent operations of the following Starfleet vessels, assigned to Starbase 364 – Narendra Station. An honorable mention to the crew of the *U.S.S. Lexington* NCC-1709 is made for its legacy to the operations of Starfleet in the Shackleton Expanse.

USS LEXINGTON NCC-1709

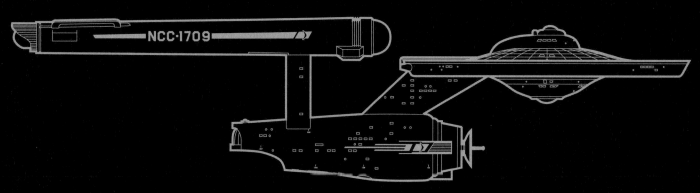

Jamie Adams	Damian Bruniany	Chris Fougere	Donavan Kienenberger	Robert Payne	Micah Sweet
Daryl Adams	Greg Burke	Michael Freeman	Josh King	John Peel	Eomer Sweet
Tim Adkins	Evan Burris	Tom Fritchman	Brian Kirchhoff	Zachary Peel	Ira Taborn
Robert Albanez	Nicholas Cardarelli	Chris Geiger	David Kitrel	Jeff Pender	Charles Tallman
Scott Atkins	Giulio Cazzoli	Adam B. Gibson	Geoffrey Lamb	Wayne Peters	Roger Taylor
Tad Atkinson	Christopher Centers	Patrick Goodman	Sean Lane	David Phillips Jr	Marcus Thelen
Daniel Atson	Mike Colello	Jeffrey Hamilton	Carl Lehmann	Jammar Prince	Blake Trebert
Ruben Ballester	Dustin Conroy	Ian Hammock	Ian Lemke	Steve Race	Joe Van Ginkel
Josh Barber	Richard Conti	Ed Handley	Jim Litmer	Christi Rainer	Dustin Ventin
Raphael Xavier Barbosa	Kevin Coons	Richard Harrison	Greg Littlejohn	Christopher Reasoner	Veto Void
Thomas Barnes	Forrest Cooper	Rob Heath	Randy Loggins	Adrienn Reed	Che Webster
Samuel Belt	Jon Crew	Steven Heller	Paul Lukianchuk	Stephen Reuille	Whitney White
Michael Berthiaume	Jeff Crowder	Danny Hensel	John Macek	Paul Ring	Raymond Whitehead
Marisa Bishop	Carlos Eduardo	Jamie Hewitt	Lisa Macek	Sebastián Riquelme	Sean Williams
Nina Blain	da Silva Leal	Jon Hines	Dennis Maciuszek	Daniel Rodriguez	Kirk Williamson
Ken Blair	Brittany Dodge	Richard Hirsch	Patrick Maes	Peter Sardinha	David Willsey
Matthew Blanchard	Dylan Downing	Nathaniel Hodgdon	Jose Ramon Marco Mata	René Schultze	Chris Wilson
David Blesa	John Eccleston	William Hostman	Jeff McArthur	Josh Shaffer	Tim Winter
Joseph Blomquist	Gerald Eidelvein	Brett Howell	Douglas McConnell	Billy Shepard	Daniel Wirth
Marcus Bockelmann	Kyrinn S. Eis	Chris Hutchinson	Brian McCutcheon	Paul Sheppard	Greg Yoder
August Bolen	Julio Escajedo	Kevin Innarelli	Robert McKittrick	Allen Shock	Michalene Yoder
Michael Boothroyd	Yancy Evans	Denver Ison	Troy Mepyans	Elbert Smith	Rachel Yoder
Bruce Boragine	Frank Falkenberg	Leo Jenicek	Tracey Michienzi	Meredith Stearns	William Yoder
Gareth Bowers	Vincent Florio	Davy Jones	John Miley	Chris Stearns	Jose Roberto Zanchetta
Matthew Broome	Bruce Ford	Mark Jurkuhn	Christopher Moore	Rachel Stearns	
Michael Brown	Ed Fortune	Antti Kautiainen	Ron Müller	Eric Stearns	
Ken Brown	Russell Foubert	Mike Kelley	Jimmy Navajo	Adam Stein	
Doug Brown	Anita Fougere	James Kerr	Vinícius Parisi	Chloe Stuberg	

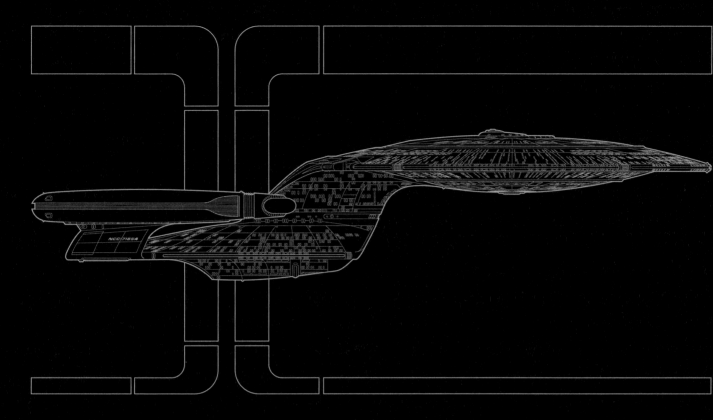

Jamie Adams
Eric Alexander
Scott Barilla
Tucker Barnes
Daniel Baruela
Doug Baumeister
Brad Bell
Trevor Benson
David Benson
Dusan Bikovski
Corwen Blaine
Matthew Blanchard
Rick Blanco
Michael Branagh
Stefan Breiner
Eric Brown
Eirik Bull
Doug Burke
Evan Burris
Mark Buschhaus
Bryan Byrnes
James Carus
Ermes Cellot
Mark ChristianScher
Michael Chumbler
Adam Coleman
Russell Coniff
Lachlan Conley
Graham Cooper
Justin Cripps
Merita Cruz
Shanna Curtis
Jim Cushman
Gene Demaitre

Tymoteusz Demel
Peter Demes
Anthony DeMinico
Marc-André Dufour
Michael Duxbury
Kaleb Falk
Greg Fehr
KC Finch
Jason Flowers
Bruce Ford
Kurtis Franks
Christopher Furness
Nick Gabbard
Christi Garrett
Keith Garrett
Tom Giblin
Joshua Gillund
John Godwin
Michael Goebel
Erik Goettsche
Al Gonzalez
Kristy Gordon
Brett Gordon
Björn Gramatke
Adrian Gramps
Daniel Gunther
Lindsay Haley
Seth Hartley
Jack R. Hetherington
Joyce Higginbotham
Katie R. Hinton
Martin Horvath
Marisa Iborra
Steven James

Rex Janeway
Eva Carolin Karl-Rückert
Sean Karraker
Courtnie Karraker
Roos Knaepkens
Astrid Knobling-Sterner
Christoph Krumm
Robin Kuiper
Timothy J. Lanza
Patrick Ledet
Gilberto Lopez
Fred Love
Chris Lovejoy
Walter Manbeck
Jason Marden
AWJ Marshall
Carlos Martinez Taco
Mathew Martini
Christine Martin-Resotko
J.J. Mason
Stephen McMillan
Greg McMillin
Simon Melmeth
Christian Moldaschl
Ghislain Morel
William Nabors
Liam Neeley
Adam Neisius
Chris Nord
Patrick Odell
Todd Olsen
Matthew Penkava
Jennifer Perez
Michael Pflugradt

Tony Pi
Laurens Plompen
Christopher Reid
Mario Richer
Peter Robben
Darcy A. S. Thornburg
Blaine Salzman
Cameron Saylor
James Schaeffer
Chris Scurfield
Troy Seward
Karaina Silvermoon
Christopher Smith
Torsten Sprunk
Daniel Stanley
Joerg Sterner
Thorsten Stichweh
Isaac Storch
Erik Stumpf
Brian Swift
Els Tercken
Edward Thater
Christopher Thompson
Jeremy Upchurch
Seth Uricheck
Spencer Utley
JW van Heerden
Rob Van Tuinen
Markus Wagner
Ross Wheeldon
Jannine Wheeldon
Jan Willms
Jeremy Wininger
Wendy Woodbury

USS THUNDERCHILD NCC-63549

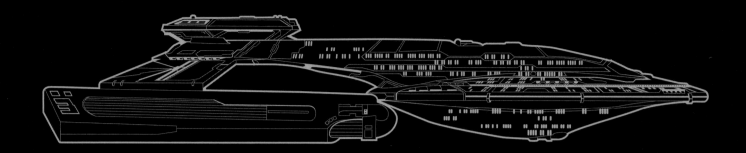

Charlemagne Abraham	Evan Burris	Kevan Elliott	Matthew Jones	Imunar Minratt	Scott Steinke
Eric Anderson	Jose Busó	Julio Escajedo	Jay Jong	David Nizamoff	Sean Tingle
Martin Antoine	Gonzalo Calvo	Remi Fayomi	Nico Kammel	Wes Odom	Tony Vodicka
Robert Arndt	Clark Campbell	Mark Garstka	John Keehn	Sara Poerschke	Shawn Walters
Christoph Balles	Malachi Carnegie	Patric Henson	Shari Khalil	John Polack	Randy Ward
Aaron Blankenship	Chris Conner	Philip Herbig	Tom Killingbeck	Mario Priesterath	
Tim Bruns	Richard Conti	Peter Holland	Michael Kirk	Chris Renshaw	
Shane Bryner	Mike DeLance	Steve Huntsberry	Conor Marshall	Mark Roberts	

AKIRA CLASS

USS BELLEROPHON NCC-74705

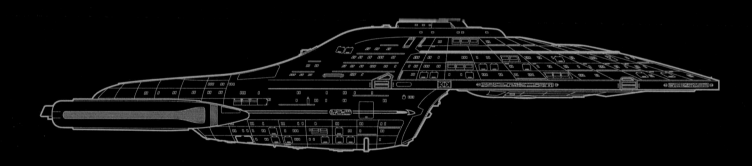

Andrea Alvisi	Jacob Cohen	Sarah Händler	Wesley Lovell	Timothy Relph	Roxanne Thompson
Josip Antolis	A Crompton	Steve Hanson	Vincent Maxera	Valentina Righi	Dominic Toghill
Gus Badnell	Tim Dalvang	Kurosch Hourfar	Mislav Mijatovic	Frank Rijckx	Kaleb Trumbly
Carsten Bärmann	Geoffrey Davis	Matthew Jackson	Walter Milani-Müller	Kevin Rolfe	Saverio Vaccari
John C Barstow	Erwin De Hondt	Kendall Jung	Nickolas R. Miller	David Rosson	Travis Weik
Corey Bass	Derek Dokter	Jan-Hendrik Kalusche	Alexander Neubert	Thorsten Sagorski	David Whitecar
Lukas Bohn	Jason Douglas	Paul Kießhauer	Christian A. Nord	Sandra Schaefer-Drapp	Michael Willett
Jason Buchanan	William Dowie	Chad E King	Juan Ignacio Oller Aznar	Stephan Settelmeier	Michael Wolf
Mareike Burggraf	Anorei Elvaster	Kai Klomann	Joerg Pechau	Jon Snodgrass	
Marcus Burggraf	Mattia Filippi	Mark LaCroix	Robin Pools	Michael Stanley	
Evan Burris	Sean Galland	Sebastien le Couriaut	Daniel Proença	Joe Sulkin	
Enrique Busó	Gaaron Gilham	Roman Lesnoy	Paulo César Ramírez	Richard Swanson	
Sam Byford	Simone Giuliani	Kevin Leung	Barry Reese	Will Thomas	

INTREPID CLASS

STARFLEET PERSONNEL FILE

NAME: _____

SPECIES: _____   RANK: _____

ENVIRONMENT: _____   UPBRINGING: _____

ASSIGNMENT: _____

TRAITS: _____

ATTRIBUTES

CONTROL ☐   FITNESS ☐   PRESENCE ☐

DARING ☐   INSIGHT ☐   REASON ☐

DISCIPLINES

COMMAND ☐   SECURITY ☐   SCIENCE ☐

CONN ☐   ENGINEERING ☐   MEDICINE ☐

VALUES

_____

_____

_____

_____

DETERMINATION   ◯ ◯ ◯

TALENTS

_____

_____

_____

_____

_____

WEAPONS

NAME/TYPE [_____] ◢ ☐

QUALITIES [_____]

NAME/TYPE [_____] ◢ ☐

QUALITIES [_____]

NAME/TYPE [_____] ◢

QUALITIES [_____]

FOCUSES

_____

_____

_____

_____

_____

_____

_____

_____

_____

STRESS

◯ ◯ ◯ ◯ ◯ ◯
◯ ◯ ◯ ◯ ◯ ◯
◯ ◯ ◯ ◯ ◯ ◯
◯ ◯ ◯ ◯ ◯ ◯

INJURIES

_____

_____

_____

OTHER EQUIPMENT

_____

_____

_____

_____

_____

_____

STARSHIP REGISTRY ENTRY

NAME: _____

SERVICE DATE: _____

MISSION PROFILE: _____

DESIGNATION: _____

SPACE FRAME: _____

REFIT: _____

SYSTEMS

ENGINES [ ] | **COMPUTERS** [ ]
BREACHES ○○○○○ | BREACHES ○○○○○

STRUCTURE [ ] | **SENSORS** [ ]
BREACHES ○○○○○ | BREACHES ○○○○○

WEAPONS [ ]
BREACHES ○○○○○

COMMUNICATIONS [ ]
BREACHES ○○○○○

POWER

CURRENT [ ] | **TOTAL** [ ]

SHIELDS

◻ ◻ ◻ ◻ ◻ ◻
◻ ◻ ◻ ◻ ◻ ◻

LAUNCH BAY

_____
_____
_____
_____

DEPARTMENTS

COMMAND [ ] | **SECURITY** [ ] | **SCIENCE** [ ]

CONN [ ] | **ENGINEERING** [ ] | **MEDICINE** [ ]

SCALE [ ]

TALENTS

_____
_____
_____
_____

CREW SUPPORT

CURRENT [ ] | **TOTAL** [ ]

WEAPONS

NAME/TYPE _____
QUALITIES _____

NAME/TYPE _____
QUALITIES _____

NAME/TYPE _____
QUALITIES _____

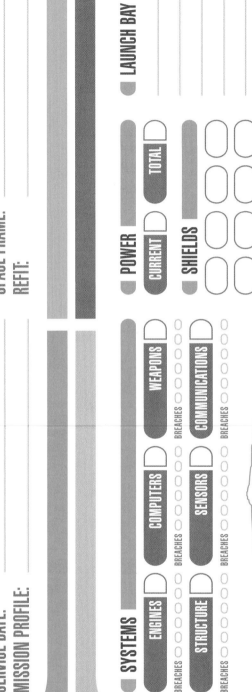
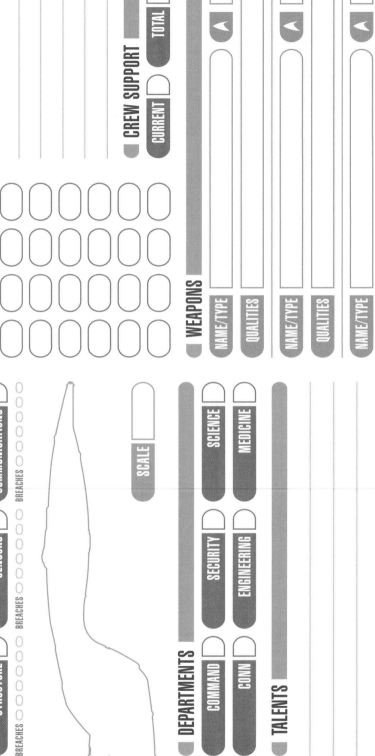
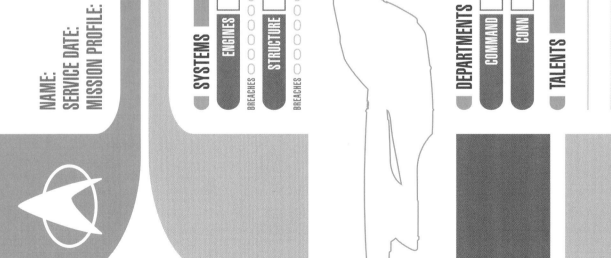

STAR TREK
ADVENTURES

FULL RANGE OF BOOKS & ACCESSORIES

NCC-1701-D Limited Edition Corebook
Away Team Edition Corebook
Command Division Book
Operations Division Book
Sciences Division Book
Alpha Quadrant Book
Beta Quadrant Book
Gamma Quadrant Book
Delta Quadrant Book
These Are The Voyages: Missions Vol.1
Strange New Worlds: Missions Vol.2
Limited Edition Borg Cube Box Set

Gamesmaster Screen
Command, Operations & Sciences Dice Sets
The Next Generation Miniatures
The Original Series Miniatures
Romulan Strike Team Miniatures
Klingon Warband Miniatures
Borg Collective Miniatures
Starfleet Away Team Miniatures
Star Trek Villains Miniatures
Starfleet Landing Party Miniatures
Starfleet Geomorphic Deck Tiles
Klingon Geomorphic Deck Tiles

Star Trek Adventures tabletop
roleplaying game takes you to the
final frontier of the Galaxy,

Books, accessories, and special
editions available now from
modiphius.net and friendly
local game stores.

MODIPHIUS.COM
STARTREK.COM

THE HYBORIAN AGE AWAITS YOU

OTHER CONAN TITLES

Conan the Adventurer
Conan the Brigand
Conan the King
Conan the Mercenary
Conan the Pirate
Conan the Thief
Conan the Scout
Conan the Wanderer

Ancient Ruins & Cursed Cities
The Book of Skelos
Horrors of the Hyborian Age
Kull of Atlantis
Nameless Cults
Conan: The Exiles Sourcebook
Conan: The Monolith Sourcebook
The Art of Conan

CONAN ACCESSORIES

Gamemaster Screen
Geomorphic Tile Sets
Q-Workshop Dice Set
Doom & Fortune Card Deck

Encounter Card Deck
Location Card Deck
Sorcery Card Deck
Story Card Deck

MŌDIPHIÜS®
ENTERTAINMENT

2D20™

CABINET

ROBERT E. HOWARD™
OFFICIAL LICENSE

HYBORIA™

modiphius.com/conan